W9-ADN-849

SHAKESPEARE'S GOD

SHAKESPEARE'S GOD

The Role of Religion in the Tragedies

by Ivor Morris

London · George Allen & Unwin Ltd

RUSKIN HOUSE   MUSEUM STREET

DALE H. GRAMLEY LIBRARY
SALEM COLLEGE
WINSTON-SALEM, N. C.

PR.
2983
M6
1972b

First published in 1972

This book is copyright under the Berne Convention. All
rights are reserved. Apart from any fair dealing for the
purpose of private study, research, criticism or review, as
permitted under the Copyright Act, 1956, no part of this
publication may be reproduced, stored in a retrieval
system, or transmitted, in any form or by any means,
electronic, electrical, chemical, mechanical, optical
photocopying, recording or otherwise, without the prior
permission of the copyright owner. Enquiries should be
addressed to the publishers.

© George Allen & Unwin Ltd 1972

ISBN 0 04 822033 7

Printed in Great Britain
in 11 on 12 point Baskerville type
by Clarke, Doble & Brendon Ltd
Plymouth

This book is dedicated
to the memory of
Dr Reinhold Niebuhr
prophet to his times

Preface

Tragedy raises more pointedly and insistently than any other form of art the question of our life's meaning. To the perplexities from which it draws its being it can provide no formal answer; and generally it must hold true that the more sensitive and accomplished the criticism of a great play, the more it will intensify the questioning.

Yet to say that the critic can no more afford to try to rise above human experience than the dramatist himself would be incorrect, since no appreciation would be possible if standards of far-reaching import were not applied to the happenings on the stage. If to criticize must be in some sense to affirm, criticism may properly contemplate a response to tragedy's ultimate challenge by the use of the most far-reaching standards of affirmation at its command : those of revealed religion.

Indeed, if there is 'truth' in tragedy – if it successfully conveys the quality of human experience – it ought necessarily to have some relation to theology, if theology's claim to provide a means of assessing man's experience in the world is itself true. But however attractive in theory, the reconciliation is difficult to achieve in practice; for, both in inspiration and in manner, drama and theology are exceedingly unlike. Far from lending insight, theological judgements can be a positive hindrance to appreciation.

It is therefore an essential concern of this study to find a basis for the theological interpretation of Shakespearian tragedy – to determine an area of compatibility, where the two disciplines speak in terms that are not mutually exclusive. As a consequence of the approach that has been adopted it has become possible, in the process of working towards an interpretation of the tragedies that should be as meaningful to a literary judgement as to a theological one, to present a systematic theological explanation of the phenomena of literary tragedy itself.

The great danger in an undertaking of this kind is an excessive resort to the subjective or the theoretical on the part of the writer. An attempt has therefore been made to treat both existing dramatic criticism and the theology that is referred to as the given facts of the situation which is being explored, and thus to ensure that the argument evolves as much from the experience of others as from the writer's personal experience. It is in accordance with this aim that ideas have as far as possible been traced to their source, or else supported by reference to other works, and

9

that disagreement with authoritative writers, where it occurs, has been made clear.

It may be considered that the discussion has been rather fully sustained throughout the work. But since a view of possibilities is being set forth which is at first sight surprising, and might even be unwelcome, to a wholly secular outlook, it has been thought better to present the case fully at all stages than to require the reader to carry its assumptions forward.

It is a pleasure to record my indebtedness to the kindness and learning of Dr M. E. Seaton, Fellow of St Hugh's College, Oxford, who supervised my earlier research. It is to her that I owe anything I have since achieved in the craft of bringing scholarship to the aid of literary appreciation. And it was the profundity of her insights into motive and attitude in Shakespeare which led me to believe there was scope for a more far-reaching appraisal of his tragedies in terms of the higher reaches of personality than had yet appeared. That I finally attempted such a study was largely due to the encouragement of the Rev. John Huxtable, Minister-Secretary of the Congregational Church in England and Wales, and I take this opportunity of expressing my gratitude to him for his wise councils in this and other matters.

For help and advice they have given in the earlier stages of this work I should like to thank the Rev. Canon H. Balmforth, Mr Ernest Martin, Professor the Rev. Canon W. M. Merchant, Professor the Rev. Canon J. R. Porter, the Rev. D. L. Powell and Mr J. H. Speirs. I am grateful to Professor Dame Helen Gardner for reading the manuscript and for her criticisms and suggestions for publication.

Mr Peter Leek, of Messrs George Allen and Unwin, Ltd, who has prepared the book for publication with skill and care, is responsible for a number of improvements in presentation.

I would like to acknowledge the assistance given by the staffs of the Reading Room of the British Museum, Stevenage Central Library and Dr Williams's Library, and the Libraries of the Universities of Cambridge, Exeter and London.

I am most grateful to my friend Mrs B. J. Borne for undertaking a complex job of typing, and doing it so splendidly, and to my wife, who has brought a scientist's accuracy and a true devotion to the formidable job of checking.

I.M.

Knebworth, Hertfordshire
14 May 1971

Contents

DALE H. GRAMLEY LIBRARY
SALEM COLLEGE
WINSTON-SALEM, N. C.

List of Abbreviations

Angl. Theol. Rev.	*Anglican Theological Review*
Conf.	*Confessiones*
Contra Jul. Imp. Op.	*Contra Julianum Imperfectum Opus*
Contra Gent.	*Summa Contra Gentiles*
I Cor.	*The First Epistle of Paul to the Corinthians*
De Agone Christ.	*De Agone Christiano*
De Civ. Dei	*De Civitate Dei*
De Cont.	*De Continentia*
De Cor. et Grat.;	
De Corrept. et Grat.	*De Correptione et Gratia*
De Dono Persev.	*De Dono Perseverantiae*
De Gen. ad Lit.	*De Genesi ad Litteram*
De Gest. Pelag.	*De Gestis Pelagii*
De Grat. et Lib. Arb.	*De Gratia et Libero Arbitrio*
De Lib. Arb.	*De Libero Arbitrio*
De Nat. Boni	*De Natura Boni*
De Nat. et Grat.	*De Natura et Gratia*
De Pat.	*De Patientia*
De Praedest. Sanct.	*De Praedestinatione Sanctorum*
De Quaest. ad Simp.	*De Quaestionibus ad Simplicianum*
De Quant. Anim.	*De Quantitate Animae*
De Serm. Dom. in Monte	*De Sermone Domini in Monte*
De Spir. et Litt.	*De Spiritu et Littera*
De Trin.	*De Trinitate*
De Vera Relig.	*De Vera Religione*
Eccl. Pol.	*Of the Laws of Ecclesiastical Polity*
E.L.H.	*English Literary History*
En. in Ps.	*Enarrationes in Psalmos*
Ench.	*Enchiridion*
Ep.	*Epistolae*
Eth. Nicom.	*Ethica Nicomachea*
Exod.	*The Book of Exodus*
Gal.	*The Epistle of Paul to the Galatians*
Galatians	*A Commentary on St Paul's Epistle to the Galatians*
Heb.	*The Epistle to the Hebrews*

In Epist. Jo. ad Parth.	*In Epistolam Joannis ad Parthos Tractatus*
Tract. decem	*decem*
In Jo. Ev. Tr.	*In Joannis Evangelium Tractatus*
In Lib. de Divin. Nomin.	*Opusculum VII In Librum Beati Dionysii*
	de Divinis Nominibus
Inst.	*The Institutes of the Christian Religion*
J.E.G.P.	*Journal of English and German Philology*
L.C.C.	*Library of Christian Classics*
Matt.	*The Gospel according to Matthew*
Metaphy.	*Metaphysica*
N.E.D.	*New English Dictionary*
Philippians	*The Epistle of Paul to the Philippians*
P.M.L.A.	*Publications of the Modern Language*
	Association
Proc. Brit. Acad.	*Proceedings of the British Academy*
Propos. ex Ep. ad Rom.	*Expositio Quarumdam Propositionum ex*
	Epistola ad Romanos
Ps.	*The Book of Psalms*
R.E.L.	*Review of English Literature*
Retract.	*Retractiones*
Rom.	*The Epistle of Paul to the Romans*
Romans	*Luther: Lectures on Romans*
Serm.	*Sermones*
S.Q.	*Shakespeare Quarterly*
S.S.	*Shakespeare Survey*
S.T.; Summa	*Summa Theologica*
Stud. Phil.	*Studies in Philology*
Titus	*The Epistle of Paul to Titus*
Wisdom	*The Wisdom of Solomon*

And chiefly Thou O Spirit, that dost prefer
Before all Temples th'upright heart and pure,
Instruct me, for Thou know'st; Thou from the first
Wast present, and with mighty wings outspread
Dove-like satst brooding on the vast Abyss
And mad'st it pregnant: What in me is dark
Illumine, what is low raise and support;
That to the highth of this great Argument
I may assert Eternal Providence,
And justifie the wayes of God to men.

I
The Theological Interpretation of
Shakespeare's Tragedies:
A Consideration of the
Literary Problems

Chapter 1

THE 'RELIGIOUS CONCEPT' IN INTERPRETATION

In his essay on 'The Absence of Religion in Shakespeare', G. Santayana makes an observation that must serve as direful epigraph to all attempts at applying theological conceptions to the study of Shakespearian tragedy. It may indeed be Shakespeare's unspoken comment upon the value of such undertakings. The metaphysical Hamlet, he says, himself sees a 'true ghost', but so far reverts to 'the positivism that underlies Shakespeare's thinking' as to speak soon after of that

> undiscover'd country from whose bourn
> No traveller returns.[1]

No inconsistency could be more glaring or more symptomatic of a secular concern; and it encourages Santayana in his impression that there are scarcely half a dozen passages in Shakespeare that have so much as a religious sound, and that even these upon examination 'should not prove to be the expression of any deep religious conception'.[2] Santayana must surely have had in mind direct reference to explicit formulations; in his conclusion that there is to be found in the plays 'no fixed conception of any forces, natural or moral, transcending our mortal energies' it is the word 'fixed' that is operative, since Shakespeare is scarcely less full of intimations than human life itself. Nonetheless, Santayana's assertion is not to be dismissed lightly. And his claim that Shakespeare wrote 'without a philosophy and without a religion'[3] is difficult to disprove by means of clear pronouncements from the plays.

The difficulty is enhanced by the attempt to overcome it. In his search for passages susceptible of ultimate interpretation, G. Boas seizes upon Prospero's prophetic lines concerning the destined end of 'The cloud-capp'd towers' and 'gorgeous palaces'. The soothing beauty of these lines, he says, has become so familiar that it requires an effort to grasp their significance.

[1] G. Santayana, 'The Absence of Religion in Shakespeare', *Interpretations of Poetry and Religion*, Chas. Scribner's Sons, N.Y., 1905, p. 149.
[2] ibid., p. 153.   [3] ibid., p. 163.

19

The end of this world is to be no dramatic event, there is to be no second coming, no trumpet summoning to a Last Judgement, no *dies irae* nor millenium. Instead, all our miracles of science and industry and art, the frieze of the Parthenon, the treasures of the Vatican, the Mauretania, the Ritz Hotel, together with the Alps and the Atlantic, are to melt into the air like vapour, and all the human emotions that played around them are to be dissolved into nothingness like dreams. It is a peaceful and not unbeautiful end.[4]

It is also, unhappily, better proof that Shakespeare wrote 'without a philosophy and without a religion' than it is of any ultimate belief. But in a further sense no apparent reference to ultimate issues is to be trusted. The very absorption in the human that constitutes Shakespeare's greatness as a dramatist precludes direct reference to conceptual systems; and this negative capability precludes also the identifying of a character's utterance with Shakespeare's own position. Though Prospero's 'cloud-capp'd towers', and 'this earthly world' scorned in its imperfection by Lady Macduff before her assassination,[5] may belong to visions of something 'transcending our mortal energies', it would be truer to say that it is the impressions of Prospero and Lady Macduff, and not of Shakespeare, that are in question. In his study of Shakespeare's tragedies in relation to Christian doctrine, R. M. Frye is impelled to the conclusion that 'Shakespeare does not speak for himself in the plays, but for the characters he has created';[6] and, according to W. Clemen, there is to be perceived in contemporary criticism a greater willingness to accept 'the impenetrability of Shakespeare's own "Weltanschauung"' and the 'ultimate mystery' of his personal beliefs.[7] If, therefore, there are religious significances in the tragedies, they are inexplicit and indirect enough to require an approach through inference. To this extent, Santayana's charge of positivism is justified.

A general inference may obviously be drawn from the religious origins of drama. Thus W. M. Merchant argues that the expansions of the story in the Mystery plays are always 'strictly congruous with the intention of the biblical narrative', and that the lively obtrusion of secular interest in the two Shepherd plays produces nothing alien or heterodox, but dramatic episodes that are 'complementary in their serious exploration of man's fallen nature . . . taken up into the joy of redemption'.[8] The point is well made, for there is nothing in the secular story of Mac the Shepherd's supposed child which does not give new interest and meaning to

[4] 'Shakespeare and Christianity', *The Shakespeare Review* I, 1929, p. 94.
[5] IV. ii. 72–5.
[6] *Shakespeare and Christian Doctrine*, London, 1963, p. 270.
[7] 'Shakespeare and the Modern World', *S.S.* XVI, 1963, pp. 59, 60.
[8] *Creed and Drama*, 1965, pp. 29, 31.

the announcement of the Christ-child's birth. Such consistency as this, and the clear line of derivation from the worship and the preaching of the Church that constrains Elizabethan tragedy to make the human soul the true centre of its action, enable Merchant to declare with confidence that Marlowe's *Faustus* is 'in series with the late medieval Morality', and to demonstrate the fraudulent nature of Faustus's intellectualism, and the blasphemous reversal of values by which Marlowe indicates his hero's condemned state.[9] But the assumed similarity between a Faustus lured into damnation by his gifts of intellect, and Hamlet's vision of the creature man who, though 'infinite in faculties', is yet but a 'quintessence of dust', is less convincing: for the one conception is related to a clearly-defined heaven and hell, and the other is not. A ready identification is possible, therefore, between the Elizabethan play and its predecessors, with the reservation that – as O. J. Campbell puts it – 'The bare outlines of the dramatic type have been overlaid and often obscured by the fullness of the plot and the intricacies of the relationship between the characters.' Thus Campbell is able to assert that *King Lear* follows the Morality pattern in structure and the medieval homiletic tradition in content:[10] he sees Lear as an Everyman, rewarded by the discovery of the spiritual values he seeks just before Death's awful summons comes to him at the close of what is essentially 'a sublime morality play'.[11]

A similar reasoning lies behind W. Farnham's relating of Elizabethan tragedy to the medieval tragic pattern,[12] and is to be found in Theodore Spencer's attempt to show that the tragedy is based upon the medieval Contempt of the World theme,[13] and in E. M. W. Tillyard's tracing primitive rituals of renewal through destruction through the Christian beliefs which replaced them, and finding in both the true being of tragedy.[14] Of the former endeavour, it has been pointed out that A. C. Bradley wrote in awareness of Shakespeare's medieval heritage in tragedy but affirmed that 'Shakespeare's idea of the tragic fact is larger than this idea and goes beyond it';[15] and concerning the latter, S. Barnet argues that to interpret the drama in the light of its origins and analogues 'is to engage in the reductive fallacy and to see the product as containing no more than the source'.[16] To say that Shakespeare's tragedy is related to medieval drama is one thing; to assume that its nature was bestowed upon it by the drama that preceded it is another. A great artist does not become

[9] ibid., pp. 33, 39, 45–6.   [10] 'The Salvation of Lear', *E.L.H.* XV, 1948, p. 108.
[11] ibid., p. 94.
[12] *The Medieval Heritage of Elizabethan Tragedy*, University of California Press, 1936, p. 71.
[13] *Death and Elizabethan Tragedy*, Harvard University Press, 1936.
[14] See e.g. *Shakespeare's Problem Plays*, 1957, pp. 14–17, 26, for the view that the regenerative is essential to the tragic.
[15] H. Weisinger, 'The Study of Shakespearian Tragedy since Bradley', *S.Q.* VI, 1955, p. 392; Bradley, *Shakespearean Tragedy*, 2nd edn, pp. 8–9.
[16] 'Some Limitations of a Christian Approach to Shakespeare', *E.L.H.* XXII, 1955, p. 81.

absorbed in his heritage, but rather converts it to his own uses :[17] as it was once said of man's soul, that 'Her nature is peculiar and her own', so the nature of Shakespearian tragedy is proper to itself.

Yet there can be detected in the tragedies sufficient allusion to theological concepts to make possible a literary criticism based on a strict religious orthodoxy. W. M. Merchant cites T. S. Eliot's judgement of *Macbeth* as being a story of sin and expiation that shows hell and the state of damnation to consist in the absence of the beatific vision.[18] The storm in *King Lear* is for Merchant a presentation both of the Fall by which all creation was involved in tragedy and of the final cataclysm to which it is doomed; the uttering of a 'Nothing will come of nothing' within the created order is a blasphemy, as is the relating of love to a graded reward amidst creatures redeemed by the love of God.[19] He points out the theological precision inherent in 'The fear of the sin, unconfessed and unrepented at the point of death' at the prayer scene in *Hamlet*, and in the purgatorial condition of its Ghost; and his argument that, following our ignoring of the 'frame of orthodoxy' which encloses and illuminates the diseased social order of *Hamlet*, 'the homogeneity of Hamlet's attitudes, the consistency of moral reprehension, also tends to elude our recognition', is both cogent and timely.[20] There is no doubting in these examples the force and acuteness attainable by criticism so inspired. Yet many critics would not share Merchant's confidence that, by the reference to 'the promis'd end', the tragic end of *King Lear* 'is given its final import by its setting within a traditional eschatology',[21] since, whatever import the words may have, they bring no clear finality to that terrible conclusion. It may on the contrary be held of this play that, far from asserting orthodoxy, 'No work of art has ever articulated more closely man's interrogation of the Gods'.[22] Indeed, its reference to 'the promis'd end' appears to R. B. Sewall to imply despair :

> The Christian hope is shattered. The promised Judgement confuses evil and good, and both perish.[23]

In this critic's judgement, there is nothing Christian in Lear's response to the terrible fact of Cordelia's death. The heaven he invokes as he carries her in is 'deaf indeed'; and the final scene speaks nothing of salvation, but shows only 'a wan restoration, after great loss, of a kind of order'.[24] The claim that the structure of Shakespeare's drama 'is

---

17 See Weisinger, op. cit., p. 394. 18 *Creed and Drama*, p. 53.
19 ibid., p. 52.
20 'Shakespeare's Theology', *R.E.L.* V, 1964, pp. 81–3.
21 ibid., p. 78.
22 R. Speaight, *Nature in Shakespearian Tragedy*, 1955, p. 113.
23 *The Vision of Tragedy*, Yale University Press, 1965, p. 73.
24 ibid., pp. 77–8.

integrated by the credal assumptions of his age'[25] is justified only provided that it is not taken to exclude other integrating elements, and that it in no way implies an outcome, in terms of event and meaning, that is dictated by, or limited to, the scheme of reference to which such assumptions belong.

If this provision is not accepted, a ready-made standard of judgement must be introduced. Indeed, the abundant references to a supernatural order in the plays must then invalidate a secular criticism : concepts like heaven and hell, or the working of angels and devils, must inevitably transcend and disqualify the more limited and mundane principles by which the characters live. It could further be demonstrated that Shakespeare's characters act in accordance with religious concepts : that Hamlet's distrust of the Ghost, and Macbeth's of the dagger, are based on the sound belief that

> The devil is so crafty a spirit, that he can ape and deceive our senses. He can cause one to think he sees something, which he sees not, that he hears thunder or a trumpet, which he hears not.[26]

They would seem to display a proper theological apprehension of the devil's power to 'betray' and 'abuse' mankind into damnation; that evil agencies

> are alwaies buzy to procure our destruction : that they go about the earth, that they bee neuer away from vs, that they bee euer feeling meanes to get into vs, and that as soone as they finde neuer so small a breach, they enter into vs to throwe vs into endlesse destruction.[27]

Hamlet's appeal to 'angels and ministers of grace' at the Ghost's sudden appearance is an appropriate confidence that

> when the devil intends to hurt us, then the loving holy angels resist and drive him away,

in obedience to God's command that they should preserve mankind.[28] And the devil's propensity to affright people in their sleep

> with heavy dreams and visions, so that the whole body sweats in anguish of heart,

or to lead them, sleeping,

> out of their beds and chambers up into high dangerous places, so that if, by the loving angels who are about them, they were not preserved, he would throw them down, and cause their death,[29]

[25] *Creed and Drama*, p. 56.

[26] *The Table-Talk of Martin Luther*, tr. W. Hazlitt, London, 1883, dcviii.

[27] *Calvins Sermons on Job*, tr. Arthur Golding, London, Dec. 1573, p. 19a. See *Macbeth* I. iii. 122–6, and *Hamlet* II. ii. 606–11.

[28] Luther, op. cit., dlxxi; *Hamlet* I. iv. 39.   [29] ibid., dxcviii.

is not without evident recognition in the tragedies. Even Hamlet's reference in the quickness of banter to the cherubim glowing with knowledge (IV. iii. 50)[30] can demonstrate an acute grasp of religious lore.

It is not upon the presence of these concepts, however, but upon their effectiveness within their context, that literary judgement must be founded. This is the point of a cautionary observation by Miss Helen Gardner upon the insistent mention of the supernatural order in *Othello*.

> It has been suggested that the frequent references to Heaven and Hell, angels and devils make a theological interpretation necessary. On the contrary, their very frequency deprives them of any imaginative potency.[31]

Such a pronouncement as 'Thou art a soul in bliss' (IV. vii. 46) is meaningful in *King Lear*, she argues, because of its unusualness;

> But Heaven and Hell are bandied about too lightly in *Othello* for the words to have any but a flat ring.[32]

The less frequently these concepts appear in the words of the play, the more significant, it seems, they are likely to be. Miss Gardner is not alone in reaching a conclusion of this sort. S. L. Bethell notes that the diabolic images in *Othello* outnumber even those in *Macbeth*, 'which recognizedly treats the theme of supernatural evil', the numbers being sixty-four to thirty-seven.[33] Since none of these images occurs in Cinthio's *novella*, it must have been Shakespeare's intention 'to develop poetically a theological theme'; but Bethell, who is not unsympathetic to the idea of a theological concern in Shakespeare, finds this theme subordinate to that preoccupation with deceitful appearances which is the play's true theme. 'The play', he declares, 'is a solemn game of hunt the devil';[34] and these supernatural concepts do not bring in considerations that transcend the play's world:

> The diabolic images we have considered do not carry us away from the characters into a world of metaphysical speculation in which they have no part. Rather they serve the true purpose of poetic drama, to show the underside, as it were, of ordinary life. It is precisely in such sordid and – to the outsider – trivial domestic quarrels that the Devil is busiest.[35]

If there is indeed a theology at work in *Othello*, it is not explicit, but rather one of suggestion; it may inform, but it does not dominate. Bethell

[30] Helen Gardner, *The Business of Criticism*, Oxford Paperbacks, 1963, p. 56.
[31] 'The Noble Moor', *Proceedings of the British Academy* XLI, 1955, p. 191.
[32] ibid.
[33] 'The Diabolic Images in *Othello*', *S.S.* V, 1952, p. 68.
[34] ibid., pp. 71–2.   [35] ibid., p. 79.

might easily have stated his conclusion in the words later used by R. M. Frye:

> Shakespeare's concern as an artist was for the life of man as he exists in the world of human society, and when his theological references point beyond the realm of time and death, they do so to illumine the state of mind or course of action of a dramatic character who is both presented within, and to be judged in terms of, a purely human situation.[36]

This judgement is in accord with that of A. C. Bradley, who, commenting on the words God, hell, devil and heaven in Shakespeare's plays, declared:

> these ideas do not materially influence his representation of life, nor are they used to throw light on the mystery of its tragedy.[37]

The inexplicitness of theological reference in Shakespearian tragedy, and the free scope that is afforded for secular judgement, are an obstacle in the path of affirmation. The obstacle seems less formidable in *Macbeth*, with its greater abundance of religious vocabulary and its aptitude for religious analogy; yet so accomplished a critic as Miss M. C. Bradbrook, though able to declare, from her study of Shakespeare's sources, that (in terms of James's *Daemonologie*) Macbeth had sinned against the Holy Ghost in doing what he knew to be evil while detesting what he did and foreseeing his punishment, nevertheless speaks with reserve concerning a theological interpretation. She notes that critics are not agreed whether there is religious significance in the play, and herself observes that

> although Macbeth's career recalls a descent into hell, it is not presented openly as a descent into hell.[38]

And her demonstration that the feelings of Shakespeare's Tarquin and Lucrece are 'identical with the central core of feeling in *Macbeth*' confirm her in her conclusion that, in the drama, 'the overt theological issue is never bluntly put'.[39]

The argument, on the contrary, that the overt theological issue is always being put – that 'The explicitly Christian quality of *Macbeth*, the fact that it is an imaginative exploration of evil in Biblical terms, is the key to the tragedy'[40] – is put forward in a penetrating study of the play's

[36] *Shakespeare and Christian Doctrine*, London, 1963, p. 57.
[37] *Shakespearean Tragedy*, p. 25.
[38] 'The Sources of *Macbeth*', *S.S.* IV, 1951, p. 43.
[39] ibid., pp. 43, 45.
[40] '*Macbeth*, King James and the Bible', *E.L.H.* XXII, 1955, p. 180.

sources and allusions by Mrs. J. H. Jack. She claims that the story is told less in terms of the notion of order and degree than in the spirit of Old Testament histories of kings whose reigns are good or bad according to their allegiance to false prophets or the true God. Shakespeare removes the motive for Macbeth's regicide that Holinshed's account gives, and makes Macbeth's motive a trust in the weird sisters consequent upon spiritual unpreparedness to resist temptation. By his ability to act contrary to the restraints of human nature and of religion through the destruction of his own conscience, Macbeth is revealed as a damned soul; the early scenes of the play show the rejection of the values that 'become' a Christian by a man who would 'jump the life to come' and its laws, and who is restrained from murder only by 'prudential fears and a natural disinclination to kill a virtuous old man'. The presence of the witches at the beginning of the play is 'a device which gives good and evil a transcendental position in the tragedy'; the contrast between Scotland and an England 'full of grace' enhances this effect; and the almost 'impossibly extensive' miseries of Macbeth's domain read like the havoc wrought by the 'acts of God'.[41]

Mrs Jack bases this interpretation primarily upon the 'vivid pattern of references to Scripture' by which Shakespeare conveys the nature and power of evil – upon the wealth of such memorable expressions as 'Nor heaven peep through the blanket of the dark', 'jump the life to come', 'In the great hand of God', 'heaven's cherubims', 'Are you so gospell'd' and 'the grace of Grace'.[42] But she bases it also upon impressive analogies from the writings of King James and from the Bible: from *Basilikon Doron*, which treats of the conscience that can become 'a great torture to the wicked', and of the *'cauterized conscience . . .* become senseless of sinne';[43] from the *Daemonologie*, where it is maintained that the devil can only deceive 'such as first wilfully deceiue themselves, by running vnto him', and where the assurance of wicked prophesyers, 'No euill shal come vpon you', foreshadows the Witches' 'Fear not, Macbeth' (V. iii. 6);[44] and from *A Fruitfull Meditation*, whose statement that 'the wicked are euer the greatest part of the world' may be the origin of the words of young Macduff to his mother (IV. ii. 54–6).[45] Amongst some Biblical parallels of much interest, the protestation of David to Saul,

Vnderstand me, and se, that there is nether euil nor wickedness in me, nether haue I sinned against thee . . . The Lord be iudge betwene thee & me (*I. Samuel* xxiv. 10–12),

---

[41] ibid., pp. 180–6.   [42] ibid., p. 179.
[43] ibid., pp. 176–7.   [44] ibid., p. 181.
[45] ibid., p. 187.

is convincingly shown to be related to the interview between Malcolm and Macduff: 'But God above/Deal between thee and me' (IV. iii. 120–1).[46]

The case is impressive. Apart from its undeniable congruences, it raises the question whether a dramatist can make creative use of concepts derived from the dominating religion of his times without his imagination being conformed to the scheme or the outlook of which they are part: will he be bound to set human nature in relation to theology, or will he remain free as an artist to summon theology to the aid of his vision of human life? To this question there can be no standard answer; yet it should in the first place be asserted as a truth that the artistic imagination is extraordinarily free, and that the artistic intention must be chiefly determinative. Macbeth's evolving state of mind will obviously come within the scope of theological definition; and R. M. Frye is probably correct in asserting Shakespeare's intention:

> In Macbeth, Shakespeare has created one of the most magnificent presentations of the degeneration of the human soul which our culture affords, and he has done so in reference to Christian theology, but his purpose is still to keep the mirror up to human nature and to show the course of human life in this world.[47]

The comment of theology, and the course of human life in this world, may often grow into an identity; but any claim that theological interpretation is essential for this play must first demonstrate that the experience of Macbeth is beyond the reaches of the secular imagination of man.

Sources and analogies within a theological scheme or its concepts are only one among many forms of literary analogy; and although it may be argued that religious values are more pervasive than others, it is nevertheless as perilous to conceive of literary works as determined by their analogies as it is to regard their nature as settled by their predecessors. By the use of precisely the same method Mrs Jack applies to *Macbeth*, it could be shown that some of the most significant moments of *King Lear* belong to familiar Christian concepts and experience, and that the play has 'an explicit Christian quality' needing theological interpretation. Thus it could be argued that from the moment of his afflictions Lear is driven to assert, and also to question anew, that relationship with the gods that he had before characteristically assumed, so that his sufferings take place under the eye of heaven:

> You see me here, you gods, a poor old man,
> As full of grief as age

(II. iv. 272–3).

---

[46] ibid., p. 185. [47] *Shakespeare and Christian Doctrine*, p. 255.

He can at one moment suspect that it is the gods who 'stir these daughters' hearts/Against their father' (II. iv. 274-5), and at another call upon the heavens,

Make it your cause; send down and take my part! (II. iv. 192).

But he is concerned throughout with the high and hidden purpose of the great gods,

That keep this dreadful pother o'er our heads
(III. ii. 49-50);

and in doing so he is within the domain of that Christian teaching which exhorts,

if wee bee afflicted, we must not think it happeneth without reason, but rather that God hath iust cause to do it.[48]

For the afflicted Lear, the winds and fires of heaven are eloquent of the regal prerogative of the heavens over their subject; Lear's state of mind can be expressed in the devout belief that

as wee bee so loth to come to him: he is faine to summon vs, & to shew what authoritie he hath ouer vs: like as whē a prince seeth his subiect slow to do his dutie, he sendeth his officer to summon him. So also God . . . prouoketh vs and summoneth vs.[49]

The Scriptural belief (*Ps.* civ. 4)

that the windes be Gods heraulds to execute his will, and that the lightning haue like nature[50]

finds dramatic expression in the 'hurricanoes' and the 'thought-executing fires' which, in striking at 'ingrateful man', carry out their divinely-ordained task against God's enemies (III. ii. 1-9).

In the thoughts of Job, as they are expounded in Golding's translation of Calvin's *Sermons*, lie some very close correspondences to the words of Lear. There is a similarity in the reactions of both men to the assaults of the 'summoners':

Iob was prouoked to say, what a thing is this? Men are agaynst mee, and God hath made himselfe mine enemie. For from whence come these hideous windes. It is sayd that the windes are Gods messengers to execute his commaundements as though they were Heraulds. It is sayd, that the fire of heauen is as it were a signe of his presence. Iob therefore might haue concluded thus: I see how God warreth against

48 *Calvins Sermons on Job*, 1573, p. 35b.
49 ibid., p. 33a.   50 ibid., p. 30a.

me on the one side, and men on the other, and there is neyther heauen nor earth with me, but all is agaynst mee. Alas, whither may I goe?[51]

Lear's view of his situation bears a marked resemblance to Job's at this point:

> here I stand, your slave,
> A poor, infirm, weak, and despis'd old man.
> But yet I call you servile ministers,
> That have with two pernicious daughters join'd
> Your high-engender'd battles 'gainst a head
> So old and white as this. O! O! 'tis foul
>
> (III. ii. 19–24).

Just as Lear's resort under affliction is to a preoccupation which might be termed theological, so his complementary concern with man's nature is in keeping with Calvin's exposition of the duty of Christians.

> Also as ofte and as long as wee wante the goodes of this worlde, or indure hunger and colde, or bee nipped with anye aduersitie, and haue no reliefe: let vs bethinke vs of oure byrthe, and let vs consyder our selues, bothe what wee bee, and whence wee come.[52]

Lear appears to act in accordance with this urging when the appearance of 'unaccommodated man' in the person of poor Tom provokes the expression of a growing concern with the whole state of mortal man:

> Is man no more than this? Consider him well
>
> (III. iv. 101).

Affliction, declares Calvin, is instituted by God

> to the ende that by trying what is in vs, we also might knowe what our estate is. Moreouer it is good and profitable, that the faythfull, when God afflicteth them, should enforce themselues to thinke, who am I? what am I? and wherefore am I thus afflicted?[53]

With this instruction should be compared the effect upon Lear of the revelation of his own impotence and Goneril's malignity:

> Does any here know me? This is not Lear:
> Does Lear walk thus? speak thus? Where are his eyes?
> Either his notion weakens, his discernings
> Are lethargied. Ha! waking? 'tis not so.
> Who is it that can tell me who I am?
>
> (I. iv. 225–9).

[51] ibid., p. 29b.   [52] ibid., p. 33b.   [53] ibid., p. 32b.

The assertion that

> it beccommeth vs too suffer paciently the losse of our goodes and ryches, when so euer wee bee berefte of them[54]

could have given rise, as J. F. Danby has tried to show,[55] to a great deal in Lear's oft-repeated wish,

> You heavens, give me that patience, patience I need! (II. iv. 271).

And the thought that we must not become angry against God,

> but wee must rather call vpon him, according as it is sayde: let him that is sorrowfull pray,[56]

may be found in Lear's resolve,

> I'll pray, and then I'll sleep
> (III. iv. 27).

Yet the manner of Lear's prayer must be noted. It is not addressed to God: it is addressed to the 'Poor naked wretches', and to himself. Job's stripping himself of his clothes was an act of piety and obedience to God –

> For Iob could not make a better proofe of his pacience, then in determining too bee starke naked, syth it was God's good pleasure that hee shoulde bee so,

the rending of clothes being

> a signe of repentance among the men of olde tyme.[57]

No such purpose informs Lear's casting aside of his 'lendings'. A burning zeal for truth and honesty he may have; but by no stretch of the imagination is a passion for moral and intellectual honesty to be equated with an act of worship. For, in the words of Scripture,

> 'Job rose up, and rent his clothes, and shore his head, and cast himselfe to the grounde, and vvorshipped. /And sayde, Naked I came out of my mother's vvomb, and naked I shall returne againe: the Lord hath giuen, and the Lord hath taken avvay: Blessed be the name of the Lorde.' (*Job* i. 20–1).[58]

This is the chord which is not struck in Shakespeare's play. If Shakespeare was familiar with Calvin's exposition, he has in employing it removed from it all that is strictly of religious import, and thereby produced an ending that a Dr Johnson would perforce find unendurable.

[54] ibid., p. 33b.
[55] '*King Lear* and Christian Patience', *The Cambridge Journal* I, 1947–8, p. 305.
[56] Calvin, op. cit., p. 63a.   [57] ibid., p. 32b.   [58] ibid., p. 30a.

Shakespeare may therefore be attributed with the use of Christian concepts and significances towards a secular purpose; and it may be said in consequence that, in the immediate sense, a dramatist's imagination need by no means become conformed to the religious system whose concepts he employs. In support of this view may be cited H. B. Charlton's observation that even where phrases occur which 'seem to connote a more deeply penetrating body of Christian sentiment', Shakespeare appears to throw around them 'a more general and a more indefinite atmosphere': by the use of such expressions as 'mine eternal jewel' and 'the common enemy of man', for example,

> Macbeth's sense of the corruption of his spiritual nature comprehends all such evil in general, and is not restricted to the diagnostic terminology of any particular school of spiritual pathology.[59]

There may however remain an ultimate sense in which the writer's understanding is claimed by a system whose concepts have no hold over him in detail. Mrs Jack's explanation of *Macbeth* is thus not invalidated by the foregoing mention of *King Lear*; but it may be held to emerge from what has been said that, no matter how close the sources and analogies may appear to a dramatist's work, they are no assured guide to its significance, and that any residual or ultimate effect theological concepts may exert will, in the absence of explicit indications within the drama, remain too inferential to be the subject of assertion.

If search be made in the sentiments of Shakespeare's characters for likenesses to the commonplaces of Christian exordium, a positive embarrassment of analogies will arise. Albany's fear of his wife's disposition on the principle,

> That nature, which contemns its origin,
> Cannot be border'd certain in itself
>
> (IV. ii. 32–3),

will be found to be in keeping with Calvin's pronouncement that the child who unnaturally disdains his parent 'is a monster and every man will abhor him'.[60] Lady Macbeth's weary reflection,

> Nought's had, all's spent,
> Where our desire is got without content:
> 'Tis safer to be that which we destroy
> Than by destruction dwell in doubtful joy
>
> (III. ii. 4–7),

---

[59] *Shakespearian Tragedy*, 1948, pp. 146–7.
[60] *Sermons on Deuteronomy* (v. 16), tr. A. Golding, London, 1583, p. 213, as quoted by R. M. Frye, op. cit., p. 123.

could be seen as a rendering of Luther's view on this subject:

> Even if [the wicked] were to gain possession of everything that they wished, what sweet and pure enjoyment could they have if their conscience was not at rest? Is there an evil more cruel than the unrest caused by a mordant conscience?[61]

Hamlet's resolve to 'speak daggers' to Gertrude but use none (III. ii. 402) is in striking accord with Luther's advice to the righteously censorious.

> You should so inflict the wound that you can both mitigate and heal it; you should be so severe as not to forget to be kind.[62]

In all such instances it must never be forgotten that the incomparable expression of that 'Which oft was thought' is a standard of literary excellence which applies no less to Shakespeare than it does to the eighteenth century. The fact that Hamlet's

> Sure he that made us with such large discourse,
> Looking before and after, gave us not
> That capability and god-like reason
> To fust in us unus'd
>
> (IV. iv. 36–9),

has an exact parallel in Luther's *Lectures on Genesis*[63] is no cause, as R. M. Frye observes, for our jumping to the conclusion 'that Hamlet's soliloquy on Fortinbras's army is a Christian statement'. Even the precision with which Claudius treats the subject of forgiveness, and echoes the well-known teaching that there can be no relenting of God's wrath

> till recompense and restitution to man accompany the penitential confession we have made to Almighty God,[64]

has as its primary object the characterizing of Claudius. As Frye argues in another context, we have no right to assume that because Shakespeare anywhere demonstrates an apt and accurate knowledge of an elementary point in theology, he is therefore talking in theological terms.[65] That Shakespeare breathed the intellectual air of his times, and used the common coin of any of its realms of thought in dealing with human experience, is a matter of inevitability, as it is of fact – but it does not

---

[61] 'Comforts for the Weary and Heavy Laden', *Reformation Writings of Martin Luther*, ed. B. L. Woolf, London, 1956, II, p. 36, quoted by Frye, op. cit., p. 176.

[62] *Exp. Gal.* (iv. 16), Weimar Edition, II, p. 546, as quoted by Frye, op. cit., p. 155.

[63] See Frye, op. cit., p. 205.

[64] R. Hooker, *The Laws of Ecclesiastical Polity* VI. v. 7, quoted by Frye, p. 241.

[65] op. cit., p. 48.

mean that a play is to be regarded as either a thesis or a descant upon a doctrine it may echo.

So to regard it is the temptation of those who, through general or specific analogy, endeavour to show that a single religious concept a play may contain is in fact its ruling concept, and thus to overcome the difficulty all must face who seek to bring mere likeness into the province of interpretation. The beginning of such an endeavour is to be found in G. Boas's sense of Desdemona's absolute moral superiority over those who wrong her: for as long as Othello lives on, he does so not as victor, but rather as the victim of her 'innocent meekness'. In this impression Boas can distinguish the play's theme:

Innocence in the end conquers suspicion not by expostulation or complaint, but by merely remaining itself and bearing no malice. Surely it is in such a sense as this that Christ meant that the meek shall inherit the earth?[66]

On the basis of the analogy, Desdemona's love can be termed 'unearthly', and her spirit can be seen 'to walk secure upon a higher plane' amidst the turbulence of events;[67] Boas here does not adduce the play's references to her 'blessedness' of disposition, though he might have done. With this assessment of Desdemona's behaviour few could fail to sympathize; but to find in the religious analogy the key to the play's interpretation would surely be going too far. As a recent critic has said of Boas's attempt,

he is reconstructing the play and shaping it into something which Shakespeare probably would have agreed with but did not write.[68]

This charge must always threaten those who would interpret a great play in terms of a single moral or religious emphasis; it can be levelled the more readily, the more specific the concept is upon which the play is claimed to be patterned. Thus J. F. Danby, through the analogy of Christian patience as he finds it outlined for example in Coverdale's *A Spiritual and Most Precious Pearl*,[69] seeks to show that *King Lear* is largely an essay upon this virtue. He identifies two kinds of patience: that which stems from 'the natural hope', which is a gift and benefit of God to mankind that limits despair and encourages men to wait; and that derived from 'the other hope, which the spirit of God doth newly inspire through faith'[70] – a hope which under adversity tames human nature into mildness and generosity, and which can never falter, since it is nurtured by obedience to God's commandments and by the promise

[66] 'Shakespeare and Christianity', *The Shakespeare Review* I, 1929, p. 92.
[67] ibid.
[68] S. Barnet, 'Some Limitations of a Christian Approach to Shakespeare', *E.L.H* .XXII, 1955, p. 87.
[69] '*King Lear* and Christian Patience', *The Cambridge Journal* I, 1947–8, p. 305.
[70] ibid., pp. 311, 313.

B

of the life to come. Danby finds that, apart from the times when they yield to despair, both Lear and Gloucester alternate between the two hopes, the natural and the divine, and the kinds of patience that each brings. In spite of the utterance, 'As flies to wanton boys are we to the gods', Danby affirms that 'Gloucester's course over the heath is lit repeatedly from within by this light of Christian patience'; his pilgrimage is held to 'zigzag' less widely than Lear's, which is the more given to extremes.[71]

This reading of a clear measure of Christian faith, from the nature of the type of patience he exhibits, into the character of Gloucester – to say nothing of that of Lear – must be regarded as venturesome. Few claims, in fact, could better illustrate the essential dissimilarity between formal theological precept on the one hand and drama's intense and living moment on the other – or the hazards which accompany the attempt to bridge this gulf of incompatibility. Whether or not *King Lear* embodies or echoes the concept of patience so defined, conceptual criticism must nonetheless 'reshape' the play into something its author did not write; for the drama contains a host of significances so various and so extensive as to express in its total meaning far more than this concept can comprehend. The difference of quality between the teeming apprehension of the playwright and the deliberate formulations of the moralist implies a difference of attitude between playwright and conceptual critic : the one would appear to be intent upon responding to and creating a vision of life, while the other appears to be under the necessity of thinking that he is dealing with an interpretation of life. And since the two categories, while not mutually exclusive, are yet very far from being identical, over-simplification is bound to result from a failure to distinguish between them.

This could be said of a similar attempt to show that *King Lear* is 'a play about Christian folly, which is paradoxically to be interpreted as a kind of wisdom',[72] as it is in Paul's well-known reference to the folly and weakness of Christians in the eyes of the world, and his counselling the man seeking spiritual advancement to 'become a fool, that he may be wise'.[73] It is shown that Shakespeare's contemporaries would have received such exhortations as are to be found in the *Homilies,* to 'cast them from the wits of their braines' and 'to renounce the wisedome and policy of this fond world'; and an analogy to Lear's 'I am old and foolish' (IV. vii. 84) is found in *Ecclesiastes'* 'Better is a poor and a wise child than an old and foolish king, who will no more be admonished' (iv. 13).[74] Thus the argument is advanced that Lear, while he is sane, must suffer the painful

[71] ibid., p. 318.
[72] C. S. French, 'Shakespeare's "Folly": *King Lear*', S.Q. X, 1959, p. 524.
[73] ibid., p. 524; *I Cor.* i. 18–31, ii. 18.   [74] French, op. cit., p. 525.

wisdom of the Fool, and during his madness must endure the no less painful flashes of reason in madness which occur while he has taken upon him the guise of being his own fool, becoming, in his own words, 'The natural fool of Fortune' (IV. vi. 194); and thus Cordelia replaces the Fool when Lear has accepted with sane mind the truths he accepted in his madness.[75] Lear, it is true, does come to see the shallowness of his former wisdom and its standards, no less than of the standards of man's world. But that 'folly' and 'weakness' of Christians which is in truth the height of wisdom and strength consists in their trust in God and the things of God; and though Lear does attain new and profound insights, no relation to convictions beyond the secular is asserted for them – apart from what may be understood from the term 'God's spies' (V. iii. 17) – and no act or deliberation of religious purport can be ascribed to him at the end of the play. Here again, therefore, whether or not there is to be found some use of the concept, the play is strictly not 'about Christian folly'.

As well as its over-simplification, conceptual criticism shows a tendency to ascribe significance over and above the literal to features of a play not clearly requiring such enhanced emphasis, or even capable of sustaining it. The tendency is most clear in the idealization of certain characters already apparent in Boas's references to Desdemona. In the study of Lear just mentioned, the Fool is seen as a person with 'innate ability to reveal hidden mysteries of the spirit'.[76] It is true that he is an enigmatic figure, and has a Chorus-like function; but this exalted idea of the matter of his discourse should be compared with the suggestion of K. Muir that the Fool represents 'worldly common sense'.[77] Similarly, J. F. Danby, while observing that 'almost everyone' makes Cordelia verily her father's daughter, will not 'strain to detect in her the traces of her father's pride', since he sees her more as a personification than a person:

> Cordelia when she says nothing is the sheep before the shearers that must be dumb. She is quite simply the truly patient woman and daughter. If we read Coverdale's 'patience . . . of Christians' we can see clearly the relation between his abstract description and Shakespeare's living presentation.[78]

Too much can certainly be made of the thought of Cordelia's likeness to Lear, but in the stubborn clinging to principle a resemblance may be observed between them. So it may in their forthrightness; whether or not she be classed as patient, it is hard to see how someone characterized as dumb at one moment can be so thoroughly outspoken, not to say pointedly sarcastic, at the next – a point as disturbing to Danby's attempt

[75] ibid., p. 527. [76] ibid.
[77] K. Muir, ed., Arden Edition, 1963, Introduction, p. lxiii.
[78] op. cit., p. 314.

to personify as it was to Bradley's somewhat idealized view of Cordelia's womanhood.[79] In support of his attempt Danby urges the manner in which Cordelia is described by others:

> The habitual terms applied to her in the play would be extravagant in respect of a mere woman. They are quite natural when applied to a woman who is conceived as a Griselda or a Beatrice.[80]

This argument ignores the fact that, in Cordelia's absence from the scene of events, it is a matter of dramatic necessity that the beauty of her grief and the strength of her love should be represented with the poet's full power. It ignores also that terms no less 'extravagant in respect of a mere woman' are applied to Cleopatra, and are not found unnatural in their context: to whatever extent Cleopatra is held to symbolize the eternal allure of womankind, those terms are earned and appropriate in that queen upon whom can be conferred no higher title of praise than the term, 'a lass unparalleled'. This attributing a superhuman significance to a character is part of a process which can give undue emphasis to anything that seemingly supports a conceptual interpretation. Thus Danby, while admitting that there is 'no overt Christian reference' in Edgar's 'Ripeness is all' (V. ii. 11), can claim that 'The Nature which ripens man through adversity is, by implication, the Christian rather than the heathen thing'.[81] But the expression is obscure, and forms part of an utterance in haste. In the preceding words that 'Men must endure /Their going hence, even as their coming hither', the reference is to man's lot as being one of suffering; the conclusion that what follows is 'more nearly Stoic than Christian'[82] must be regarded as the best, if a conclusion is to be reached at all. The implication Danby speaks of derives less from the lines themselves than from the concept that is being used for the play's interpretation.

The innate unlikeness between the dramatist's creation and formal precept must therefore bring under suspicion of unwarranted emphasis all attempts to interpret Shakespeare's tragedies in terms of religious concepts. Such attempts can be of value in their ability to distinguish and emphasize the moral tone pervading a play; but the inevitable danger that the rigidly Christian interpretation 'forces a tragedy to fit ideas which Shakespeare doubtless held but did not dramatize' is well pointed out by S. Barnet. He writes:

> Such interpretations are not based on a total appreciation of the tragedy, but on individual lines which are related to a preconceived context. Shakespeare presents such full worlds that it is possible, with

[79] *Shakespearean Tragedy*, p. 322.   [80] op. cit., p. 314.
[81] ibid., p. 319.
[82] R. M. Frye, *Shakespeare and Christian Doctrine*, p. 139.

a little ingenuity and effort, to find in him almost any theory which the researcher wishes to discover. It is perhaps better to accept the immediate impressions yielded by the plays, and to see in these dramas not explicit eternal theological verities, portrayed on a canvas stretching from hell-mouth to heaven, but a picture of man's achievements and failures, hopes and fears, life and death.[83]

The richness of texture of Shakespeare's plays is such as to afford place for verbal and conceptual associations of great profundity; and the effect for the critic can surely be summed-up in words which Miss Helen Gardner has applied to recent trends in Biblical criticism :

If patterns are what we are interested in, and patterns are what we are looking for, patterns can certainly be found.[84]

This applies the more strongly to theological 'patterns', since much that is in accord with theological concepts can have its origin in the ordinary human experience to which it mainly refers. The ability of secular experience to attain insights identical with those of theology has already become evident; and this impression is powerfully reinforced by the research of R. M. Frye into the status of the secular life in the eyes of the theologians of the Reformation. He finds Luther, Calvin and Hooker unanimous in asserting that the laws of reason and nature enable man to discover God's will, since, in Hooker's words, '[the] law of nature and the moral law of Scripture are in the substance of law all one'.[85] Thus Hooker can maintain that the virtues belonging to 'moral righteousness and honesty of life . . . are not proper unto Christian men, as they are Christian, but do concern them as they are men';[86] and Frye shows that, in the thought of Calvin, such concepts as faith in Divine justice, the mercy of God, prayer, retribution, and the need for sincerity in sacrifice, were all attainable by the pagan consciousness. His conclusion is that 'the religious insights which Shakespeare grants to his pagan characters had theological warrant for being within the reach of pagan men',[87] and that for the critic to find sanction in a universal rather than an exclusively Christian system of ethical values would thus be in accordance with the position of the major theologians of the Reformation.[88] This conclusion should be considered together with an earlier and complementary observation that any mirror held up to reflect all of man's life will reflect instances of theological interest even though theology does not dominate the drama.[89] The critic endeavouring to interpret the

---

[83] 'Some Limitations of a Christian Approach', p. 92.
[84] *The Business of Criticism*, 1963, p. 122.
[85] *Eccl. Pol.* III. ix. 2, quoted in *Shakespeare and Christian Doctrine*, p. 105.
[86] *Eccl. Pol.* III. i. 7, quoted by Frye, op. cit., p. 109.
[87] op. cit., pp. 168–9.   [88] ibid., p. 108.   [89] ibid., p. 113.

tragedies according to religious concepts must therefore demonstrate that the concepts he identifies are exclusively theological, not only in their origin, but in their ultimate reference as the drama as a whole embodies and asserts it, before he sets about interpreting a play with their aid. Such demonstration is not easily achieved.

A way of escape from so rigorous an obligation is to be found in pleading, not so much the religious concepts to be found in the text, but the condition of mind of those to whom the text was addressed. This is the method of P. N. Siegel in an analysis of *Othello*.[90] Shakespeare, he argues, was writing for an age accustomed to think analogically; he therefore simplified the great Christian scheme of things into the pattern of events of the dramatic action, appealing to the imaginations of his audience rather than trying to outline the scheme of things in detail in the manner of the morality plays. For an Elizabethan consciousness, words like heaven, hell, angel, devil, soul, grace, repentance and sin would carry implications reaching far beyond the play's events; and the characters themselves, in following the old pattern of temptation, sin and retribution, recall 'the archetypes of erring humanity, divine goodness, and diabolic evil'. And while attention is centred upon the present world, in which the struggles of the characters take place, there is suggested to the imagination of the audience 'a heaven and hell above and beneath them, each awaiting the outcome of this struggle and ready to receive them.' The qualities of soul of the characters, therefore, would have had for the audience no loosely metaphorical meaning :

> Desdemona, who in her forgiveness and perfect love, a love requited by death, is reminiscent of Christ, would have represented Christian values; Iago, who in his envious hatred and destructive negativism is reminiscent of Satan, would have represented anti-Christian values. The choice that Othello had to make was between Christian love and forgiveness and Satanic hate and vengefulness . . . his fall was reminiscent of that of Adam.[91]

So long as it limits itself to its proper function of suggesting possible associations in the minds of the Elizabethan audience, this theory is virtually unassailable. Trouble arises when the religious susceptibilities of the age are made to creep subtly into the mind of the playwright, and the theory is used as an open invitation to infer from the text a detailed conformity to the Christian scheme of salvation and reprobation. Thus Desdomona's concern at Emilia's cheerful protestation of readiness to proceed to marital infidelity, expressed in such questions as, 'Wouldst thou do such a deed for all the world?' becomes part of a 'temptation

[90] 'The Damnation of Othello', *P.M.L.A.* LXVIII, 1953, p. 1068.
[91] ibid.

scene' in which 'We are reminded of Christ's rejection of the temptation to possess the world';[92] her assuring of Cassio that she would rather die than give his cause away 'reminds us of the steadfastness of Christ in sacrificing himself for mankind'.[93] In similar vein, the career of Cassio in the play – and particularly, one suspects, his drunken protestation of a hope to be saved – is held to suggest the 'possibility of the ordinary man . . . achieving salvation through faith and repentance';[94] and Emilia's last words, 'So come my soul to bliss as I speak true', indicate that 'she has won her soul'.[95] Othello's last words, on the other hand, are spoken 'with the resolution of one who knows his irrevocable fate and with the regret of one who knows the preciousness of what he has lost'[96] – for he is doomed to damnation.

It is evident from these judgements that the play is being wrenched into a preconceived context. Whatever the analogies attainable by an audience of Shakespeare's contemporaries, the immediate impression of the play in its swift progress is of human relationships; and any subsequent inference which is not in complete accord with those relationships will tend to produce a false criticism. We do not, in fact, see Cassio as a signpost to salvation for the common man; and Desdemona as she appears in her dealings with Emilia and with Cassio is a gracious and admirable woman, but not Christ remanifested. As for Othello's resolution and regret, they can proceed from much other than the certainty of damnation: the nearness of death alone can concentrate a man's mind wonderfully. One is increasingly aware that in his concern to detect the outlines of a religious scheme the critic is adapting the play rather than responding to it.

The account Siegel gives of the moments before Desdemona's murder may be cited as an example of this deadening of critical response:

> In the mood of elevated pity in which he offers Desdemona the last opportunity to confess her misdeeds lies Othello's last hope for escaping damnation. 'This sorrow's heavenly' indeed. When he says 'amen' in reply to Desdemona's 'Then Lord have mercy on me', Desdemona cries, 'And have you mercy too!' But Othello cannot call up from within him the forgiveness of Christ and, forgetting the Lord's Prayer and Christ's injunction (*Matt.* vi. 15), 'If ye forgive not men their trespasses, neither will your Father forgive your trespasses', loses his claim to God's mercy.[97]

[92] ibid., p. 1073.   [93] ibid., p. 1076.
[94] ibid., 1075.   [95] ibid., p. 1074.
[96] ibid., p. 1072. For examples of a similar criticism by unqualified inference from Biblical analogy, see R. W. Battenhouse, 'Shakespearean tragedy: A Christian Interpretation', *The Tragic Vision and the Christian Faith*, ed. N. A. Scott, N.Y., 1957, pp. 56–94.
[97] op. cit., p. 1071.

The critic, proceeding by reference to religious concepts, assumes that the character is doing so; instead of an analysis of his state of mind, we are given one of his theological situation; motive is replaced by religious concept – and emotion is left out of the account altogether. That there is a strain of elevated pity in Othello at this stage is quite certain; but his mention of the 'heavenly' nature of his sorrow is far from being a testimony to its theological virtue. Its reference is, characteristically, to himself and not to Desdemona; it is, in him, part of a process of presumption through which, by the accompanying inhumanity of a 'sorrow' which 'strikes where it doth love', he aspires to place himself

In seate of judgement in th'Almighties stead.[98]

As for his 'forgetting' the Lord's prayer and Christ's injunction at the point where Desdemona cries, 'And have you mercy too!' it must be said that neither the remembering nor the forgetting of such things is here in question. What is uppermost in Othello's mind, and dictates his action, is his strong emotion, his compelling purpose, his evidence of the handkerchief and his growing sense of the irresponsibility of Desdemona's exclamations concerning it. The effect of what Othello is about may subsequently be related to the theological text-book; but Shakespeare did not construct that situation by reference to such a text-book, but according to the full range of human passions – to which passions this critic, in his preoccupation with conceptual notions, is failing to respond. The pursuit of ideas 'which Shakespeare doubtless held but did not dramatize' must indeed result in failure to achieve 'a total appreciation of the tragedy'.[99]

Further instances of the disabling effect which a pre-eminent concern with theological concepts may have upon critical response are afforded by a writer for whom Shakespearian drama is a 'uniquely true and powerful *mundane* vision of human life from the *Christian* standpoint'.[100] This conviction enables him to trace the working-out of theological principles in what may be thought very unlikely moments of Macbeth's career. Thus, in the presence of the gracious Duncan (I. iv.), Macbeth

experiences an intense contrition which can lead to real repentance, to the 'doing' of everything he ought to do by way of service to his king in a humble, 'safe' (sane and healthy) spirit of loyal devotion.[101]

The 'supreme opportunity for such repentance' offered 'providentially' by Duncan's proclamation of Malcolm is allowed to slip; Macbeth's

---

[98] Spenser, *Faerie Queene* V, st. xi.
[99] S. Barnet: see p. 36 above.
[100] G. R. Elliott, 'Shakespeare's Christian, Dramatic Charity', *Theology* LVI, 1953, p. 461.
[101] *Dramatic Providence in 'Macbeth'*, Princeton University Press, 1958, p. 49.

acknowledgement of his 'black and deep desires', and of a will to do what 'the eye fears, when it is done, to see', is not encouraging :

> But we know that his present mood, occasioned by a sudden and unforeseen crisis, need by no means be final. The fact that he recognizes so plainly the blackness of his desires is promising.[102]

After Duncan's murder, the prospect of repentance opens widely upon the 'complete confession' represented by his acknowledgement of Banquo's royalty of nature, and the fell character of the deed that has put rancours in the vessel of his peace for the benefit of another;

> But pride intervenes, along with that other deadly sin (in the Christian viewpoint) . . . namely despairing unbelief in God's mercy. Macbeth resents, instead of submitting to, the divine punishment inflicted upon him through Banquo's aloof and just attitude.[103]

Last among other essays or gestures of penitence is Macbeth's declining to fight with Macduff – not out of fear, but out of

> willingness to sacrifice his lust of fame by way of compensating for the evil he has done.

Macduff, 'somewhat astonishingly', offers him the life of humiliating captivity that is essential 'if his penitence is to become real repentance'. But this final 'providential opportunity' is rejected 'only too naturally' by Macbeth's 'resurgent pride'.[104] The degree to which this critic misconstrues the passions of the moment is governed by his absorption in superimposing upon events, through the agency of the concepts he brings to them, a spiritual drama of his own creation.

It would appear, therefore, that while religious allusions and significances – assuming that they are what they appear to be – may be noted, and may be brought into interpretation in company with other significances, the attempt to make them the yardsticks of interpretation is misguided. As far as is possible – for the critic, like the dramatist, must be free to use all the resources that the experience of his age affords – the play must be judged by what it is in itself. An instance of this necessary restraint is to be found in a study of *Julius Caesar* by E. Schanzer.[105] He notes that, although the invitation Caesar addresses to those who will soon be his assassins,

> Good friends, go in, and taste some wine with me;
> And we, like friends, will straightway go together
> II. ii. 126–7),

---

[102] ibid., p. 52.   [103] ibid., p. 113.   [104] ibid., p. 26.
[105] 'The Problem of *Julius Caesar*', S.Q. VI, 1955, p. 297.

is probably inspired by Plutarch's coupling of Caesar's hospitality with his courtesy, the lines 'also call up memories of the ceremonial sharing of wine before another betrayal, memories which are strengthened by the kiss which Brutus gives to Caesar in the Capitol . . . and later by Antony's reproach of Brutus at Philippi:

> In your bad strokes, Brutus, you give good words.
> Witness the hole you made in Caesar's heart
> Crying "Long live! hail Caesar!"
>
> (V. i. 30ff.)

("And forthwith he came to Jesus, and said, Hail, master; and kissed him" [*Matt.* xxvi. 49]).'[106] The analogy is very suggestive, but Schanzer in considering it does not make it the key to the play's interpretation. To have done so would have been to ignore the fact that any assassination, as a betrayal and crucifixion of man, can arouse memories of that other crucifixion. Insistence upon the analogy must have brought embarrassing consequences; Shakespeare's Caesar, for example, can hardly be regarded as Christ-like – and if Brutus be a Judas, Mark Antony is certainly not a Peter or a Paul. Shakespeare may certainly have employed the analogy to bring home the full significance and horror of the deed; but if analogy is turned into an absolute, its wealth of significance will simply distort what the play contains. And it is also worth remembering that the resemblance might be quite accidental.

When, through the operation of any theory or method whatsoever, a true critical restraint is overborne, and a play is made over for interpretation in accordance with the religious significances it is held to embody, the ensuing criticism, falling short of the wholeness needed for true appreciation, can display more than most other forms of criticism a capacity for seeing meanings that are not there and for missing those that are. A single-minded attempt to relate *Antony and Cleopatra* to Christian concepts is made by Miss D. G. Cunningham, whose preliminary assumption is that Shakespeare habitually imposes Christian principles on manifestly pre-Christian material, pagan tradition having in any case been 'absorbed by Christianity a great many centuries before Shakespeare'.[107] She has no difficulty in distinguishing Christian concepts in the 'explicit statements of characters within the play' – notably in the words of Enobarbus, the 'accurate, reasonable commentator', who, in his condemnation of Antony for allowing his will to make itself lord of his reason, and his valour to prey upon reason, gives vent to 'the familiar Christian commonplace that men sin through being ill disposed towards

---

106 ibid., p. 304.
107 'The Characterization of Shakespeare's Cleopatra', *S.Q.* VI, 1955, p. 9.

their proper ends as rational beings'.[108] On the other hand, the sentiments of the lovers tend – like Antony's characteristic 'Let Rome in Tiber melt' – to involve a 'defiant inversion of traditional values'.[109] Antony confesses to Cleopatra that 'Thy beck might from the bidding of the gods /Command me', and proclaims that his will has been subservient to one 'whose bosom was my crownet, my chief end'. In so doing, Miss Cunningham declares,

> Antony clearly defines his tragedy in terms of the Christian moral finalism which has defined the action from the beginning . . . Cleopatra's bosom was his chief end – that is, his God. Surely the Christian implications are deliberate, for Antony is saying that he has substituted lust for the will of God, that he has made a principle out of defect of principle.[110]

Similarly, Cleopatra's protestation that 'Eternity was in our lips and eyes, /Bliss in our brows bent' is replete with impious suggestion :

> But any schoolboy knew that eternity was no such place, and that heavenly bliss was not to be found in earthly love of any kind, least of all in this kind which has already been condemned as irrational lust. The complete fusion of sensual love with religious terms in the language of this passage is repeated throughout the play and is especially characteristic of Cleopatra. The lovers' perverse location of the absolute in themselves and their love amounts in itself to an easily recognizable parody of the Christian life.[111]

The using of religious terminology to give expression to a human love is thus by definition to blaspheme. One wonders what reproof is implicit in Romeo's wish to 'make blessed my rude hand' (I. v. 54) by touching the hand of his beloved, or to 'steal immortal blessing from her lips' (III. iii. 37) – or, indeed, in the protestation of any human lover.

What takes place toward the end of the play, according to Miss Cunningham, is an attempt in Cleopatra to forsake the authority of the senses for the values of a permanent order; and her trying, in fact, 'to prepare for death by means of Christian repentance' accounts for the change in her character. Her efforts to die better than she has lived are analogous, we are told, to the familiar steps of the discipline of repentance inherited from the Middle Ages – the steps being 'the conviction of sin, the contrition of the heart, the faith that God will forgive sin, and the firm purpose of amendment of life'.[112] Cleopatra's actions in the last act are in their outlines comparable to those of the penitent Christian : she has achieved 'the humility and hard lesson that mortality is subject to

[108] ibid., p. 10.   [109] ibid., p. 13.   [110] ibid., p. 12.
[111] ibid., p. 13.   [112] ibid., p. 14.

43

the accidents of temporal life'; her resolve to do what is brave and noble after the high Roman fashion 'expresses faith in the possibility of a better life'; and in the weapons of defiance against Caesar that she names to Proculeius in the words,

> Sir, I will eat no meat, I'll not drink, sir;
> If idle talk will once be necessary,
> I'll not sleep neither. This mortal house I'll
>   ruin
>
> (V. ii. 49–51),

are to be found 'the penitential disciplines of fasting and mortification'.[113]

However, no rash pretension is made that all is well: it is noted that 'pride of life, dignity of royalty, and the old, extravagant yearning for Antony' intrude upon her pious intent. She unhappily keeps thinking about her lover, flirts with Dolabella and enslaves him 'by her famous charms', and

> maneuvers unscrupulously against Caesar and is out-maneuverd. To what end these maneuvers are directed, it is difficult to say.

They are indeed not exercises in piety. Nonetheless, in the 'immortal longings' to which she utters testimony lies a wish to 'put off the body of this death for the permanence of immortality and the crown of eternal life';[114] in that passage 'the essential conflict of the whole action is transferred to Cleopatra' – the conflict in fact consisting in the

> opposition between the 'pagan' concept of irrational sensuality and the central Christian concept of the reasonable soul, which embraces the noble Roman qualities by which Enobarbus and the soldiers measure Antony.[115]

Under this judgement, Cleopatra would have done better to transfer her affections to Caesar, who is the embodiment of that 'reasonable soul' which permits neither will nor valour to prey upon it, and is therefore presumably to be accounted the more worthy personage of the twain. However, Cleopatra embraces neither Caesar nor piety. 'Her movement toward eternity', Miss Cunningham declares, 'is recurrently imperiled by her baser life'.[116] She misguidedly construes death itself as a sensuous experience, in the concepts of a lover's pinch and the sweetness of balm; upon each of her renunciations 'the image of Antony intrudes itself'; and she is at length guilty of the final indecorum of conceiving Antony's kiss as her heavenly reward, and of the most unseemly of all haste in rushing to claim it in advance of Iras.[117] Because of these things, Miss Cunning-

113 ibid., p. 15.   114 ibid.   115 ibid., p. 16.
116 ibid.   117 ibid.

ham makes no claim that the final actions of Antony and Cleopatra 'conform to Christian teaching as to how men should meet death', but asserts that their deviation is constantly measured against that teaching – that it is

> the traditional scheme of Christian ethics which provides the standards of realism for judging the character of Cleopatra and the entire dramatic action.[118]

If this interpretation were true, *Antony and Cleopatra* would be the tragedy of unfulfilment, and its conclusion would be sombre. But in fact there can be few tragedies with so triumphant an ending. No audience would have Cleopatra other than she is. She retains her fascination not only to her last breath, but beyond it; even in death she appears to Caesar

> As she would catch another Antony
> In her strong toil of grace
>
> (V. ii. 344–5).

Her ending of her own life is effected as an achievement, and with a sense of rejoicing in which the audience shares; no less for them can it be said of the deed that

> It is well done, and fitting for a princess
> Descended of so many royal kings
>
> (V. ii. 324–5).

In recognition of her essential and moving royalty Charmian and Caesar concur; and it is fitting that the final tribute of Caesar should be his use of love's own terminology in celebration of the principle by which she has lived, and is to be immortalized:

> No grave upon the earth shall clip in it
> A pair so famous
>
> (V. ii. 356–7).

This interpretation of *Antony and Cleopatra* in accordance with religious concepts must be judged to have resulted in such mincing of the limbs of tragedy as was executed by the rugged Pyrrhus upon the unfortunate monarch of Troy.

[118] ibid., p. 17.

Chapter 2

TRAGEDY'S SECULAR APPEAL

It can therefore be said of religious significances in Shakespearian tragedy that they are difficult to identify, as they are not easy to apply once they have been distinguished. There is a general lack of definiteness in their expression, and little that could be regarded as clearly systematic in their use; and the essential difference between the dramatic and the conceptual is in itself a formidable barrier to religious interpretation. The attempt to interpret a play, therefore, as the embodiment of a religious concept or scheme readily produces narrowing and distortion, just as to regard a character as the embodiment of a principle is to do him, and the play, little justice – both tendencies being part of a single way of thought. That there are suggestions in the tragedies that could be termed religious is beyond doubt; but the wiser course would appear to be to assess the individual play, as a continuum of interwoven thought and action, on the level of 'immediate impression', rather than to try to relate it, through the suggestions it inspires, to the scheme of thought, or the reading of life, to which those suggestions appear to belong. The point at which the suggestion hardens, in the critic's mind, into the theological principle would appear to form part of the boundary and true limit of sound criticism.

In support of this judgement might be adduced an emphatic comment by G. Wilson Knight concerning the stage production of Shakespearian tragedy. He accepts the presence of profound theological ideas in *Othello*, and will go so far as to say that, in symbolic terms, 'Othello, Desdemona and Iago are Man, the Divine, and the Devil'. But he will not allow these significances to be directly conveyed by the dramatic presentation:

> The symbolic effects . . . are all in the poetry: Iago knows he is in league with hell-forces and often says so, while Desdemona is clearly equated imagistically with divinity. But the moment any of this is allowed to interfere with the expressly domestic and human qualities of the drama, you get disaster.[1]

[1] *Principles of Shakespearian Production*, 1936, p. 151 (not p. 57 as given; 1964 edn, p. 104), quoted by M. Rosenberg, 'In Defense of Iago', *S.Q.* VI, 1955, p. 151.

Whilst it cannot be affirmed that what is true of the theatre must necessarily apply to the work of the critic, it can be argued that the critic's
proper task is to judge a play 'With the same spirit that its author writ',
and that Shakespeare's chief purpose centred upon the stage rather than
upon the study, and involved the 'imitation'[2] rather than the explanation
of humanity. His clear intention is to create, not personifications, but
people – people realized so completely within the limits of the art form
that the strongest bonds of identification and sympathy may exist between
them and an audience. From this point of view it may be urged that

> We would not spare much pity for the troubles of Divinity; but we
> weep for the frail and lovely woman who was Desdemona; and in the
> same way we are strangely stirred by the wickedness of the man
> Iago.[3]

Similarly, Shakespeare's main intention in the plays themselves is to
convey and represent the process of life itself, as human experience finds it
to operate; to give

> the very age and body of the time his form and pressure[4]

and not to interpret it. And while such representation need not preclude
interpretation, and may indeed grow towards it, the ultimate meanings
which the dramatist may see must be held as incidental to his purpose;
and it is to the manifest purpose of the writer that the critic should in
the first place address himself. In fulfilling that purpose Shakespeare
achieved a great deal; it need not follow that his achievement ranged
beyond his clear intent. It cannot be denied that poetry's art of imitation
– its 'speaking picture', as Sidney describes it – is affirmed to have as its
object teaching as well as delight – that beneath the appearance of its
'conjectured likelihood'[5] are to be discerned the generalized principles of
human behaviour. But if those principles belong to ultimate truth, they
are themselves neither its measure nor its explanation. Poetry's consummate understanding of the human heart is not unaware of man's seeking
for truth and faith, yet need not know what is beyond man, or subscribe
to any system of belief. It may be that the height of Shakespeare's art
consists in his ability to 'buckle and bow the mind unto the nature of
things'[6] in the manner of the scientist's rationality; it need not follow
that his vision of human life contains intimations of the means whereby
it may be transcended, or even mastered. For this reason, Pope's dictum
must apply. What Shakespeare fails to assert, the critic must be wary of

[2] See *Hamlet* III. ii. 35.   [3] M. Rosenberg, op. cit., p. 151.
[4] *Hamlet* III. ii. 24–5.
[5] *An Apology for Poetry*, ed. G. Shepherd, 1965, pp. 101, 110.
[6] Francis Bacon, *The Advancement of Learning*, ed. W. A. Wright, 1920, II. iv. 2.

asserting; and though questions naturally spring from Shakespeare's work, the critic must avoid that remote parody of Lear's earnestness which would ask, in his penetrating yet abstracted vein,

> First let me talk with this philosopher.
> What is the cause of thunder?
>
> (III. iv. 151–2.)

Indeed, it is precisely because of the questions that are inherent in the plays that such theological echoes and significances as they contain can be held to be unrelated to any theological view or intention in their author. Thus W. Clemen can find in *King Lear* no assertion of meaning, but on the contrary an insistent questioning; the play is for him a perfect example of 'this art of Shakespeare's of raising questions but not answering them'.[7] In that play, he argues, far from taking over traditional beliefs and employing them as underlying principles of the action, Shakespeare is calling these traditional values in question.[8] This statement of Clemen's is a legitimate comment upon the failure of theological concepts within the play manifestly to dominate and direct the action. Here, and in his impression that a positive affirmation is made – though it appear as a glimmering upon the play's horizon[9] – Clemen is in agreement with L. C. Knights, for whom this affirmation 'is one which takes up into itself the questioning: it is an affirmation "in spite of" '. What the play constrains us to accept are such insistences as that, without love, human life is 'a meaningless chaos of competing egoisms'; they are 'fundamentally Christian';[10] but they are reached only

> by an act of profound individual exploration: the play does not take them for granted; it takes nothing for granted but Nature and the natural energies and passions.[11]

This impression that the mind of the playwright had no prepossessions – that, in all his human sensitivity and sympathy, his imagination remained disinterested and pure – has convinced many great critics that Shakespeare is not a religious writer – that the ideal world of his creative imagination was the world of man and morality rather than that of the gods and of theology,[12] and that his greatness consists in the unswerving fidelity to its secular appearance of a mind of extraordinary power.[13] Thus the judgement of *King Lear* must be founded, according to D. G. James, upon that play's inevitable claim to be a just rendering of mortal life as it is seen, not through the eyes of faith or of intellect, but through

---

[7] 'Shakespeare and the Modern World', *S.S.* XVI, 1963, p. 60.
[8] ibid., pp. 61–2. [9] ibid.
[10] *Some Shakespearian Themes*, 1959, pp. 117–18. [11] ibid., p. 91.
[12] H. B. Charlton, *Shakespearean Tragedy*, 1948, p. 232.
[13] A. C. Bradley, op. cit., p. 25.

those of 'the most powerful secular imagination the world has yet known'.[14] For the product of the artistic imagination issues from 'a peculiar labour of knowing', and its merits are those of a genuine exploration of experience; the imagination of a Shakespeare belongs fully to the life of reason; and, far from being devoted to titillating agreeable or other emotions,

> it may proceed with all the impersonality, the bleak labour of discovery, which animates the scientist or the philosopher; it has its own rational life; and the only desire which masters it is the desire shared by saint, philosopher, and scientist, to see things as they really are.[15]

Shakespeare trusts to his imagination as to an agency of truth, and, for this reason, will not for a moment abate his craftsmanly secularity:

> Shakespeare is precisely not a religious dramatist; he is committed to being loyal to his art; he will not make any facile surrender to faith; he will not feign 'the successes and issues of actions more just', as Bacon said, 'in retribution, and more according to revealed providence'; his job is to discover and see and show.[16]

From Shakespeare's dispassionate assessment of man's lot James will admit some transcendent, if not religious, values to emerge; he maintains that in *King Lear* the 'wholly good' is shown to be 'altogether proof against all that is brought against it'.[17] But for J. J. Lawlor this impression is not only unreliable in its subjectivity, but marks a failure to appreciate the massive truthfulness which is the ground both of Shakespeare's stature and his secularity. No matter what Lear has learned from the intimations that come to him, Lawlor argues,

> do we not feel, a moment later, when the last stroke falls, our obliviousness of all that has gone before? Repentance and forgiveness are the greatest goods; but it is act and consequence that play the decisive part: and with both sets of terms we are made to turn away, for once, from the gods above to man on this earth.[18]

The whole art and integrity of Shakespearian tragedy, according to this point of view, consists in this: that intimations of greater truths are only forthcoming through the dramatist's disciplined self-limitation to the mundane which is drama's proper field of inquiry; that 'act and consequence' are not made to yield to 'repentance and forgiveness', but retain a dominion that accords with the condition of human life; and that the significance of 'repentance and forgiveness' is left for the conscience

[14] *The Dream of Learning*, 1951, p. 80. [15] ibid., pp. 78–80.
[16] ibid., p. 90. [17] ibid., p. 124.
[18] *The Tragic Sense in Shakespeare*, 1960, p. 174.

of the reader to determine rather than made a basis for the events of the drama. If this be so, great tragedy conforms to what T. S. Eliot regards as the function of all artistic creation

> in imposing a credible order upon ordinary reality, and thereby eliciting some perception of an order *in* reality, to bring us to a condition of serenity, stillness and reconciliation; and then to leave us, as Virgil left Dante, to proceed toward a region where that guide can avail us no farther.[19]

Impressions arising from the tragedy may therefore bear out religious teaching without making the play an embodiment of theological formulations; and indeed, with such a play as *King Lear*, it would be unsafe to say anything other than that man is there set in the strictest relation to the forces that are naturally within and around him. As has recently been argued, if Lear learns his own limitations and the true values of humility and love, it is manifestly through the operation neither of conceptual thought nor of supernatural agency; on the contrary,

> It is the disciplining of this wilful man by all the conditions of life that we witness – by the consequence of his own deeds, by age and physical weakness, and by the powers of nature embodied in the storm.[20]

Whatever religious concepts may be held to spring in Lear's apprehension, or to be echoed in the play's situations, they cannot be observed to direct the drama's world.

This conviction forms the basis of Dr Johnson's disapproval. The fate of Cordelia, he declares, is 'contrary to the natural idea of justice, to the hope of the reader, and . . . to the faith of chronicles'; but it is interesting to note his admission that it may constitute 'a just representation of the common events of human life'.[21] Johnson's criticism is eloquent testimony to the playwright's main concern as being to represent human life rather than to explain or interpret it; Shakespeare, he writes,

> is so much more careful to please than to instruct, that he seems to write without any moral purpose. From his writings indeed a system of social duty may be selected, for he that thinks reasonably must think morally; but his precepts and axioms drop casually from him; he makes no just distribution of good or evil, nor is always careful to shew in the virtuous a disapprobation of the wicked.[22]

Johnson would never have written to the effect that Shakespeare was sufficiently far from being a conscious moralist as to be true to life in his

[19] *Poetry and Drama*, 1951, p. 35.
[20] J. W. Bennett, 'The Storm Within: the Madness of Lear', *S.Q.* XIII, 1962, p. 152.
[21] *Johnson on Shakespeare*, ed. W. Raleigh, 1957, p. 161.   [22] ibid., pp. 20–1.

writing, yet these lines might be held to contain a suggestion of such a heresy. For, either in the general or the specific sense, it is difficult to view the tragedies as related to, or eloquent of, a moral. A primary obstacle is the ambiguous status, from the standpoint of religious affirmation, of the heroes themselves. Johnson evidently did not expect that the heroes should be men of faith; he would have agreed with Harbage's impression that the virtues they seek and exercise relate almost exclusively to success in man's world,[23] though he might have questioned the judgement that 'even in Shakespeare's good men, devotion to the more transcendental virtues is apt to appear as disabling'.[24] It is not to be denied, however, that aspirations towards piety and saintliness are not commonly to be found in them; indeed, the absence of these aspirations might be held largely to constitute their essential and representative humanity. In this respect the comment of S. Barnet is very much to the point. Shakespeare's heroes are 'heroic' : that is, they are

> duly concerned about their strength and reputation, and have little in common with the heroes of Christianity . . . Altering Alcuin, we might well ask, 'Quid enim Othello cum Christo?'[25]

In this estimate of Othello, Barnet may be speaking more truly than he knows; but the ambiguity that is here evident extends to the plays which present these examples of humanity to us :

> Othello is a great man, but he performs an abominable deed. Aware of his crime, he enjoins the public to remember his honorable deeds (an action which, from a Christian point of view, might seem to show undue pride), and then kills himself. What is the moral? Is the play merely a parable acted out? Does Shakespeare draw a simple moral? Does he even wish us to draw one?[26]

The questions are well put. To them might be added the observation that the mind of the average beholder at the conclusion of one of Shakespeare's great tragedies is very far from being disposed to point the moral. Even after reflection and study, the process is not easy. To say that the moral of *Othello* is that husbands and wives should trust each other would be to put the tragedy in the category of the cautionary verse; to say that Shakespeare writes there in support of the ten commandments is from a literary point of view quite untrue. And can it be intellectually honest to describe *King Lear* as an essay upon the true nature of love, in the consciousness that the play investigates with such compelling and terrible

23 'Shakespeare's Ideal Man', *J. Q. Adams Memorial Studies*, Washington, 1948, p. 72.
24 ibid., p. 75.
25 'Some Limitations of a Christian Approach', *E.L.H.* XXII, 1955, p. 87.
26 ibid., p. 88.

power the nature of human existence? The more one tries to formulate an adequate moral, the greater grows the impression that one is confronting life itself, and that the endeavour is absurdly platitudinous.

A similar difficulty must arise if the status of characters within the play is viewed in the light of anything more far-reaching than a secular ethic. For the ethics of Christianity extend to a realm which drama cannot penetrate, and in which, by all appearances, it could scarcely subsist; and to apply them with any consistency is to require that the plays of Shakespeare should, in Barnet's phrase, be 'acted out to Judgement Day'.[27] The embarrassment attending such a position has already been evident in the case of Cleopatra; her tragedy becomes lamentable indeed. The same can be said of Othello : his fate, in traditional terms, must be not only death but damnation. The issue has been variously decided by critics;[28] but the reaction of an audience to the character concerned cannot possibly be conceived as varying. This is true whether the play is seen as an enactment of eternal truth on the pattern of the moralities or as strictly related to the ethics of Christianity : the beholders will not suddenly transpose their thinking to the secular level in order to allow the hero to escape reprobation and hell-fire;[29] their consistency in that respect will be related to the consistency of the author. The conclusion appears inescapable that Shakespeare 'does not treat suicide in a consistent Christian manner';[30] for although a case might be made out for Othello's damnation, it is hard to imagine that in the persons of Romeo and Juliet we are studying, in dramatic terms, the earthly careers of damned spirits. And if a decision is not possible in so clear-cut an instance as this, similar decisions are hardly possible elsewhere :

> If we are unwilling to apply to Shakespeare's characters the universal condemnation of suicides . . . then we must abandon the entire process of theologizing Shakespeare's plays on any consistent basis.[31]

Similarly, the status of the person and virtues of Cordelia may be inferred in the beholder's conscience, but they may not be judged by the critic in strict accordance with a Christian ethic : any such judgement is out of keeping with the drama's own consistency, and can be shown to clash with it. Thus O. J. Campbell, in facing the problem raised by Cordelia's murder and Lear's grief, insists that what is of eternal significance in Cordelia is of primary significance for the dramatic critic :

> It is not what the earthly creature Cordelia *is*, but what she *represents* that is important for the meaning of the play. It is her spirit not her

---

[27] ibid.
[28] See ibid. for a list of critics at variance on this point.
[29] ibid.   [30] ibid.
[31] R. M. Frye, *Shakespeare and Christian Doctrine*, London, 1963, p. 24.

bodily presence that redeems her father . . . she is hanged, as Christ was crucified, so that mankind might be saved.[32]

Barnet's method of questioning this judgement is to show that it is not related to the working-out of the play :

he fails to explain just how her death saves the King, and why it is necessary when her mere presence had (as Campbell says) already restored health of soul to the King.[33]

Another instance arises from the apparent utterance of joy which Lear makes with his dying breath. Basing what he says upon the pattern of the morality play as well as upon the true meaning of Cordelia's virtues, Campbell maintains that the joy in question springs from Lear's having discovered

in her unselfish God-like love the one companion who is willing to go with him through Death up to the throne of the Everlasting Judge.[34]

Barnet's response is that this evaluation is dramatically inadmissible :

But Cordelia is very dead, and Lear's discovery is a mistake, not a poet's allegorical statement that love is eternal . . . [Lear's] joy is the product of an error, and the audience feels not merely relief for his death but also horror for his ultimate false perception.[35]

To apply a Christian ethic consistently to persons and to virtues in the tragedies is to be driven, not only to allegory, but to the ignoring of a drama's proper sequence and immediate effect – not to mention such proliferation of Christ-figures in the plays as would rank Timon of Athens with Cordelia, Desdemona, and the Duke in *Measure for Measure*.[36] The attempt to moralize upon the basis of a transcendental system, in that it tends to set the critic at a distance from the full impact of the drama, emphasizes that in Shakespeare dramatic creation was neither inspired nor sustained by adherence to a formal scheme of belief and value; for

the ethics of the plays partake of Christian ethics, but they are not based, as Christian ethics in fact are, upon the eschatology of the Christian system.[37]

Shakespeare's preoccupation is with man as a phenomenon; it cannot be said of him that he is concerned with man as a creature in the sense

---

[32] 'The Salvation of Lear', *E.L.H.* XV, 1948, p. 107.
[33] op. cit., p. 91.
[34] op. cit., p. 107.
[35] 'Some Limitations', p. 91.
[36] G. Wilson Knight, *The Wheel of Fire*, 1949, pp. 236, 82.
[37] Barnet, op. cit., p. 87.

that it can be said of a Dante or a Milton. If it could, he would never in the first instance have achieved the height of tragedy; for the tragic belongs to the secular, and must appear insubstantial in that unearthly light which would dissolve the conflict on which its significance depends.[38] So must the characteristic undertakings of Shakespeare's heroes; they are impelled in their careers by loves which reach but to dust – as Sidney expressed it, and Hamlet came to understand: from the viewpoint of eternity they were all pestilent complete knaves, and Othello a direct villain. But in Shakespearian tragedy, it would appear, as in life itself,

> this eternal blazon must not be
> To ears of flesh and blood.[39]

A 'just distribution of good or evil' and an enactment of the 'faith of chronicles' is not to be found in the tragedies – and it is scarcely to be achieved by criticism. The critic may assess the qualities, motives and purposes of the characters, and trace cause and effect and all inter-relationships; but if he seeks to point the moral with finality, he does so in accordance with his own schemes of thought rather than Shakespeare's. And he does so also, it might be argued, through his ignoring the proper function and limits of the tragic:

> Tragedy does not claim to offer the whole truth, nor does it require an act of faith to be believed. It sets forth a kind of experience which every man knows, presenting suffering and death as the hard facts which most men feel them to be.[40]

[38] Una Ellis-Fermor, *The Frontiers of Drama*, 1945, p. 5.
[39] *Hamlet* I. v. 21–2.
[40] Barnet, op. cit., p. 86.

Chapter 3

THE ROLE OF THE EXPERIENCING MIND

It is the quality of life, rather than its meaning, that tragedy endeavours to bring to definition. But the statement that 'it does not claim to offer the whole truth' requires a certain qualification. In the first place, in the process of presenting suffering and death, the joys, the achievements, and the very being of man are also displayed. Very much more is shown to us, therefore, than a mere aspect of life. To manifest the world which humanity experiences is not necessarily to explain it; but it is to give rise to the question whether the meaning of life is deducible from its very quality. And in this respect it is further to be noted that part of the appreciation of tragedy is the heightened, if not exhilarating, sense of meaning and significance which it induces: the knowledge it conveys is, in Sidney's term, 'heart-ravishing'.[1] This response cannot be ignored, since it represents in all probability the 'motive and the cue' for criticism as it does the essence of the poet's achievement. Whilst, therefore, the critic may be wrong in attempting to deduce from the inner harmony and organization of the tragedy a system of value by which the qualities and events both of the play and of life in general may be judged, it may well be that from the phenomenon of tragedy itself, as from a kind of intense reflection of the life man knows, some revelation of meaning is to be gained. The aim of the critic, in short, may be misdirected in its ignoring the uniqueness and the integrity of the artistic creation, as also in the characteristically human preference for minute dissection as opposed to consideration of the whole; but the aim in itself is legitimate, as it is probably inevitable. The more tragedy is a realization of 'the kind of experience which every man knows', the more it must give rise to ultimate questions. The one thing the critic must beware of is the assumption that because a play shows a knowledge of

> all qualities, with a learned spirit,
> Of human dealings,[2]

[1] *Apology*, ed. Shepherd, p. 98.
[2] *Othello* III. iii. 259–60.

it must therefore be constructed upon principles which transcend, or even explicate, the human.

This assumption lies, tacitly or otherwise, behind much Shakespeare criticism. If it is put aside, there is room for a consideration which, though it appears paradoxical at first sight, might yet show the way to a proper religious evaluation. There is a sense in which the resolute secularity of Shakespearian tragedy not only keeps it 'true to life', but makes it a confirmation, in the wider sense, of the Christian truths it never explicitly affirms. In its determined adherence to the 'hard facts' of the human condition – a propensity which it shares with other tragedy – lies a possible means of reconciliation. Though Shakespeare does not affirm the truths of the Christian religion, writes J. J. Lawlor, there is nothing in his universe that appears to contradict them :

> There is in *King Lear* nothing to impugn any doctrine of repentance and forgiveness. We see only what our unthinking acceptance of such a doctrine may mean . . . and has commonly meant, the illusion that we have made an end of the offence when we have repented the offending. . . . This, of course, far from constituting any divergence from Christianity, might be called a profoundly Christian truth; the guilt of sin and the fact of sin – wrong-doing as carrying consequences for our fellow-men, creatures set like us in time – have ever been held inseparable in practical Christian teaching. . . . Shakespeare preserves truth by refusing the fiction in the soul.[3]

Christianity is a religion revealed and manifested in history and through human experience; a strict adherence to the 'hard facts' of human experience can never, if it is true, do it injustice or mischief. It is, on the contrary, the attempt to cast a transcendental light upon that experience – to show what the experience means, rather than what it is – that might be held to constitute the greater danger to a Christian perspective, though, ironically enough, Christian teachings will be employed for the purpose. For it must be the peculiar effect of applying a system of theological credence either to the creation of great tragedy or to its criticism, and thereby endeavouring in thoroughgoing manner to

> raise and erect the mind, by submitting the shows of things to the desires of the mind,[4]

that it abstracts both the play and the beholder from the mortal world of 'doing or suffering'. The incongruity between theological concept and the process of dramatic creation is apparent; the attempt in itself to reconcile settled formulation with raw event must needs impose such a

[3] *The Tragic Sense in Shakespeare*, 1960, p. 175.
[4] Bacon, *Advancement of Learning* II. iv. 2.

degree of order upon disorder, and detachment upon involvement, as is never to be met with in real life; and the outcome, if it please the theologian or the moralist, must do so at the expense of the vitalities and dynamisms of man's world. For that world, though it be the basis of a natural theology, precisely does not bear witness to a system of Christian theology – and the endeavour to make it do so must consequently be termed a 'fiction in the soul'. Any attempt to bring to bear upon the human life represented in drama conditions other than those secular existence imposes upon it is by definition a shrinking from history and from fact, and must create a 'feigned history' beyond Bacon's meaning;[5] and the question is whether such shrinking and feigning can be as great a help to a true Christian perspective as its contrary. For Christianity consists neither in a doctrinal code nor a philosophy nor a system of ethics, however much use it makes of these things; it is, on the contrary, as intimately bound up with the process of living and experiencing as is tragedy itself. To direct the operation of tragedy in accordance with theological formulations in order that it might be their exemplar, and constitute a kind of prologue of Heaven – to urge, as it were, the beholder to

Lay thy finger thus, and let thy soul be instructed – [6]

though it be of benefit to man's understanding, must withhold and belie the intensities of man's experience in his world.

Christian experience, it is true, is inclusive of such intimations from a realm beyond mortality as must change a human perspective; and there is in drama a *genre* which avowedly uses the mundane as a symbol of the eternal, and patterns the seemingly secular upon the truths of the world to come. Yet this drama, particularly in its proneness to rely upon a formulated system of thought, might perhaps be said to find its being in response to what has been apprehended and not in the apprehension itself: to concern itself with the content of Christian experience rather than with its living intensity. Miss Ellis-Fermor's comments on so-called 'religious' drama bear out this impression. It is not an accident, she writes, that the main body of medieval 'religious' drama and of much that succeeds it

is not concerned with any essential part of religious experience but preoccupied instead either with illustrating the dogmas or ethics incidental to some specific form of organized belief, or with presenting some aspect of the conflict set up by the claims of this ethic and other passions which actually form the main tissue of the play. There are several hundred plays of this kind, but how often do we find a play in which the fire and illumination that is the essence of religious experience becomes the central force?[7]

5 ibid.   6 *Othello* II. i. 221–2.   7 *Frontiers*, p. 5.

It is with the intensities of the secular rather than the ostensibly religious life that drama is overwhelmingly successful. And since the essential Christian awareness is embedded in, and part of, our ordinary mortal experience, the drama that is a just representation of the 'common events of human life' – which not only urges upon the beholder, 'Expose thyself to feel what wretches feel', but ensures that he is so exposed – may in this sense have a rightful claim against the drama which, in the assumed interests of a higher truth, sets forth a world that never was. The criticism which has essayed a religious interpretation of Shakespearian tragedy has tended to seek in it correspondences with Christian formulations; but in so doing it has been the representative of only one of what might be called two divergent impulses or urges in Christian thinking. The one (which could be said to be partly Classical in inspiration) seeks to place the human world and man's powers and endeavours in such relation to a universal scheme as must proclaim a harmony and create in man assurance of the relevance of his condition to ultimate being and truth. The other (which it could be argued is in its inspiration more strictly Biblical) insists upon the ultimate disparity between the realm, powers and ambitions of man and the life and things of the spirit, and proclaims that the way to harmony, and to assurance for man, lies in the over-coming of 'the world' through an enabling from beyond it. And while the categories of 'the world' employed in these two emphases may differ, and thus show a way out of the apparent contradiction, the emphases themselves are extremely unlike, and may point to a real division in the human mind.[8] The peculiar concern of tragedy is with what must be 'overcome'. In that great tragedy, therefore, reveals to the beholder the nature both of mortal man and of his world – in that its greatness, indeed, consists in proportion to its giving a clear and just estimate of the forces within the secular human condition – it may through devotion to the secular be in its way a better instrument for bringing the questing soul to the attainment of ultimate truth than a drama constructed upon overtly religious principles. The latitude which Bacon allowed poetry for the ordering of human actions and events 'more according to revealed providence'[9] is precisely that 'handling of final causes, mixed with the rest in physical inquiries' that he deprecated in contemporary scientific investigation;[10] and it may be that the purity of approach he recommended, which he was confident would remove obscurity and lead in the end to an understanding of those final causes which were not to be assumed or engrafted from another discipline, should extend to drama as to natural philosophy. And as for the reasoning that the contemplation of the mundane world through the drama, in the exclusion of what has

[8] See Section II, pp. 99–100.
[9] *Advancement* II. iv. 2.   [10] ibid., II. vii. 7.

been revealed from beyond it, must itself be a distortion, the words Bacon used concerning the physical sciences might in return be applied to tragedy : that the mingling of revealed with natural truth

> undoubtedly will make an heretical religion, and an imaginary and fabulous philosophy.[11]

It may therefore be said that it is of the essence of tragic drama, and ultimately speaking its true task, to reveal the natural human condition, rather than to set forth something 'imaginary and fabulous' by way of interpreting it. The very secularity of tragedy would thus constitute its religious potential; or, as it has been somewhat differently expressed by a modern writer,

> It is perhaps the highest function of tragedy to hold steadily before us those 'realities we should like to forget, if forgetting would abolish them'.[12]

What Sidney said about the disparagement heaped upon the poetry of the Bible because of its secular appeal is no less applicable to tragic poetry's objectivity :

> But they that with quiet judgement will look a little deeper into it, shall find the end and working of it such as, being rightly applied, deserveth not to be scourged out of the Church of God.[13]

Tragedy insists that 'security /Is mortals' chiefest enemy' : it reveals to them their acquiescence in their own shortcomings and in the terms of a strictly mortal existence. In demonstrating the scope and limitations of the reality to which men commit themselves, tragedy performs an exercise which is thoroughly in keeping with its religious origins. But its origins are human no less than religious : it springs from secular life as it does from religion, since man is inescapably involved in the tragic as he is necessarily caught up in relationship to the Divine. Thus the dispassionate inquiry into man's secular condition, as it is the proper undertaking of the tragedian, must also be a true religious function. This is a perception which K. Muir comes close to proclaiming. Despite Shakespearian tragedy's being 'manifestly secular', he writes,

> Tragedy is necessarily concerned with man (as Newman says) 'implicated in some terrible aboriginal catastrophe'; and from the very nature of man Shakespeare rediscovers what he may not, as a poet, assume.[14]

He also comes to the realization that the religious import of tragedy is to be sought, not so much in a play's concepts and literary content, but

---

[11] ibid., II. vi. 1.   [12] Lawlor, *The Tragic Sense*, p. 180.
[13] *Apology*, ed. Shepherd, 1965, p. 99.
[14] 'Shakespeare and the Tragic Pattern', *Proc. Brit. Acad.* XLIV, 1958, p. 158.

in the awareness of the audience that experiences it. The thoughts of Macbeth, considered in the fullness of their imaginative appeal, would indicate that life is meaningless;

> In fact the meaninglessness is transcended, not for Macbeth but for us – we realize, that is, that life is not 'a tale /Told by an idiot, full of sound and fury, /Signifying nothing' because we know that Macbeth has destroyed the significance of life by his own acts. The moral retribution which has overtaken him reinforces for the audience the conviction that life is full of meaning, that a moral order exists however much the individual may violate it.[15]

It is from such an understanding of the nature of tragedy's outlook upon the mortal world that profound conclusions can be reached by a criticism that will in itself venture little further than a consideration of material cause and effect. Thus R. Speaight, perceiving Macbeth to be destroyed by the counter-forces he had himself set in motion, and holding that 'the poet's personal beliefs are indistinct', is yet constrained to admit, from the play's revelation of good springing from evil, that 'no ending in Shakespeare is more profoundly theological'.[16] The question must arise, however, whether similar affirmations can be made of tragedies whose conclusions are unrelieved by evidence of a moral order that makes a 'just distribution' of good and evil, but reveal only a rough justice, or an order that appears unpleasing and harsh to mortal eyes.

From this position – if it is accepted – it is at once clear that the search for religious meaning in Shakespeare's plays does not come to an end the moment it is decided that they are devoted to man's secular experience. Muir either declines to adopt the position he comes near, or is not concerned to explore the possibilities it reveals, but remains content with the assertion of secularity. Shakespeare, he concludes, always refused to impose an ideological pattern on his material; the only pattern that finally emerges is an artistic one :

> As a poet he was primarily concerned with imposing order on chaos, with extracting the maximum significance from the situation with which he was dealing. He might, if the material allowed, show that crime does not pay, or reveal that pride is destructive and self-love suicidal. But such morals are not imposed on his material : they emerge as the simple facts of life.[17]

Muir is sure that significance is there; but he does not undertake to show what it is. He will only go so far as to say that if Shakespeare had a

---

[15] ibid., p. 159.
[16] *Nature in Shakespearian Tragedy*, 1955, p. 68, quoted by I. Ribner, '*Macbeth*: the Pattern of Idea and Action', *S.Q.* X, 1959, p. 148.　　　　[17] op. cit., p. 162.

theory of tragedy, it would have been that its function was didactic : for the plays reveal in him a concern

> to hold the mirror up to nature, to present particular examples of disaster, caused partly by human error and evil, and, by stripping them of accidentals, to offer both a mirror for magistrates and a commentary on human existence, in all its terror and in all its glory.[18]

Two questions arise immediately from this conclusion. The first concerns the exact whereabouts of the commentary and the precise nature of its message. A mirror, of course, cannot comment, and there is a sense in which Shakespeare's plays merely reflect; but there is a sense also in which the intense realization of life which Shakespeare's creative imagination achieved must needs reveal, and it is this which Muir recognizes. The question is, what is revealed, and whether it can be formulated. The categories that Muir rests upon, it is to be noted, are 'nature', 'examples of disaster', 'human error and evil', and 'human existence, in all its terror and in all its glory' – to which might be added what is contained in his observation that the tragic hero falls through 'Fate, his own faults, and evil in others'.[19] The second question is related to the first : whatever the commentary is, how can it not have theological implications? If it is in any way concerned with 'nature', 'disaster', 'faults', 'evil' and 'fate' – and it is difficult to understand how it could avoid them – its affirmations must partake of the theological and the metaphysical, in that they must raise the subject of ultimate standards and ultimate reality, and bring in the more immediate connotations which those words have in human experience.

What is quite clear is that tragedy must at least raise ultimate questions, if it does not answer them : that a revelation of the 'terror' and the 'glory' of human existence is also by its nature an appeal for further revelation. Its impression of waste, as Bradley has noted, brings that profounder sense of mystery which makes it a type of the mystery of the whole world, and evokes from us the cry, Why does man exist 'if this beauty and greatness only tortures itself and throws itself away?'[20] It also becomes evident that the more a tragedy is felt to approximate to a true commentary upon human existence, the more difficult it becomes to extract and formulate its message.[21] The immediate explanation may be a literary one : excellence in tragic achievement, and the true tragic eloquence, may subsist in the function of reflecting and the refusal to transcend the medium. But the question of its 'commentary' and significance then remains unresolved. Can it not be that the truest intimations

---

[18] *Shakespeare : the Great Tragedies* (Writers and their Work), Longmans, 1961, p. 38.
[19] ibid. [20] *Shakespearean Tragedy*, p. 23.
[21] See p. 73–5 below.

reach man as experience rather than as intellectualized concepts; that the 'commentary' so assuredly postulated of Shakespearian tragedy lies precisely in Muir's vouchsafed categories of nature, disaster, error, evil, fate, terror and glory; and that, in fact, the best, and ultimately the only, commentary upon the life of mortal man is the life of mortal man itself? And can this be in part the reason why formal concepts are not compatible with, and must ultimately distort, what Shakespeare is presenting? May it not, in short, be the strict task of tragedy to enable us to rediscover 'from the very nature of man' what we ourselves, as mere men, have through choice or indifference come to ignore?

This is by no means to say that important meanings are not manifest in Shakespearian tragedy; it is simply to insist that they 'are not imposed on his material', but 'emerge as the simple facts of life'. If the principles upon which the characters act thus derive from the natural human propensities rather than from metaphysical evaluations of those propensities, the emergent meanings can be of ultimate import only in so far as the secular existence of man is eloquent of ultimate meaning. The 'commentary on human existence' therefore lies in its finality in the plays themselves and can scarcely be separated from them; and it is this realization that their reading of life is 'coextensive with the plays themselves' which leads Miss Ellis-Fermor to declare that their meaning can be grasped only 'by a lifetime spent in their world'.[22] Their theological significance, further, will come as intimation rather than as concept or doctrine, and derive from the effect of the whole rather than from the explicit comment of a part. If the secularity of the tragedies is accepted, however, a new significance attaches itself to any intimations thus gained : they are seen, not as the result of the playwright's committal and formal tribute to certain doctrines, but as revelations from life itself – as a confirmation, and not an exemplification, of a theological understanding, and therefore if anything of greater moment, though of less precision. Thus Lear's turning, in his need to comfort his child at the onset of unknown perils, to a view of existence which transcends and scorns the merely mortal under the impulsion of his love, or Macbeth's inability to pronounce amen and his conviction of having murdered sleep, are suggestions of great power because of the circumstances of their utterance and their deriving from the very instinct of man's awareness. But they remain suggestions only. The derivation that invests them with significance prevents their being detached from the play and turned into principles by which the dramatic action may be said to be ruled. Their import can thus only be known to the experiencing conscience of the beholder through their relation to the play as a whole – as G. Wilson Knight is aware in laying it down as a principle that 'At every moment

[22] *Shakespeare the Dramatist and other papers*, ed. K. Muir, 1961, p. 11.

the production itself should seem *aware* of the whole play's meaning'.[23] It is not so much in particular meanings, therefore, but in the presenting life to the living, that tragedy must make its appeal, and establish its truth.

Such particular meanings as become clear, for instance in the examples given above, though they may be held to harmonize with Christian concepts, will not be explicitly Christian; and they will come within the scope of R. M. Frye's warning that

> Shakespeare's total dramatic structure could as well be supported by the ethics of the virtuous heathen as by those of the Christian church.[24]

If the limited task of tragedy is to reveal the mortal world, however – if its very secularity is indeed its religious potential – the virtues that come to light can hardly be other than secular, and acceptable to the heathen. The ethics that are in question emanate from a human situation which both pagans and Christians experience, and which is the very bed-rock of Christianity. Not only was that situation the ground and the means of Christianity's inception, but it is the basis also of Christian conviction: for if the secular experience of man bore no strict relation to the Christian order and experience, upon what ground could the unconverted and converted alike find Christianity relevant to the quality and condition of the existence they know? The transcendent requires that there be something to transcend, and that what is to be transcended should bear some relation to, and play some part in, the transcending. If the virtues that arise from a secular situation are found to approximate to those required by a theological understanding of life, they may in their achievement constitute a foreshadowing of Christian truth, and in their shortcoming provide a demonstration of its necessity. For worldly experience is the arena within which Christianity must prove itself; and virtues and actions which cannot be identified as being directed according to a Christian ethic or concept are not for this reason outside the scope of a Christian interpretation – provided the attempt is not made to base such interpretation upon definitions offered by the plays, for they offer none. Even so outstanding an act as the sacrifice which Cordelia makes for her father, though it be seen as one upon which 'The gods themselves throw incense' (V. iii. 21), could nonetheless be the work of a 'virtuous pagan'. In evident disproof of this judgement, G. F. Danby argues cogently that the elaborate procedure by which Edgar undertakes to 'cure' his father's despair arises from doctrinal concepts. Quoting Coverdale's *A Spiritual and Most Precious Pearl*, he notes the instruction to Christians under adversity to 'banish all manner of heavy, sorrowful, and desperate fancies and imaginations of the mind', and claims that Edgar's conduct in assur-

---

[23] *Principles of Shakespearian Production*, 1936, p. 54.
[24] *Shakespeare and Christian Doctrine*, London, 1963, pp. 94–5.

ing the blind Gloucester that he has jumped from the cliff and been miraculously preserved is consistent with the purpose of inducing in his father 'a right judgement and opinion of all things that happen and chance'. Of Edgar's reference to the work of 'the clearest gods' (IV. vi. 74), Danby concludes,

> of course, it might be that Edgar's deception is the means taken by the clearest Gods to intervene. In the realm of real spiritual advancement the end justifies the means.[25]

Yet this deed too might have been the action of human kindness rather than of Christian conformity – in spirit akin to the substitution of a painted leaf on a wall for a last autumnal leaf, effected by a ne'er-do-well artist to allay the despair, and speed the recovery, of a sick girl.[26] Both actions in origin and by category might not be Christian: yet they relate powerfully to Christian experience, whether they are the work of pagans or not, in that they arise from, and are eloquent of, man's life in his world, showing the conditions upon which Christianity must operate. From this point of view, whether the event or the virtue is susceptible of categorical definition may not be the most important thing about its religious significance. The critic proceeding by theological concept may in fact be likened to the moral philosophers whom Sidney pictures as 'casting largesse as they go of definitions, divisions, and distractions' in their scorn of secular writing. For, like them, the conceptual critic is inclined soberly to doubt

> whether it is possible to find any path so ready to lead a man to virtue as that which teacheth what virtue is – and teacheth it not only by delivering forth his very being, his causes, and effects, but also by making known his enemy, vice, which must be destroyed, and his cumbersome servant, passion, which must be mastered, by showing the generalities that containeth it, and the specialities that are derived from it; lastly, by plain setting down, how it extendeth itself out of the limits of a man's own little world to the government of families, and maintaining of public societies.[27]

It is to the attitude that a demonstration of man's possibilities in his situation, if it is just, must in some way contribute to the Christian cause, that G. Boas finally came in his attempt to link Shakespeare's drama with Christianity. He states his conviction in terms which closely resemble those used by Muir in declaring Shakespeare's intention in tragedy:

> Surely it would be making of religion a very narrow thing to see no element of it in Shakespeare merely because he does not talk the

---

[25] 'King Lear and Christian Patience', The Cambridge Journal I, 1947–8, p. 313.
[26] O. Henry, 'The Last Leaf', The Best of O. Henry, ed. 'Sapper', London, 1960, pp. 285–93.
[27] Apology, ed. Shepherd, 1965, p. 105.

language of ecclesiasticism or concern himself with problems of theology which are outside his purpose. If to bring home to men, with unparalleled sanity and sensibility and power, the beauty and majesty of the universe, the immense significance of human life, the vast occasions it affords for good and evil, the horrors which folly and crime bring in their train, and the loveliness of simple virtue: in fact, to vindicate throughout that what matters is not the chances and mis-chances of fortune but the spiritual qualities which they bring forth to meet them: if this is not furthering in its widest sense the cause of religion, religion is a very different thing from what Christ intended it to be.[28]

Boas goes further than he has warrant: the tragedies in themselves are very far from vindicating that chances and mischances do not matter; and the 'significance' of human life they simply do not show – they are concerned with its fact and its features. But he recognizes, as Muir does in a different way, that tragedy, which concerns itself with what is univer-sally human – which presents humanity to itself – must be related to Christianity, and that the relation is to be found through experience rather than in concept. The emphasis towards which both writers come is that the religious activity of tragedy lies in what it is as a revelation of man's life, and in its direct apprehension by the experiencing mind rather than in anything it formally says. A similar realization that the highest truth must be lively in nature, and a subsequent concern with man as experiencing rather than with formulations from experience, is to be met with in contemporary philosophy. As a commentator on the writings of Edmund Husserl puts the matter,

> The truth about existence is not something to be grasped in abstract concepts: 'we are inside the truth, and evidence is experience of the truth'.[29]

If the impress upon us in the witnessing of tragedy is that of life itself – if during the 'two hours' traffic' we are with our kindled sympathies and intensified perceptions 'inside the truth' – our experience must in some sense be of a religious character. Tragedy's peculiar attribute of the stately and the solemn is universally recognized; the phenomenon itself, though set in various traditions, makes an unfailing appeal; and there is a readi-ness, even among those whose approach to religious interpretation is more strictly doctrinal, to acknowledge the presence of

> structural and thematic elements in Jacobean drama . . . which relate Shakespeare to the Wakefield Master – and to Sophocles.[30]

[28] 'Shakespeare and Christianity', *The Shakespeare Review* I, 1929, pp. 96–7.
[29] P. B. Rice, 'Existentialism and the Self', *The Kenyon Review* XII, 1950, p. 308.
[30] W. M. Merchant, 'Shakespeare's Theology', *R.E.L.* V, 1964, p. 73.

But if the kinship of all tragedies in their approach to ultimate meaning is recognized, the precise grounds of relationship are hard to determine; and, it might be added, the attempt to find affinities from religious concepts within the plays must tend to obscure the possibility that likeness springs from the sharing of a common religious function rather than a common body of belief. Be that as it may, the criticism of Shakespearian tragedy which A. C. Bradley made on the basis of Aristotle's definitions has, as H. Weisinger points out, exercised great authority, if indeed it has not been more felicitous than any other. The fact may be held to witness to the truth

> that, as a consequence of the nature of tragedy in general, both Aristotelian theory and Greek practice are germane to the consideration of what Shakespeare wrote, even assuming that he knew nothing at all about them. What is missing is a bridge, valid on aesthetic, historical, and ideological grounds, which can link Athenian and Elizabethan tragedy together in such a way as to close the gap in Bradley's treatment. Such a link would have to fit the pattern of Athenian tragedy, retain its vitality in the Middle Ages, and appear again as central to Shakespearian tragedy. Moreover, it would have to include within itself the possibility of a valid parallel between the Greek idea of *hybris* and the Christian doctrine of sin; it would have to be able to create a pattern of tragic action applicable both to Sophocles and to Shakespeare; and it would have to be able to take into account the parallel dialectical transformation of Greek myth into Greek tragedy and of Christian exemplum into Elizabethan tragedy.[31]

The 'bridge' that is required must be a common system of religious affirmation – if tragedy in Shakespeare can be shown to be founded upon religious concepts. But if, on the other hand, the function of his tragedy be a just reflection and revelation of the world of man, the 'bridge' must consist of a common experience and apprehension of the human condition that is true in itself, and can thus become the basis for a reaching toward ultimate conclusions.

[31] H. Weisinger, 'The Study of Shakespearian Tragedy since Bradley', *S.Q.* VI, 1955 p. 396.

Chapter 4
POETIC CREATION AND CONCEPTUAL THINKING

The difficulty of identifying theological concepts within Shakespeare's tragedies, and the dangers that beset the attempt to make them the standards of interpretation, have already appeared from the discussion, and have indicated the essential unlikeness between the formal concept and the process of dramatic creation. This unlikeness may be the cause of an initial hesitancy to discuss possible religious significances in the tragedies which W. M. Merchant has observed in many critics, who have reacted

> as though the existence of credal assumptions in a dramatist's work implied a crippling limitation of his creative power.[1]

Their impression may be seen as arising not from the mingling of disciplines in itself but from an awareness of the artist's manner of working, and of the exceedingly personal nature of literary creation. As W. B. Yeats has observed,

> All art is founded upon personal vision, and the greater the art, the more surprising the vision; and all bad art is founded upon impersonal types and images, accepted by average men and women out of imaginative poverty and timidity.[2]

To the creation both of the vision and of the personality the impersonal formulations of theology may have contributed; but to the transmuting power itself they are alien, nor can their categories readily be thrust upon the 'rich and strange' product of the artistic experience. The dynamic vision to which a great dramatist responds, and the 'high-flying liberty'[3] of his response, are not of a nature to pause for reference before conceptual formulations of possibility. What the artist does constantly refer to is the form which gives expression to his work and constitutes the true limitation of its thought. Through that form the vision is both sustained

[1] 'Shakespeare's Theology', R.E.L. V, 1964, p. 72.
[2] W. B. Yeats, Plays and Controversies, 1923, p. 154.
[3] Sidney, Apology, ed. Shepherd, 1965, p. 99.

at its intensity and enabled to be communicated; yet it is itself the product of the vision it substantiates. It can be said of literature as of other realms of artistic activity that

> There seems to have been a pre-existing affinity between the form and its content as though they were afore-prepared for marriage.[4]

It is precisely this 'marriage' between form and content in artistic creativity – this absolute mutual reference – which is unknown to the theological formulation and renders it an intruder. Miss U. Ellis-Fermor has defined poetry as

> that apprehension of beauty which irradiates the mind of the poet, presenting order or form as an aspect of truth, and distinguishing it at that point from the mind of the philosopher or of the saint.[5]

It is this necessary and fruitful harmony, no less than its personal inspiration, that gives art its integrity and constitutes its unlikeness to conceptual thought.

That unlikeness subsists, further, in the consequent independence of art. The relevance of other intellectual pursuits can lie only in their relation to what already is; but the poet,

> disdaining to be tied to any such subjection, lifted up with the vigour of his own invention, doth grow in effect unto another nature,[6]

in that the object of his labours is a thing in itself, relevant first in its uniqueness and fashioned upon its own laws, the imagination being able, as Bacon observed, to join and to dissever with a freedom unknown to nature.[7] The freedom of the poet's mind in its creative activity becomes evident, for example, in the study of the sources out of which Shakespeare creates, in *Macbeth*,

> a vast and comprehensive whole – a single structure, though of Gothic design.[8]

The unity and integrity of the new creation applies to thought as it does to event and character: if there is little resemblance to original fable in this 'Gothic design', what resemblance to formal doctrine is to be assumed from such reference to theological concept as the play may be held to make? The dramatist, as he is engaged in his dual task of exploring the nature of life in this world and challenging the imagination of his audience, may in his own way come to exemplify these ideas, but he is under no obligation either to relate them to their origins or to follow them to their conclusions; his obligation is to employ them, in imagina-

[4] H. S. Coffin, *The Public Worship of God*, London, 1950, p. 43.
[5] *Shakespeare the Dramatist*, 1961, p. 7.   [6] Sidney, *Apology*, ed. cit., p. 100.
[7] *Advancement of Learning* II. iv. 1.
[8] M. C. Bradbrook, 'The Sources of *Macbeth*', *S.S.* IV, 1951, p. 35.

tive freedom and under the exigencies of artistic creation, as part of a new and unique structure – and it is in terms of this structure alone that their significance is to be judged. The attempt thus has to be made to adapt theological concept for dealing with what W. M. Merchant terms 'this dramatic cosmos'; to recognize

> the freedom and autonomy of the artist's realm, the new order which a work of art brings into being,[9]

the peculiar consistency, and even moral validity, that a work of high imagination embodies. Whether so far-reaching an adaptation is possible may be doubted; Merchant himself, though insisting that a didactic aim does not necessarily affect the artist's integrity, recognizes that

> rarely can an affirmation be abstracted in a systematic way without impairing the integrity of any art form.[10]

It would appear to be the effect of that 'intensity' which Keats declares to be the height of art, not only to make 'all disagreeables evaporate',[11] but to triumph over the kind of logic that inheres in conceptual thinking. The quality of the imaginative logic of great drama is well exemplified in Miss Ellis-Fermor's analysis of the action of Shakespeare's tragedies :

> The art of the dramatist has been engaged not in presenting a closely locked and logically coherent action that points irresistibly to a certain deduction, but in selecting those fragments of the whole that stimulate our imaginations to an understanding of the essential experience, to the perception of a nexus of truths too vast to be defined as themes, whose enduring power disengages a seemingly unending series of perceptions and responses. It would seem that the imagination of audience or reader is thrown forward, by the immense impact of such scenes, to come to rest upon the next scene at the moment of its curving flight at which it can alight without interference or loss of momentum, to be projected again upon another movement, there to be similarly received, diverted, and flung out again upon its track of discovery. And this proceeds with economy and harmony as do the forces of gravitation at work upon the movements of bodies in a solar system.[12]

In its concern thus to project us into the intensity of experience, Miss Ellis-Fermor declares, the action of great drama orders itself 'not by demonstrative but by poetic logic'.[13] Whether conceptual thought can

[9] 'Shakespeare's Theology', *R.E.L.* V, 1964, pp. 74–5.
[10] *Creed and Drama*, 1965, p. 3.
[11] *The Letters of John Keats*, ed. M. Buxton Forman, 1952, p. 70, quoted by J. Lawlor, *The Tragic Sense in Shakespeare*, 1960, p. 11.
[12] 'The Nature of Plot in Drama', *Essays and Studies* XIII, 1960, pp. 78–9.
[13] ibid., p. 80.

exist in any systematic way in the context of such imaginative activity is unlikely; the probability, indeed, is that such thought, if and where it exists, is subordinated, like the action, to the purpose of guiding our imaginations 'to an understanding of the essential experience', rather than to the judging of that experience. Certainly, the activity of judging is precluded from a true response to the tragic:

> When we are immersed in tragedy, we feel towards dispositions, actions, and persons such emotions as attraction and repulsion, pity, wonder, fear, horror, perhaps hatred; but we do not *judge*. This is a point of view which emerges only when, in reading a play, we slip, by our own fault or the dramatist's, from the tragic position, or when, in thinking about the play afterwards, we fall back on our everyday legal or moral notions. But tragedy does not belong, any more than religion belongs, to the sphere of these notions; neither does the imaginative attitude in the presence of it. When we are in its world we watch it for what it is, seeing that so it happened and must have happened, feeling that it is piteous, dreadful, awful, mysterious, but neither passing sentence on the agents, nor asking whether the behaviour of the ultimate power towards them is just. And, therefore, the use of such language in attempts to render our imaginative experience in terms of the understanding is, to say the least, full of danger.[14]

The question whether the truest intimations do not reach man as experience rather than as intellectualized concepts has already arisen with regard both to faith and to the appreciation of tragedy.[15] It can evidently apply no less to tragedy's inception: though the purport of conceptualized notions may emerge from the creative process, the notions themselves are not akin to a process grounded, as L. C. Knights argues, upon 'intense living experience'. Knights will admit that traditional ideas of law and nature are to be found in *King Lear*, and concepts derived from the Schoolmen in *Macbeth*:

> But the point is that these ideas are never merely accepted and applied; they are re-lived; their adequacy is tested in a full and personal exposure to life, and only then are they assimilated into a work of art with a life of its own.[16]

It is because the plays are created out of living experience that the pressure of life can be apprehended in them, and that they are themselves able to create experience in an audience – and in the critic.[17] The recognition that the true basis for criticism can only be experience thus conveyed and

---

[14] A. C. Bradley, *Shakespearean Tragedy*, pp. 32–3.   [15] See pp. 56–7, 61–2 above.
[16] 'On Historical Scholarship and the Interpretation of Shakespeare', *Sewanee Review*, LXIII, 1955, pp. 223, 236.   [17] ibid., p. 237.

recreated lies behind Knights's insistence that Shakespeare's plays cannot be reduced to illustrations of past systems of thought, and his warning against substituting accumulated 'Knowledge about' for what he terms 'a living responsiveness'.[18] The peril that arises for criticism

> if, instead of starting with Shakespeare's plays, your own direct experience of Shakespeare's plays, and working back to what most deeply nourished them in the thought, the mental habits and the tradition of the time, you invoke a conceptual framework which you proceed to show the plays as illustrating,[19]

does not consist merely in an apparently fool-proof ideal, and a fixed meaning; there is a corresponding danger of

> the failure of imagination that seems almost inevitable when the critic works too persistently and exclusively in terms of formulable ideas.[20]

The tendency of a preoccupation with conceptual notions to hinder a full response in the critic and to distort his interpretation of a play has been clear in some preceding instances. It is a necessary outcome, both of human nature and of the nature of great drama, that

> A mind which is concerned with being right, which is nervously anxious not to be taken in, which sits in judgement, and approaches works of passion and imagination with neatly formulated demands, is inhibited from the receptiveness and disinterestedness which are the conditions of aesthetic experience.[21]

The truth about a play is thus completely bound up with the experiencing of it, and whatever makes experience subordinate will falsify. The problem directly confronts those who endeavour to bring historical evaluation into the interpretation of Shakespearian tragedy, and thus to bring in standards not derived from a direct appreciation of the plays. According to R. Ornstein, it has been found that

> while scholarship can make the interpretation of Shakespeare more scientific, it cannot make of interpretation a science based upon factual information. The dichotomy of scholarly fact and aesthetic impression is finally misleading because the refined, disciplined aesthetic impression *is* the fact upon which the interpretation of Shakespeare must ultimately rest: that is to say, all scholarly evidence outside the text of a play is related to it by inferences which must themselves be supported by aesthetic impressions. . . . The attempt of historical criticism to recapture (in so far as it is possible) Shakespeare's own artistic inten-

[18] ibid., pp. 238, 234.   [19] ibid., p. 229.   [20] ibid., p. 227.
[21] Helen Gardner, *The Business of Criticism*, Oxford Paperbacks, 1963, p. 13.

71

tion is, or should be, the goal of all responsible criticism. But we must insist that the intention is fully realized in the play and can be grasped only from the play.[22]

If concepts deriving from external systems of thought can thus be destructive of a true response, those derived from theology can be peculiarly so. For theology is the theory, in terms suited to the human intellect, of the process of the Divine self-revelation, nature and design. It is a guide to salvation, and a means of achieving relationship to God; but, despite its having relevance to them, it is not essentially an instrument for judging human relationships and attitudes. If theological concepts are so employed, whether in man's society or in the realm of art, a means vouchsafed for spiritual progress is being utilized for an inferior end: the critic, ignoring the Divine resources of wisdom, love and mercy in the exercise of what he takes to be a precise and all-inclusive system, employs the things of God in constituting himself the judge of his fellow men. The result is a legalism more potentially severe than that imposed by any other conceptual system. Its effects have been demonstrated upon Othello and Cleopatra; the danger it holds even for the most cautious of critics is apparent in what R. M. Frye has to say about Lear's protestation,

> I am a man
> More sinn'd against than sinning
> (III. ii. 59–60).

Citing the apostle Paul, and with apposite quotation from Calvin and Luther, Frye declares Lear's impatience and his comparison of himself with others to be, theologically speaking, reprehensible; and he concludes that

> Lear was surely not speaking in Christian terms when he declared himself more sinned against than sinning, but that after all is quite appropriate, for Shakespeare characterizes Lear as a pagan.[23]

At the risk of unfairness in dwelling thus upon an isolated lapse, it could be observed that Lear's statement is both true and justified, and that by it he reveals some affinity with the manner of Job's devotion to his God:

> I will not refrain my mouth; I will speak in the anguish of my spirit; I will complain in the bitterness of my soul (vii. 11).
> Oh that I knew where I might find him! that I might come even to his seat! I would order my cause before him, and fill my mouth with arguments (xxiii. 3–4).

[22] 'Historical Criticism and the Interpretation of Shakespeare', *S.Q.* X, 1959, p. 3.
[23] *Shakespeare and Christian Doctrine*, London, 1963, pp. 252–3.

For, as R. B. Sewall observes, the protest embodied in *The Book of Job* 'came not from fear or hate, but from love';[24] and Lear is not necessarily farther removed from piety than Job in the choosing to maintain his own ways before his Creator (xiii. 15). Theology here leads the critic into a judgement that is unfitting and narrow, and tempts him, for a moment, into assuming the mantles of Eliphaz, Bildad and Zophar.

The particular inappropriateness of conceptual thought to drama may owe a great deal to drama's incapacity – more than is to be found in any other form of art – to transcend the medium of its operation. In its function of reflecting, of presenting life to the living, may be found the reason for Santayana's judging Shakespeare's drama to subsist in the absence of a philosophy or a religion. It is what Miss Ellis-Fermor calls 'the differentiating quality of drama'[25] – its preoccupation with the life and activity of man – that makes the operation of thought peculiarly difficult to discern. Though the writer's theme may be universal, she argues, his subject remains man's experience, and what he says or implies must be stated in terms of this medium:[26] though he plumb the depths of a veritable ocean of experience, he is bound to reveal his perceptions

> in terms of that efflorescence upon the surface which is made up of the words and deeds of his characters.[27]

In this sense, dramatic character and plot are images on a grand scale; and the function of imagery is to evoke perceptions which are aspects of an underlying reality, rather than to present a statement or abstract of the reality that is perceived.[28] The law of drama is that the larger inferences which the playwright draws from his experience of life can be expressed only implicitly:

> In so far as he does in fact depart from this law, itself an inference from the differentiating characteristic of drama, in so far does he depart from the strict dramatic mode.[29]

Drama, like other art, is the result of a tension between the ultimate nature of what is apprehended and the finitude of the means both of apprehension and expression; like other art, it is necessarily a symbolism. The artistic perception can therefore be equated with the Christian consciousness in that, as Reinhold Niebuhr puts it, time and what is contained in time is real only as it gives expression to principles and powers which lie outside it;

> Yet every suggestion of the principle of a process must be expressed in terms of the temporal process, and every idea of the God who is

---

[24] *The Vision of Tragedy*, Yale University Press, 1965, p. 11.
[25] *Shakespeare the Dramatist*, 1961, p. 5.
[26] ibid., p. 8. [27] ibid., p. 40.
[28] ibid., p. 23. [29] ibid., p. 10.

the ground of the world must be expressed in some term taken from the world.[30]

Art is more closely related to religion than science is, Niebuhr declares, since it does not describe the world in terms of its exact relationships, but falsifies these relationships in order to express their total meaning.[31] There is a corresponding sense in which drama departs from an exact rendering of life, since

> Only by abandoning the apparent safeguards of verisimilitude can drama . . . become the vehicle of the deepest-hidden truth.[32]

But such abandonment of verisimilitude must, in great tragedy, serve only to intensify the impression of real and actual experience : the inquiry that begins with man's world must end with it. It is this necessity, perhaps, which can lead the critic to think that dramatic poetry, and indeed all poetry, is by nature anthropocentric :

> the poets must be pardoned a preference for what they know in some sense to what is in no sense known, for the present obvious and precious person to the obscure and conjectured essence of the whole. The spiritual principle to which our loyalty is due – where is it to be seen at work except among men? Not until he finds it within him does he search for it without.[33]

Whether it is indeed all that he knows or whether it is simply his sole means of expression, human experience in its intensity must be created and shown forth by the tragedian, and concept must be eschewed. The identification and involvement of the beholder with the created object that is to be discerned in all art is here at its height, and it is at this point that the conceptual vanishes. As Miss Ellis-Fermor points out,

> We remain continuously immersed in the character's experience; we never cease to be Macbeth; we are never invited to observe him. This is in fact the essential difference between 'Guilty creatures sitting at a play' and those sitting at a sermon.[34]

The tension of art therefore exists in great tragedy in its extreme form. The more profound and far-reaching the intimations which come to the tragedian's consciousness, the less explicit can his expression of them be : the more a critic is aware of a profundity of meaning in a tragedy, the more difficult will it become for him to extract the significance from the experience that avouches its presence. The dramatist, concerned as a

[30] *Beyond Tragedy*, London, 1947, p. 5.   [31] ibid., p. 6.
[32] Una Ellis-Fermor, op. cit., p. 31.
[33] W. Macneile Dixon, *Tragedy*, 1929, pp. 180, 184.
[34] op. cit., p. 37.

poet to make manifest the truth of things, creates in each play he writes
a symbol of his vision of life:

> and as he goes on, the symbols become more expressive and less
> translatable; more and more they render their great object as it really
> is.[35]

The truth that intense personal experience of life is both the beginning
and the end of great drama carries with it the paradox that the life of
art here implies the death of concept. The force of this paradox is evident
in Miss Ellis-Fermor's insistence that the 'reading of life' which informs
tragedy is coextensive with the plays themselves;[36] and its operation has
been finely analysed and described by D. G. James:

> What we have, or so it seems to me, in these great tragedies, is a state
> of affairs in which any conceptual schemes, any mere significances,
> never quite break out from the presented situations; they are held, if
> only barely, in solution; and they are not precipitated in our appre-
> hension of the plays. That is to say, the state of affairs is strictly one
> of symbolism, not of allegory; one of involvement, not of explication.
> There is indeed a certain tension between what is imaginative and
> what is intellectual; but the tension never comes to a break: it never
> snaps the mind into two and concurrent apprehensions. We are never
> merely concerned with meanings. What is exhibited is charged with
> meaning; but it does not *carry* it. Now this state of affairs, which is
> not one of allegory proper, is yet one in which intellectual formulation
> is nearly breaking out from the imaginative unity of the play; the
> imagination only just succeeds in keeping its supremacy; the ally
> pressed into service is all but in revolt, but is always just held; and
> it is in works like *Othello* and *King Lear* where there is almost intoler-
> able tension of this kind, and where the artistic consciousness comes
> near to breaking and to losing its autonomy, that we are aware of the
> very highest artistic power.[37]

Shakespeare's achievement at its height therefore defies conceptual
analysis, and requires from the perceptive critic a reticence, if it does
not exact a bafflement: there is a profound sense (which earlier discussion
may have helped to distinguish) in which a search for the highest meanings can be synonymous with a flagging of response. To this awareness
Miss Ellis-Fermor gives expression in saying that

> If we look for a theme in Shakespeare's plays, we find none, other
> than the bottomless and endlessly extending wisdom that asks of his
> readers a lifetime's consecration to explore;[38]

[35] D. G. James, *The Dream of Learning*, 1951, p. 123.   [36] op. cit., p. 11.
[37] op. cit., pp. 88–9.
[38] *Shakespeare the Dramatist*, 1961, p. 7.

it makes possible the terms of praise that Miss H. Gardner addresses to Miss Lascelles:

> The success of her book is that it does not arrive finally at 'the meaning of *Measure for Measure*';[39]

and it is the begetter of Charles Williams's expostulation that 'the trouble about Shakespeare is that he is both Christian and non-Christian, and it is fatal to call him either', and of his *cri du cœur*,

> Let us – O let us leave that great ambiguous figure, his own ambiguity! . . . We ought to remain content with 'half-knowledge'; the 'irritable reaching' after identity of doctrine is as dangerous on one side as on the other. The plays are the cloudy frontier where much meets, and their definitions are always and only in themselves.[40]

Whether or not the presence of theological formulation is ultimately in question, therefore, the perils of 'reaching after' it are assured by the nature of tragedy itself. Even if tragedy permitted it to be distinguishable to any degree, its relation to complex and developing event would make its identification hazardous: a particular instance in a play might by its emphasis bestride the religious categories of its own age, or even of any age, at the promptings of its dramatic situation. As W. M. Merchant observes,

> in the tragedies and the problem plays, if any equation between dramatic argument and personal belief has validity, Shakespeare is exploring metaphysical problems which the orthodox believer is rarely called upon to investigate. At these points of creative inquiry his precise ecclesiastical affiliation . . . is of marginal relevance.[41]

The theology of these agonized instances is hardly susceptible of definition; one wonders indeed what an orthodox believer would make of such matters as the status and the injunction of the ghost of Hamlet's father, or of Hamlet's attitude toward Claudius and his killing, or toward suicide, quite apart from the problem of what attitude might be said to exist toward them by definition from the play itself. A similar problem of interpretation must exist, as has been noted, even in instances where doctrinal terminology could be said to be clear in itself: terminological clarity bears no discourse to the dramatic use to which terminology is put, use being the arbiter of the significance of all conceptual terms, whether in their clarity or in their proliferation.[42] And though the importance of these terms might be seen to lie in their bringing a par-

---

[39] *The Business of Criticism*, 1963, p. 154.

[40] 'Two Brief Essays on Shakespearian Topics', *The Image of the City and Other Essays*, 1958, p. 39.

[41] 'Shakespeare's Theology', *R.E.L.* V, 1964, p. 74.   [42] See pp. 24–5 above.

ticular scheme of reference into the imaginative possibilities of the play – as indeed they do – interpretation according to the scheme requires that no considerable event or vitality within the play can resist being attributed to it, and that there are to be found, in thought, image or act, no other possible systems of reference. In the face of such requirements, the conclusion that great drama is a 'cloudy frontier' must seem inescapable. But there is a further requirement if the possibility is maintained that theological concepts, rather than the exigencies of secular life, direct the unfolding of events in tragedy: it is 'the note of rejoicing', which S. Barnet insists should in that case come from the playwright's knowledge that all things are working for good, and should echo through the tragedy. That note is never heard; and if the tragedian wished to sound it, he could scarcely do so. His concern is with nature, disaster, error, evil and fate; and the mood proper to the consideration of such matters is not rejoicing, but sorrow.

It is not impossible to derive from tragedy inferences which could properly be called religious, in that they refer to a scheme of values which transcends those of mortal life, and those, seemingly, of the play itself. Thus A. C. Bradley, in what he terms 'impressions beyond the tragic', can apprehend Lear and Cordelia as being strangely untouched by the world in which they appear – can

find, perhaps, the suffering and death counting for little or nothing, the greatness of soul for much or all,

and the judgement of the world – indeed, the evident reality of the world itself – to be a lie.[43] It is significant that these perceptions, if they be truth, belong to the experiencing mind; that they come, not strictly from the play's events, but as it were in spite of them – not from formal pronouncement within the play, but from that awareness in the beholder's conscience which the play creates; that they constitute a 'rediscovery', both by author and audience, 'from the very nature of man', of what, from the nature of tragedy itself, they cannot assume.[44] The secularity of tragedy might here indeed be regarded as its religious potential; but it is manifestly here also the means by which it may be itself. For Bradley, aware as he is of the importance of these intimations, is the first to insist upon their danger for the critic, and himself declines to dwell upon them. Taken beyond a certain point, he declares, the impression which is thus recorded will 'destroy the tragedy';

Pursued further again, it leads to the idea that this world, in that obvious appearance of it which tragedy cannot dissolve without dissolving itself, is illusive.[45]

[43] *Shakespearean Tragedy*, pp. 323 ff.   [44] K. Muir; see p. 59 above.
[45] op. cit., pp. 327–8.

For great tragedy to attempt to show what is beyond itself is to destroy itself before the attempt were made. As I. A. Richards states the matter,

> Tragedy is only possible to a mind which is for the moment agnostic or Manichean. The least touch of any theology which has a compensating Heaven to offer the tragic hero is fatal.[46]

For the ordinary spectator of drama, a suspension of disbelief for a moment is required; but the religious spectator of tragedy requires also a suspension of belief[47] – and man in his purgatorial state of devout worldliness, grieved at the waste of good and the suffering of the innocent, finds no difficulty in thus relapsing from religious conviction. The fact, therefore, that the possibility of a reality beyond the mortal can come only by mere impression and inference from beyond what is objectively presented, is an indication that theological concepts are not in control of the drama. Joy does not abound. What is evident at the close of tragedy is the playwright's true task throughout : well might he declare,

Our present business
Is general woe.[48]

It therefore becomes evident that, whatever of religious significance may inhere in Shakespearian tragedy, it is generally not to be dealt with in terms of theological concept; and the conclusion must be drawn that, if Shakespearian tragedy's kinship in religious intimation with Greek tragedy is to be found, it must be sought in a secular experience commonly shared.[49] It has already been suggested that great tragedy, in its dispassionate inquiry into the nature of human experience in this world, merits the status of philosophy in Bacon's sense as part of the domain of reason; and the illegitimacy of imposing theological conclusions upon it may finally be seen as related to his division of human knowledge into what descends from above and what springs from beneath, 'the one informed by the light of nature, the other inspired by divine revelation'.[50] In that tragedy, by its proper devotion to the secular, may come to such

> knowledge or rudiment of knowledge concerning God, which may be obtained by the contemplation of his creatures,[51]

it may rise to a 'natural theology'; but the limit of this knowledge, according to Bacon, is 'that it sufficeth to convince atheism, but not to inform religion' – for the works of God can 'show forth the omnipotency and

---

[46] *Principles of Literary Criticism*, 1926, p. 246, quoted by S. Barnet, 'Some Limitations of a Christian Approach to Shakespeare', *E.L.H.* XXII, 1955, p. 85.
[47] F. L. Lucas, *Tragedy in Relation to Aristotle's 'Poetics'*, 1953, p. 45.
[48] *King Lear* V. iii. 319-20.   [49] See p. 66 above.
[50] *The Advancement of Learning* II. v. 1.   [51] ibid., II. vi. 1.

wisdom of the maker, but not his image'.[52] It may therefore be thought wise to concur in the judgement that the imposition upon a human knowledge, grounded on the contemplation of the natural world, of assurances concerning the points of faith is unsafe : that

> we ought not to attempt to draw down or to submit the mysteries of God to our reason; but contrariwise to raise and advance our reason to the divine truth.[53]

It would thus appear as the condition of the inquiry into secular experience, as it does of the inquiry into the physical universe, if it is to be true to itself and its function, that it impose upon itself a proper discipline and finitude :

> for the contemplation of God's creatures and works produceth (having regard to the works and creatures themselves) knowledge, but having regard to God, no perfect knowledge, but wonder, which is broken knowledge. And therefore it was most aptly said by one of Plato's school, *That the sense of man carrieth a resemblance with the sun, which (as we see) openeth and revealeth all the terrestrial globe; but then again it obscureth and concealeth the stars and celestial globe: so doth the sense discover natural things, but it darkeneth and shutteth up divine.*[54]

If tragedy attains higher truth, such knowledge must therefore appear to man's experience through tragedy's limitations, and as it were by contradiction, as 'an affirmation "in spite of" '[55] – must have its origin in 'wonder'. Tragedy must not be credited with conceptions to which it cannot aspire.

This is not to disparage the religious significance of tragedy; theology owes its very existence to the fact that religious experience cannot be readily formulated, as tragedy may owe its deepest appeal to its spiritual intimations. It is the application of tragedy that is really the issue. Critics have generally assumed that it must piece out its view of man's world with perceptions belonging to revelation, and have not considered the possibility that tragedy's religious import might lie in its very subjection to the mundane. This understanding – or rather misunderstanding – of tragedy stands in some relationship with the attitude of 'the ungodly', who, according to Calvin,

> having alienated themselves from God and his household, do not understand that they are still within the reach of God's hand.[56]

[52] ibid.   [53] ibid.
[54] ibid., I. i. 3.   [55] L. C. Knights; see p. 48 above.
[56] *Commentaries* (*Heb.* xii. 4–6), ed. J. Haroutunian (L.C.C. XXIII), 1958, p. 212.

The absence of theological reference in tragedy is in keeping with its absence from the mortal world: neither situation is incompatible with the highest of purposes, and with the working of providence itself. Bacon observes in his profundity that

> as in civil actions he is the greater and deeper politique, that can make other men the instruments of his will and ends, and yet never acquaint them with his purpose, so as they shall do it and yet not know what they do, than he that imparteth his meaning to those he employeth; so is the wisdom of God more admirable, when nature intendeth one thing, and providence draweth forth another, than if he had communicated to particular creatures and motions the characters and impressions of his providence.[57]

What providence may 'draw forth' of the phenomenon of tragedy may indeed perplex those who approach it from the direction of formulable concept. Their approach in itself, in its conviction that, like poetry in general, great tragedy gives assurance of 'some participation of divineness',[58] is part of a universal human awareness; their error is in their failure to grasp that in the natural world it is man, and not God, who speaks in theological terms: and in seeking the 'characters and impressions' of revelation in the world of nature and reason they may well miss what revelation there is. The very purpose which creates great tragedy, revealing man to himself, may not fall short, as Miss Ellis-Fermor observes, of 'some participation' of divine truth – for that participation relates more to method than to message. It is in tragedy's freedom from prepossession, in the steadiness and impartiality of its gaze, that the means of assurance is to be found:

> 'This even-handed justice', this universal sympathy which has at once the balance of impersonal detachment and the radiance of affection, gives to the record made and to the reading of life implied a power of assurance beyond that of any utterance short of the affirmation of the mystic. . . . For it is this which, operating without bias, reveals in the mind of a man the shadow of the divine attribute of immanence and transcendence.[59]

The necessary process by which man apprehends a God from the natural world, and from his own being and powers, no less than the assurance to which this process of experiencing gives birth, is intensified by the very workmanship of the phenomenon that presents before him life as it corresponds to his deepest natural awareness of it. What can be revealed by the phenomenon itself must be the subject for further inquiry.

[57] *Advancement* II. vii. 7.   [58] ibid., II. iv. 2.
[59] *Shakespeare the Dramatist and Other Papers*, ed. K. Muir, 1961, p. 19.

Chapter 5
THE SEARCH FOR COMMON GROUND

Great tragedy must therefore be seen as devoted to the secular in its concern with revealing afresh the conditions of mortal existence and in its arising from the intense personal experience which it tries to recreate in the beholder. Whatever conceptual notions may be of moment in a tragedy are transmuted in the creative process – in James's metaphor, they are held in solution, and not precipitated; and since it is experience of life, and not intellectual formulation, that is essential in tragedy's inception, the undiscriminating use of theological concepts in its interpretation must be held as correspondingly inimical. It is, in fact, a perilous proceeding in criticism to regard any significance that arises, conceptual or otherwise, as transcending the sphere of the play's investigation and as providing an ultimate explanation of the life it embodies. If so profound a message is at all to be discovered, it must come from the impact of the play as a whole; and it is to be sought, not in explicit pronouncement, but rather in the conscience of the beholder exposed to the full effect of the tragedy. The task of the critic, therefore, is to interpret the play in terms of itself rather than in terms of theological presuppositions to which it may apparently make reference. Such significances as may be conceptualized, or equated to concept, are to be seen as operating locally and momentarily as part of the multitudinous impressions of the drama. They are to be regarded as inseparable from the interaction of consciousness with consciousness that drama truly is, and to be referred as closely as possible to its centre. It should never be assumed that apparent conceptual references are systematically used, or that their absence or accumulation is significant in itself, or that they must in their presence mediate direction for the creative artist who adopts them.

Yet in the latter respect the possibility remains of a residual claim upon the dramatist's sensibility of a system of belief whose concepts have no hold over him in detail:[1] while the influence of religious formulation can in no way be proved, in this sense the idea of its retaining some ultimate effect cannot be entirely dismissed, despite its being even less susceptible of proof. The critic must therefore take due note of those

[1] See p. 31 above.

instances in which the awareness or inner conflict of a character appears in any degree as a dramatization of a distinctive moral awareness vividly pointing beyond the emotions of the moment – an awareness, for example, that makes pity, for Macbeth,

> like a naked new-born babe,
> Striding the blast
>
> (I. vii. 21–2),

or an instance so charged with what appear to be perversions of a traditional Christian understanding as Oswald's drawing his sword upon the defenceless Gloucester with the words,

> That eyeless head of thine was first fram'd
> flesh
> To raise my fortunes
>
> (IV. vi. 228–9).

That instances of this sort can come close to making explicit reference to religious standards and concepts is evident in Hamlet's wish that the Everlasting had not set 'His canon 'gainst self-slaughter', and in the thoughts respecting forgiveness in Claudius's attempt to 'try what prayer can do'. There are, further, points where doctrinal presuppositions evidently obtrude into a play and dictate its form. The effect of the elder Hamlet's being murdered in an 'Unhousel'd, disappointed' and unconfessed state might be seen as one of them; the attitude to 'damned incest' could be another; and both Hamlet's self-contempt (if a religious leaning could be inferred in it) and his trust in Providence can conceivably be interpreted in this way. It would, however, beseem the critic to be aware that these instances are in general not exclusively Christian, but part of the religious consciousness of all the ages – that the 'unhousel'd' Hamlet is in much the same case as the unburied Polynices – and that the religious consciousness, being part of the human condition, will necessarily find reflection in tragedy. The impressions beyond the tragic which arise in Bradley out of his experience of the plays, as opposed to particular items of their content, will in this respect be more deserving of attention. All these things are to be taken into assessment, provided that they retain for the critic their true status of suggestion, and are not understood by him as an open invitation to bring in schemes of value that lie outside the play; they are relevant only in so far as they are held within the bounds of immediate dramatic impression and of relationship to the play as a whole. Granted these conditions, however, suggestions which tend beyond the immediate secular context must be allowed their proper degree of weight. For though the proper concern of tragedy must be with the secular, it would be the height of presumption in the critic, as well as an abandonment of responsible criticism, to attempt arbitrarily to limit the imaginations of those who create or those who experience tragedy to the confines of a universe as secular as the conditions of the form of art which claims them. It is not for the critic to ignore, as it is not for him to impose: his unvarying task is full and sensitive response.

Tragedy is eloquent of man's state in the world. The conditions of its creation ensure an incongruity with conceptual thought. And a true criticism must therefore be as close as possible to the dramatic immediacies of thought, impression and event. For all these reasons, the bringing of theological concepts into the detailed interpretation of tragedy must be held in general to be precluded. But if experience arising from the contemplation of tragedy, rather than formulations within it, be regarded as the proper ground in the search for religious significance – if, from the phenomenon itself, in its devoted rendering of the secular condition of man, some revelation of further meaning may be gained – a basis is found for bringing theological concepts into relation with tragedy. What tragedy has to say about the human condition, in fact, may be brought into comparison with what theology has to say about it. If tragedy, from a religious point of view, can be said to deal with the state of affairs above which the man of faith is empowered to rise, theology, in the process of defining the principles of faith, and of applying them, cannot but make reference to the conditions of human existence in which faith takes root. It is therefore not accidental that in the greatest of Christian philosophers are to be discerned the widest of human sympathies: the truths of theology which they formulate are intimately associated with the realities of their experience as men. The attempt will therefore be made to see whether the human condition as it has appeared in Christian thinking can approximate to the experience of life which the great tragedies have shared, and Shakespearian tragedy reveals.

II

The Human Condition:
Theology's Assessment of the
Medium of Tragedy

Chapter 6

MAN AS A CREATURE

The chief characteristic of man's life on earth, according to traditional Christian thinking, is its tragic involvement in its own evil. The question of Paul the apostle, 'Who shall deliver me from the body of this death?' (*Rom.* vii. 24), far from being a cry in extremity, is normative for the human situation where men in their best endeavours do, not the good that they wish, but the ill that they will not. The words that Shakespeare's Claudius applies to himself could well have been used by the apostle to state the spiritual position of all men:

> O limed soul, that struggling to be free
> Art more engaged![1]

Goodness cannot lie in men. The category of a good man Augustine is prepared to recognize, despite his assertion that there is no man 'that in some things yields not unto the concupiscence of the flesh'; but such goodness, in its failure to inspire men to the labour of admonishing and reforming the wicked, condemns itself. The virtuous of this world tolerate the deeds of their evil fellow-creatures; therefore,

> because they wink at their damnable exorbitances, by reason they fear by them to lose their own vain temporalities, justly do they partake with them in the punishments temporal though they shall not do so in the eternal.[2]

The good and the wicked endure a common scourge because they share a love of this world; but they share also a common evil that renders any man's claim to be 'purely separate'[3] from all other faults an absurdity. 'What man is he', asks Augustine, 'who, weighing his own infirmity, dares to ascribe his purity and innocency to his own strength'? The evil that a man has not done is to be ascribed solely to the grace of God.[4]

The misery in which human life is plunged is partly due to a tragic liability to deception by bodily or mental sensations resulting from the constant state of struggle against evil in which man finds himself engaged,

---

[1] *Hamlet* III. iii. 68–9.   [2] *De Civ. Dei* I. ix.
[3] ibid.   [4] *Conf.* II. vii. 15.

and which is itself proof of the essential evil of his condition.[5] Flesh strives against spirit; and though the resistance of the flesh be good, yet the strife itself is evil,[6] and is eloquent of the situation that gives rise to it. The never-ending struggle

> testifies that there is evil in us, and that we are in evil. It teaches us that it is evil to assent unto sin, and good to avoid it. But yet neither can prudence nor temperance rid our lives of that evil which they forewarn us of and arm us against. And what of justice, that gives every one his due? and the just order of nature is that the soul be under God, the flesh under the soul, and both together under God. Is it not plain that this is rather continually laboured after than truly attained in this life?[7]

The evil of the Christian conflict is inseparable from the evil of man's life.[8] Evil desires may be fought and lessened, but not eliminated:[9] they will trouble a man 'until the body is revived and death is swallowed up in victory'.[10]

For worldly man is self-betrayed by an insatiable desire for power that is itself an evil, and incapacitates him in his strivings toward the good. Rightly directed, the will to power is legitimate: man's blessedness, according to Augustine, consists in willing well and being able to do as one wills.[11] But to pursue the principle of power in neglect of that of righteousness is the besetting folly both of man and of devil, since righteousness is the condition of power – as was evident in the righteousness of Christ, which disabled Satan and could confer power on men.[12] But men imitate Satan in that they are 'lovers of might', scorning first to attain a good will in the prior conquest of their own vices:

> It is to be wished, then, that power may now be given, but against vices, to conquer which men do not wish to be powerful, while they wish to be so in order to conquer men; and why is this, unless that, being in truth conquered, they feignedly conquer, and are conquerors not in truth, but in opinion?[13]

In all his achievements, therefore, worldly man proclaims himself the victim of his own evil – in the irrelevance of his joys, his pursuit of trifles,[14] his rejoicing in novelties; in his taking more pleasure in learning that knowing, in the battle than in the victory; and above all in his

---

[5] *Ench.* vii. 21. [6] *De Cont.* viii. 19.
[7] *De Civ. Dei* XIX. iv. [8] ibid., XXII. xxiii.
[9] *Serm.* cli. 5, quoted by J. Burnaby, *Amor Dei*, 1949, p. 58.
[10] *Propos. ex Ep. ad Rom.* xxxv. [11] *De Trin.* XIII. xiii. 17.
[12] *De Trin.* XIII. xiv. 18. [13] *De Trin.* XIII. xiii. 17.
[14] *De Vera Relig.* xlix. 95; liii. 102.

compulsion to order his life in accordance with his desires: for the end of man's desires is not the desires.[15] Truth and the precepts of truth, he ignores, and his life is evil; yet evil there would not be if the soul recognized its Creator and subjected itself to Him.[16]

But is spiritual deadness – the being 'sunk in trifles and baseness'[17] – inappropriate in those who have inherited 'spiritual death'?[18] Man's nature and human custom stems from original sin and the habit of repeated sinning,[19] which make him liable 'to that death, torture of the affections, and corruption which we all feel now'.[20] From birth to death man as a creature stands condemned and depraved; for, since men were all propagated from one source, for the purpose of human sociability and future concord, the nature of Adam and Eve, 'being hereby depraved, was so transfused through all their offspring in the same degree of corruption, and necessity of death';[21] or, as Calvin puts it, 'rotten branches came forth from a rotten root, which transmitted their rottenness to the other twigs sprouting from them'.[22] Thus *'shapen in iniquity'*[23] and conceived in sin man may be washed clean of the sin of guilt, but not of that of punishment; he remains subject to that which is in itself a plurality of sins,[24] which mars him with a loss of all uprightness, a proneness to evil, a loathing of the good, a disdain for wisdom but fondness for error, and a contempt for good works but an eagerness for doing evil.[25] The mind and heart are so completely alienated from God's righteousness that they can conceive nothing but what is corrupt; and whatever apparent good may be produced, they are yet but 'works of the flesh';[26] and mind and heart remain enveloped in hypocrisy and bound by inner perversity.[27]

The condition of humanity, then, is indeed *'wearisome'*; spiritually speaking, it is one of ineradicable vice. Yet this creature, though *'created sicke,'* is *'commanded to be sound'* : born under the law of flesh, his being is committed to that of spirit.[28] The universe, embodying the laws of the almighty Creator, lays upon the soul the inexorable demand of allegiance to Him and the good use of its powers, and visits suffering upon it if it fails to pay what is due:

> Either it pays this by the good use of what it has received, or else by the loss of what it refuses to use well. Hence if it does not pay by acting

---

[15] ibid., liii. 102.   [16] ibid., xx. 39.   [17] ibid., xlix. 95.
[18] 'A Treatise of Christian Doctrine', *The Prose Works of John Milton*, (Bohn) 1853, IV, p. 266.
[19] *De Quaest. ad Simplicianum* I. i. 10.
[20] *De Civ. Dei* XIV. xii.   [21] ibid., XIV. i.   [22] *Inst.* II. i. 7.
[23] *Conf.* I. vii. 12.   [24] *Ench.* xii. 45, 46.
[25] Luther, *Lectures on Romans* (v. 12), tr. W. Pauck, L.C.C. XV, 1961, pp. 167–8.
[26] *Inst.* II. i. 8.   [27] ibid., II. v. 19.
[28] Fulke Greville, *Mustapha*, Chorvs Sacerdotvm (Bullough edn., II, p. 136).

justly, it will pay by suffering unhappiness, for the word 'debt' applies to both. Thus what has been said could also have been formulated as follows: If a soul does not pay by doing what it ought to do, it will pay by suffering what it ought to suffer.

The soul's failure thus to pay back to God the existence it had received from Him is not God's fault; rather, it is a matter for praise that the soul should suffer as it ought.[29] Aquinas writes similarly of the concept of man's debt to his Creator:

> Now it is evident that all things contained in an order are, in a manner, one, in relation to the principle of that order. Consequently, whatever rises up against an order, is put down by that order or by the principle thereof. And because sin is an inordinate act, it is evident that whoever sins, commits an offence against an order: wherefore he is put down, in consequence, by that same order, which repression is punishment.[30]

The demand is simple, but absolute; and absolute compliance is impossible for man out of his own flawed powers. His very status as a creature, as Aquinas makes clear, is synonymous with shortcoming: man cannot side-step his imperfections. For in the first place, since the good or evil of a human act is determined by its end, and secondary ends are desirable only as they are ordered towards the last end, no human end can be acceptable that is not directed toward the love and service of God.[31] In the second place, Creation is a 'descending from',[32] and a creature as such 'is characterized by a certain deficiency in the degree and mode of being';[33] and on the principle that 'Operations and actions are like the beings that perform them', man, 'as a defective and imperfect being, is bound to perform incomplete and defective actions, and therefore good and bad are always combined in them, though in variable proportions'.[34] In the third place, though all being is good, the multiplicity in creatures requires no lack in any creaturely power or instrument, and any such lack in the fullness of being will result in evil.[35] To which might be added Augustine's observation that man's falling away from God resulted in the multiplicity both of the temporal forms around him and of his own sensibilities, so that abundance became laborious and his needs became abundant;[36] and as it was with Augustine, so it is with all men,

---

[29] *De Lib. Arb.* III. xv. 44, 46.   [30] *S.T.* Ia IIae lxxxvii. 1, *ad R.*
[31] E. Gilson, *The Philosophy of St Thomas Aquinas*, tr. E. Bullough, Cambridge, 1924, p. 259; *S.T.* Ia IIae xviii. 6, *ad R.*
[32] *Summa Contra Gentiles* IV. vii, quoted by Gilson, op. cit., p. 131.
[33] *In Lib. de Divin. Nomin.* I. i, quoted by Gilson, ibid.
[34] *De Malo* ii. 4, *ad R.*; *S.T.* Ia IIae xviii. 1, *ad R.*; quoted by Gilson, ibid., pp. 248-9.
[35] *S.T.* Ia IIae xviii. 1, *ad R.*   [36] *De Vera Relig.* xxi. 41.

that 'while turned from Thee, the One Good, I lost myself among a multiplicity of things'.[37] Only one outcome is possible. Whether through failure in the choice of the highest end in all things, or through the imperfection inherent in creatureliness, or through some deficiency in an instrument of the soul, or through the bewildering multiplicity of temporal forms in and around him (to say nothing of his inherent state of sin), man will fail in paying his due; and it is therefore his destiny that every inordinate affection shall be its own punishment.[38] The present sin, Aquinas maintains, can be the punishment not only of the preceding sin, but of itself.[39]

Any desire or longing short of the desire for God, or temporal pleasure unqualified by aspiration toward the divine, is a vice and an enslavement – for a man is a slave to as many masters as he has vices:[40] he is necessarily enslaved by whatever means he seeks to be happy. He follows them wheresoever they lead, and fears anyone who seems to have the power to rob him of them. And if a spark of fire, or a tiny animal, or any one of unnumbered adverse possibilities does not deprive him of them, time itself will come and snatch his loves away.[41] Thus men's worldly desires lead them into a realm of fearful and tragic delusion: ungodly man is engaged in a veritable dance of death:

> To those who make a bad use of so good a thing as the mind, desiring visible things outside the mind which ought to remind them to behold intelligible things, to them will be given outer darkness. The beginning of this darkness is fleshly knowledge and the weakness of the bodily senses. Those who delight in strife will be aliens from peace and involved in frightful difficulties. . . . Those who want to hunger and thirst, to burn with lust and be weary, so that they may have pleasure in eating and drinking, in lying with a woman, and in sleeping, love indigence which is the beginnng of the greatest woes. What they love will be made perfect for them, for they will be where there is weeping and gnashing of teeth. . . . Those, who love the journey rather than the return home or the journey's end, are to be sent into distant parts. They are flesh and spirit continually on the move and never reaching home.[42]

The 'outer darkness' thus decreed for those dedicated to imperfect desire might be said to resemble the condition of man set forth in literary tragedy; and the resemblance becomes closer where Augustine considers

---

[37] *Conf.* II. i. 1.
[38] *Conf.* I. xii. 19.
[39] *S.T.* Ia IIae lxxxvii. 2, *ad R.*
[40] *De Civ. Dei* IV. iii.
[41] *De Vera Relig.* xxxviii. 69.
[42] *De Vera Relig.* liv. 104, 105.

the inevitable conflict which must arise from the errant desires of those inclined to evil. For

> both doth each one injure himself, and all injure one another. For they desire that, the love which is fraught with death, and which may easily be taken away from them; and this they take away from one another, when they persecute one another. And so they, from whom things temporal are taken away, are greatly pained, because of their love of them: but they who take them away, rejoice. But such joy is blindness and supreme misery: for this very joy involves the soul the more, and leads it unto greater torments.[43]

The will 'To aske, and haue: commaund, and be obeied',[44] with its accompanying conflict, sums up many a tragical history.

Frustration in the external sphere does not alone constitute the punishment: wrongful desire also corrupts the nature that entertains it, and the resulting inner perversion is if anything the more terrible, for thereby the soul cannot gain from any reality it apprehends. Just as food is changed into the likeness of the body, so the personality is transformed by the evil habits that feed on it:[45]

> But Thou avengest what men commit against themselves, seeing also when they sin against Thee, they do wickedly against their own souls, and *iniquity gives itself the lie*, by corrupting and perverting their nature, which Thou has created and ordained.[46]

By its self-concern the soul brings about its own perversion. For human self-love can properly have no other basis than righteousness centred in the love of God; and the unrighteous love of self, retained by those with minds unattuned to the divine love, may rather, because of its destructiveness to its possessor, be termed a self-hate. 'It is indeed a fearful delusion by which, though all men desire their own advantage, so many do only what works their ruin'.[47] The desires of a natural but incorrect self-love produce loves which the mind cannot quell, and errors from which it can see no escape.[48] This atrophy of mind and character – Augustine's *infirmitas* – springing from man's desire for a mutable good, leads to an ignorance of what is needful, and a concupiscent wish for what is hurtful,[49] over and above what is already innate in human nature. For in the process of 'doing wickedly against his own soul', every unrighteous emphasis brings a corresponding weakening of a man's nobler

---

[43] *De Agone Christ.* vii. 8.
[45] *De Agone Christ.* ii. 2.
[47] *De Trin.* XIV. xiv. 18.
[49] *Ench.* viii. 23, 24.

[44] Marlowe, *Tamburlaine* (Part I) I. v. 767.
[46] *Conf.* III. viii. 16.
[48] ibid.

powers. As Augustine declares, it is the most just punishment for sin

> that man should lose what he was unwilling to make a good use of, when he could have done so without difficulty if he had wished. It is just that he who, knowing what is right, does not do it should lose the capacity to know what is right, and that he who had the power to do what is right and would not should lose the power to do it when he is willing.[50]

The perversion of the soul produced by the atrophy of its powers ensures that sin will tend to produce further sin: human acts tend to produce like acts, Aquinas argues, and a man's sins therefore must occasion a diminutation of his natural inclination to virtue.[51]

Just as the loving fulfilment of God's will is by definition union with Him, so sin means separation of man from God; and the enduring state of separation from his Creator is, for Augustine, the weight of sin that every man bears.[52] This punishment manifests itself, and largely consists, in the mind being ruled by passion, and thereby losing its ability to judge between false and true, and to attain consistency, and therefore confidence, in its own discernments, amidst the storms of emotion that now shake man's being.

> Wherever he turns, avarice can confine him, self-indulgence dissipate him, ambition master him, pride puff him up, envy torture him, sloth drug him, obstinacy rouse him, oppression afflict him, and countless other feelings which crowd and exploit the power of passion. Can we think this no punishment at all, which, as you see, all who do not cling to wisdom must necessarily suffer?[53]

The refusal to pay back to God the existence it owes him, in the express breach of His commandments, is ruinous for the soul of man.[54] In his treatise 'Of True Religion', Augustine argues that the soul, by paying the penalty of its involvement in its sin, finds the difference between the neglected precept and the committed sin, and thus learns through its suffering, and that therefore the moral difficulty ensuing from vice is simply the penalty which it suffers.[55] If anyone could claim that he had never sinned, or that through this knowledge he had refrained from sinning, the argument might hold; but it can on the contrary be doubted whether, in view of Providence's punishing sin with sin and decreeing that sin should reign, sin can be held as having its genesis in the realm

[50] De Lib. Arb. III. xviii. 52.   [51] S.T. Ia IIae lxxxv. 1, ad R.
[52] J. Burnaby, Amor Dei, 1938, p. 186.
[53] De Lib. Arb. I. xi. 22, tr. M. Pontifex, Ancient Christian Writers, Newman Press, 1955.
[54] De Civ. Dei XIV. xiii.   [55] De Vera Relig.xx. 38, 39.

of the human will.[56] Meanwhile the universal condition of the children of men is that '*Faults* are in *flesh*, as *motes* be in the *Sunne*'.[57]

This condition is the result of mankind's attempt to live unto itself – a feat as impossible as it is absurd in a species whose means of goodness lies not in themselves. No man can have true virtue, says Augustine, who does not truly adore the one God : the virtue that is dedicated to a human glory, to whatever heights it be taken, cannot stand comparison even with the imperfect beginnings of the virtue whose hope is fixed in the grace and mercy of God :[58]

> For though there be a seeming of these things, yet if the soul and the reason serve not God, as He has taught them how to serve Him, they can never have true dominion over the body, nor over the passions : for how can that soul have any true measure of this decorum, that knows not God, nor serves His greatness, but is prostituted with the influence of the unclean and filthy devils? No, those things which she seems to account virtues, and thereby to sway her affections, if they be not all referred unto God, are indeed rather vices than virtues. For although some hold them to be real virtues, when they are desired only for their own account, and nothing else; yet even so they incur vainglory, and so lose their true goodness.[59]

Thus

> he that perversely affected a good of nature, though he attain it, is evil himself in this good, and wretched, being deprived of a better.[60]

Aquinas writes essentially to the same effect. A man's will, in order to be good, must be conformed to the Divine will; and since what can be good under one aspect may be evil under God's universal aspect, a will must be referred to the common good as an end, and formally will the Divine and universal good in addition to a particular good.[61]

In this doctrine that faith alone is the source of good, and that the apparent virtues of unbelief are really evil, Luther and Calvin concur. On the principle that the end of what is right is always to serve God, and that whatever is directed to any other end cannot merit that title, Calvin declares that 'whatever a man thinks, plans, or carries out before he is reconciled to God through faith is accursed';[62] and Luther and he echo Augustine in pronouncing that

---

[56] See A. Harnack, *A History of Dogma*, V, tr. J. Millar, Theol. Tr. Lib. X, London, 1889 p. 217.

[57] Fulke Greville, *Alaham* II. iv. 121 (Bullough edn., II, p. 173).

[58] *De Civ. Dei* V. xix.   [59] ibid., XIX. xxv.

[60] ibid., XII. viii.   [61] *S.T.* Ia IIae xix. 9, 10, *ad R.*

[62] *Inst.* III. xiv. 4.

94

the brightest virtues among the heathen, the best works among the philosophers, the most excellent deeds among men, which appear in the eyes of the world to be upright and good, and are so called, are really flesh in the sight of God, and minister to the kingdom of Satan; that is, they are ungodly, sacrilegious, and evil in every respect.[63]

Calvin argues that, in the apparently virtuous, God's providence restrains the perversity of human nature from external acts, but does not purify it within; but that, since we can have the Holy Spirit only by regeneration, all that man has from nature is carnal and unrighteous.[64]

Augustine's view of the virtues of the heathen as being vices (on the basis of *Romans* xiv. 23) has been taken to be inconsistent with his view that man's nature is good and the divine image not lost.[65] But this is to ignore Augustine's theory that, in a world of becoming, a lesser good becomes a source of evil if it is preferred to a greater; and to ignore also that, in such a world, what is admissible in the context of the mundane is not necessarily so in that of the divine.[66]

To live unto himself is for man apostasy; and by his native powers he can attain to only a meretricious virtue. Augustine can therefore write of man's true self-interest that

this nature created in such excellence, that though it be mutable yet by inherence with God that unchangeable good, it may become blessed : nor satisfies the one need without blessedness, nor has any means to attain this blessedness but God, truly commits a great error and enormity in not adhering unto Him.[67]

So to live is a continuous lie. For God is truth; and to live according to the self, and not according to the will of the Creator, is a pretension in the creature as perverse as it is laughable, for it means that he is seeking blessedness through the abandonment of the course that leads to it, and life apart from the source of all life.[68] 'Shall any be his own artificer?' asks Augustine. 'Or can there elsewhere be derived any vein, which may stream essence and life into us, save from Thee, O Lord, in whom essence and life are one? for Thou Thyself art supremely Essence and Life'.[69] With far more meaning can it be said within the realm of the spirit that the nature which seeks to

[63] *Martin Luther on the Bondage of the Will*, tr. J. I. Parker and O. R. Johnston, London, 1959, p. 253. See also Calvin, *Inst.* III. xiv. 3, 4, 8.
[64] *Inst.* II. iii. 3, 1.
[65] *De Gen. ad lit.* VIII. xiv. 31, 32; *Retract.* II. xxiv, quoted by J. Morgan, *The Psychological Teaching of St Augustine*, London, 1932, p. 41.
[66] Augustine, *De Lib. Arb.* II. xix. 53 (see p. 150 below); Martin Luther, *A Commentary on St Paul's Epistle to the Galatians* (ii. 20), ed. P. S. Watson, 1953, p. 175 (see p. 137 below).
[67] *De Civ. Dei* XII. i.   [68] ibid., XIV. iv.
[69] *Conf.* I. vi. 10.

> sliver and disbranch
> From her material sap, perforce must wither
> And come to deadly use.[70]

To the pagan soul pleading unconsciousness of God's being, it is urged that God's invisible reality is clear from visible things;[71] to the cry 'I see these things, but I do not see Him', the stern reply is that God gave us both eyes to see these things, and a mind whereby we might see Him.[72] In the government of the whole universe, and in the directing of souls themselves, God is manifest.

For the soul is in a state of blessed incompleteness: in their powers and in their incapacities alike God is ministering to His creatures. In the gifts of nature He makes them like His image; in the gift of reason, He gives them that by which they may know Him; and in the gift of grace lies the means whereby may be transcended that true sense of creaturely limitation that is the height, as it is also the commonplace, of mortal knowledge.[73] The better a man is, the greater will be his awareness that his good deserts are themselves God's gifts,[74] and that, though he may freely do evil, and fall away from God, good he cannot do without God's assistance.[75] God's gracious work in man is for Augustine what it is to Calvin: 'like the transformation of stone into flesh'.[76] God is manifest in man's helplessness – as He is in his hopelessness. For the unhappiness of man proclaims the presence of the Creator: nothing can be well with him who deserts the sole good, and so great a good as the rational nature can find no other good save God to make it happy.[77] Happiness, for a creature like man, cannot inhere in any created good, or in the goods of his own soul, capable as he is of seeking the universal good and truth.[78] God alone can satisfy man's will and constitute his happiness.

So the will in man to live unto himself, and be an end in himself, can, for Aquinas, only be the result of man's not having, in this life, a clear view of the Divine essence, and of the connexion of all particular goods with Him. Yet in his being as a creature lie the means of adherence. From the moment when created things receive the impulse which places them in a state of being external to that of the Creator, they receive also an impulse leading them back and impelling them toward their first source.[79] Part of that impulse in man is his own will to happiness: he can find no happiness in his own soul, for 'that which is in potentiality cannot be the last end',[80] and that which is in need of being brought

---

[70] *King Lear* IV. ii. 34–6.   [71] Morgan, op. cit., p. 43.

[72] 'New Year's Day, a Sermon against the Pagans' (Ben. no. 197), *Augustine: Sermons for Christmas and Epiphany*, tr. T. C. Lawler (Ancient Christian Writers), London, 1952, p. 142.

[73] *De Civ. Dei* VIII. x.   [74] *Ench.* xxviii. 107.

[75] *De Civ. Dei* XV. xxi.   [76] *Inst.* II. iii. 6.

[77] *De Nat. Boni* vii.   [78] *S.T.* Ia IIae ii. 8, *ad R.*; Gilson, op. cit., p. 260.

[79] Gilson, op. cit., pp. 226, 236.   [80] *S.T.* Ia IIae ii. 7, *ad R.*

from potency to act is as the incomplete to the complete, and, existing as it does in view of some other thing, cannot properly make itself its own last end.[81] Thus the human soul is in a state almost of deprivation – or is, rather, an 'incomplete perfection', tending and needing to complete itself. But it has no means to make its own potency actual: the operation needed to bring completeness remains beyond its own powers.[82] Hence the cry of Augustine,

> Therefore is *my soul like a land where no water is*, because as it cannot of itself enlighten itself, so can it not of itself satisfy itself.[83]

Just as the soul is the life of the body, so, for Augustine, God is the life of the soul, and must both animate and dominate man, just as the soul does the body.[84] For the soul has no principle of life, no divine spark, in itself. Its real immortality is in its participation in the life of God, and therefore the soul can die, and can be dead in a living body.[85] The life of the soul is its righteousness; and

> Man's righteousness therefore is this: to have God his Lord, and himself His subject, his soul master over his body, and his reason over sin, either by subduing it or resisting it: and to entreat God both for His grace for merit, and His pardon for sin, and lastly to be grateful for all His bestowed graces.[86]

Among all those matters which are the objects of men's faith and belief, Augustine argues, those and no others come into the prospect and realm of hope which find expression in the Lord's Prayer. For ' "Cursed is every man that putteth his hope in a man (*Jer.* 17.5)", and consequently any man who puts his hope in himself is involved in the meshes of this curse'.[87]

In the meshes of this curse worldly man is fully involved; and in a universe divinely ordained and governed, every incident of mundane life must work to teach and convince us that 'we are nothing with all our gifts, be they never so great, except God assist us'. Human life can be no more than the tragedy of mortal hopes and aspirations.[88]

---

[81] Gilson, op. cit., p. 259.   [82] ibid., p. 164.
[83] *Conf.* XIII. xvi. 19.   [84] J. Burnaby, *Amor Dei*, 1938, p. 149.
[85] ibid., pp. 151–2, quoting *Serm.* lxv. 4f.   [86] *De Civ. Dei* XIX. xxvii.
[87] *Ench.* xxx. 114.
[88] Luther, *A Commentary on St Paul's Epistle to the Galatians* (ii. 13), ed. P. S. Watson, 1953, p. 121.

D

Chapter 7

THE CREATED UNIVERSE

If its own creaturely needs do not instruct it in its dependence, therefore, the soul's adventures in the external sphere must demonstrate its limitations. For the essential unreality of the soul in itself is matched by that of the world to which it turns for the purpose of self-assertion. In the thought of Augustine the Platonic concept of the unreality of what is 'becoming' receives a Christian emphasis. The created universe has come into existence out of the will of God; by that will it is sustained; from that will alone, and not from any quality apparently proper to itself, does it derive its reality. Thus, if in his search for self-validity man is led to seek validity in existences set over against himself, he is doubly betrayed.

> For whithersoever the soul of man turns itself, unless toward Thee, it is rivetted upon sorrows, yea though it is rivetted on things beautiful. And yet they, out of Thee, and out of the soul, were not, unless they were from Thee. They rise, and set; and by rising, they begin as it were to be; they grow, that they may be perfected; and perfected, they wax old and wither; and all grow not old, but all wither. So then when they rise and tend to be, the more quickly they grow that they may be, so much the more they haste not to be. This is the law of them.[1]

All that exists is incomplete and mutable; permanence lies only with the purpose that decreed that they should be mere portions towards the completion of a universe. In them is no true existence; when sought,

> they abide not, they flee; and who can follow them with the senses of the flesh? yea, who can grasp them, when they are hard by?[2]

Had man's intellectual capacity not been precluded, for his punishment, from comprehending the whole, and restricted to a part of it, he would wish that all mortal existence should pass away;[3] in the interim, all things that gave pleasure were to be an occasion for God's praise: they were to be loved in God, in Whom alone they were firmly established, and for Whom alone a human love was fit.[4] Otherwise chaos was come

---

[1] *Conf.* IV. x. 15.   [2] ibid.   [3] ibid., IV. xi. 17.   [4] ibid., IV. xii. 18.

again: the possession of worldly means of happiness without the hope centred in God 'is a false beatitude, and a most true misery'.[5]

Almost in the same breath, Augustine can both deprecate and admit the love of 'the world, [and] the things that are in the world'. What saves him from self-contradiction is his overriding concern for the quality of man's love for the things of the world: 'God forbids you not to love them, but he will not have you seek your bliss in them'. An inordinate esteem for them, that leaves no room for the thought of the Creator, has the character of a lust.[6] For the mind is fashioned according to what it lives by; and, in this life, the very mind that seeks conformity with God must needs use and traffic with corporeal things. To place our end in such good things is to become conformed to this world; the true and admissible love for them is that

> whatever we do rationally in the using of temporal things, we may do it with the contemplation of attaining eternal things, passing through the former, but cleaving to the latter.[7]

The view that 'The world-renouncing and world-accepting temper both meet in S. Austin'[8] needs qualification if it is not to suggest that life in the world has value only as it is preparation for what is to come, and to obscure a resolution in Augustine's thinking. Augustine insists upon a correct appraisal of the world; and in his estimation, a true acceptance of created things involves a forsaking. To accept worldly forms for what they are not is not acceptance: to assume value and reality in what has no abiding permanence is infatuation. Only by accepting the world for what it truly is does it become possible – since it is inevitable – to forsake it. The things of the world have only a conditional existence: God alone truly is. Things are good in that they are of God, but they are not God in that they are not supremely good; and they are liable to vitiation for the reason that by themselves they are nothing.[9] The Christian perception of mundane existences is

> that they neither altogether are, nor altogether are not, for they are, since they are from Thee, but are not, because they are not, what Thou art. For that truly is, which remains unchangeably.[10]

The will for true existence must lead men away from the temporal. Both before they exist, and after they have passed away, temporal things have no existence, and even as they come into existence they pass away. It is for the lover of existence, therefore, to appreciate these things so far as they exist, and to love that which exists eternally.[11] Augustine thus

[5] De Civ. Dei XIX. xx.   [6] In Epist. Jo. ad Parth. Tract. decem ii. 11.
[7] De Trin. XII. xiii. 21.
[8] J. N. Figgis, The Political Aspects of S. Augustine's 'The City of God', 1921, pp. 67, 56.
[9] De Vera Relig. xix. 37.   [10] Conf. VII. xi. 17.   [11] De Lib. Arb. III. vii. 21.

99

comes to anticipate the thought of Berkeley, that the existence of the external universe springs from its comprehension in the mind of God:

> We therefore see these things which Thou madest, because they are: but they are, because Thou seest them.[12]

The inordinate love, in its attempt to gain pleasure and validity from created things, is characterized precisely by its forsaking God, and its self-involvement in delusion: the position of worldly man is that

> Things held me far from Thee, which, unless they were in Thee, were not at all.[13]

Thus the very loveliness of the Creator's handiwork is as it were a prophetic message of God's being and greatness to the soul of the beholder, not an opportunity given him for selfish enrapturement. Whoever craves gratification and permanence in the creature in contempt of the Creator – who seeks, and fights, for pleasures and certainties and advancement in the world of men – is guilty, apart from his folly, of a spurious aestheticism which prizes form without content and words without meaning, and is rewarded at the end with the emptiness it has seized upon.[14] The life that lusts after things that are born and pass away, labours to acquire them, rejoices in their abundance, and fears lest they should perish, can neither see nor cleave to the Truth, unchangeable and undefiled;[15] and its failure to possess the kingdom of God involves the loss of all its unrighteous loves:

> for by loving inferior things it is given a place among the inferior creatures, being deprived of its pleasures and afflicted with grief. What is bodily grief but the sudden loss of integrity in something which the soul has made a bad use of, so rendering it liable to corruption. And what is spiritual grief but to lose mutable things which the soul enjoyed or hoped to be able to enjoy? This covers the whole range of evil, i.e. sin and its penalty.[16]

It would be true to say also that it covered the whole range of tragedy.

In turning to goods of the external order, whether to assert its native vitalities or make good its own deficiencies by laying hold of seeming realities without, the self-deluded soul is mocked by its environment. External goods cannot make a man good or better; rather, such apparent goods are made good by the manner in which they are used – and only a good man can use them rightly. For the love of God prevents him from loving them with the love that would make them members of his own soul, and he is thus their master, ready to possess and control them, but still more ready to lose or forsake them.[17] His love for them thus corres-

---

[12] *Conf.* XIII. xxxviii. 53.   [13] ibid., X. xxvii. 38.   [14] *De Lib. Arb.* II. xvi. 43.
[15] *De Agone Christ.* xiii. 14.   [16] *De Vera Relig.* xii. 23.   [17] *De Lib. Arb.* I. xv. 33.

ponds with their true nature, and he is enabled to extend to them the true acceptance that involves forsaking. But the loves of the ungodly and unregenerate are capable of no such temperance; theirs can only be the tragic plaint

> that not in Him, but in His creatures – myself and others – I sought for pleasures, sublimities, truths, and so fell headlong into sorrows, confusions, errors.[18]

The created universe is evanescent, but it is not deceptive, save only to an unrighteous will. The decay of temporal things enables the future to follow the past and the beauty of the ages to unfold. Under the eternal law, which sustains all (not least the mind of man) in due order, created things act in accordance to what has been given them; and in accordance with the measure of their being they pay their debt to their Creator.[19] Time and space are not illusions; nor are they independent or real principles, since they depend on the Creator's will. The Divine order of the universe is that which gives us both existence and limitation, the condition of existence; in all causes God is present, and the fortuitous is that whose cause is hidden from us.[20] It is for man to learn the measure of his being in the order to which he is subject; and the demand upon him is the knowing and loving of God. In the activity of this quest, and in the unity thus created of man redeemed and predestinated to God's universal purpose, lies reality, as far as man can experience it; in the effort of self-realization, where the self is seen as in opposition to the Divine order of things – where the will 'turns from the unchangeable and common good and turns to its own private good or to anything exterior or inferior'[21] – lies disunity and unreality.[22] It is not the scheme of things that is unreal; it is rather the perverse will which opposes the Divine purpose in the created order that converts all it touches to its own unreality.

Worldly man may well oppose the Divine will; but frustrate it he may never. Indeed it must be within the scope and purpose of divine providence that its will should be so opposed.

> He . . . having left neither heaven, nor earth, nor angel, nor man, no nor the most base and contemptible creature, neither the bird's feather, nor the herb's flower, nor the tree's leaf, without the true harmony of their parts, and peaceful concord of composition; it is no way credible, that He would leave the kingdoms of men, and their bondages and freedoms loose and uncomprised in the laws of His eternal providence.[23]

[18] *Conf.* I. xviii. 31.   [19] *De Lib. Arb.* III. v. 16; III. xv. 42; I. vi. 15.
[20] *Retract.* I. i.   [21] *De Lib. Arb.* II. xix. 53.
[22] For this paragraph see C. N. Cochrane, *Christianity and Classical Culture*, 1940, pp. 479–88.
[23] *De Civ. Dei* V. xi.

Neither to God nor to creation as a whole can anything be evil, since there is nothing that can break in and corrupt the order He has appointed. If some parts of creation are accounted evil through their disharmony with others, the more extensive harmony in which they are involved establishes their ultimate goodness.[24]

The evil will, no less than any other created will, is under God's control. If the devils have any power or can do anything at all, Augustine argues, it is no more than God's secret providence permits them to do;[25] and because of the bounds that are assigned to their power the beauty and order of the universe is undisturbed.[26] All wills serve Divine providence : the just man serves freely as a son, the unjust in fetters as a slave. Though one do good and the other do evil, yet both do well, for of the actions of good and evil alike is done what is just; and 'that which is done justly is done well'.[27] No created nature can be harmed unjustly. The harm occasioned by the sinner is of course unjust, but the power by which he is permitted to do harm is from God, who knows, though the sinner does not, what ought to be suffered by those whom He permits him to harm.[28]

For the action of God in his secret working and in his self-manifestation is to transform evil into good; it is on this principle that Augustine can maintain that God 'judged it better to bring good out of evil than to preclude evil from existing'.[29] There can be no possible limitation to God's transforming power. Though something may be done contrary to His will, it is not done in spite of His will, for He would not permit it if He did not will it;

> nor, being good, would he permit an evil act, if he were not by his omnipotence able even of the evil to make a good effect.[30]

Even were the very foreknowledge of God to be confounded by a sudden act of sin, the 'inexpressible force of God's power' would be strong enough to permit nothing unbecoming to exist in His dominion;[31] so that whatever the depravity of the will that used created goods amiss, the justice of God would be manifest in using that evil well[32] –

> either by pardoning, or by healing, or by fitting and turning unto the profit of the pious, or even by most justly taking vengeance. For all these are good, and most worthy a good and Almighty God : and yet they are not made save of evils.[33]

[24] *Conf.* VII. xiii. 19.   [25] *De Civ. Dei* II. xxiii.
[26] See E. B. Pusey, ed., *Conf.* (V. ii. 2), A Library of Fathers, Oxford, 1838, quoting *De Gen. ad Lit.* I. xi. 21.
[27] *De Agone Christ.* vii. 7.   [28] *De Nat. Boni* xi.   [29] *Ench.* viii. 27.
[30] ibid., xxvi. 100.   [31] *De Lib. Arb.* III. xii. 35.
[32] *De Nat. Boni* xxxvii.   [33] *De Cont.* vi. 15.

God's rewarding the good and punishing the bad is a process entirely beneficial – but the punishments are evils to those who suffer them :[34] the pleasures of life can be known and acquired only through difficulties, so that 'The greater joy is ushered in by the greater pain'.[35] Though Augustine never agrees with Plotinus to the extent of justifying evil as being necessary to good,[36] he can justify the operation of evil by its contributing to the working out of good :

> Consequently, although things which are evil, in so far as they are evil, are not good, yet that there should exist not only good things, but also evil things, is a good thing.[37]

The contribution made by evil (under Divine direction) to the 'marvellous beauty of the universe'[38] is not apparent to human reason; but reason can relate the seeming chaotic ugliness of evil to the operation of the Divine justice, upon which that beauty must be founded.

> For order, is a good disposition of discrepant parts, each in the fittest place, and therefore the miserable (as they are miserable), are out of order, wanting that peaceable and unperturbed state which order exacts. But because their own merits have incurred this misery, therefore even herein they are imposed in a certain set order howsoever.[39]

Sin and consequent evils invoke and manifest the justice of God : the souls that justly become unhappy because of the sin they have willed contribute to the perfection of the whole, and are comprehended within it.[40] But lest it appear to impugn the justice of God that he should punish sins that are necessary for the perfection of Creation, Augustine insists that the sins themselves, or the unhappiness or the evil itself, 'are not necessary for the perfection of the whole; but the souls are necessary as souls.[41] He refrains at this point from arguing that the capability of sinning is a necessity for the souls' progression, implanted in them by God in His wisdom; but he insists that if sins were committed and no unhappiness were to ensue, the order of things would be stained with injustice.[42] But as ever in the thought of Augustine it is in the purpose of God, and not in the means to His purpose, that reality is to be found; and thus sin and the punishment of sin are said to be not of themselves substantial things, but rather the states of substantial things, the former being voluntary and the latter being penal.[43] For God's handiwork is good; and what is itself non-being, uncreated by Him, can never effectually mar what is substantial :

[34] *De Lib. Arb.* I. i. 1. [35] *Conf.* VIII. iii. 7, 8. [36] Burnaby, *Amor*, p. 195.
[37] *Ench.* xxiv. 96. [38] ibid., iii. 10. [39] *De Civ. Dei* XIX. xiii.
[40] ibid. [41] *De Lib. Arb.* III. ix. 26.
[42] ibid. [43] ibid.

It is a better order that a thing [*natura*] should suffer punishment justly than that it should rejoice in sin with impunity. So long as it retains some measure, form and order there is still some good in it no matter into what extremity it may come.[44]

As for the sufferings of the innocent, not only will they be as nothing when they are past, but none can know what ample compensation may be in store for those afflicted.[45] But the suffering itself is not outside the scope of God's providence. For by the very act of avoiding pain and seeking pleasure, all life in creation confesses that it shuns division and seeks unity. What troubles us in inconsistency is precisely that it has no unity;

Hence it is clear that everything, whether it inflicts harm or suffers harm, whether it causes pleasure or is given pleasure, suggests and proclaims the unity of the Creator.[46]

The sorrow of mankind is a confession of its craving for unity, goodness and love – of its yearning for its God and its blessedness.[47] This insight might be reflected in the words of Lear to his weeping child:

Thou art a soul in bliss (IV. vii. 46);

but it might be apprehended far more widely in the scope of Shakespearian tragedy itself.

Harm can thus come to man neither unjustly nor unprovidentially; and if it does come, then so long as within the bounds of a brief and transitory existence a mortal man be not compelled to acts of iniquity or injustice, it will do no harm.[48] The justification of any unperfectness either in human nature or in the created universe is that the good are in reality unassailable:

And therefore not at all do [the evil] injure the good; seeing that they take from them this which they love not: for that which they love, and whence they are blessed, no one can take away from them. But bodily torture miserably afflicts evil souls, but the good it strongly cleanses.[49]

The doctrine is clear: whatever man who has overcome his own vices cannot be overcome by any other man – for what resides with him is that which cannot be taken away from him.[50]

Such a man, as long as he is in this life, uses his friend to repay favours received, his enemy to cultivate patience, anyone at all in order to cultivate beneficence, and all men as objects of benevolence. Though he does not love temporal things, he uses them rightly himself, and

---

[44] *De Nat. Boni* ix.   [45] *De Lib. Arb.* III. xxiii. 68.
[46] ibid., III. xxiii. 70.   [47] *S.T.* Ia IIae xxxvi. 3, *ad R.*
[48] *De Civ. Dei* V. xvii.   [49] *De Agone Christ.* vii. 8.   [50] *De Vera Relig.* xlvi. 86.

takes thought for men according to the lot of each, if he cannot treat them all alike. . . . He is not made sorrowful by the death of anyone, for he who loves God with all his mind knows that nothing can perish for him unless it perish also in the sight of God. But God is the Lord of the living and the dead. He is not made unhappy by the unhappiness of another, any more than he is made just by the justice of another. As no one can take from him God and justice, so no one can take from him his happiness.

In all laborious duties he cherishes the certain expectation of rest to come, and so is not crushed. What can harm him who can make good use even of an enemy? He does not fear enmities because he is guarded and protected by God who has given both the command and the ability to love enemies. In tribulation he feels it a small thing not to be saddened. Rather he even rejoices, knowing that 'tribulation worketh patience, and patience experience, and experience hope, and hope maketh us not ashamed, because the love of God is shed abroad in our hearts by the Holy Spirit, which is given to us' (*Rom.* v. 3–5). Who can hurt such a man? Who can subdue him?[51]

The tragic involvements of mortal life can neither harm the good nor disturb the harmony of the universe. For in all these cases there is no evil except sin and sin's penalty: that is, a voluntary abandonment of the highest being and involuntary toil among inferior beings.[52] And if health and goodness are to be found in no man; if in the agonies of a punitive existence a man were to cry, as all men have to cry,

But if *I was shapen in iniquity, and in sin did my mother conceive me,* where, I beseech Thee, O my God, where, Lord, or when, was I Thy servant guiltless?[53]

his consolation lies in those very sufferings, in which the working and the righteousness of the Divine purpose is manifest. Righteous no man may be; but God is faithful. The beauty of created order must lie above all in this: that man in his unrighteousness is unfailingly confronted by the righteousness of God.

The beauty of the created universe is free from all fault because of these three things – the condemnation of sinners, the proving of the just, and the perfecting of the blessed.[54]

In the evils, as well as in the joys, of creaturely existence, is the hand of God to be discerned, and His blessings apprehended.

The resolution of Milton's Satan in Hell, 'Evil, be thou my good' (IV. 110), is a masterpiece of angelic intuition and apostate folly. For

[51] ibid., xlvi. 91, 92.
[52] ibid., xl. 76. See p. 93 above.
[53] *Conf.* I. vii. 12.
[54] *De Vera Relig.* xxiii. 44.

105

it is both an imitation of God's government and an apprehension of the salutary potential of evil. The defiance of God, however, not only destroys the desired potential but precludes the knowledge that evil's operation is conformed to the will of the Deity thus defied. In the determination 'out of good still to find means of evil' (I. 165) God will therefore be no less obeyed; and all Satan's endeavours

> served but to bring forth
> Infinite goodness, grace and mercy shown
> On man by him seduced, but on himself
> Treble confusion, wrath and vengeance
> poured   (I. 217–20).

For the tragedy which Satan, by God's permission and through frail human will, inflicts on mankind is a blessing; the tragedy which by his own will he inflicts on himself is a damnation; but the process itself by which both take place, in its good and its evil alike, is by the will of God a revelation.

For a humanity involved in sin and beset with evils, the question of the nature of evil is of the greatest importance. The starting-point for any inquiry, where once the Christian revelation has been taken into account, is the sentiment of Augustine:

> whatsoever is, is good. That evil then which I sought, whence it is, is not any substance: for were it a substance, it should be good.[55]

The evil of something is by definition a vice in it; and to blame the vice of any thing or being is nothing else than to praise the nature of the thing whose vice is blamed – for the vice is what is opposed to that nature in its goodness.[56] Evil therefore is the lack or privation of good, the absence of health:[57] for if the being and the perfection of any nature are goods, then evil, as opposite to good, can have neither being nor perfection, can be neither an essence nor a reality.[58] In the absence of positive and real existences to be its vehicle it cannot conceivably be present in the universe, for it is no substance, but negation within a substance, a deprivation or corruption of the good that is its support – for it can only be said to exist where there is some good.[59] That good, however, it can never wholly corrupt, since it would thereby consume itself.[60] Its subsistence within good as in its natural subject shows that it must necessarily have a cause. But only being can be a cause; and since all being is good, good itself is the only possible cause of evil.[61]

---

[55] *Conf.* VII. xii. 18.   [56] *De Lib. Arb.* III. xiv. 41.   [57] *Ench.* iii. 11.
[58] Gilson, op. cit., pp. 132–3; *S.T.* I. xlviii. 1, *ad R.; Summa Contra Gentiles* III. vii.
[59] Gilson, op. cit., p. 133; *S.T.* I. xlviii. 3, *ad R. Ench.* iv. 12, 13.
[60] Gilson, ibid.; *S.T.* I. xlix. 3, *ad R.*
[61] Gilson, op. cit., p. 134; *S.T.* I. xlix. 1, *ad R. Ench.* iv. 14, 15.

According to Aquinas, it is the goodness of the universe that is the cause of evil. The universe is a reflection of its Creator; and since His goodness cannot be adequately represented by one creature alone, its perfection consists in the diversity and variety of creatures necessary to express as nearly as created things can the resemblance to their God.[62] Plurality involves inequality; for creatures to be formally distinct, it is necessary for them to be unequal. Aquinas derives this doctrine of formal distinction from Aristotle (*Metaphy.* viii. 10), urging that 'the forms of things are like numbers in which species vary by addition or subtraction of unity', and that these forms can therefore be regarded in terms of superiority and inferiority.[63] Thus the Divine wisdom, in willing the distinction of things for the sake of the perfection of the universe, becomes the cause of inequality – in a universe which is excellent as a whole, its parts being strictly speaking excellent in their proportioning.[64] For the universe to be perfect, every grade of goodness has to be found within it – including that grade which can fail, as well as goodness that is incorruptible. The requirement for corruptible beings means that some should be able to fall short of their degree of perfection. So to fall short is the very definition of evil; and thus the existence of corruptible beings within the universe 'brings inevitably in its train the presence of evil'.[65] All that remains unaccounted for in this scheme is the origin of the will to corruptibility in the beings concerned. For God, though by this scheme manifestly the author of the evil which is penalty, is not the author of the evil which is fault.[66]

The existence of corruptible creatures – indeed, the status of being a creature implies defect – is required for the perfection of the universe. Is this to imply that evil is necessary for good? Aquinas, though willing to point out that many good things would be taken away if there were no evil, will not go so far.[67] Yet the existence of corruptibility is clearly God's purpose, and the quantitative nature of formal distinction, if it is true, lies subject to His will. The reason for this will is not, and cannot be, explored. In the words of Etienne Gilson,

to determine why God has willed these imperfect and defective creatures, is an impossible quest.[68]

[62] Gilson, op. cit., p. 127; *S.T.* I. xlvii. 1, *ad R.*
[63] *S.T.* I. xlvii. 2, *ad R.*; Gilson, pp. 128–9.
[64] *S.T.* I. xlviii. 2, *ad 3*; Gilson, p. 129.
[65] Gilson, p. 130; *S.T.* I. xlviii. 2, *ad R.*
[66] *S.T.* I. xlviii. 6, *ad R.*; I. xlix. 2, *ad R.*
[67] *S.T.* I. xlviii. 2, *ad 3*.   [68] Gilson, op. cit., p. 131.

Chapter 8

THE HUMAN WILL

Of these imperfect and defective creatures, man is the chief. In him, corruptibility has resulted in corruption; but the source of evil in him lies in no imperfection of his created being and nature, but rather in the perverse preoccupation with the self and the inferior desires of 'a will most incorrect to heaven'.[1] It is in the condition of our wills, declares Augustine, that is to be sought the demarcation between men and angels:

> It is not our earthly, bodily habitation but our unclean carnal affection, that causes separation between them and us.[2]

The body, though corruptible, 'does not burden the soul' and cause it to sin, but rather, it is the sinning soul which makes the flesh corruptible; to think otherwise would be to ascribe sinlessness to the Devil, who has no flesh.[3] The soul is superior to what is corporal, in the way gold is to silver; and just as gold becomes adulterated by the admixture of silver which is pure in itself, so the soul of man becomes tarnished through its desire for the things of the earth, though the earth itself is clean in its own nature and level.[4] Consequently,

> We should not therefore wrong our Creator in imputing our vices to the flesh: the flesh is good, but to leave the Creator and live according to this created good, is the mischief: whether a man chooses to live according to the body or the soul or both, which make the full man, who therefore may be called by either of them. For he that makes the soul's nature, the greatest good, and the body's the greatest evil, does both carnally desire the soul, and carnally avoid the flesh: conceiving of both as human vanity, not as divine verity teaches.[5]

There are lawful delights for all our bodily senses; indeed, a contempt for *res humanae* is no less than contumely toward God.[6] Thus sin in man is due to a corruption of the soul, not of the body.[7]

This distinction Aquinas preserves. If the Devil may be said to work

---

[1] *Hamlet* I. ii. 95. [2] *De Civ. Dei* VIII. xxv. [3] ibid., XIV. iii.
[4] *De Serm. Dom. in Monte* II. xiii. 44. [5] *De Civ. Dei* XIV. v.
[6] *Serm.* clix. 2, and *Ep.* cclviii. 2, quoted by J. Burnaby, *Amor Dei*, p. 113.
[7] See also *De Vera Relig.* xx. 40.

through the imagination and the sensitive appetite to persuade men to sin, it is due to the fact that the corporal nature has a necessary aptitude (being subordinate) to be moved locally by the spiritual nature.[8] The principle appears to be reflected in the situation of man with respect to original sin :

> What accrues to the soul from the corruption of the first sin, has the character of guilt, while whatever accrues to the flesh, has the character, not of guilt but of punishment : so that, therefore, the soul is the subject of original sin, and not the flesh.[9]

Original sin thus affects the will before it affects the other corporeal powers.[10]

What Augustine and Aquinas say here is in strict accord with Biblical doctrine. Of the four meanings of 'flesh' that can be adduced from Scriptural usage – the living body, the strictly human existence, the corporeal element, and corporal relationship or kinship – none is identified with evil, though the sense of 'perishable' may apply. And the unfavourable meaning which the term conveys in the Pauline writings relates rather to the natural state of man than to what is distinctively fleshly in him.[11]

In apparent contradiction to the distinction they make are various other pronouncements. Thus Augustine can argue that the corruptible body burdens even that soul which is subjected to God, and that the soul is always liable to domination by bodily lusts.[12] Aquinas, though pointing out that sorrow can be a virtuous and useful good, admits that sorrow or pain do burden or depress the soul when the evil concerned appears unavoidable.[13] In its desire for the sensible good, concupiscence, though belonging to the united soul and body, lies, properly speaking, in the sensitive appetite;[14] and bodily or concupiscent pleasures, considered in relation to ourselves rather than as in strict comparison with intellectual pleasures, are more vehement than the intellectual, since pleasures from sensible things are better known, and produce bodily alteration, and are sought as remedies for bodily griefs.[15] Bodily pleasure, further, positively hinders the use of reason – by distracting it, or by being directly contrary to the order of reason, or even by fettering the reason through bodily disturbance.[16] If such statements as these do not amount to an admission

[8] *S.T.* Ia IIae lxxx. 2, *ad R.*   [9] ibid., Ia IIae lxxxiii. 1, *ad R.*
[10] ibid., Ia IIae lxxxiii. 3, *ad R.*
[11] See J. Laidlaw, *The Bible Doctrine of Man*, Edinburgh, T. & T. Clark, 1905, ch. VI, pp. 109–20.
[12] *De Civ. Dei* XIX. xxvii; *De Lib. Arb.* I. iii. 8; cited by J. Morgan, *The Psychological Teaching of St Augustine*, 1932, p. 189.
[13] *S.T.* Ia IIae xxxix. 2, 3, *ad R.*; xxxvii. 2, *ad R.*
[14] *S.T.* Ia IIae xxx. 1, *ad R.*   [15] *S.T.* Ia IIae xxxi. 5, *ad R.*
[16] *S.T.* Ia IIae xxxiii. 3, *ad R.*

that bodily imperfection is a cause of sin, they do recognize in creaturely frailty itself a powerful means by which sin may be induced – for hereby any initial incorrectness in the will is provided with formidable allies.

Of such allies, passion is the chief. The deterioration of the personality through congruence with evil habits and the atrophy of neglected faculties leads to its being tyrannized by disordered passions. But the beginning of the process lies in inferiority of desire; and the passions in their very tyranny retain their characteristic of wrongful will:

> for there is a will in them all: nay, they are all direct wills: what is desire, and joy, but a will consenting to that which we affect: and what is fear, and sorrow, but a will contrary unto what we like? But when we consent to the desire of anything, that is desire: and when we consent in enjoying anything, this is delight. So, when we dislike a thing, and would not have it come to pass, this will is fear: when we dislike it being come to pass, this is grief or sorrow. And thus according to the variety of the things desired or avoided, as the will consents, or dislikes, so are our diversity of passions.[17]

The absence of passions which disturb the mind and resist reason is a good thing; but to attempt, with the Stoics, to abandon all mental passions is stupidity worse than sin.[18] For passions, though admittedly an affliction to the evil, are necessary to the good. Christians do indeed fear, and desire, and rejoice, and sorrow. 'But', says Augustine, 'their love being right, straightens all those affections'.[19] They fear eternal pain, desire eternal joy, sorrow for the present, and rejoice in their hope. Augustine does not mention anger here but Luther adds his own testimony:

> I never work better than when I am inspired by anger; when I am angry, I can write, pray, and preach well, for then my whole temperament is quickened, my understanding sharpened, and all mundane vexations and temptations depart.[20]

His conclusion is certainly that of Augustine: 'then has a bad life bad affections, and a good life good ones'.[21] The passions may become evil, and may lead to evil – but they cannot be in themselves the source of evil in the sinning soul.

Aquinas likewise relates the goodness or badness of the passions to the will's control of them, and permits their being regarded as disturbances of the soul and diseases only when they are not controlled by reason[22]– reason being for him, as for Augustine, the means to bring the motions of the soul into conformity with eternal law.[23] But since the passions are

---

[17] *De Civ. Dei* XIV. vi.   [18] ibid., XIV. ix.   [19] ibid.
[20] *The Table-Talk of Martin Luther*, tr. W. Hazlitt, London, 1883, cccxix.
[21] *De Civ. Dei* XIV. ix.   [22] *S.T.* Ia IIae xxiv. 1, 2, *ad R*.
[23] *De Lib. Arb.* I. viii. 18.

constituted by the sensitive rather than the intellectual appetite, they are properly part of man's corporeal endowment;[24] and qualifications similar to those applied to the other bodily faculties are to be found concerning the part played by the passions in the incidence of sin. Aquinas concedes that, although in theory they cannot do so, in practice the passions of the sensitive appetite can indirectly move the will to sin. The reason and the will naturally tend to follow these passions; and by distracting a man from his knowledge; by simply opposing a man's knowledge; by producing bodily encumbrance; or even by their own sheer intensity, the passions can draw the reason to judge in particular in defiance of the knowledge it has in general.[25] In the man in whom passion predominates, the sensitive appetite holds sway, so that the irascible and concupiscible powers can move the will;[26] and, in such a man, reason can become completely engrossed, and the will entirely moved by passion.[27]

Further – and far more serious – the passions and the temptations of the Devil, being alike causes of sin, are impeded only by the help of Divine grace. God's withdrawing of His grace as a punishment for sin allows the passions to overcome, and thus to be the cause – though accidentally – of further sin. Aquinas of course makes the distinction that one sin cannot essentially be the cause of another because sin in its essence must proceed from the will.[28] But his consideration of the matter *per accidens* reveals two causes stronger than the human will, and identifies passion as a direct cause of sin. It can therefore be said that the doctrine of the priority of the will in human sinning, in its treatment by Augustine and Aquinas, is not set forth without apparent qualification; that even in theory the appropriate functioning of the will appears to be imperilled by certain features of man's imperfect physical endowment; and that in practice, to be human must inevitably be to err. The question of the origin of human sin and that of the potentiality and scope of the human will are thus intimately related to each other.

The supremacy of the human will in the powers of the soul derives, in the thought of Augustine, from the analogy with the third hypostasis of the Trinity in its dynamic function as the principle of cosmic motion. Thus, in the trinity in the human soul which he bases on the soul's self-knowledge, in which the mental 'word' is begotten of knowledge and love, love is not begotten of the mind, as knowledge is, since it is the motive of seeking for self-knowledge, and therefore appears as the superior principle.[29] Similarly, in the trinity based upon sense-perception (object, sense-organ's perception and mental attention) and that based upon the

[24] *S.T.* Ia IIae xxii. 2, 3, *ad R.*
[25] *S.T.* Ia IIae lxxvii. 1, 2, *ad R.*
[26] *S.T.* Ia IIae ix. 2, *ad 1, 3.*
[27] *S.T.* Ia IIae x. 3, *ad R.*
[28] *S.T.* Ia IIae lxxxvii. 2, *ad R.*
[29] *De Trin.* IX. ix. 14; IX. xii. 17, 18.

functioning of imagination (memory, inward vision and will), the will is in both the linking and enabling agency.[30] Because of the will's control over the process of acquiring knowledge, even a man's awareness of God cannot pass into knowledge without its consent or desire; but all knowledge whatsoever, whether of the reason or of the senses, is dependent on the soul's volition.[31]

The concept of the will's ascendancy enables body and soul to be seen as part of a single process, to the extent of a fine material substance being postulated as the link between the two. The physical roots of human nature are no less spiritual for their being corporeal, since the soul takes part in the activity of sensation.[32] Will is the one efficient cause of human activity; love is to the mind what weight is to the body :

My weight, is my love; thereby am I borne, whithersoever I am borne.[33]

Physical or corporeal causes in themselves are negative, and in no sense are to be seen as efficient in influencing the activity of will.[34] By nothing save its own will and free choice is the mind made to give way to desire.[35]

For Aquinas too the principal holds good. The will, having as its object the good in general, moves all the powers of the soul to their respective acts.[36] Further, since a more perfect form eliminates a previous form while possessing all that the previous form possessed, the intellectual soul both contains and transcends the sensitive soul.[37] Absolutely speaking, intellect is superior to will; but in its inclination to the general good, will is the nobler.[38] Thus Aquinas would subscribe to Augustine's doctrine that no inferior thing can deprave the will, unless the will first depraves itself by inordinate choice.[39] For both, will, not intellect, is the centre of personality; the appeal of truth is neither to reason nor to emotion, but to will. Thus the sovereignty of will, and the significance of its 'love' or inclination, makes it possible to speak of all the endeavours of the soul as desire or appetite.[40] Augustine's higher and lower desire, the latter endeavouring to make a final good of the things perceived by the body, is reflected in Aquinas's two appetitive powers, will and sensuality.[41]

In principle, the will being sovereign, it lies in a man's own power whether he is to have, or not to have, the good will which is the most

---

[30] ibid., XI. ii. 5; XI. iii. 6, iv. 7; XI. v. 9.

[31] ibid., XI. xi. 18; Morgan, *Psychological Teaching*, p. 145.

[32] *De Gen. ad Lit.* VII. xv. 21, quoted by Morgan, op. cit., p. 128; Cochrane, *Christianity and Classical Culture*, p. 445.

[33] *Conf.* XIII. ix. 10.

[34] *De Civ. Dei* V. ix.

[35] *De Lib. Arb.* I. xi. 21.

[36] *S.T.* I. lxxxii. 4, *ad R.*

[37] Gilson, op. cit., p. 171; *S.T.* I. cxviii. 2, *ad 2.*

[38] *S.T.* I. lxxxii. 3, *ad R.*; Gilson, p. 227.

[39] *De Civ. Dei* XII. vi.

[40] *S.T.* I. lxxx. 1, *ad R.*; *De Cont.* xiii. 28.

[41] *De Trin.* IX. viii. 13; XII. x. 15; *De Veritate* XV. iii, *ad R.*, quoted by Gilson, op. cit., p. 217.

precious human possession. He can acquire it, in principle, with such ease, that to wish for it is the same as to possess what he wishes.[42] But in practice man does not have this free choice of will. Through 'ignorance', or through 'the resistance of carnal habits, which have become second nature as a result of the unrestraint handed on in human heredity', man sees and wills what he ought to do, but cannot carry out what he wishes. For the nobler powers of the sinning soul degenerate, and ignorance and difficulty are the two punishments that justly torment it.[43] Yet these two afflictions are to be looked upon as 'an encouragement to progress and a beginning of perfection'; the refusal so to progress under this stimulus is justly seen as sin.[44] Thus, despite the depredations that original sin and consequent corruptions have made upon human nature, the principle of choice is maintained. Man's punishment for his disobedience consists in his disobedience to himself: the emotions that now seize upon him against his will could not do so if his nature were wholly obedient to his will.[45] Yet even here, despite the weight of man's imperfections and sins, the will's sovereignty is not denied. Apart from the disobedience of man's nature to his will, the suggestion can be made of a disobedience within the will itself causing a failure of its authority: that the will disobeys itself because

it willeth not entirely: therefore doth it not command entirely.[46]

The happy potentiality is never lost sight of.

Though Augustine may speak of habits as becoming a second nature, they may do so only by reference to the will. A man is not punished for the faults of his nature, he declares, but rather for the fault of his will, since what appears to be a vicious nature in him, and has become so through the force of habit, has its origin in a corruption of the will.[47] The process is described in the *Confessions*:

My will the enemy held, and thence had made a chain for me, and bound me. For of a froward will, was a lust made; and a lust served, became custom; and custom not resisted, became necessity.[48]

Here lies the beginning of Aquinas's developed doctrine, in which habit becomes 'a dynamic element of progress and organization' within the soul, and a necessary instrument of the intellect.[49] For the soul, being a form that can operate in diverse ways, needs complementary powers

---

[42] *De Lib. Arb.* I. xii. 25; I. xiii. 27, 29. [43] ibid., III. xviii. 52.

[44] ibid., III. xx. 56. (Pontifex tr. Burleigh reads: 'If that is so in the case of souls that are born, ignorance and toil will not be punishment for sin but a warning to improve themselves, and the beginning of their perfecting.')

[45] *De Civ. Dei* XIV. xv. [46] *Conf.* VIII. ix. 21.

[47] *De Civ. Dei* XII. iii. [48] VIII. v. 10.

[49] Gilson, op. cit., p. 246.

which can dispose it to its operations; and these powers, or habits, may be described as dispositions in relation to a thing's nature, and to its manner of working or its end, which influence it towards either acceptance or rejection.[50] As far as they act according to reason, the sensitive powers possess habit, but its seat is more properly said to be in the intellect.[51] And it is principally related to the will, since, on the principle that every power implies and possesses a habit, habit is simply *'that which one uses when one wills'*.[52] Thus the quality of habit, like that of passion, stands in direct relation to that of the presiding will; it may be said to be simply a means by which a being realizes his own definition, and to be good or bad according as it approximates him to, or removes him from, his ideal type, at the dictate of his will.[53] Thus, despite the formidable power of habit and custom within the soul, the ultimate supremacy of will is not impaired: 'Use', as Aquinas defines it, 'is, properly speaking, an act of the will'.[54]

Thus it comes about that the anomaly of the will's being opposed by other of man's creaturely powers is provided with a resolution: for the opposition of sense, passion or habit may be regarded in some ultimate sense as subsidiary manifestations of the will's opposition to itself. Yet even so an anomaly remains, since the will's self-opposition must have some cause. And in so far as the creaturely powers concerned are not commonly treated as aspects of the will, but instead are referred to as in distinction from it, the weight of usage itself would indicate the need for a category by which these strong recalcitrant forces, of whatever origin, might be distinguished. For the more an absolute moral potentiality in the human will is insisted upon, the more a seemingly absolute disparity is made manifest. If, on the one hand, it is urged that nothing in the external order, or in the inner world of man, or in the very nature of evil itself, can overcome the will's autonomy, it becomes clear on the other hand that the creaturely condition of man is one in which there exist such fearsome potentialities for error as must challenge the will in the severest manner if they do not directly or indirectly contradict its autonomy; and, further, that man's condition, if he rely on his own powers, must approximate to that involvement in sin and evil which fact and experience show to be reigning in his world. For human experience is of the good that cannot be done through the will, and of the evil that is committed in the will's despite.

The solution to the dilemma is found in the Biblical doctrine of the Fall. The will of unfallen man was sovereign in that, though influenced in the direction of God, it had the choice of willing what was right or

<hr/>

[50] *S.T.* Ia IIae xlix. 4, *ad R.*; *ad 1.*   [51] *S.T.* Ia IIae lx. 3, 4, *ad R.*

[52] *S.T.* Ia IIae lx. 5, *ad R.*

[53] Gilson, op. cit., p. 244; *S.T.* Ia IIae xlix. 2, *ad R.*   [54] *S.T.* Ia IIae xvi. 1, *ad R.*

wrong.[55] Will in man was therefore the originator of evil, and all subsequent evil is correspondingly due to a free choice in the will.[56] For free will man retains – but the will to choose freely what is right he does not. The freedom of the will to do right was present in man's original state; but when the free will of man is referred to, the reference is to his present state, which is that of punishment –

> not the nature of man as he was made, but the punishment to which he has been condemned. When we speak of the freedom of the will to do right, the freedom of which we speak is that in which man was made.[57]

His devolution to his present punishment lies in this: 'that seeing he would not what he might, now he cannot what he would'.[58] The free will that man now possesses is a necessary tendency to sin, itself the result of tendencies which have vitiated human nature, and which are in turn the punishment of sin committed without necessity.[59] With this position of Augustine, Calvin is in full accord. Man, he says, sins voluntarily:

> Yet so depraved is his nature that he can be moved or impelled only to evil. But if this is true, then it is clearly expressed that man is surely subject to the necessity of sinning.[60]

By the grace of God this necessity for evil choice may be removed, and liberty be enjoyed completely, a complete necessity for error on the part of the will being replaced by the absolute necessity of the will's co-operation with God.[61] But through mere strength or supremacy of human will there can be no righteousness. Human free will at present is thus either a mere innate self-activity or power to choose, or an utter incapacity to resist sin or originate a good impulse.[62] The will of fallen man, of its own powers, can produce nothing save what is evil.

The present meaning of free will is slavery to sin; the true meaning of free will is freedom from sin's distortion, and harmony between the will of man and the will of God. It is, in fact, the service of God, in which there is no freedom to sin[63] – for in its true nature the will of man is in complete harmony with the will of God.

[55] J. Morgan, op. cit., p. 148; *De Civ. Dei* XIV. xii-xv; *De Cor. et Grat.* xi. 32.
[56] *De Lib. Arb.* III. i. 2; *Retract.* I. xiii. 5, cited by Morgan, op. cit., p. 148.
[57] *De Lib. Arb.* III. xviii. 52, quoted by Burnaby, *Amor Dei*, p. 188.
[58] *De Civ. Dei* XIV. xv.
[59] *De Nat. et Grat.* lxvi. 79; lxvii. 80, quoted by Morgan, op. cit., p. 153.
[60] *Inst.* II. iii. 5.
[61] *De Nat. et Grat.* lxvi. 79, quoted by Morgan, op. cit., p. 153.
[62] Morgan, op. cit., p. 154.
[63] *De Cor. et Grat.* xi. 32; xii. 33, quoted by W. Cunningham, *S. Austin and his Place in the History of Christian Thought*, Cambridge, 1886, p. 95.

For between the will of the Divine nature, which is set on the good of His creatures, and the will of the true human nature there is no necessary conflict; the depraved will, blinded by passion and enslaved by lust, does indeed rebel against God: but not so the will of the man who has attained to Freedom: he has come to see things as God sees them, and to will as God wills; just for the very reason that he is at length free, the discord between the human will and the divine is at an end, since the two natures are reconciled.[64]

The freedom of the human will under its present necessity of sinning and of dependence upon God for any good act, is likened by Augustine to that of an eye in darkness needing light.[65] Under such a similitude, the will (subject to the grace of God) may still be seen as the source of human virtue.[66]

Augustine's teaching concerning the human will is of decisive importance for the subject of the Divine omnipotence, according to W. Cunningham. For Augustine, man is not free to do good because he is enslaved and blinded by lust and passion; whereas for Calvin, man is not free to do good because he is predetermined.[67] The distinction is an acute one, but it provokes a bigger question than it settles: that of the relationship between man's state of enslavement and God's foreknowledge of his enslaved state, and, consequently, that of the relationship between man's will and God's almighty will.

Knowledge does not imply control; and the foreknowledge of God does not influence man's decisions. Just as a man's memory does not compel those of his deeds which are past, Augustine argues, so the foreknowledge of God does not compel the doing of things which are in the future.[68] Even where Holy Writ speaks of God's stirring up men's spirit, Augustine asserts the freedom of the wills thus stirred.[69] No action can take place unless God in the first instance gives the power by which it may do so:

But the giving of power is not the imposition of necessity: the David who received the power to slay Saul, chose to spare and not to strike. Thus we understand that the evil receive power for the condemnation of their evil will, but the good for the proving of their good will.[70]

All indeed obeys the will of God, and it can thus be said that the wills of men who do not know His will are none the less conformed to it; but God may will things without effecting them:

[64] Cunningham, op. cit., p. 96, citing *De Trin.* XIII. vii. 10.
[65] *De Gest. Pelag.* iii. 7, quoted by Morgan, op. cit., p. 154.
[66] *De Quant. Anim.* xxxiii. 73, cited by Morgan, op. cit., p. 162.
[67] op. cit., p. 105.　　　　　[68] *De Lib. Arb.* III. iii. 6, 7, 8; III. iv. 11.
[69] *De Grat. et Lib. Arb.* xxi. 42, quoted by Cunningham, op. cit., p. 86.
[70] *De Spir. et Litt.* xxxi. 54.

116

For the saints do will many things that are inspired with His holy will, and yet are not done by Him, as when they pray for any one, it is not He that causes this their prayer, though He do produce this *will* of prayer in them, by His Holy Spirit . . . God wills it and yet works it not.[71]

The relation between the willing and the working, the matter of the reconciliation between the primary and the subordinate cause, is not explored, but the distinction between them is insisted upon: the idea of compulsion is held to eliminate not only moral responsibility but also the will itself. God is therefore considered to be the preparer of the will, acting without encroaching upon personality;[72] but the concept terminates in what is clearly related to paradox, if it is not paradox itself:

What the soul is to possess, *what* it is to receive, pertains to God: the receiving and possessing, necessarily to him who receives and possesses.[73]

Aquinas accepts the position that it is God who in the first place moves the will to will but that this operation introduces no necessity into the will's voluntary acts. The movement God imparts is morally indeterminate:

God so moves it, that He does not determine it of necessity to one thing, but its movement remains contingent and not necessary, except in those things to which it is moved naturally.[74]

The only necessity the will may be said to exist under is that of desiring the good as such, since the will cannot will the contrary of beatitude:[75] toward the object that is good under all aspects the will must necessarily tend.[76] But for every particular good man has the choice of means, and in all other respects his will is not obliged to will that which it does will.[77]

The very act of free will, however, is for Aquinas traced to God as to a cause,[78] and from this fact it necessarily follows that what happens from the exercise of a free will is subject to Divine providence. Since providence produces every grade of being, there exists both necessity and contingency: Divine providence has prepared [*sic*] necessary causes for the former, and contingent causes for the latter;[79] again,

whatsoever divine providence ordains to happen infallibly and of necessity happens infallibly and of necessity; and that happens from

---

[71] *De Civ. Dei* XXII. i-ii.

[72] *Contra. Jul. Imp. Op.* I. ci; *Serm.* clxix. 13; quoted by Burnaby, *Amor Dei*, p. 228.

[73] *De Spir. et Litt.* xxxiv. 60, quoted by Burnaby, op. cit., p. 229.

[74] Gilson, *The Philosophy of St Thomas Aquinas*, Cambridge, 1924, pp. 231-2; *S.T.* Ia IIae x. 4, *ad R.*

[75] *S.T.* Ia IIae xiii. 3, *ad R.*   [76] *S.T.* Ia IIae x. 2, *ad R.*

[77] *S.T.* I. lxxxii. 2, *ad R.*; Ia IIae xiii. 6, *ad R.*

[78] *S.T.* I. xxii. 2, *ad R.*   [79] *S.T.* I. xxii. 4, *ad R.*

contingency, which the plan [*sic*] of divine providence conceives to happen from contingency.[80]

Predestination is a part of providence, and men are predestined; but it does not follow that predestination places anything, as it were, in those affected: the force of predestination is in the predestinating mind.[81] Thus the minds of those predestined remain free. God produces effects through secondary causes; and since there is 'no distinction between what flows from a secondary cause and from a first cause', it can be said that no distinction exists between the products of free will and predestination:

Wherefore, that which flows from free will is also of predestination.[82]

Thus nothing in the reprobate or in the predestinate affects their free will, since God's will does not take away any power of the person concerned.[83]

It is at this point that Augustine's problem of the relationship between God's willing and His working recurs most forcefully in Aquinas's thought, for neither the will of God nor the free will of man can be conceived as being inoperative in a situation which requires the operation of both. Thus the impossibility of the reprobate's obtaining grace 'must not be understood as implying absolute impossibility; but only conditional impossibility'; and the predestined must necessarily be saved,

yet by a conditional necessity, which does not do away with the liberty of choice. Whence, although one reprobated by God cannot acquire grace, nevertheless that he falls into this or that particular sin comes from the use of his free will.[84]

Though predestination be certain, yet free will is unaffected, and contingency persists. As for the Divine knowledge and will,

they do not destroy contingency in things, though they themselves are most certain and infallible.[85]

The paradox is complete and unresolved, and expresses itself in verbal self-contradiction as explicit as it is significant.

Augustine had carefully preserved a distinction between God's foreknowing and his predetermining: God's use of predetermining means is consequent upon a foreknowledge of the operation of those means in the individual:

It is because God foresees what man will do, that He predestines; and thus it is by the use of the means of grace that human beings accomplish the destiny which He has foreseen.[86]

[80] *S.T.* I. xxii. 4, *ad 1.*   [81] *S.T.* I. xxiii. 2, *ad R.*   [82] *S.T.* I. xxiii. 5, *ad R.*
[83] *S.T.* I. xxiii. 3, *ad 3.*   [84] ibid.   [85] *S.T.* I. xxiii. 6, *ad R.*
[86] Cunningham, op. cit., p. 127, citing *De Dono Persev.* xiv. 35 and *De Praedest. Sanct.* xvii. 34.

The distinction is hard to preserve, however, since 'what man will do' of good is in Augustine's thought itself entirely dependent on God's prior act:

When God crowns our merits, He crowns nothing but His own gifts.[87]

If merits are the fruit of grace, election cannot be a matter of the knowing of future merits on God's part, and God's foreknowledge must be that of His own intentions. This is the objection of Aquinas to what Augustine had taught, which he likens to a king giving a horse to a soldier because he knows he will make good use of it:

It is, however, manifest that what is of grace is the effect of predestination; and this cannot be considered as the reason of predestination, since it is contained in the notion of predestination. Therefore, if anything else in us be the reason of predestination, it will be outside the effect of predestination.[88]

Aquinas therefore subjects both human free will and Divine grace to the order of predestination:

whatsoever is in man disposing him towards salvation, is all included under the effect of predestination; even the preparation for grace. For neither does this happen otherwise than by divine help.[89]

In considering the words of *I Tim.* i. 9–10, that the faithful have been saved and called to a holy calling 'not according to our works, but according to his own purpose and grace', Calvin declares the gift of grace to be

nothing other than the predestination by which we are adopted to become sons of God.[90]

He does so in apparent conformity with Aquinas's position, and with such of his pronouncements as,

predestination implies a relation to grace, as of cause to effect, and of act to its object.[91]

It is on the necessary and crucial question of the cause of will that the problem of the relationship between Divine necessity and human free will becomes most urgent. That God is cause, in the sense of giving power, is for Augustine and Aquinas beyond question;[92] but the idea that the movement He imparts to the soul is morally indeterminate, so that the good are enabled to prove their good will and the evil to be self-condemned by their own evil will, must receive qualification from

---

[87] *Ep.* cxciv. 19, quoted by Burnaby, *Amor Dei*, p. 238.
[88] *S.T.* I. xxiii. 5, *ad R.*   [89] ibid.
[90] *Commentaries*, tr. J. Haroutunian, L.C.C. XXIII, 1958, p. 310.
[91] *S.T.* I. xxiii. 2, *ad 4.*
[92] *S.T.* Ia IIae ix. 4, 6, *ad R.*; ix. 6, *ad 3*; x. 4, *ad R. De Spir. et Litt.* xxxi. 53, 54.

the doctrine that 'the good will itself is wrought in us by the will of God'.[93] The activity of God is no less evident in reprobation. Although Aquinas can argue that 'guilt proceeds from the free will of the person who is reprobated and deserted by grace',[94] it must likewise be said that

> the cause of grace being withheld is not only the man who raises an obstacle to grace; but God, Who, of His own accord, withholds His grace. In this way, God is the cause of spiritual blindness, deafness of ear, and hardness of heart.[95]

The blindness so caused is directed to the damnation of those who are blinded, for the sake of the whole universe, and in particular of the good.[96] Similarly, as has been seen, the sin which follows from God's withdrawal of grace, in allowing the passions to overcome, is accidentally the cause of further sin.[97] The activity of the Divine will is the 'something more' than foreknowledge that for Aquinas is included in predestination:

> as predestination includes the will to confer grace and glory; so also reprobation includes the will to permit a person to fall into sin, and to impose the punishment of damnation on account of that sin[98]

The activity of the Divine will, for all that it may be held to leave the human will free, is clearly more than a mote to trouble the mind's eye.

If God is the cause of a good will, what is the cause of an evil will? The question is insistent, as it is inevitable: for if all is *ex nihilo*, and God is supremely good, how can motion away from Him arise?[99] This is a question which Augustine more than once declines to pursue, for reasons which he gives eloquently in *The City of God*:

> Let none therefore seek the efficient cause of an evil will: for it is not efficient but deficient, nor is there effect but defect: namely falling from that highest essence unto a lower, this is to have an evil will. The cause whereof (being not efficient but deficient) if one endeavours to seek it, it is as if he should seek to see darkness, or to hear silence: we know them both, this by ear, and that by the eye: but not in any forms of theirs, but in privation of forms. Let none seek then to know that of me which I know not myself.[100]

Aquinas likewise will not admit an efficient cause of an evil will. Good is the only possible cause of evil; yet God, the cause of all good, is not the cause of evil.[101] In the realm of corruptible things God may be seen

[93] *De Quaest. ad Simplicianum* I. ii. 12. [94] *S.T.* I. xxiii. 3, *ad* 2.
[95] *S.T.* Ia IIae lxxix. 3, *ad R.* [96] *S.T.* Ia IIae lxxix. 4, *ad R.*; *ad 1–4*.
[97] *S.T.* Ia IIae lxxxvii. 2, *ad R.* [98] *S.T.* I. xxiii. 3, *ad R.*
[99] See W. A. Christian, 'The Creation of the World', *A Companion to the Study of St Augustine*, ed. R. W. Battenhouse, N.Y., 1955, p. 336.
[100] *De Civ. Dei* XII. vii; see also *De Lib. Arb.* III. xvii. 49.
[101] *S.T.* I. xlix. 1, *ad R.*; Gilson, op. cit., p. 135.

as cause, since out of the will for the good order of the universe arises the necessity for things that can fail which is the accidental cause of corruption. Thus He is the author of the evil of penalty in creatures that sin; but of the fault in the acting being, be it defect of action or defect of agent, He is not the cause.[102] The failure of the will to subject itself to its proper rule is a deficiency :

> This defect, however, is not a fault, but fault follows upon it from the fact that the will acts with this defect.[103]

Evil in the acting will is deficiency, in the same way as evil itself is nothing; and deficiency, being insubstantial, can have no cause. The cause of evil, therefore, as Gilson puts it,

> reduces itself to the tendency of some things to return to non-being.[104]

If, however, there can be no cause of evil apart from the will, and evil in the will is in the strict sense uncaused, the question arises as to the cause of the tendency. It does so, however, in the process of an infinite regress which must result, sooner or later, in silence.[105]

It is precisely upon the point of the relation between the willing of God and the effective working of His will upon those to whom it is directed, that Luther writes with most emphasis. The lack of emphasis upon that relationship in the thought of Augustine and Aquinas had been largely due to their concern to preserve the concept of human free will; Luther's insistence is that in all matters affecting the things of God and the relation of man to God, the will, grace and providence of God is a matter of His prior initiative and direct rule upon the human soul :

> Do you suppose that He does not will what He foreknows, or that He does not foreknow what He wills? If He wills what He foreknows, His will is eternal and changeless, because His nature is so too. From which it follows, by a resistless logic, that all we do, however it may appear to us to be done mutably and contingently, is in reality done necessarily and immutably in respect of God's will.[106]

The idea of human independence in spiritual matters will alike be affected by the doctrine that destroys contingency. 'The foreknowledge and omnipotence of God', Luther declares, 'are diametrically opposed to our "free will" ';[107] and Calvin follows him in insisting that, in preparing the way for His providence, God inclines and moves men's wills both inwardly and externally, so that their choice in all its liberty remains subject to His will.[108]

[102] *S.T.* I. xlix. 2, *ad R.*   [103] *S.T.* I. xlix. 1, *ad 3.*   [104] op. cit., p. 136.
[105] See D. E. Roberts, 'The Earliest Writings', *A Companion*, p. 122.
[106] *Martin Luther on the Bondage of the Will*, tr. Parker and Johnston, London, 1959, p. 80.
[107] ibid., p. 217.   [108] *Inst.* II. iv. 7.

The discussion of the concept of free will in Augustine and Aquinas had taken place, in the main, at a theoretical level, concerning itself with human nature as it ideally was rather than as it stands distorted after the Fall. In the latter category, free will for Augustine is a necessary tendency to sin, and an incapacity for doing the good that is willed – an incapacity from which man may be liberated, but only by the grace of God.[109] It is from this existential situation that Luther chooses to argue, the essence of free will for him being that it is not free: that it 'is nothing but the slave of sin, death and Satan, not doing anything, nor able to attempt anything, but evil'.[110] The theory of a capacity for willing good without the ability to use it appears to him as a contradiction: what is ineffective power but, in plain language, no power?[111] Why, in view of the frequency of such Biblical statements as 'they are all gone out of the way, there is *none* righteous, *none* that doeth good, no, not one', should contradictory statements have won acceptance?[112] Why, he asks, do we cling so tenaciously to an empty word?

> By thus misusing language, anyone can boast that he has anything: for instance, that he is lord of heaven and earth – if God would give him that distinction! But such talk is more appropriate to actors and confidence tricksters than to theologians.[113]

What man is able to do of his own strength towards the winning of righteousness Luther likens to the ability of the earth to procure for itself seasonable rain – a similitude not unlike Augustine's example of an eye in the dark.[114] Thus in things relating to salvation or damnation, man has no free will, but is a centre for the contention of spiritual agencies:

> So man's will is like a beast standing between two riders. If God rides, it wills and goes where God wills. . . . If Satan rides, it wills and goes where Satan wills. Nor may it choose to which rider it will run, or which it will seek; but the riders themselves fight to decide who shall have and hold it.[115]

This pronouncement in its severity is not distinctive to Luther; it recalls a vision in the thought of Augustine, where

> the entire contest of human life is fittingly conducted by the unchanging providence of God who allots different rôles to the vanquished and the victorious, the contestants, the spectators, and the tranquil who contemplate God alone –

---

[109] See p. 115 above. [110] *Bondage*, p. 301. [111] ibid., p. 104.
[112] ibid., p. 298; *Rom.* iii. 10. [113] *Bondage*, p. 106.
[114] *A Commentary on Paul's Epistle to the Galatians*, ed. Watson, 1953, p. 23; Augustine, *De Gest. Pelag.* iii. 7.
[115] *Bondage*, p. 103. See also Calvin, *Inst.* II. iv. 1.

though Augustine is careful to add the qualification that the evil will in man is voluntary.[116]

Yet the same providence which overrules all human initiative in spiritual matters, Luther argues, has decreed that man by his very nature should be involved in this contention: man is created and preserved for the purpose that he may work with God, and God with him, whether by His general omnipotence or the special power of His spirit.[117] God does not work in us without us:

> Note, however, that if we meant by 'the power of free will' the power which makes human beings fit subjects to be caught up by the Spirit and touched by God's grace, as creatures made for eternal life or eternal death, we should have a proper definition. And I certainly acknowledge the existence of this power, this fitness, or 'dispositional quality' and 'passive aptitude' (as the Sophists call it), which, as everyone knows, is not given to plants or animals. As the proverb says, God did not make heaven for geese![118]

Neither the Divine initiative in matters spiritual, nor the immediate pressure of the Divine omnipotence, nor the human enslavement to sin, invalidates, for Luther and Calvin, the operation of man's will, or denies his responsibility. As Calvin puts it, the human reason remains, though it is 'partly weakened and partly corrupted'; and although he is deprived of supernatural talents,

> in man's perverted and degenerate nature some sparks still gleam. These show him to be a rational being, differing from brute beasts, because he is endowed with understanding. Yet . . . they show this light choked with dense ignorance, so that it cannot come forth effectively. Similarly the will, because it is inseparable from man's nature, did not perish, but was so bound to wicked desires that it cannot strive after the right.[119]

Thus sin for Calvin, equally as for Augustine,[120] is the defect of a good nature; and despite the activity of the Providential will, the sin committed proceeds from the will of man – the ordination of God which applies the destiny of sinning being guided by an equity unknown to us:

> For even though by God's eternal providence man has been created to undergo that calamity to which he is subject, it still takes its occasion from man himself, not from God.[121]

[116] *De Vera Relig.* xl. 76. [117] *Bondage*, p. 267.
[118] ibid., p. 105. [119] *Inst.* II. ii. 12.
[120] In contradiction to Cunningham, *S. Austin and his Place*, 1886, p. 83.
[121] *Inst.* III. xxiii. 9; in contradiction to Cunningham, op. cit., p. 105: see p. 116 above.

Further, the absolute nature of the Divine omnipotence does not imply an 'apparently arbitrary power of the Divine Will' for the thought of Luther and Calvin.[122] Augustine's position that the apparently arbitrary acts of God rest on reasons which we shall eventually understand should be compared to Luther's statement that the light of glory (as opposed to that of nature and grace) 'will one day reveal God . . . as a God whose justice is most righteous and evident', and to Calvin's that God's secrets cannot be known to us at this day because we have 'too small a capacitie', and that we must be content to know in part 'vntill full knowledge be disclosed to vs at the latter daye'.[123] It is to be admitted, however, that the Divine reason, present in the knowledge given to the saints and effecting the completion of human reason, does appear to be more mysterious for Luther and Calvin than it is for Augustine and Aquinas.

This brief account of the scope and possibilities of the human will as they have appeared in Christian thinking reveals three major facts to a greater or lesser degree unreconciled. The first is an inevitable and ineradicable tendency of men to sin despite their own will. The second is the supreme importance of human decision, and the consequent need to preserve the idea of the validity and capacity of the functioning will. The third is the subjection of the human will in its sinning and its choosing – for the one seems inseparable from the other – to the omnipotent will and purpose of God. If these three contradictory facts cohere in one universe, as Christian experience says they do, then they must also cohere in one process.

[122] Cunningham, p. 104, quoting *Inst.* III. xxi. 1.

[123] *Bondage*, p. 317; *Calvins Sermons on Job*, tr. A. Golding, 1573, p. 24b; Augustine, *De Grat. et Lib. Arb.* xxiii. 45.

Chapter 9

THE HUMAN INTELLECT

The potentialities of the human will, according to Aquinas, can be nobler than those of the intellect only with respect to the movement toward the good that is willed; but in all other respects the intellect is the superior of the two higher faculties of the soul.[1] This judgement is based on the traditional doctrine that man's distinctiveness and eminence as a creature lies in his powers of understanding; that

> God made man according to His image and likeness, giving him a soul whereby in reason and understanding he excelled all the other creatures, that had no such soul.[2]

The rationality that distinguishes man from beast is partly concerned with the bodily life, and this Augustine makes the 'lower' reason. In the Fall the lower reason, of which Eve is the personification, had revolted against the higher; and in this present world men take for preference to the active, lower form of rationality which Augustine distinguishes by the title of knowledge, and forsake the higher, contemplative form which for him constitutes wisdom:[3]

> the intellectual cognizance of eternal things belongs to wisdom, but the rational cognizance of temporal things to knowledge.[4]

Thus he retains in some measure the Platonic distinction between intuitive knowledge of the good, and discursive thinking, as the higher and the lower functions of the human mind in the intelligible world. The tragedy of worldly man consists very largely in his will to attain to knowledge; for in thus exercising his mind upon external fact he is able, not only to pursue worldly desire, but to procure also a confirmation of his own creaturely existence.

> For when he neglects the love of wisdom, which remains always after the same fashion, and lusts after knowledge by experiment upon things

---

[1] *S.T.* I. lxxxii. 3, *ad R.* [2] *De Civ. Dei* XII. xxiii.
[3] *De Trin.* XII. iii. 3, vii. 9–12. [4] ibid., XII. xv. 25.

temporal and mutable, that knowledge puffeth up, it does not edify : so that the mind is overweighed and thrust out, as it were, by its own weight from blessedness.[5]

The 'image and likeness' of God in man does not lie in the rational nature that man possesses, but rather in man's power to use that rationality.[6] The human mind, in its trinity of self-remembrance, self-understanding and self-love, is God's image in its manifest capacity to know Him;[7] but the mind's own self-love is of that image only in that it has power so to remember, understand and love its Creator. Otherwise its self-love is folly. In the worship of God alone lies wisdom – for such worship is a partaking by the mind of the Divine light.[8] Wisdom is not of man.

Faith, therefore, though belonging to the order of knowledge,[9] is a condition for the true exercise of reason and the gaining of understanding. Authority's prior demand of faith does not constitute a denial of that reason 'by virtue of which He has made us superior to other animals'.[10] Faith and reason are complementary activities of the mind, in that they both apprehend an 'unmoved' principle in and behind phenomena, and thus are alike validated by a principle at once beyond them and in them. Both empower and encourage man to seek for a truth that discursive reason could never attain to. For the constructions that discursive reason places upon things are relative to the creaturely faculties and being of the observer. But the intimations of wisdom derive from the Creator; and though faith and reason lead man to seek them, they are different in quality and kind from his active mental processes.[11]

Luther, concerned as he is to emphasize the directness and completeness of man's dependence upon God's grace for the achieving of all good, intensifies the distinction between the insights gained by human reason and those bestowed by God's direct and gracious revelation to the faithful.[12] Thus he can argue that 'The teachings of human experience and reason are far below the divine law', and that 'Philosophy understands naught of divine matters' and should not be mixed up with divinity.[13] Man's soul has the light of reason, but it is through the spirit that he attains things eternal and otherwise incomprehensible; and unless the spirit, lightened with faith (itself a work of God, not of man) controls the light of reason, the soul will remain in darkness and error.[14] The

[5] ibid., XII. xi. 16.   [6] ibid., XIV. iv. 6.   [7] ibid., XIV. viii. 11.
[8] ibid., XIV. xii. 15.   [9] ibid., XIII. xix. 24; XIV. i. 3.
[10] *Ep.* cxx. 3, quoted by Cochrane, *Christianity and Classical Culture*, p. 401.
[11] For this paragraph see Cochrane, pp. 400–15.
[12] B. A. Gerrish, *Grace and Reason: a Study of the Theology of Martin Luther*, 1962, p. 136.
[13] 'The Papacy at Rome', quoted in *A Compend of Luther's Theology*, ed. H. T. Kerr, Philadelphia, 1943, p. 4; *Table-Talk*, xlviii.
[14] 'The Magnificat', quoted in *A Compend*, p. 78.

natural reason of man is sufficient for worldly matters, but unless checked it will carry into the realm of the spirit concepts deriving from its own limited humanity and worldliness. But God in creating faith creates anew the reason and natural wisdom of man; and reason thus resuscitated becomes conformed to the mind of God and the nature of the spiritual realm by adopting concepts derived from God's own Word.[15] Thus does the natural instrument, formerly hurtful, become wholesome:

> The natural wisdom of a human creature . . . is altogether in darkness. . . . But in a faithful person, regenerate and enlightened by the Holy Spirit, through the Word, it is a fair and glorious instrument.[16]

Thus faith is the completion of reason in a sense which would appear to include that wisdom which was for Augustine largely beyond the capacities of mortal man.

It is Aquinas who comes closest to identifying the human reason with the Divine. The goodness of the will, he argues, depends on its object – and it is the reason which proposes the object to it.[17] But it is by God's decree that the reason rules the will:

> Now it is from the eternal law, which is the Divine Reason, that human reason is the rule of the human will, from which the human will derives its goodness;[18]

and since the second cause acts only in virtue of the first,

> It is therefore evident that the goodness of the human will depends on the eternal law much more than on human reason.[19]

Such is the dignity of reason that every will at variance with it, whether right or erring, is always evil.[20]

Reason thus understood is not to be divorced from the attaining of intelligible truth. Man achieves knowledge of intelligible truth by advancing from one thing to another by rational process, and thus reason and intellect appertain to the same power. Intellect is both the beginning and the end of the reasoning process:

> Reasoning, therefore, is compared to understanding, as movement is to rest.[21]

Augustine's 'higher' and 'lower' reason, the one seeking the eternal, the other the temporal, are two distinct forces, Aquinas argues, but part

---

[15] *Table-Talk*, ccxciv; Gerrish, op. cit., p. 170.
[16] *Table-Talk*, ccxcvi   [17] *S.T.* Ia IIae xix. 3, *ad R.*
[18] *S.T.* Ia IIae xix. 4, *ad R.*   [19] ibid.
[20] *S.T.* Ia IIae xix. 5, *ad R.*   [21] *S.T.* I. lxxix. 8, *ad R.*

of one process, since 'one of them' – the lower – 'is the means of knowing the other'.[22]

The corporeal element in intellectual activity, however, if it does not imply a qualification in Aquinas's position, is nevertheless to some degree an apparent anomaly. For Aquinas as for Augustine, body and soul are a true unity, and, despite their inequality, their union is a beneficent linking.[23] But it is precisely because it requires a body for its proper operation that human intellectuality is inferior to that of the angels; for the body is not of the essence of the soul, though the soul by its essence can be united to the body.[24] Since it is thus constrained to seek for the intelligible within the sensible, the human is 'the lowest in the order of intelligence and most remote from the perfection of the Divine intellect' – though man is like all creatures in that his soul is not an intellect but only a principle of intellect,[25] the Creator alone being intellect in essence.[26] But on the general principle that the nobler a form is, the higher it rises above corporeality, the human soul therefore

> excels corporeal matter in its power by the fact that it has an operation and a power in which corporeal matter has no share whatever. This power is called the intellect.[27]

The union of soul and body is necessary to intellect; but the soul's excellence, namely its intellect, is conceived as lying in its very remoteness from the corporeal.

The excellence of the soul's cognitive activity appears to derive from what Aquinas, following Aristotle, terms the active intellect. The human intellect, having to pass from potentiality to act with regard to things intelligible, is in the beginning passive; the active intellect, by abstracting the species from material conditions, is the power by which things are rendered intelligible.[28] This power is not something external to man, but operates within the soul; nonetheless, it draws its being from the mind of its Creator, in which it participates and from whence it derives its intellectual light.[29] If, therefore, the intellectual light which is in man is, as Aquinas puts it,

> nothing else than a participated likeness of the uncreated light, in which are contained the eternal types,[30]

22 S.T. I. lxxix. 9, ad R.

23 Gilson, op. cit., pp. 162, 7; Contra Gent. II. lvii; J. Morgan, The Psychological Teaching of St Augustine, 1932, p. 114.

24 Gilson, op. cit., p. 161; S.T. I. lxxv. 7, ad 3.

25 S.T. I. lxxix. 2, ad R.; Gilson, p. 173.

26 S.T. I. lxxix. 1, ad R.   27 S.T. I. lxxvi. 1, ad R.

28 S.T. I. lxxix. 2, 3, ad R.   29 S.T. I. lxxix. 4, ad R., ad 5.

30 S.T. I. lxxxiv. 5, ad R.

it would follow that intelligibles are within man's reach. This in one sense Aquinas appears to admit : on the principle that one thing is said to be known in another as in a principle of knowledge (as we might say that we know in the sun what we see by its light), he declares that 'we must needs say that the human soul knows all things in the eternal types'. But he qualifies this statement with the thought that man needs also intelligible species derived from things for his knowledge of material things, and concludes by quoting Augustine to the effect that the eternal types themselves are seen only in the vision of the holy and the pure – adding no further comment of his own.[31] The inference to be drawn here is that, despite the previous reasoning, active intellect in man is not so excellent as to be able to attain the realm of intelligibles in the absence of all that is involved in the concept of blessedness. The inference is confirmed by Aquinas's statement elsewhere that

> Higher intelligible things [than 'those we can come to know through the senses'] the human intellect cannot know, unless it be perfected by a stronger light, viz. the light of faith or prophecy which is called the *light of grace*, inasmuch as it is added to nature.[32]

Thus it is not directly through intelligible species themselves, but through the active intellect's rendering intelligible of material things by abstraction from the phantasms, that human knowledge is derived.[33] The sensitive powers are essential to the judgement of intellect, for the phantasms are strictly related to the senses, albeit that the sensitive soul is subsumed under the rational.[34] As for the first principles of knowledge, they are by no means innate ideas; these germs of knowledge are formed by the human intellect in its first contacts with the sensible, and the intervention of the sensible is necessary to their creation.[35] Thus humanity can have neither actual nor habitual knowledge of the infinite, for the infinite exists only potentially in material things and in our own minds.[36] Immaterial substances in themselves the mind cannot understand. Both passive and active intellects extend to material things only; and the active intellect (despite the high derivation previously claimed for it) 'is not a separate substance; but a faculty of the soul' like its passive partner.[37] In consequence of this, and of the fact that 'there is no proper and adequate proportion between material and immaterial things'[38] (a concept implicit in Aquinas's view of the relation between soul and body in intellectual

[31] ibid.   [32] *S.T.* Ia IIae cix. 1, *ad R.*
[33] *S.T.* I. lxxxiv. 6, 7, *ad R.*
[34] *S.T.* I. lxxxiv. 8, *ad R.*; Gilson, op. cit., pp. 205, 222–3; *De Anima* iv, *ad 5.*
[35] Gilson, pp. 201–2; *Contra Gent.* IV. xi. [36] *S.T.* I. lxxxvi. 2, *ad R.*
[37] *S.T.* I. lxxxviii. 1, *ad R.*   [38] *S.T.* I. lxxxviii. 2, *ad 1.*

E

activity), no direct or perfect understanding of immaterial substances is possible to man.[39] If the human intellect – as Gilson puts it – is

faced by the supreme intelligibles, it remains blinded and bewildered like the owl which does not see the sun before its eyes.[40]

Thus in different ways the three writers referred to formulate the incapacity of the unaided human intellect to attain to eternal truth, and indicate (explicitly or otherwise) a difference in quality and in operation between the reason of man and the Divine reason. To the aid of a feeble will, therefore, man can only bring an imperfect understanding: as he is unable truly to grasp the good by his natural will, so he has not the means truly to apprehend it by unaided intellect. In the inadequacy of these higher powers is summed up the other faculties of an imperfect nature; and it can therefore be said of worldly man, with all his creaturely imperfections upon him, and beset as he was with the hosts of spiritual dangers and temptations, that he must tend insistently towards evil – that

you cannot do anything but sin, do what you will[41] –

unless his will be corrected and his understanding enlightened by God's grace. At the end of all man's resources lies his need for God.

[39] *S.T.* I. lxxxviii. 2, 3, *ad R.*; Gilson, p. 210.   [40] op. cit., p. 211.
[41] Luther, 'Gospel Sermon, First Sunday in Advent', quoted in *A Compend of Luther's Theology*, ed. H. T. Kerr, Philadelphia, 1943, p. 105.

Chapter 10

THE GRACE OF GOD

What is remarkable about the Apostle Paul's use of the word 'spirit', as denoting the highest principle, is that a term is made applicable to man which relates primarily to God. As it is used of men the term does not represent the element of God-consciousness within them. Nor is it any faculty which can be singled out; on the contrary, it may involve all the human faculties while not belonging to them. But whether, in Biblical usage, the term refers to the regenerate or spiritual life of man as in the New Testament, or to the Divine origination of man's life as in the Old, it refers to a potentiality rather than a quality: to a God-given principle rather than to a life element.[1] In employing a term that is common to God and to man, the Bible asserts that they are both spirit; but its emphasis where man is concerned is that he is spiritual in so far as he acts according to his origin. And the Bible's view of the human situation may be said to be that the fulfilling of this Divine potentiality is impossible without Divine help. The traditional Christian view finds expression in the words of Augustine:

> Our nature, corrupted by sin, produces citizens of earth: and grace freeing us from the sin of nature, makes us citizens of heaven.[2]

Man cannot rise towards God by his own will. For the will of mortal man is a slave to sin; and unless it is set free from its slavery by the grace of God, and given help to overcome its creaturely vices, a man cannot live an upright or devout life.[3] Thus, apart from any good that he has done, Augustine can ascribe to God's grace whatever he has not done of evil.[4] Aquinas concurs in the doctrine that man cannot avoid sin, or rise to God, without God's gift of grace,[5] as he does in the belief that the recovery of the true free will, lost in Eden, can only be effected through the intervention of Him who first bestowed it.[6] Free will is

[1] See G. S. Hendry, *The Holy Spirit in Christian Theology*, S.C.M. Press, 1965, pp. 101–17.
[2] *De Civ. Dei* XV. ii. For this paragraph, see J. Laidlaw, *The Bible Doctrine of Man*, Edinburgh, 1905, ch. VIII, pp. 164–5; IV, pp. 93–8.
[3] *De Lib. Arb.* II. xviii. 51; *Retract.* I. ix. 4.   [4] *Conf.* II. vii. 15.
[5] *S.T.* Ia IIae cix. 7, 8, *ad R.*
[6] *De Civ. Dei* XIV. xi; Aquinas, *S.T.* Ia IIae cix. 2, *ad R.*

therefore truly and utterly in God's command; the free will that man naturally possesses can be turned to God only when God turns it toward Himself;[7] and when it is thus the captive of His grace, it

> shall be more free from being freed from the delight of sinning to an undeclinable and steadfast delight of not sinning.[8]

In the general sense, the dependence of creatures on God's power, and the concept of God as first mover, can give rise to the idea of the whole of man's existence, including his very being, as due to God's grace.[9] As Augustine puts it, 'We could neither will nor run unless he stirred us and put the motive-power in us';[10] or in Calvin's words,

> we could not stand one minute of an houre, if wee were not preserued by the grace of God.[11]

But more particularly the doctrine of the grace of God relates to man's salvation. Without grace, says Augustine, men do nothing good when they think or wish or love or act;[12] for

> the good will itself is wrought in us by the will of God.[13]

We are thus saved through grace; and in this sense Augustine will admit faith as being a direct gift of God.[14] By the gift of grace man is not only enlightened, but he is empowered to do lovingly the good that is revealed.[15] Thus all good in man derives from the gracious will of God:

> Even if men do good things which pertain to God's service, it is He Himself that brings it about that they do what He commanded.[16]

That which perfects human nature derives from a source utterly beyond the human. If God may be said to co-operate with us by His grace, says Augustine, it is only because he is perfecting what He began by operating in us:[17] all subsequent grace is the strengthening of a humanity which was first healed by the Divine prevenience.[18] Aquinas similarly relates what is distinctively human in the operation of grace to a subordinate level.

> God does not justify us without ourselves, because whilst we are being justified we consent to God's justification (justitiae) by a movement of

---

[7] S.T. Ia IIae cix. 6, ad R., ad 1.   [8] De Civ. Dei XXII. xxx.
[9] A. C. Outler, 'The Person and Work of Christ', A Companion to the Study of Augustine, p. 359.
[10] De Quaest. ad Simplicianum I. ii. 21.   [11] Sermons on Job, tr. Golding, 1573, p. 22b.
[12] De Corrept. et Grat. ii. 3, quoted by Aquinas, S.T. Ia IIae cix. 2, sed contra.
[13] De Quaest. ad Simp. I. ii. 12.   [14] Ench. viii. 30, 31.
[15] De Corrept. et Grat. i. 2, quoted by Aquinas, S.T. Ia IIae cix. 4, ad R.
[16] De Praedest. Sanct. x. 19, quoted by D. M. Baillie, God Was in Christ, 1963, p. 114.
[17] De Grat. et Lib. Arb. xvii. 33, quoted by Aquinas, S.T. Ia IIae cxi. 2, sed contra.
[18] De Natura et Grat. xxxi. 35, quoted in S.T. Ia IIae cxi. 3, ad R.

our free-will. Nevertheless this movement is not the cause of grace, but the effect; hence the whole operation pertains to grace.[19]

In no sense can a creature be a cause of grace.[20] Unless a man receive the gratuitous help of God, he cannot prepare himself for the light of grace:[21] though *Proverbs* xvi. 1 may declare it to be the part of man to prepare the soul, 'yet it is principally from God, Who moves the free-will'.[22] As no man can merit for himself the first grace, so, even after he has been healed, each man needs grace to be moved to act rightly.[23] Even in his perfect state, man needed grace for acts of surpassing good; in his present state, though some limited natural good (like building houses) he may do, the perfectly natural task of loving God he cannot perform apart from the grace of God.[24]

It is by the act of God, therefore, and in no substantial sense by the activity of man, that those who were once the slaves of sin are thus set free from sin, and become the slaves of righteousness (*Rom.* vi. 17, 18). The teaching of Augustine is here explicit:

> he that is set free may not glory in his own deserts, nor he that is condemned make complaint except of his own deserts. For it is grace alone that separates the redeemed from the lost: for a cause common to both, a cause derived from their origin, had compacted them both into one mass of perdition . . . that thus every mouth of such as would glory in their own merits should be stopped, and that he that glorieth should glory in the Lord.[25]

Any merit in man is a gift of grace. Only in a secondary and consequential sense is it possible to regard men's works as gaining God's grace, for men's good deeds are the fruit of a righteousness not their own. When Luther, defining grace as 'an extraneous righteousness which . . . comes from heaven', urges *Romans* ix. 16 in his support – 'So then it is not of him that willeth, nor of him that runneth, but of God that showeth mercy'[26] – he is quoting what Aquinas and Augustine had already quoted on this subject.[27] For through the operation of grace, Aquinas declares, men 'are given a new being out of nothing, i.e. not from merits'.[28] The salvation of man derives from a supernatural gift creating a new nature, and crowns a goodness beyond man both in its origin and its substance:

> God gives grace to none but the worthy, not that they were

---

[19] *S.T.* Ia IIae cxi. 2, *ad* 2.   [20] *S.T.* Ia IIae cxii. 1, *ad R.*
[21] *S.T.* Ia IIae cix. 6, *ad R.*   [22] *S.T.* Ia IIae cxii. 2, *ad R.*
[23] *S.T.* Ia IIae cxiv. 5, *ad R.*; cix. 9, *ad R.*
[24] *S.T.* Ia IIae cix. 2, 3, *ad R.*   [25] *Ench.* xxv. 99.
[26] *Lectures on Romans*, L.C.C. XV, 1961, pp. 4, 5.
[27] *S.T.* Ia IIae cix. 2, *sed contra*; *Ench.* ix. 32.
[28] *S.T.* Ia IIae cx. 2, *ad* 3.

previously worthy, but that by His grace He makes them worthy.[29]

The experience of Paul, delivered from an existence of compulsive evil and spiritual corruption by the act of God that made him incorporate in Christ, with no merit of his own,[30] is recalled in Augustine's confession of a God who plucks him out of evil involvement by the operation of His grace.[31] That confession is a commonplace of Christian witness. In the words of a poet of a later age,

> What is the chaine which drawes us backe againe,
> And lifts man up unto his first Creation?
>
> It is a light, a guifte, a grace inspired,
> A sparcke of power, a goodnesse of the good,
> Desire in him, that never it desired,
> An unitie where desolation stood;
> In us, not of us; a spirit not of earth,
> Fashioninge the mortall to imortall birth.[32]

The concern of Luther and Calvin was to restore the idea of the primacy of man's dependence upon God for all good, and of the good will in man as being the result of God's work within him, in the face of a penitential system which emphasized the concept of the meritorious act. This concept, while not denying Divine prevenience, so concerned itself with the part played by human free will in the process of justification as to indicate, within the process, an independent human will or deed in no way necessitated by God for man, or performed by God in man, but carried out by man acting in some sense apart from God.[33] The Reformers' insistence was that no such action is possible, and that the ground of justification can be neither man's volition nor his action, but God's gracious act alone. In the matter of our justification, says Calvin, two questions are involved:

first, whether the glory of our salvation is to be divided between ourselves and God; and second whether as in the sight of God our conscience can with safety put any confidence in works.[34]

These questions Luther had approached from four main positions. In the first place, he urges the sovereignty and predestinating power of God's

---

[29] *S.T.* Ia IIae cxiv. 5, *ad 2*. See H. Wheeler Robinson, *The Christian Doctrine of Man* Edinburgh, 1958, p. 98.

[30] *Philippians* iii. 9.   [31] *Conf.* X. xxxiv. 53.

[32] Fulke Greville, 'A Treatise of Religion', st. 2, 3, *The Remains*, ed. G. A. Wilkes, Oxford, 1965, p. 203.

[33] Luther, *Bondage*, ed. Parker and Johnston, 1959, Introduction, p. 51.

[34] 'The Necessity of Reforming the Church', *Theological Treatises*, tr. J. K. S. Reid, L.C.C. XXII, 1964, p. 199.

will against the idea of any area where the operation of contingency might admit human initiative in spiritual matters. If for example, as in *Matthew* xxv. 34, those on the right hand of God are to inherit a kingdom prepared for them from the foundation of the world,

> How do they *merit* what is already theirs, and was prepared for them before they were in existence? We could more accurately say that it is rather the kingdom of God that merits its possessors; so putting the merit where our opponents put the reward, and the reward where they put the merit.[35]

Both merit and reward, therefore, are worked by God.[36] In the second place, Luther opposes a Divine grace freely bestowed to the idea of the attainment of grace by a prior human endeavour. If it is true (*Romans* iii. 21–5) that all have sinned, that the redemption which is in Christ is freely bestowed by God's grace upon those otherwise no different from sinners, and that eternal life is imparted with this righteousness, then there can be no such thing as merit at all.

> Where is your endeavour now? and your effort? and your good works? and the merits of 'free-will'? What use are they?[37]

In the third place, the greatness of the Person and work of Christ is opposed to the idea that human works can be spiritually significant:

> For if our sins may be taken away by our own work, merits and satisfactions, what needeth the Son of Man to be given for them?[38]

The complementary notion that the power of sin may in some sense be overcome by human effort is similarly challenged:

> Therefore here is to be marked the infinite greatness of the price paid for it, and then it will appear evidently that the power of it is so great, that by no means it could be put away, but that the Son of God must needs be given for it.[39]

In the fourth place, the doctrine that the free will of man in matters spiritual is entirely subject to God's grace is reasserted, and any reservation is branded as incompatible with humility and redolent of arrogance. Grace, Luther argues, can only be received in humility;

> But a man cannot be thoroughly humbled till he realizes that his salvation is utterly beyond his own powers, counsels, efforts, will and works, and depends absolutely on the will, counsel, pleasure and work of Another – God alone. As long as he is persuaded that he can make

[35] *Bondage*, p. 182.   [36] ibid., p. 185.   [37] ibid., p. 292.
[38] *A Commentary on St Paul's Epistle to the Galatians* (i. 4), ed. P. S. Watson, 1953, p. 47.
[39] ibid.

even the smallest contribution to his salvation, he remains self-confident and does not utterly despair of himself, and so is not humbled before God.[40]

The humiliation of man, in fact, is the beginning of his election. The reprobate not only resist the means of their humiliation, but condemn the teaching of self-despair. As Luther puts it, 'they want a little something left that they can do for themselves', and remain secretly proud and enemies of God's grace.[41] Calvin is no more receptive to the doctrine that fallen man, though unable to act aright, yet possesses, if aided by the grace of God, 'something of his own and from himself which he may contribute'; he will admit that the human will acts freely under the guidance of the Holy Spirit, but will not allow in man the ability to act aright that would empower him 'to ascribe to himself no less than to God the glory of his justification'.[42]

The Reformers thus see whatever is praiseworthy in their deeds as proceeding from the grace of God, and will ascribe not the least portion to themselves. Man is justified, 'not without works yet not through works'.[43] Works, says Luther, are indeed included among the necessities of our life in this world:

> nevertheless we are righteous not in these, but in the faith of the Son of God.[44]

From the use of the word 'reward' it is not to be inferred that our good works are the cause of salvation: the kingdom of heaven, Calvin declares, is not the stipend of servants, but the inheritance of children.[45] He goes further than Augustine in laying it down that no action even of a pious man, viewed by the scrutinizing eye of Divine justice, would be above condemnation;[46] but he is with him in the thought that human deeds are never acceptable to God unless the person who performs them has found favour in His sight.[47] There can be no deed of man apart from God which has even the relish of salvation in it.

Luther resists the argument of Jerome that Paul's condemnation of 'works of the law' refers only to the ceremonial law, and shows by his exegesis that Paul has in mind all human efforts towards righteousness.[48] The teaching that a good work before grace (being worthy of God's reward) may obtain the grace of congruence, and that works following the grace so obtained are bound to receive the reward of everlasting life

---

[40] *Bondage*, p. 100.   [41] ibid.

[42] 'The Necessity of Reforming the Church', *Theological Treatises*, L.C.C. XXII, p. 198.

[43] Calvin, *Inst.* III. xv. 3, xvi. 1.

[44] 'A Treatise on Christian Liberty', quoted in *A Compend*, ed. Kerr, p. 104.

[45] *Inst.* III. xviii. 2.   [46] ibid., III. xiv. 11

[47] ibid., III. xiv. 8.   [48] *Galatians* (ii. 16), p. 128.

through their power of condign merit, Luther terms 'the divinity of the Antichristian kingdom' because of its ignoring the death and victory of Christ.[49] It is precisely because faith apprehends and possesses 'this treasure, even Christ present', that Luther rejects the doctrine that charity is the lively completion of faith's bare outline.[50] He will not make a human sinlessness the precondition of salvation : a Christian is not one who has no sin, or feels no sin, but one to whom God does not impute his sin because of his faith in Christ.[51] Those who seek to link the process of salvation with the attaining of merit, Luther declares,

> make of the law grace, and of grace the law, of Moses Christ, and of Christ Moses.[52]

The proper function of 'the law' in the general sense is to challenge, accuse and condemn the unreflecting, and demonstrate that they are subject to God's wrath.[53] Its function is not to delineate tasks that men may meritoriously perform. That a meritorious task may be performed on the basis of man's natural powers Luther cannot admit. The plea that God does not require more than man can do, and that, though human nature is corrupt, the qualities of that nature are sound and uncorrupt, prompts Luther to make a definition recalling an earlier one of Augustine :

> We do not deny that these sentences are true in the corporal kingdom : but if ye bring them into the spiritual kingdom and the presence of God, I utterly deny them; for there, as I said, we are clean overwhelmed and drowned in sins.[54]

In the spiritual kingdom we can plead nothing save what God has done : thus Luther understands Paul's reference to Abraham's faith being reckoned to him as righteousness. Faith, far from being a mere assent of man's reason, bears for Luther the connotation of Augustine's worship; and therefore as the gift and creation of God, faith is the equivalent of the wisdom which stands opposed in Augustine's thought to the knowledge that is the product of a mere human reason :[55]

> faith is an almighty thing, and . . . the power thereof is infinite and inestimable; for it giveth glory unto God, which is the highest thing that can be given unto him. Now, to give glory unto God, is to believe in him, to count him true, wise, righteous, merciful, almighty : briefly, to acknowledge him to be the author and giver of all goodness. This reason doth not, but faith. . . . To be able to give that glory unto

[49] ibid., pp. 129–30.   [50] ibid., pp. 134–5.   [51] ibid., p. 138.
[52] ibid. (ii. 17), p. 146.   [53] ibid., p. 151.
[54] ibid. (ii. 20), p. 175; *De Civ. Dei* XIX. xxv; see p. 94 above.
[55] *De Trin.* XIV. xii. 15; XII. xv. 25. See p. 125 above.

God, it is the wisdom of wisdoms, the righteousness of righteousnesses, the religion of religions, and sacrifice of sacrifices.[56]

The righteousness of man consists in giving glory to God; in rendering the tribute due, the height of human endeavour manifests itself in a complete humility – and the sins that remain are not laid to the sinner's charge.[57]

The unregenerate reason of man, bringing inordinately into the spiritual realm the concepts of worldly experience, conceives of a God who is angry with sinners. Luther points to a Biblical tension that refutes such an understanding:

How then can these two contradictories stand together: I am a sinner and most worthy of God's wrath and indignation; and yet the Father loveth me? Here nothing cometh between, but only Christ the mediator.[58]

The Person of Christ is a revelation of the Divine reasoning which utterly transcends the retributory suppositions with which an unregenerate reason tries to do honour to the idea of God. And it utterly disproves the idea that salvation is to be attained through men's worthy deeds: for by its light unregenerate reason is shown to be confusing the principle of what we ought to do with that of the means by which we are made righteous.

We deny not but that the faithful ought to follow the example of Christ, and to work well; but we say that they are not justified thereby before God. . . . In this matter we must set nothing before our eyes, but Jesus Christ dying for our sins and rising again for our righteousness; and him we must apprehend by faith, as a gift, not as an example. This, reason understandeth not.[59]

For Luther, therefore, the Person of Christ stands opposed to an unregenerate reason which despite its professed aspirations remains the servant of evil and is therefore

the greatest and mightiest enemy of God: for reason despiseth God, denieth his wisdom, justice, power, truth, mercy, majesty and divinity.[60]

The true sacrifice therefore for man is to abandon those principles that make for his distinctive humanity: to conform his reasoning to the reasoning of God – in fact, to

kill reason and believe in Christ.[61]

---

[56] *Galatians* (iii. 6), p. 221.   [57] ibid., p. 227.   [58] ibid., p. 228.
[59] ibid. (iii. 9), p. 239.   [60] ibid. (iii. 6), p. 223.
[61] ibid., p. 227. See Augustine, *De Trin.* XII. xi. 16, on the necessary abandonment of the human.

By this argument which restores the full priority in spiritual matters of the grace of God, Luther seeks to attribute to the act of God whatever virtue and merit had been postulated of human deeds. A man's good deeds do not constitute his righteousness, but are rather his prayer for righteousness;[62] in fact,

> All things which are attributed to works, do properly belong unto faith. For works must not be looked upon morally, but faithfully and spiritually.[63]

He alone truly does the bidding of the law who has first received the Holy Ghost through faith in Christ, and through the power God has imparted to him has begun to love God and to do good to his neighbour :

> So this word 'to do' must comprehend also the faith which maketh the tree, and when the tree is made, then follow the fruits.[64]

Spiritually speaking, there is no righteous deed apart from the grace of God by which alone we are righteous. Arguing from *Romans* iii. 20 and viii. 5–13, Luther attacks a doctrine which he regards as pernicious as it is flattering :

> For we are not made righteous by doing righteous deeds but we do righteous deeds in so far as we are righteous;[65]

and again,

> Works and actions do not produce virtue, as Aristotle says, but virtues determine actions, as Christ teaches.[66]

Thus Luther extends the absolute distinction Augustine had made between a human and a pious virtue to the conduct that relates to those virtues : what Augustine does for the virtue, Luther does for the deed :

> Wherefore we must ascend up higher in divinity with this word 'doing' than in nature or philosophy, so that it may be made altogether new... it must have a quite new signification, and must require a right judgement of reason, and a good will, not morally, but divinely. . . . Here 'doing' is a new thing, unknown to reason, to philosophers, to lawyers, and unto all men : for it is a 'wisdom hidden in a mystery' &c (*I Cor.* ii. 7). Therefore in divinity the work necessarily requireth faith itself going before. . . . Therefore, when we that are divines speak of doing, we must needs speak of that faithful doing.[67]

---

[62] *Lectures on Romans* (iii. 5), tr. W. Pauck, L.C.C. XV, 1961, p. 84.
[63] *Galatians* (iii. 10), p. 257.   [64] ibid., p. 247.
[65] *Lectures on Romans* (iii. 20), p. 108.
[66] ibid. (viii. 5–13), p. 228. Aristotle, *Eth. Nicom.* II. i.
[67] *Galatians* (iii. 10), p. 254. See p. 94 above.

A man living according to man, and not according to God, Augustine had declared, is like the devil; and the achiever of any natural good, though he attain it, is evil and wretched in that good.[68] Luther applies the sole sufficiency of Christ to every area of human endeavour.

> Forasmuch then as Christ reigneth by his grace in the hearts of the faithful, there is no sin, no death, no curse: but where Christ is not known, there all these things do still remain.[69]

Since human righteousness is of God's creation, and neither men's thinking nor their actions can conform to God's will except through His prior gift of grace, clearly it is only through what is above him that man can lay hold of the Gospel. The proclamation of everlasting life freely given in Christ, says Luther, is a kind of doctrine that is not attained by man's diligence or wisdom, but is revealed to him by God Himself, first through the external Word and then by the working of God's Spirit.[70] Faith therefore is for Luther what it is for Calvin, a special gift of God.

> Our mind is too rude to be able to grasp the spiritual wisdom of God which is revealed to us through faith; and our hearts are too prone to distrust or to perverse confidence in ourselves or in other creatures to rest of their own accord in God. But the Holy Spirit by his illumination makes us capable of understanding those things which would otherwise far exceed our grasp, and brings us to a sure persuasion by sealing the promises of salvation in our hearts.[71]

Man by his own reason and strength cannot anticipate God and move Him to be gracious: God must first come and seek us, since we may not pursue Him.[72] Faith in God lies therefore in acceptance and trust; in such trust, Luther observes, is the beginning, middle and end of all works and righteousness.[73] Far from being mere belief, it is that whereby one may

> put my trust in Him, surrender myself to Him and make bold to deal with Him, believing without doubt that He will be to me and do to me just what is said of Him.[74]

It consists, says Calvin, in

> a light of the Holy Spirit through which our understandings are en-

---

[68] *De Civ. Dei* XIV. iv; XII. viii.

[69] *Galatians* (iii. 13), p. 274.   [70] ibid. (i. 16), p. 121.

[71] 'The Catechism of the Church of Geneva', *Theological Treatises*, tr. J. K. S. Reid, L.C.C. XXII, 1954, p. 105.

[72] Luther, 'Treatise on the New Testament'; 'Epistle Sermon, Twentieth Sunday after Trinity'; quoted in *A Compend*, ed. Kerr, Philadelphia, 1943, pp. 32–3.

[73] 'Treatise on the New Testament', ibid.

[74] 'A brief Explanation of the Ten Commandments, the Creed, and the Lord's Prayer', quoted in *A Compend*, p. 33.

140

lightened and our hearts confirmed in a sure persuasion which is assured that the truth of God is so certain that he can but accomplish that which he hath promised through his holy word that he will do.[75]

This trust, entirely the work of God, also relates entirely to God; similarly the righteousness that accompanies faith relates to God, not to man.[76] We are justified by faith,

> not in the sense that we receive righteousness, but because the righteousness of Christ is credited to us, entirely as if it were really ours, while our iniquity is not charged to us, so that one can truly call this righteousness simply the remission of sins.[77]

Both the faith of man, and the righteousness consequent upon it, consist solely in God's gracious act.

The attributing of all spiritual good, and therefore all real good, entirely to the grace of God is traditional in Christian theology, as it is necessary in Christian experience. It springs from a transcendent sense of God's bounty towards His Creation and mercy toward mankind that must drive men to their knees. This sense Kierkegaard expresses in the thought that whoever with true thankfulness comes to realize the disparity, divinely speaking, between his own activity and all that he must accept as a gift, will not spoil the beauty of the gift or the certainty of the bestowing grace by taking his own merit into account, but will be instructed by the excessiveness of the gift in the quiet gladness which is not importunate in its unremitting activity, but humble even in its gratitude.[78] But this humility springs no less from an understanding of the true nature of the love between God and man. A man can do no more than to love God; but that love falsifies the relationship between man and God which subsists on a basis of man's thankfulness:

> for even the one who is always willing to return thanks, still loves according to his perfection, and a man can truly only love God when he loves Him according to his own imperfection. What is this love? It is the love born of repentance, which is more beautiful than all other love; for in it you love God! It is more faithful and more inward than all other love; for in repentance it is God who loves you.[79]

The spiritual enabling of man is always truly seen, not in the fact that we loved God, but in the fact that He loved us.

[75] *Instruction in Faith*, tr. P. T. Fuhrmann, Lutterworth Press, 1949, p. 39.
[76] *Inst.* III. xi. 23.
[77] *Instruction in Faith*, p. 40.
[78] Søren Kierkegaard, 'The Expectation of an Eternal Happiness', *Edifying Discourses*, tr. D. F. and L. M. Swenson, Minneapolis, 1950-3, III, p. 96.
[79] Kierkegaard, 'Every Good and Perfect Gift is from Above', ed. cit., I, pp. 51-2.

But the attribution of man's advancement solely to the grace of God has a further ground, which has been investigated. It is entirely appropriate to an understanding of the human condition in this world. By his natural powers a man is able to do no more than plunge into sin – so far distant is he, in himself, from the possibility of blessedness, and from peace, both within him and round about him. The situation of man in his wordly tragedy may be seen to develop, not merely from error or limitation of creaturely faculty, but more radically from his God-forsaking, and state of forsakenness. A precursor of the Elizabethan tragic hero can thus speak of his own fate in terms of an underlying tragedy of the spirit:

> For noble blood made me bothe prince and pere
> yea pereless to had reason purchast place
> And god with gyfts endowed me largelie here
> but what availes his gyfts where failes his grace?[80]

[80] Thomas Sackville, *The Complaint of Henry Duke of Buckingham*, 1563, ed. M. Hearsey, Yale University Press, 1936, st. 82 (3), p. 61.

Chapter 11

THE JUSTICE OF GOD

It is not only the goodness of man which, according to traditional Christian concepts, is not germane to himself. His very being, and his ultimate destiny, stem alike from a principle that is infinitely beyond him. It follows consequently that in his creaturely existence he is endowed with a good beyond all possible merit. Augustine's pointing out that the goodness of God gives life, sustenance and power both to fallen angels and to evil men[1] is echoed in Aquinas's teaching that God's justice and mercy is evident in His giving to all existing things what is appropriate to them, and preserving the nature of each one in the order and with the powers that properly belong to it.[2] For nothing is due to creatures; their existence – and man's being man – depends upon God's goodness.

> So in every work of God, viewed at its primary source, there appears mercy.[3]

A further consequence also appears, however. It is that the nature and circumstances of man's mortal existence cannot possibly be judged by creaturely standards of appropriateness: that man's own purposes, and sense of what is just, cannot fittingly be applied to the purpose and the justice of God.

Whether they concern his own evils or the evils that are apparent in the world, therefore, man's most inspired observations do not readily attain at the truth. Thus the doctrine that the power that God imparts to His human creatures is morally neutral, and that the wills of men alone are responsible for converting that power to evil, raises a further question that is beyond the wit of man:

> Why then does He not alter those evil wills which He moves? This question touches on the secrets of His Majesty, where 'His judgements are past finding out' (cf. *Rom.* xi. 33). It is not for us to inquire into these mysteries, but to adore them. If flesh and blood take offence here, and grumble, well, let them grumble; they will achieve nothing;

---

[1] *Ench.* viii. 27.   [2] *S.T.* I. xxi. 1, *ad R.*   [3] *S.T.* I. xxi. 4, *ad R.*

143

grumbling will not change God. And however many of the ungodly stumble and depart, the elect will remain.[4]

Calvin on this point acquiesces in the pronouncement of Augustine:

'God could turn the will of evil men to good because he is almighty. Obviously he could. Why, then, does he not? Because he wills otherwise. Why he wills otherwise rests with him.'[5]

Man must trust in that judgement of God that deemed it better to bring good out of evil than to preclude evil from existing,[6] and in the righteousness of that judgement whereby permission is given for the doings that are evil. What is evil is obviously not good; but that evil things should exist is, in the scope of God's providence, a good thing.[7]

The Divine providence is, however, apparent to the godly understanding in its condemnation of sin in the world. If mercy be taken to mean the removal of any kind of defect, Aquinas argues, then mercy and truth are necessarily found in all God's works;[8] or, as Augustine puts it,

The righteousness of God's wrath is closely concerned with whatever it is that by blind and uncontrolled concupiscence evil men do wilfully, and with whatever by manifest and apparent penalty they suffer unwillingly.[9]

The justice and mercy of God appear similarly in the punishment of the just in this world,

since by afflictions lesser faults are cleansed in them, and they are the more raised up from earthly affections to God.[10]

The just are not without sin; and the heavenly physician, Calvin declares, 'restrains our unrestrained flesh with the remedy of the cross'.[11] By being chastened through adversity the elect are freed from the condemnation of the world;[12] by the demonstration of our frailty, God shows us that he saves us 'not by our merits but by sheer election and his immutable will'.[13] Indeed, the world's inescapable evils are the very foundation of piety:

For this we must believe: that the mind is never seriously aroused to desire and ponder the life to come unless it be previously imbued with contempt for the present life.[14]

---

[4] Luther, *Bondage*, tr. Parker and Johnston, London, 1959, p. 204, 208.
[5] *Inst.* III. xxiv. 13, quoting *De Gen. ad Lit.* XI. x. 13.
[6] Augustine, *Ench.* viii. 27. [7] ibid., xxiv. 96. [8] *S.T.* I. xxi. 4, *ad R.*
[9] *Ench.* viii. 27. [10] *S.T.* I. xxi. 4, *ad 3.* [11] *Inst.* III. viii. 5.
[12] ibid., III. viii. 6.
[13] Luther, *Romans* (viii. 28–39) L.C.C. XV, 1961, p. 247. [14] *Inst.* III. xi. 1.

Expedient though man's punishment be, its basis is not a merciful expediency, but a justice more comprehensive. For mankind is utterly involved in sin. Apart from each individual's deserts and doings,

> in one man originally and so to speak radically the whole human race came into condemnation;[15]

and it was condemned by a judgement of God so righteous, that even if not a single man were delivered from it, no one would have grounds for complaint against it.[16] Thus it comes about that

> except by unmerited mercy no man is delivered, and except by merited judgement no man is condemned.[17]

God may indeed turn an evil will to good effect (or conversely confirm an evil will in its iniquity) :

> But when he does this, it is through mercy that he does it : when he does not do it, it is through judgement that he does not : for he hath mercy upon whom he will and whom he will he hardeneth (*Rom.* ix. 18).[18]

The reason why God elects some and rejects others, says Aquinas, is to manifest his goodness in men – by his mercy in respect to those whom he predestines, by his justice in respect to those he reprobates – in a universe requiring a multiformity of grades to express His own undivided goodness.[19] The reprobate cannot complain, for they have their deserts : they may be told, '*Take what is thine, and go thy way*'.[20] The potter has power over the clay; and the reprobate are saved through no merit of their own, that they may glory only in the Lord.[21] But the reason for God's choice in particular cases no man may know :

> Yet why He chooses some for glory, and reprobates others, has no reason, except the divine will. Whence Augustine says (*Tract.* xxvi. *in Joan.*) : *Why He draws one, and another He draws not, seek not to judge, if thou dost not wish to err.*[22]

Calvin's conclusion upon the matter is to the same effect as those of his predecessors :

> To sum up : by free adoption God makes those whom he wills to be his sons; the intrinsic cause of this is in himself, for he is content with his own secret good pleasure.[23]

[15] *Ench.* xiv. 48.   [16] ibid., xxv. 99.   [17] ibid.
[18] ibid., xxv. 98.   [19] *S.T.* I. xxiii. 5, *ad 3.*   [20] ibid., quoting *Matt.* xx. 14.
[21] *Ench.* xxv. 99, 98.   [22] *S.T.* I. xxiii. 5, *ad 3.*   [23] *Inst.* III. xxii. 7.

In making 'vessels of perdition from the lump of the impious', Augustine declares, God, apart from enabling some to obtain mercy, demonstrates his power.[24] In raising up a reprobate tyrant, says Luther, God manifests His own agency and control in and over all things, and thus strengthens the faith of His chosen ones.[25] For it is not by taking refuge in any strength of his own, but in the revelation of the omnipotence of God's will, that a man may find comfort. Nothing is due to man; but

> It is due to God that there should be fulfilled in creatures what His will and wisdom require.[26]

Thus in all things the sovereign will of God is manifest to the faithful; and God,

> whether through his compassion he has mercy upon whom he will, or through his judgement he hardens whom he will, neither does anything unrighteously nor does anything at all unless he wills it.[27]

It is with such an understanding of the will of God that Calvin can say that the salvation of the elect is 'without regard to human worth' and the reprobate are condemned 'by his just and irreprehensible but incomprehensible judgement'.[28]

The love of God to all men, says Aquinas, consists in His wishing them all some good. But He does not wish all good to them all; and some, to whom He does not wish the good of eternal life, He may be said to hate or reprobate.[29] These words are symptomatic of a difficulty in reconciling the mercy and judgement of God experienced in contexts indicating a universality in God's will to save or in the appeal of the Gospel. Both Augustine and Calvin interpret *I Tim.* ii. 1–4 as referring to all classes of men rather than to all men.[30] Augustine further interprets 'Who will have all men to be saved' as meaning that only those obtain salvation whom it has been His will should be saved; or, he says,

> it can be understood in any way whatever, so long as we are not induced to think that it was the will of almighty God that something should be done and it has not been done.[31]

Similarly, Calvin interprets the announcement of salvation to all men indiscriminately in a manner that is restrictive:

> For by so promising he merely means that his mercy is extended to all, provided they seek after it and implore it. But only those whom

[24] *De Quaest. ad Simplicianum* I. ii. 18.
[25] *Bondage (Exod.* iii. 19–20), p. 211.
[26] *S.T.* I. xxi. 1, *ad 3.*
[27] *Ench.* xxvi. 102. See also *De Quaest. ad Simp.* I. ii. 16.
[28] *Inst.* III. xxi. 7.
[29] *S.T.* I. xxiii. 3, *ad 1.*
[30] *Ench.* xxvii. 103; *Inst.* III. xxiv. 16.
[31] *Ench.* xxvii. 103.

146

he has illumined do this. And he illumines those whom he has predestined to salvation.

The universality of the offer is to demonstrate to the pious that nothing but their faith separates them from sinners, and to the wicked that they reject the sanctuary which is offered them.[32]

Any unease in this respect arises from its being quite clear that God, Who is supreme over all wills, wills to save some and condemn others[33] – 'that is, he has or has not mercy on whom he will', as Augustine puts it.

> Let us believe [he continues] that this belongs to a certain hidden equity that cannot be searched out by any human standard of measurement, though its effects are to be observed in human affairs and earthly arrangements.[34]

Calvin concurs in the thought that 'the reason of the Divine righteousness is higher than man's standard can measure',[35] and Luther asserts that its incomprehensibility is entirely as it should be – that

> inasmuch as He is the one true God, wholly incomprehensible and inaccessible to man's understanding, it is reasonable, indeed inevitable, that His justice also should be incomprehensible.[36]

In such questions as the permitting of men's evil acts, or of man's original sin in Eden, it is sufficient to regard the will of the Creator, since all other grounds are subordinate to it in its righteousness.

> God is He for Whose will no cause or ground [ratio] may be laid down as its rule or standard. . . . What God wills is not right because He ought, or was bound, so to will; on the contrary, what takes place must be right, because He so wills it. Causes and grounds are laid down for the will of the creature, but not for the will of the Creator – unless you set another Creator over him![37]

The questioning of that will is a presumption that is unpleasing to God. Luther can urge those so motivated, 'speculate not with thy damnable queries', and he quotes Christ's reply to Peter as being relevant to all such inquiries: 'thou shalt know hereafter'.[38] In so doing he echoes Augustine's words:

> Then it will appear in the bright light of wisdom, what now the faith of the godly has hold upon even before it appears in open recognition, how sure and immutable and effective is the will of God.[39]

[32] *Inst.* III. xxiv. 17.
[33] ibid., III. xxi. 1, xxiv. 4.
[34] *De Quaest. ad Simplicianum* I. ii. 16.
[35] *Inst.* III. xxiii. 4, xxiv. 17.
[36] *Bondage*, p. 315.
[37] ibid., p. 209.
[38] *Table-Talk*, lxvi.
[39] *Ench.* xxiv. 95.

Until the coming of that light, the justice of God must remain beyond man's comprehension, and the strange liberty of evil must continue mysterious. To the regenerate consciousness, good and evil alike, and every happening in man's mortal existence in which they are alike involved, and every joy and every grief deriving from them, may be apprehended as a revelation of the justice of the Divine providence. But to the unregenerate it must appear that men in their afflictions are teased for the sport of the powers that are above them.

Chapter 12

THE TRAGEDY OF MAN

It is the just decree of God that man should not be saved by any creaturely power or happiness: that he should be a living paradox, and his estate both proud and wretched. The corporeal good that he seizes upon is but founded

on many a thousand grains

That issue out of dust.[1]

His formidable powers of will can find expression only in a compulsive urge to sin. His intellect, albeit admirable in its scope and working, is yet blind and ignorant where essential knowledge is concerned. If he can be saved from sin, and can do good, it is only in spite of his own nature. And he himself (no less than the universe round about him) can be real only in so far as he serves a principle above him. It is for him to pay what is due to God in the choice between the true acceptance of created good which involves renunciation, and the false acceptance which is assertion; between Augustine's two cities of the love of God in contempt of oneself, and self-love in contempt of God; between being a living testimony to God's glory, and attempting to be his own creature. A proper understanding of his nature can only lead him to 'a relinquishing and forgetting' of that nature:[2] the natural, declares Augustine, exists only for the sake of the supernatural.

For as it is not of the flesh, but above the flesh, that animates the body; so it is not of man, but above man, which beatifies the mind of man, yea, and of all the powers of the heavens.[3]

His words are a final comment – indeed they are an epitaph – on the fitful fever of man's life on earth. For the spontaneous wish of mankind is like that of Milton's Mammon in his new situation, the quest of the false beatitude which would

rather seek

Our own good from our selves

(II. 252–3).

---

[1] *Measure for Measure* III. i. 20–1.
[2] Edward Reynolds, *A Treatise of the Passions and Faculties of the Soule of Man*, 1640, p. 42.
[3] *De Civ. Dei* XIX. xxv.

149

It is good that man chooses, not evil; but the choice of the lesser good in preference to the greater is itself the 'foul disproportion' that is the beginning of all evil, and the prelude to the Divine displeasure. The will of man sins, says Augustine,

> if it turns away from the unchangeable good which is common to all, and turns to a private good, whether outside or below it. It turns toward a private good when it wishes to be its own master – outside, when it is anxious to know the private affairs of someone else, or whatever is not its own concern, and below it, when it loves bodily pleasure. Thus a man who becomes proud, curious and self-indulgent is caught up in another life, which compared to the higher life is death. . . . Evil is the turning of the will away from the unchangeable good, and towards changeable good. Since this turning from the one to the other is free and unforced, the pain which follows as a punishment is fitting and just.[4]

There is admittedly in this concept an identifying of being and value which appears to do scant justice to ethical goodness as distinct from the natural goodness of being.[5] Its associating of evil with non-being rather than with sin is clearly derived from its basis in the Platonic doctrine of the unreality of matter.[6] However, it is to be noted that Augustine's attention is directed to the will that makes the choice rather than what is actually chosen;[7] and also that the lesser nature of the good involved in the choice is a necessary accompaniment of a perversion in the acting will. Aquinas, following Augustine in making the direct cause of sin an adherence to a mutable good, states the latter point with great emphasis :

> Now the fact that anyone desires a temporal good inordinately, is due to the fact that he loves himself inordinately.[8]

The love of self involves the choice of the lesser good, since it is externally characterized by its trying to make the part into the whole. It does this presumably because it must reject as irrelevant or non-existent all that does not appear to concern it, and because such a perverse rejection of the whole is the very process whereby self-love creates itself. It is the absurdity of the choice, as Augustine sees it, that proclaims the ethical quality of the will that makes it.

> For the soul loving its own power, slips onwards from the whole which is common, to a part, which belongs especially to itself. And that

---

[4] *De Lib. Arb.* II. xix. 53.   [5] J. Burnaby, *Amor Dei*, 1938, p. 40.

[6] ibid., p. 42. See S. R. Hopper, 'The Anti-Manichaean Writings', *A Companion to the Study of St Augustine*, N.Y., 1955, p. 186.

[7] See H. W. Robinson, *The Christian Doctrine of Man*, Edinburgh, 1958, p. 177.

[8] *S.T.* Ia IIae lxxvii. 4, *ad R.*

apostatizing pride . . . by seeking something more than the whole, and struggling to govern this by a law of its own, is thrust on, since nothing is more than the whole, into caring for a part; and thus by lusting after something more, is made less.[9]

Thus the deficiency in substance of the good that is chosen is matched – in a Divine universe – by the insubstantiality of the evil in the acting will:

I inquired what iniquity was, and found it to be no substance, but the perversion of the will, turned aside from Thee, O God, the Supreme, towards these lower things, and *casting out its bowels*, and puffed up outwardly.[10]

The choice of the lesser good, and inordinate love of self, are therefore part of one process: they constitute the conversion to creatures that is for Aquinas the material part of sin, whose 'formal aspect and complement' is the aversion from God most fully expressed in the sin of pride. For whereas other sins are a fleeing from God, and partake of the aversion by consequence, aversion belongs to pride by its very nature and definition.[11] And to the extent that by its operation other sins may be directed to its end of self-magnification, and indeed made possible through its removing the obstacle of respect for the Divine law, pride may be seen as having 'somewhat of a generic character' as the beginning of the other sins, in Eden and thereafter.[12] The distinguishing feature of human pride is, in fact, the definition of all evil, a tendency towards non-being and nothingness. Man was lessened in excellence upon his Fall, declares Augustine, through his inclining to himself. His nature indeed derives from God, yet it falls from God in that it was made of nothing, and its excellence can lie only in adherence to God:

whom he leaving, to adhere to, and delight in himself, he grew (not to be nothing, but) towards nothing.[13]

Those who refrain from praising and thanking God through a concern for their creaturely excellence become 'empty in their thoughts', emptiness being 'the peculiar disease of men who deceive themselves in the belief that they are something, when they are nothing'.[14]

Man, desiring more, becomes less. Like the evil angels, he falls from an all-sufficient God through the perverse choice of being sufficient in himself. The act of pride is an overstepping of right reason, which requires that man's will should tend to what is proportionate to him: it is that whereby a man 'aims higher *(supra)* than he is'[15] – or in Augustine's words,

9 *De Trin.* XII. ix. 14.
10 *Conf.* VII. xvi. 22.
11 *S.T.* IIa IIae clxii. 6, *ad R.*
12 *S.T.* IIa IIae clxii. 2, *ad R.*; clxiii. 1, *ad R.*
13 *De Civ. Dei* XIV. xiii.
14 *De Spir. et Litt.* xix. 12.
15 Aquinas, *S.T.* IIa IIae clxii. 1, *ad R.*

what is pride but a perverse desire of height, in forsaking Him to whom the soul ought solely to cleave, as the beginning thereof, to make the self seem the one beginning.[16]

The image and likeness of God, by which God has honoured man, is not preserved except in relation to Him who first impressed it, which relationship involves the forsaking of what is peculiarly one's own.[17] But the sinning soul, apprehending its divine origination, desires the more to possess what appears to be its own in its will to self-aggrandizement:

through the desire of making trial of his own power, man by his own bidding falls down to himself as to a sort of intermediate grade. And so, while he wishes to be as God is, that is, under no one, he is thrust on, even from his own middle grade, by way of punishment, to that which is lowest, that is, to those things in which beasts delight.[18]

Thus it comes about that an evil will in the creature is inescapably a proclamation of the Creator. Even in the height of its sin the soul seeks a sort of likeness of God: the thief, being as a creature a prisoner of God's law, mimics a freedom he does not possess in his desire to do with impunity things not permitted him, and thus creates 'a darkened likeness of Thy Omnipotency'.[19] An erring will sets forth an imitation of God in its desire for goods and qualities that are present supereminently in God himself;[20] and therefore there is a pointer toward humanity's true happiness

in the search for rank and excellence, even in the pride and vain pomp of this world. For what else does a man seek in this case but to be if possible the sole lord of all things, perversely imitating Almighty God? If he submissively imitated him by living according to his commandments, God would put all other things under him, and he would not reach such deformity as to fear a little animal even while he wants to rule over men. Pride in a manner seeks unity and omnipotence, but in the realm of temporal things, where all things are transient like a shadow.[21]

The process of pride is the search for a terrestrial beatitude – what Augustine calls 'vain temporalities'. It is the will to possess as an end what is the means to an end, to make those significances appertain to the self that properly belong to the will and purpose of God. In it the soul seeks to deny what it is and to be what it cannot be; to possess what it cannot have and to destroy what it cannot establish; to yield to the insensate folly of biting the hand that feeds it. It is an essay in irresponsibility in which the soul acts as if it has forgotten itself. Thus

[16] *De Civ. Dei* XIV. xiii. [17] *De Trin.* XII. xi. 16. [18] ibid.
[19] *Conf.* II. vi. 14. [20] ibid., II. vi. 12. [21] *De Vera Relig.* xlv. 84.

It sees beauties of the inward realm, belonging to that transcendent reality which is God. Its duty is to stand fast for the enjoyment of them; but because it would ascribe them to itself, and instead of being a derived likeness of God, derive from itself the being that is his only, it turns away from him, loses its stability and sinks into something constantly diminishing, in the fancy that it is constantly increasing. For neither can it suffice itself, nor can aught else suffice it if it withdraw from him who alone suffices.[22]

The exercising of any will to transcendence or to creaturely excellence in any form in the realm of the temporal which is not dedicated and bound to the service of God beyond any concern for the self is the very definition of the greatest of the sins. It is also the most characteristic human will and activity. It is the beginning of the mundane afflictions registered in the historical process; and it is featured most prominently in the art of literary tragedy.

The essence of tragedy is a choice seriously made in certain given circumstances which must inevitably result in suffering and defeat.[23] The circumstances themselves need be no more than indifferent or neutral; but in the situation of man on earth, the oppression of circumstances might itself be said to give rise to a tragedy of frustration and loss. For man's desire for happiness is like nothing more than the desire of the moth for the star. Though a certain participation of happiness may be obtained in this life, says Aquinas, perfect and true happiness is impossible. Whether they derive from the ignorance of intellect, the affections of the appetite, bodily infirmity or whatsoever cause, evils abound and cannot be avoided. Likewise man's natural wish for the goods he enjoys in this life to be abiding must inevitably be disappointed.[24] And the true happiness, which consists in the vision of the Divine essence, is unobtainable by man in this life – for the knowledge of God by means of any created similitude is not the vision of His essence, and man's soul can know only what has a form in matter, or can be known by such a form.[25] Thus man is caught up in the sombre irony that, by the very creaturely endowments that provoke in him a desire for happiness that is as compelling within him as it is universal, the attainment of perfect happiness is precluded.

But the participation of happiness that Aquinas mentions is not restricted to that attainable by his own powers. Man is not abandoned to himself in the universe, unless he himself wills the abandonment: something of the happiness that belongs to participation in the eternal he can know, since truth has been revealed to him. Happiness, for

---

[22] *De Trin.* X. v. 7.
[23] See O. Mandel, *A Definition of Tragedy*, N.Y., 1961, p. 20.
[24] *S.T.* Ia IIae v. 3, *ad R.*   [25] *S.T.* Ia IIae v. 5, *ad R.*; I. xii. 11, *ad R.*

Augustine, is 'truth-given joy';[26] it is a relation of knowledge and love which binds us to Reality – and shows the soul its sinfulness. The desire for happiness is by definition the desire for beatitude; and since there is no worldly happiness without alloy, and death must end all such happiness, to wish to be happy is a wish for immortality – for in heaven alone can the soul of man 'have all that he wants, and want nothing wrongly'.[27] But a perverse humanity seizes upon the first of these desires, and ignores the latter : the beatitude that it seeks to raise up is a terrestrial one, and the being to which it would do honour is the creature, not the Creator. Sinning man chooses 'vain temporalities' in preference to the eternal; and that serious choice of his will, in the circumstances that God has ordained, must lead to his earthly suffering, and constitute his tragedy.

> For in the worlds corrupted trafficke here,
> Goodnesse puts onely tincture on our gall,
> The light of Truth, doth but in clouds appeare,
> Hardly discern'd, and not obey'd at all :
> *No man yeelds glory vnto him that makes him,*
> *For if he doe, he sees the world forsakes him.*

> Now in this *twilight* of Deliberation,
> Where Man is darke, because he will not see :
> Must he not trust to his selfe-constellation?
> Or else grow confident, he cannot be?
> Assuming this, hee makes himselfe his end,
> And what he vnderstands, that takes to friend.

> In which strange oddes, betweene the earth and skie,
> Examine but the state of euery heart;
> Flesh feeles and feares strong inequality;
> Horrors of sinne cannot be free'd by art :
> Humours are mans religion, Power his lawes,
> His Wit confusion, and his Will the cause.[28]

The life of man on earth is a 'hell', says Augustine, because of his 'profundity of ignorance' and his 'love of things vain and noxious' :[29] his existence is unhappy because – in the self-adulation that is contempt for God and His laws – he makes it so. The desire for happiness that is the source of all the strife and effort in human life is really a desire for immortality[30] – but man, rejecting immortality, is left to a hopeless struggle in the face of annihilation. His abandonment is of his own seeking; and

---

[26] *Conf.* X. xxiii. 33, quoted by Burnaby, *Amor Dei*, p. 49.   [27] *De Trin.* XIII. v. 8.
[28] Fulke Greville, 'An Inqvisition vpon Fame and Honovr', st. 10–12, *Poems and Dramas*, ed. G. Bullough, 1939, I, pp. 194–5.
[29] *De Civ. Dei* XXII. xxii, quoted by Burnaby, op. cit., p. 57.
[30] *De Trin.* XIII. viii. 11.

what he covets as a bliss is in truth his own purgatory. Thus it comes about that, by God's decree and man's choice,

the whole life of mortal man is a punishment.[31]

Upon the mortal existence of man no happiness can be established. The peace that we have on this earth, declares Augustine, be it public or private, can only bear the character of a solace to our wretchedness. Such happiness on earth as is vouchsafed us by the peace proceeding from goodness will be seen, when it is compared to the true happiness, to be plain misery.[32] In human strength of any kind there is no salvation: the appearance of power is the possession of evil men, and that power is really a 'ridiculous weakness'.[33] Nor can any human faculty be a refuge; for it can be said of man's greatest gifts, that

the greater help they afford him against anguish, dangers, and griefs, the surer testimonies are they of human miseries.[34]

The world's prosperities are darkened by the fear of adversity and of the corruption of our joys; the pains of its adversities threaten to shatter our endurance, and their stern lessons are lost in a fond longing for renewed worldly prosperity.

Is not the *life of man on earth all trial,* [asks Augustine] without any interval?[35]

Nothing can save us from afflictions and sorrows. And the true virtue makes no pretence of being able to do so; it aims at this alone, that human life, perturbed as it is with extremes of sorrows, should be made a partaker of safety and of felicity in the life to come. The happiness of man in this life, as Paul has maintained *(Rom.* viii. 24), is both con-stituted and confirmed by the hope which by the grace of God he may bear.

Wherefore as we are saved, so we are blessed by hope, and as we have no hold on our safety, no more have we of our felicity, but by hope, patiently awaiting it; and being as yet in a desert of thorny dangers, all which we must constantly endure until we come to the paradise of all ineffable delights, having then passed all the perils of encumbrance.[36]

There is not to be found in the thought of Augustine the concept, implicit in that of Luther and Calvin, of the Kingdom of God breaking into and transforming history, and the social order – the possibility that

[31] *De Civ. Dei* XXI. xiv, quoted by Burnaby, p. 202.
[32] *De Civ. Dei* XIX. xxvii; XIX. x.   [33] *De Trin.* XIII. xiii. 17.
[34] *De Civ. Dei* XIX. iv.   [35] *Conf.* X. xxviii. 39.
[36] *De Civ. Dei* XIX. iv.

the justice and stability that belonged to what he regarded as the only true society on earth, the City of God, might become more generally implanted in the secular world.[37] Secular history was for him unprogressive – it was the spectacle of a humanity perpetually engaged in chasing its own tail; however, his view that the true history of the human race, and the real progress, is to be found in 'the process of enlightenment and salvation by which human nature is liberated and restored to spiritual freedom'[38] can bring him into accord with modern views.[39] It is most probable that his view of the unreclaimable nature of human society is influenced by the Platonic and even the Manichaean dualism. Nonetheless, it is not inconsistent with the tragic situation of man which Christian thinking has set forth, and has the effect of depicting the more graphically and literally the abdication essential to the Christian experience – that rejection of what is distinctively human, and of all purely natural good, that is implied alike in the Elizabethan poet's

> *God comes not till man be ouerthrowne;*
> *Peace is the seed of grace, in dead flesh sowne,*

and in Augustine's, *'the friendship of this world is fornication against Thee'.*[40] And in so far as his reference is to the society of worldly men, Augustine is not alone in seeing it involved in their pride, their evil and their doom :

> Wherefore if man serve not God, what justice can be thought to be in him? seeing that if he serve not Him the soul has neither lawful sovereignty over the body, nor the reason over the affections : now if this justice cannot be found in one man, nor can it then in a whole multitude of such like men.[41]

While it is perfectly true of Augustine that he nowhere asserts in so many words 'that human society is a bad thing',[42] it would also be true to say that he finds human society acceptable only in the sense that it may be journeyed through. The solaces it affords him who travels hopefully, that is to say, are transformed into poisons for him who undergoes the delusion that he has arrived. What gives its goodness and its comfort to man's society on earth is the process of leaving it : that one is

---

[37] *De Civ. Dei* II. xxi. See T. J. Bigham and A. T. Mollegen, 'The Christian Ethic', *A Companion to the Study of St Augustine*, p. 393.

[38] G. Dawson, 'St Augustine and His Age', *A Monument to St Augustine*, 1934, p. 71.

[39] See Reinhold Niebuhr, *Faith and History*, London, 1949, pp. 31, 65, for a view of history as a 'realm of endless possibilities of renewal and rebirth', rather than as progressing or determined.

[40] Fulke Greville, *Caelica* xcvi, ll. 47–8 (Bullough edn, I, p. 142); *Conf.* I. xiii. 21.

[41] *De Civ. Dei* XIX. xxi.

[42] J. N. Figgis, *The Political Aspects*, 1921, p. 65.

here on the way, there in our fatherland. Now therefore my brethren, let us sing, not for our delight as we rest, but to cheer us in our labour. As labourers are wont to sing, sing, but keep marching.[43]

It is harder for Augustine, under the Platonic influence, to see the highest good in terms of personal encounter, and to find the grace of God in the meeting of persons, than it is for other thinkers.[44] A declaration such as, 'If we are ablaze with love for eternity we shall hate temporal relationships', must be regarded as extreme;[45] but it derives from a transcendent vision of God's unique reality that must be the outcome of any Christian pondering on the estate of man in relation to his Maker:

> For the true honour of man is the image and likeness of God, which is not preserved except it be in relation to Him by whom it is impressed. The less therefore that one loves what is one's own, the more one cleaves to God.[46]

What is to be despised in relationships is their merely human aspect. It is not that we may not love people; but we should truly love in them what is real, and what is real in them is of God.[47] Thus is borne out his statement that 'All are related who have one God for their father and who love him and do his will'[48] – and his conviction that man, loving God, does not in the strict sense need his neighbour any more than he needs himself in the face of God's sufficiency:

> He needs God alone, by cleaving to whom he is happy. No one can take God from him.[49]

Man is truly man, and truly lovable, only by virtue of the love of God. He is human through what is entirely above humanity, and falls below humanity in any reliance upon human power. The conception is not unfamiliar in modern theology;[50] and it is implied in Aquinas's teaching that secondary ends, in man, are truly desirable only as they are ordered toward the last end which is the first of all desirable objects.[51]

But the secondary ends of worldly man are not so ordered: the city of man is the city of self-love in contempt of God, doomed to the Divine displeasure, in which reigns a will that is self-indulgent, self-congratulating and self-destructive. The fatal egoism upon which mortal society is

[43] *Serm.* cclvi. 3, quoted by R. Hazleton, 'The Devotional Life', *A Companion*, p. 410.
[44] See Bigham and Mollegen, op. cit., in *A Companion*, p. 381.
[45] *De Vera Relig.* xlvi. 89.   [46] *De Trin.* XII. xi. 16.
[47] *De Vera Relig.* xlvi. 88.   [48] ibid., xlvi. 89.
[49] ibid., xlvii. 90. Augustine here seems to dismiss not only half of 'all the law and the prophets' (*Matt.* xxii. 40), but the self which is to be the subject of happiness and love.
[50] J. Baillie, *Our Knowledge of God*, Oxford Paperbacks, 1963, pp. 41–2.
[51] E. Gilson, *The Philosophy of St Thomas Aquinas*, tr. E. Bullough, Cambridge, 1924, p. 259; *S.T.* Ia IIae i. 6, *ad R.*

founded finds insidious expression in a manifold urge to aggrandizement, a *libido dominandi*[52] self-procreating in strife and vitalized by the very disaster it brings down : for its operation can only be in defiance of God, and the things that are of God, and must inevitably result in the violation of good principle.[53] The social life of unredeemed mankind can therefore be no more than a vast injustice, and human society itself only a 'vale of mortal miseries'.[54] Injustice lies at the very beginning of the kingdoms of the world : the conqueror and the robber are indistinguishable apart from the scale of their operations;[55] and as for the triumph of one man or faction in conflict with another, human victories are empty – there can be no just war,

> for it is other men's wickedness that works his cause just that he ought to deplore, whether it produce wars or not,

and exultation in his just victory can be the action only of one devoid of 'the natural feeling of a man'.[56] The society of unregenerate man is the realm that forsakes God and is forsaken by him, being in its career of blind instinct and vicious worldliness both the punisher and the punished :

> But woe is thee, thou torrent of human custom! Who shall stand against thee? How long shalt thou not be dried up? How long roll the sons of Eve into that huge and hideous ocean, which even they scarcely overpass who climb the cross?[57]

Mortal man in this world, declares Augustine, experiences a 'dying life . . . or living death';[58] man's life is, for Calvin, a sepulchre, a prison, and a place of exile;[59] for Luther, 'this present evil world'

> is the kingdom of the devil. For there is nothing in it but ignorance, contempt, blasphemy, hatred of God, and disobedience against all the words and works of God. In and under this kingdom we are.[60]

And thus it is that the wisdom of the just man in mortal society lies solely in the cry,

> Lord, take me out of all my troubles.[61]

The act of God alone is man's deliverance from the body and the land of death, from the 'frail and foul-browed world'[62] that is mankind's tragic abode.

---

[52] *De Civ. Dei* XIV. xxviii; XIX. xii. [53] ibid., XV. iv. [54] ibid., XIX. viii.
[55] ibid., IV. iv. [56] *De Civ. Dei* XIX. vii.
[57] *Conf.* I. xvi. 25. [58] ibid., I. vi. 7. [59] *Inst.* III. viii. 7.
[60] *Galatians* (i. 4), ed. P. S. Watson, 1953, p. 53.
[61] *De Civ. Dei.* XIX vi.
[62] ibid., XIX. x. For this paragraph see J. N. Cochrane, *Christianity and Classical Culture*, 1940, p. 492.

But the 'shattered and bleeding soul'[63] can, by God's grace, begin to find its deliverance in this world: mortal man may, through a due obedience to God's law, performed in faith, make his peace with immortal God, and be purified by the hope that he is able to bear:[64]

You purify yourself in uniting your will to God. You purify yourself, not by yourself but by him who comes to dwell within you.[65]

Man can know no happiness greater than that which is vouchsafed to him from beyond himself in despite of the outward circumstance which had appeared to be the means of his pleasures. For such things as honour, fame, power and bodily good are delusory, Aquinas argues, in that they are unrelated to the last end.[66] Creatures attain their last end in the measure of their participation in the Creator's likeness; and, because of the degree of their intelligence,

man and other rational creatures attain to their last end by knowing and loving God.[67]

It is perhaps a commentary upon their failure to show the implementation of the Divine will in the world of man that Augustine and Aquinas should make the means to this knowledge and love of God not an utter transformation of the human will, but an utter renunciation of it; that having insisted upon the validity of human free will in matters spiritual, they should make the beholding and enjoying of truth conditional upon the will's quiescence. For Augustine, the activity of the will is but the path to man's peace; and when the vision of truth, produced from above, comes to it, the will fulfils its final task in remaining silent before the working of revelation.[68] In this life however there must be continuous exertion by the struggling soul: it is in the life to come that perfect contemplation, as

the end of all actions, and the everlasting fullness of joy,[69]

is promised us. For Aquinas also, the perfect happiness which consists in the vision of the Divine essence is identified wth the end of all desire:[70] it is the complete contemplation only possible in the life to come, as opposed to the incomplete contemplation, intermingled with the operations of the practical intellect, that is the highest that man can achieve on earth.[71] The operation of the practical intellect makes the human mind proportionate to God's, but by the operation of the speculative

[63] *Conf.* IV. vii. 12.   [64] *De Civ. Dei* XIX. xiii.

[65] *In Epist. Jo. ad Parth. Tract. decem* iv. 7.

[66] *S.T.* Ia IIae ii. 2–6, *ad R.*

[67] *S.T.* Ia IIae i. 8, *ad R.*; E. Gilson, *The Philosophy of St Thomas Aquinas*, Cambridge, 1924, p. 258, citing *Contra Gent.* III. xxv.

[68] *De Trin.* I. x. 20.   [69] ibid., I. viii. 17.

[70] *S.T.* Ia IIae iii. 8, *ad R.*   [71] *S.T.* Ia IIae iii. 5, *ad R.*

159

intellect man's mind reaches out to God's mind and attains union with it.[72] Thus for Aquinas also the act that constitutes beatitude must be speculative in nature. This trend toward the abstract, and toward extatic self-abnegation in the relinquishing of the will and identification with the being of God, is at variance with the concept of love (by Augustine identified with will) by which the human may be reordered and conformed to the Divine, and through which God may indeed be immediately known: which by its proper virtue can ensure that a man may both believe and hope as he should,[73] and can bring him into God's presence with its innate affirmation that

If God is love, whoever loves love, loves God.[74]

There is in fact a possible failure to appreciate the full force of the commonplace that the peace of God passes all understanding. It may well be that the loving and willing service of God constitutes not only perfect freedom for man, but also his true peace, and a true participation of a beatitude yet to be completed. But in whatever terms the knowledge, love and adoration of God are expressed, and whatever contradictory aspirations these terms may embody, they are eloquent of a single assurance: that the love of God, which is man's deliverance and his salvation, comes to him from beyond him, as the work of a love infinitely greater than his own. In this assurance lies the resignation that goes properly with the thought of human blessedness:

In Thy Gift we rest; there we enjoy Thee.
Our rest is our place.[75]

[72] *S.T.* Ia IIae iii. 5, *ad 1, 3*. See Gilson, op. cit., p. 262.   [73] *Ench.* xxxi. 117.
[74] *In Epist. Jo. ad Parth. Tract. decem* ix. 10.   [75] *Conf.* XIII. ix. 10.

Chapter 13

THE USES OF ADVERSITY

In a Divine universe, every human aspiration short of the desire for God must come to naught. Those who seek, not in Him, but in his creatures, for pleasures, sublimities and truths must, through the insubstantiality of the goods they desire, fall headlong into sorrows, confusions and errors.[1] That perverse will in man which, through inordinate self-love, 'makes himselfe his end' in contempt of God, engineers with its feverish activity not its happiness but its tragedy. In this process, the nature of the universe is at one with the Divine love which created it: for how can the love of God deal with the aspirations of the sinning will save by defeating them? Worldly men will naturally bewail the overthrow of their creaturely assurances and pleasures;

> whereas if they had any judgement, they would rather attribute these calamities and miseries of mortality, all unto the providence of God, which useth to reform the corruptions of men's manners, by war and oppressions, and laudably to exercise the righteous in such afflictions.[2]

Where creatures mistakenly seek their own good from themselves, it is only through the destruction of that apparent good that they will be awakened to the presence of the good that belongs to an order above themselves – for no good that they have previously known, properly speaking, was attainable without the grace of the Source of all good, in whom alone man's true purpose and happiness can reside, and apart from whom no happiness can subsist. It is not in their earthly joys, but in the death of their joys, that God will be perceived by an erring mankind. No pleasure without alloy is discoverable, cries Augustine,

> save in Thee, O Lord, who *teachest by sorrow*, and woundest us, to heal; and killest us, lest we die from Thee.[3]

The assurance and comfort of man lies neither in his own strength nor his own being but in his omnipotent Creator; nor is the providence of God to be seen solely in the good and the joyous, but it is equally apparent in the phenomena of evil and grief in man's world.[4] The wisdom and

---

[1] ibid., I. xviii. 31.
[2] *De Civ. Dei* I. i.
[3] *Conf.* II. ii. 3.
[4] See pp. 144, 148 above.

the will of God, which of necessity must be fulfilled in His creatures,[5] must, amidst a sinful humanity, justly be discerned in the phenomena of affliction.

Augustine, therefore, considering the tragic loss and defeat that is inseparable from the human condition, concludes that affliction, far from being an enigmatic and harrowing anomaly, is the very assurance of God's loving care for His creatures; that

> all the evils of this world, and the griefs and labours of men, although they come from the deserts of sins, and especially of original sin, whence life itself too became bound by the bond of death, yet have fitly remained, even when sin is forgiven; that man might have wherewith to contend for truth, and whereby the goodness of the faithful might be exercised; in order that the new man through the new covenant might be made ready among the evils of this world for a new world, by bearing wisely the misery which this condemned life deserved, and by rejoicing soberly because it will be finished, but expecting faithfully and patiently the blessedness which the future life, being set free, will have for ever. . . . And those evils which the faithful endure piously, are of profit either for the correction of sins, or for the exercising and proving of righteousness, or to manifest the misery of this life, that the life where will be that true and perpetual blessedness may be desired more ardently, and sought out more earnestly. But it is on their account that these evils are still kept in being, of whom the apostle says: 'For we know that all things work together for good in them that love God, to them who are called to be holy according to his purpose.'[6]

His exasperation against the Roman populace lay in the fact that, though they had been made miserable by their oppressions, their inordinate affections rendered them irreformable, and deprived them of what he termed 'the benefit of affliction'.[7] A benefit that he dwells on particularly is affliction's testing and proving a man in his self-knowledge and his love for God: temporal afflictions exist that the righteous soul

> may be proved and fully known whether it hath so much godly virtue as to love God freely, and for Himself alone.[8]

That man who makes spiritual progress amidst prosperity learns through adversity what progress he has made. His not trusting in the abundance of the passing goods of this world is confirmed by their withdrawal: in their departure he discovers the sort of person he is[9] – and, largely, the kind of person that the tragic situation of man has helped to make him.

[5] S.T. I. xxi. 1, ad 3.   [6] De Trin. XIII. xvi. 20.   [7] De Civ. Dei I. xxxiii.
[8] ibid., I. ix.   [9] De Vera Relig. xlvii. 92.

As for the action of evil in the afflictions of mankind, Augustine can turn to his own experience in declaring its healthfulness. Through the decree that each wrongful affection should be its own punishment, he can confess himself justly punished for his own sin, and instructed by his very evil:[10]

> For Thou didst grant me Thy discipline, while I was learning vanities; and my sin of delighting in those vanities Thou has forgiven.[11]

The evils produced by the purposed and malicious will of one soul against its fellows are none the less brought about by Providence, using the agency of inferior beings who find pleasure in their task and who never know the good that is being done through their actions. Through the perverse dealings of those who delight in the misery and destruction of others, the good, says Augustine, are 'admonished and exercised, and they are victorious, triumphant and regal' in that process in which the bad are deceived and tortured.[12] In no instance of human malice would Augustine have sought to deny what had been confirmed to him in his own life, that

> Thou, Lord, Governor of all in heaven and earth, who turnest to Thy purposes the deepest currents, and the ruled turbulence of the tide of times, didst by the very unhealthiness of one soul, heal another.[13]

The act of evil is thus consistent with the purpose of almighty God, as indeed is every other temporal adversity, whereby, in the words of Calvin,

> in the very act of afflicting us with the cross he is providing for our salvation.[14]

For the subtle and persistent will of man's soul is to seek a temporal felicity. With a 'brutish love', says Calvin, devolving from a 'blind love of self',

> the whole soul, enmeshed in the allurements of the flesh, seeks its happiness on earth;[15]

and the 'fittest means' by which it may be dissuaded from cleaving too tenaciously to that love is an involvement in the miseries that follow from it. Therefore a beneficent God permits his human creatures 'to be troubled and plagued either with wars or tumults, or robberies, or other injuries';[16] with exile, famine, or fire. They may be troubled with depraved wives, or humbled by evil offspring, or afflicted with bereavement – or,

---

[10] *Conf.* I. xii. 19. [11] ibid., I. xv. 24. [12] *De Vera Relig.* xl. 75.
[13] *Conf.* IX. viii. 18. [14] *Inst.* III. viii. 11. [15] ibid., III. viii. 3; ix. 1.
[16] ibid., III. ix. 1.

if not through these, they are instructed by other 'diseases and perils' in the unstable and fleeting nature of the goods that are subject to mortality :

> Then only do we rightly advance by the discipline of the cross, when we learn that this life, judged in itself, is troubled, turbulent, unhappy in countless ways, and in no respect clearly happy; that all those things which are judged to be its goods are uncertain, fleeting, vain, and vitiated by many intermingled evils. From this, and at the same time, we conclude that in this life we are to seek and hope for nothing but struggle; when we think of our crown, we are to raise our eyes to heaven.[17]

Mortal affliction teaches a humbled humanity to rest upon God alone.[18]

A tragic involvement in adversity, suffering and destruction is the necessary lot of man on earth. His natural endowments and capacities, and his creaturely promptings and ideals, must speed him alike to this conclusion. For the good and the evil, the elect and the reprobate, there is no distinction in the evils of circumstance, as they are themselves undistinguished by any good that is properly their own. Yet they, and the adversities from which they cannot separate themselves, serve a Providential purpose of good amongst mankind: worldly man, and his tragedy, are manifestations of a love, wisdom and justice superior to a mundane understanding. The depths of that paradoxical goodness cannot be known; but its operation in the mortal world, as the Christian awareness gives feature to it, can be said to unperplex the living contradictions in the mortal state of a creature who, though hurled in endless error, must yet be the judge of truth. For in the process of adversity the depravity of man's will, the dignity and validity of its power of choice, and its subjection to the omnipotence of God's will – the seemingly irreconcilable trinity of fact which dominates the human condition – find coherence and affirmation. The general nature of man's tragic involvement points to apostasy and irresponsibility equally universal and ineradicable, a will turned away from truth toward the 'proud imaginations' of self-concern.[19] The remedy of adversity is indeed the 'fittest means' to counter this depravity in that it permits and safeguards the operation of human choice though the will choose to overthrow all reason and violate all good; and it therefore points to the integrity of man's will as being of ultimate importance. And in the inevitability of the tragic outcome, the requirements both of God's justice and of His love for man, the nature of the universe He ordained in his purpose of love, and the permitted perversity of the apostate will in mankind, combine in the working out of that necessity in which the Divine will's omnipotence is to be apprehended.

[17] ibid. [18] ibid., III. viii. 3. [19] *Paradise Lost* II. 10.

In this coherence, and its intimations of an underlying harmony, lies another, equally gladdening : the recognition that

in the very harshness of tribulations we must recognize the kindness and generosity of our Father towards us, since he does not even then cease to promote our salvation.[20]

It is in the tragic necessity of human life that Christianity finds its very being, and the means of its assurance, and takes all human experience unto itself.

For the Lord has ordained that those who are one day to be crowned in heaven should first undergo struggles on earth in order that they may not triumph until they have overcome the difficulties of war, and attained victory.[21]

Those among mankind whose earthly bliss has been destroyed are the more likely to be graced with the creation of 'A paradise within thee, happier far'[22] – for it will be the work, not of themselves, but of a God who has come to dwell with them, and cannot be taken away from them.[23] The human condition and earthly predicament is such as to incite the mind of faith to gain life and courage only from hope : and otherwise to consign the apostate will to gleaning what resolution it can from inevitable loss and despair. For its terms are such as must bring any secular ambition within the compass of disaster.

[20] Calvin, *Inst.* III. viii. 6.
[21] ibid., III. ix. 3.
[22] *Paradise Lost* XII. 587.
[23] *De Vera Relig.* xlvi. 90.

III

The Tragic Phenomenon:
Literary Tragedy as the
Secular Enactment of
Theological Principle

[II]

The Tragic Phenomenon:
Literary Tragedy as the
Secular Enactment of
Theological Principle

Chapter 14

THE TRAGIC NECESSITY

In considering the order which lies behind Shakespeare's tragedies, and of which they are to be seen as manifestations, A. C. Bradley writes in the presence of dilemma. The tragic order cannot be benevolent because of the suffering it inflicts, yet it cannot be indifferent to good because those beholding its operation are not left in despair.[1] The cause of the tragic outcome is invariably evil, and indeed moral evil;[2] yet we are scarcely witnessing a moral order asserting itself against attack or want of conformity because of our certainty that its evil agents are its parts and expressions – that 'in their defect or evil *it* is untrue to its soul of goodness', and that in their suffering it suffers itself.[3] The appearance of tragedy is for Bradley that of

> a world travailing for perfection, but bringing to birth, together with glorious good, an evil which it is able to overcome only by self-torture and self-waste.[4]

In the face of the dilemma Bradley is not prepared to assert that the tragic picture is incompatible with the existence of a personal and kindly God, and therefore with the Christian faith, but his position is yet by no means far removed from such pronouncements of later criticism.[5] That the presence of evil within the universe should be a stumbling-block to mortal evaluation is not surprising; nor is it surprising that, in the overriding concern of literary criticism to relate the phenomena of tragedy to a moral universe, the intimations of a spiritual universe should receive a certain neglect. For the moral is consistent with the self-centredness of man as it is with his greatness; and to convert the reality of its standards into finality is to obscure the reality of sin, of the soul, and of God. It is to take a creaturely view of those capacities and inclinations which, to a Christian understanding, must lead necessarily to frustration and loss in a creature dedicated to apostasy. Nothing, according to this understanding, can be well with him who does not adhere to the sole good:[6]

[1] *Shakespearean Tragedy*, 2nd. edn, p. 26. [2] ibid., p. 34.
[3] ibid., p. 37. [4] ibid., p. 39.
[5] See C. Leech, *Shakespeare's Tragedies, and Other Studies in 17th-Century Drama*, 1950, p. 18.
[6] (Section II, p. 96.)

169

the secular condition is, to the mind of faith, almost synonymous with the tragic.

If Shakespeare's tragic heroes can in any sense be said to share a common vocation, it is for each man to be 'his own artificer':[7] in no man of them – with one exception – is to be found a manner of living that would '[yeeld] glory vnto him that makes him'.[8] They exist and strive in what, to the spiritual discernment, must be a state of 'great error and enormity'.[9] Unreadiness to forsake worldly desire and ambition is a rejection of the blessedness that alone can constitute desire's fulfilment.[10] Only by a forsaking can human life be properly directed to the glory of Him who is its beginning; and, without such direction, it must relapse into a condition more unhappy than that of any of the brutes.[11] The primary instinct of the tragic hero is the assertion of the self; but, by Christian definition, the first duty of man is self-denial:

> We are not our own: let not our reason nor our will, therefore, sway our plans and deeds. We are not our own: let us therefore not set it as our goal to seek what is expedient for us according to the flesh. We are not our own: in so far as we can, let us therefore forget ourselves and all that is ours. Conversely, we are God's: let us therefore live for him and die for him. We are God's: let his wisdom and will therefore rule all our actions. . . . Let this therefore be the first step, that a man depart from himself in order that he may apply the whole force of his ability in the service of the Lord.[12]

A man's gifts of body and mind are not his to possess; they are entrusted to him on the condition that they are used for the benefit of his neighbours.[13] If he receive evil from his fellow men, he is to contemplate, not their wickedness, but the Divine image within them, and respond with a love that obliterates their faults.[14] And in the life of him who thus finds all desirable good in the Divine benediction there will be no passionate striving for possessions and honours,[15] and not even a variation in response to the various accidents of mortal existence. Happiness, health, want, suffering, disappointment and the receipt of evil must alike be the occasions of thanksgiving.[16] By such standards as these is human activity in the world to be assessed – and condemned.

[7] Augustine, *Conf.* I. vi. 10.

[8] Greville, 'An Inqvisition vpon Fame and Honovr', st. 10, *Poems and Dramas*, ed. Bullough, 1938, I, p. 194.

[9] *De Civ. Dei* XII. i.   [10] (Section II, p. 95.)

[11] Calvin, 'Catechism of the Church of Geneva', *Theological Treatises*, tr. J. K. S. Reid, L.C.C. XXII, 1954, p. 91.

[12] *Inst.* III. vii. 1.   [13] ibid., III. vii. 5.

[14] ibid., III. vii. 6.   [15] ibid., III. vii. 9.

[16] Søren Kierkegaard, 'Every Good and Perfect Gift is from Above', *Edifying Discourses*, tr. D. F. and L. M. Swenson, Minneapolis, 1950–3, I, pp. 48–9.

The abandonment of the self is scarcely possible in this life. Even in the faithful, the flesh, the world and the devil hinder and harass faith; and the striving of flesh against spirit in the saints testifies to man's infirmity. No man can claim more, says Luther, than that he is beginning to be leavened:[17] in the tragedy of unfulfilment which is the human lot the pious also share, being distinguished by little save a 'blessed hope'.[18] Yet the light of this hope is enough to expose all merely human validities as fraudulent:

> If we could fully assure ourselves, and constantly believe that God is our Father, and we his sons and heirs, then should we utterly contemn this world, with all the glory, righteousness, wisdom, and power, and with all the royal sceptres and crowns, and with all the riches and pleasure thereof. We should not be so careful for this life: we should not be so addicted to worldly things, trusting unto them when we have them, lamenting and despairing when we lose them; but we should do all things with great love, humility, and patience. But we do the contrary; for the flesh is yet strong, but faith is feeble, and the spirit weak.[19]

Because of human faithlessness, the world is a theatre for assertion and suffering rather than a temple for worship. Worldly man seeks dominance, in a misguided instinct for the imitation of God; yet it is through the submission of worship that man attains the truest resemblance to Him. Man and God do not resemble each other directly, but conversely; only when God has become the eternal object of worship, and man the constant worshipper, do they resemble each other:

> If a man wishes to resemble God through the fact of ruling, then he has forgotten God, then God has gone away, and the man plays ruler in His absence. And paganism was like this, it was human life carried on in God's absence.[20]

This is the condition and quality also of the life that is set forth in Shakespeare's plays. It is with human society and its ordinances, and not with God, that the tragic heroes have made their covenant: Macbeth is not alone in wishing to pay his debt to 'time and mortal custom'. The worldly bond is constantly threatened and broken by corruption within and without – by man's limited wisdom, his tainted morality, the waywardness of chance, and the decay of institutions; and the attempts of the members

---

[17] *A Commentary on St Paul's Epistle to the Galatians* (iii. 25), ed. P. S. Watson, 1953, p. 338.

[18] *Titus* ii. 13; Hardy, 'The Darkling Thrush'.

[19] Luther, op. cit. (iv. 7, 8), p. 378.

[20] Søren Kierkegaard, 'The Glory of our Common Humanity', *The Gospel of Suffering and the Lillies of the Field*, tr. D. F. and L. M. Swenson, Minneapolis, Augsburg Publishing House, 1948, p. 212.

of the tragic society to defend and strengthen it can be seen as desperate strivings in a state which is truly penitential:

> These are all, in a sense, acts of penance, that is, acts whose deepest intent is to purge us of guilt and the fear of being abandoned.[21]

This fear in tragic man has its origin in his adherence to the worldly passion or desire that Augustine declares to be the evil principle: 'the love of those things which each of us can lose against his will'.[22] By it, order is disrupted, not only in the individual soul, but in the society formed by such souls.[23] The fate of those in a Divine universe who dedicate themselves to imperfect desire can only be exile from God and enslavement in evil:[24] both the fear and the fact of tragic circumstance are commensurate with Godlessness.

The suffering of tragedy can appear to derive from man's sin in his own sphere against the rationality that sustains the universe, and has its origin in the very will of God.[25]. It is to be adduced not only in law Divine and human, and in man's own reason, but in universal nature, which God uses as an instrument for His high purposes.[26] By following reason (in the universe as the Elizabethan mind could conceive it) man exercised an autonomy that was only apparent; ultimately he was following and co-operating with God.[27] And in rejecting reason in the choice and act of sinning he was doing something

> which cannot be done without the singular disgrace of Nature, and the utter disturbance of that divine order.[28]

The definition and significance of evil is to be sought in its relation to God, and not to man, in a universe where the debt of creatures is to achieve resemblance to God 'in the constancy and excellency of those operations which belong unto their kind'.[29] The overcoming of reason in a spiritual universe must produce consequences in nature out of all proportion to the act through which it takes place. In Shakespearian tragedy it can be seen to effect 'a macrocosmic translation of Lear's inner chaos' in the storm on the heath;[30] to embody in the individual 'Rebellion against one's self, loss of all nature, lapse into chaos';[31] and to release an

---

[21] J. Stampfer, 'The Catharsis of *King Lear*', S.S. XIII, 1960, p.9.

[22] *De Lib. Arb.* I. iii. 8; I. iv. 10.   [23] *De Civ. Dei* XIX. xxi.   [24] (Section II, p. 91.)

[25] *S.T.* Ia IIae lxxxvii. 1 *ad R.*; Hooker, *Eccl. Pol.* I. iii. 1; quoted by J. L. Rosier, 'The Lex Aeterna and *King Lear*', *J.E.G.P.* LIII, 1954, p. 574.

[26] *Eccl. Pol.* I. iii. 4, quoted by Rosier, op. cit., p. 574.

[27] P. Munz, *The Place of Hooker in the History of Thought*, London, 1952, quoted by Rosier, op. cit., p. 575.

[28] *Eccl. Pol.* I. vii. 7.   [29] ibid., I. v. 2. quoted by Rosier, op. cit., p. 575.

[30] Rosier, op. cit., p. 579.

[31] J. F. Danby, *Shakespeare's Doctrine of Nature*, 1949, p. 25, quoted by Rosier, op. cit., p. 575.

'all-embracing destructive force of evil which touches every area of God's creation'.[32] The God-given means of existence and possibility become, in their overthrow, their own antithesis.

The tragic isolation of man and its consequences can thus, through the emphasis of Aquinas, be seen from the viewpoint of human initiative; it can no less readily be regarded from that of the Divine. The worst thing that can happen to a man, according to Calvin, is to live without God:[33] the contemning of God's word is, for Luther, the forerunner of God's punishments[34] – and to these punishments worldly man is infallibly committed. The sins which go on with power in human life, and by which God is displeased, are many and various; but they are as nothing compared to that contemning of God's word out of which they arise.[35] For where man is not steadfastly the servant of God's word and command, he must as resolutely be the servant of his own – and the devil's – will.[36] Devotion to any principle that falls short of the worship of God is faithlessness; and the works of infidelity can only issue forth in idolatry. No man, Luther declares, now makes calves like Jeroboam's;

> but upon whatsoever a man depends or trusts – God set aside – this is the calves of Jeroboam, that is, other and strange gods, honoured and worshipped instead of the only, true, living, and eternal God, who only can and will help and comfort in all need. In like manner also, all such as rely and depend upon their art, wisdom, strength, sanctity, riches, honour, power, or anything else, under what title or name soever, on which the world builds, make and worship the calves of Jeroboam. For they trust in and depend on vanishing creatures.

The inclination to idolatry comes easily to man by natural inheritance;[37] and by the faith they place in 'things temporal and mutable', the tragic heroes may be said to share in a common mind of man that is 'thrust out by its own weight from blessedness'.[38]

The wrath of God is to permit in man the self-love and isolation that he chooses. When God punishes sinners, He inflicts no evil of His own upon them, but leaves them to that which is theirs.[39] There can be no greater anger than the silence of God;[40] for apart from His word and purpose, no reality is to be found by mortal creatures in an evanescent

[32] I. Ribner, 'Macbeth: The Pattern of Idea and Action', S.Q. X, 1959, p. 147.
[33] Theological Treatises (tr. Reid; L.C.C. XXII) p. 91.
[34] The Table-Talk of Martin Luther, tr. W. Hazlitt, London, 1883, xxxi.
[35] ibid., ccxlvii.
[36] ibid., cxii.
[37] ibid., clxxv.
[38] Augustine, De Trin. XII. xi. 16.
[39] En. in Ps. v. 10, quoted by Burnaby, Amor Dei, p. 210; see Section II, pp. 95–7.
[40] Luther, Table-Talk, lxxxiii.

universe. For creatures in self-love to presume upon what they are is truly no more than a self-hatred.[41]

> We are nothing worth with all our gifts and qualities, how great soever they be, unless God continually hold his hand over us : if he forsake us, then are our wisdom, art, sense and understanding futile. If he do not constantly aid us, then our highest knowledge and experience in divinity, or whatever else we attain unto, will nothing serve; for when the hour of trial and temptation comes, we shall be despatched in a moment.[42]

For the life that is lived in Christ, there is no sin, no death, and no curse; where Christ is not known these things remain.[43] The possession of worldly glory is 'a false beatitude, and a most true misery';[44] or, in the words of Luther,

> He that has not God, let him have else what he will, is more miserable than Lazarus, who lay at the rich man's gate, and was starved to death.[45]

What appear to a mortal gaze to be strength of will or stature of soul are in reality the attributes of a 'confounded, corrupt and poisoned nature' that of itself can do nothing but sin.[46] Godless man is, in himself, a cripple – indeed, a slave, and doubly so : he is enslaved not only by the desires which he follows, but by the evil agency which inhabits them, and establishes a tyranny within him from which there can be no escape :

> the devil will not be driven but by devils, much less by men, or by man's strength, but only by God's spirit and power. Hence, if the devil be not driven out through God's finger, then the kingdom of the devil subsists there.[47]

In the state of human weakness, no man can afford not to call upon God for his help in the face of diabolical temptation :

> For both our mind by its native vanity is susceptible to his frauds, and our will, which is always more inclined to evil, would forthwith surrender to him.[48]

The condition of mankind is that God sustains His faithful, and deprives of His grace, strikes with blindness, and abandons to a reprobate mind

---

[41] (Section II, p. 92.) [42] Luther, *Table-Talk*, lxxxvii.
[43] *A Commentary on St Paul's Epistle to the Galatians*, ed. P. S. Watson, 1953, p. 274.
[44] *De Civ. Dei* XIX. xx; see Section II, p. 99. [45] *Table-Talk*, ci.
[46] ibid., cclxii. [47] ibid., cclxiii; see also dxcvi.
[48] 'Catechism of the Church of Geneva', *Calvin: Theological Treatises*, tr. J. K. S. Reid, L.C.C. XXII, 1954, p. 128.

and to the assaults of temptation, those who have forsaken Him and are deemed worthy and needful of punishment.[49] From this condition it is not to be postulated that Shakespeare's tragic hero, or any other category of mortal man, is in some manner exempt.

There is to be perceived in the tragic human condition much that is good – but it is not, in Bradley's term, 'glorious good'.[50] In the light of glory, and of truth, it is impossible to see anything that is not 'impure, profane, and abominable to God' in the works of an intellect blind and wrapped in error, a will full of corrupt affections, and a corporeal endowment that ever tends toward iniquity.[51] Mortal man is caught up in brutish loves, and his abode is the devil's kingdom;[52] yet the subjection of man to Satan is part of his reformation. It is decreed 'to the ende that wee should know our owne wretchednesse',[53] and for the reason that the righteousness of God must defeat the aspirations of the erring will.[54] The tragic waste in man's world is proportionate to its sin :

> There is greate reason why God shoulde chastyze men. For how greate are our sinnes? the number of them is infinite. Agayne, if wee looke vpon our lustes, there is also a very bottomlesse gulfe, which hath neede to bee mended. God therefore muste mortifie vs.[55]

The gladness of man, declares Augustine, is but wickedness unpunished : the misery of man is the proof of his guilt.[56] And, by the same token, literary tragedy is indicative of men's spiritual condition. This truth the Elizabethans were able to recognize : in their appraisal the chief task of tragedy was reformative. For Puttenham, its purpose was to remind men of 'the mutabilitie of fortune, and the iust punishment of God in reuenge of a vicious and euill life';[57] for Fulke Greville, the tragedy which appeared on the contemporary stage had as its aim to 'point out Gods revenging aspect upon every particular sin, to the despaire, or confusion of mortality';[58] and for Sir Philip Sidney it is

> the high and excellent Tragedy, that openeth the greatest wounds, and showeth forth the ulcers that are covered with tissue . . . that . . . teacheth the uncertainty of this world, and upon how weak foundations gilden roofs are builded.[59]

[49] ibid.   [50] *Shakespearean Tragedy*, p. 39.
[51] Calvin, *Instruction in Faith*, tr. P. T. Fuhrmann, Lutterworth Press, 1949, p. 21.
[52] Luther, *Galatians* (i. 4), ed. P. S. Watson, 1953, p. 53.
[53] *Calvins Sermons on Job*, tr. A Golding, 1573, p. 18a.
[54] ibid., p. 25a.   [55] ibid., p. 63b.
[56] *Serm.* clxxi. 4; *Contra Jul. Imp. Op.* xxvii, quoted by J. Burnaby, *Amor Dei*, 1949, pp. 202–3.
[57] George Puttenham, *The Arte of English Poesie*, ed. G. D. Willcock and A. Walker, 1936, p. 33.
[58] *Life of Sir Philip Sidney*, 1652, ed. Nowell Smith, 1907, xviii, p. 221.
[59] *An Apology for Poetry*, ed. G. Shepherd, Nelson, 1965, p. 117.

The difference between that age and the present is well illustrated in the words of a recent critic who, considering the irremediable suffering which Elizabethan tragedy presents, can deduce from 'this alleged didactic or reformative value of the drama' of those times that

> the writers themselves were not clear what they were doing in writing tragedy.[60]

The phenomenon which is to the mind of faith an assurance of God's loving care is to the secular imagination a proof of God's indifference, or non-existence.

A worldly wisdom, writes Kierkegaard, which ponders the matter of ultimate reality, will be 'repeatedly answering the question of where the way is'; it will remain ignorant of the fact 'that, spiritually understood, the way is: *how* it is traveled'.[61] For by the will of God, and in the testimony of the Scriptures, 'the way of perfection is in afflictions';[62] or, as Calvin puts it, the path to heaven can be trodden by fallen man only through the discipline of the Cross.[63] At the heart of the mystery of the human condition springs the fact – no less mysterious – of the Christian hope, which can instruct the believer, in the expectation of disaster and fear, 'When this happens, then lift up your heads'.[64] For Kierkegaard, the fact that humanity must endure affliction is 'a joyful thought':

> For then it is indeed immediately clear what the task is. Doubt wishes to make the sufferer wonder whether it might not still be possible for the affliction to be taken away, and he still continue to walk on the same way – without affliction. But if the affliction is the way, then it is indeed impossible for it to be taken away, and the way still remain the same.[65]

Affliction being the way, the afflicted can be assured of progress, and even of preferment.[66] If that which appears to obstruct humanity in its course becomes the very means of furthering it,[67] there is indeed matter for rejoicing. And this, despite the grief and dread of suffering; for suffering does not truly have the capacity to overwhelm mankind. Neither the affliction nor the fear is of superhuman magnitude; in the strict sense, it is rather he that suffers it who rises above his condition:

> when the affliction is most terrible, the believer is taller by a head, a head taller, aye, he is indeed a head taller, as he rises above the afflic-

60 C. Leech, *Shakespeare's Tragedies, and Other Studies in 17th-Century Drama*, 1950, pp. 26–7.

61 Kierkegaard, 'The Joy in the Thought that it is not the Way which is Narrow, but the Narrowness which is the Way', *The Gospel of Suffering and the Lillies of the Field*, tr. D. F. and L. M. Swenson, Minneapolis, 1948, p. 99.

62 ibid., p. 101. 63 *Inst*. III. ix. 1.

64 Kierkegaard, op. cit., p. 116. 65 ibid., p. 106.

66 ibid., pp. 111–15. 67 ibid., p. 115.

tion. And when affliction is the way, then is the believer also above the affliction; for the way *on which* a man goes certainly does not go over his head; no, when he walks on it, then he plants his foot on it.[68]

The world's gladness flatters the ear, but is abhorrent to the soul; but the true voice of consolation – 'this voice which trembles in pain and yet proclaims the gladness'[69] – strengthens the man of faith to find joy in the depths of sorrow.

According to Aquinas, the sorrow of mankind is both a craving for the unity which a creature cannot attain, and a proof that it exists.[70] It is with such an understanding as this that Augustine can assert that our Master has commanded us to be beaten, and that the whole of this mortal life is our stroke and chastisement. Many have grown so callous as not to feel their strokes:

> But to those who have been made sons, has been given the sense of pain: they feel that they are chastised, and they know who has commanded their chastisement.[71]

The inability, in the ungodly, to understand that they are within the reach of God's hand is the result and proof of their alienation from Him; to them He is a wrathful judge, as in His afflictions he is a loving Father to the elect. For they, being claimed by the truth, can be aware of the evil of their condition, and thus reach toward a higher destiny:

> we cannot taste the love of God in our afflictions, unless we are persuaded that they are rods with which our Father chastises us for our sins.[72]

For those who are constrained by tragic circumstance to come to terms with the reality of their mortal condition, and are enabled in the process to come close to the Divine love, the tragic fact can hold no true terror:

> If, being innocent and of good conscience, we are stripped of our possessions by the wickedness of impious folk, we are indeed reduced to penury among men. But in God's presence in heaven our true riches are thus increased. If we are cast out of our own house, then we will be the more intimately received into God's family. If we are vexed and despised, we but take all the firmer root in Christ. If we are branded with disgrace and ignominy, we but have a fuller place in the Kingdom of God. . . . For, if heaven is our homeland, what

[68] ibid., p. 116.
[69] 'The Lord Gave, and the Lord hath Taken Away, Blessed be the Name of the Lord', *Edifying Discourses*, tr. Swenson, Minneapolis, 1950–3, II, pp. 23–4.
[70] *S.T.* Ia IIae xxxvi. 3, *ad R.*
[71] *En. in Ps.* cxxii. 6, quoted by Burnaby, *Amor Dei*, p. 202.
[72] *Calvin: Commentaries*, (*Heb.* xii, 4–6) tr. J. Haroutunian, L.C.C. XXIII, 1958, p. 212.

else is the earth but our place of exile? If departure from the world is entry into life, what else is the world but a sepulcher? And what else is it for us to remain in life but to be immersed in death? If to be freed from the body is to be released into perfect freedom, what else is the body but a prison?[73]

It is not in their creaturely joys, but rather in their destruction, that a sinful humanity, abandoned to self-will, can perceive God and the things of God. In itself the earthly life is not to be despised; it is to be hated only in comparison to the life that is to come. But man in his worldly existence is like a sentry at his post, which he must guard and endure without repining until he is recalled; but in the midst of life the faithful must be resolute and zealous for the end of mortal pleasures, and for the coming of death.[74] The post at which he is stationed, however, is one which confirms and promises in its very harshnesses the blessedness of the forthcoming release. Through its imposed suffering, the self receives assurance 'of its own tangibility', and the spirit comes to the 'sense of its mass and substance':[75] in the consciousness of mortal limitation comes the awareness of the full dimensions of man's being, and the intimation of that infinite Being in whose necessity these dimensions reside.[76]

Literary tragedy has been described as poetry's point of implication with philosophy and religion;[77] and the description is fitting, since, as a representation of the common experience of human life, tragedy must provoke the questions, and reflect the significances, that human life itself does. If suffering is a preliminary, or a means, of revelation, literary tragedy must be found able to suggest as much. And in fact it is widely agreed that great tragedy cannot come into being unless it has access to, and itself conveys, a sense of transcendent possibility. It is through what he calls a 'community of expectation' and a 'light of larger reference' which plays upon the thoughts of the characters that, according to G. Steiner, the height of Shakespearian tragedy is realized;[78] and the decline of tragedy in any age bears for him an intimate relation to 'the decline of the organic world view'.[79] The paradox emerges that great tragedy, while limited by its very nature more strictly to the secular existence of man than most other forms of art, succeeds also by its very nature in suggesting modes and possibilities of being that contradict the standards it sets forth. What produces the tragic moment, declares R. B. Sewall, is the conflict of a 'growing secularist imagination' with a 'foregone conclusion'.[80] According to H. Weisinger, tragedy can exist only 'in

---

[73] Calvin, *Inst.* III. viii. 7; ix. 4. [74] ibid., III. ix. 4.
[75] M. de Unamuno, *The Tragic Sense of Life*, tr. J. E. Crawford Flitch, London, 1931, p. 205.
[76] ibid., pp. 207, 212. [77] Macneile Dixon, *Tragedy*, 1929, p. 8.
[78] *The Death of Tragedy*, 1961, pp. 319–20. [79] ibid., p. 292.
[80] *The Vision of Tragedy*, Yale University Press, 1965, p. 55.

an atmosphere of sceptical faith'.[81] T. Spencer similarly affirms a clash between the secularist and the transcendent principle to be essential to the creation of tragedy; what is needed, he says, is

> first, a convenient pattern of belief and behaviour, and second, an acute consciousness of how that conventional pattern can be violated.[82]

Miss Una Ellis-Fermor terms this requirement 'the equilibrium of tragedy':

> tragedy depends most intimately upon the preservation of a strict and limiting balance between two contrary readings of life . . . the intense awareness of evil and pain . . . [and] the intuitive and often undefined apprehension of another universe implying other values.[83]

It contrives to hint at a possible reconciliation between those opposing worlds, or at some interpretation in terms of good; yet the conflict is at first sight unresolved, and must give rise to a sense of mystery.[84] Attempts to resolve it result in the diminution of tragedy: the assurance of religious revaluation or of the efficacy of social readjustment on the one hand, or of an evil or irremediable world order on the other, must destroy the tragic balance and create in the beholder the impression of an incomplete reading of life.[85] For either emphasis is untrue to what is essential in man's apprehension of his world:

> The balance between the evil that is observed and the good that is guessed at is so common a part of human experience as to be perhaps its highest common factor. It is because tragedy reveals directly this equilibrium of conflicting thought and emotion that it has its enduring power.[86]

Tragedy's constant obligation – apart from anything it may suggest – to produce the impression of immediacy in the beholder ensures that the indications it may give of 'the interpenetrating world of spiritual reality' are generally of a subordinate kind. But a phase can arise where

> deed and event are, it would appear, primarily significant as images which make visible and manifest the reality which was hidden but immanent.[87]

But a religious predominance which would interpret the phenomena as merely 'appearances' is incompatible with the tragic.[88] Miss Ellis-Fermor

---

[81] *Tragedy and the Paradox of the Fortunate Fall*, London, Routledge and Kegan Paul, 1953, p. 268.
[82] *Death and Elizabethan Tragedy*, Harvard University Press, 1936, p. 53.
[83] *The Frontiers of Drama*, 1945, pp. 127–8.   [84] ibid., p. 128.
[85] ibid., pp. 136–8.   [86] ibid., p. 144.
[87] ibid., p. 145.   [88] ibid., p. 146.

would have approved R. B. Sewall's definition of Christian tragedy as one in which the certainties of revealed Christianity must lose the substance of faith and become only tantalizing possibilities, hovering above the action, but not defining it, in a world of multiplied alternatives that is terrible in its inconclusiveness.[89] Precisely because of its close identification with life in this world, tragedy cannot invoke or proclaim ultimate things. The account it gives has therefore to be incomplete; and,

> Precisely because it is an interim reading of life, it speaks to the condition of all but a few at some period of their lives; for it reveals that balance, that uncertainty, which seeks two worlds of being and cannot wholly accept either.[90]

The high duty of tragedy, in fact, is to present the situation that faith must overcome. With that situation every mind must sooner or later wrestle, and in the conflict exercise a will which mysteriously retains an integrity and sovereignty despite all the necessities to which it appears to be bound. In this respect tragedy might appear to carry out a theological task; and in the process of doing so – in that restraint proper to its nature by which it must ever be concealing the ultimate under the appearance of the mundane – it could be said to share in a theological necessity. For in the theatre of the universe, the ultimate is similarly obscured from man, and similarly perceived amidst suffering :

> That there may be room for faith, therefore, all that is believed must be hidden. Yet it is not hidden more deeply than under a contrary appearance of sight, sense and experience. Thus, when God quickens, He does so by killing; when He justifies, He does so by pronouncing guilty; when He carries up to heaven, He does so by bringing down to hell. As Scripture says in *I Kings* ii, 'The Lord killeth and maketh alive; He bringeth down to the grave and bringeth up' (*I Sam.* ii. 6) . . . Thus God conceals his eternal mercy and loving kindness beneath eternal wrath, His righteousness beneath unrighteousness . . . the impossibility of understanding makes room for the exercise of faith.[91]

In the spectacle of great tragedy, philosophy and religion indeed converge : the proclamation of Aeschylus, that 'Wisdom comes alone through suffering',[92] is at one with that of the writer of *The Book of Job*, that

> He delivereth the poor in his affliction, and openeth their ears in oppression (xxxvi. 15).

The testimony of tragedy is of the beauty of created things, of the wondrous potentiality of the human spirit, of the reality of that spirit's

[89] op. cit., p. 68.   [90] U. Ellis-Fermor, op. cit., p. 147.
[91] *Martin Luther on the Bondage of the Will*, tr. J. I. Parker and O. R. Johnston, 1959, p. 101,
[92] *Agamemnon*, 177.

choice, and of the severe limitations of its earthly dwelling. In so far as it directs men's thoughts toward the need to transcend their mortal existence, and shadows forth the nature of a reality beyond it, it may be said to instruct men to 'depend upon invisible things'.[93] And in its demonstration of the truth that there can in this life be no pleasure without alloy – that, in common experience as in literary fable, 'evere the latter ende of joye is wo'[94] – it can be held to be in itself a work of the providence of a God who teaches by sorrow, and wounds us to heal, and kills us, lest we die away from His presence.[95] The spectacle of the frailty and the transience of human life which it presents is such, declares Schlegel, that

> every heart which is not dead to feeling must be overpowered by an inexpressible melancholy, for which there is no other counterpoise than the consciousness of a vocation transcending the limits of this earthly life.[96]

The anguish which tragic event kindles in human sympathies by its demonstration of the fleetingness of all things can bring about at the same time perceptions of the imperishable. As Unamuno expresses it,

> this anguish itself reveals to us the consolation of that which does not pass away, of the eternal, of the beautiful;[97]

or, in the terms of another definition,

> the core of greatness in tragedy, the mark by which it may be recognized [is] the sense of assurance, achieved through suffering, of rational order.[98]

That it is possible through considerations such as these to place a Christian interpretation upon the rôle of literary tragedy has been affirmed by T. R. Henn. Tragedy so viewed, he writes, may be seen as moving

> on a lower plane but parallel to, the religious experience which selects, as the material for suffering, the examination of the crooked questions, and the origin of the divine spark in man. The awakening of pity seems the first step ... to a sense of Christian charity : that of fear, a necessary state of mind to our readiness to consider the idea of the numinous; both together forcing us to confront a series of ethical problems which

---

[93] Luther, *Table-Talk*, tr. Hazlitt, 1883, lxxvii.

[94] Chaucer, 'The Nun's Priest's Tale', *Canterbury Tales*, Fragment VII, 1.3205 (Group B², 1.4395).

[95] Augustine, *Conf.* II. ii. 3.

[96] *Lectures on Dramatic Art and Literature*, tr. J. Black, rev. A. J. W. Morrison, A.M.S. Press, Inc., N.Y., 1965, p. 45.

[97] op. cit., p. 203.

[98] H. Weisinger, *Tragedy and the Paradox of the Fortunate Fall*, London, 1953, p. 266.

181

have their solution only in faith. The groundwork of that faith is to be found in the moments of awareness of a unity . . . which is derived from all great art.[99]

If this opinion – and the understanding of life that lies behind it – is correct, the question must arise whether the Scriptural assertion, 'Blessed is the man whom thou chastenest, O Lord' (*Ps.* xciv. 12) can in any way be supported by evidence derived from the phenomena of tragedy.

The secular approach must always tend to deny this possibility. Modern tragedy itself, deprived of a cosmic pattern of the kind which could be present to an Elizabethan conjecture, possesses what has been termed a 'quality of absurd incomprehension'.[100] But it is hard in any age for man to derive confidence from his own defeat. A similar bewilderment, and doubt concerning man's relation to the ultimately real, is to be sensed at the end of *King Lear*, and indeed in almost all tragedy; and to a secular criticism it must appear as a dominating feature. It can for example readily be held that the poignance of *King Lear* lies in great measure in the fact that while its issues are central to Christianity it is denied the mitigation that could be offered by a doctrine of supernatural salvation.[101] In the deaths at the end, therefore, Shakespeare can be interpreted as 'confronting chaos itself, unmitigated, brutal, and utterly unresolved',[102] and as inspiring in the audience a fear that they inhabit an imbecile universe dominated by 'malignity, intransigence or chaos'.[103] For death is the end of man's province, and no purely moralistic interpretation can spell comfort to an understanding which remains within its bounds; indeed, the 'moralists', as Macneile Dixon calls them, stand revealed as traitors, both to man and the art they presume to discuss:

> If this be piety it is at the same time the destruction of tragedy, and such surrender – hateful word – surrender to the downfall of Oedipus, the sufferings of Cordelia – is the greatest betrayal, in the chiefest degree inhuman, infamous and unnatural; no less than to embrace our fetters and put a final end to ourselves. Antigone, Desdemona, Brutus, Hamlet, for all their affection, for all their nobility, have gone down into the dust.[104]

The true quality of this kind of appraisal, however, is to be inferred from one of Stampfer's remarks on the unrelieved conclusion of *King Lear*. At this point, he suggests, if the universe of the play contained a transcendent providence,

[99] *The Harvest of Tragedy*, 1966, pp. 290–1.
[100] W. M. Merchant, *Creed and Drama*, 1965, p. 114.
[101] J. Stampfer, 'The Catharsis of *King Lear*', *S.S.* XIII, 1960, p. 1.
[102] ibid., p. 2.   [103] ibid., p. 10.
[104] *Tragedy*, 1929, p. 220.

it should act as in the closing movement of *Hamlet*, mysteriously to redeem a society unable to redeem itself.[105]

The careers of Kent and Edgar, and the growth in principle and stature of an Albany,[106] might well qualify the view that society is shown to be unable to redeem itself; but more important is the sense in which the term redemption is employed. There can be no doubt that the providence here invoked is challenged on the basis of a terrestrial good, and called upon for conformity to a creaturely will. The question might be asked whether such an agency would merit so august a title. And the assertion that providence should redeem society also gives rise to the question whether it might not with more propriety be called upon to redeem the souls it has created – and whether, indeed, the tragedy does not show this task being effected. To a merely human understanding, which cannot give credence to what Francis Bacon affirms to be 'the divineness of souls',

> the earth with men upon it . . . will not seem much other than an ant hill whereas some ants carry corn, and some carry their young, and some go empty, and all to and fro a little heap of dust.[107]

A secular criticism cannot but be insensitive to the positive intimations of tragedy.

Those, however, who are not prepared to limit significance to the bounds of a mortal existence are able to discern in literary tragedy something of what Augustine called 'the benefit of affliction'.[108] Amidst the suffering and waste which it presents emerge some intimations of a larger truth; but their appearance in tragedy indicates that they are not germane to the world in which they are manifested. Their values, far from being a guarantee of success in that world, are perceived in spite of it: the good of a transcendent order, indeed, becomes visible only in the destruction of the apparent good of the existing order. In Karl Jasper's words,

> By watching the doom of what is finite, man witnesses the reality and truth of the infinite.[109]

What persists and recommends itself to man in despite of his ruin – what smells sweet and blossoms in the dust of mischance – is by definition of a nature to transcend; and the ultimately real is to be known only by such persistence, and by its impress upon a material inferior, refractory and evanescent. It is upon a basis such as this, according to L. C. Knights, that *King Lear* makes a transcendent affirmation.

[105] op. cit., p. 9.
[106] See L. Kirschbaum, 'Albany', *S.S.* XIII, 1960, esp. p. 29.
[107] 'Advancement of Learning', *Philosophical Works*, ed. J. M. Robertson, 1905, pp. 71-2.
[108] *De Civ. Dei* I. xxxiii; see Section II, p. 162.
[109] *Tragedy is Not Enough*, tr. H. A. T. Reiche *et al.*, London, 1953, p. 78.

What Lear touches in Cordelia . . . is, we are made to feel, the reality, and the values revealed so surely there are established in the face of the worst that can be known of man or Nature. To keep nothing in reserve, to slur over no possible cruelty or misfortune, was the only way of ensuring that the positive values discovered and established in the play should keep their triumphant hold on our imagination, should assert that unconditional rightness which . . . we are bound to attribute to them.[110]

The very starkness of the tragedy, therefore, is the means of enlightenment:

It is because the play has brought us to this vision of horror – seen without disguise or palliation – that the way is open for the final insights.[111]

The existing order is destroyed, however, not only in the external world, but in the deepest consciences of Lear and of ourselves. Before what is ultimately real can be received, there must be a forsaking of all untruth; and the play is a process of the successive stripping away of the layers of appearance, that the true and the real may be left open to discovery. In *King Lear* it takes the form of the love and forgiveness of Cordelia; and before he can approach it, Lear has to earn it by

the achievement of honesty and humility, the painful shedding of all that is recognized as incompatible with the highest good.[112]

Erring man lives upon illusion: the reward of perversity is to be deceived by appearances. But in his seeking to impose illusion upon others, he is enabled, in the midst of the confusion and suffering that he brings down on others and himself, to apprehend a higher order that interpenetrates both the outside world and his own inner being.[113] In the tragic conflict he is confronted with the salutary harshness of fact:

he sets in motion a sequence of events that finally brings him face to face with an actuality that can be neither denied nor disguised.[114]

Actuality does not inhere in the material order. Man's undue reliance upon that order obscures it, yet it is his only means of apprehending it: his knowledge of higher things can come only through his senses.[115] In this paradox lies the tragic necessity. In tragedy's fires of suffering, observes K. Muir, all the characters of *King Lear* are refined, and develop; in that play,

[110] *Some Shakespearean Themes*, 1959, p. 117.
[111] ibid., p. 99.   [112] ibid.
[113] J. Lawlor, *The Tragic Sense in Shakespeare*, 1960, pp. 127–8.
[114] Knights, op. cit., p. 94.   [115] See Section II, pp. 128–30.

The image of the tortured body expresses the suffering, not merely of Lear, but of Man; and the suffering is more important than the causes. That is the significance of the continual references to patience and endurance.[116]

King Lear may be understood as a consideration of the problem of the inherent guilt of the flesh, and, at the same time, of its potential for revelation; the flesh, argues W. M. T. Nowottny, is there a symbol of guilt, of begetting, of suffering, and of knowing: 'all a man can know is what he knows through the flesh'.[117] It is through the suffering of the flesh that the afflicted Lear, throwing off the protection of man-made 'lendings', seeks to attain to truth:[118] in the smell of mortality, rather than in human achievement, lies the means of perception and hope. In the thought of the play, the flesh is where evil things breed, yet flesh dissected will reveal the truth: the whole play moves toward 'revelation through suffering'[119] in a creature both wondrous and frail.

Something of the same trend is to be observed in all great tragedy. In tragic conflict is born the impression of possibility – the impression, as R. B. Sewall states it, that suffering could lead 'to the discovery of a higher level of being'. Tragic suffering, on the whole, 'shows progression toward value, rather than denial of it'; the suffering of Job and Oedipus, of Orestes and Antigone and Medea, 'makes a difference'.[120] Our final impression of Sophocles' Oedipus, full of concern for his daughters even as he faces a wretched future, is in sharp contrast to the over-confident and slightly pompous figure of the opening scenes. He is in no sense 'born again' – but he has 'enlarged his domain as a human being'.[121] At the conclusion of tragedy we are at least nearer to truth: in Sophoclean tragedy, Sewall observes, each action 'reveals the doer more clearly for what he is, and the world he lives in more clearly for what it is'.[122] And we are nearer also to hope. Lear ends in some sense victor as well as victim; 'new and saving qualities appear':

The counter-action qualifies the terrible implication and reveals possibilities which make the whole bearable.[123]

The victim of tragic circumstance is not seen to be blessed; but, through and in him, the boundaries of significance are found to have been extended – particularly by those who are able to place some reliance upon 'invisible things'.

[116] *Shakespeare: The Great Tragedies* (Writers and Their Work), 1961, pp. 29–31.
[117] 'Lear's Questions', *S.S.* X, 1957, p. 92.
[118] ibid.   [119] ibid., pp. 93, 95, 97.
[120] *The Vision of Tragedy*, Yale, 1965, p. 48.
[121] ibid., p. 42.   [122] ibid., p. 37.   [123] ibid., p. 74.

Chapter 15

THE TRAGIC PARADOXES

(a) TRUTH FROM CONFUSION

The threat which literary tragedy must ever be making to 'affright the eyes' of humanity with its 'black-visaged shows', and to stifle their hearts with 'true sense of misery', is identical, in Marston's terms, with its promise to reveal 'what men were and are'.[1] The claim of truth is the primary justification for the pleasure that stems from the tragic experience; according to Aristotle, it is the delight which is inseparable from coming to grips with reality, and which is evident in the instinctive processes of imitation and learning, that constitutes the origin of poetry itself.[2] Any theory that seeks to identify the satisfaction derived from the tragic with the beholder's isolation from the turmoil it presents before him is guilty of mistaking the means for the end. Art does indeed make a game of life;[3] and it is true that the sense of calm which is one of the emotional effects of tragedy owes much to

> that philosophic detachment which comes from watching with the aloofness of ghosts or gods the feverish struggles of humanity.[4]

In order to see the picture of life in its wholeness, it is necessary to stand back from it; but there the usefulness of the metaphor ends. For greater detachment is in this case the preliminary to greater involvement – to a concern with life more intense than that which the beholder usually undergoes, albeit different in quality.

The shows of tragedy satisfy a craving for experience. We go to tragedy, it has been said, not to get rid of emotions, but to have them more abundantly[5] – whatever may be the mechanics of their alleged subsequent purgation.[6] The catharsis may indeed be seen as a liberation not from the tyranny of the emotions, but from the tyranny of the self: as the coming of a new-born sympathy, a 'blessed transformation of our merely defensive capacity to bear the ills of others',[7] an

[1] Prologue to *Antonio's Revenge*, 1599, quoted by F. L. Lucas, *Tragedy in Relation to Aristotle's 'Poetics'*, 1953, p. 22.

[2] Aristotle, *Poetics*, iv.

[3] W. Macneile Dixon, *Tragedy*, 1929, p. 5.

[4] Lucas, op. cit., p. 29.

[5] ibid., p. 52.

[6] *Poetics*, vi.

[7] Lawlor, *The Tragic Sense in Shakespeare*, p. 173.

escape from personal preoccupations and anxieties into the larger life of sympathy with the whole human clan.[8]

But the emotions of tragedy are not incited by spurious means; tragedy can be the embodiment only of an action of some importance or seriousness,[9] and the beholder's reactions to it are those which the greatest issues in life would evince in him. In the tragic is to be understood, above all else, 'something fundamentally true to life',[10] a discerning

for an instant through its mists the sheer mountain-face of life.[11]

A predominant emotion in the appreciation of tragedy, in fact, is the exhilaration that is at one with the discerning of profound meaning.[12] F. L. Lucas would therefore define man's response to tragedy as

the pleasure we take in a rendering of life both serious and true;

and he declares it to be 'Tragedy's one end and aim' to investigate and display the strengths and weaknesses of the creature man.[13]

It is not to be doubted that the compelling power of tragedy is in ✓ its laying bare and making clear – in its shattering of illusion in the protagonists, and in its exemplifying of man's abilities and nature. The entire action of *King Lear* is in this sense a search for truth; and the message of the play, as J. J. Lawlor observes, may well be taken to be that, in the face of typical human misunderstanding, 'The only hope lies in undisguised word and act'.[14] The main themes of the play have all to do with veracity : the theme of trial and sentence, in which a corruptible justice essays to deal with a vicious humanity; the theme of outward show, where rank, act and garment conceal the true nature; the theme of blindness and illusion, where a will to see what is not prevents the seeing of what truly confronts;[15] and the theme of plain speaking, which is to be found not only in Cordelia and Kent, and in the fruitful labour of the Fool's jesting, but in the very kingliness of manner of Lear himself.[16] The play proclaims that all disguises must, for humanity's well-being, be torn away; but man is here 'loop'd and window'd' also that his very being may be probed by the tragic action.[17] It is probed to the depths : the passionate will is observed to go below the level of beasts, to assume the form of nameless monsters. In this play, as in all tragedy, humanity may be seen to be engaged in its proper study; the conclusion is unavoidable that 'Nothing less than the limits of man's nature is under scrutiny'.[18]

The question is, however, whether tragedy, in its relentless devotion to truth, does not in that just estimation of 'Nature and the natural

[8] Dixon, op. cit., p. 118.
[9] *Poetics*, vi.
[10] Lucas, op. cit., p. 53.
[11] ibid., p. 54.
[12] (Section I, p. 55.)
[13] op. cit., pp. 54–5.
[14] *The Tragic Sense*, p. 155.
[15] ibid.
[16] ibid., p. 161.
[17] ibid., p. 155.
[18] ibid., p. 165.

187

energies and passions' to which it is limited,[19] enable the beholder to range further in understanding – whether, from the evident quality of life, ultimate meaning is not to be inferred.[20] Overt statement in the midst of tragedy is precluded: tragedy, through its necessary discipline, can in its formal structure constitute no more than an appeal for further revelation. It is only in its ability to create experience – to place the beholder 'inside the truth' – that the means of further understanding is to be found.[21] That understanding will have its beginning in the conscience's acquaintance with the depths of fact and the depths of sorrow; and it will arise from suggestion that persists in the destruction of what might appear to sustain all possible hope and certainty. If tragedy does give access to an ultimate truth, a 'higher level of being', or an exalted 'possibility',[22] it can only be through the response to the tragic fact of the mind that is subjected to it. And those impressions must necessarily be, as Bradley observes, beyond the tragic.[23]

Bradley defines these intimations of higher possibility in terms that are compatible with a theological view of the human condition. What is most pronounced in his experience of literary tragedy

> is the impression that the heroic being, though in one sense and outwardly he has failed, is yet in another sense superior to the world in which he appears; is, in some way which we do not seek to define, untouched by the doom that overtakes him; and is rather set free from life than deprived of it.[24]

That the nature and destiny of man is higher than that of the temporal condition in which he is placed is almost the definition of the religious view; but the idea of man's essential immunity to the force of outward circumstance corresponds to Augustine's teaching that sin and its punishment in man – including the fact of death – are not in themselves substantial things, but rather states of the soul, which is truly substantial. The sins themselves, which are voluntary, and the punishment and unhappiness itself, which is penal, are not necessary for the perfection of the whole; but the souls as souls are necessary to its perfection, and therefore sin and its penalty help in the forming of a harmony and a beauty within it.[25] Death, therefore, is indeed a release: for, as Augustine observes, when the suffering is past, it is as nothing to those who have endured it.[26] He would thus have approved Bradley's feeling concerning Cordelia, that

[19] L. C. Knights, *Some Shakespearean Themes*, 1959, p. 118; see Section I, p. 48.
[20] (See Section I, p. 55.)   [21] ibid., pp. 61–2, 65.
[22] See p. 185 above.   [23] *Shakespearean Tragedy*, 1956, p. 324.
[24] ibid.
[25] *De Lib. Arb.* III. ix. 25, 26; see Section II, p. 103.
[26] ibid., III. xxiii. 68.

what happens to such a being does not matter; all that matters is what she is.[27]

An accompanying impression of Bradley's – one which, if developed, would he is convinced transform the tragic view of things – is that sense of the incompleteness of human perception that tragedy quickens in us.

It implies that the tragic world, if taken as it is presented with all its error, guilt, failure, woe and waste, is no final reality, but only a part of reality taken for the whole, and, when so taken, illusive; and that if we could see the whole, and the tragic facts in their place in it, we should find them, not abolished, of course, but so transmuted that they had ceased to be strictly tragic, – find, perhaps, the suffering and death counting for little or nothing, the greatness of the soul for much or all.[28]

A corresponding impression of the partial and restricted nature of the human outlook in consequence of man's penitential state, and of the joyful nature of the reality he does not see, is to be gained from Augustine:

But had the sense of thy flesh a capacity for comprehending the whole, and not itself also, for thy punishment, been justly restricted to a part of the whole, thou wouldest, that whatsoever existeth at this present should pass away, that so the whole might better please thee.[29]

A final impression is created by the scandal of the disproportion between prosperity and human goodness. It

flashes on us the conviction that our whole attitude in asking or expecting that goodness should be prosperous is wrong. . . . The 'gods', it seems, do *not* show their approval by 'defending' their own from adversity or death, or by giving them power and prosperity. These, on the contrary, are worthless, or worse; it is not on them, but on the renunciation of them, that the gods throw incense. They breed lust, pride, hardness of heart, the insolence of office, cruelty, scorn, hypocrisy, contention, war, murder, self-destruction. . . . But . . . adversity, to the blessed in spirit, is blessed. It wins fragrance from the crushed flower. It melts in aged hearts sympathies which prosperity had frozen.[30]

This conviction in Bradley could well summarize Augustine's teaching on the disproportionate suffering of the good in this life, and of the benefit of adversity and of the forsaking of a world that conforms to a purpose far more exalted than itself :

whatever affliction good men and bad do suffer together in this life, it doth not prove the persons indistinct, because so they both do jointly

[27] op. cit., p. 325. [28] ibid., p. 324.
[29] *Conf.* IV. xi. 17. [30] op. cit., pp. 326–7.

endure like pains; for as in one fire, gold shineth and chaff smoketh, and as under one flail the straw is bruised, and the ear cleansed; nor is the lees and the oil confused because they are both pressed in one press, so likewise one and the same violence of affliction, proveth, purifieth, and melteth the good, and condemneth, wasteth, and casteth out the bad. And thus in one and the same distress do the wicked offend God by detestation and blasphemy, and the good do glorify Him by praise and prayer. So great is the difference wherein we ponder not what, but how a man suffers his affects. For one and the same motion maketh the mud smell filthily, and the unguent smell most fragrantly.[31]

Thus out of the tragic fact comes forth an intimation

that somehow, if we could see it, this agony counts as nothing against the heroism and love which appear in it and thrill our hearts . . . that these mighty or heavenly spirits who perish are too great for the little world in which they move.[32]

It is this sense of the greatness of soul, and the littleness by contrast of destructive circumstance, that 'sweeps our grief away'.[33] It makes it possible for one caught up in the experience of the tragic to cry of an Emilia, dying in the accomplishment of her loyalty,

Why should she live? If she lived for ever she could never soar a higher pitch;[34]

and to urge the forsaking of the goods of the mortal condition in terms no less appealing than those the theologian would employ:

The judgement of this world is a lie; its goods, which we covet, corrupt us; its ills, which break our bodies, set us free. . . . Let us renounce the world, hate it, and lose it gladly.[35]

A Luther would wish to see such utter contemning of this world, with all its glory, righteousness, wisdom, power, riches and pleasures, established in mankind.[36] But it is an attitude which can be sustained only in the consciousness of a greater reality – of a full assurance of the Fatherhood of God, and the constancy of His truth. Such a faith, Luther declares, must be born in the strength of the spirit and the weakness of the flesh. The truth of the tragic action, in its setting forth the nature and the limitations of man and his world, may therefore be the means of a greater truth. In its encompassing the destruction of those attitudes in mankind that are distinctively human, literary tragedy may enable man to glimpse what is beyond himself.[37] It may be an instrument in the

31 *De Civ. Dei* I. viii.   32 Bradley, op. cit., p. 38.   33 ibid., p. 198.
34 ibid., p. 242.   35 ibid., p. 327.   36 See p. 171 above.
37 See Section II, p 138.

hands of that Providence which confounded humanity with the scandal of Calvary:

> For, overturning that good opinion which we falsely entertain concerning our own strength, and unmasking our hypocrisy, which affords us delight, the cross strikes at our perilous confidence in the flesh. It teaches us, thus humbled, to rest upon God alone, with the result that we do not faint or yield.[38]

(b) JOY IN SORROW

The question of tragedy's imparting of truth, both by what it enacts and what it intimates, is necessarily bound up with its imparting of pleasure. That pleasure is to be experienced in the receiving of truth for its own sake is both fact and platitude; but a bitter truth, which concerns them nearly, bringing a fearful message of grief and destruction to their alarmed humanity, is no more acceptable to men at large than it was to King Lear – for in the tragic hero we see ourselves. This identity, and the powerful bond of emotion which it creates, must bring under suspicion of falsifying our response those theories which would ascribe the pleasure of tragedy to the spectator's self-congratulation at his own immunity. The essence of literary tragedy, as Augustine observed, is a sorrow which the beholder shares with the protagonist:

> and this very sorrow is his pleasure. What is this but a miserable madness? . . . For the auditor is not called on to relieve, but only to grieve: and he applauds the author of these fictions the more, the more he grieves. And if the calamities of these persons (whether of old times or mere fictions) be so acted, that the spectator is not moved to tears, he goes away disgusted and criticizing; but if he be moved to passion, he stays intent, and weeps for joy.[39]

To weep for joy is a trick of behaviour acceptable to human experience; but to rejoice in sorrow – though it be a sorrow evoked by the conviction of the frail and miserable condition of human life – must be the occasion for puzzlement. Aristotle's theory of catharsis, which would explain this rejoicing in terms of involvement in suffering rather than detachment from it,[40] appears to dispel the contradiction. The exciting of the emotions of pity and fear in the beholder has the effect of releasing him from their tyranny: they are called forth in excess,

> that, surfeiting,
> The appetite may sicken, and so die.

[38] Calvin, *Institutes* III. viii. 3.
[39] Macneile Dixon, *Tragedy*, 1929, pp. 1–2, quoting *Conf.* III. ii. 2.
[40] *Poetics*, vi.

Pity and terror expire, as it were, in their own too much – and in the pleasure experienced by the liberated conscience, it is as if it were congratulating itself on the disappearance of the spectres and scourges of its mental being, and saying, with Macbeth, in its gratification,

> Why, so; being gone,
> I am a man again
> (III. iv. 107–8).

It might be questioned whether the method of dispelling these spectres of the mind is to raise them, and to allow their full scope and sovereignty; Socrates' dictum, that poetry feeds and waters the passions, instead of drying them up,[41] might be held to apply more truly to the experience of tragedy, particularly since the tragic pleasure does not make a subsequent appearance, but is at its height while pity and fear are at their full intensity. But Aristotle's theory is open to the less technical but more far-reaching charge that it both belittles the stature of tragedy and belies our response to it. It draws attention to the order of man's emotions at the expense of those intimations which tragedy makes to his understanding. The satisfaction that is to be derived from the phenomenon, Macneile Dixon argues, is of such nature that the phenomenon itself cannot be put in the Aristotelian category of an agreeable medicament:

> Pity and fear – how do, or how can these emotions provide the lofty satisfaction of tragedy? There is a gap in the argument. He would have this medicine restore us to the normal, to health, but surely it is an elixir not a remedy, and the function of tragic drama is to exalt not to cure us.[42]

The failure of Aristotle – that 'intellect incarnate', as Macneile Dixon calls him – lies in his missing the quality and substantial nature of the joyful response, and of the truthfulness that evokes it – in there being 'not enough of the poet or mystic in him'.[43] He explains the effect of tragedy in terms of a human nature which he knows; but he cannot relate its impression upon the human condition to a truth above that condition, for he knows of no such truth. The resort to the physiological is in some sense, therefore, a refuge from the dignity and the mystery of the tragic – from the supreme paradox

> That from its poverty we extract sustenance, from its wretchedness satisfaction, from its discouragement, confidence.[44]

Tragedy's power to exalt, if it is in any way bound up with a power to shadow forth a larger truth, can find no explanation in Aristotle's philosophy.

[41] *Republic*, 606 A, quoted by Dixon, *Tragedy*, p. 119.
[42] op. cit., p. 127.   [43] ibid., p. 128.   [44] ibid., p. 145.

To do justice to Aristotle, the exaltation is not easily accounted for. It can be affirmed at the outset that the pleasure deriving from tragedy is in part an impression of harmony – an impression so compelling that it is possible to take an aesthetic view of the emotion it imparts. Thus it has been pointed out that the ending of *Othello* is devoid of all suggestion of wider import:

> No circumstances point away from this close. No living Fortinbras or Malcolm, no dead Goneril and Regan allow us to speak of a purged realm or of the justice of the heavens. There is nothing but 'the tragic loading of this bed' and the comment of the generous Cassio: 'For he was great at heart'. Yet in this terrible end there is so solemn a sense of completeness that it might well be called the most beautiful end in Shakespearian tragedy.[45]

But the sense of completeness applies to more than the inevitable outcome of the interaction of forces, however wonderfully they are wrought out in the poet's imagination. The tragic outcome carries the implicit consent of the audience, and this acquiescence embraces both the universe of the play and the human experience of those who observe it. The harmony that establishes itself therefore cannot be without moral import: a feeling of 'completeness' is not enough, of itself, to describe what must be a precursor to joy. The comment of J. J. Lawlor is more central to the problem:

> The final characteristic of tragic experience is 'rightness', a sense that what is done, though it may be surprising and may well seem disproportionate to the offence or weakness to which it is related, is nevertheless acceptable.[46]

This acceptance, however, is the more mysterious in that it appears to assert itself in defiance of the natural wishes, and the moral standards, of the audience. There can be no willed acquiescence, for example, in the final events of such a play as *King Lear*; yet the terrible nature of those happenings, and the no less dreadful doubts and fears which they raise, are seemingly no obstacle to the tragic pleasure; and it is by no means immediately clear whether this satisfaction derives from the ultimate order which tragedy shows in operation, or from the worthiness of the play itself, or from a sense of the worth and dignity of the personages of the play. For the three are interconnected, and the tragic pleasure must relate to them all, since otherwise a disharmony would exist, and the claim of a general 'rightness' could not be made. It is to this unity of the tragic experience that W. M. Merchant calls attention in summing up the effect of *King Lear*:

[45] H. Gardner, 'The Noble Moor', *Proc. Brit. Acad.* XLI, 1955, p. 202.
[46] *The Tragic Sense*, 1960, p. 53.

G

We are left at the conclusion of the play with the profound intuition that there is neither rational explanation nor any mitigation in this tragic view of life, but that the impact of the play's nobility leads to a sense of exaltation.[47]

The attempt to separate man from the order which afflicts him – the plea that the consolation of literary tragedy derives from the evidence which it affords of human qualities that are admirable in themselves – is made by F. L. Lucas. He argues that the stature and integrity of the tragic hero, and the integrity also of the poet's mind, which grapples with existence and 'faces life as it is', are able to counteract what is implied in that necessity of evil and suffering which tragedy can do nothing but assert.[48] This unflinching courage and honesty Lucas would have to be 'man's answer to this universe that crushes him',[49] and the source of our pleasure; but what can give so ineffectual an answer, one must suspect, can bring only a desperate pleasure, and certainly not exaltation. It is perfectly true that the sense of rejoicing extends to, and is concerned with, the strictly human qualities that are revealed in tragedy; the problem is how the rejoicing survives the lamentable deaths of those in whom these qualities appear, and the message of general doom that is conveyed. Thus, though the logic of the process is not clear, the assertion may rightly be made that

In some way or other 'the human spirit' is validated and vindicated,[50]

and the mood of exaltation thereby captured. But in the manifest defeat and destruction of humanity, positive affirmations can only come from the order of which humanity is a part: that vindication of human qualities, the strange assurance of their value, their truth, and their enduring power that alone can make for pleasure, must come from association with a higher truth than the tragic action sets forth. The conviction that the joyful intimations of tragedy are not simply impressions of human worth, but must derive from beyond the secular condition – the realization, indeed, that the effect of tragedy is not the creation of despair – forces Bradley, despite his professed incomprehension, to link the destiny of tragic man to an ultimate order making for good:

the fact that the struggle does not leave us rebellious or desperate is due to a more or less distinct perception that the tragic suffering and death arise from collision, not with a fate or blank power, but with a moral power.[51]

---

[47] *Creed and Drama*, 1965, p. 53.

[48] *Tragedy in Relation to Aristotle's 'Poetics'*, 1953, p. 57.   [49] ibid., p. 58.

[50] N. A. Scott, 'The Tragic Vision and the Christian Faith', *Anglican Theological Review* XLV, 1963, p. 34.

[51] *Shakespearean Tragedy*, p. 36.

Though the adequacy of the term 'moral' might be doubted, Bradley's instinct surely does not err. The pleasure in human worth, if it endure beyond the stark fact of human transience, can do so only through the apprehending of some power, order or truth of exalted nature: the sense of joy concerning tragic man, though it derive largely from what he is, must reach to what is beyond him. This impression is one which Bradley shares with A. W. Schlegel:

> The satisfaction . . . which we derive from the representation, in a good tragedy, of powerful situations and overwhelming sorrows, must be ascribed either to the feeling of the dignity of human nature, excited in us by such grand instances of it as are therein displayed, or to the trace of a higher order of things, impressed on the apparently irregular course of events, and mysteriously revealed in them; or perhaps to both these causes conjointly. The true reason, therefore, why tragedy need not shun even the harshest subject is, that a spiritual and invisible power can only be measured by the opposition which it encounters from some external force capable of being appreciated by the senses.[52]

Schlegel identifies the 'spiritual and invisible power' more with the ultimate status of man than with what ultimately confers that status upon him; and he can conceive it to be the theoretical purpose of tragedy to embody the truth

> that to establish the claims of the mind to a divine origin, its earthly existence must be disregarded as vain and insignificant, all sorrows endured and all difficulties overcome.[53]

The 'miserable madness' of literary tragedy, its paradoxical phenomenon of joy in sorrow, is acceptable to the human understanding only if the tragic fact is seen as confirmation of a larger truth.[54]

In giving expression to the opinion that

> There is some soul of goodness in things evil,
> Would men observingly distil it out,[55]

Shakespeare may have had in mind the insights of his own plays, and their observed effect. If so, he would have been apprehending, like Aeschylus, some ultimate and reconciling truth within the tragic process – a sense of the 'inflexible solidarity' of things, and of a divine purpose in Zeus which could enable sorrow itself to be turned to account.[56] These impressions are not remote from everyday life, but are part of its very

---

[52] *Lectures on Dramatic Art and Literature*, rev. A. J. W. Morrison, N.Y., 1965, p. 69.
[53] ibid.
[54] The phenomenon may be seen to incorporate the absolute necessity which, according to Occam's formula, is the sole ground for postulating the existence of something not otherwise known to exist.
[55] *Henry V* IV. i. 4–5.   [56] Dixon, *Tragedy*, pp. 76–81.

texture – though the work of art gives heightened expression to their mystery. Macneile Dixon quotes Garibaldi's offering only suffering and death to those who would follow him, and declares,

> Explain to me the force of this appeal, why it warms and not chills the heart, and I will listen to you when you speak of tragedy.[57]

What is in all probability its real explanation is vouchsafed by A. P. Rossiter :

> Garibaldi offered strength to overcome the world, if only in will.[58]

In accepting the invitation to overcome the world, man, for all his short-coming and blindness, is responding to his true destiny; and in forsaking, for a while, the pursuit of pleasure and advantage in the beholding of tragedy, he is enabled to hear the true voice of consolation – the voice which trembles in pain and yet proclaims the gladness.[59] Nothing short of a realization that, for mortal man, the way to reality and happiness is through suffering and loss, can account for the tragic emotion in its full-ness. Tragedy is restful, says Anouilh in his *Antigone*, because hope has no part in it : those enmeshed in it are kingly, in that there is no struggle to escape. His Antigone asserts that her father was at peace, and became beautiful, from the moment that he knew that nothing could save him; and it is with this conviction that she spurns Creon's 'filthy hope'.[60] Anouilh here speaks with an eloquence that is perhaps literary before it is tragic, and thus approaches the very centre of paradox. The hope that is rejected is 'filthy' because it is of this world, and therefore beneath the true dignity of man, as it is necessarily a departure from truth itself. It is, in fact, an escape from a process which indeed exalts, and Antigone is right to despise it – though she does not do so with the formal pro-nouncement that 'the way of perfection is in afflictions'.

The pleasure that is felt in the witnessing of tragedy can therefore be regarded as proportionate to tragedy's capacity to reveal. It is a partici-pation of that happiness which for Augustine can only be 'truth-given joy' – a product of relationship with reality.[61] Like the truth that is mani-fested, it must arise from grief and destruction, and persist in the absence of what might appear to sustain it; it must be imparted at once through the agency of the material order and in its despite, and can exist only in the conscience – perhaps the very deepest and secret conscience – of him who beholds and experiences. It must have its beginnings in an acknow-ledgement of the necessary predominance of tragic affliction over man's

---

[57] ibid., p. 159.   [58] *Angel with Horns*, 1961, p. 273.

[59] See p. 177 above.

[60] *Antigone*, ed. W. M. Landers, London, Harrap, 1966, p. 84; cited by Merchant, *Creed and Drama*, 1965, p. 17.

[61] (Section II, p. 154).

world – that in the recognized frailty of the corporeal attributes of mankind, their perversity of will can do nothing but bring disaster upon them. Such recognition is the only possible reason for the acceptance which must be the forerunner of pleasure; but the pleasure itself can, in the assumption of a spiritual universe, be understood to spring from the number of those things which separate men from their God. It can come into being from the very fact that in the destructiveness of tragedy is found a new means of discernment – that the good of a transcendent order can become evident in the overthrow of the lesser goods of an inferior order. It can be a rejoicing in the overthrow itself; for worldly man lives in *'labyrinths of error'*[62] beneath the artificial heaven of his own understanding, engaged in the pursuit of things which can be lost against his will and the building of happiness upon vanishing creatures, the unhappy possessor of a 'false beatitude and most true misery'.[63] The order that mankind recognizes seeks to found assurance upon limitation; and in tragedy's inevitable justice, which destroys mundane power and breaks up a living untruth, and institutes its salutary process of disillusionment and its accompanying pain, there may be found to lie the seeds of assurance, a sense of rightness, and of joy. Such rejoicing might be termed the ending of a punishment; for what tragic man chiefly desires, the being his own arbiter and his own artificer, is the substance of the Divine doom and sentence upon him. What is destroyed by the tragic dispensation of a providential universe are those idols of his imagination – those 'calves of Jeroboam' – which he has in misguided zeal set up against his own comfort, and his progress to happiness and truth. The tragic pleasure, therefore, may derive from a sense of liberation, and of opportunity.

It could spring equally from a revelation of the human state of sin: man's misery in tragedy may be the proof to him of his own guilt – as Augustine affirms that it should.[64] It may be understood to unmask what Calvin calls the hypocrisy of mankind, and, in dispelling the illusion of human strength, reveal at once the perilous nature of the progress that they had previously made with such assurance in the world, and the extent of the means of succour that is available to them, if they will but rest upon it.[65] The observed consequences of sin, also, may be a source of affirmation and even of exultation, in their confirming both the absoluteness and the righteousness of Divine decree – that 'ruin lies in the express breach of God's precepts'.[66] And they may, furthermore, serve to establish His nearness; for the conviction of sin and the assurance of the presence of God have ever been part of the same process. In God's affliction of mankind – in all that follows from the abandonment to a

[62] Fulke Greville, 'An Inqvisition vpon Fame and Honovr', st. 1, *Poems and Dramas*, ed. G. Bullough, 1938, I, p. 192.
[63] Augustine, *De Civ. Dei* XIX. xx.
[64] See p. 175 above.
[65] *Inst.* III. viii. 3; viii. 2; vii. 8, 9.
[66] *De Civ. Dei* XIV. xiii.

reprobate mind and to the assaults of temptation[67] – there is inevitability, but not impersonality : the punishments of God, in Christian experience, are never applied in isolation from His love :

> For whom the Lord loveth he chasteneth, and scourgeth every son whom he receiveth.[68]

The apprehension of sin and punishment may, therefore, through the operation of a Providence which teaches by sorrow, give assurance of a closeness to God. Or if suffering indeed is the way for apostate man, there can at least appear in him the feeling of irrelevance having in some way been removed and purged – an assurance, perhaps, of the diminishing of exile or of enslavement, or a new sense of confidence that can reveal him as 'triumphant and regal' upon the tragic stage of the theatre, as it can in Augustine's testimony upon that of the world.[69] In the chastening and refining of a Lear may be understood the working of that salutary experience endured by those who are favoured, in which, to use the terminology of Aquinas,

> by afflictions lesser faults are cleansed in them, and they are the more raised up from earthly affections to God.[70]

Even where benefit is not received or even seen in the pain of tragedy, the sufferings themselves for once make manifest the operation in the world of a purpose whose power and righteousness alike are normally obscured from humanity's sight by their condition of sin.[71] For, whatever the level of discernment in protagonist or audience, there must come upon the consciousness the impression of a potentiality in the compelling power and logic of the tragic event that is above the human, though it ministers to it – of a justice, and a necessity, which must be submitted to in defiance of a merely human understanding. In beholding the tragic stage man has lively evidence of a reality greater than himself; and in this fact can be seen to lie half, at least, of a theological perspective. For to the insistence that man is not the highest reality, theology adds the further emphasis that man's assurance lies, not in his own strength, but in the will and purpose of a God in whose sight he is justly condemned.[72] Concerning that greater necessity to which the Shakespearian tragic hero is apprehended at every stage to be subject, and to which every spectator is subdued, it may well be possible to say, in the outcome, that

> the justice of it pleases[73] –

[67] See p. 174–5 above.
[68] *Calvin: Commentaries*, ed. Haroutunian, L.C.C. XXIII, 1958, p. 211.
[69] *De Vera Relig.* xl. 75; see Section II, p. 163.
[70] *S.T.* I. xxi. 4, *ad 3*; see Section II, p. 144.
[71] (Section II, p. 106.)   [72] (Section II, p. 146.)   [73] *Othello* IV. i. 212.

though this is a subject which must merit further consideration. But if the tragic suffering indeed 'makes a difference', and can indeed lead to the perception of wider possibility, and to 'the discovery of a higher level of being',[74] then whatever categories are employed to describe the new hope, there must be occasion for joy. The perception of a new order or dispensation; the acknowledgement of its all-embracing power; the intimation that present ills are in some sense but temporary; and above all, the consciousness that the 'mighty or heavenly spirits' of the tragic world, though they be not of heavenly birth, are truly of no mundane destiny – all these things can make up the substance of the tragic pleasure. The joy in human greatness itself, through this realization, is transformed into intimation and assurance of the power and goodness of the ultimate order.

Such assurance as this, which is here considered as the only begetter of the pleasure found in the experience of tragedy, is quite beyond a worldly understanding. But equally it must be true that a human estimate of what is fitting is not to be applied to God's purpose and justice in the mortal world, which tragedy must in some measure reflect.[75] No human purpose would ordain the possibility of evil, or conceive or compass the greater good of bringing good out of the very evil that would seem to deny and defeat it. It is the characteristic of a lesser being than God to covet a limited good, and to desire no knowledge of its own unrighteousness. The human standard of what is appropriate, Luther declares, is that

> our Adam's flesh and blood must have good and easy days, and suffer nothing. How may these agree together? Our flesh is given over to death and hell.[76]

The absurdity of man's judgement devolves from his mode of living no less than from his reprobate condition. To live according to his own will, rather than in accord with the God whom he was created to serve, and in whose will lies both the truth and the blessing that he desires, is the overturning of all reason and responsibility; and it is on the basis of this confusion that humanity sets forth its judgements.[77] It judges in the light of its desires; but those desires, falling short of the desire for God, cannot be other than depraved and vicious, and the means, not of enlightenment, but of a darkness and enslavement that must ever keep it, despite its strivings, from its true home and happiness. In the insensate demands which they make of life, men are the victims of their own energies: self-concern brings self-perversion, and 'iniquity giveth itself the lie' by removing the ability to consider the eternal in those who will regard only

[74] See p. 185 above. [75] (Section II, p. 143.)
[76] *Table-Talk*, tr. W. Hazlitt, London, 1883, cxvii.
[77] *De Civ. Dei* XIV. iv.

what is temporal.[78] In tragic circumstance, therefore, humanity can see nothing but deprivation and mischance :

> The highest wisdom of the world is to busy itself with temporal, earthly and ephemeral things; and when these go ill, it says, Who would have thought it?[79]

Neither is it for worldly man to perceive that the things of earth are not only perishable, but even at variance with themselves, and must therefore share a dissolution in time with the affections that confer a spurious reality upon them. A mortal judgement of what is appropriate for man can therefore be nothing but an enormous and sacrilegious folly. For, apart from the earthiness of the human understanding, to lay down a standard in condemnation of what God has decreed is, as Luther observed, virtually to set up man as a Creator above Him.[80] The contradictory nature of such a creaturely judgement is evident even as it is made. As Kierkegaard pronounces upon him who makes it,

> You wished that God's ideas about what was profitable to you might be your ideas, but you also wished that He might be the almighty Creator of heaven and earth, so that He might rightly fulfil your wish. And yet if He were to share your ideas, then must He cease to be the almighty Father. You would in your childish impatience, as it were, corrupt God's eternal Being.[81]

Amidst an apostate humanity, incomprehension of the tragic pleasure is of a piece with its repining over tragic pain.

In Luther's terms, it is entirely reasonable that the justice of the one true God should be incomprehensible to a creaturely reason. Man's reason can see no need for a contemning or a forsaking of the life that he leads; but if the condition for perceiving and trusting 'invisible things' is indeed a 'contempt for the present life', then tragic affliction, though it be evil, is transformed into a good :

> When we see no way or means, by advice or aid, through which we may be helped in our miseries, we at once conclude, according to our human reason : now our condition is desperate; but when we believe trustingly in God, our deliverance begins. . . . To be suppressed and troubled, is to arise, to grow, and to increase.[82]

The standard for judging human life, and the tragic fact, cannot be a human one, since humanity is not to be isolated from the universal order of which it is a subordinate part : a proper estimate of the mortal condition is one which can measure its capacity to bring about 'the condemnation of sinners, the proving of the just, and the perfecting of the

---

[78] (Section II, p. 92.)   [79] *Table-Talk*, cxlvii.   [80] (Section II, p. 147.)
[81] 'Every Good and Perfect Gift is from Above', *Edifying Discourses*, tr. D. F. and L. M. Swenson, Minneapolis, 1950–3, I, p. 41.   [82] *Table-Talk*, cxvi.

blessed'.[83] No such assessment can come of unaided human power, for man's intellect is limited in terms, not only of scope, but of sin. Before God, man is always in the wrong;[84] and that acceptance of the tragic that is comprised in the tragic pleasure is an acceptance also of the infallible errancy of the human understanding. In the harmony of the tragic outcome Hegel surely did well to sense a deeper reconciliation: as it was once satirically observed of his position, with an acuteness which may happily have been inspired,

> By putting the Individual in the wrong, we put the Universe in the right.[85]

Hegel's impression must, at first glance, necessarily appear as unusual and ill-defined as it does unfounded: for the meaning of literary tragedy, like that of the more extensive tragedies of human existence upon earth, is not to be found at the centre of human experience and consciousness, but is to be sought at its periphery if it is to be found at all. The workings of history, Reinhold Niebuhr affirms, can reveal nothing of ultimate significance to a creaturely examination:

> The points of reference for the structure of the meaning of history in the Christian faith are obviously not found by an empirical analysis of the observable structures and coherences of history. They are 'revelations', apprehended by faith, of the character and purposes of God. The experience of faith, by which they are apprehended, is an experience at the ultimate limits of human knowledge.[86]

It is for this reason that Miss Ellis-Fermor affirms that the positive reading of life which constitutes one side of the tragic balance, the intimation of another universe and its standards which tragedy can impart and which Hegel presumably received, must ever be 'intuitive and often undefined'.[87]

Hegel's theory of 'reconciliation', though it may diverge at certain points in concept, and particularly in terminology, from the view of tragedy that has been considered, nevertheless bears an essential compatibility with it. The vision which Hegel sees in tragedy of a world that is a battlefield for spiritual powers and ethical substances,

> Warring within our breasts for regiment,[88]

does not, it is true, square with a Christian appraisal. Similarly, the idea of one right, or ideal, being asserted, in the tragic situation, against

---

[83] Augustine, *De Vera Relig.* xxiii. 44; Section II, p. 105.

[84] Søren Kierkegaard, 'The Joy in the Thought that in Relation to God a Man always Suffers as Being Guilty', *The Gospel of Suffering and The Lillies of the Field*, tr. D. F. and L. M. Swenson, Minneapolis, 1948, pp. 71, 91–4.

[85] J. S. Smart, 'Tragedy', *Essays and Studies* VIII, 1922, p. 17.

[86] *Faith and History*, London, 1949, p. 155.

[87] *The Frontiers of Drama*, 1945, p. 128.　　　　[88] Marlowe, *Tamburlaine* I, 1.870.

another equally justified in itself, and both, in their inerrancy, being disciplined by a superior Rationality in proportion to the absoluteness that they claim for themselves,[89] cannot be regarded as germane to the thinking of an Augustine or a Luther. Yet the experiencing, above the claims of creaturely fear and tragic sympathy, of a feeling of reconciliation which tragedy instils by virtue of its apprehending the work of some lofty and eternal justice – the perception which lies at the centre of Hegel's theory[90] – could in itself form part of a Christian response to tragic occurrence. Hegel's picture of necessary conflict amongst spiritual agencies goads A. C. Bradley justifiably into protest;[91] but a Christian view of man's world is one which can accommodate the conflict which must arise amongst men through their choice of inferior principle, and that which is imposed upon their world by God's inexorable judgement and condemnation. It recognizes in all instances of discord and suffering that

> The righteous wrath of God is closely concerned with whatever it is that by blind and uncontrolled concupiscence evil men do wilfully, and with whatever by manifest and apparent penalty they suffer unwillingly.[92]

The wider harmony that Hegel apprehends can exist only by virtue of a justice that is as infallible as it is exalted. This understanding of the Divine justice, which conceives of the universe – despite all its contradictory scenes of wretchedness and strife that are due to inordinate assertion – as of a vast theatre of beauty, reconciliation and peace, is also present to Christian thinking. Augustine can say, as he surveys the turbulence of his misguided fellows, that no happening can either mar or fail to promote the ultimate harmony and good:

> And behold, the universe with them is fair, though they are foul. And how have they injured Thee? or how have they disgraced Thy government, which, from the heaven to this lowest earth, is just and perfect? . . . But they fled, that they might not see Thee seeing them, and blinded, might stumble against Thee . . . withdrawing themselves from Thy gentleness, and stumbling at Thy uprightness, and falling upon their own ruggedness.[93]

Hegel's conception diverges from Augustine's chiefly in its impersonality; but otherwise the two are not unlike. And Hegel's argument, finally, that the tragic characters should acknowledge the justice of their fate,[94] should be compared with Augustine's assertion that the universal order is un-

---

[89] See A. C. Bradley, 'Hegel's Theory of Tragedy', *Oxford Lectures on Poetry*, 1941, pp. 71–3, and W. Macneile Dixon, *Tragedy*, 1929, pp. 161, 165.

[90] Macneile Dixon, op. cit., p. 163.

[91] op. cit., p. 83. [92] Augustine, *Enchiridion* viii. 27.

[93] *Conf.* V. ii. 2. [94] Dixon, op. cit., p. 164.

blemished in that the misery of the miserable has been incurred by their own merits.[95] The medium for misdeed is for the theologian not some atmosphere of spiritous 'rationality', but a world where a Providential reason and wisdom assigns such bounds to wills of whatever sort as ensure the inviolable proportion, harmony and order of the whole. Here again it is the impersonality of Hegel's system that prevents a fuller accord; and the introduction within it of a personal principle would, it is suggested, have the effect of making up the difference between the acquiescence which is all that in Bradley's estimation Hegel's universal justice could summon forth from human nature, and the exultation that he demanded it must be able to inspire.[96]

A confident rejection of the commonsense claims of a temporal understanding is also to be found in the theories of Schopenhauer and Nietzsche. Both regard the destructiveness of tragedy to be in itself a means of discernment; and both trace the tragic satisfaction to the overthrowing of the imperatives and idols of a false order. In neither theory does there emerge a realization of the conviction of sin, or a sense of submission to a just punishment; but in both there is an eager perceiving of profound and compulsive error and misunderstanding in human worldliness, and the prospect of a pleasurable awakening into enlightenment. And the joy of tragedy is in each case centred upon the apprehension of the truth of a higher order : upon its all-embracing power, and the absoluteness of its standards, if not of their righteousness; upon its capacity to render insignificant all creaturely ills; and upon the certainty it imparts of a larger destiny for man.

The promise of the ultimate order in Hegel extends to the present, but in Schopenhauer it is largely concerned with the future; therefore, what for the one carries a message of reconciliation moves the other toward resignation and renunciation – attitudes which are both acceptable to a theological interpretation of human destiny, and correspond to characteristic emphases of the human mind which have made themselves evident in Christian thought.[97] Schopenhauer intensifies the difference between the higher truth and the present reality. For him, the purification afforded by tragic suffering takes the form of a rejection of the will to live; what we see in the tragedies, he affirms, is that

the noblest men, after long conflict and suffering, at last renounce the ends they have so keenly followed, and all the pleasures of life for ever, or else freely and joyfully surrender life itself.[98]

In the moment of the tragic catastrophe the conviction dawns upon all who are caught up in experiencing it that life is a bad dream from which

[95] *De Civ. Dei* XIX. xiii; see Section II, p. 103.
[96] *Oxford Lectures*, p. 84.   [97] (Section I, p. 58.)
[98] *The World as Will and Idea*, tr. R. B. Haldane and J. Kemp, London, 1883, I, p. 327.

they have to awake. It is this awakening to the knowledge that life in the mundane world can afford men no true pleasure, and is consequently not worthy of their attachment, that bestows upon literary tragedy its peculiar tendency towards the sublime.[99] Thus, Schopenhauer argues, the tragedy of the Christian era

> shows the surrender of the whole will to live, joyful forsaking of the world in the consciousness of its worthlessness and vanity.[100]

It has been objected to this theory that tragedy shows no such thing. 'Is Macbeth, in any interpretation of the word, resigned, or Othello?' asks Macneile Dixon. The tragic heroes, like the heroes of the ancient Greeks, appear to be made of sterner stuff : 'they seem to have mounting spirits and an amazing care for the things of this world';[101] they appear to affirm, rather than deny, the will to live, and consequently both they and their beholders are at a good distance from 'Schopenhauer's mood of withered submission'.[102] Schopenhauer, it is true, is forced into the admission that Attic tragedy shows the human race under the rule of chance and error but not under that of the resignation that should derive from it; but the charge that, in postulating a response of resignation in the beholders of ancient tragedy rather than in the protagonists, he was resorting to an attempt 'to save his doctrine',[103] may arise from a misunderstanding of what he was trying to convey concerning the tragic impression. He is at pains to emphasize that the will to resignation might be only brief in duration, and would be experienced at the deepest levels of man's being; that it receive literary expression is therefore not essential to his theory. And the abandonment of the 'will to live' does not, for him, signify impermanence and despondency, but rather continuity and life : renunciation – as in the Christian experience – is the prelude to a greater acquiring, the entering into a higher truth. Persistence in 'the will to live', so understood, is a perverse absenting from felicity, the product of that 'stupid and empty confidence in the flesh'[104] which (according to Schopenhauer no less than to Calvin) the afflictions suffered by man in his mortal state reveal in all its worthlessness, and which must be overcome in us before we can enter into our true being.

Although, then, the ancients displayed little of the spirit of resignation, the turning away of the will from life, in their tragic heroes themselves, as their frame of mind, yet the peculiar tendency and effect of tragedy remains the awakening of that spirit in the beholder, the calling up of that frame of mind, even though only temporarily. The horrors upon the stage hold up to him the bitterness and worthlessness of life, thus the vanity of all its struggle. The effect of this impression must be

[99] ibid., III, pp. 212–3.   [100] ibid., p. 214.   [101] op. cit., pp. 198–9.
[102] ibid., p. 197.   [103] ibid., p. 195.   [104] *Institutes* III. viii. 2.

that he become conscious, if only in obscure feeling, that it is better to tear his heart free from life, to turn his will from it, to love not the world nor life; whereby then, in his deepest soul, the consciousness is aroused that for another kind of willing there must also be another existence.[105]

Tragedy's 'exhibition of the most terrible side of life, brought before our eyes in the most glaring light' is a summons 'to turn away the will from life'[106] – from the world and the flesh. It is a summons which is made upon the perception, through the very aspect of disaster, of a higher order of things, and which is therefore a clarion call to joy.

The conviction of the inadequacy of a mortal existence, which is so strong in Schopenhauer's view of literary tragedy, becomes even more pronounced in that of Nietzsche: the will to the renunciation of an existence that has no inherent worth there gives place to a positive delight in its destruction. For this delight an analogy is scarcely to be found in a Christian attitude toward the tragic. The worthlessness that attends life in this world relates, in Christian thinking, not to human existence itself, but to the aims and pleasures that are peculiar to it, and are made the objects of wrongful ambition. An emphasis upon the worthlessness of creaturely being is legitimate only if it is made by way of comparison with the glory and worth of the life that is to be. Reality, it is true, is in God alone; but it inheres also in His purposes, which confer reality upon all acceptance of them within the bounds of a finite universe. Matter, time and space, therefore, are not hindrances to the attaining of the real, but instead, in the presence of faith, are the means by which reality may be apprehended and grasped.[107] The creatures of the material order enjoy a conditional existence, in that

> they neither altogether are, nor altogether are not, for they are, since they are from Thee, but are not, because they are not, what Thou art.[108]

So far as they exist, they may be enjoyed; but the inordinate love, seeking to assign permanence to the things it would make an end in themselves, confers, as it were, illusion upon them. It is not that the best, in Voltaire's phrase, is the enemy of the good, but that it can be made so by men who are no better than they ought to be. Man, as a creature dedicated to what is beyond him, is bound to a relinquishing in acceptance. He must not decline, on the one hand, to a fleshly desire for material good; but he must not presume, on the other hand, to desire spiritual good out of a motivation which is carnal, or to a spiritual disdain for the flesh itself.[109] Wordsworth's conclusion upon the extinction of the Venetian republic must, it would appear, apply in some sense to the Christian

[105] op. cit., III, p. 214.   [106] ibid., p. 215.   [107] (Section II, p. 101.)
[108] Augustine, *Conf.* VII. xi. 17.   [109] (Section II, pp. 100, 108.)

appreciation of the tragic in its hinting at a qualification needful to the condition of those who are yet creatures:

> Men are we, and must grieve when even the shade
> Of that which once was great is passed away.

Worldly existence is not decreed for the sole purpose that it may be abandoned, or even despised. In likening the life of man on earth to the duty of a soldier at his post, Calvin asserts a proper emphasis.[110] And although there are to be found in Christian tradition instances of such relinquishing as might be regarded as a will for the abandonment of the duty of mortals in its flight from worldly joys and satisfactions, they are to be regarded as reactions to ill-moderated desire that themselves verge upon excess, rather than as constituting criteria from which Nietzsche's position of willed destructiveness is to be judged.

The basis of Nietzsche's joy in tragic fact is the revelation which tragedy makes 'Of something far more deeply interfused' – of a greater potentiality, a level of being above the human. Tragic myth, he declares, through the figure of the hero,

> delivers us from our avid thirst for earthly satisfaction and reminds us of another existence and a higher delight.[111]

A no less powerful source of pleasure is Nietzsche's consequent assurance of the absurdity of a temporal judgement. The Apollonian principle in art, in its orderliness and serenity, proffers an apparent redemption that is founded upon illusion; but the unruly principle of Dionysus in literary tragedy

> breaks the spell of individuation and opens a path to the maternal womb of being.[112]

That sense of creaturely limitation, which is the proper outcome of all human knowledge and at the same time the beginning of the spiritual life, is present to Nietzsche in the tragic phenomenon. There man is for him revealed, in Gilson's phrase, as a 'defective and imperfect being'[113] destined never to succeed in its struggle to find happiness in the created good of its environment or even of its own nature. Yet, in his incompleteness, the will to happiness is part of an exalted impulse which must lead him back to his first source. It proves to him that he cannot be his own last end; and it proves also that the means by which perfection of being is to be realized does not lie within his own powers.[114] The 'spell of

---

[110] See p. 178 above.

[111] *The Birth of Tragedy*, tr. F. Golffing, N.Y., Doubleday, 1956, p. 126.

[112] ibid., p. 97.

[113] *The Philosophy of St Thomas Aquinas*, tr. E. Bullough, Cambridge, 1924, p. 248; *S.T.* Ia IIae xviii. 1, *ad R.*; Section II, p. 90.

[114] (Section II, p. 95.)

individuation' is for Nietzsche what the will for 'a private or external or inferior' good, in the soul turned away from God, is for Augustine;[115] and the latter's confession that the aspiring soul is

> like a land where no water is, because as it cannot of itself enlighten itself, so it cannot of itself satisfy itself[116]

may contain the essence of Nietzsche's 'immortal longings'. Both can see in the creature's resolve to live unto the self the inevitable ruin of its mortal hopes and joys; and there may possibly be understood in Nietzsche's flight from the living lie of human self-sufficiency some apprehension of that curse which, in holy writ, must come upon all who would put their trust in a man. The experience of the tragic must release in the beholder a complete self-renunciation :

> How can he bear, shut in the paltry glass bell of his individuality, to hear the echoes of innumerable cries of weal and woe sounding out of the 'vast spaces of the cosmic night', and not wish, amidst these pipings of metaphysical pastoral, to flee incontinent to his primordial home?[117]

The conviction of human inadequacy is accompanied by the sense of the inadequacy of temporal pleasures unqualified by higher aspiration that is also part of a Christian view of life. The tragic fact is evidence of the impermanence of created things, and therefore of the delusive nature of worldly joys : Dionysiac art, Nietzsche affirms,

> makes us realize that everything that is generated must be prepared to face its painful dissolution.[118]

The transience of the material order which tragedy impresses upon him ensures that he will not be one of those consigned to the 'outer darkness' decreed for the multitudes dedicated to the pleasures of the senses :[119] he will precisely not be one of those who must ever be trying to follow fleeting delights with 'the senses of the flesh'[120] in an arena of futile endeavour reserved for

> Those, who love the journey rather than the return home or the journey's end.[121]

It might on the contrary be said of Nietzsche that his desire for the end of the journey was too pronounced; that in his impatience with the process which Augustine describes as the use of temporal things with the contemplation of attaining eternal things, 'passing through the former,

115 De Lib. Arb. II. xix. 53.   116 Conf. XIII. xvi. 19; see Section II, p. 97.
117 op. cit., p. 127.   118 ibid., p. 102.
119 Augustine, De Vera Relig. liv. 104; see Section II, p. 91.
120 Conf. IV. x. 15; See Section II, p. 98.
121 De Vera Relig. liv. 107.

but cleaving to the latter',[122] he showed a disdain more reprehensible in a creature than a worldly lust. In a Christian understanding, man is to learn the measure of his being from the order in which he is placed : it is not for him to rebel. Nonetheless, there is to be understood in the 'primal Dionysiac delight',[123] which is for Nietzsche the tragic pleasure, that joy in the destruction of a false order – in the tumbling of gilden roofs about their weak foundations – which is part of the salutary lesson of suffering in a spiritual universe, and which must indicate a purpose, if not a justice, that is too exalted for man's wit to comprehend, but yet makes demands in which he must acquiesce. The spectator of tragedy, Nietzsche says,

> will have responded profoundly to the events presented on the stage and yet fled willingly into that which passes understanding. He will have considered the action of the hero justified and yet felt an even greater exaltation when these very actions brought about his destruction. He will have shuddered at the suffering about to befall the hero and yet divined in them a higher, overmastering joy.[124]

Nietzsche's response to the tragic, it has been said, is evidence of 'a secret instinct for annihilation'[125] in his philosophy. That this instinct also lies in the deepest recesses of the human conscience is a possibility to which Bergson has given memorable expression in defining the nature of pity :

> True pity consists not so much in fearing suffering as in desiring it. The desire is a faint one, and we should hardly wish to see it realized; yet we form it in spite of ourselves, as if Nature were committing some great injustice and it were necessary to get rid of all suspicion of complicity with her.[126]

This definition, as T. R. Henn points out, is 'a great deal less than Christian'; but the impulsion towards destructiveness out of which it arises may be a testimony to the fact that, amidst the works of godless men, the best must indeed appear as the enemy of the good. The necessity, in the impermanence of the external order, for the relinquishing of all within it that remains undevoted in the will's aspiration towards truth, is an essential part of Christian experience;[127] and in the apprehension of the 'need for sacrifice', which Miss Helen Adolf takes to be the origin of literary tragedy,[128] may lie humanity's dim acknowledgement and figuring forth of the forsaking which must be accomplished before man may

[122] *De Trin.* XII. xiii. 21; see Section II, p. 99.
[123] op. cit., p. 143.   [124] ibid., p. 132.
[125] Macneile Dixon, *Tragedy*, 1929, p. 205.
[126] *Time and Free Will*, tr. F. L. Pogson, London, 1910, p. 19, quoted by T. R. Henn, *The Harvest of Tragedy*, 1966, p. 13.
[127] See Section II, pp. 98–101.
[128] 'The Essence and Origin of Tragedy', *Journal of Aesthetics and Art Criticism* X, 1951–2, p. 123.

draw near to reality, and which Christianity expresses in the figure of the taking up of a cross. If the tragic is so interpreted, both the sadistic and the masochistic theories which have been adduced to explain the pleasure it imparts are set in a context of profounder possibilities: both appear as the unconscious recognition of a sacrificial principle at work in the world.[129]

The sacrificial principle evident in Nietzsche's appreciation of tragedy may be seen to originate – much as it does in Christianity – in a desire for the attainment of the very height and truth of the being that man may enjoy. A feature of that being is the capacity of the mind to be conformed to the principle it lives by. Just as the likeness of God is for the Christian preserved only through a relationship with Him who confers it which must involve a forsaking of what is peculiarly one's own,[130] so Nietzsche is moved by a passion for conformity with the ultimate: he echoes, in effect, the dictum of Augustine that 'it is not of man, but above man, which beatifies the mind of man'.[131] To say that in this he is the embodiment of humility must surely be questionable; but he is the exemplar of an attitude which appears far removed from humanity's characteristic vice of pride. There is an evident abandonment of that will to a mutable or lesser good which is the direct cause of sin, and which, in its compulsive nature, betokens an inordinate self-love battening upon what can create the illusion of its supremacy.[132] The seeking, by a soul 'loving its own power', to govern by a law derived from the self a reality that is superior to the individual will, and thus, through lusting after 'something more', being 'made less',[133] is here precluded. Far from the soul trying with perverse energy to make the self seem its own beginning,[134] there is the desire only to cleave to its true beginning. There is thus in Nietzsche the seeming opposite of that will to set up in man and his world some form of creaturely transcendence which is most characteristic of mankind both in its sins and in its tragedy.[135] In this refusal to turn a means into an end, Nietzsche appears to wish to bring to a conclusion that incessant tragedy of frustration and loss which pervades human life, in which man seeks to gain in an earthly medium a happiness which it is incapable of accommodating or conveying.[136] That wish for immortality, which by Augustine's definition is the true essence of the wish for happiness, is Nietzsche's own. Worldly man seizes upon the desire to 'have all that he wants', and disdains to 'want nothing wrongly':[137] but the latter desire Nietzsche appears to respect in such a manner as must lead toward the

129 See Henn, op. cit., pp. 43–58.
130 Augustine, *De Trin.* XII. xi. 16; see Section II, p. 152.
131 *De Civ. Dei* XIX. xxv; see Section II, p. 149.
132 Aquinas, *S.T.* Ia IIae lxxvii. 4, *ad R.*
133 *De Trin.* XII. ix. 14.   134 *De Civ. Dei* XIV. xiii.   135 *De Trin.* X. v. 7.
136 *S.T.* I. xii. 11, *ad R.*   137 *De Trin.* XIII. v. 8.

209

ultimate order in which – though it is far from Augustine's heaven – a will so uncreaturely alone can flourish. The categories of good and evil, which in Christianity are of a force to transcend, have for Nietzsche no relevance in the ultimate context – no more, indeed, than does mortal existence itself; and he must needs dismiss 'the ineradicable love of existence and our reluctance to part with it'[138] as further irrelevance, founded upon the errors of the earth-bound intellect. His resulting doctrine that the terrestrial life of man is to be regarded merely as an aesthetic spectacle[139] is in contradiction to Christian thought, and is indeed a travesty of it : but it holds undeniable correspondences with it.[140]

Thus, in the three writers considered, the outcome of the tragic is a rejoicing in an order beyond the mortal that its suffering reveals. In them it is not a testimony to Christian truth; but it may be seen, broadly speaking, as a confirmation of Christian experience.

(c) GREATNESS IN FAILURE

The action of literary tragedy renders its hero the victim of overwhelming and irremediable suffering, and of death. But the cause of his sorrows is seen to be principally in himself. Circumstances, in their demand upon him, help to bring about his defeat; but in the upshot it is nothing other than his own greatness which is fatal to him. As Bradley states the matter,

> To meet these circumstances something is required which a smaller man might have given, but which the hero cannot give.[141]

This alarming paradox is the source of that sense of waste, and of mystery, which Bradley describes as the centre of the tragic impression : the spectacle of beings whose power and intelligence affirms their worth perishing and destroying themselves as if they had come into being for no other end.[142] It is at this point that, in company with many critics, he turns to ponder the nature of the order behind the tragedies. For they indicate 'a fundamental antinomy'. The universe produces a human greatness, which must therefore be natural to it; yet this same greatness seems, in tragedy, to be an unnatural intruder into the world in which it appears.[143] Tragic man finds that the universal order which has created him has become his antagonist. What Virginia Woolf says of Henchard, in *The Mayor of Casterbridge*, applies also to the Shakespearian tragic hero :

[138] Dixon, op. cit., p. 214. [139] ibid., p. 206.
[140] For the above paragraph, see Section II, pp. 149–53.
[141] *Shakespearean Tragedy*, p. 21. [142] ibid., p. 23.
[143] A. P. Rossiter, *Angel with Horns*, 1961, p. 264.

[He] is pitted, not against another man, but against something outside himself which is opposed to men of his ambition and power.[144]

The apprehending in the order in which man is set of an agency which is antagonistic to human distinction is part of the response to all tragedy; it is present in the Greek myths, where success itself seems to be the precursor to disaster, to be dangerous to man and an offence to the gods.[145] In what Reinhold Niebuhr affirms to be 'the purest conception of tragedy',

> the hero defies malignant power to assert the integrity of his soul. He suffers because he is strong and not because he is weak. He involves himself in guilt not by his vice but by his virtue.[146]

The tragic hero dies because of his very strength. In that strength, admittedly, he is not entirely free from fault, since he is only human; and this consideration prompts Bradley to wonder whether the ultimate order might not be bent on nothing short of good in perfection, and be ruthless in its demand for it.[147] But the supposition will not hold for the full range of our response – it cannot account for the impression that, in the violent casting out of defect, the tragic order

> has lost a part of its own substance – a part more dangerous and unquiet, but far more valuable and nearer its heart, than that which remains.[148]

Both in the tragic fact, therefore, and in the attempt to detect a moral purpose in the order which gives rise to it, there is apparent self-contradiction. Can it be that there is a 'double heart' at the centre of things, asks Rossiter, with that which is the good of the one God being the evil of the other, in a quasi-Manichaean universe?[149] This more ultimate division would at least explain the precariousness of human greatness in the inferior realm, the uncertainty of the right to admiration and respect which it can claim under one aspect of the tragic, beneath the pressure of that mocking commentary upon human finitude which interposes to predominance under another.[150] All decision and achievement in the tragic heroes is accompanied by a 'sense of vertiginous insecurity'[151] devolving from some ulterior paradox; and in the achievement of the self-imposed purposes to which their greatness drives them, they find that their very gain is their loss. In tragedy, Rossiter declares, Fate is revealed as being 'a sardonic *farceur*' – a malicious agency which seem-

---

[144] 'The Novels of Thomas Hardy', *The Common Reader*, 2nd Ser., 1932, p. 255, quoted by Rossiter, op. cit., p. 265.
[145] Dixon, *Tragedy*, p. 83. [146] *Beyond Tragedy*, London, 1947, pp. 160. 156.
[147] op. cit., p. 35. [148] ibid., p. 37, quoted by Rossiter, op. cit., p. 265.
[149] *Angel with Horns*, p. 266. [150] ibid., pp. 266–9. [151] ibid., p. 272.

ingly takes the hero at his own word, only to betray him in deepest consequence.

> The final alarmingness is not the loss of life (with no promise of any after-life); nor the injustice of excessive or too widespread retribution: but the threat of indignity, of the loss of heroic *existence*, by the mocking devaluation of those very qualities by which the hero commands our admiration.[152]

The greatness of the tragic hero is inseparable from his failure. But that failure is in two quite opposite senses a commentary upon him. It finally demonstrates his inadequacy; but it is necessary in the first place for the revelation of the greatness which is so soon to be called into question. It is in the error and fall of the hero that, in Bradley's words, we are made 'vividly conscious of the possibilities of human nature';[153] yet we may be no less assured that the fall itself produces a 'sense of contrast, of the powerlessness of man'.[154] That these two impressions, though contradictory, should not be mutually exclusive, is a mystery within the tragic mystery of evident waste. F. L. Lucas includes both impressions, without any sense of inconsistency, within a single sentence:

> What was tragedy to Aeschylus? A means of uttering his exultation in human greatness and heroism, his troubled groping to find the gods behind the gods, the hidden springs of the justice of the world.[155]

The celebration of human greatness in tragedy leads to, and is involved in, the failure through which greatness is revealed. The two are inseparable; and their strange coherence must necessarily lead to the consideration of the order under which these irreconcilables are produced, and come by the means of unity. But it must also raise the larger question of the veracity both of the greatness and of the failure evident to the earth-bound and erring understandings of men.

In tragedy, strength and weakness are mingled and confused. Great suffering is premissed; and the suffering can only be that of a great nature. But the suffering, the greatness, and the failure itself, are limited; and it is the function of tragedy, in presenting their full extent to our sympathies, to make evident also their finitude. The highest quality of a tragedian, declares J. S. Smart, is his ability to direct a human gaze toward the horizons of the infinite:

> It is the power to suggest something illimitable, to place life against a background of eternity, and to make the reader feel the presence of problems which he cannot solve. That this vision of the incomprehensible may lead to a pessimistic philosophy is true; but it has not always

---

[152] ibid. [153] op. cit., p. 22. [154] ibid., p. 10.
[155] *Tragedy in Relation to Aristotle's 'Poetics'*, 1953, p. 35.

done so; and spirits are not finely touched but to fine issues. *L'âme s'ennoblit dans le voisinage des mystères insondables; elle puise, dans ce travail d'exploration, avec le sentiment de sa petitesse, celui de sa grandeur.*[156]

A concluding irony of Faustus's last minutes on earth is his turning his eyes in despair towards the heavens which were made for him, and which now display the true means of man's fulfilment. He had used every resource of intellect, and every conceivable adjunct to human power, in the establishment of a creaturely eminence; now he realizes, as the claims of a spiritual universe exert themselves upon him, that he has been engaged in a diminution of the being he had been so zealous to augment, and would now indeed bring that process to its logical conclusion of willed dissolution in the face of impending doom. Having sought to become great, he has been made least : and having loved his life, he must now lose it. Earthly standards of loss and gain, greatness and littleness, success and failure, happiness and wretchedness, are confounded in the acknowledgement of a spiritual principle. In the destruction of a worldly greatness, therefore, may lie the means of true stature – of a birthright to which all other forms of ennoblement, or aspirations toward permanence, are in comparison worthless :

> Whoever is attached to this world deprives himself of heavenly life, to which we cannot be heirs unless we live as strangers and sojourners in this world. Hence it is that anyone who is too anxious for his security in this world is an alien to the Kingdom of God, or the true life.[157]

The success, and the greatness, of King Lear, according to this understanding, will lie in his knowledge – brought about by degradation – that he is 'old and foolish', and not in the conscious delight in

> power,
> Pre-eminence, and all the large effects
> That troop with majesty (I. i. 130–2).

Whoever aspires to an earthly greatness trusts in 'vanishing creatures', and devotes God-given energies to tasks which, though they may enhance his consequence in men's eyes, bear no real relationship to his being. To gain worldly success, he must adopt the world's garb, its manners, and its coin; but his devotion to the ephemeral can only bring forth the meretricious : he must remain a stranger to real greatness –

> To others, wonder; to himselfe a rod.[158]

---

[156] 'Tragedy', *Essays and Studies* VIII, 1922, p. 36.
[157] *Calvin: Commentaries*, L.C.C. XXIII, p. 319.
[158] Fulke Greville, 'A Treatise of Religion', st. 6, *The Remains*, ed. G. A. Wilkes, 1965, p. 204.

Success in the external sphere, therefore, may be the measure of littleness, and defeat the means of greatness, in a universe which is Providential :

> he who has only the standard of the temporal existence goes down with the temporal, and perhaps does not even last as long. Even if one's life passes quietly and peacefully, events may still take place which his experience has not exhausted. If this happens to a man, he becomes the prey of despair. And, on the other hand, if he succeeds in slipping through life without any such dispensation of Providence upsetting his calculations, then, if he has learned nothing higher in life, he is still a child of the temporal existence, for whom the eternal does not exist.[159]

Destiny's apparent contempt for distinction in man must call attention to what is real, and of true worth, in human personality. It must qualify, and indeed unmask, the instinct of creaturely self-adulation which is at work in the beholders of tragedy, who see in the hero

> power, intelligence, life and glory, which astound us and seem to call for our worship.[160]

If reality is in God alone, no lesser or created good, whether in himself or elsewhere, can be worthy of man's unqualified respect. In a universe of becoming they are means to an end; and it is in the progress towards the end rather than in the means of progress that reality must inhere. It is no mere accident, therefore, that prompts Augustine to make the will rather than the intellect the centre of personality, and to assign the appeal of truth in the last resort neither to reason nor to emotion, but to human volition.[161] According to this understanding, the true character of personality must depend, not upon creaturely attribute and peculiarity, however impressive they may be, but upon the nature of the end to which the mind is striving,[162] and its progress along a pilgrimage which all men must make in common. All human impulses and motives are therefore eloquent of the state of the soul, since they cannot exist apart from it : external influences and inner compulsions alike can gain dominance only through the consent of the will.[163] And the primacy of will itself consists, not in its dignity as an attribute, but in its capacity for the attaining of truth.[164] Human personality, therefore, is not an object, or to be seen as an object, or as a thing in itself : it is rather the expression of potentiality and movement. It has true being, but only in a limited sense :

[159] Søren Kierkegaard, 'The Expectation of an Eternal Happiness', *Edifying Discourses*, tr. D. F. and L. M. Swenson, Minneapolis, 1950–3, III, pp. 104–5.

[160] Bradley, *Shakespearean Tragedy*, p. 23.

[161] J. Morgan, *The Psychological Teaching of St Augustine*, 1932, pp. 176–7.

[162] ibid., p. 141.

[163] See D. E. Roberts, 'The Earliest Writings', *A Companion to the Study of St Augustine*, ed. R. W. Battenhouse, N.Y., 1955, p. 119.

[164] *De Trin.* XIV. iv. 6; Section II, p. 126.

its being lies in process and progress towards God. Man, like the universe itself, is in a condition of becoming, and his reality lies in his tendency towards his Creator. The glories of our blood and state are indeed not substantial; and they can appear as substantial only to the recreant and apostatizing vision of a humanity involved in itself. The will, then, in its relationship to God, is in the strictest and highest sense determinative of human character; there alone lies what may be glorious in man, and all other glories are more apparent than real. But who, it may be asked, has not come short in will? Man is the worthy object, not of awe, but of pity – a 'shattered and bleeding soul',[165] able to be delivered in no wise save by an unmerited mercy from the 'mass of perdition'[166] in which he subsists. Such a being is involved in failure before ever he attempts an earthly goal; and his success in it can only confirm his wretchedness.

This is the state of affairs – and perhaps the verdict – which literary tragedy presents to us. There, man's inevitable defeat, and the contradictory joy that it inspires, may be an enactment of the maxim that man's misery is proof of his guilt and apostasy.[167] For drama is able to present the operation of the will with a clarity not in any other way vouchsafed to human experience, in that lively microcosm of the mortal world which is the play's own society. The great creator of character, writes P. Ure, fulfils the promise that lies in drama's constant traffic between inner and outer of giving his audience a God-like view of the individual, with the certainty that they have at their disposal a plenitude of evidence such is rarely available in ordinary life. The dramatist's concern is with the human will:

> with action and the motives for action; with what happens to the personality as a result of its commitment to a course of action.[168]

These, as Bradley observes, are actions in the full sense of the word. They are not things done in a state of undiscerning, but acts or omissions that are fully expressive of the doer. The centre of the tragedy is thus 'action issuing from character' or 'character issuing in action', for the actions are 'characteristic deeds'.[169] And the result of the actions of these great personages, which are so expressive of the state of their wills – and their souls – is their inevitable downfall: greatness and failure go hand in hand. The conclusion cannot be avoided that the heroes' downfall, because of their obvious contributing to it, is strictly speaking a judgement upon them – and it is for this reason that Fulke Greville could see in the tragedies of his age the exemplification of God's revenge on each particular sin.[170] But, in a vision such as his, the categories of success and

---

[165] Augustine, *Conf.* IV. vii. 12.   [166] *Enchiridion* xxiv. 94.   [167] See p. 175 above.
[168] *Shakespeare and the Inward Self of the Tragic Hero*, 1961, p. 4.
[169] op. cit., p. 12.
[170] *Life of Sir Philip Sidney*, ed. Nowell Smith, 1907, p. 221.

failure would have very limited application. For within the Christian universe, humanity's greatness may not be greatness, its success may not be success, its failure may not be failure. And the tragic destiny that mocks at its seemings and pretensions can reveal itself as the agent of salvation:

> *Afflictions* water cooles the heate of *sinne*,
> And brings soule-health.[171]

(d) MIGHTY OPPOSITES

It is a dangerous thing, Hamlet observes, for a lesser being to come

> Between the pass and fell-incensed points
> Of mighty opposites
>
> (V. ii. 61–2).

Yet the sufferings of tragic man are largely due to his involvement, in his puny and unprotected state, in the clash of those mighty and opposing principles that rend his world and destroy him. Hamlet is himself perhaps the most notable instance of this characteristic misfortune of the protagonist, whose compulsion to act must bring upon him, and engender within him, the warring of forces greater than he. It is the misfortune of mankind at large : Hamlet, declares Miss Helen Gardner,

> is the quintessence of European man, who holds that man is 'ordained to govern the world according to equity and righteousness with an upright heart', and not to renounce the world and leave it to its corruption. By that conception of man's duty and destiny he is involved in those tragic dilemmas with which our own age is so terribly familiar. For how can man secure justice except by committing injustice, and how can he act without outraging the very conscience which demands that he should act?[172]

It is not only modern man's destiny to live beneath this paradox : the problem confronting Hamlet is essentially the same as that which Sophocles' Antigone faces. For Hegel, the tragic dilemma shows the discord of principle being resolved at last into a higher harmony. Both Creon and Antigone are right in the principle they assert; their wrongness consists in their being too emphatic and partial in their righteousness.[173] Goethe rejects the idea that Antigone is in any sense wrong, and puts the blame squarely upon Creon's shoulders on the principle that 'We should never describe any action as public morality which is contrary to

---

[171] John Davies of Hereford, *Microcosmos*, Oxford, 1603, p. 79.

[172] *The Business of Criticism*, Oxford Paperbacks, 1963, p. 50.

[173] See A. C. Bradley, *Oxford Lectures on Poetry*, 1941, p. 73; F. L. Lucas, *Tragedy in Relation*, 1953, p. 40.

morality in general'[174] He is perfectly right, but far too abstract. The institution of the state, through its human servant, may have erred; but the institution itself is a worthy principle in the life of man, and its security, together with the security of those to whom it ministers, is an important consideration at any time. In asserting the right of the state in that particular historical context, Creon may be perversely hiding an evil action beneath a good principle : but the clash of principles is none the less real. And it is inevitable at almost any stage of history. The coercive power of government, Reinhold Niebuhr observes, is never – as ideally it should be – established by the whole society and held strictly accountable to it, because of the exigencies of military power, or priestly prestige, or through the special skills that government itself requires. Government is thus 'at once the source of order and the root of injustice in a community'. But to overturn it by way of response to an injustice may be to commit greater injustice in the resulting disorder; for

there is life as well as death, virtue as well as sin, in these social and political configurations.[175]

The tension and conflict that exists between the individual conscience and the state is part of the duality and conflict of principle that is to be observed throughout human life.

The sense of duality is to be found in Nietzsche's vision of a world in conflict, subjected to the alternate illusion of Apollo and disillusion of Dionysus.[176] His vision, if it can be accused of lacking objectivity, can claim at least a subjective reality in its reflection of the struggle in man between the thought of the splendour of human life and life's promptings to despair. These feelings are symptomatic of the opposite potentialities and emotions which in human existence are locked in seeming oppugnancy, of the balance upon which every essay of life or mind must be constructed. The pleasure of tragedy has been attributed to that equilibrium between opposing forces which its form and nature requires, to its 'organic sense of the coexistence of apparent opposites',[177] or to the 'balance or reconciliation of opposite and discordant qualities' which it effects.[178] The *catharsis* of tragedy lies in their union, and the consequent 'sense of release, of repose in the midst of stress, of balance and composure'[179] It is not to be doubted that this sense of balance exists, and that satisfaction arises from it; the question is whether what is manifested at the aesthetic level does not have affinities with the metaphysical. The endeavour of M. Krieger is to keep the two separate. The 'tragic vision' he con-

[174] Eckermann's *Gespräche mit Goethe*, 28 March, 1827, quoted by J. S. Smart, 'Tragedy', *Essays and Studies* VIII, 1922, p. 20.

[175] *Faith and History*, London, 1949, pp. 249–51.   [176] Lucas, op. cit., p. 47.

[177] Lawlor, *The Tragic Sense in Shakespeare*, 1960, p. 12.

[178] I. A. Richards, *Principles of Literary Criticism*, 1925, pp. 245–6, quoted by Lucas, op. cit., p. 49.   [179] Lucas, op. cit., p. 49.

signs to the tragic hero; the 'tragedy' is for him the literary structure itself[180] – and this, as the exemplification of a comprehensive and formal principle, becomes a force for affirmation, and, in consequence, for exaltation. Balance, however, though it be a salutary thing, is not enough; the fact that it should be needed is more to the point. The contrarieties that are locked in conflict may be 'the life of one another'; yet in the same breath it has to be admitted that they 'destroy one another'.[181] It is through conflict that tragedy is born, and subsists :

> Though all desire good and only good, yet from the struggle for its various forms and appearances arise evils and tragedies. Over against the individual stands Nature, over against him also stands the community : tragedy is the measure of their differences and conflicting purposes.[182]

The conflict may express itself in a clash between the individual and his society; it may be seen in the opposition between law and custom and those creative vitalities which they try to control; or it may take the form of collision between a human reason which would bring all things into orderly relationship, and a passionate imagination which would break all prudential restraints in seeking a fulfilment in some larger destiny.[183] The unresolved conflict in the heart of Greek tragedy, according to Reinhold Niebuhr, is its not knowing whether the real centre of life is in law or in vitality;[184] but the unresolved conflict of all tragedy, it may be said, is the antagonism of apparent goods. In the process of asserting the full dimension of his own being in the championing of a particular good or principle, the tragic hero incurs the hostility of other or opposite goods or principles.

One thing at least is clear in the mystery of clashing goods : that if they were ultimately good they could not come into conflict, and that therefore they must be lesser goods, and not suitable subjects for finality. The paradoxical state of conflict in tragedy points to the paradox maintained in Christian thinking, in particular through the doctrine of grace, of an incompatibility in principle between the mundane and the spiritual worlds, and of the insubstantiality of worldly qualities of goodness. Mankind's suffering, in the thought of Augustine, has its beginning in their refusal to pay back in duty to God the existence they owe him.[185] Men would live unto the self – but there can be no goodness in themselves. Those things which the soul accounts to be virtues, should they not all be

---

[180] 'Tragedy and the Tragic Vision', *Kenyon Review* XX, 1958, p. 283, quoted by N. A. Scott, 'The Tragic Vision and The Christian Faith', *Anglican Theological Review* XLV, 1963, pp. 35–7.

[181] Macneile Dixon, *Tragedy*, 1929, p. 111, quoting Sir Thomas Browne.

[182] Macneile Dixon, op. cit., p. 108.

[183] Reinhold Niebuhr, *Beyond Tragedy*, London, 1947, pp. 161–4.

[184] ibid., p. 165.   [185] *De Civ. Dei* XIV. xiii; Section II, p. 93.

referred to God, 'are indeed rather vices than virtues';[186] and whoever exults in the possession of a natural good

is evil himself in this good, and wretched, being deprived of a better.[187]

This teaching, that what is good under one aspect may be evil under God's universal aspect,[188] is present in the manner of Luther's rejection of the idea that the qualities of human nature may be sound and uncorrupted, despite the corruption of human nature itself. Luther declares it to be 'true in the corporal kingdom', but false in 'the spiritual kingdom and the presence of God'.[189] The Reformers renew Augustine's insistence that mortal men cannot live upright lives without being set free by God's grace from their slavery to sin;[190] but if they are correct in the extension of their judgement from the virtues of the heathen to their works as well, and in asserting that those works 'must not be looked upon morally, but faithfully and spiritually',[191] then Luther's conclusion that 'we do righteous deeds in so far as we are righteous'[192] must apply. The deeds of the unrighteous must exemplify their unrighteousness: they can only be as 'ungodly, sacrilegious, and evil in every respect'[193] as the will which performs them, and as the principles upon which those wills act. It is a matter for the gravest doubt whether bad trees can bring forth fruit which, though impure and abhorrent under the eternal order, can be pronounced wholesome under the mundane.

The dichotomy which Augustine perceives is rediscovered by Luther in the writings of Paul. From the *Epistle to the Romans* Luther receives the argument that

all that is wrought and done among men is either righteousness or sin in God's sight: righteousness, if faith is with it; sin, if faith is lacking. With men, indeed, it is the case that actions in which men who owe nothing to each other confer nothing on each other are called 'intermediate' and 'neutral'. But the ungodly man sins against God, whether he eats, or drinks, or whatever he does, because he abuses God's creation by his ungodliness and persistent ingratitude, and does not from his heart give glory to God for a moment.[194]

Faith is the condition of virtue, as it is of understanding. Just as the natural reason of man is 'altogether in darkness',[195] and his own intellect

---

[186] *De Civ. Dei* XIX. xxv.   [187] ibid., XII. viii.

[188] *S.T.* Ia IIae xix. 9, 10, *ad R.*; Section II, pp. 94–5.

[189] *A Commentary on St Paul's Epistle to the Galatians* (ii. 20), ed. P. S. Watson, 1953, p. 175; Section II, p. 137.

[190] *Retract.* I. ix. 4.   [191] *Galatians* (iii. 10), p. 247.

[192] *Lectures on Romans*, tr. W. Pauck, L.C.C. XV, 1961, p. 108.

[193] *Martin Luther on The Bondage of the Will*, ed. Parker and Johnston, London, 1959, p. 253. See Section II, p. 139.

[194] *Bondage (Rom.* iii. 21–5), p. 290.   [195] Luther, *Table-Talk*, ccxcvi.

'blinded and bewildered' by the light of ultimate truth,[196] so, as Augustine argues, 'true virtue can be in none in whom there is no piety', and the greatest gifts present in men

> do . . . not promise any people in whom they are, any assurance from suffering temporal sorrows.[197]

The same emphasis is present in Calvin. Faith, the means of virtue, is first the means of order both in the individual and his society:

> It is vain to cry up righteousness without religion. This is as unreasonable as to display a mutilated, decapitated body as something beautiful. Not only is religion the chief part, but the very soul, whereby the whole breathes and thrives. And apart from the fear of God men do not preserve equity and love among themselves.[198]

Desires which are not virtuous – which are not dedicated and bound to the service of God beyond any concern for the self – are by definition sinful;[199] and it is in the nature of these desires for the lesser good that they should come into conflict, and involve those who entertain them. Thus

> both doth each one injure himself, and all injure one another. For they desire that, the love of which is fraught with death, and which may easily be taken away from them; and this they take away from one another.[200]

Man must therefore be the victim in the clash of mighty opposites – a clash whose necessity lies precisely in the fact that the opponents, though mighty, are not almighty. The conflicting principles are part of his being, and their limited yet considerable worth helps to exalt his own stature, so that he may appear to the spectator of tragedy, or even to his neighbour, as a princely 'piece of work' worthy of the acclaim of a conqueror. But the heroes of tragedy are in truth the victims of their desires; and,

> being in truth conquered, they feignedly conquer, and are conquerors not in truth, but in opinion.[201]

Despite the inherent nobility of the powers he is endowed with, man is not a god, for all that he may appear God-like. His calling is that of a renegade; he lives in a condition that is penitential; and he is the exemplar of desires that are discordant and unholy. In this must lie the answer to Bradley's despairing question,

[196] E. Gilson, *The Philosophy of St Thomas Aquinas*, tr. E. Bullough, Cambridge, 1924, p. 210.
[197] *De Civ. Dei* XIX. iv; see also XIX. xxi, quoted in Section II, p. 156.
[198] *Inst.* II. viii. 11.   [199] (Section II, p. 153.)
[200] Augustine, *De Agone Christ.* vii. 8; see Section II, p. 92.
[201] *De Trin.* XIII. xiii. 17.

Why is it that a man's virtues help to destroy him, and that his weakness and defect is so intertwined with everything that is admirable in him that we can hardly separate them even in imagination?[202]

The warring contrarities present in the historical process, and in the human soul, are the product of seeming virtues which in reality are vices: the standards of earth are not those of heaven, and with the best of wills man can but sin, and become involved in the consequences of his sin. Faith and love are scarcely to be found among men; and the gilden roofs of human excellences are built upon such weak foundations as must quickly betray their unperfectness. Human history is a defiance of God, and tragedy is the merit of defiance, and the evidence of man's aversion from his God.

In its profounder moments the Church has known that Pilate and the priests are symbolic of the fact that every majesty or virtue, which is tenable in history, is involved in the crucifixion of a 'prince of glory' who incarnates a love which is normative for, but not tenable in history. That love which could not maintain itself in history becomes the symbol both of the new beginning which a man could make if he subjected his life to the judgement of Christ, and of the mercy of God which alone could overcome the fateful impotence of man ever to achieve so perfect a love. . . . Thus Biblical faith . . . ends by seeing human history perpetually, and of every level of its achievements, in contradiction to the divine.[203]

The clashing principles of human life come out of aspiration for good. But it is lesser goods, not the greatest, which a perverse humanity desires; and to these goods they impart a wrongful absoluteness, in the process of an idolatrous quest of a personal integrity and predominance, in a medium which must betray them to the extent that they betray themselves.

(e) REALITY IN TRANSIENCE

In the depths of our being, according to Schopenhauer, we receive from tragedy a sense of the worthlessness of life, and the spectacle it places before us frees us from the will to live.[204] Yet our more conscious reaction is a conviction of the worth of existence. Tragedy is a force for affirmation; and from its sombre shows we derive satisfaction and confidence.[205] In the tragic event we are conscious of both pleasure and of pain, of

[202] *Shakespearean Tragedy*, 1956, p. 29.
[203] R. Niebuhr, *Faith and History*, London, 1949, pp. 162–3.
[204] *The World as Will and Idea*, tr. Haldane and Kemp, London, 1883, I, p. 327; III, pp. 212–14.
[205] See p. 192 above.

despair and of hope : our appreciation of its meaning must be bounded on one side by a knowledge of the perils with which human existence is beset, and on the other by a feeling of assurance deriving from the witnessed operation of those very perils. At the moment of catastrophe life appears

> infinitely fragile, yet never more intensely ours.[206]

The interpenetration of opposite responses and emotions has produced contrasting theories : we can be said to derive a largely malicious pleasure from tragedy, or to find in it the opportunity for indulgence in a luxury of sympathy.[207] Or the terrible and the joyous can be reconciled as the opposite extremes of a single scale of human experience, so as to make the difference between the painful and the pleasant a matter of degree[208]– and the art of tragedy a massive exercise in aesthetic discretion. Or there can arise a negative or subjective attitude, which recognizes tragedy's potentialities of insecurity and terror as well as its instances of the pleasureable, without attempting a reconciliation – which will limit the tragic pleasure to the mind's activity in that imaginative and creative comprehension of life which can venture into its more intense and terrible possibilities.[209] In all these theories there is the same endeavour to find the basis for a unitary response to an experience which must manifestly call forth diverse emotions.[210]

The diversity of response to life is not only evident in the minds of the beholders. It may be sensed in the very texture of tragic poetry – in that relationship between mankind and the principle of life and organic growth in the natural world in which man is set, that finds expression in Shakespeare's verse. According to L. C. Knights, nature and men's values are felt as intimately related, and at the same time as antagonistic. Humanity is evidently not entirely at home in the world of nature, and appears in some ways to be set over against it; yet there is abundant evidence in the poetry of the plays that the human mind can find itself in nature, and thereby come into its own.[211] The question of the principle by which reconciliation can be effected must thus present itself; and Knights finds the principle in a human goodness devolving from acknowledgement of the supernatural character of its own humanity :

[206] F. L. Lucas, *Tragedy in Relation to Aristotle's 'Poetics'*, 1953, p. 45.

[207] For the sadistic and masochistic theories, see T. R. Henn. *The Harvest of Tragedy*, 2nd edn, 1966, pp. 46–58.

[208] Le Bovier de Fontenelle, 'Reflexions sur la Poetique' xxxvi, *Oeuvres*, Paris, B. Brunet, 1758, III, pp. 163–4.

[209] David Hume, 'Of Tragedy', *Essays Moral, Political and Literary* (1741–2), O.U.P., 1966, pp. 225–6.

[210] For this paragraph see Lucas, op. cit., pp. 37–9.

[211] *Some Shakespearean Themes*, 1959, pp. 124–9.

The mind . . . contains within itself elements corresponding to non-human life – Blake's tiger and lamb. So long as these natural forces are not integrated by the specifically human principle they are, or are likely to become, chaotic and destructive. Given that principle, they may be sublimated and transformed, but they are not disowned; they are freely accepted as the natural sources of life and power. So too with the external world of nature : it is only the man who recognizes his own humanity, and that of others, as something essentially other than a product of the natural world, who is really open to nature; neither fascinated nor afraid, he can respond creatively to its created-ness, and, paradoxically, find in nature a symbol for all that is natural in the other sense – that is, most truly human.[212]

A similar conception of the principle by which external nature is rendered acceptable and akin to man's own nature and purposes is to be found in Augustine's thought. The knowledge of nature is made possible by God, and the natural world is indeed His handiwork; yet the appearances of nature in all its complex forms will obscure reality, and the perception of God, in that soul which is to be found

> without-doors, dwelling in the eye of my flesh, and chewing the cud by myself.[213]

A true and reconciling loveliness is to be apprehended through the evidence of things that are made, and through the ministry of the outer man to the inner man by the means of the body's senses. The confession of these outward things is, 'We are not thy God, seek above us',[214] and their voice is neither restricted nor in any way unclear :

> Nay, verily, it speaks unto all; but they only understand it who compare that voice received from without by the senses, with the truth which is within.[215]

Only where the spirit of God is present within can His handiwork be discovered in nature without, and a reconciliation be effected; otherwise a true appreciation is not possible. The failure to acknowledge a supernatural principle is a denial of the Creator which must in its turn ensure that men will 'use the creature with lust instead of temperance' :[216] by their inordinate inclination to the external they will not only confer a spurious reality upon things that proclaim rather than possess reality, but render themselves unfit to receive a true impression :

---

[212] ibid., p. 132.
[213] Conf. III. vi. 11. (W. Watts' translation, 1631, in Loeb Classical Library, 1919).
[214] ibid., X. vi. 9.   [215] ibid., X. vi. 10.
[216] In Epist. Jo. ad Parth. Tract. decem ii. 11.

by inordinate love of them, they make themselves subjects unto them : and subjects are not fit to judge.[217]

The want of a spiritual principle thus afflicts both external nature and the perceiving mind with a loss of truth and a threat of the terrors of unreality which must qualify all that is good and joyous in creation. In their striving to wrest pleasure and permanence out of the limited reality they know, men do but set themselves at greater distance from what is real, and cling to emptiness. The desire for the joys of existence therefore can properly be nothing short of a will for the relinquishing of the temporal – for that alone can be substantial which is in accordance with God's will :

> The more you love to exist, the more you will desire . . . that your inclinations be not temporal. . . . These earthly things have no existence before they exist, and while they exist they pass away, and when they have passed away they will exist no more. When they are still in the future, they do not yet exist, and when they are past they are now no more. How then shall we hold them lastingly, seeing that the beginning of their existence is their passage into non-existence?[218]

The soul which seeks to found its being upon fleeting existences rather than upon the will and purpose which decreed them must lose distinction in its joys; time, decay, and the fact of evil must give the universe a hostile appearance, and transform its pleasures into sorrows, its loves into terrors :

> Life which delights in material joys . . . will not possess the kingdom of God, and what it loves will be snatched from it. It loves what, being matter, is less than life, and, on account of the sinfulness of so doing, the beloved object becomes corruptible, is dissolved and lost to its lover, even as it, in loving a material thing, has abandoned God . . . for by loving inferior things it is given a place among the inferior creatures, being deprived of its pleasures and afflicted with grief.[219]

Its grief is the very loss, failure or transformation of those mutable things which it had enjoyed, or hoped to enjoy; and the sufferer is led to a desperate certainty that he is one of many who

> Have sat in taverns, while the tempest hurled
> Their hopeful plans to emptiness, and cursed
> Whatever brute and blackguard made the world.[220]

---

[217] *Conf.* X. vi. 10 (Watts' translation). For this paragraph see R. E. Cushman, 'Faith and Reason', in *A Companion to the Study of St Augustine*, N.Y., 1955, pp. 293–4.
[218] *De Lib. Arb.* III. vii. 21.   [219] *De Vera Relig.* xi. 22; xii. 23.
[220] A. E. Housman, *Last Poems*, ix.

The conviction of the worth of existence becomes a sense of the worth-lessness of life. But for him who adheres to God, the created universe can be a means of enlightenment and joy: aspiration toward the true love places in proportion all lesser loves, and sets up a harmony of loveliness which unites man and the natural order with their Creator, speaking through all temporal forms and pleasures of a state of being

> where there shineth unto my soul, what space cannot contain, and there soundeth, what time beareth not away, and there smelleth, what breathing disperseth not, and there tasteth, what eating diminisheth not, and there clingeth, what satiety divorceth not.[221]

This harmony, in which the joys of earth may be loved even in their limitation, and may be received as an earnest of joys that are to come, does not reach the ears of tragic man. Finding a good in himself and in the created universe, he seeks to build his pleasures upon mortality, for-saking the only source of life and happiness. Whatever other matters may be incidental to his downfall, in this one fact lies the assurance of his defeat:

> The good that you love is from Him; but it is good and pleasant through reference to Him, and justly shall it be embittered, because unjustly is any thing loved which is from Him, if He be forsaken for it.[222]

Augustine's conclusion therefore embraces the entire tragic experience of mankind:

> There is no rest, where ye seek it. Seek what ye seek; but it is not there where ye seek. Ye seek a blessed life in the land of death; it is not there. For how should there be a blessed life, where life itself is not?[223]

[221] *Conf.* X. vi. 8. (Pusey tr.)   [222] ibid., IV. xii. 18.   [223] ibid.

Chapter 16

THE TRAGIC FLAW

A sense of disparity is an essential part of the response to the tragic. The degree of the hero's responsibility for events and the extent to which accident plays a part will vary; but in the disproportion between intention and outcome, and in the ultimate misery itself, there must always be the impression of injustice. In his concern to find the presence of a moral order in tragedy, A. C. Bradley must admit, concerning Lear, that 'to assert that he deserved to suffer what he did suffer is to do violence not merely to language but to any healthy moral sense'; and he is constrained to 'put aside the ideas of justice and merit' in considering the nature of the ultimate order.[1] In doing so he appears to share the intuition of Aristotle, who lays it down that the cause of the tragic occurrence must not be a vice, but rather some great error,[2] and thus contrives for the ultimate powers an indeterminate rôle, and for himself the avoidance of the moral issue. His justification is that in Greek tragedy the scale of the tragic heroes' involvement in their fate ranges from clear initiative in evil-doing to doomed and helpless innocence.[3] And it may also be found in that yearning of the human mind to believe the universe not utterly immoral which he himself expresses in the injunction that morally good or 'decent' people must not be shown in the 'disgusting' situation of passing from prosperity to misfortune.[4]

Criticism is faced with the difficulty of having to make a choice in the matter of the moral responsibility for tragedy. It must decide whether tragedy involves the ideas of justice and retribution, or whether it treats simply 'Of fate and chance, and change in human life'.[5] F. L. Lucas recognizes that the tragic error often has been moral, and argues that it either may or may not be so, since the error is based primarily on artistic and logical considerations, and the mistakes of Shakespeare's tragic heroes serve 'to make their fate not just, but logical and convincing'.[6] There is no question that chance is always present in Shakespeare's tragedies as 'a fact, and a prominent fact, of human life',[7] and that the idea of

[1] *Shakespearean Tragedy*, pp. 32–3.
[2] *Poetics*, xiii.
[3] Lucas, *Tragedy in Relation*, 1953, pp. 100–1.
[4] *Poetics*, xiii.
[5] *Paradise Regained*, IV, 1.265.
[6] op. cit., p. 102.
[7] Bradley, op. cit., p. 15.

226

Fortune is always present to Shakespeare's mind: Lear's 'I am even / The natural fool of fortune' (IV. vi. 191–2) does but echo Romeo's 'O! I am Fortune's fool' (III. i. 135).[8] Neither the imaginative experience of tragedy nor the words in which it is couched suggest that moral guilt alone is at its root; the idea is advanced

> by philosophers rather than by the poets themselves. The latter are more often satisfied with fragmentary and vivid glimpses of reality; but the philosophers seek to survey all things and co-ordinate them.[9]

Critics are thus torn between the Hebraic intuition which can see in tragic event 'a specific moral fault or failure of understanding', and the Greek apprehension that the forces that make for tragedy are beyond reason and justice, and that 'Outside and within man is *l'autre*, the "otherness" of the world' that mocks and destroys.[10]

Whereas the Greek protagonists act and suffer as if they are in the presence of a higher power, Elizabethan tragedy concerns itself with the particular frailty of a particular man.[11] In its development toward inclusiveness, to a wider rendering of all that man's experience presents for observation, drama has become increasingly concerned with presenting character at the expense of action – and at the expense, it may be argued, of mystery. Destiny has become identified with the personal:[12] it has been noted of Shakespeare that

> always he draws his characters in such a way that there is clearly only one line of conduct possible for them in the situation in which they find themselves: for them it is the doom-in-the-character rather than the doom-in-the-house.[13]

Human character is invaluable to the dramatist in its striking a note of kinship and of recognition, and in its being a field of limited knowledge in a realm of limitless possibilities. But to give chief priority in the tragic situation to what must necessarily loom large in a human perspective is to imperil true proportion, and to make men's individual differences obscure the profounder fact of their resemblances and their common destiny. The power of tragedy to inspire pity and terror lies, not in differentiation of character or exemplification of the means through which events occur, but in event and happening itself.[14] It can thus be argued that, to the extent that tragic suffering is traced to some frailty which bechances human nature or personality, and tragedy's grasp is widened

---

[8] J. S. Smart, 'Tragedy', *Essays and Studies* VIII, 1922, pp. 10–11.
[9] ibid., p. 16.   [10] G. Steiner, *The Death of Tragedy*, 1961, pp. 6–9.
[11] Dixon, *Tragedy*, 1929, pp. 33–6.
[12] C. E. Vaughan, *Types of Tragic Drama*, 1908, pp. 17–18.
[13] C. Leech, *Shakespeare's Tragedies, and Other Studies*, 1950, p. 17.
[14] Dixon, op. cit., pp. 99–101.

to include the technicalities of character and motive, the mind is withdrawn from its contemplation of the central issue of tragedy, and the issue itself is obscured. For tragedy's real concern is with

> the workings of a great, incalculable, natural force; that great Necessity, whatever it be, which brought us into being, governs us and removes us from the scene.[15]

A concern with character can more readily accommodate the idea that a moral order is at work; but where it is seen as an instance of mankind's destiny, tragedy appears as rooted in the incalculable.[16]

The conclusion is unavoidable that defect of character can only be a partial explanation of the tragic, and one which avoids the deeper questions. Character, though it provide the means of destruction, does not rule in the tragic universe; as K. Muir argues, Macbeth, like all Shakespeare's tragic heroes, is destroyed by fate as well as by the particular weakness through which fate is able to work.[17] But a more particular reason for the lesser importance of character as an explanation of the incidence of tragedy is to be found in the necessary identification between the tragic hero and his beholders. Though his choice be seen to be determined by his qualities, the failing which proves his downfall is in no way remote from their experience: it is common in a thousand cases. But what is usually of little consequence is in this instance disastrous, bringing down upon itself the disproportionate weight of the universe.[18] However exalted in capacity the hero may be, the ultimate order is seen to operate not against the exceptional but against the common failing, from which none can claim to be immune. It is thus that tragedy preserves what Lawlor calls its 'mythic power' – the ability of the hero to stand as substitute for the spectator, and his story to be symbolic of the human situation.[19] The greatness of Shakespeare's characters, as Bradley has observed, consists not in a uniqueness of endowment, but in 'an intensification of the life they share with others'.[20] Ethically and spiritually speaking, they are in no way superior to those who throng the theatre. Tragedy possesses a true vision: as humanity is magnified on the stage, so its weaknesses become correspondingly clear; and as the heroes are revealed in all their potentiality, truth is always insisting to the onlooker, 'tush, man, mortal men, mortal men'. In the scope of tragedy, therefore, man must ever be patient as well as agent, and his earthly task is to endure a destiny whose operation appears to lie beyond his personal motives.[21]

---

[15] ibid., p. 66.   [16] ibid., p. 42.
[17] *Shakespeare: The Great Tragedies* (Writers and Their Work), 1961, p. 35.
[18] J. Lawlor, *The Tragic Sense in Shakespeare*, 1960, p. 121.
[19] ibid., p. 147.   [20] op. cit., p. 20.   [21] Lawlor, op. cit., p. 147.

It is true that if the critic sees in the disproportion between the 'offence' and the disaster that follows from it a warning to banish from his consciousness the demand that the tragic victims should 'deserve' what befalls them, he may point to a kind of justice which, if it is not concerned with 'a nice balance of deserts and rewards',[22] is at least not beyond reason. According to this view, we see in tragedy the enactment of a law of cause and effect which preserves justice precisely by refusing the demand for a poetic justice made by those who expect reality to answer their bidding.[23] Act and consequence are therefore supreme:

> The justice of the gods consists simply in the natural law that every act must have its consequence and that the consequence will be determined by the act and its context.[24]

This formula appears to be closer to the experience of tragedy, and more in keeping with the disproportion of disaster, than any moralistic one. And it can claim the Biblical sanction of *Ecclesiastes'*

> the race is not to the swift, nor the battle to the strong, neither yet bread to the wise, nor yet riches to men of understanding, nor yet favour to men of skill; but time and chance happeneth to them all (ix. 11),

and of Job's outcry on the inequality of mortal existence:

> One dieth in his full strength, being wholly
> at ease and quiet . . .
> And another dieth in the bitterness of his
> soul, and never eateth with pleasure
> They shall lie down alike in the dust, and
> the worms shall cover them (xxi. 23–6).

It would also have the effect of putting an end to the 'hamartia-hunting'[25] which has been a source of great misrepresentation in criticism, as, indeed, it falsifies human life. For the insistence that man is the victim of his own act, and the demand for perfection of judgement, can scarcely relate to one who is

> launched weak, unskilled, ignorant, upon a sea full of reefs and dangers, terribly limited in time as in knowledge.[26]

In an incalculable world, to act and to blunder are one. To explain the fate of the heroes in terms of their having taken a wrong path, made the

[22] C. Leech, op. cit., p. 14.   [23] Lawlor, op. cit., p. 170; Dixon. *Tragedy*, p. 137.
[24] C. Leech, op. cit., pp. 14–15.   [25] A. P. Rossiter, *Angel with Horns*, 1961, p. 263.
[26] Dixon, op. cit., p. 69.

wrong choice, given too free a reign to their passions, yielded to temptation or neglected some duty, as if wiser or better heroes might have met
the demands of the hour, is to reduce tragedy to the status of morality.
Hamlet thus becomes an exemplar of sloth, Lear of senility and wrath,
Othello the embodiment of primitive and brutal passions – and *Romeo
and Juliet* an object lesson in the dangers of falling too deeply in love.
But it may more truly be said that all these are instances of that falling
into the power of evil which, through some accident or mis-step, may
happen to the wisest and best of men, and which threatens each and all
alike.[27] Yet the theory of 'act and consequence', however attractive, will
not suffice. It does not square with the common observation that the
main source of the tragic convulsion 'is in every case evil' and 'in almost
every case . . . plain moral evil'.[28] The paradox must remain that although
a moralistic 'tragic flaw' does not do justice to the characters, they are
not innocent of responsibility for what happens: the problem of the fate
of the tragic hero is not the same as that of the guiltless sufferer. And the
theory of 'act and consequence', also, must raise greater doubts and fears
than it settles. It consigns man to a justice which is 'terrible', leaving him

> as questioner, naked, unaccommodated, alone, facing mysterious
> demonic forces in his own nature and outside, and the irreducible
> facts of suffering and death.[29]

The 'tragic flaw' theory asserts that the universe is moral; the 'act and
consequence' theory would concede that it is meaningless.

The suffering and destruction of an Antigone, a Hamlet or a Cordelia
might seem to bear out Socrates' verdict upon the universe that its evils
can never pass away, since 'there must always remain something which is
antagonist to good';[30] yet what is 'antagonist to good' has helped to
create these persons, since it is part of their universe, and in their deaths
it proclaims what they are. A justice and a good to which evil circumstance is subjected is to be observed in their creation and preservation;
but for a reconciliation of the fact of good with what is antagonist to
good in the tragic conclusion there is required a justice and a good over
and above events in the historical process. What would thus remove
finality from tragic happenings would also diminish the charge of responsibility which they must make against the tragic hero. It would also smooth
the way for Augustine's assertion that 'Suffering is to be judged not by
its own character but by the character of him who bears it'.[31] The same
understanding of life may be found in Kierkegaard's insistence that the

---

[27] Lawlor, op. cit., p. 170.   [28] A. C. Bradley, op. cit., p. 34.
[29] R. B. Sewall, *The Vision of Tragedy*, Yale U.P., 1965, p. 5.
[30] Plato, *Theatetus* clxxvi, quoted by Dixon, op. cit., p. 178 (*Dialogues*, ed. Jowett, 1875, IV,
p. 326).   [31] *De Civ. Dei* I. viii.

effect of a man's encounter with Christ is the discovery that his fate is not dependent on the incongruities of mortal existence but rather upon the way in which he goes forward to meet them.[32] Christianity affirms the operation of a dual justice in the universe. It discerns the working out of moral judgements in man's world, but appreciates that they cannot be made with precision because of their relation with the morally irrelevant fact of power. The Divine supremacy over history is compatible with evident inexactness; but above and beyond the rough judgements of worldly events there is apprehended a future history and an end of history that qualifies and redeems facts observable in the world:[33]

> There are, in short, tangents of moral meaning in history; but there are no clear or exact patterns. The moral obscurities of history must either tempt men to the despairing conclusion that there is no meaning in the total historical enterprise and that history is merely a bewildering confusion of 'death for the right cause, death for the wrong cause, pæans of victory and groans of defeat', or that it is under a sovereignty too mysterious to conform fully to the patterns of meaning which human beings are able to construct. Yet this sovereignty is not pure mystery, since the experiences of life, in which egotism and self-worship are punished, are in rough and inexact relation to an ultimate judgement upon the self, perceived by the self in the experience of repentance and faith.[34]

Suffering innocence itself, which proclaims the moral ambiguity of events within the human condition, can, for this faith, display a relationship to a justice which, if it does not promise to overcome what is contradictory in man's existence, promises to resolve it.

Instances of unmerited suffering there may be; but man in himself is not innocent. The web of tragedy is woven not only out of mischance, but also out of the desires and passions of a fallen creature; and the means of the penalizing judgement that is inflicted upon him is his own world, which must needs partake of what he is. Such intervals of peace as mankind establish on earth can therefore only mediate solace to their true state of wretchedness, and to that innate liability to the tragic to which both their natures and their history bear witness. In our life on earth, Augustine declares,

> our peace is as uncertain, as we are ignorant of their hearts, with whom we hold it, and though we nigh know today what they would do, tomorrow we shall not. Who should be greater friends than those of

[32] See P. L. Holmer, 'Søren Kierkegaard: Faith in a Tragic World', *The Tragic Vision and the Christian Faith*, ed. N. A. Scott, N.Y., 1957, p. 186.
[33] R. Niebuhr, *Faith and History*, London, 1949, pp. 143–8.
[34] ibid., p. 150.

231

one family? yet how many secret plots of malice lie even amongst such, to expel security? . . . So, then, if a man's own private house afford him no shelter from these incursions, what shall the city do. . . ?[35]

Augustine's undertaking in *The City of God* is to show that the security and justice which appeared to have been guaranteed by the Roman Empire are in fact not to be sought on earth, and are a treasure, not of the body, but of the soul.[36] Only the final triumph of the City of God can give meaning to life in what is otherwise a 'vale of mortal miseries'.[37] For it is peopled by a natural humanity, wounded by the Fall and by their sins, by nature yet creatures of God, but capable of all the perversities implied in their ultimate perversity of Godlessness.

According to R. B. Sewall, the moral inadequacy of the tragic hero's position is not only to be sensed by an audience, but is an indispensable part of the hero's own apprehensions:

The suffering is not so much that of physical ordeal (although this can be part of it) but of mental or spiritual anguish as the protagonist acts in the knowledge that what he feels he must do is in some sense wrong – as he sees himself both good and bad, justified yet unjustified.[38]

The clue to the protagonist's degree of responsibility within the tragic downfall is surely to be sought in that destruction of kindness and naturalness which is common to the careers of Shakespeare's great tragic heroes. All, in the process of the action, must overcome the force of natural affection, and obstruct the 'compunctious visitings of nature' which bring to human affairs a gladness and a healing otherwise unattainable.

To make possible the tragic waste, all occasion of tenderness must be decisively rejected; the current must be finally earthed. So Ophelia is thrust from Hamlet's path; so, too, Lear is separated, by his own decree, from his natural daughter. Once the 'natural' is excluded, we are sadly confined within the range of the possible; and that limitation points only one way. Only one course is open, the assertion of 'I am I', the descent from the illusion of power to self-destroying powerlessness.[39]

For this assertion that, in Shakespeare, 'the greatest good is the holding of the natural bond',[40] Lawlor can find abundant testimony in the plays themselves, as well as in the pronouncements of critics. Indeed, where the absence of the mitigation of an ultimate moral order is most keenly felt, the good of the natural bond is most in evidence. Thus J. Stampfer, for

[35] *De Civ. Dei* XIX. v.
[36] J. N. Figgis, *The Political Aspects of S. Augustine's 'The City of God'*, 1921, pp. 32–6.
[37] *De Civ. Dei* XIX. viii.   [38] op. cit., p. 47.
[39] Lawlor, *The Tragic Sense in Shakespeare*, 1960, p. 117.
[40] ibid., p. 181.

whom the message of tragedy is chaos and negation, is able to his own surprise to find one source of assurance :

> Strangely enough, however, while the denouement seems to destroy any basis for providential justice, it would seem to vindicate Cordelia with regard to the bond of human nature. . . . It would seem, then, by the denouement that the universe belongs to Edmund, but mankind belongs to Cordelia. In a palsied cosmos, orphan man must either live by the moral law, which is the bond of love, or swiftly destroy himself.[41]

The quelling of kindness, and the assumption of self-hood with which it is associated, appears in the course of the tragic action to be what Miss M. C. Bradbrook calls 'a sort of suicide'.[42] In *Macbeth* the violence that is resorted to is most readily seen to be self-violence, and the protagonist's real victim to be himself;[43] but in his fate he speaks for all Shakespeare's tragic heroes. The tragedies reveal 'the inadequacy of man setting up on his own'[44] – that the will to live unto the self is inimical to human good, and the path to baleful obsession :

> The proposition 'I am I' is incapable of moderation; thus a world of individuals is in the last resort a world which destroys itself. To choose 'I am I' is finally not to be.[45]

It is thus, declares Lawlor, that the matter of justice is shown not to be the ultimate question in tragic experience. The will to isolation in the individual hero betokens a humanity permanently wrapped in illusion – and punishment is hardly to be predicated of those who fail to achieve realization. The tragic hero's punishment can only be the knowledge of the waste he has brought about by the separate existence he has willed.[46] Shakespearian tragedy thus shows

> the utter punishment of separate existence, on the one hand; and on the other, the endlessly fruitful possibilities once the human circle holds. . . . The power of the natural bond is the only final reality; and as such it illuminates and sustains all else.[47]

The natural bond is clearly a good; whether it may be described as 'the only final reality' is a larger question. In a purely moral context it may be so. But it may well be asked whether the moral is not rather eloquent of the spiritual state of man : it is not to be ignored that Macbeth's destruction of 'that great bond' is associated with an inability to pronounce 'Amen' (II. ii. 30). In Lawlor's view, the adopting of the position

---

[41] 'The Catharsis of *King Lear*', *S.S.* XIII, 1960, pp. 6–7.
[42] 'The Sources of *Macbeth*', *S.S.* IV, 1951, p. 46.
[43] ibid.   [44] Lawlor, op. cit., p. 181.
[45] ibid., p. 169.   [46] ibid., p. 171.   [47] ibid., p. 182.

'I am I' is the consequence of the banishing of natural affection; but a spiritual understanding would make it the cause. Thus, to Fulke Greville, it is man's urge to 'trust to his selfe-constellation' which creates the confusion and inhumanity of his world[48] – and the taking of the fatal position 'I am I' is itself caused by man's spiritual blindness and apostasy. For in a God-centred universe there can be no divorce between moral and spiritual: by Aquinas's definition,

> The ultimate basis of the moral law is the eternal law, which is nothing else than the divine reason or will issuing its commands to respect the natural order and forbidding it to be disturbed on pain of punishment.[49]

There can be no scorning of human kindness which is not first a defiance of God.

Nor, in the human condition, can human kindness long be sustained without the acknowledgement of the Creator. The soul of man, according to Augustine, is faced with clear and fateful alternatives:

> It must serve its Master, lest it be trodden down by its own servant.[50]

For him, as for Aquinas, the goodness of a human act is dependent upon the end to which the will is directed; and consequently no action can be good, or come to good, which is performed with an object short of God's glory.[51] This does not mean that man must avoid involvement in the created order: if a creature is loved with reference to the Creator, that love is charity, and not cupidity; but those human loves 'not having God, but the will itself for their end'[52] are in themselves evil, and must produce evil. The good or evil of an action may not be externally apparent. The delivering up of Christ by God and of the man Jesus by Judas may appear similar; yet one is charity and the other is treachery:

> You see, we have to look, not at what a man does, but with what mind and will he does it.[53]

An act committed with good intention is 'light', though its outcome, in a world where outcomes must be uncertain, may be 'darkness'. In a bad intention, even the light is darkness. And

> if the very intention of your heart, by which you do what you do and of which you are conscious, is tarnished by a craving for earthly and temporal things and as a result blinded, how much more is the

48 (Section II, p. 154.)

49 B. Roland-Gosselin, 'St Augustine's System of Morals', *A Monument to St Augustine*, Sheed and Ward, 1934, p. 237.

50 *In Jo. Ev. Tr.* xxiii. 5. 51 *S.T.* Ia IIae xviii. 4, *ad R.*

52 *De Civ. Dei* XIV. xi; XIX. xii. 53 *In Epist. Jo. ad Parth. Tract. decem* vii. 7.

action whose outcome is uncertain, tarnished and enveloped in darkness.[54]

The final outcome of the doctrine is Luther's distinction between the corporal and the spiritual realms in the judging of men's qualities and deeds, and his insistence at the same time that the inner and the outer in man, like the two realms that he dwells in, are interrelated. Thus,

all knowledge and virtue and whatever good we desire and search for in reliance upon our natural possibilities will turn out to be evil kinds of good, because they are not measured according to God's standard but according to that of the creature, i.e. according to our selfish ends. For how can one refer anything to God if one does not love him above everything else? And how can one love him if one does not know him? How can man know him if, by fault of his first sin, he is bound to darkness in all his thinking and feeling? So then, unless faith enlightens him and love sets him free, man cannot will or have or do anything good – he can do only evil even in case [*sic*] he does good.[55]

Without God there is no righteousness. Thus a creaturely aspiration, manifest in the will to selfhood of the embattled tragic hero, is the cause rather than the product of his violence; and the natural bond which he breaks, far from being the one final reality, is sustained only by service to a greater.

This greater reality, in the evidence of their will to creaturely absoluteness no less than in their deeds, Shakespeare's tragic heroes do not serve. Their actions are eloquent of a 'friendship of this world', and the goals they set themselves have to do with the pride of life, and the lust of the eye and of the flesh. Their passions are in keeping with their preoccupations; they are compounded of the hatred, debate, emulation, wrath, contentions, envyings and murders which Paul describes as the works of the flesh manifest in those who are not to inherit the kingdom of God,[56] and which Augustine would include among those '*darkened* affections' which signify removal from His presence.[57] The degree of passion to which they are provoked points to a cause in themselves rather than in outward circumstances:

People who impute their anger or impatience to what injures or troubles them, talk foolishly. For tribulation does not make anyone impatient but it brings to light the impatience that was or is in him. Thus everybody can learn in tribulation what kind of a man he really is.[58]

[54] *De Serm. Dom. in Monte* II. xiii. 46.
[55] *Lectures on Romans* (viii. 1–4), tr. W. Pauck (L.C.C. XV), 1961, p. 218.
[56] *De Civ. Dei* XIV. ii; *Gal.* v. 19–21.
[57] *Conf.* I. xviii. 28.   [58] Luther, *Romans*, p. 156.

The extremes of conduct to which passion drives them are marks of the domination within them of concupiscence, through whose tyrannous demands the victim 'considers good whatever he desires, even if this judgement contradicts the universal judgement'[59] of reason's 'safer guides'. But it is perhaps in their not scrupling to 'hurl their hatred at others for any reason whatever' that the heroes above all show what Calvin terms 'the mentality common to the children of this world'.[60] For the love which the law of God demands bestows itself without regard for the recipient's merit; but the world's children deny the claim to be

> neighbour'd, pitied, and reliev'd[61]

of those whom they deem to be unworthy of their friendship. The hatred of any creature of God betokens the 'unsoundness' of the self. Life will offer many an occasion for dispute; but

> in a quarrel for earth, turn not to earth. Whoever hates his brother may not say that he walks in the light . . . if you hate your brothers, what and where are you?[62]

But the deed which Shakespeare's heroes must characteristically yearn to accomplish, and which brings tragedy upon them, is evidence for its own condemnation. Both morally and spiritually it will not stand scrutiny. The sum of the ten commandments, Luther declares, is

> 'What thou wouldest have done to thyself, the same do thou to another'. God presses upon this point, saying: 'Such measure as thou metest, the same shall be measured to thee again'. With this measuring line has God marked the whole world.[63]

By this same measuring line, the deeds of Shakespeare's tragic heroes, like those of men in general, are revealed as 'ungodly, sacrilegious, and evil in every respect'.[64] And the quality of their virtues becomes evident in the question whether Othello would like his treatment of Desdemona to be applied to himself, or whether Lear would be dealt with as he deals with Cordelia. Their actions, in human terms, are only too understandable; but, considered in themselves, they betray a state of mind of appalling depravity and arrogance. For God alone has the right to visit condign judgement upon his creatures; yet so little akin is such procedure to the pattern of goodness, that

> He that might the vantage best have took,
> Found out the remedy.[65]

59 E. Gilson, *The Philosophy of St Thomas Aquinas*, 1924, p. 252; *S.T.* Ia IIae lviii. 4, 5, *ad R.*
60 *Commentaries*, L.C.C. XXIII, p. 331.   61 *King Lear* I. i. 119.
62 *In Epist. Jo. ad Parth. Tract. decem* i. 11.   63 *Table-Talk*, xlii.
64 *Bondage*, tr. Parker and Johnston, 1959, p. 253.   65 *Measure for Measure* II. ii. 74–5.

The inhumanity of the heroes is the inevitable outcome of presumption; in the scope for savagery which they arrogate to themselves may be seen the will to build in their own imaginations what Augustine calls 'a darkened likeness of Thy Omnipotency'.[66]

That this will is so little evident to the spectators must be due in some measure to their sharing, in their humanity, the state of mind and spirit of the hero. It is due also, however, to the relative gradualness with which it assumes possession of him, and the excellence of the qualities and delights which otherwise centre upon his experience. The beginning of his apostasy is not a revolt, but a straying:

> Woe to those who wander away from Thy paths, who love Thy foot-prints rather than Thyself. . . . The elements of happiness which they still find in their works of the flesh they owe to the radiance of Thy light, but the darkness they love weakens their eyes and renders them incapable of supporting Thy sight. The night of sin gradually enfolds their conscience. Through no longer regarding as evil what flatters and enchains them, they at last cease to be willing to recognize either the True or the Good.[67]

The particular stages in the tragic hero's motion toward spiritual downfall are not easy to discern; indeed, the enormity of the conclusion must be for many the first sign of something radically amiss:

> For as a snake does not creep on with open steps, but advances by the very minutest efforts of its several scales; so the slippery motion of falling away from what is good takes possession of the negligent only gradually, and beginning from a perverse desire for the likeness of God, arrives in the end at the likeness of beasts.[68]

As in every approach towards evil, it is always a good that is sought, and the goodness of what is desired tends therefore to obscure the true quality of the seeking. The good which Macbeth seeks is obviously one from which he is disqualified; but Lear seems to wish nothing for himself, but only to see gratitude in others, and Othello's desire for chastity and honourable dealing is blameless. Their characteristic wills, however, are restricted to the mundane – and in this they are corruptible:

> our soul becomes tarnished through our desire for the things of the earth, though the earth itself is clean in its own nature and level.[69]

But failure to recognize the hero's depravity of will may finally reside in unwillingness to acquiesce in the judgement that comes upon it. Doubt

[66] Conf. II. vi. 14.
[67] De Lib. Arb. II. xvi. 43, quoted by B. Roland-Gosselin, 'St Augustine's System of Morals', A Monument, 1934, p. 239.
[68] De Trin. XII. xi. 16.   [69] De Serm. Dom. in Monte II. xiii. 44.

concerning the justice of God can arise, according to Augustine, from moral dishonesty, as well as from intellectual perplexity: there can be amongst mankind a refusal to acknowledge sin and to face its consequences – for in the truth revealed in God's punitive act all are condemned, and many hate the condemnation.[70] In this respect there is evident in criticism a marked reluctance to reject the virtues for which the hero is admired, and an attitude of reverence – if not of 'worship'[71] – toward them, that must inevitably raise the matter of ultimate loyalties.

For man must be a dweller in one of two cities – the *civitas terrena*, with its love of the self in contempt of God, and the *civitas caelestis*, loving God in contempt of the self[72] – and he must choose between the two loves:

> The one is holy, the other foul; the one social, the other selfish; the one thinks of the common advantage for the sake of the higher association, the other reduces even the common good to a possession of its own for the sake of selfish ascendancy; the one is subject to, the other a rival to God; the one is peaceful, the other turbulent.[73]

The love of Shakespeare's tragic heroes is earthly and selfish; and they are therefore to be numbered among the ungodly who, trusting in their own powers rather than in the power of God, can see only ruin when their hopes are ruined.

> For their hope was no hope, but a crooked and presumptuous trust in their own works and their own righteousness.[74]

In their attitude of 'I am I', and the desperate harshnesses which it drives them to, is to be found evidence of that 'sink[ing] downwards into our own keeping'[75] which is the beginning of apostasy and tragedy alike.

In the course of the tragic action the hero may become concerned with many things; but his true concern is with himself. N. A. Scott, in an account of the tragic experience based upon much recent work on the subject, sees in the protagonist 'a man who has taken upon himself the full burden of his own destiny'.[76] The posture is not basically God-like, since it is part of an attempt to deal with unquiet and discordant forces which threaten his own existence; but it is essentially not God-seeking, since the will to alleviation, or to defiant assertion, is at the same

[70] J. Burnaby, *Amor Dei*, 1938, pp. 198–9, quoting *Contra Jul. Imp. Op.* III. xxiv, and *In Jo Ev. Tr.* xc. 2.
[71] A. C. Bradley, *Shakespearean Tragedy*, p. 23.   [72] *De Civ. Dei* XIV. xxviii.
[73] C. N. Cochrane, *Christianity and Classical Culture*, Oxford, 1940, p. 489.
[74] Luther, *Romans* (v. 5), L.C.C. XV, p. 161.   [75] *De Trin.* IX. vii. 13.
[76] 'The Tragic Vision and The Christian Faith', *Anglican Theological Review* XLV, 1963, p. 29.

time a seeking to impose upon external incongruities the pattern of a justice and order peculiar to the self. The hero, in fact, is driven to the self-choosing to which in truth he aspires;[77] and the *hubris* which, according to Scott, is involved in the choice, is to be defined as

> that extreme passion with which the tragic man hurls himself against the boundaries of his existence in an effort to summon out of the innermost depths of reality some promise of the possibility of his being finally accommodated.[78]

Both the reality which impels him, however, and the reality to which he resorts, do not extend beyond a temporal good; and thus it comes about that the inordinate desire of a temporal good is both the means and the expression of an inordinate self-love.[79]

The hero's self-affirmation must therefore lead to his whole-hearted pursuit or assertion of a value or ideal which is a partial and limited good; and the endeavour

> has the effect of throwing his life out of gear with certain facets of reality which also have a valid claim upon him.[80]

Instead of a concern that the self should conform to the widest reality that can be ascertained, there is an assumption that reality is somehow comprised within the bounds of the self. Thus 'the whole slant and bias of the authentically tragic drama . . . is humanistic'.[81] Man, seeking as it were something more than the whole, and striving to govern it by a law of his own, comes inevitably to care for a part, and to be made less.[82] He comes to 'delight in himself', to be a 'pleaser' of himself.[83] The mind 'grows over-occupied with its own dealings and the restless pleasures gathered from them';[84] and the glory that it seeks is human.

In the quest for meaning, the tragic hero turns, fatally, to himself. In the absence of a larger vision, must he not, indeed, make

> himselfe his end,
> And what he vnderstands, that [take] to friend?[85]

But his trust is thereby placed in what is his principal disadvantage; for in so choosing himself and shouldering the burden of his own destiny, he is committed, simply by reason of his humanity, to an understanding that

---

[77] ibid.   [78] ibid.
[79] *S.T.* Ia IIae lxxvii. 4, *ad R.*   [80] Scott, op. cit., p. 30.
[81] H. J. Muller, *The Spirit of Tragedy*, N.Y., 1956, p. 18, quoted by Scott, ibid.
[82] *De Trin.* XII. ix. 14.   [83] *De Civ. Dei* XIV. xiii.   [84] *De Trin.* X. v. 7.
[85] Greville, 'An Inqvisition vpon Fame and Honovr', st. 11, *Poems and Dramas*, ed. G. Bullough, 1938, I, p. 194.

is something less than the whole truth.[86] He draws in the horizons of reality to accommodate a truth which he can compass, and makes a world of his own – and thus turns aside a good which is incommunicable and common to pursue a good which is private and inferior.[87] In doing so, he is guilty; for his action is the very definition of sin. His resort to the standards and means of a transient satisfaction – the unqualified desire for a personal happiness – is lust; and his disregard of the Source of everlasting value, and the flouting of its decrees, is pride.[88] The predominance which mortal man may desire involves both power and righteousness; the tragic hero, in a fashion characteristic of fallen mankind, desires the former before he attain the latter.[89] The soul seeks a likeness to God, not by the true course of submission, but by the perverse path of imitation. In its striving toward the highest, it

also looks at its changeable self and in some sense comes into its own mind. The reason is simply that it is distinct from God, and yet is something capable of causing itself pleasure after God. It is better if it forgets itself through love of the unchangeable God, or despises itself utterly in comparison with Him. But if, so to speak, it goes out of its way to produce a false imitation of God, and to will to take pleasure in its own power, then the greater it wishes to become the less it becomes in fact. And that is *pride, the beginning of all sin*; and *the beginning of the pride of man is to fall off from God* (*Ecclus.* x. 13, 12).[90]

The defect in the tragic hero, therefore, is not some flaw of character which might possibly be remedied, but that by which humanity as a whole is defective – that is, his creaturely finitude. Once he has chosen to be the artificer and arbiter of his own destiny, he is impelled to other choices which may be the immediate causes of tragic event;

But since there would be no guilt – and hence no suffering – had not the protagonist committed himself to some partial and limited good, and since this is a commitment that he would not have undertaken had he not been attempting through it to affirm his humanity, it must be concluded that the fundamental cause of his guilt is that act of transcendence whereby he 'chose himself'. The ultimate offense, in other words, of the tragic man is his very existence as a limited and conditioned creature . . . [and] his presumptuousness in daring to speak out at all in his own behalf.[91]

[86] Scott, op. cit., p. 30.

[87] Augustine, *De Lib. Arb.* II. xix. 53; Cochrane, op. cit., p. 488.

[88] Aquinas, *De Malo* viii. 1, *ad R.*; quoted by W. O. Cross, 'The Problem of Human Evil', *Anglican Theological Review* XLV, 1963, p. 21. [89] (Section II, p. 88.)

[90] *De Lib. Arb.* III. xxv. 76. [91] Scott, op. cit., p. 31.

Scott's conclusion echoes that of Schopenhauer:

> The true sense of tragedy is the deeper insight, that it is not his own individual sins that the hero atones for, but original sin, *i.e.* the crime of existence itself.[92]

To be alive is no sin; the error is in the attempt to transform a creaturely existence into a creaturely transcendence. In trying to fashion his world according to his desires, man would invest them with an absoluteness. But 'the end of all these desires' cannot possibly be in the desires themselves.[93] In all his aspirations man remains a creature, and his sin arises from his not being satisfied to remain so. He seeks to realize himself by turning his creatureliness into infinity; whereas his salvation depends upon his subjecting his creaturely weakness to God's infinite good. The life that he trusts in is the way of death: for God is the life of his soul, and in His wisdom must show Himself to be the enemy and judge of every human pretension which transgresses the limits of human finiteness.[94] Any such pretension comes under the curse ordained for him

> that trusteth in man, and maketh flesh his arm, and whose heart departeth from the Lord (*Jer.* xvii. 5),[95]

or the *nemesis* which decrees that

> misfortune from heaven shall overtake men who forget to think as mortals.[96]

The sin of which history is a record, declares Reinhold Niebuhr,

> is the consequence of man's abortive effort to overcome his insecurity by his own power, to hide the finiteness of his intelligence by pretensions of omniscience and to seek for emancipation from his ambiguous position by his own resources. Sin is, in short, the consequence of man's inclination to usurp the prerogatives of God, to think more highly of himself than he ought to think, thus making destructive use of his freedom by not observing the limits to which a creaturely freedom is bound.[97]

Niebuhr's seeing in the continuous drama of human existence, not so much a contest between good and evil forces in history, as an unceasing contest between all men and God,[98] is in keeping with Augustine's judgement of man's history as being 'one of continuous and persistent self-

---

[92] *The World as Will and Idea*, London, 1883, I, p. 328.

[93] Augustine, *De Vera Relig.* liii. 102.

[94] R. Niebuhr, *Faith and History*, London, 1949, p. 117.

[95] Augustine, *Ench.* xxx. 114.

[96] W. Macneile Dixon, *Tragedy*, 1929, p. 86.

[97] op. cit., p. 137.   [98] ibid., p. 141.

abuse'[99] through the vain dream that he can usurp the place of the Creator, and the consequent penalty which he brings upon himself by his violation of the inexorable laws of the universe. To this tragedy which natural man destines upon himself in his striving for a creaturely realization and completeness is to be contrasted the faith of the New Testament, that God's love and power will confer upon man a completeness which the soul of itself has not the means of attaining, and overcome the evil introduced into human life through man's attempt to achieve wholeness by his own strength.[100] The choosing of the self, and the striving to preserve it, are destructive for man because they are a denial of his true nature and destiny. In a Christian perception,

> It is recognized that the true self has a dimension, transcending its contingent historical existence, and that it could destroy itself in that dimension by trying too desperately to keep alive.[101]

Whoever saves his life will lose it; but he who will subject his life to the 'losing' implied in the recognition of a truth, and the claim of a love, that go beyond the demands of self, will save it.

> Agape is nevertheless the final law of human existence, because every realization of the self which is motivated by concern for the self inevitably results in a narrower and more self-contained self than the freedom of the self requires. Consequently the highest forms of self-realization are those which are not intended or calculated but are the fruit of some movement of 'grace', which draws the self out of itself despite itself into the love of God and the neighbour.[102]

In the apostate and self-regarding will of man lies what Max Scheler calls the 'necessary bond between good and evil',[103] and the cause of the tragic nature of existence itself. The good and the evil among mankind are not distinguished by what befalls them in their lives, but share one tragic fate because they are at one in manifesting a love which is worldly and self-appraising:

> For they both endure one scourge, not because they are both guilty of one disordered life, but because they both do too much affect this transitory life; not in like measure, but yet both together.[104]

These words are applicable to the tragic hero in Shakespeare. Richard and Macbeth are clearly villainous; and, as Bradley reminds us, 'it is

[99] Cochrane, *Christianity and Classical Culture*, p. 241.
[100] Niebuhr, op. cit., p. 163; see Section II, pp. 96–7.
[101] ibid., p. 199.   [102] ibid., p. 198.
[103] *On The Eternal in Man*, tr. B. Noble, London, 1960, p. 234.
[104] *De Civ. Dei* I. ix.

important to observe that Shakespeare does admit such heroes',[105] and thus contradicts Aristotle's precept.[106] Bradley absolves the rest of the heroes from 'conscious breach of right',[107] but he can recognize some apprehensions of error in them that are less conscious and less pronounced; and it is to be wondered indeed how much room for consciousness of error may exist in an attitude like Lear's

> Better thou
> Hadst not been born than not to have pleas'd
> me better
>
> (I. i. 234–5).

What emerges, however, is that it is not necessary for Shakespeare's heroes to be good, but to be great.[108] Greatness Macbeth shares with the rest; and the question must arise to what extent he is otherwise an exception. For in their self-choosing, and their will to creaturely transcendence, they are all akin. In the one case, the nature of the chosen means betrays the quality of the will behind it – but a similar will may be apprehended in the others:

> To go beyond the limits of humanity (and this again we shall see in *King Lear*) is to place oneself outside the sphere of humanity. It is, in fact, the ironic fulfilment of Lady Macbeth's invocation to the dark powers; she and Macbeth both are to be made unnatural. . . . It is an attempt to reach beyond the human condition.[109]

The human condition is one of man's essential inadequacy, and his need for strength from without. In this state, a consciousness of power, and a creaturely self-reliance, must be founded upon illusion – and the more they are persisted in, the greater the illusion must become. In the character of Iago an underlying dread of littleness can be seen to start the process of self-magnification:

> Mostly he defends himself from the awareness of this self-contempt by transferring his hostility into furious fantasies of his great power.[110]

A similar necessity may be at work in the claim of the upstart Tamburlaine – made with a degree or so of justification – to

> hold the Fates bound fast in yron chaines,
> And with my hand turne Fortunes wheel about;[111]

[105] Bradley, *Shakespearean Tragedy*, 1956, p. 22.
[106] *Poetics*, xiii.   [107] Bradley, op. cit., p.22.   [108] ibid.
[109] Lawlor, *The Tragic Sense*, 1960, p. 120.
[110] M. Rosenberg, 'In Defense of Iago', *S.Q.* VI, 1955, p. 153.
[111] I, 11. 369–70.

and the process may even be adduced amidst the endearing uncouthness of a Dogberry, when the possibility of his inadequacy first impinges upon his apprehension:

> I am a wise fellow; and, which is more, an officer; and, which is more, a householder; and, which is more, as pretty a piece of flesh as any is in Messina; and one that knows the law, go to; and a rich fellow enough, go to; and a fellow that hath had losses; and one that hath two gowns, and everything handsome about him.[112]

There is no difference in principle between Dogberry's two gowns and the

> large effects
> That troop with majesty;

and if there is a difference in principle between the folly of a Lear and the witlessness of a Dogberry, there is none in effect.

Shakespeare's great tragedies have been called 'tragedies of obsession';[113] they could as well be referred to as having their basis in the illusion of adequacy. Each hero places an absolute trust in some characteristic 'great power' to whose operation he commits his own and others' destinies in the confidence that it affords him the measure of reality. Their confidence does not arise from mere imagination: their 'power' may consist in political eminence, or in personal ability, or in a moral excellence, ideal or righteousness which has considerable basis in fact. This they assert with 'extreme passion' against whatever threatens their security; but the possibility exists that, if the fierce inner compulsion with which their action is associated does not indeed draw its energies from a deep and necessary sense of their simple human inadequacy, its very fierceness witnesses to the smallness of the power or the quality they trust in. And there is the further possibility that the actions to which they are impelled in their tragic career may be, like the actions of Iago, a restless and compulsive attempt to force the bounds of consciousness away from a true self-knowledge – and humility – towards the world of action, or towards some self-congratulating notion or image of adequacy, or of a creaturely excellence. It can certainly be said that the self-estimate of a Lear or an Othello is responsible for their being driven to their self-destructive ends through the assault of 'furious fantasies' – and that there is to be found in Shakespeare's tragic heroes what has been termed a 'will to self-assertion, to unlimited self-hood',[114] which is the beginning of all evil. For in prizing, and seeking to impose, a righteousness derived from their own creaturely strength and vision, they are precluded from

112 *Much Ado* IV. ii. 81–7.
113 A. P. Rossiter, *Angel with Horns*, 1961, p. 259.
114 ibid., p. 218.

244

the 'weighing of their own infirmity' which results from a spiritual vision, and thus denied the saving knowledge that

no man is able by his own works or his own power to put away sins.[115]

Their histories may well serve as confirmation of Augustine's teaching that the soul which aspires no higher than to a human glory must necessarily err; that

those things which she seems to account virtues, and thereby to sway her affections, if they be not all referred unto God, are indeed rather vices than virtues;[116]

and that, where God is not known,

all the gifts, either of the body or of the mind, which thou enjoyest, as wisdom, righteousness, holiness, eloquence, power, beauty, and riches, are but slavish instruments of the devil, and with all these thou art compelled to serve him, and to advance his kingdom.[117]

The will to righteousness, in those whose loyalties are earthly, carries within it greater peril than a declining into manifest evil. The 'white devil', which forces men to commit spiritual sins in a quest for apparent righteousness, is far more dangerous, as Luther sees it, than the 'black devil' which impels them to those deeds of the flesh which all the world acknowledges to be sin.[118] They are enticed, not to those things of body, mind or circumstances that may be equally desired by others, but toward the very works which belong properly to the good.[119] Their works, however, 'incur vainglory, and so lose their true goodness',[120] because the soul that covets them wills above all

to think of the works of righteousness as its own, acquired by itself for itself.[121]

The means for the service of God becomes a means for the soul's self-worship; the soul itself, by this process, may be transformed into an idol:

Some worship the soul in place of the most high God, the first intellectual creature which the Father made by means of the truth, that it might ever behold the truth.[122]

But the greatest and best of qualities may, through the depraved soul's 'perverse desire of height',[123] become the object

of a damnable and vain glorious end, a joy in human vanity.[124]

---

[115] Luther, *Galatians* (i. 4), ed. Watson, 1953, p. 53.
[116] *De Civ. Dei* XIX. xxv.   [117] Luther, *Galatians* (i. 4), p. 54.   [118] ibid.
[119] *De Spir. et Litt.* xi. 18.   [120] *De Civ. Dei.* XIX. xxv.   [121] *De Spir. et Litt.* xi. 18.
[122] *De Vera Relig.* xxxvii. 68.   [123] *De Civ. Dei* XIV. xiii.   [124] *Conf.* III. iv. 7.

The legitimate aspiration of a lofty spirit towards pre-eminence in human affairs may become a brutalizing lust for the 'golden round' of political predominance; it can allow itself to be entranced by the 'pomp, pride and circumstance' of its worldly occupation, and the qualities created in its discharge, into forgetting the humanity upon which these splendours are raised; or it can assume that the eminence of the place it occupies in the world will extend to its own nature, and make it 'ague-proof'. In the most selfless of employments the temptation will always be strong to do 'the right deed for the wrong reason',[125] to yield to the sinister and empty joy of wishing, through heroic endeavour, 'to be feared and loved of men'.[126] Even in a generous mind's finding 'great love'[127] in those who are subject to it, there must remain the suspicion of its exulting in a confirmation of its own worth – of its being

> pleased at being loved and feared, not for Thy sake, but in Thy stead.[128]

Modern man chooses to ignore what Reinhold Niebuhr calls the simple but profound truth that 'man's life remains self-contradictory in its sin, no matter how high human culture rises';[129] but the Elizabethans were assured of the spiritual perils that beset the noble and aspiring soul – that

> it is to be feared that where maiestie approcheth to excesse, and the mynde is obsessed with inordinate glorie, lest pride, of al vices most horrible, shuld sodainely entre and take prisoner the harte of a gentil-man called to autoritie.[130]

Their apprehension was firmly based upon Christian teaching. Augustine classes the love of praise and glory, and ambition, as irrational passions.[131] For Aquinas, no human excellence may in itself be a source of pleasure, since all honour for it is due to God, and pleasure in honour received should relate only to a man's consequent ability to do good to others. In this definition, and in the characterization of an inordinate desire for honour, may be seen the beginning of more than one tragic hero's downfall:

> Now the desire of honour may be inordinate in three ways. First, when a man desires the recognition of an excellence he hath not. . . . Secondly, when a man desires honour without referring it to God. Thirdly, when a man's appetite rests in honour itself, without referring it to the profit of others.[132]

---

[125] T. S. Eliot, 'Murder in the Cathedral', *Collected Plays*, 1962, p. 30.
[126] *Conf.* X. xxxvi. 59. [127] *Othello* II. i. 205.
[128] Augustine, op. cit., X. xxxvi. 59.
[129] R. Niebuhr, *Beyond Tragedy*, London, 1947, p. 18.
[130] Sir. T. Elyot, *The Gouernour* II. iv (Everyman edn, 1937, p. 126).
[131] *De Lib. Arb.* I. viii. 18. [132] *S.T.* IIa IIae cxxxi. 1, *ad R.*

Where there exists a creaturely will to excellence, or a delight in it, which is not dedicated to God's service beyond any concern for the self, or where there is to be found a reliance upon the self which does not devolve from a submission to God, there exists a 'canker of our nature' which can only enlarge itself in further evil. The ordinary human state of self-congratulation is in itself tragic. It is tragic in its inevitable destiny of evil consequence, but also in its present untruth and illusion – and it is in this sense that the psalmist can promise that it shall

soon be cut down like the grass, and wither as the green herb (xxxvii. 2).

In appearance, human pride exalts; but to a spiritual discernment, though it 'vaunt aloud', yet it is 'rack'd with deep despair', and carries within itself the seeds of both illusion and destruction. A catastrophic outcome is thus an incidental happening, and less truly noteworthy than what precedes it; and even where catastrophe does not occur, the downfall already exists, and those skilled in the spirit may be, with the poet, 'Doubting sad end of principle unsound'.[133] For the pride of man is its own defeat :

In humility therefore there is this to be admired, that it elevates the heart : and pride in this, that it dejects it. This seems strangely contrary, that elevation should be below, and dejection aloft. But godly humility subjects one to his superior : and God is above all; therefore humility exalts one, in making him God's subject. But pride the vice, refusing this subjection, falls from him that is above all, and so becomes more base by far (than those that stand) fulfilling this place of the Psalm : 'Thou hast cast them down in their own exaltation'. He says not when they were exalted, they were dejected afterwards : but in their very exaltation were they cast down, their elevation was their ruin.[134]

Their virtues are their vices; and the vision and the powers that they have put their trust in are small enough. They will be rendered even smaller by that self-concern which will impose limitation upon their natures, and confirm in them a preoccupation with things that have little reality. They are lost before they can act; and, when the tragic perplexity comes upon them, they can only, like the violet in the sun,

Corrupt with virtuous season.[135]

It is the illusion of adequacy, and the perverse choosing of the self, which, according to A. P. Rossiter, is most evident in the tragedy of *Macbeth*. In that play, he writes, Shakespeare symbolizes the forces that

---

[133] Spenser, *Faerie Queene* V. xi. 2.   [134] Augustine, *De Civ. Dei* XIV. xiii.
[135] *Measure for Measure* II. ii. 168.

operate in every moral conflict. In the depths of all such conflicts we are brought to the contemplation of something of fearful implication that is both alien and familiar –

> of something powerful, anomalous and apparently ungraspable. I call that an impulsion, and use the name *will* for it for lack of a better : meaning thereby something less intellectual and consciously scheming, less argumentative, belonging more to the blood and the elementary passions, than we commonly think of when we use the term. It is the passionate will to self-assertion, to unlimited self-hood, and especially the impulsion to force the world (and everything in it) to *my* pattern, in *my* time, and with my own hand.[136]

This self-assertive impulse Shakespeare presents as a force promoting disorder – 'in man, in nature, in everything'. Rossiter will not 'call the trend to order "love", and the trend to disorder "hate" or "evil" – though it is evil', on the grounds that to do so would be a 'Christian simplification', and that Shakespeare himself goes beyond any such simplification. The plays confine themselves to the human plane, and demonstrate how, at that level, the results of 'hard-willed assertion' develop into success, insensibility, separateness, remorse and monstrousness, in a world where

> every thing includes itself in power,
> Power into will, will into appetite,

and humanity preys upon itself like monsters of the deep.[137] The greatness of *Macbeth* lies in its displaying powers of the mind that are present in all human beings, and particularly in the universality of those 'inchoate all-or-nothing forces' which, in the individual and in the world, tend towards 'isolation, oppugnancy, negativeness and chaos'.[138] Macbeth is in himself a manifestation of the truth that

> the ruthless impulse of self-assertion, the blind urge to dominate through power, make a desolation in which all men are enemies; and enemies not only to one another, but to all nature; enemies even to themselves.[139]

It is a truth which Augustine would have characterized as that instinctive self-love which in the godless is transformed into a self-hate :

> the man who does not love God, though he retains the love of self which belongs to his nature, may yet properly be said to hate himself when he does what is contrary to his own good and behaves to himself

---

[136] *Angel with Horns*, pp. 217–18.
[137] ibid., p. 218.   [138] ibid., p. 219.   [139] ibid., p. 226.

as an enemy. It is indeed a fearful delusion by which, though all men desire their own advantage, so many do only what works their ruin.[140]

The innate and universal character of man's will to transcendence makes irrelevant the search for a particular weakness of character in the tragic hero. If the worldly existence of man is in its entirety flawed, it is scarcely realistic to require a 'tragic flaw' peculiar to the protagonist. It is surely for this reason that Miss Helen Gardner deprecates, in the criticism of *Othello*, the

> searching for some psychological weakness in the hero which caused his faith to fail, and whose discovery will protect us from the tragic experience by substituting for its pleasures the easier gratification of moral and intellectual superiority to the sufferer.[141]

Miss Gardner will therefore not try to explain why Othello found it impossible to reply for a second time to the thought of his wife's inconstancy, 'My life upon her faith'; and she would certainly not consider doing so in terms of a flaw in the hero, or in the nature of the love he bears to Desdemona. If there is a flaw, it is so subtly implanted that no spectator can have been aware of it; but in seeking for it we set ourselves at a distance from Shakespeare's predominant concern:

> What matters to the tragic dramatist is wherefore, not why: not what causes suffering, but what comes of it. We distract ourselves, and to no purpose, by asking insoluble questions such as: Why 'seems it so particular to Hamlet?'[142]

But, having determined not to seek for a particular cause, Miss Gardner finds it impossible not to seek for a cause at all. She rejects the idea that the play is a study in pride, egoism or self-deception, and affirms that its subject is sexual jealousy – but before long she is asking why sexual jealousy should 'seem so particular' to Othello. She finds the reason in a significant disinclination, which Othello shares with the other heroes, to come to terms, in his human limitation, with the limitations of the human life about him – a strenuous and passionate insistence upon a personal standard or ideal, and attempt to impose it upon his world, that can lead to the hero's being treated as a moral warning:

> Let Hamlet remember that 'Vengeance is the Lord's', allow the world to go its own way and mind the business of his own soul. Let Lear recognize that it is a law of life that the young should thrust out the old, and moderate his demands for love. . . . Let Othello remember

---

[140] *De Trin.* XIV. xiv. 18; see Section II, p. 92.
[141] 'The Noble Moor', *Proc. Brit. Acad.* XLI, 1955, p. 198.   [142] ibid.

that perfection is not to be looked for, that though two may at times feel one, at other times they will feel very much two.[143]

In Hamlet's staying at his post, therefore, Lear's going out into the storm, Macbeth's perseverence in his course of action while yet 'knowing the deed', and Othello's resolve to destroy what he must desire but cannot honour, is to be found the 'tragic responsibility', the soul's almost superhuman self-committal to the principle by which it destroys, and is destroyed. Mingled with all that is primitive in the murder of Desdemona, there is that 'agonizing renunciation' through which the heroic proportion is reached.[144] It is indeed a renunciation of human joys; but it is also a rejection, not only of moral restraints, but of the creaturely condition itself in an overmastering desire for transcendence, which makes Desdemona's murder 'heroic in its absoluteness, disinterestedness, and finality':

The tragic hero usurps the function of the gods and attempts to remake the world. This *hubris*, which arouses awe and terror, appears in an extreme form in Othello's assumption of the rôle of a God who chastises where he loves, and of a priest who must present a perfect victim.[145]

In the play's concluding enormity is to be found the familiar pattern of self-choosing and inhumanity, and the handiwork of the 'inchoate all-or-nothing forces' which drive the human mind to isolation, oppugnancy, negativeness and chaos, making men enemies to nature, to one another, and to themselves. It may even be found in Othello's suicide. In the speech that precedes it and in the act itself Bradley finds the expression of

a triumphant scorn for the fetters of the flesh and the littleness of all the lives that must survive him

which must sweep our grief away and impress us with the power of 'love and man's unconquerable mind'.[146] But it may also be seen to display the logical outcome of a will to self-assertion and self-transcendence, akin in spirit to the self-blinding of Oedipus:

The act seems compounded of opposite elements: egotism and altruism, self-loathing and self-glorification. . . . Whatever he may have thought he was doing, the act stands in the play as his culminating act of freedom, the assertion of his ability to act independent of any god, oracle or prophecy.[147]

---

[143] ibid., p. 199. [144] ibid., p. 200. [145] ibid., p. 201.
[146] *Shakespearean Tragedy*, p. 198.
[147] R. B. Sewall, *The Vision of Tragedy*, Yale U.P., 1965, p. 41.

In the same manner, Othello may be held to assert his own soul's predominance in the destruction of that very self which has imposed limitation upon the self, just as he had destroyed the being who had dispelled the dream of his own glory and subjected his soul to limitation and doubt. As, at the end, Iago utilizes in his silence the last means of self-assertion left to him, so Othello may be understood to employ his self-murder. If this is true, master and servant are to be seen throughout the play, not as absolute opposites, but as strangely allied in an impious assertiveness of spirit. Indeed, the white devil which has enticed Othello to bloodshed may be regarded as having shown itself to be far more dangerous than the black devil which Iago has served with conscious depravity.

In company with all the evils which men bring upon themselves, tragedy is to be regarded as the consequence of a creaturely self-centredness and perverse will to predominance which disturbs the harmony of existence.[148] The tragic hero's unnaturalness and inhumanity, which, as has been argued, is the clue to his spiritual condition, is also of necessity the tangible effect of his revolt:

> The life which seeks to transcend its creatureliness and make itself the centre of existence offends not only against God, who is the centre and source of existence, but against other life which has a rightful place in the harmony of the whole. Security through power means insecurity for those who lack power.[149]

The hero's dealings with his fellow men must reveal his true quality: those who begin from a perverted straining after the likeness of God will be seen to assume amidst their fellows the likeness of beasts.[150] That likeness witnesses to the fact that, in its concern for self-realization, the soul is destroying itself in the dimension where its being truly lies – and that the goodness it seeks or tries to preserve, be it of the body or of the spirit, is as limited as the creature that seeks it. Opposed to the creaturely ethic of the hero, which would make all revolve around himself, there is the 'impossible ethic' of Christianity, whose function is to drive man away from himself to his Creator, and to make him rely for truth and substantiality upon that movement of grace which draws him into the love of God and his fellows in despite of the self and its peculiar virtues. The effect of grace is to eliminate the self-choosing which is the chief barrier between man and God – and the chief function of tragic man. Self-choosing is self-destruction. Reliance upon a creaturely strength results in the tragic impotence and loss, just as the attempt in man to be moral defeats itself, and leads to Pharisaism instead of real goodness;[151]

---

[148] R. Niebuhr, *Beyond Tragedy*, London, 1947, p. 166.
[149] ibid., p. 102.   [150] *De Trin.* XII. xi. 16; see p. 237 above.
[151] D. M. Baillie, *God was in Christ*, Faber and Faber, 1963, pp. 116–21.

251

but as the strength of Jesus can be seen to come entirely from dependence upon the will of God, so also can it be said that in Him, righteousness stands at an opposite extreme to the heroic : that

> His sinlessness consists in His renouncing all claim to ethical heroism.[152]

In Jesus's forsaking of self-choosing – in the precise opposite of what Jung has called the 'God-almightiness' that the creature man prizes in his heroes – is implied the world's rejection and contempt. In the saints, according to Luther, is seen an acceptance of creaturely limitation, and an acknowledgement both of their impotence and their unrighteousness :

> The saints are at the same time sinners while they are righteous because they believe in Christ whose righteousness covers them and is imputed to them, but they are sinners because they do not fulfil the law and are not without concupiscence. They are like sick people in the care of a physician : they are really sick but healthy only in hope. . . . Nothing could be so harmful to them as the presumption that they were in fact healthy, for it would cause a bad relapse.[153]

Man, created sick, is commanded to be sound; but the means of soundness do not lie in himself. The tragic heroes presume upon their souls' health, strength and righteousness; and their tragedy is their relapse.

[152] ibid., p. 127.
[153] *Lectures on Romans* (vii. 25), L.C.C. XV, 1961, p. 208, quoted in Introd., p. xlv.

Chapter 17

THE TRAGIC DREAD

The assertion of the self in literary tragedy is accompanied by a feeling of dismay. The preliminary to Troilus's embittered resolve that neither fate, nor obedience, nor the hand of Mars should hinder him in his chosen course is his conviction, and resulting fear, that

> The bonds of heaven are slipp'd, dissolv'd,
> and loos'd
>
> (V. ii. 153).

For all the tragic heroes there must be this sense of 'a rift in the realm of ultimate reality'[1] – of a world 'out of joint', or one where

> all the operation of the orbs
> From whom we do exist, and cease to be

has evidently failed in its effect, leaving men bewildered and beset by anomalous forces. Above the impression of cosmic failure and mortal disorder, there is that of injustice: there is present to the mind of the heroic individual the

> discrepancy between the facts of his situation and the requirements of justice and right reason,[2]

and a grievance which can express itself in outcries against the unseen powers of the universe. Thus Lear can suspect it is the heavens themselves who 'stir these daughters' hearts /Against their father' (II. iv. 274–5), and can upbraid the ministers of an erring justice (III. ii. 21–4); Hamlet can regard himself as the victim of a 'cursed spite' in having to oppose a personal righteousness against a flawed world (I. v. 189–90); and Othello apprehends a similar curse and injustice in the fact

> That we can call these delicate creatures ours,
> And not their appetites
>
> (III. iii. 269–70).

[1] N. A. Scott, 'The Tragic Vision and the Christian Faith', *Angl. Theol. Rev.* XLV, 1963, p. 27.
[2] ibid.

253

Their response to their situations recalls that of Camus' metaphysical rebel who 'blasphemes primarily in the name of order, denouncing God as the father of death and as the supreme outrage'.[3] Harmony has gone from the universe, and what is left is the jarring of irreconcilable forces and the appearance of 'things rank and gross in nature'. Threatened as he is by discord and confusion, the tragic protagonist is above all

> uncertain as to the relation in which he stands to the transcendently real;[4]

and as he sets about his feverish task of trying to impose upon the frame of things a reality springing from his own vitalities and vision, he experiences, with regret and dread,

> a sense of separation from a once known, normative, and loved deity or cosmic order or principle of conduct.[5]

Having tried to comprehend reality and truth within a creaturely will and understanding, he now exclaims, with creaturely dread,

> O! now, for ever
> Farewell the tranquil mind; farewell content![6]

The tragic dread derives, therefore, from acquiescence in the personality's existence in its human condition and environment without the ability – or the desire – to see beyond the finitude of its present being. The tragic hero asserts his existence as his reality, and declares,

> For mine own good
> All causes shall give way;[7]

but in a spiritual universe, mere existence cannot be ultimately meaningful, and the good of existence itself must soon pass into non-existence. The inordinate trust in temporal good amongst mankind incurs the penalty that what they love will be made perfect for them: that those who love the journey rather than the return home or the journey's end, will be sent into distant parts, and will feel as flesh and blood must feel which is continually on the move, and never reaches home.[8] The tragic dread is the emotion of those without a resting-place: the fate of those who abandon God is ever to walk in a circle.[9]

This emotion, according to W. O. Cross, is widely experienced by modern man. It finds expression in his literature, where he is to be seen as a being afflicted with cosmic dread, and in the existentialist metaphysic,

---

[3] ibid., p. 27.　　　　　[4] ibid., p. 28.
[5] R. B. Sewall, *The Vision of Tragedy*, p. 44.
[6] *Othello* III. iii. 348–9.　　　[7] *Macbeth* III. iv. 135–6.
[8] Augustine, *De Vera Relig.* liv. 104–6, lv. 107; see Section II, p. 91.
[9] *De Civ. Dei* XII. xiii; *Ps.* xii. 8.

which insists that man's very anguish is his true essence, and makes him the estranged inhabitant of an absurd universe, a creature whose assertion of his own being is as meaningless as his destiny.[10] The contemporary doubt as to the validity of man's existence is accompanied by scepticism about the merit of his rational powers. To the threat of the frustration of the psychic vitalities by complex causes, psychology adds a death-wish that may counter man's instinct for fullness of life by implying in all that he does a desire for his own failure and annihilation; and existentialism would substitute for the life of reason and the will to fulfilment, as constituting man's true being, the strength of subconscious impulsions, and the will for death itself. Humanity appears to contemporary eyes to be confronted by the problem of a demonic urge to destruction within itself; of forces within the psyche that are contrary to rationality, and to the development of the individual's potentiality of being; and of a chronic apprehension which is both effect and cause of the others. In the process, therefore, of asserting selfness and identity, the will of modern man appears to himself to be self-destructive.[11]

The concepts of good and evil are now replaced by those of being and non-being. A denial or perversion of the human potential for existence is evil; but there is the recognition that the forces making for disruption are not truly uncreative, but are 'abortive and anarchic energy that is at its heart a good'.[12] Where order has been imposed upon this energy and it has been made submissive to a wholeness of personality, it flows out as a purposive urge to sustain and nourish the being of others – as a natural love that seeks expression in social relationship. But this love, which is a characteristic and outcome of being, cannot prevail against the anxiety bred in the heart by an ultimate threat of non-being –

> a haunting occult fear bred of man's knowledge of death, that brings cold terror to his heart and wrings him white in fear and trembling and sickness unto death.[13]

From a Christian point of view, a creaturely fear must exemplify the quality of the good whose desire is its origin. Being is what is desired; but mortal being can be no other than a subordinate good. For

> Being was not *Manns* creations end;
> But to be happy in a high degree :
> And therefore al *men* al their *forces* bend,
> T'inioy that *Good*, that *Beeing* doth cōmend.[14]

The happiness which is mankind's legitimate aspiration is beyond the realm of creaturely being; but the aspiration of modern man is entirely

---

[10] 'The Problem of Human Evil', *Angl. Theol. Rev.* XLV, 1963, pp. 4–5.
[11] ibid., pp. 7–9.   [12] ibid., p. 14.   [13] ibid., pp. 16–17.
[14] John Davies of Hereford, *Microcosmos*, Oxford, 1603, p. 58.

within it. It is for this reason, therefore, that Tillich affirms the unknown fear to be identical with finitude; his biological fear of extinction and his social fear of meaninglessness properly derive from creaturely limitation.[15] But the fear of guilt, which Tillich finds to be another element in the modern apprehension, in its congruence with despair at the loss of destiny, must point to a potentiality in man transcending the human, which man, in the assertion of his own existence as reality, will not admit to his consciousness. He would make himself his own end; but, in the terms of Aquinas, a will which is not formally directed to our last end is sinful, and cannot prevail.[16] The concept of creaturely being as ultimate good denies the power of will and of moral choice, and imparts to man a false helplessness in a false world. The irrationality that threatens what is potential in man proceeds not so much from the depths of his psychic constitution as from perversity; and, in this context, anxiety is no mere neurosis but the outcome of a salutary realization both of human littleness and of a failure to respond to what is ultimately good that merits the category of sin – for it is

> a fear of not gaining happiness, of not being able to fulfil one's self, of failing in perfection.[17]

The evil of anxiety is in this case the result of good, and is also good in itself. It is revealed as

> a growth or by-product of love, love being a natural consonance with value, and anxiety a fear of not obtaining the value, whether the value be survival or God. Human love being imperfect and lacking serenity, man's acts become anxiously frantic, deviant, ruthless, greedy and lustful.[18]

Not possessing the means of its own completion, a natural love declines to perverse self-love and self-choosing, and dread accompanies its every step. Thus the contemporary experience of life bears out Aquinas's teaching that love itself may be the cause of fear, where love of a good makes its deprivation evil, and thus feared.[19] A creaturely will, desiring unlimited good, but in the limitation implied in self-choosing denying itself the means, brings upon itself by its own endeavours an inescapable anxiety.

Modern man's sense of his own irrationality surely does him credit. There is to be seen in him a will towards a desired finitude together with an awareness that finitude is, in the higher meanings of the word, undesirable : man's 'being' is therefore truly his 'non-being'. The fear of incapacity to attain to true being becomes a principle of assertion. As

---

[15] *Systematic Theology*, London, Nisbet, 1955, I, pp. 212–13; *The Courage to Be*, Chap. II; quoted by Cross, op. cit., pp. 17, 18.

[16] *De Malo* iv. 2, *ad R.*, quoted by Cross, op. cit., p. 21.

[17] Cross, op. cit., p. 22.   [18] ibid.   [19] *S.T.* Ia IIae xliii. 1, *ad R.*

J.-P. Sartre declares, man's attempt at self-definition is founded upon a primary nothingness:[20] man's evil – his own creaturely insubstantiality – becomes his good. Like Milton's Satan in that choice, he is doomed to an agony of unfulfilment in a nightmarish world – the traditional state of the proud and the unredeemed.[21] A good has produced this evil; for man's being, which is his means of perversely desiring finitude, is good: but that the evil of the desire for finitude should have been produced is also a good thing, in that it demonstrates to man the inadequacy of his creaturely state, and impels him to seek beyond it. In man's self-choosing, whether in literary tragedy or in mortal life, it becomes evident that

> All natural inclinations are either without God or against God: therefore none are good.[22]

In the tragic dread, and man's apprehension of discord, abandonment, impotence and loss, may be seen the hand of a Providential discipline:

> As they arrogate to themselves more than what is right, and even inebriate themselves with delusions, he strips them naked, that after having known that all they think they have either from nature, or from themselves, or from other creatures, is a mere phantom, they may seek true glory.[23]

For the tragic or the cosmic dread springs from the soul's inability to accommodate itself within the temporal, and from its lack of the good that bears proportion to its true nature. The discipline of tragedy is inseparable from that of mortality itself, varying only in accordance with the degree to which temporal or creaturely good is trusted or asserted, but coming necessarily to the sense of loss and abandonment that betokens separation from God:

> So, when the *Soule* finds here no true content,
>   And, like *Noah's* doue, can no sure footing take;
> She doth returne from whence she first was sent,
>   And flies to *Him* that first her wings did make.[24]

The tragic dread is expressed most fully in the philosophy of existentialism, since existentialism is synonymous with self-choosing. The will of mankind, Luther has written, is either presumptuous or despairing;[25] the protagonist of tragedy and the existentialist thinker share the distinc-

---

[20] *Existentialism and Humanism*, tr. P. Mairet, London, 1966, p. 28.

[21] Augustine, *Conf.* II. i. 1; *Paradise Lost*, I, 11. 213–20.

[22] *Table-Talk*, cclvii.

[23] Calvin, *Commentaries on Jeremiah and Lamentations*, tr. and ed. J. Owen, Calvin Translation Society, Edinburgh, 1850, I (*Jer.* ix. 24), pp. 498–9, quoted by Frye, *Shakespeare and Christian Doctrine*, London, 1963, p. 201.

[24] Sir John Davies, 'Nosce Teipsum', 1599, *Complete Poems*, ed. A. B. Grosart, 1876, I, p. 87.

[25] *Table-Talk*, cclx.

tion of being able to combine the two categories in a single attitude, in their attempt to identify the boundaries of reality with those of the self. According to P. B. Rice, the earliest stage of Edmund Husserl's philosophy was a descriptive phenomenology – an attempt to get to the truth about human experience

> by suspending belief in a world outside experience and by describing or analyzing what is immediately given to consciousness, including its intentions of going beyond the given.[26]

The ultimate phase, however, is a realization of the failure of the attempt, and of the necessity of an order beyond that of human existence:

> Essences cannot really be divorced from existence; existence is always claiming them . . . 'the greatest lesson of the phenomenological reduction is the impossibility of a complete reduction'.[27]

Jean-Paul Sartre's idealistic view of phenomenology does not take account of this lesson. It sees the world outside the self as a mere inert matter which consciousness organizes, and against which, indeed, the self is set in opposition. In order to realize itself it must adopt negative attitudes to other being; its very essence, and the whole activity of consciousness, lies in the process of *néantisation*.[28] Whereas the Christian self, acknowledging that its vital principle derives from beyond itself, is able to accept what appears irrelevant or inimical to its being both in nature and in itself, and thus turn its own being into a part of a larger harmony, the existentialist self denies the reality of anything beyond it. The medium, or 'space', in which the individual finds himself is an undifferentiated medium, a pure *dehors*, from out of which he constructs a system of relations centred upon himself and his projects. The idea of a world in space is rejected; and instead the self substitutes a space 'for itself'.[29] It trusts in, and makes, in Greville's term, a 'self-constellation', in the fear that otherwise it might cease to be.

Thus there can be no human nature because there is no ultimate order against which to measure it or supreme Being to have a conception of it, and the definition of man can be nothing except what he makes himself. Nothing exists before the self projects itself; and man himself attains existence only when he is what he purposes to be.[30] The essence of his being is that (like Milton's Satan) he is his own Creator.[31] This

[26] 'Existentialism and the Self', *Kenyon Review* XII, 1950, No. 3, p. 307.
[27] Rice, ibid., p. 308.
[28] I. W. Alexander, 'Jean-Paul Sartre and Existential Philosophy', *The Cambridge Journal* I, 1947-8, pp. 722-3.
[29] ibid., p. 724.
[30] J.-P. Sartre, *Existentialism and Humanism*, p. 28.
[31] R. Niebuhr, *Faith and History*, London, 1949, p. 196.

principle of the soul's self-creation is seen at work in the tragic hero's purposive pursuit of a value, ideal or desire which is identified with the height of his existence, and which must be asserted in the process by which the tragic self seeks to govern the reality it knows by a law of its own.[32] In whatever this will to ideal selfhood may be found to lie – whether it be Hamlet's craving for his thoughts to be bloody, or Macbeth's resolve to put into act the firstlings of his heart; whether it lie in Othello's love for Desdemona or for his own passionless 'stillness' of disposition, or in Lear's remorseless determination that his power must confirm his sentences – the threat of its frustration in the tragic hero is felt as a death to his soul, and is grappled with as if it were his bitterest foe.

But self-assertion, in existentialism as in the tragic protagonist, must bring in creaturely fear. Through the very humanity of the self which has been chosen, there is a committal to a truth that is less than the whole truth; and in the disparity between the two must reign that which would be feared. The self strives to make its being its reality, to reach the state where its being is being-in-itself;[33] but only a power beyond the self can give it its integrity and true existence. The service of any other good or principle will involve it in the loss of its integrity of being. And humanity's devotion to the principle of its own being is a metaphysical contradiction, and a living lie. It means that any attitude that is adopted is limited to reference to the self, and that consequently the individual's emotions must be a conscious pretence or affectation, since otherwise he tends beyond the self towards *le dehors* and ultimate nothingness, and is transformed into a thing. In consciousness, therefore, there is an element of untruth which is bound up with the condition of human existence; for since to recognize a validity beyond the self is to destroy the basis for the assertion of the self, man's consciousness cannot, without destroying itself, maintain any position it has received or acquired.[34] It is therefore characterized by a feverish instability and dread; its state of freedom is coextensive with the 'nothing' which man is, and partakes of the dread that must predominate in his lack of confidence in his ability to choose rightly.[35] Hence his sense of his freedom is inseparable from that of his anguish – man's liberty is a condemnation:

> Ordinary or objective fear is directed towards external events over which I have no control; anguish is fear of myself, of my own freedom, of not finding myself on the other side of the rendezvous which I have made with myself. . . . The pathos of the human situation is found in the striving of being-for-itself to become being-in-itself, man's craving to be the cause of his own actions and to become something definite.

[32] Augustine, *De Trin.* XII. ix. 14.   [33] Alexander, op. cit., p. 724.
[34] ibid., p. 730.   [35] ibid., p. 726.

Since this craving is doomed to frustration, 'man is a useless passion'.[36]

The cosmic or tragic dread, therefore, must persist in one who, having chosen himself, now bears the solitary burden of a choice in which there can come to him no help, from the world or from his fellows or even from his own past.[37] The artist alone (rather than the saint) is able, in his transcending of human existence, to escape the condemnation of freedom. For this freedom, which consists in the negating by the consciousness of man's situation as it is, in order to constitute itself an end in itself, independent of all other being and motive,[38] ends – as it only can – by condemning the being which subjects it to such arrogant abuse. The philosophy of Sartre would give to man what the tragic hero in truth aspires to – the power to create and to determine which is the prerogative of God.[39]

The existentialism of modern man is, by Kierkegaard's definition, at one with the old world of paganism and the imaginary one of literary tragedy: it is 'human life carried on in God's absence'.[40] It has been assessed by Reinhold Niebuhr in the following terms:

Lacking a faith which sees a higher coherence beyond the immediate incoherences, it seeks nevertheless to assert the meaning of the present moment and the present experience in defiance of the chaos of existence. Its islands of meaning in the sea of meaninglessness are, however, tiny and periodically inundated. Existentialism is a desperate affirmation of meaning within the framework of despair. It is a very accurate index of the spiritual crisis in contemporary culture.[41]

It is also an index of spiritual crisis in the tragic hero, and indeed in every individual. The wish to convert the immediately real into ultimate reality, to make

the be-all and the end-all here,
But here, upon this bank and shoal of time,

and jump the life to come, is man's most characteristic desire, the outcome of a perverse self-love. With the love of self that is natural and morally neutral, and can be seen as in instinct for self-protection and an aim towards well-being, every man, says Augustine, is endowed. But the true love of self, which is the love of God and neighbour, is too rarely to be found amidst a worldly humanity.[42] They are possessed instead by the false self-love, the *amor suae potestatis*, the desire to escape from God's rule, and to become the principle of their own existence.[43] It is not surprising that they are soon also possessed by bafflement and dread:

[36] P. B. Rice, op. cit., p. 315.
[37] Alexander, op. cit., p. 729.
[38] ibid., p. 733.
[39] ibid., pp. 733, 736.
[40] See p. 171 above.
[41] *Faith and History*, p. 184.
[42] *In Jo. Ev. Tr.* lxxxvii. 1, quoted by Burnaby, *Amor Dei*, p. 117.
[43] *De Civ. Dei* XIV. xiii, quoted by Burnaby, op. cit., p. 119.

Whoever lets God go and loves himself, letting God go *in* loving himself, remains not even in himself but goes out of himself too. He is exiled from his own heart through contempt of the inward and love for the outward.[44]

The 'demonic urge to self and social destruction' which is present, and is recognized, in the modern consciousness is in essence akin to that occult 'tendency of some things to return to non-being'[45] which is the ultimate definition of evil, and the definition by inference of a will to depart from the One Good, the source of all being. The consequence of apostasy can only be, in man's imagination, the tragic or cosmic dread, and, in his world, the tragic threat and fact of non-being. From the evil and waste of tragedy, however, arises a Providential judgement and a redeeming. To the ungodly, who blind themselves to the perception of truth, tragedy comes as punishment. They hate the truth for reproving and revealing them:

Whence she shall so repay them, that they who would not be made manifest by her, she both against their will makes manifest, and herself becometh not manifest unto them. Thus, thus, yea thus doth the mind of man, thus blind and sick, foul and ill-favoured, wish to be hidden, but that aught should be hidden from it, it wills not. But the contrary is requited it, that itself should not be hidden from the Truth; but the Truth is hid from it.[46]

But to those who will acknowledge their God, the light which tragedy casts, though at first it dismay them, brings self-knowledge and blessing:

Euen so *Man's Soule* which did God's image beare,
　　And was at first faire, good, and spotlesse pure;
　　Since with her *sinnes* her beauties blotted were,
　　Doth of all sights her owne sight least endure:

For euen at first reflection she espies,
　　Such strange *chimeraes*, and such monsters there;
　　Such toyes, such *antikes*, and such vanities,
　　As she retires, and shrinks for shame and feare . . .

And while the face of outward things we find,
　　Pleasing and faire, agreeable and sweet;
　　These things transport, and carry out the mind,
　　That with her selfe her selfe can neuer meet.

[44] *Serm.* cccxxx. 3; xcvi. 2; quoted by Burnaby, op. cit., p. 120.
[45] E. Gilson, *The Philosophy of St Thomas Aquinas*, Cambridge, 1924, p. 136; Section II, p. 121.
[46] Augustine, *Conf.* X. xxiii. 34.

> Yet if *Affliction* once her warres begin,
> And threat the feebler *Sense* with sword and fire;
> The *Minde* contracts her selfe and shrinketh in,
> And to her selfe she gladly doth retire . . .

> If ought can teach vs ought, *Afflictions* lookes,
> (Making vs looke into our selues so neere,)
> Teach vs to *know our selues* beyond all bookes,
> Or all the learned Schooles that euer were.[47]

Adversity must afflict a diseased mankind. The remedy of the cross of tragedy is a bitter and dreadful medicine; but it is the means of health – and the way of light, truth and grace – in them who believe.

[47] Sir J. Davies, 'Nosce Teipsum', *Complete Poems*, ed. A. B. Grosart, 1876, I, pp. 21–3.

Chapter 18

THE TRAGIC DESTINY

The two poles of the tragic world, according to A. W. Schlegel, are an inward liberty and an external necessity.[1] He was discussing the tragedy of ancient Greece, which emphasized the remoteness from the world of man, both in sympathy and in concept, of the ultimate powers. Man's individual liberty, and his subjection to some higher necessity, are seen to operate in all tragedy; but more often they are seen to operate simultaneously, as part of one process, and to be proclaimed, as it were, in the same breath. Thus it can be argued that the tragic impression consists not only in what arises from the destruction of the hero, but equally in the sense of his being fated to destruction; that

> If we do not feel at times that the hero is, in some sense, a doomed man; that he and others drift struggling to destruction like helpless creatures borne on an irresistible flood towards a cataract . . . we have failed to receive an essential part of the full tragic effect. . . . They fight blindly in the dark, and the power that works through them makes them the instrument of a design which is not theirs.[2]

Yet the feeling that the hero is fated proves not to be incompatible with the feeling that he is free. The tragic impression can be held to be constituted as largely by man's freedom as by his subordination to necessity:

> The notion of man as a responsible agent, freely choosing disaster, is essential to all tragic experience; for it is the foundation of that fortitude in the chooser which answers to the spectator's sense of man as 'splendid in his ashes'.[3]

Not only is the tragic impression able to sustain the contradiction, but it provides, in the intimation of a comprehensive destiny, the very means by which its contradictory assertion of man's free initiative can be made – for the extent of the hero's freedom cannot be known except as, in literary tragedy, it faces the ultimate test of self-destruction. But the question of

[1] *Lectures on Dramatic Art and Literature*, tr. J. Black, rev. A. J. W. Morrison, A.M.S. Press Inc., N.Y., 1965, p. 67.
[2] A. C. Bradley, *Shakespearean Tragedy*, p. 27.
[3] Lawlor, *The Tragic Sense in Shakespeare*, 1960, p. 109.

man's being free or fated, however urgent it may be felt to be, must yield place to a further consideration to which tragedy also gives rise: the evidence from the life of the tragic character that he is under a necessity to accommodate and submit himself to a disposition of things transcending the standards of fitness entertained by his own personal vision and will. In the light of this necessity, as J. J. Lawlor argues, the matter of whether man is free or fated, agent or patient, appears to be of somewhat lesser significance:

> He would have himself the agent of all that he possesses, rules, and claims as his own, for authority and for honour alike. Conversely . . . he will plead himself the patient of all that goes against his intention, counters his hopes, and diminishes him in revealing the limits of his power. But the spectator may see what Lear himself, like Hamlet, does not see: that man is the patient of what he would ignore or evade. It is acceptance that confers freedom; truly, the 'Ripeness is all'.[4]

Tragedy gives evidence of a larger truth than can be comprehended within the individual existence, of a reality so august that man's freedom is in the last resort to be defined in terms of conformity to it. There may be discerned within the operation of tragedy, therefore, a certain rough correspondence to what, in terms of theological definition, was earlier described as a trinity of fact governing the human condition: the freedom of the will as real and vital in man, the incapacity of the unaided will to escape the necessity of evil-doing and its consequences, and the entire subjection of man's will and his world to Providential disposition, in conformity to which man finds his true freedom.[5] It remains to be seen whether the idea of man's freedom implied within the tragic necessity can be reconciled to a theological estimate of the activity of the human will under Providence.

It is scarcely to be denied that Shakespearian tragedy does not present a study of fatalism in its obvious forms[6] – that its heroes have evident scope for both good and evil choice, and that, where an evil course is chosen, or an evil deed done, it is 'an evil deliberately willed and persisted in'.[7] In the great heroes there is the same purposeful overthrowing of what lies in their way, and unflinching acceptance of the consequences of self-assertion, that is innate within Macbeth's preparedness to

> let that be
> Which the eye fears, when it is done, to see.
>
> (I. iv. 52–3.)

In Macbeth's desire to 'trammel up the consequences' of his proposed deed, however, there lies an ironically partial understanding of man's

---

[4] ibid., p. 171.   [5] (Section II, pp. 116,124.)   [6] Bradley, op. cit., p. 29.
[7] L. C. Knights, *Some Shakespearean Themes*, 1959, p. 137 (of Macbeth).

scope for action in the conditions to which life subjects him. His grasp
of consequence is appropriate to one dedicated to external happenings;
although he can talk of judgement here, he must dismiss the signs of a
deeper judgement that already appear to his consciousness, and serve
notice upon him of a limitation of his freedom in the order of his own
being more severe than any that could be imposed from without. For,
as L. C. Knights has observed, just as there is a human equivalent – in
the qualities of loyalty, trust and liking – to the benevolence of the natural
order that may be discerned in Shakespeare's verse, so there is to be
found in nature's 'sub-moral world' a counterpart to 'cursed thoughts' in
man. If man disregards the kindliness of nature and chooses its 'mischief',
the consequent disorder impairs the freedom he has exercised. He 'unties
the winds'; and nature's powers, becoming autonomous in the human
sphere, 'swarm upon' their host. Macbeth and his queen, therefore, in
surrendering their intellectual integrity, make themselves wilfully blind,
and thus become the prey of the 'black agents' of the night,[8] and –
whether they be naturally or metaphysically conceived – of the 'spirits
/That tend on mortal thoughts'.[9] From the time when he first entertains
his characteristic ambition, there is evident in Macbeth a continuous
lessening of his freedom :

> One feels that in proportion as the good in him diminishes, his liberty
> of free choice is determined more and more by evil inclination and that
> he cannot choose the better course. Hence we speak of destiny or fate,
> as if it were some external force or moral order, compelling him against
> his will to certain destruction.[10]

The play therefore presents Macbeth as the slave of his own sin, and as
the possessor of a freedom of will which in effect is freedom only to do evil.
He is not without a desire for love and honour among his fellows; but he
is without the will to act in pursuance of this desire, and so in his compulsive career manifests the state of fallen man,

> that seeing he would not what he might, now he cannot what he
> would.[11]

In Augustine's terms, the servant of sin is free only for sinning; and the
bearer of a depraved nature can only do evil until he is set free from
bondage.[12] And if, in their self-choosing and presumptuous will to a
creaturely supremacy, the great tragic heroes all lose sight of the essential

---

[8] ibid., pp. 136–9.

[9] See P. H. Kocher, 'Lady Macbeth and the Doctor', *S.Q.* V, 1954, pp. 347–8, for the argument that the reference here and in the 'murdering ministers' is to the animal spirits of
contemporary psychology.

[10] W. C. Curry, *Shakespeare's Philosophical Patterns*, Baton Rouge, Louisiana State University
Press, 1937, p. 105, quoted by Knights, op. cit., p. 140.

[11] *De Civ. Dei* XIV. xv; see Section II, p. 115.   [12] *Enchiridion* ix. 30.

inadequacy of their condition, and rely upon illusions of personal strength or righteousness, they are as like Macbeth in their inspiration as they are in their overthrow, and must be subject to a similar necessity. The evil to which they incline must, in their own souls and in the external realm, impose limitation and constraint upon them. In their purpose of self-assertion, the tragic heroes, desiring fullness of being, embrace the means of their destiny and doom. Of their own will they contrive the ruin that must inevitably come upon them, and are both free and fated, the authors and the victims of their own tragedy, in a world of which, though they would be so in pretension, they are neither creators, arbiters nor masters.

If the medium of existence itself, and of cause and effect, did not call it into question, the destiny beneath which the tragic hero appears to serve and to suffer must raise the matter of the ultimate order behind the tragedies. By the necessity which he sees to operate through events, Bradley is driven to subsume, under the category of 'fate',

> the whole system of order, of which the individual characters form an inconsiderable and feeble part; which seems to determine, far more than they, their native dispositions and their circumstances, and, through these, their action; which is so vast and complex that they can scarcely understand it or control its workings; and which has a nature so definite and fixed that whatever changes take place in it produce other changes inevitably and without regard to men's desires and regrets.[13]

Bradley's view of the order, in its omnipotence, its imposition of necessity, and its inscrutability of working, bears a resemblance to the Christian idea of the ultimate. It clearly differs from it in its impersonality; but the underlying difference is in its taking the created universe to be of the nature of ultimate truth, and its not admitting a spiritual level of being and good above and beyond the evident good of creaturely being. It therefore does not share the ability of a spiritual order to reconcile or resolve the anomalies that tragedy brings into prominence. It can offer no explanation of the order's yielding a place to evil while being essentially averse to it.[14] It is aghast at the order's destruction and waste of its own good in the tragic paroxysm. It must leave as absurdity the beholders' being neither crushed nor rebellious as the order exercises its devastating prerogatives,[15] and lets fall its 'horrible pleasures' upon subject humanity. It knows no means whereby men's lives, which appear diminutive and puny in comparison to the order, can yet appear as significant within it. It cannot account for the transformation of tragic man's intention and act into the opposite of itself, and the apparent disproportion between what is thought or done and its effect in the tragic world. It

---

[13] *Shakespearean Tragedy*, 1956, p. 30.   [14] ibid., p. 37.   [15] ibid., p. 26.

can see no reason why a man's virtues should help to destroy him[16] – and is not at all inclined to search for one. And that the order should determine men's actions while at the same time safeguarding their freedom of choice it would not believe if it could escape from its own observations. The view of the ultimate order which Bradley puts forward as arising from tragic experience within a merely human awareness is, in short, quite unable to explain the tragic fact and necessity – as he himself is the first to admit.[17]

That man is both free and fated points for its resolution, in the experience of tragedy and in Christian experience alike, to a reality that is beyond man's world, and an understanding that is above the human. In Christian experience it takes the form of a Providence which works through human wills without frustrating or compelling their activity. In decreeing its infallible purpose, it preserves the distinction amidst its human creatures that it 'wills it and yet works it not';[18] that its predestinating of men places nothing in those affected, so that they conform to what is ordained for them without the operation of constraint.[19] Yet the freedom which it bestows in no way hinders it from having all human wills under its control; for although the necessity involved in the relationship between the will of God and that of man may be described as conditional by an Aquinas or in terms denoting ultimacy by a Luther,[20] there is no denying of its reality for either. The dependence of mankind upon Providence is both the source of the blessedness they seek and the means by which necessity is imposed upon them; for the turning away from God is the definition of loss of being and sin, and the creaturely aspiration of fallen humanity exercises an alternate destiny upon them of persistence in evil. But in good or evil they remain dependent, needing what Calvin calls

> the universal activity of God whereby all creatures, as they are sustained, thus derive the energy to do anything at all.[21]

Whatever be the origin or the cause either of the good or of the evil will in them, men are helpless to put their wills into effect until they receive power from above; the evil receive power that their evil will may be condemned, and the good that their good will may be proved.[22] That power, whether it be creaturely vitality or the grace necessary for the doing of good, may be withheld; and in the latter event

> it is properly said that he blinds, hardens and bends those whom he has deprived of the power of seeing, obeying, and rightly following.[23]

---

[16] ibid., pp. 27–9.   [17] ibid., p. 38.   [18] De Civ. Dei XXII. ii.
[19] Aquinas, S.T. I. xxiii. 2, ad R.; see Section II, p. 117.
[20] (Section II, pp. 118, 121.)   [21] Inst. II. iv. 2.
[22] Augustine, De Spir. et Litt. xxxi. 54; see Section II, p. 116.
[23] Calvin, Inst. II. iv. 3. See also S.T. Ia IIae lxxix. 4, ad R.; Section II, p. 120.

Or God may enhance or increase the power that already exists, in wills good or evil, quickening their intent and strengthening their endeavours, that their purposes may act in conformity to His omnipotent decree. Those who will not obey Him as sons and free men must perforce serve him as slaves, and in fetters;[24] bounds will be assigned to their power, and a God who creates good out of evils will transform their intentions while confirming them in their error.[25] As Augustine lays it down,

> The fact that men sin is their own doing; that they by sinning do this or that comes from the power of God, who divides the darkness as he pleases.[26]

In God's directing of an evil will, therefore – in His hardening the hearts and minds of those who put absolute trust in their own powers – can be seen the operation of a tragic destiny.

The necessity that is laid upon worldly man has its origin, according to Luther, in that Divine bestowing of energy whereby all who think and act do so in dependence upon God's power. Whether He works apart from the grace of His Spirit, or visits His grace upon those whom He has justified, the result is the same:

> He works all things in all men, even in the ungodly; for He alone moves, makes to act, and impels by the motion of His omnipotence, all those things which He alone created; they can neither avoid nor alter this movement, but necessarily follow and obey it, each thing according to the measure of its God-given power. Thus all things, even the ungodly, co-operate with God.[27]

When the Divine impulsion operates in evil men, evil deeds ensue; but though God's action thus produces evil, the cause of the evil thus produced lies in the evil instruments, which God does not allow to be idle:[28]

> God's omnipotence makes it impossible for the ungodly man to escape the action upon him of the movement of God; of necessity he is subject to it, and obeys it; but his corruption, his turning of himself from God, makes it impossible for him to be moved and made to act well. God cannot suspend his omnipotence on account of man's perversion, and the ungodly man cannot alter his perversion. As a result he sins incessantly and inevitably until he is set right by the spirit of God.[29]

---

[24] *De Agone Christ.* vii. 7; see Section II, p. 102.

[25] *De Nat. Boni* xxxvii; quoted by Burnaby, *Amor Dei,* p. 194.

[26] *De Praedest. Sanct.* xvi. 33; quoted by Calvin, *Inst.* II. iv. 4.

[27] *The Bondage of the Will,* tr. Parker and Johnston, London, 1959, p. 267. See also Calvin, *Inst.* II. iv. 2; Section II, pp. 116–17.

[28] *Bondage,* p. 204.   [29] ibid., pp. 204–5.

In this process can be discerned the means by which man retains his free will while remaining subjected to God's power.[30] All creatures are necessarily obedient to God's working;

> But He works according to what they are, and what He finds them to be : which means, since they are evil and perverted in themselves, that when they are impelled to action by this movement of the Divine omnipotence they do only that which is perverted and evil.[31]

If this process of the hardening of the ungodly be understood to operate within the action of tragedy, the sense of the protagonist's being at once free and fated, and the wilful contriver of his own downfall, is more readily explained. And the impression of a profoundly personal responsibility for disaster within the tragic hero is similarly accounted for. The conviction that there must be a flaw or defect of nature or of intent in the hero which is centred in his very being, and which arises from those very qualities that constitute his greatness, evokes from every beholder of tragedy the question,

> why is it that a man's virtues help to destroy him, and that his weakness or defect is so intertwined with everything that is admirable in him that we can hardly separate them even in imagination?[32]

An answer may be found in the dubious quality of a virtue that is directed toward nothing more than a worldly end, and in that will for a creaturely predominance that may be found both in the hero of literary tragedy and in the worldling who according to Luther undergoes the penalty of hardening in his sin. The chief characteristic of the ungodly man is to be wholly turned to self, and to his own :

> He does not seek God, nor care for the things of God : he seeks his own riches, and glory, and works, and wisdom, and power, and sovereignty in everything, and wants to enjoy it in peace. If anyone stands in his way, or wants to detract from any of these things, he is moved with the same perverted desire that leads him to seek them, and is outraged and furious with his opponent. He can no more restrain his fury than he can stop his self-seeking, and he can no more stop his self-seeking than he can stop existing – for he is still a creature of God; though a spoiled one.[33]

The impulsion of God, which 'goes on presenting and bringing pressure to bear', enhances and confirms the natural fault in the sinner, and prompts him to trust in and assert his strength, wealth, power or vainglory until he is 'inflated and uplifted by the idea of his own greatness'.[34]

[30] Augustine, *De Grat. et Lib. Arb.* xxi. 42. [31] *Bondage*, p. 204.
[32] A. C. Bradley, op. cit., p. 29. [33] *Bondage*, p. 205.
[34] ibid., p. 207.

269

In this confirming almost to the point of frenzy and delusion of the inclination within the sinner by which he is to be cast down may lie the cause of the peculiar ferocity of will that is evident in the heroes of tragedy; as Bradley observes, 'desire, passion or will attains in them a terrible force'.[35] It may also explain their intense self-preoccupation, the compulsive nature of their acts and their responses to life's happenings, and that obsessive insistence upon a good or an ideal that they identify with the principle of their being which appears to Bradley to be the fundamental tragic trait.

> In almost all we observe a marked one-sidedness, a predisposition in some particular direction; a total incapacity, in certain circumstances, of resisting the force which draws in this direction; a fatal tendency to identify the whole being with one interest, object, passion, or habit of mind.[36]

The tendency to one-sidedness, and to the assertion of a particular value, is characteristic of the hero or sinner; but it grows to engulf the nature that entertains it as external resistance is met and overcome, and engineers its ruin by hindering the access to reality and truth. In Luther's words,

> As of themselves they are turned away from God by the very corruption of their nature, so their antipathy greatly increases and they grow far worse as their course away from God meets with opposition or reversal.[37]

The tragic dread, the insecurity, and even the instability of mind which is frequently come upon in Shakespearian tragedy, may be seen to be rooted in this 'corrupting and perverting' of the afflicted natures that is consequent upon their alienation from God in self-concern. Shakespeare's heroes can be said to incur, within the tragic action, the two penalties which according to Augustine befall every soul that sins: the loss of the knowledge of what is right, and of the power to do it.[38] Their destiny may be held to show, indeed, the transformation of a creaturely self-love into a true self-hate, and to confirm that necessity whereby

> the mind that forsakes the God above it becomes so feeble and darkened that, through loves it cannot quell and errors out of which it sees no way of return, it falls miserably away from itself into the things which are alien and inferior to itself.[39]

But the corruption of the understanding and the enhancing of the force of will finds its principal expression – in the sinner, as it does in the

---

[35] op. cit., p. 20.   [36] ibid.   [37] *Bondage*, p. 205.
[38] *De Lib. Arb.* III. xviii. 52; see Section II, p. 93.
[39] *De Trin.* XIV. xiv. 18.

tragic hero – in the predominance of passion. The pressure of God's movement upon Pharaoh in his hardening is thus said to have

> allowed his own ungodly corruption, under Satan's sway, to blaze with anger, to swell with pride, to boil with rage and to advance along the path of scornful recklessness.[40]

The disorder which self-assertion creates in the soul finds in passion the natural means for its outward expression. The afflicted personality

> cannot but hate what opposes him, and trust to his own strength; and he grows so obstinate that he will not listen nor reflect, but is swept along in the grip of Satan like a raving madman.[41]

Hamlet's reverence for the man who is not passion's slave contrasts oddly with his own desire for passion to possess him; Othello's apprehension lest blood and passion overwhelm his 'safer guides' is justified in the wallowing in emotion that follows; and Lear, from the moment he has made his tragic decision, appears almost as the embodiment of wrath and fury. Slaves of passion the heroes most certainly are; but it is a question whether, in their passion, they are not to be regarded as slaves of Satan. For here, as elsewhere in the Christian estimate of man, the passions are strictly related to the will, being its instruments or masters according to its spiritual condition. They are indeed wills in themselves, the creation of that presiding will in man which sets in motion all the powers of the soul, yet passing beyond its control as Divine grace is withdrawn and satanic agencies centre upon them. In the righteous, the passions are a means of health and strength;

> But the city of the impious that sail after the compass of carnality, and in their most divine matters, reject the truth of God, and rely upon the instructions of men, is shaken with these affections, as with earthquakes, and infected with them as with pestilent contagions.[42]

In the process of tragedy, and of hardening, the state of man suffers the nature of an insurrection. The mind of hero and sinner is ruled by passions, which

> rage like tyrants, and throw into confusion the whole soul and life of man with storms from every quarter, fear on one side, desire on another, on another anxiety, or false empty joy, here pain for the thing which was loved and lost, there eagerness to win what is not possessed, there grief for an injury received, here burning desire to avenge it.[43]

[40] *Bondage*, p. 206.   [41] ibid., p. 207.
[42] *De Civ. Dei* XIV. ix.   [43] *De Lib. Arb.* I. xi. 22.

271

The condition which Augustine describes applies to the whole range of tragic event.

The virtues and strengths which come into evidence as the sinner is confirmed in his sin are in reality signs of weakness. Many of them are the effects of passion; all of them are the means of judgement and of downfall. The state of creaturely exaltation is itself that of tragic loss: catastrophe can only be the outward sign for something already concluded.[44] It can therefore be said of any tragic hero at any point in the action, as it was said of Macbeth toward the end, that he

> Is ripe for shaking, and the powers above
> Put on their instruments
>
> (IV. iii. 237–8).

The heroes are ensnared by something which, though ordinarily of little consequence, is at its particular time of happening the object of a fatal inability; as Bradley asks,

> what is it that brings them just the one problem which is fatal to them and would be easy to another, and sometimes brings it to them just when they are least fitted to face it?[45]

If the downfall of the tragic hero and the hardening of the sinner are kindred processes, the answer must be sought in the providence of God, and the susceptible state of a wrongful inclination of will. God confronts the sinner, Luther declares, 'at an appropriate moment':[46]

> For though one go scot-free, for awhile, yet at last he will be snapped, as the Psalm says: 'God is indeed still judge on earth'. Our Lord God suffers the ungodly to be surprised and taken captive in very slight and small things, when they think not of it, when they are most secure, and live in delight and pleasure, leaping for joy.[47]

In the Divine control over an evil will, therefore, is to be found a resolution of the problem which tragedy presents of man being simultaneously free and fated. The will of the man being hardened in his sin

> is not under unwilling constraint, but by an operation of God consonant with its nature it is impelled to will naturally, according to what it is (that is, evil).[48]

The tragic sense of an inflexible destiny which disregards creaturely categories, however, is one where evil and good alike are seen as subjected; and the tragic pleasure is to be seen as in part a recognition of a spiritual order which strangely and lovingly presides over the freedom it bestows,

---

[44] *De Civ. Dei* XIV. xiii, quoted on p. 247 above.
[45] op. cit., p. 29.   [46] *Bondage*, p. 207.
[47] *Table-Talk*, ccl.   [48] *Bondage*, p. 212.

controlling all wills through the operation of its inscrutable providence, and working nothing but good through the evil it permits. The mundane world is the scene of operation of spiritual forces; and, according to Luther, the natural reason of man, if questioned closely, would have to deny the theological concept of 'free-will' even if there were no Scriptures to aid it:

> For all men find the following convictions written in their hearts, and acknowledge and acquiese in them (albeit unwillingly) when they hear them propounded: *first*, that God is omnipotent, not only in power but also in action . . . and would be a ludicrous God were it not so; *second*, that He knows and foreknows all things, and can neither err nor be deceived. These two points being allowed by the hearts and minds of all men, they are at once compelled by irrefutable logic to admit that we are not made by our own will, but by necessity, and accordingly that we do not do anything by right of 'free-will', but according to what God foreknew and works by His infallible and immutable counsel and power.[49]

This deeper recognition and awareness it may be held the proper and religious task of tragedy to enforce. And the problem of the exact relationship between the free will of man and the will of the order to which he is subject, if it is beyond the capacity of the human creature to determine,[50] is perhaps best seen in the light of a comment of Luther which may well be man's best and final word upon the subject:

> What does it matter to me that 'free-will' is not under compulsion, but does what it does willingly? It is enough for me that you grant that its willing performance of what it does will come to pass necessarily, and that if God has thus foreknown it, then it cannot be otherwise.[51]

Dr Johnson's comment that Hamlet appears in the play 'rather as an instrument than an agent' voices an impression relating to every victim of tragic circumstance. For whether man appears on his brief stage as a horse with two riders,[52] or as a creature upheld only by grace against the flesh and the devil,[53] or as freed from an unfree free will by an irresistible grace for submission to a service which is perfect freedom,[54] there must arise in his world, as within the microcosm of the theatre, a sense of the compelling power of tragedy as the arena of ultimate forces, and the impression of a destiny inexorably harsh, yet uplifting. Man's self-contradictory acquiescence in the justice that tragedy enacts may

[49] ibid., p. 218.   [50] (Section II, pp. 117–24.)
[51] *Bondage*, p. 221.   [52] ibid., p. 103.
[53] Aquinas, *S.T.* Ia IIae lxxix. 4, *ad R*; I. xxiii. 3, *ad R*.
[54] Augustine, *De Corr. et Grat.* xii. 38.

273

spring from the profoundest understanding, and deepest kinship with his fellows in a common failing; for

In this sense shall we say that all men are hardened, for there is none that does not sin, and none would sin did not Divine long-suffering bear with him![55]

But the impression of an all-embracing destiny; that

There's a divinity that shapes our ends,
Rough-hew them how we will;[56]

that

The works of the Lord are not so constituted that a creature in the freedom of choice which has been given him may overcome the will of the Creator, even though he act against the Creator's will,[57]

must ever be the teaching of tragedy, and its consolation. The tragic necessity cannot but compel the wandering attention of man to a recognition that

the entire contest of human life is fittingly conducted by the unchanging providence of God who allots different rôles to the vanquished and the victorious, the contestants, the spectators, and the tranquil who contemplate God alone.[58]

[55] *Bondage*, p. 210.   [56] *Hamlet* V. ii. 10–11.
[57] Augustine, *En. in Ps.* cx. 2, quoted by Burnaby, *Amor Dei*, p. 194.
[58] *De Vera Relig.* xl. 76.

Chapter 19

THE TRAGIC CONSTRAINING

According to L. C. Knights, the play *King Lear* compels us to recognize the 'ruthless honesty' which has stripped its hero of every rag of illusion,[1] and must make us pause over his most emphatic pronouncement upon the world and its inhabitants: the 'three-times repeated reference to the birth-cry'[2] that is at its most forceful in Lear's description of man's world as

this great stage of fools
(IV. vi. 184).

The thought, as Knights points out, resembles Augustine's reference to our birth in *The City of God*, 'We begin our life with tears, and therein predict our future miseries',[3] and may have Biblical origin;[4] and while he warns against taking it as a summarizing comment emerging from the play as a whole, he insists that we must not seek to avoid its powerful effect:

> Whatever the physiological reasons, the baby's cry at smelling the air (and nothing can deprive that phrase of its disturbing wholesomeness) is commonly taken as a cry of fright and protest – 'Helpless, naked, piping loud'. As such it is analogous to the protest, the frightened movement towards headlong regression, of the adult who is called upon to undergo a radical transformation of consciousness.[5]

The fact that this image which Lear finds for the world 'is partly at least a projection of his own folly'[6] is in keeping with tragedy's making manifest of all that before was unclear, and with its demand upon the hero that he shed the layers of untruth that are implied in his mere humanity.[7] The tragic insecurity, declares J. S. Smart, arises from a sense of mystery concerning the individual's present and future state and the ultimate position of man himself, and the meaning of his values and his very existence. But what also afflicts the victim of tragedy is a sense

---

[1] *Some Shakespearean Themes*, 1959, p. 111.
[2] ibid., p. 113.   [3] XXI. xiv.   [4] *Wisdom* vii. 3.
[5] op. cit., p. 113.   [6] ibid.   [7] See p. 184 above.

275

of change which is unacceptable to the mind;[8] and it may be that this 'radical transformation of consciousness' which tragedy shocks him into making, and which shatters the creaturely standards to which he has in the past paid tribute, is in truth a new birth, with its necessary accompaniment of reluctance, fear and pain. The human consciousness which has bruised itself with the wordly, the temporal and the ephemeral must, when these things go ill, and before it has learned to trust in a truer life, cry out in dread and alarm, 'Who would have thought it?'[9]

In human experience, as in theological estimation, man, despite all his gifts and at the end of all his achievements, remains a creature with no ultimate good in himself, needing the God who is his one good. In terms of this need – or hope, as it may be – every merely human assessment is fraudulent. The realization of God's fatherhood would lead mankind to the utter contemning of all the glory, righteousness, wisdom and power of its world;[10] if the thought of the greatness of God's grace were to occur to a man in its eternal validity,

> it would at once nullify all his wordly thinking, imagining and desiring, and turn everything upside down.[11]

The world of man, not being reality, must deceive those who rely upon it. Whoever trusts in its 'vanishing creatures' is but another Lazarus, lying at the rich man's gate while being starved to death;[12] and its limited and apparent orderliness and good can be turned into confusion at any time, and bring grief, impotence and disillusion upon its inhabitants. Yet this chastisement and desolation of mankind, to which through compulsive error their whole lives are dedicated, is the way of their perfection, and means of their 'better life'.[13] The perfection of man lies in his sense of the need for God; and for this reason it can be affirmed that

> the highest of human tasks is for a man to allow himself to be completely persuaded that he can of himself do nothing, absolutely nothing.[14]

What is thus theologically desirable, however, can only come about in the consciousness of imperfection, the destruction of men's confidence in their own power; and there must thus arise, in that intense awareness of evil and pain which tragedy brings, an 'undefined apprehension of

---

8 'Tragedy', *Essays and Studies* VIII, 1922, p. 26.

9 Luther, *Table-Talk*, cxlvii, quoted on p. 200 above.

10 Luther, *Galatians* (iii. 25), ed. P. S. Watson, p. 338; see p. 171 above.

11 Kierkegaard, 'Man's Need of God Constitutes his Highest Perfection', *Edifying Discourses*, tr. Swenson, Minneapolis, 1950–3, IV, p. 12.

12 Luther, *Table-Talk*, ci, quoted on p. 174 above.

13 See pp. 176–7 above.   14 Kierkegaard, op. cit., p. 22.

another universe with other values'.[15] The larger truth cannot be received or accommodated by the temporal reality in which man tries to make his home, and it is through the pain of the destruction of his wordly joys that he is able to attain the rebirth that lies in the perception of the things of God. The theological task of tragedy is to strike at 'our perilous confidence in the flesh',[16] to enable human eyes to see 'without disguise or palliation', so that the 'final insights' may be apprehended.[17] God is the God of truth; and

> When life under the providence of God forces a man out of the shelter and security of its routine and elects him to be strengthened in this annihilation, the experience is one which knows no illusion and permits no evasion.[18]

He is a God, also, not of the strong and haughty, but of 'humble and perplexed hearts, who are in need, tribulation, and danger':

> God shows his power in our weakness; he will not quench the glimmering flax, neither will he break in pieces the bruised reed.[19]

Thus, while literary tragedy will fulfil its duty by destroying creaturely illusion and self-confidence, it may also possibly display, in those elected 'to be strengthened in this annihilation', the process in which

> by affliction lesser faults are cleansed in them, and they are the more raised up from earthly affections to God.[20]

The Providential constraining of man is to be seen at work in the disillusioning and the quickening that tragic affliction can bring upon the human mind. These are the two conditions, the negative and the positive, which, according to Max Scheler, are necessary to the individual's experience of his God.

> The negative is what I have called disillusion with idols, i.e. removal from the centre of the *absolute* sphere . . . of all finite things and finite goods, with a consequent release from conscious or subconscious self-identification with any finite object of 'faith' and love. The positive condition is . . . that the spiritual person should be *independently* active and active of its own spontaneous accord. . . . For *wherever* man judges rightly and truly, has a clear and unadulterated vision of

15 U. Ellis-Fermor, *The Frontiers of Drama*, 1945. p. 128; see p. 179 above.
16 *Inst.* III. viii. 3; see p. 191 above.
17 L. C. Knights, op. cit., p. 99; see p. 184 above.
18 Kierkegaard, op. cit., p. 24.
19 *Table-Talk*, dcxliii.
20 Aquinas, *S.T.* I. xxi. 4, *ad 3*.

truth, wherever he grasps and wills the objective good, this positive condition applies.[21]

In whomsoever this detachment and enlivening is accomplished,

> the person *necessarily* attains at one and the same moment, in an *indivisible and indestructible unitary experience*, to its substance in *God*, while in it the reality of God as a person becomes simultaneously discernible.[22]

The first of these conditions corresponds to the need in man for a true self-knowledge, which, as Kierkegaard explains it, is based upon, and expressive of, that need for God which is the chief principle of his being. The prudential self-knowledge, or the worldling's concept of his own nature and identity, is in the deeper sense delusion, since it is a knowledge of man's self in relation to something else rather than to himself. This kind of knowledge of the self is ultimately a dubious thing, since it is a relation between a doubtful self and an uncertain 'other' – be it one's own gifts or the external order – which can at any instant suffer alteration, leaving the deceived personality to bid farewell to whatever creaturely excellence it had taken pride in,[23] and to the comfortless reflection,

> Lord! we know what we are, but know not what we may be.[24]

Yet there would be greater deception if his false self-estimate had not been taken from him, because the entire meaning of his life would have been based upon untruth.[25] Thus, from the point of view of man's perfection, it is necessary for him to emancipate himself from the 'calves of Jeroboam' which he has previously served. It is a difficult and complicated proceeding:

> And it is also a terrifying occupation, because the deeper self-knowledge begins with that which one who refuses to understand it must call an anxiety-breeding deception. For instead of the entire world he gets merely himself; instead of being master of his fate he becomes a needy petitioner; instead of being able to do everything he can do nothing at all.[26]

In this way he is afflicted with dread, and with impotence. Every understanding of life, in terms of which he can understand himself, is revealed

---

[21] Max Scheler, *On The Eternal in Man*, tr. B. Noble, S.C.M., 1960, pp. 27–8.
[22] ibid., p. 28.
[23] 'Man's Need of God Constitutes his Highest Perfection', *Edifying Discourses*, ed. Swenson, Minneapolis, 1950–3, IV, p. 30.
[24] *Hamlet* IV. v. 43–4.
[25] Kierkegaard, op. cit., p. 30.   [26] ibid., p. 31.

278

to him as a misunderstanding, so that he becomes as nothing in his own eyes:

> This is man's annihilation, and this annihilation is his truth. This knowledge he will find it impossible to evade; for he is his own witness, his own accuser, his own judge.[27]

This negative condition, the understanding of which Kierkegaard declares to be the highest task for any human being, is the essential experience of the tragic hero. Lear's conscious sense of an exalted identity – that he is every inch a king – is founded upon the assumed reality of those 'accommodations' with which men's society and institutions dignify their lives, and upon an estimate of his nature derived from his 'place', no less than from his personal gifts. He embraces the means of delusion; yet from the start he has a characteristic awareness of the 'close pent-up guilts' of human life, and its 'simulars of virtue', that enables him later to see his own error in the context of the brittleness of all worldly strengths and virtues, and the incapacity of 'robes and furr'd gowns' to bestow either righteousness or identity. He is left, therefore, amidst the terrifying effects of disillusion, a weak and needy petitioner for his own being:

> Who is it that can tell me who I am?
>
> (I. iv. 229).

Hamlet's petition is in effect the same, but it arises from a different cause. From the outset he is in a state of disillusionment with the self: the action of the play shows that he has no concept of himself in relation to external good or to creaturely qualities, but that he constantly tries – and fails – to attain one. In pursuit of his revenge, therefore, he is also in quest of his identity; his diet is indeed 'of the chamelion's dish' as one resolve or attitude succeeds another. But his impotence, though different in quality from Lear's, is no less real, and his self-accusation is no less bitter than Lear's burning shame at the thought of his error and unrighteousness. For both, there is no evasion of true self-knowledge; they are their own witnesses, accusers and judges; and their self-preoccupation, whether in madness or in melancholy, makes it possible for either to be bounded in a nut-shell and count himself a king of infinite space, were it not for his bad dreams. Instead of the entire world, they get only themselves; and while not having attained identity, they are at least liberated from the idols of their own creation.

Scheler's positive condition for the personality's finding its substance in God – that it should be quickened into independent activity – corresponds to that reaching out towards his perfection which for Kierkegaard is implicit in man's desire for a true autonomy of being. The being in which a worldly man takes pride, and which must impress an external

[27] ibid., p. 24.

279

contemplation, does not truly derive from the self, but as it were gains its energies from the external things to which it is dedicated. A man might, in fact, be 'The glass of fashion and the mould of form', but his glory is the consequence of his mind's being 'attuned to a hymn of conquest', and his purpose's being dictated by the things he purposes.

> But if he is unwilling to be a weapon in the service of unclarified cravings, aye, in the world's service, because the world upon which he fixes his desire itself awakens this desire; if he is unwilling to be a stringed instrument played upon by unclarified moods, or rather, played upon by the world, because the movements of his soul are determined by the manner in which the world plucks the strings; if he does not wish to be a mirror that reflects the world or in which the world reflects itself; if he is unwilling to play this passive rôle, but desires first to control the eye before it marks out something that it desires to conquer, in order that the eye may belong to him and not he to the eye . . . then all is changed; the power is taken away from him and the glory.[28]

The beginning of the mind's spontaneity, in the tragic hero, lies in affliction itself: the threat of loss of being inculcates a corresponding desire for true being. The immediate resort of this desire is to the defiant assertion of the identity and being that has hitherto been known. Hamlet's retort to Rosencrantz and Guildenstern is really an address to the tragic world which threatens to dominate him:

> 'Sblood, do you think I am easier to be played on than a pipe? Call me what instrument you will, though you can fret me, you cannot play upon me (III. ii. 374-7).

This is the cry of every tragic hero. It is present in Macbeth's 'valiant fury' at the close, and in the quiet utterance of Webster's heroine, 'I am Duchess of Malfi still'. It is present no less in Othello's 'Soft you; a word or two before you go': the music of these words proclaims that Othello is at the last able to re-enter and reassert, though only for a moment, the being that he once had known, and thought had been destroyed. But Lear and Hamlet, in their desire for fullness of being, must pass beyond the first reaction of self-assertion, for the idols of their earlier devotion, or of their present seeking, have been revealed in all their unworthiness. True being, for them, is no longer to be found within the self; rather, theirs is now the search to find it for the self. In that activity of the soul – in the very 'tempest in the mind' occasioned by disillusion and suffering, and the despairing rejection of all forms of comfort – lies its rebirth, and its acquisition of spontaneity, if not of hope. It can lead

[28] ibid., pp. 23–4.

one who prided himself on his exalted state willingly to annihilate whatever reflected a false identity upon him, and, equalling himself with wretches in the search for reality, to come at last to the contempt for his former self implied in his scorn for the great ones that 'ebb and flow by the moon', and, in utter selflessness, to enter upon true identity. It can enable Hamlet to see his own condemnation in the world's unperfectness, and to swing from a desire for absolute loss of being to a readiness to lose his being in a Being greater than his own. But the mind's independence and vitality is not achieved in a moment. The former self is not easily dismissed; and the stresses of external conflict induce greater contentions within the individual. And,

> where the greater malady is fix'd,
> The lesser is scarce felt.[29]

The individual no longer strives with the world, but with himself. In the Shakespearian tragic hero, as in the soul moving towards God, there comes into being an 'inward struggle'[30] more significant than anything that occurs in the outward sphere :

Behold him now. His powerful figure is held in a close embrace by another equally powerful figure. They enfold one another so fast, they press upon one another with such equal suppleness and strength, that the wrestling cannot even begin; for it is as if the other figure would instantly overwhelm him. But this other figure is himself. Thus he can do absolutely nothing.[31]

The soul thus locked in conflict with itself is unpregnant of its cause. It has to choose between suppressing the deeper self by plunging it into oblivion or allowing its voice to be drowned in the world's changes, and admitting that the deeper self is right.[32] In the process of decision the soul is aware that the moment of happiness or success must be seized, or it will be too late;[33] but on the other hand there is no eloquence on earth that is able to confound the deeper self once it is permitted to give itself expression.[34] In the dilemma, says Kierkegaard, there is a great temptation 'to fall into dreams';[35] and one may conjecture that the fighting soul may show such severe alternations of mood and purpose as may correspond to the strength of its self-opposition, spurring itself into worldly activity with thoughts of self-righteousness, justice, revenge and honour,

---

[29] *King Lear* III. iv. 8–9.
[30] A. C. Bradley, *Shakespearean Tragedy*, 1956, p. 18.
[31] Kierkegaard, 'Man's Need of God Constitutes his Highest Perfection', *Edifying Discourses* IV, p. 24.
[32] ibid., pp. 31–2.   [33] ibid., p. 33.
[34] ibid., p. 32.   [35] ibid., p. 31.

only to relapse into the consideration of its own essential emptiness. Amidst all its frantic efforts, however,

> the deeper self sits there thoughtful and serious, like a physician at the bedside of the sick. But it also wears an air of translucent gentleness, because it knows that this sickness is not unto death but unto life.[36]

In the soul's self-confrontation, the deeper self is not passive, however: the physician must wrestle with the patient in its purpose of healing. It frustrates the characteristic movement outwards of the first self towards the surrounding world which is its object;[37] and in order to overcome that yearning for the external, the deeper self makes the world reveal itself for what it really is, in all its uncertainty and precariousness, so that the first self may acquiesce in its recall:

> The deeper self thus proceeds to picture the outer world, with its elusiveness and its mutability, in such terms that it no longer seems desirable to the first self.[38]

The characteristic activity of the disillusioned tragic hero is to withdraw from the world which has been the scene of his triumphs at the promptings of an imagination which transforms its glitter to dross. The world may appear as a stage of fools, where the justice is no better than the thief, the usurer hangs the cozener, and the beadle lusts to use the whore in the kind for which he whips her; or it may seem as an unweeded garden, producing the seed of rank and monstrous growth, or as a foul prison for the soul, or as a snare for it, a place where honesty and good meaning are at the mercy of treachery, malice and presumption. The awakening to self-knowledge is at one with the gaining of a knowledge of the world: for the soul's self-illusion is the product of the world's fraudulent claims and appearances. In both, disillusionment is the soul's quickening to truth.

This disintegration of the personality, and its affliction with impotence and dread, is fearsome to sufferer and beholder alike; yet it is more truly cause for rejoicing:

> When something of this kind takes place in a man's soul, does it not mean that this [sic] mind is beginning to give way? Ah no, it means something quite different, it means that the child is about to be weaned.[39]

The destruction of temporal certainties and felicities is the prelude to rebirth; it denotes, in the individual, that he is moving towards his

---

[36] ibid., p. 32.   [37] ibid., p. 31.   [38] ibid.
[39] ibid., pp. 33–4.

perfection – for in the sense of creaturely imperfection that comes with profound self-knowledge lies the means of the fullest being. Man arrives at the pitch of perfection, declares Kierkegaard, when, through being nothing in himself, he becomes 'suited to God' : [40]

> whoever knows in himself that he can do nothing, has each day and each moment the desired and indubitable occasion to experience the living God.[41]

As Scheler puts it, in the mind's release from idols, and its assumption of true spontaneity, the personality attains to its substance in God while God's reality at the same time becomes discernible to it. And failure to have this experience, according to Kierkegaard, must therefore be due to the soul's residual trust in its own powers.[42]

The becoming suited to God must necessarily involve unsuitability to the world, and tend in consequence to plunge the pilgrim soul deeper into temporal affliction : greatness, in the ultimate sense, is not measured by capacity to adapt or to shape the world, but by capacity to transcend it. It is perhaps for this reason that Lear can appear to Bradley as, in some indefinable way, 'greater than the world in which he appears'[43] – though reduced to being 'old and foolish' in its own terms, and by its own operation. Similarly, Hamlet, knowing 'in himself that he can do nothing',[44] must throughout the play appear naked in Claudius's king-

---

[40] ibid., p. 26.   [41] ibid., p. 42.

[42] ibid. The process of the worldly personality's destruction and its re-formation into higher being, as Scheler and Kierkegaard describe it, and as it appears in the experiencing of literary tragedy, bears a certain resemblance to concepts in psychoanalytical practice. Thus R. Morrell is able to see in the impact of tragedy a therapeutic function similar in kind and degree to treatment administered to the neurotic patient, and explains the tragic pleasure in terms of the personality's healing. The psyche which experiences a considerable shock from without in the ordinary course of life undergoes an upset of equilibrium until the impact is absorbed through the setting up of a more complex structure within the personality. The function of tragedy is to complicate and strengthen the psyche of the onlooker, just as that of the patient may be restored by the administration of mild and preventive shocks from outside his experience which make possible a reorganization and progress from his old life to a fuller one. This process of renewal towards maturity is 'the very principle of life itself'.

In pathological fixation, the psyche shrinks from the process by turning aside to a fantasy world rather than facing the world of fact; but the same tendency in the theatre audience is countered by the individual spectator's adjusting himself to real life as his fantasy life dies with the hero. In the case of the deeply afflicted patient, the treatment must be to confront him with the full depth of the terror by which he is threatened, and which he has struggled to evade; and only if the psychoanalyst is able to lead his patient to a climax of resistance ending in a painful temporary collapse can the necessary adjustment be eventually achieved. See 'The Psychology of Tragic Pleasure', Essays in Criticism VI, 1956, pp. 26–34.

If it be accepted that the experience and ambitions of unregenerate man constitute in their entirety a fantasy life within the soul, an analogy with the disintegration of the personality in tragic and spiritual experience is possible.

[43] Shakespearean Tragedy, p. 324.   [44] Kierkegaard, op. cit., p. 42.

dom, and the victim, despite all his qualities, of the fact of power. Hamlet's failure, as Rossiter observed, must be seen as a failure to come to terms with the world : 'Yet [his] fineness is noble, though all life refutes its efficacy'.[45] It is appropriate that Hamlet, who is less subject than Lear to temporal and creaturely illusion, and freer from the self-assertion characteristic of the tragic hero and of man in the world, should reach the refuge of a declared trust in Providence. His declaration has the suddenness which the fulfilling of Scheler's two conditions would seem to imply for it, and which Kierkegaard affirms must be so in him who attains to man's highest pitch of perfection. To such a man, God comes

> more quickly than the light that penetrates the darkness, swifter than the thought that dispels the fog; present as promptly as only He can be, who was already there.[46]

Hamlet's state of mind, and experience in the play, indeed appear peculiarly suited to the apprehending of God :

> When everything again becomes uncertain, when the thoughts seethe in a welter of confusion, when memory threatens to give notice and refuses any longer to serve, when the past comes before the mind only in the form of fearful anguish, when even the most sincere purpose is through the treason of anxiety transformed into insincerity toward oneself – then one understands again that a man can do absolutely nothing of himself. But in and with this understanding God is immediately present.[47]

In his readiness to confess in a breath his own impotence and a reliance upon the activity of God, Hamlet appears as one who, in Kierkegaard's terms, 'throws himself into the arms of God in unspeakable wonder over God who can do all things'.[48] But it may be said of Lear no less than of Hamlet that he learns

> more and more to die away from the world, learns to cling less and less to external things, to that which life brings and takes away, to that which it is given him outwardly to accomplish – but learns also to care more and more for the things of the inner man.[49]

In both is to be seen a manifest preparedness to relinquish vanishing creatures : the scorn for the temporal which can proclaim that,

> Since no man has aught of what he leaves what is't to leave betimes?
> (V. ii. 223–4)

[45] *Angel with Horns*, 1961, p. 185.
[46] Kierkegaard, 'Man's Need of God Constitutes his Highest Perfection', *Edifying Discourses* IV, p. 43.
[47] ibid., p. 44.   [48] ibid., p. 37.   [49] ibid., p. 46.

284

and the desire in Lear, born of disaster but also of wisdom, to live as one of 'God's spies' (V. iii. 17) among men – perhaps as one of

> Those Angell-soules in flesh imprisoned,
> Like strangers liuing in Mortalitie,[50]

in trustful expectation of a life to be.

Because of Lear's subjection to the idols of self-sufficiency, the constraining power of tragedy will produce in him rage and bewilderment, rather than the despair and irresolution it creates in Hamlet. The preoccupation for Hamlet is with the impermanence or relativity of all known goods and standards, even those within the personality; but Lear is more typical of the tragic hero in his concern with the fact of change itself, and its clashing with the mind's concept of its identity. Exclamations of astonishment or incredulity mark his progress through the earlier part of the play's action; and their effect has been likened to

> that produced by a man persistently running into an invisible wall, through which he stubbornly but vainly tries to pass.[51]

But in these 'questions of surprise and bafflement', and the attempts to 'evaluate experience with obsolete terms',[52] there is to be perceived the beginning of the same declension to impotence, and to conflict within the self, as is to be observed in Hamlet – and the developing of those 'powers of self-diagnosis'[53] which are a mark of the mind's quickening into spontaneity in the search for being. In the 'annihilation' of his former self-estimate, Lear, like Hamlet, comes upon knowledge that he finds it impossible to evade, and is as prone as he to self-accusation and self-judgement. As D. C. Hockey argues, Lear in the play is himself both the 'dreadful summoner' and the prisoner at the bar.[54] The burden of accusation is the presence of love; it is to be found in the first scene no less than in the grotesque enactment on the heath, and Lear's restoration to sanity is coincident with self-judgement: 'If you have poison for me, I will drink it' (IV. vii. 72). Lear's re-creation, however, is through forgiveness and love rather than through the sharpness of a will for personal justice or for the world's condemnation;[55] yet it may be said that

> From the start, Lear's story has been a trial in which he was judged, punished and restored.[56]

---

[50] Fulke Greville, *Alaham*, Prologue, 11. 66–7, *Poems and Dramas*, ed. G. Bullough, 1938, II, p. 140.
[51] M. Weidhorn, 'Lear's Schoolmasters', *S.Q.* XIII, 1962, p. 308.
[52] ibid.   [53] ibid., p. 314.
[54] 'The Trial Pattern in *King Lear*', *S.Q.* X, 1959, p. 391.
[55] ibid., pp. 391–3.   [56] ibid., p. 395.

Out of the disintegration of suffering, self-conflict and self-accusation a new Lear is fashioned. His annihilation has been his strengthening. He emerges

> with an awakened sense of humanity, unselfishness, and love for his fellow-creatures . . . he has risen nearer to his true strength as a man and the magnanimity and wisdom of a king. Lear has approached, through inward and outward suffering, self-realization and attainment of right relationship with life.[57]

The 'radical transformation of consciousness' demanded alike by the pangs of birth and of tragedy has been achieved. He is ' "naked" before the truth',[58] and enters upon new self-consciousness in the abandonment of all illusions of personal sufficiency, or of that of the world of man. As a creature he is 'old and foolish'; but there may be recognized in his achievement something which is altogether beyond what is creaturely. His loving communion with Cordelia, declares P. Ure, is

> the most positive achievement of an imagination enlarged and altered by its vision of the great world wearing out to naught. His giving of love here is as absolute as his demanding of it had been before; what was a self-gratifying appetite has become a selfless generosity.[59]

When challenged, earlier, by forces conflicting with his self-estimate, Lear's response is to ask the question, 'Doth any here know me?' But the basic question of *Hamlet*, as J. J. Lawlor has observed, is 'can man ever know himself?'[60] The 'nothingness' with which tragedy afflicts the individual is not here imposed by the tragic, but rather arises out of one of the 'thousand natural shocks /That flesh is heir to', and is consequent upon one of life's sterner demands.[61] And far from attempting to cling to and impose some principle or notion that is identified with the self's true being, Hamlet can find no absolute principle of selfhood to assert – apart from the duty of revenge, which he swears shall replace all pre-existing features of character and will, and thus transform him into the embodiment of a single purpose. The severity of this resolution – which is more thorough-going than Othello's oath to revenge – typifies his entire approach to life; it is evidence of the fact that 'in a sense Hamlet is in search of a satisfactory attitude toward experience', and that, in thought or in action, he is consciously – indeed, self-consciously – adopting 'a posture toward the universe'.[62] Hamlet as we know him is not able, in Scheler's words, to identify himself 'with any finite object of "faith" and

---

[57] J. L. Rosier, 'The Lex Aeterna and *King Lear*', *J.E.G.P.* LIII, 1954, p. 579.
[58] ibid. [59] *Shakespeare and The Inward Self of The Tragic Hero*, 1961, p. 17.
[60] *The Tragic Sense*, 1960, p. 45.
[61] See Bradley, op. cit., pp. 118–20.
[62] T. Greene, 'The Postures of Hamlet', *S.Q.* XI, 1960, p. 357.

love'.[63] In his detachment he is a man seeking his own identity – and aware, in his quickness of spirit, of larger possibilities beyond himself, and beyond all human speculation. His worldly purpose forces him in impatience to spurn these possibilities, and to assume such being and resolve as he can muster; but he can never really escape the sense of creaturely inadequacy. It is this, according to A. P. Rossiter, that accounts for the universality of Hamlet's experience. He paraphrases the 'To be, or not to be' soliloquy in these terms:

> Life is a burden, a bitter mortification of the spirit, and a long insult: we bear it because we do not ever certainly know what we are. In our sceptical moments we retain a wavering dream of eternal things; and in our faith, a dream that we are but burdened beasts that die and perish; and only fear persuades us not to act. . . . So it is that our very awareness thwarts all our resolutions.[64]

The quest for being itself hinders the gathering together of an earthly identity and purpose.

The inevitable outcome of Hamlet's detachment from external absolutes, and his 'large discourse' and apprehension, is division in the soul – a division made acute by the demand of momentous decisions and actions. Spontaneous action is not possible for Hamlet, Rossiter declares, not only because of an intense moral confusion, but because of 'the mind's own lack of togetherness and coherence'.[65] Hamlet's own disharmony is echoed forth in the play itself 'with relevant disharmonies and manipulated discords of tone', until it finds recognition in the beholder:

> Shakespeare knows that Hamlet often does not know Hamlet; and part of our deeper experience of the play is the awareness of that not-knowing.[66]

Hamlet, in fact, is a tragedy of

> self-awareness so acute that there is no self, but only selves;[67]

and in planning any course of action, Hamlet is burdened by the knowledge that the impulse of the consummate self is as often wrong as right, and that the selfhood he can attain is perhaps a denial of true selfhood, a by-product of circumstances.[68] His purpose, that is to say, would be dictated by the things he purposes, and he must consent to being, in Kierkegaard's words, 'a weapon in the service of unclarified cravings, aye, in the world's service'.[69]

If it be agreed that there are two selves in Hamlet, it will not be debated

[63] See p. 277 above.   [64] *Angel with Horns*, 1961, p. 176.   [65] ibid., p. 172.
[66] ibid., p. 175.   [67] ibid., p. 178.   [68] ibid.
[69] See p. 280 above.

that it is the 'deeper self' which keeps him from action, and which, to overcome his yearning for external goals, presents the world to him as undesirable. He cannot come to a firm estimate of himself, since the external order appears to him as uncertain and shifting. As Rossiter affirms, in Hamlet Shakespeare gives us a keen and philosophic mind placed in circumstances which behave as if nothing were absolute, everything relative, conditional and accidental – with the result that he becomes 'a man essentially divided within and against himself';[70] or, as D. G. James states it, Hamlet's world has crumbled to shifting sand :

> Everywhere in the play there is uncertainty and doubt; everywhere also there is incalculable and incredible conduct. In belief as in conduct nothing is firm and clear.[71]

Consequently, unlike Horatio, Hamlet can neither accept his fortune nor remain master of himself in the situations which face him. Both passivity and action are for him passion merely – whatever he is about, 'judgement is not in it'.[72] His self-conflict, and the treacherous appearance of the world, reduce him to impotence; and his acute perception helps to make him

> a mind so torn and dragged between the betrayal of action and the failure of non-action (a different betrayal) that he can call himself a coward.[73]

But the malady – if so it is to be called – is at a far deeper level than the matter of valour or cowardice : Hamlet's thoughts (Rossiter declares) are infinite, but his acts are subject to limit, 'so that any act must be a falsifying limitation of the mind'.[74] His condition is that of the helplessness which Kierkegaard described in the soul moving toward its perfection,

> when even the most sincere purpose is through the treason of anxiety transformed into insincerity toward oneself.

To this state of impotence in the divided personality, Kierkegaard affirms,

> God is immediately present.[75]

Critics are on the whole repelled by the idea of a divine conclusion to the play. It is the very voice of Hamlet's sloth, for Rossiter, that transfers his task to Providence; and in that voice is heard, not the resonance

---

[70] op. cit., p. 179.　　[71] *The Dream of Learning*, 1951, p. 52.
[72] ibid., p. 44.　　[73] Rossiter, op. cit., p. 176.　　[74] ibid., p. 177.
[75] 'Man's Need of God Constitutes', *Edifying Discourses*, tr. Swenson, Minneapolis, 1950-3, IV, p. 44.

of faith, but a 'weary fatalism'. And, for good measure, Rossiter adds the apposite thought,

> What right has a man of his keen wit to find a shaping divinity in all that he has seen in rotten Denmark?[76]

What may at any time be true of Denmark, however, applies to the world itself, as Hamlet's thoughts bear some relation to those of mankind in general. But Rossiter is left with the reflection – at once uncomfortable and unaccountable – that 'Hamlet is, as we all recognize, so much too good for his fate'.[77] This clash between the essential fineness of Hamlet and the meanness of the forces which destroy him appears to Rossiter as the play's central conflict. And he makes the moral theme of the play the further contradiction that the thinker, in order to act, must consciously come down to the world's level, accept its terms, and use men as means to an end, yet must be aware in so doing that he denies his own soul.[78] He recognizes also that, whatever ambiguities may lie in the terms 'to be' and 'to suffer', both suicide and death in attempted action are in question in Hamlet's famous soliloquy, with 'the main controlling sense' hanging upon 'the values attached to immortality'.[79] But considerations spiritual he will not in the end allow: the play as a whole embodies the eternal tragedy of man's world, the clash between 'circumstances' and 'inner values'.[80] L. C. Knights similarly finds distasteful and insignificant certain susceptibilities in Hamlet to which the term 'spiritual' might possibly be applied. His hectoring the Queen on her sin is described as 'self-righteous', and his consuming sense of his own unworthiness is termed 'neurotic': Hamlet, we are told, is possessed by 'an uncontrollable spite against the flesh'.[81] He does not recognize, in Hamlet's self-depreciation, any evidence of the phenomenon by which, according to Reinhold Niebuhr,

> The consciousness of sin and the consciousness of God are inextricably involved with each other[82] –

and indeed it would be to ask him to go beyond his province to suggest that he should consider doing so. Hamlet remains for him, as for Rossiter, a creature strangely and oddly unfitted for the world. He is a being whom life impedes, and for whom death is something positively desired – the possessor of

> a spirit which, whether 'suffering' or 'opposing', feels itself continually on the defensive against a world conceived as entirely hostile.[83]

---

[76] op. cit., pp. 180–1.   [77] ibid., p. 180.   [78] ibid., p. 185.
[79] ibid., p. 176.   [80] ibid., p. 186.
[81] 'Prince Hamlet', *Explorations*, 1946, pp. 67, 69.
[82] *Beyond Tragedy*, London, 1947, p. 12.   [83] Knights, op. cit., p. 70.

The possibility that the world's conceived hostility may be part of that process of the 'shattering of idols' in which the journeying soul 'turns from its whoremongering in spontaneous quest of its proper object, the idea of God',[84] must be the subject of further consideration. But Hamlet's reaction to the world around him may simply be due to the fact of its evil, as G. Wilson Knight, amidst others, is prepared to recognize; and the same critic points to a significance within the play which, if it is more than seeming, must raise the whole matter of proportion and value in the mind of the beholder :

> We properly know Hamlet himself only when he is alone with death : then he is lovable and gentle, then he is beautiful and noble, and, there being no trivial things of life to blur our mortal vision, our minds are tuned to the exquisite music of his soul.[85]

In his address to the Ghost, in the 'To be, or not to be' discourse, and in the graveyard scene we meet the real Hamlet;

> Here, and when he is dying, we glimpse, perhaps, a thought wherein death, not life, holds the deeper assurance for humanity.[86]

In his search for fullness of being and reality, and his consciousness of the deceptive nature of the goods of the external world, Hamlet is at one with Anouilh's Antigone. It could be said of them, as Antigone says of herself and her father,

> Nous sommes de ceux qui posent les questions jusqu'au bout. Jusqu'à ce qu'il ne reste vraiment plus la petite chance d'espoir vivante, la plus petite chance d'espoir à étrangler.[87]

Just as Oedipus became calm and beautiful when he knew that nothing could save him, so Hamlet appears as his true self – lovable, gentle, beautiful and noble – when he is 'alone with death'. In these moments he is close to the tragic experience, and considers its tidings of suffering and loss, its annihilation of worldly man. The things of life, and the hope that can be derived from them, then appear 'trivial' to him, as they do to us – for may not imagination trace the noble dust of Alexander till it find it stopping a bung-hole, just as it may ascribe the acquiescence in mundane finitude of a Creon to his possessing *des têtes de cuisiniers*? The kingliness of those enmeshed in tragedy may be regarded as due to their freedom from both life's alarms and its hopes, for a response to either can now be seen as beneath the soul's dignity, and as departure from truth. Tragic affliction extends to man a perfecting, and a strange par-

[84] Scheler, *On The Eternal in Man*, 1960, pp. 267–8.
[85] *The Wheel of Fire*, London, 1949, pp. 45–6.
[86] ibid., p. 46.   [87] *Antigone*, ed. W. M. Landers, Harrap, 1966, p. 84.

ticipation in joy; it may also be conceived as putting an end to the soul's whoremongering, and understood, in the process of its constraining, to be bringing before the soul, as its proper object, the idea of God.

The individual's disillusionment with himself and his world cannot be without reference to the ethical in its highest reaches. That which detaches man from a false self-estimate, creates in him a true activity of spirit, and empowers human eyes to see without disguise, cannot but bring into contempt the merely human virtues. This necessity may be the origin of the peculiar character of the good which the Shakespearian tragic hero may be observed to seek, and to fail to find, amongst men – that yearning for righteousness to which both Lear and Hamlet appear to be dedicated. There can be seen in them a preoccupation with the disparity between the apparent and the real, the outer and the inner, and a horror at the untruth and vice which it betokens. Hamlet's first substantial utterance of the play begins with his swift 'I know not seems'; and his prizing of 'that within which passeth show' and contempt for 'actions that a man might play' may be held to correspond with Lear's scorn for 'that little seeming substance' which he has found to cover up a deeper insincerity. Hamlet's mock wonder at men's change of attitude to Claudius on his assumption of the crown – that

> those that would make mows at him while my father lived, give twenty, forty, fifty, an hundred ducats a-piece for his picture in little (II. ii. 369–71) –

is virtually Lear's emphasis that 'A dog's obeyed in office', and implies his denunciation of the scurvy politician, who, with the 'glass eyes' of flattering self-advantage, dedicates himself, and the lives of others, to falsehood (IV. vi. 171–3). In human dealings, both men seek 'the thing itself'. It is not 'the body of contraction', but its 'soul', that concerns Hamlet; he is aghast lest plausible actions on the surface of affairs should

> but skin and film the ulcerous place,
> Whiles rank corruption, mining all within,
> Infects unseen
>
> (III. iv. 147–9).

Lear in his madness would have the 'warp'd looks' of the wicked proclaim what store their hearts are made on (III. vi. 54–5). He is dominated by the thought of the readiness with which the depths of human depravity can be concealed by outward conformity to the standards of a creaturely righteousness, and wills the gods of this world to afflict mankind with the demands of a righteousness of a higher order, which will 'Rive' their 'concealing continents' and bring to light the 'undivulged crimes, /Un-whipp'd of justice' (III. ii. 52–8). Disillusionment with man thus makes

291

way for standards that are beyond his own; or it may equally be held that it is the light of a higher truth which first makes such disillusionment possible.

This awakened sense of the difference between mortal and eternal standards of righteousness is compatible with a general spiritual awakening. According to Calvin, it is a sign of the total claim which God's law makes upon the soul. A mortal lawgiver's supervision extends only to outward conduct, and his ordinances are not violated unless actual crimes are committed. Human laws may determine with what intent such crimes have been committed; secret thoughts, however, they do not search out.

> But God, whose eye nothing escapes, and who is concerned not so much with outward appearance as with purity of heart, under the prohibition of fornication, murder, and theft, forbids lust, anger, hatred, coveting a neighbour's possessions, deceit, and the like. For since he is a spiritual lawgiver, he speaks no less to the soul than to the body. But murder that is of the soul consists in anger and hatred; theft, in evil covetousness and avarice; fornication, in lust.[88]

It is by a spiritual vision that the great image of human authority is dispelled, and man perceives that he must strip his own back for punishment. Such a vision may be thought to be consistent with the impression of man's condemnation in Hamlet and Lear, and with the charity that emerges from it – the sense that 'We are arrant knaves, all', and a consequent determination to use no man after his deserts, for none is without fault :

> None does offend, none, I say none; I'll able 'em.[89]

For, as Calvin argues, though no one would deny that a conformity is demanded of man

> not only to outward honesty but to inward and spiritual righteousness,[90]

very few take due note of the fact because of the worldliness of their preoccupation :

> This happens because they do not look to the Lawgiver, by whose character the nature of the law also is to be appraised.[91]

It is not asserted here that Lear and Hamlet are the possessors of a pious intent, but rather that there may be seen in them evidence of the constraining of tragedy within a Providential universe. There is a sense in which tragedy's destruction of humanity's assurance in its own powers,

---

[88] *Inst.* II. viii. 6.   [89] *Hamlet* III. i. 129; *King Lear* IV. vi. 169.
[90] *Inst.* II. viii. 6.   [91] ibid.

292

its shattering of the 'perilous confidence in the flesh', is a preparation for the Christian faith, and indeed does its work. According to Reinhold Niebuhr,

> Such a faith can of course only be held on the ground of a view of life which makes all human virtue problematic and sees all historic achievement as ambiguous. Its basis is repentance. Yet it can be negatively validated by the simple process of recognizing the problematic character of all human virtues and the ambiguous character of all historic achievements.[92]

This further negative condition for the dawning of faith, which corresponds to Calvin's formula that we never truly glory in God until we have entirely renounced all glory of our own,[93] the tragic constraining may be regarded as having fulfilled in Lear and Hamlet.

The possibility of a Providential universe must bring into question the reality of the tragic experience. A concept of the tragic process which would include it within a Divine plan and the operation of grace appears to make of man's world a proving ground, and of the catastrophe itself no final disaster. In fact, the statement can then be made that

> every one of man's basic experiences ceases to be tragic in a Christian context.[94]

The pronouncement of G. Steiner, however, that 'The Christian view knows only partial or episodic tragedy',[95] must be judged the more acceptable. For the accomplishment to which the gospel bears witness is experienced by the believer very largely through anticipation. He stands in the interim between disclosure and fulfilment, and he remains liable to all that may befall a limited being in a tragic world.[96] The tragic suffering therefore represents for the Christian beholder his experience as mortal man; but it can reflect also sufferings unknown to the worldly: the agony of decision, and of rebirth in faith.[97] Further, the terror of his own weakness in faith may be enhanced by fellow-feeling with the sufferer, and by the manifest extent of all that faith must overcome. The temptations and penalties for the human spirit which literary tragedy bodies forth are the more fearsome to those who know that they must succumb – should they do so – in full knowledge of what they betray,

[92] *Faith and History*, London, 1949, p. 225.
[93] *Inst.* III. xiii. 2.
[94] Karl Jaspers, *Tragedy is Not Enough*, tr. Reiche, Moore and Deutsch, London, 1953, p. 40.
[95] *The Death of Tragedy*, 1961, p. 332.
[96] N. A. Scott, 'The Tragic Vision and The Christian Faith', *Angl. Theol. Rev.* XLV, 1963, pp. 38–40.
[97] R. B. Sewall, *The Vision of Tragedy*, Yale U.P., 1965, p. 51.

and that their sinning is not against themselves alone.[98] These considerations, and the fact of drama's power to involve the spectator in the experiences of the life it sets upon the stage, are not to be excluded from the Christian understanding of the tragic.[99] Nor is it to be overlooked that this understanding, while no less appreciative of the joys and vitalities of mortal existence than many others, can yet not accept them without certain qualification. Indeed, in so far as it recognizes the inevitability of evil's presence in the height of human achievement and enterprise, the Christian consciousness can be regarded almost as an aid to the appreciation of the tragic. Only in its conviction that evil is not inherent in existence itself, but ultimately under the dominion of a good God, does Christianity provide an area of human experience that is free from the tragic claim.[100]

Christianity offers a resolution of the problem of suffering in its concept of the humility of the Incarnation and the agony of the Cross. The confession of Christ as Lord is at the same time an acknowledgement that patience and suffering are God's ways of dealing with man in the world and an example and encouragement for the individual.[101] The thought that his involvement in the tragic life of the world is a participation in the suffering of God has in all ages been a consolation to the Christian; as Calvin expresses it,

> How much more can it do to soften all the bitterness of the cross, that the more we are afflicted with adversities, the more surely our fellowship with Christ is confirmed! By communion with him the very sufferings themselves not only become blessed to us but also help much in promoting our salvation.[102]

The faithful sacrifices which men make are in God, and God's sacrifice is in them. The eternal covenant of identification and offering in the grace of the risen Christ is the message and the means by which the tragic may be transformed,[103] and the problem of the suffering of the innocent resolved. In the guiltlessness of Christ is the reproof of those who would champion a peculiar virtue; and in the crucifixion, the sovereignty of God is expressed in suffering love rather than in power, and incorporates the tragic experience of man into the solution.[104] The Christian triumph itself, therefore, is centred upon pain, defeat and pity:

> The Cross is not tragic but the resolution of tragedy. Here suffering is carried into the very life of God and overcome. It becomes the basis of salvation. Yet it has tears of pity for those who do not understand life

[98] ibid., p. 52. [99] T. R. Henn, *The Harvest of Tragedy*, 1966, p. 291.
[100] R. Niebuhr, *Beyond Tragedy*, London, 1947, Preface, x–xi.
[101] Scott, op. cit., p. 41. [102] *Inst.* III. viii. 1.
[103] Scott, op. cit., pp. 42 ff. [104] Niebuhr, *Faith and History*, p. 161.

profoundly enough to escape the chaos of impulse and chance by which most lives are determined.[105]

The revelation that it is God's nature to swallow up evil in Himself and destroy it reveals that life is in its deepest essence good.[106] Yet it points directly to the tragic as a means of revelation and assurance for mankind, and asserts God's ordaining of conflict for those whom He loves: that those who are one day to be crowned in heaven must first undergo struggles on earth.[107] As D. M. Mackinnon argues, the Passion of Christ itself, in which the believer finds at once the judgement and the redemption of the world, is

> a desperately human occasion fraught, not with a great, but with an ultimate, significance. But it is also failure; and that not in the language of devotion, but in that of literal fact. It is in the figure of Judas Iscariot that the failure of Jesus is focused, and the tragic quality of his mission becomes plain. . . . There is no solution here of the problem of moral evil; there is nothing moreover which the Easter faith somehow obliterates. For it is to his own, and not to the world, that the risen Christ shows himself; and even those who accept as factual the record of the empty tomb admit that in itself that emptiness is no more than a sign pointing.[108]

The reality that is to be does not effect a lessening of the realities of the present.

The tragic is thus an instrument in the hands of a God who teaches by sorrow, and wounds men in order to heal them;[109] and it is inherent in the very existence of man as a creature. For man could not be, if God were not hidden from him; and the goodness of God which brings him into being is to be seen in that very imposition of limitation, and of distance from his Creator, that makes possible his entering upon creaturely identity. The ways of God are not man's; and in his love God must remove Himself from man's presence. In Kierkegaard's words,

> it is precisely Thy greatness which makes Thee invisible. For Thou art too far removed from the thoughts of men in Thy wisdom that they should see Thee; and Thou are too near men in Thy omnipresence to permit them to see Thee. Thou dost conceal Thyself from man in Thy goodness, and Thy omnipotence causes him not to see Thee, for then he would himself become as nothing![110]

[105] Niebuhr, *Beyond Tragedy*, pp. 155–6.   [106] ibid., p. 168.
[107] Calvin, *Inst.* III. ix. 3.
[108] 'Theology and Tragedy', *Religious Studies* II, 1967, pp. 168–9.
[109] Augustine, *Conf.* II. ii. 3.
[110] 'Man's Need of God Constitutes his Highest Perfection', *Edifying Discourses*, tr. Swenson, Minneapolis, 1950–3, IV, pp. 25–6.

Yet separation from God, by which man comes into existence, is truly a diminution of being; and his predicament is the more tragic in that the exercise of creaturely powers and initiatives, if not directed to the attainment of being of a higher order, must necessarily increase that separation, and undermine the very means of his creaturely identity. If, therefore, he does not renounce the limited goods of mortal existence, they will renounce themselves in inflicting tragic defeat upon him; yet his creaturely state of sin is such that the pains of affliction alone can bring him to realize the imperfection of the being he enjoys, and make for his acquiescence in that death of what appertains to the creature that is the prelude to rebirth into higher truth. Worldly man is wrapped in a dream of existence, rather than in existence itself; and unless he is disturbed in his temporal dwelling, his thoughts of higher things will also be as the dreams of one who is but a 'speculator of divinity'.[111] Not until it is imbued with a 'contempt for the present life', therefore, is the mind of man 'seriously aroused to desire and ponder the life to come;[112] or, in Luther's words,

> It is impossible for a human heart, without crosses and tribulations, to think upon God.[113]

The cause is not merely limitation and ignorance, but the active perversity inherent in man's self-congratulation – this 'beast which is called vain glory', which only affliction can beat down and suppress.[114] The fact of death presents to the worldly the tidings of annihilation; and

> Though it fills man with terror and crushes him with despair, yet this thought is necessary for us in order that, being divested of our own righteousness, having given up faith in our own power, being rejected from all expectation of life, we may learn from the understanding of our poverty, misery, and infamy, to prostrate ourselves before the Lord.[115]

Nothing is better for us, declares Luther in characteristic manner, than to be covered over with the shovel.[116]

The eloquence of death is in its constraining towards the thought of the necessity of higher being. To the worldling who will not permit this thought, death betokens the frustration of life, and a final unreason at the heart of things. To him, as O. Mandel points out, death is the blight of life, and the proof of its futility; indeed, the less tragic his life has been, the more tragic does the fact of death appear to him. But death

---

[111] Luther, *Table-Talk*, tr. W. Hazlitt, London, 1883, lxii.
[112] Calvin, *Inst.* III. xi. 1.   [113] *Table-Talk*, dcxxxviii.
[114] Luther, *Galatians* (v. 25), ed. P. S. Watson, 1953, pp. 530–1.
[115] Calvin, *Instruction in Faith*, tr. P. T. Fuhrmann, Lutterworth Press, 1949, p. 23.
[116] *Table-Talk*, lxxiv.

is not necessarily an evil.[117] To the mind of faith, death is itself reassurance, and a confirmation of the triumph of an exalted purpose over the seeming imperfections and disharmonies of the created order. The justice of God, Luther asserts, is inexplicable in mortal terms; but

> a summary explanation . . . is found in a single little word: *There is a life after this life; and all that is not punished and repaid here will be punished and repaid there; for this life is nothing more than a precursor, or, rather, a beginning, of the life that is to come.*[118]

The wisdom of paganism is summed up in Aristotle's saying, that 'Death is a dreadful thing, for it is the end';[119] in terms of the Christian understanding, the doctrine that holds that there is no life after this is 'Of all stupidities . . . the most foolish, the basest, and the most pernicious'.[120] To the latter awareness, tribulations come to confirm the faith of man and display the power of God; and the true function of tragedy can be seen to be the same as that of the greater poetry of existence itself: to display the beauty and evanescence of mortal forms, that the beholder may become

> a passionate lover of that unspeakable and everlasting beauty to be seen by the eyes of the mind, only cleared by faith.[121]

The affirmation that suffering and death are not final requires that the terrors of life should be revealed in their fullness.

Tragedy may possibly be held not to effect anything deserving the title of a radical transformation of consciousness in either hero or beholder. Its assault upon creaturely self-confidence may be understood rather to confirm human strengths and glories; and instead of the apprehension of another universe with different values, the human consciousness may be driven to even greater attachment to its own world. Nonetheless, tragedy may serve a purpose of revelation in its urging of certain essential truth upon the mind which experiences it. It makes clear the goodness of good and the evil of evil.[122] Goodness in tragedy, as J. J. Lawlor affirms, is distinguished and recommended 'by the fact of human solidarity', whereas evil 'shows itself merely individualistic, incapable of combination save for severely limited ends'.[123] The main source of the tragic convulsion in Shakespearian tragedy Bradley declares to be 'in

[117] *A Definition of Tragedy*, N.Y., 1961, p. 168.
[118] *Bondage*, tr. Parker and Johnston, London, 1959, p. 316.
[119] Quoted by W. Macneile Dixon, *The Human Situation*, 1938, p. 299.
[120] Dante, *The Convivio*, ed. P. H. Wicksteed, Temple Classics, Dent, 1903, p. 97.
[121] Sir Philip Sidney, *An Apology for Poetry*, ed. G. Shepherd, 1965, p. 99.
[122] See R. B. Sewall, *The Vision of Tragedy*, p. 79.
[123] *The Tragic Sense in Shakespeare*, 1960, p. 100.

every case evil', and in almost every case 'plain moral evil', to the extent that the demand that tragedy appears to make is for 'nothing short of good in perfection'.[124] Evil, on the other hand,

> exhibits itself everywhere as something negative, barren, weakening, destructive, a principle of death. It isolates, disunites, and tends to annihilate not only its opposite but itself. That which keeps the evil man prosperous, makes him succeed, even permits him to exist, is the good in him. . . . When the evil in him masters the good and has its way, it destroys other people through him, but it also destroys *him*.[125]

The evil that is displayed in tragedy conforms to the definition of something which could have no existence apart from the good which is its only support, and which, since it must consume itself if it could exhaust the good whence it claims its being, is in the last resort to be regarded as deficiency rather than entity:[126]

> It must be the implacable enemy of all that is ordered, submissive and co-operating, 'Whatever is begotten, born and dies': and in this lies its fatal weakness.[127]

Tragedy also impresses the supreme good of personality. At the conclusion of the action, according to K. Jaspers, the tragic perception sees in all human accomplishment 'an inescapable nexus of guilt and doom', from which a deliverance may lie in the 'elemental' fact of human courage.[128] In the character of Macbeth, L. Abercrombie sees something which appears capable of transcending the evil both of its condition and of its own creation within itself. Macbeth has striven and lost all in a cause which now appears to him in its true futility:

> But he seizes upon the appalling moment and masters even this; he masters it by knowing it absolutely and completely by forcing even this quintessence of all evil to live before him with the zest and terrible splendour of his own unquenchable mind.[129]

In Jasper's terms, Macbeth's action would reveal, 'together with its steadfastness, reality':[130] the horror of evil, and the goodness of being in general, are outmatched in impressiveness by that aspect of being which is the human spirit even as it succumbs to the forces of destructiveness. That this can be so is both a joy and a mystery – and, according to

---

[124] *Shakespearean Tragedy*, pp. 34–5.   [125] ibid., p. 35.
[126] Aquinas, *S.T.* I. xlviii. 2, 3, *ad R.*; I. xlix. 3, *ad R.*
[127] Lawlor, op. cit., p. 100.
[128] *Tragedy is Not Enough*, pp. 96, 78.
[129] *The Idea of Great Poetry*, 1925, p. 176, quoted by V. Y. Kantak, 'An Approach to Shakespearian Tragedy: The 'Actor' Image in *Macbeth*', *S.S.* XVI, 1963, p. 45.
[130] op., cit. p. 78.

W. B. Yeats, its demonstration constitutes the height of tragedy's achievement:

> The arts are at their greatest when they seek for a life growing always more scornful of everything that is not itself and passing into its own fullness, as it were, ever more completely as all that is created out of the passing mode of society slips from it; and attaining that fullness, perfectly it may be – and from this is tragic joy and the perfectness of tragedy – when the world itself has slipped away in death. We, who are believers, cannot see reality anywhere but in the soul itself, and seeing it there we cannot do other than rejoice in every energy, whether of gesture, or of action, or of speech, coming out of the personality, the soul's image.[131]

The tragic catastrophe would seem to establish the insignificance of the human spirit; but it is on the contrary the significance of human personality that is established in the experiencing mind.

If the human condition is to be transcended, it must be through a principle which belongs to a higher order, and a personality which has an existence beyond the temporal, and can find its place in such an order. The principle concerned can only be goodness in the fullest and highest sense, which extends to others as it does to the self. And the personality can only be one perfected by love for renewed and nobler life. Tragedy therefore directs attention to certain necessary means or conditions for transcendence – but only in the process of revealing the human world to which it is bound. That world is seen to have no power to transcend itself, and the conclusion of literary tragedy must therefore be 'general woe'. But even in its conclusion, tragedy makes clear what Christian experience affirms: that for the true completion both of the principle of goodness in man and of the significance of his own spirit, the working and the grace of a higher order is necessary. And those to whom faith is present may find in tragedy's brief history of perturbation, mischance and defeat in the mortal undertakings of man's spirit the confirmation of its loftier need and potentiality: the truth that

> Thou madest us for Thyself, and our heart is restless, until it repose in Thee.[132]

[131] 'The Play, The Player, and The Scene', *Plays and Controversies*, 1923, pp. 123–4.
[132] Augustine, *Conf.* I. i. 1.

IV

A Theological Interpretation of
Shakespearian Tragedy:
The Heroic Predicament as the
Operation of the
Apostate Will Beneath
Providential Ordinance

Chapter 20

INTRODUCTORY

From the foregoing study it may be concluded that a correspondence exists between the manifestations of literary tragedy and a theological estimate of the human condition and its possibilities. The tragic phenomenon appears not only to be in accord with a religious understanding of man's life on earth, but both necessary in its incidence and predictable in its unfolding. Yet although drama and theology may find grounds of reconciliation in their approach to the tragic fact, as disciplines they remain distinct. Theology has its beginning in what is beyond man, but literary tragedy is a human creation, inspired by mortal appearances and limited by its nature to secular terms; and, despite any more far-reaching congruity or relevance it may show, it is only to be judged in accordance with its nature. The correspondence with theological teaching that has become evident does not therefore imply an appropriateness in the systematic use of theological categories for the criticism of drama; but it raises instead the larger question of whether, in a Divine universe, the significance of secular existence and event can remain limited to themselves.

If the correspondence is real, there should be discernible in the heroic failing scope for error of a kind that is more grievous and profound than must appear to a wholly mundane appraisal, and meaning in all the happenings of tragedy that is more lively and edifying. That literary criticism at its best goes far towards meeting this requirement, and establishing amidst the secular an awareness that tends beyond it, is apparent from the studies that have been adduced; but it has also often been clear that significances which tend beyond man's world will nonetheless be restricted to a purely human experience of life by a criticism which lacks the means of discerning their true nature, and of bringing them into the task of appreciation with the necessary accuracy. Such criticism cannot be blamed for failing to find, in the sense of heightened meaning which tragedy bestows, an approach to the transcendental. Just as the function of tragedy lies in its exemplifying the human condition rather than explaining it through concepts which tend beyond it, so it is ideally the purpose of criticism to re-present what the dramatist sets forth in a way that enhances its appeal and rekindles in the reader the

powers of appreciation. But if its concern, like that of the drama it relates
to, is with immediate experience rather than ultimate truth, its vision
of the concrete instance can scarcely be without relation to the depth
of the understanding which entertains it. And, further, if a concern for
the integrity of his art constrains a critic to avoid an absoluteness of
judgement, both the wide prerogatives and the inescapable duty of his
calling – to say nothing of human nature itself – must always promote
in him a reaching toward finality. A secular estimate of a secular art-
form will not be invalid; on the contrary, it will have immediate
relevance, and penetration and insight no more limited than man's
imagination itself. But there must remain room for doubt, once it is conceded that the laws of tragedy do not operate apart from a Providential
system, whether that literary criticism can achieve completeness, and
in the highest sense justice, which is remote from all theological awareness. Indeed, a criticism deriving from its author's acquiescence in the
mode of life which is content to pay its debt to 'time and mortal custom',
despite all the perceptions which may be incidental to such a purpose,
may from an ultimate point of view be as misleading as Macbeth's
characteristic intent.

The tragic hero is heroic only because he is in the first place representative: what is true of him in his attitude to the world is therefore
no less true of his worldly critic. They share a mystification at a universe
which appears now benevolent and now unuttterably harsh, and which
at all times shows itself as beyond a mortal comprehension. They share
also, nonetheless, a will to impose a human estimate upon experience that
points beyond humanity: to approach life in terms of creaturely predominance, and the assumed absence of the God in the light of whose
truth all creaturely standards and suppositions are revealed as empty.
If the hero, in dismissing Divine truth from his awareness, typifies a
common mind in mankind that is 'thrust out by its own weight from
blessedness', he speaks no less for his critic; and if the critic brings to
the assessment of tragedy the knowledge of modes of happiness and being
that do not range beyond what is mortal, he is merely applying the
yardstick of a 'false beatitude',[1] which would do better to recognize its
own confusion in the tragic downfall. The more far-reaching effect of
man's subjection to misfortune may be to convince him of his Godlessness
and guilt; but the greater part of what issues from this needful knowledge
must be unattainable by a Godless criticism – for,

where the Iudge is false, what truth abides?[2]

[1] Augustine, *De Civ. Dei* XIX. xx.
[2] Fulke Greville, 'A Treatie of Humane Learning', st. 51, *Poems and Dramas*, ed. G. Bullough,
1938, I, p. 166.

If the world's gladnesses are tokens of a wickedness unpunished, and its miseries are proof of its guilt – if, in fact, literary tragedy declares the spiritual condition of mankind – the worldly critic is in little better position to recognize it than the tragic hero. It does not follow that his inability will hinder others in this recognition; but in no sense will it help them.

It may perhaps be too much to ask of any critic that he should see in tragedy the effects of a Divine chastisement that an audience as a whole scarcely begins to appreciate; indeed, an interpretation of this order, if it be admitted, can come only as the culmination of every other kind and quality of perception. But there must be available to him an awareness that is not restricted to the categories of flesh and blood, action and passion, time and chance. For great tragedy is able to convey an impression of transcendent possibility in despite of its natural terms; it cannot in fact achieve the rank of greatness if, within its workings, a tension does not exist between the reality it sets forth and an exalted reality which interpenetrates it. This tension or balance the drama will recreate in the mind of the beholder; and the mind of the critic must be capable of maintaining it as he turns to judgement. Only as he does so will he be able to bring a true response to what is in itself an 'interim reading of life';[3] and only the readiness to assume the reality of God and all that devolves from it in mortal affairs can create a response of this quality. What is easy for the spectator of great tragedy is thus a severe responsibility for the critic – though it can be met the more readily in the mind which is alive to the full potentialities of the human spirit.

It cannot be met by the critic whose approach is determinedly secular. If, to use Schlegel's terms, the interpreter of tragedy can give no personal credence to intimations of 'a vocation transcending the limits of this earthly life',[4] and can admit no assurance of rational order through the circumstances of loss and pain, the drama will bring him little more than the melancholy tidings of an imbecile universe. For what has ultimate value has no permanent relation to the tragic world; and the sense of abiding truth that can come only with the destruction of mortal forms and hopes is beyond the ordinary capacities of those for whom reality is limited to what is mortal. For others, the unfolding of tragedy does extend the boundaries of significance, and bring new insights; but the quality of those insights cannot be adequately assessed by a criticism which hesitates at the brink of the spiritual. Through the very force of its discipline tragedy is an appeal for further revelation; and a critic who cannot in himself relate the present happening to what stands beyond the present will not normally be empowered to sustain that appeal by

[3] U. Ellis-Fermor, *The Frontiers of Drama*, 1945, p. 147.
[4] *Lectures on Dramatic Art and Literature*, tr. J. Black, rev. A. J. W. Morrison, N.Y., 1965, p.45.

his interpretation of the tragic event. Even an imagination like A. C. Bradley's, fired by the realization of the strange immunity of the good from what is outward, and of the incompleteness of an understanding that cannot concede the salutary effect of misfortune upon human nature,[5] can permit his criticism to glean from these things no more than marginal – if not indeed questionable – meaning.

It is not surprising, therefore, that tragedy's harvest of joy in the human spirit, though variously explained by the secular mind, remains bewildering in its power to exalt. The critic of real perception is impelled away from the processes that lie within man to the consideration of an order of existence beyond him, being obliged to acknowledge that the tragic joy is finally commensurate only with some measure of revelation. But although rhyme and reason is seen in the destruction of artificial and imperfect human attitudes as a means of apprehending and approaching reality – although it be asserted that 'Breakdown and failure reveal the true nature of things', and that in the approach of the tragic hero towards his doom may be understood 'a movement toward man's proper essence'[6] – these insights are customarily obscured by a lesser criticism, and fail to attain, even in the ablest hands, their final penetration and dignity. The terms 'reality' and 'essence' have in the last resort small meaning if they are used apart from the knowledge of a Divine order mediated by revelation. Only a criticism applied in the recognition of such an order can enable the reader to distinguish in tragic happening the joy-imparting and Providential process in which the barriers of human apostasy are swept away.

What applies to the paradox of tragic pleasure applies to every moral or evaluative pronouncement which criticism may attempt concerning the phenomenon in general or the details of its enactment. There can be no full comprehension of either tragic pleasure or tragic pain, no adequate vision of purpose or justice in the tragic world, in minds which do not attain further than a creaturely knowledge and the wisdom that is built upon it. The human propensity is to covet a limited good, and to judge in terms of mortal desires; and these endeavours of a reprobate self-concern can only envelop their objects in the perversity from which they sprang. An understanding whose chief and most insistent preoccupation is, in Luther's phrase, to busy itself with temporal, earthly and ephemeral things[7] will perceive, when those things go amiss, not

A mercy still in everything,
And shining through all mysteries,[8]

[5] *Shakespearean Tragedy*, 1956, pp. 326–7.
[6] Karl Jaspers, *Tragedy is Not Enough*, tr. H. A. T. Reiche *et al.*, London, 1953, p. 41.
[7] *Table-Talk*, tr. W. Hazlitt, London, 1883, cxlvii.
[8] From the hymn 'O blessed life!', by W. T. Matson.

but mere mischance. It is manifest, however, that finality of perception cannot be expected where happenings in the human sphere are accounted for in isolation from the universal order of which they are part – where the human condition is judged from considerations which cannot tend beyond it. An entirely secular approach to the interpretation of tragedy must be held to deny itself the means of thorough-going evaluation. But any judgement whatsoever, even in the common categories of good and evil, right and wrong, greatness and littleness, success and failure, must presuppose in the critic reference to some system of ultimate standards, or a degree of trust in the good or otherwise of certain values which would merit the use of the term 'faith'. Every emphatic statement of critical appraisal, therefore, must carry with it the overtones of meta-physical connotation. A critic who is not 'religious' in some sense of the term can hardly exist.

Even if a critic of this order could be produced, he would face the disadvantage of the invariable conduct of the tragic heroes themselves, whose every ambition and desire embodies a challenge to the highest consciousness and idealism of those who consider them. All critics face the need to distinguish among the varieties of human desire, and the differing conceptions of good that are to be found in the pattern of the tragedy; and they must also confront the mystery of the clash of good with good, and the hero's destruction by what is evidently fine in his personal qualities and his soul's aspirations. From this jarring of worthy principles the worldly critic is no more able to escape than the tragic hero, neither is he better able to identify surpassing and positive good, until he can relieve the weight of mortal mystery by resort to mysteries of the spirit. Only by the resulting acknowledgement of continuity be-tween the moral and the spiritual can it be apprehended that what is good under one aspect of existence is evil in terms of a higher aspect – that human qualities and their material enactment can become vicious in quality and effect when they are not dedicated to the final end of all creaturely activity. No outlook which is less than religious can envisage a resolution of the conflict between apparent and rival goods – or of other tragic anomaly that ranges from the liberty of evil and the fact of evident waste to the working of an inflexible destiny within the manifest scope of human freedom. The challenge which tragedy makes to the spirit of man can be re-emphasized as it can be muted by a criticism limited to secular experience; but if it is in any way the task of an accomplished criticism to set forth the challenge in its completeness, or to equip the reader for the fullest response, a religious awareness in the critic is indispensable.

The challenge of tragedy expresses itself most compellingly in the characteristic ambition of the tragic hero which brings about his over-

307

throw. A secular criticism can name the over-reaching pretension with objectivity and ease, can assess the deadly consequences of its breaking the bond of humanity, and the dire effects of the rule of passion. But to the significance of the heroic preoccupation with a mortal beatitude it cannot but be insensitive. In this preoccupation, and the accompanying darkened affections, it may not readily see the signs of spiritual alienation, nor distinguish a self-love that descends to acts of blasphemous horror in perverse imitation of Divine omnipotence. For all that emerges from the purpose of converting creatureliness into infinity, if not for the purpose itself, there will tend to be critical adulation rather than critical apprehension. Like the heroes themselves, the worldly critic will presume upon the health of the embattled soul; and in its predicament he will see the evidence, not of spiritual relapse, but of earthly misfortune. For both are caught up in the tragic mortal state of self-congratulation: and neither will find, in disaster itself, or in the personality's disintegration and disillusion under the blows of mischance, a purposive constraining within a Providential universe. In the very instance of tragedy's most urgent approach to the conscience of man, a criticism devoid of theological perspective will, lacking a vital element in experience, fall short in its apprehension of meaning.

The correspondence that has been shown to exist between a theological estimate of the human condition and the course of literary tragedy therefore indicates the need for a degree of theological awareness in any thorough criticism of Shakespeare's tragedies, or of any great tragedy; and the need is at its greatest where consideration is given to the nature of the hero's failing and its consequences within his personality. A theological interpretation of Shakespeare's main tragedies – if it be possible, and if it is to be successful – must devote itself in particular to the profoundest possible analysis of the state of will and quality of motive in the tragic hero. Beneath the secular or prudential level of his awareness, which manifests the operation of ambition or jealousy, or the workings of passion, or the grip of obsession, it must be able to distinguish an underlying state of radical guilt, 'some form of inordinate selfinterest',[9] a pride or a *hubris* of gross and baleful aspect which must corrupt the purposes played out on the tragic stage. It must be able, in short, to show that the hero's error, and his disordered affections, are the symptoms of a disease of personality which a secular criticism lacks the means to diagnose. In the studies of Shakespeare's tragedies which follow, the attempt will be made to reach the heart of tragedy, and to test the correspondence that has been indicated at a more theoretical level, by determining whether there may be detected – through a literary approach

[9] R. W. Battenhouse, 'Shakespearian Tragedy : A Christian Interpretation', *The Tragic Vision and the Christian Faith*, ed. N. A. Scott, N.Y., 1957, p. 84.

that is undivorced from religious awareness – a kind of significance within mortal thoughts which cannot be bordered within mortal considerations, and which in itself is inimical to humanity: a desire in the tragic hero for that depravity of existence comprised in the choice of the city of man in contempt of God.

Chapter 21
MACBETH

The villainy of Macbeth sets a problem for any criticism that falls short of being a purely aesthetic appraisal. As J. Markels has noted, following a similar comment in Bradley, the play is one of the few masterpieces whose protagonist grows in depravity without diminishing our pity for him.[1] Bradley's right to treat Macbeth as a tragic hero rather than a hero-villain has been questioned by Miss L. B. Campbell. She points out that Macbeth is a character who, in C. V. Boyer's definition,

> deliberately opposes moral law from wilfulness, and for the purpose of advancing his own interests, recognizing at the same time the sanction of the law he defies.[2]

The evil of the means which Macbeth uses to break the bond with his fellows speaks for itself; and the beneficence – indeed, the sacredness – of all that is 'strong against the deed' is widely acknowledged. In his scorning of human kindness Macbeth is seen to make war against humanity and the natural order,[3] if not to set up a defiance of God;[4] and the assertion can strongly be made that it is his

> knowing and deliberate denial of God and his rejection of the law of nature which set him apart from the heroes of *Hamlet, Othello* and *Lear*.[5]

His recognized depravity can lead the critic to regard the play as a study of evil in all its manifestations, and to see in it, more than in any other play, 'a reflection of Shakespeare's view of evil's operation in the world'.[6]

Yet sympathy would scarcely extend to Macbeth if he were so balefully distinguished, and Bradley surely displays a profounder discernment in ranking him with the others. He does not see them all as sharing a

---

[1] 'The Spectacle of Deterioration : *Macbeth* and the "Manner" of Tragic Imitation', *S.Q* XII, 1961, p. 293.

[2] Lily B. Campbell, 'Concerning Bradley's *Shakespearean Tragedy*', *Huntingdon Library Quarterly* XIII, 1949–50, p. 1; Boyer, *The Villain as Hero in Elizabethan Tragedy*, London, 1914, p. 6.

[3] T. Spencer, *Shakespeare and the Nature of Man*, 1943, p. 156.

[4] I. Ribner, '*Macbeth* : The Pattern of Idea and Action', *S.Q.* X, 1959, p. 150.

[5] ibid., p. 147.   [6] ibid.

renegade calling, and pursuing, like mankind at large, the unholy desires of a penitential destiny;[7] but in Macbeth's making himself his end and the world his means he doubtless saw that kinship in common aspiration with natural man which links him with his tragic peers – and which is the main origin of the audience's sympathy, as it is the true beginning of Macbeth's evil. A further source of pity, however, is that fact that, for all his conscious resolution, Macbeth is to a degree unaware of what he is doing. He sets aside the moral law – but he is blind to what setting aside the moral law means: as Bradley puts it, he cannot accept 'as the principle of his conduct the morality which takes shape in his imaginative fears'.[8] His instinctive preference for the worst evokes in the spectator the response which Iago's compulsive cynicism calls forth in Desdemona: 'O heavy ignorance!' (II. i. 143.) Macbeth is deluded by appearances, and is truly the victim of the means he employs; the entire play, according to I. Ribner, is a statement of the deceptive nature of evil:

Not until the very end of the play does Macbeth learn how evil works.[9]

If, therefore, all men are involved in evil, and may be distinguished as they know and acquiesce in it, or are blind and suffer for it, or see their own evil and fly from it, Macbeth's state extends to the second category; and Shakespeare's drawing the beholder's attention from the crime's effect on its victim to its effect on its perpetrator[10] is in keeping with an estimate of Macbeth as the classic victim of error. If he chooses villainy, therefore, he is certainly without the 'illness' that should attend it: the blood on his hands, despite its being a pledge of his ambition's success, must remain 'a sorry sight'. Nothing can make him forget, in Bradley's words, 'what he once was and Iago and Goneril never were'.[11]

It is customary to observe in Lady Macbeth a nature limited to the practical and the matter-of-fact. Her literalness of mind can conceive of courage as screwed to the sticking-place, memory as a fume, the receipt of reason as a limbeck, blood as a filthy witness, and the sleeping and the dead but as pictures. This concreteness of vision becomes Macbeth's own. He will judge of men as if their thoughts were determined by tangible qualities which Nature has 'clos'd' within them (III. i. 98–9); so must he judge also of sickness of mind or spirit, willing that physic may be able to 'pluck', 'raze' and 'cleanse' the 'perilous stuff' that weighs upon the heart (V. iii. 41–5). Like his wife, he must be able to see all realities as concrete, and himself the master of them. Intangibles are 'brainsickly' notions; 'good' becomes for them the crown and the means to it, and 'evil' is what stands in the way.[12] This tendency Bradley

[7] (Section III, p. 220.)   [8] *Shakespearian Tragedy*, 2nd edn, 1956, p. 357.
[9] op. cit., p. 152.
[10] J. Markels, 'The Spectacle of Deterioration', *S.Q.* XII, 1961, p. 298.
[11] op. cit., p. 365.   [12] ibid., p. 370.

characterizes in Lady Macbeth as want of imagination; once only, he declares, is she able to glimpse the future and perceive conscientious scruple has the power to 'make us mad'.[13] Yet in the narrowness which is hers, and which her spirit confirms in her husband with a persistent 'Consider it not so deeply', may be seen an underlying impulsion to draw in the horizons of the understanding in order to make reality correspond to a mundane and creaturely purpose.[14]

The aggrandizement of the self is the only doctrine which Macbeth and his wife are able to understand – or to conceive as ruling the wills of any save Duncan. This assumption of universal self-seeking accounts for the peculiar and laboured quality of their insincerities. They must give assurance of the overbalancing of personal gain: Macbeth's service and loyalty to Duncan, 'In doing it, pays itself'; the labour that is delighted in, 'physics pain'; and if Banquo will

> cleave to my consent, when 'tis,
> It shall make honour for you
> (II. i. 25–6).

As H. B. Charlton declares, 'No bribe was ever more flagrantly confessed'.[15] These are the involuntary confessions of natures devoted to their own advancement, whose habitual thoughts and aims are all of station and power.[16] They are akin to Macbeth's involuntary starting at the pronouncement of the Witches; Macbeth, declares Coleridge, had been 'rendered temptible by previous dalliance of the fancy with ambitious thoughts', and both his starting and his soliloquy show 'the early birth-date of his guilt'.[17] The will of a practical and narrow understanding is swiftly directed to the means of its ambitions: Coleridge compares the 'eagerness' of Macbeth at the tidings with 'the easily-satisfied mind of the self-uninterested Banquo'.[18] Macbeth sees his course immediately. His questions to the 'imperfect speakers' are completely to the point: they concern the manner of the forthcoming events, the source of the Witches' knowledge and the purpose of their action. The promise made by this 'supernatural soliciting' (though soliciting it is not)[19] cannot be 'ill' since it denotes prosperity. As Charlton points out,

> The metaphysical question is irrelevant. He is preoccupied with the sense that the kingship is very near his grasp.[20]

His thoughts fly to the means which may crown him; and, once he is decided, he gives evidence of such zest for practical achievement, and

---

[13] ibid., pp. 373–4. [14] (Section III, pp. 239–40).
[15] *Shakespearian Tragedy*, 1952, p. 174.
[16] Bradley, op. cit., p. 350.
[17] *Lectures and Notes on Shakespere*, ed. T. Ashe, (Bohn) 1904, pp. 371–2.
[18] ibid., p. 372. [19] Bradley, *Shakespearean Tragedy*, p. 344.
[20] op. cit., p. 164.

such fierce joy in the deeds he has planned, as must make Iago's self-congratulation seem almost genteel. It is the assertion of one who has made himself his own end – and who thereby preoccupies himself with a particular and limited good. The kingship is his divinity, and the world his kingdom. To attain the one and to rule the other he will 'jump the life to come' and cast away his 'eternal jewel'. He is zealous only to

> live the lease of nature, pay his breath
> To time and mortal custom
>
> (IV. i. 99–100).

To a common-sense ethic this is no singular design; only in the consequences will it see a perverse will declining upon a part of reality, and, seeking to be more, being made less.[21]

The origin of Macbeth's will it may with perhaps greater justification fail to determine, for the question of the presence and the powers of the Witches admits of no easy answers. It is not possible to take refuge in the thought that they may be of the same origin as Macbeth's air-drawn dagger, for Banquo has seen and talked with them. Dr Johnson emphasizes the exactness with which Shakespeare has followed popular accounts and common traditions; and he makes an observation concerning Shakespeare's presentation of them which should not be ignored. Witchcraft or enchantment, he says, 'though not strictly the same, are confounded in this play'.[22] The confusion which Shakespeare allows points to his acquiescence in his audience's uncertainty – a probability which has not escaped the modern critic. K. Muir concludes that

> He left it to the audience to decide whether the weird sisters were witches, or devils disguised as witches, and whether Lady Macbeth, when she deliberately chose evil, was literally, or only metaphorically, possessed by demons.[23]

The Witches may testify to the dramatist's ability to plumb depths inaccessible to the merely realistic, and to his belief in a supernatural reality; yet it is significant that in *Macbeth*, where the 'metaphysical' is most fully in evidence, the centre of interest remains the realistic. Equivocation in the Witches, as J. J. Lawlor argues, answers to equivocation first in the heart and then in the act of man. He sees Macbeth's as a willed downfall, and the progress of the tragedy as the infection of the will by a disease which he would diagnose as impatience with time and lack of ripeness.[24] The rôle of the Witches he takes to be, from the stand-

---

[21] (Section II, p. 151.)

[22] *Johnson on Shakespeare*, ed. W. Raleigh, 1957, pp. 167, 170.

[23] *Shakespeare : the Great Tragedies* (Writers and their Work), Longmans, 1961, p. 36.

[24] *The Tragic Sense in Shakespeare*, 1960, pp. 151–2.

point of choice, a demonstration that disaster must inevitably dog the footsteps of double-dealing.[25]

Yet their unequivocal presence must raise the subject of their influence. The contrast with Banquo confirms Bradley in the belief that Macbeth's actions are not forced upon him.[26] Temptation was clearly already within him, and the idea of Duncan's murder is his own. The matter of the Witches' foreknowledge he regards as being inaccessible to critical judgement,[27] and would thus have agreed with T. Spencer that 'The problem of predestination and free-will is presented, but is left unanswered'.[28] Criticism on the whole has recognized in the weird sisters 'a power not to determine a man's fate, but to stir his imagination', and has thus insisted that the problem is not that of occult agencies but of mankind's susceptibility.[29] I. Ribner, quoting writers who, like himself, are concerned with religious patterns of thought, ascribes the impulse of evil to Macbeth. The Witches, he declares,

> simply suggest an object which may incite the inclination to evil which is always within man because of original sins [sic], and they do this by means of prophecy;

and thus while the good man, sharing in Divine grace as well as in original sin, can resist their appeal, the evil man falls.[30] Yet the suggestion of a mysterious power remains. Coleridge styles the Witches as 'the shadowy obscure and fearfully anomalous of physical nature, the lawless of human nature'.[31] Bradley yields, as it were, to the suggestion that Shakespeare dwells upon phenomena which make it seem that man in the play 'is in the power of secret forces lurking below, and independent of his consciousness and will', setting up 'a dread of the presence of evil all through and around our mysterious nature'.[32] *Macbeth* certainly presents the threat of an uncontrollable world in which man is involved: its hero's first words, uttered the moment the Witches' charm is 'wound up', partake of their earlier incantation. It may justifiably be concluded that we shall never know, and that Shakespeare does not wish us to determine, whether the weird sisters control Macbeth's fate, or whether their prophecies are a reflection of his character.[33] That he drives us to this conclusion may mean simply that Shakespeare will not claim a wisdom beyond humanity. It may point to his awareness of the strength of man's passionate endowment, his compulsive inclination to evil, and

---

[25] ibid., p. 120. [26] op. cit., p. 343. [27] ibid., pp. 344–5.

[28] *Shakespeare and the Nature of Man*, 1943, p. 157.

[29] J. Markels, 'The Spectacle of Deterioration', *S.Q.* XII, 1961, p. 298.

[30] '*Macbeth* : the Pattern of Idea and Action', *S.Q.* X, 1959, p. 151.

[31] *Lectures and Notes* (Bohn), 1904, p. 370.

[32] op. cit., p. 338.

[33] J. I. M. Stewart, *Character and Motive in Shakespeare*, 1959, p. 86, quoting R. Bridges, 'The Influence of the Audience on Shakespeare's Drama', *Collected Essays* I, 1927, p. 14.

his sense of overruling destiny that have always puzzled those who have speculated on the human will. To inquire into the cause of an evil will has been likened to seeking 'to see darkness, or to hear silence' :[34] this is a point at which humanity's inquiries vanish as breath into the wind.

If the precise origin of Macbeth's will to evil cannot be determined, its nature at least can come under scrutiny. It may be observed in that instant response to Angus's account of the previous thane of Cawdor, 'The greatest is behind'. It is present in the passionate and no less immediate response to Malcolm's proclamation as Prince of Cumberland, and in the vehemence of the words which denote the blocking of his aspirations : 'For in my way it lies'. And it is to be understood equally in the greeting of his wife as 'my dearest partner of greatness'. It is a complete assumption of right and worth, that appears to Bradley as a 'consciousness of exceptional powers and merit'[35] which is an adjunct of greatness, but which may fittingly be characterized as self-worship.

L. L. Schücking is clearly correct in saying that Lady Macbeth does not think of combating her husband's goodness of heart and moral scruples, but instead spurs him into action by taunts about cowardice and weakness of will.[36] It is not a matter of overcoming or repressing scruple, but rather of provoking resolution, and strengthening a tendency already present. It may be said that Macbeth is to an extent emboldened by his wife's visualization of a plan of action; yet the plan is in itself not remarkable, and argument in the main does not rage round its details, despite its being concluded by reference to them. Ambition is clearly a greater force. It lies in and is assumed in all that is said; yet it cannot be claimed that ambition alone is sufficient to impel Macbeth to the deed, not only because more personal and immediate pressures are manifestly required, but because ambition itself would counsel no further proceeding. As A. P. Rossiter remarks, Macbeth knows the hideousness of the proposed deed, the inadequacy of his 'vaulting ambition' and the certainty of his receiving 'judgement here'. These considerations are 'abnormal in their coexistence', and lead to the conclusion that, unlike the heroes of Greek Tragedy, 'Macbeth acts with a full realization that no good can come of it'.[37] Ambition may inhere in his mind and will; yet it is scarcely the force which alone moves him, despite reluctance and dread, to Duncan's door. Ambition, though it may inform his murder of the sleeping King, cannot account for the manner of his doing it :

The deed is done in horror, and without the faintest desire or sense of glory – done, one might say, as if it were an appalling duty.[38]

[34] (Section II, p. 120.)   [35] *Shakespearean Tragedy*, 1956, p. 352.
[36] *Character Problems in Shakespeare's Plays*, London, 1922, p. 82.
[37] *Angel with Horns*, 1961, pp. 215–16.   [38] Bradley, op. cit., p. 358.

The quality of Lady Macbeth's taunting and inciting of her husband must therefore take prominent place in the assessment of his motive. The charge of cowardice may be regarded as constituting enough in itself to provoke Macbeth into resolution. In Bradley's view, it is a taunt no man, least of all a soldier, can bear;[39] and Charlton, noting that valour appears as the supreme standard of Macbeth's Scotland, can see the accusation as 'the sharpest instrument of reproach'.[40] But it is questionable whether it is the decisive consideration. Rossiter, after surveying the disadvantages which Macbeth knows will accrue from his action, asks,

> Surely we must find it incomprehensible that a man should be aware of all this, yet commit a deadly evil because he cannot endure to be called a coward?[41]

It might be replied that the prospect of being a coward in his wife's esteem might well upset prudential calculations in any man, and that Lady Macbeth is not slow with the emphasis, 'From this time /Such I account thy love'. This consideration might be held to outweigh Macbeth's personal consciousness that he is a dauntless soldier, and even now shines in the gloss of 'golden opinions'; but neither partner of the marriage can for long be unaware that Macbeth has appeared as 'valour's minion', and is second to none in the kingdom for his martial worth. Besides, what Lady Macbeth has to say does not, when strictly viewed, appear to bear principally upon the subject of her husband's courage, or lack of it. As Thomas Whately once observed,

> The argument is, that the strongest and most natural affections are to be stifled upon so great an occasion: and such an argument is proper to persuade one who is liable to be swayed by them; but is no incentive either to his courage or his ambition.[42]

It must consequently appear that, just as other forces in Macbeth's thinking mask themselves in the concept of fear, so profounder considerations underlie the charge of cowardice – and the associated charges that Macbeth had first thought of the murder, and had sworn to carry it out. What Lady Macbeth has to say has little worth as argument; and Bradley surely comes close to self-contradiction in dismissing the reasoning she uses as 'mere sophisms' that 'could persuade no man', and declaring,

> It is not by them, it is by personal appeals, through the admiration she extorts from him, and through sheer force of will, that she impels him to the deed.[43]

[39] ibid., p. 367. [40] Shakespearian Tragedy, 1952, p. 149.
[41] op. cit., p. 216.
[42] 'Remarks on Some of the Characters of Shakespeare', 1785, in Shakespeare Criticism : A Selection, ed. D. Nichol Smith, World's Classics, 1953, p. 129.
[43] Shakespearean Tragedy, p. 367.

316

Is it by her 'personal appeals', the bond of affection, and the 'undaunted valour' which he admires in his wife, that Macbeth is finally convinced? Clearly, if it were not for her agency he would have smothered his design; and the fact therefore admits Hazlitt's cautious judgement that Macbeth 'is even made in some measure the dupe of his uxoriousness'.[44] Nevertheless, it cannot be said that in the end Macbeth yields and submits himself to the direction of another mind. If this were so, he would not only be placing himself within the company of 'women's men', but consigning away his right to heroic stature. As Rossiter argues,

> If he acts because his wife has poured her spirits in his ear and chastised him with the valour of her tongue, and for that only . . . then Macbeth has no nobility of mind and no independent strength of will. Such a man cannot be admirable, nor his fate of tragic importance.[45]

Whatever Lady Macbeth urges, therefore, must correspond to something within himself : the decision must in the fullest sense be his. The play does in fact show evidence that Macbeth's mind is made up in advance of his interview with his wife. The thought which, after the confirmation of the Witches' prophecy,

> Shakes so my single state of man that function
> Is smother'd in surmise

> (I. iii. 140–1)

is akin to the 'phantasma, or a hideous dream' in the resolved Brutus, and the 'insurrection' which his 'state of man' suffers

> Between the acting of a dreadful thing
> And the first motion

> (II. i. 63–9)

as he awaits the arrival of the conspirators. Lady Macbeth seeks to embody in fact and action what has already been resolved in spirit.

It is consequently of the greatest importance to ascertain the substance of her appeal. It concerns precisely the acting out of a personal will :

> Art thou afeard
> To be the same in thine own act and valour
> As thou art in desire?

> (I. vii. 39–41.)

Macbeth and his wife are their own creatures, recognizing no greater claim upon themselves than their own wishes. The desires of such

---

[44] 'Characters of Shakespear's Plays', 1817, *Shakespeare Criticism : A Selection*, ed. Nichol Smith, 1953, p. 280.

[45] *Angel with Horns*, 1961, p. 217.

towering self-esteem become imperatives, and failure to carry them out is humiliation. Lady Macbeth does no more than to spell out these implications to a consciousness that cannot but respond to them. She presents him, in the first instance, not with exhortations, but with the image of contempt, and with such 'self-comparisons' as must infallibly bring about self-contempt. Was the hope drunk in which he had dressed himself – was his will so weak that it had to be drugged into determination? Was he of a nature to be bold only as long as his boast remained impossible to carry out? Her love for her child would not prevent her killing it if she had sworn to do so – for were not their desires dearer pledges of their existence even than their offspring? Her husband's resolution is for her the child of his personality and the means of self-esteem; and in breaking his word he is dashing out the brains of their happiness. Lady Macbeth thus preaches the sanctity of a personal will; and she conquers by creating in her husband a response to her precedent in self-deification. She rekindles in him what Bradley recognizes as that characteristic 'passion for power and his instinct of self-assertion'[46] which is too vehement thenceforth to advance from remorse to repentance, and what Rossiter defines as a 'blind urge to dominate through power' that makes men enemies of others, of Nature, and of themselves.[47] This urge in Macbeth, Rossiter declares, is an impulsion

to assert *his* pattern on the world : to make Macbeth Scotland.[48]

He is thus able to recognize in the murderer of Duncan that will to transform a creaturely existence into creaturely transcendence, and to impose upon the external world the pattern of a justice or order peculiar to the self, which is the characteristic activity of the Godless and the proud,[49] and which a theological awareness will express in more specific terms as a 'rebellion of the perverted finite will against the mandates of the infinite will'.[50]

Lady Macbeth is from the first the embodiment of this activity. She silences her husband with the taunt, 'To alter favour ever is to fear', and conveys an intensity of misliking in terms of hatred of irresolution : 'Infirm of purpose !' She is 'sublime', according to Bradley, in that her will is never relaxed;[51] and her doctrine continues its work in her husband. It is through the quality of resolution, Macbeth declares, that a man receives

[46] op. cit., p. 352.

[47] *Angel with Horns*, p. 226; see Section III, p. 248.

[48] op. cit., p. 211.

[49] (Section III, p. 238.)

[50] W. C. Curry, *Shakespeare's Philosophical Patterns*, Baton Rouge, Louisiana State University Press, 1937, p. 112, quoted by I. Ribner, '*Macbeth* : the Pattern of Idea and Action', *S.Q.* X, 1959, p. 149.

[51] *Shakespearean Tragedy*, p. 368.

Particular addition, from the bill
That writes them all alike

(III. i. 100–1).

The insistence of an absolute personal sovereignty finds expression in
the reaction to those who deny their presence 'at our great bidding';
it is equally evident in Macbeth's fervent and passionate utterance at
the news of Fleance's escape :

Then comes my fit again : I had else been perfect;
Whole as the marble, founded as the rock,
As broad and general as the casing air :
But now I am cabin'd, cribb'd, confin'd, bound in
To saucy doubts and fears

(III. iv. 21–5).

In this response is to be discerned the seeking of a unity and an omnipotence in that realm of transient things where they are not to be found;[52]
and its perversity is manifest in a will that can

wish the estate o' the world were now undone

(V. v. 50),

and can persist, despite all knowledge, in insensate activity

though the yesty waves
Confound and swallow navigation up;
Though bladed corn be lodg'd and trees blown down;
Though castles topple on their warders' heads;
Though palaces and pyramids do slope
Their heads to their foundations

(IV. i. 53–8).

Self-adulation naturally aspires to power; for power not only corresponds to the sense of merit, but is also a reprieve from the sense of
creaturely littleness. There is a distaste in Macbeth and his wife for the
limitations of service and the subterfuges of contriving which they trust
success will wipe out; and Lady Macbeth's being transported by her
husband's letter 'beyond /This ignorant present' may be interpreted as
a longing for liberation in a wider sense. To both, witchcraft and evil are
welcome; their murdering ministers help to break the ties which limit
them, and enable them to rise superior to events. Macbeth does not fear
the Witches : he accepts their ministration with a gratified credulity, and
becomes fascinated by the dire purposes that appear to set him above
his fellows. But the quest for power over others serves only to reveal the
frailty of the self which was its beginning, and in neither sphere is

[52] (Section II, pp. 152–3.)

conquest ultimately possible. Loss of power is accompanied by loss of self-control, and the conviction that he may be betrayed not only by others, but by his own emotions. His ruffianly bearing to those around him is part of a life that has become a constant pretence; if it is self-assertion in the face of failing authority, it is also a desire to frighten those who frighten him – whose linen cheeks are 'counsellors to fear', in one who can accept naught save predominance in the outer and the inner worlds.

That the perverse will, battening upon its partial reality, must be deceived in both spheres, if it is not the postulate of criticism, can be deduced from the progress of the play. The acquiescence in the creaturely is bound to find illusion in the evanescence of the created world : Macbeth must inevitably come to see in life no more than a walking shadow and a succession of yesterdays. In the dedication to a single desire, what he loves must be made perfect for him; and the love of that which is fraught with death, and which may easily be taken from him, must bring strife and pain.[53] The play at least makes clear that disillusion in Macbeth is the consequence of self-deception. The tearing to pieces of the bonds of human sympathy for the sake of personal power must appear as a doubtful transaction : the suppression of the wish to receive the heart's thanks of friends and pledge love and health to all is a plain denial of the deepest need. The forbidding prospect that confronts his ambition – the even-handed justice that he must provoke – he is aware of; and the limitations of his personal powers are also known to him in the deceiving of his senses by the Witches and the air-drawn dagger. But these realizations are dismissed from his consciousness in the manner in which he attempts to dismiss Banquo's ghost. He thus proceeds in a wilful ignorance; the fixing upon one desire must exclude all other awareness, and itself contrive the illusion that must follow. He can enact his purpose only by blinding himself to what opposes it : the idea in the play's imagery that darkness or partial blinding is the prerequisite of evil is exemplified in its chief character.[54]

Illusion in the external sphere is, however, but an extension of illusion within. The play is almost an exemplification of the process by which the attempt to assert the individual existence, and transform being-for-itself into being-in-itself, must destroy the self that is identified with being. In his blindness to reality Macbeth appears to the audience as one of those who 'do wickedly against their own souls' – though such action may not be evident in its prior category as sin against God.[55] According to Bradley, Macbeth in the play has made mortal war on his own soul.[56] The sleep

[53] (Section II, pp. 92, 100-1.)
[54] C. F. E. Spurgeon, *Shakespeare's Imagery*, 1935, p. 330.
[55] (Section II, p. 92.)   [56] op. cit., p. 359.

that he murders is his own innocence and serenity; the work his own hands have done appears to be that of another creature. He kills part of his own personality – or, as H. B. Charlton puts it, in destroying another piece of human nature he destroys the human nature in himself.[57] The increasing restriction which 'fell deeds' impose upon Macbeth's freedom is something that an audience can sense. They will not associate it with the self-perversion of an evil nature within a Providential system, whereby the erring soul must lose the power to know and do what is right;[58] but they will appreciate the perversity, and the fearsome cost to himself, of his fight against the emotions of his own conscience. They will also understand, as Macbeth himself does not, the nature of the fears which shake him. They will see in them, and in the images which his imagination presents to him, and which he interprets as fear of consequences, 'the protest of his deeper self',[59] and 'the inward pangs and warnings of conscience'.[60] Right and wrong, though finding no reasonable expression in his mind, inhabit his true self; and thus it comes about that

> His conscious or reflective mind . . . moves chiefly among considerations of outward success and failure, while his inner being is convulsed with conscience.[61]

The will to negation that underlies the choice of evil is thus made increasingly apparent by the action of the play. Macbeth can make life tolerable only by the smothering of all moral sensibility, the grim pursuit of indifference; yet what makes life bearable for him must also undermine in him the will to live. Action becomes replaced by torpor, and desire for power yields to the will for death.[62] Macbeth appears as a soul in disintegration – and as a life cut off from the life around him, and from all springs of joy. The self that wished to subject all others to its whim finds that it is tied to itself like a bear to the stake:

> He thus attains a tragic stature which is distinctive and, in Shakespeare's practice at least, unique. Himself a 'walking shadow', he stands upon the further side of our experience, to contemplate the life we know with a longing which is without hope but can never be without desire.[63]

The bond of marriage must yield to his greater divorce: the fellowship of husband and wife is at an end, and each must die alone.[64] All consciousness can now but produce further evil. Remorse is no hindrance to

[57] *Shakespearian Tragedy*, 1952, p. 182.   [58] (Section II, p. 93.)
[59] Bradley, op. cit., p. 353.
[60] Coleridge, *Lectures and Notes on Shakespere*, (Bohn) 1904, p. 376.
[61] Bradley, op. cit., p. 353.
[62] D. Cunningham, '*Macbeth* : the Tragedy of the Hardened Heart', *S.Q.*XIV, 1963, p. 44.
[63] J. Lawlor, *The Tragic Sense in Shakespeare*, 1960, p. 128.
[64] I. Ribner, '*Macbeth* : the Pattern of Idea and Action', *S.Q.* X, 1959, p. 156.

L

new enormities. The apprehension of treachery in others must either lead Macbeth to use indignity upon the suspect, or teach treachery to his subordinates by lessening their respect for right; and he thus creates the instruments of his own downfall. The knowledge of the deep and inaccessible sources of good in human nature, and the sense of the presence of a mysterious agency for justice and goodness in the world, can only drive him to further despair and further savagery: he can now find ease for his tortured thoughts only in destruction.[65] But the policy he is settled on – or which forces itself upon him – must reveal its emptiness to those around him; he may be seen to embody the truth that evil can only inhere in good, and must annihilate itself in the destruction of what supports it. Malcolm's forces therefore meet with foes that strike beside them; and there must remain in the conscience of the beholder the impression that a religious understanding would acknowledge as truth,

that through the working out of evil in a harmonious world order good must prevail.[66]

[65] Bradley, op. cit., p. 362.   [66] I. Ribner, op. cit., p. 159.

Chapter 22

OTHELLO

Othello comes before us as a captain of men whose element is the bustling life of camp and court – yet who is sharply distinguished from those who move under his command. He is separated from them not only by station or uniqueness of gift, but by a rapturous aloofness of spirit that draws him apart from his fellows and leads him to exult in his solitariness. Despite the ease and naturalness of his bearing towards others, says Granville-Barker, Othello has been 'a man apart, alone';[1] and Bradley concludes that 'He does not belong to our world'.[2] What divides him from that world appears to be an ideal of himself, a consciousness of his soul's nobility, and a conscious pursuit of his own image – his parts, title, and perfect soul – in all his undertakings. In the cool command to assailant and friend to keep up their bright swords is evidence of a complete trust in himself. Wilson Knight remarks that Othello 'is, as it were, conscious of all he stands for';[3] and it is to be admitted that he proceeds beneath a sense of personal adequacy that, within the confines of his calling, cannot be termed illusion. He invariably assumes that he will conquer by his merits, and does in fact do so. After his speech to the Senators, the bitter and dangerous charges of Brabantio have become

> thin habits and poor likelihoods
> Of modern seeming
>
> (I. iii. 108–9);

and his appearance in the Senate house is cause in itself for the Duke's overlooking the grim-faced Senator who enters at his side.

Yet if the nature of Othello's peculiar consciousness is examined, the knowledge of what he stands for resolves itself into a consciousness of the self. He is, as Miss Gardner has observed, 'a man of faith'; yet it might be questioned whether 'his sense of the worth of the life and the causes he has chosen'[4] is not the consequence, rather than the cause, of the impressive sense of his own worth that she finds in him – whether it is not the absorption in his own imaginative vision, in the self which

---

[1] *Prefaces to Shakespeare*, 4th Ser., 1947, p. 178.
[2] *Shakespearean Tragedy*, 1956, p. 157.   [3] *The Wheel of Fire*, 1949, p. 107.
[4] 'The Noble Moor', *Proceedings of the British Academy* XLI, 1955, p. 194.

his imagination presents to him,[5] that constitutes his faith and confers a solidity and splendour upon his world. In this respect it has been noted that 'Othello in his images continually has himself in mind',[6] and that

> [his] generalizations, his expansion of his immediate situation into a wider realm of implication, are concerned with his view of himself.[7]

There is, according to the same critic, something remarkable to Othello himself about his own history,[8] for he is at his grandest when he refers to anything connected with it; and the beauty which then invests the words he speaks can appear 'to imply his belief that his life is indeed matter for poetry'.[9] Iago does not err in appraising the consciousness of worth in the man whose ruin he is to encompass: it is not without significance that his first conversation with Othello should begin with pretended anger against those who have used scurvy and provoking terms against his captain's honour.

The honour thus invoked is founded neither upon mere self-esteem nor known achievement, but upon a state of mind and soul from which they take their origin – an awareness that the higher faculties of his being are in complete control of the lesser powers and affections.[10] H. B. Charlton is surely mistaken to see in this apparent self-mastery the 'simple moral ideal' of a naturally passionate man practiced in compensating powers of restraint;[11] so to view the matter is to overlook the familiar Elizabethan identification of virtue with the triumph of reason over the passions, and to dismiss the common endeavour and understanding of Hamlet and his age, that

> he that is a perfect knight indeed, ought not onely to win the Conquest of his Enemies: but must also triumphe ouer the Passions of his owne Soule, which must be cleane, and exempt from all vnlawfull desires, or absurde and base villainies.[12]

To be one 'Whom passion could not shake' (IV. i. 268) is by definition, in Lodovico's phrase, to be a 'noble nature', and the object of admiration – as Othello indeed is the embodiment of much that is admirable. Whether it is also to be provided with the means and the right to self-admiration is something which must give the critic pause. He may not recognize the distinction that a human excellence cannot legitimately be

---

[5] J. Bayley, *The Character of Love*, 1960, p. 182.

[6] W. H. Clemen, *The Development of Shakespeare's Imagery*, London, 1951, p. 121.

[7] T. Spencer, *Shakespeare and the Nature of Man*, 1943, p. 129.

[8] ibid., p. 128.

[9] P. Ure, *Shakespeare and the Inward Self of the Tragic Hero*, University of Durham, 1961, p. 10.

[10] T. Spencer, op. cit., p. 128.

[11] *Shakespearian Tragedy*, 1952, p. 121.

[12] T. Milles, *The Treasurie of Auncient and Moderne Times*, 2 vols., 1613–19, I, p. 865.

a source of pleasure in itself, since honour for it must relate to its ultimate origin;[13] and he may not subscribe to the belief that God alone can be the source of unity and order in the soul of man – that the just order of nature requires the soul and the flesh to be 'both together under God'.[14] Yet it will be apparent to him that Othello derives his nobility out of the powers of the self, and employs it to no greater end than the purposes of the self; and in the tragic conclusion he will be able to perceive not only the spurious nature of the excellence that was assumed, but the familiar 'I am I' of the heroic wish to be its own artificer which can admit of no moderation and must end in obsession.[15] Othello will not appear as the personification of presumption, but he will instead seem in his self-sufficiency the inhabitant of a world of his own which he constructs in his imagination upon the idea of himself and his virtues; and when he has fallen into degradation and dishonour, he will be observed to feel, not that his world and his self-ideal were illusion, but that events have removed him from the imperishable truth of a real greatness – that he can still seek

> refuge from dishonour among imaged memories of a glory indefeasibly his.[16]

It will be clear that his view of himself was his reality; but his fate may not be ascribed to a creature's placing of trust in its own powers. The fact that the 'marble heaven' by which he swears, but to which he does not pray, remains 'vast, distant, separate, seen but not apprehended' – that it is 'conceived as outside his interests' – will indicate a limitation of outlook rather than an apostasy.[17]

Othello's justification must be that the glory which he senses within himself is reflected upon his consciousness by achievement, and proved in the realm of fact rather than gained through introspection. He is a man of action rather than of word and concept, and can speak little more of the great world than pertains to feats of broil and battle. His very being expresses itself in what might be termed splendid externalities – in the services he has done the signory, in the dignities of great public institutions, and in the storms of martial achievement. There he is 'in his beloved element':[18] he is 'unawed by dignities and unelated by honours',[19] for they are to him the stuff of existence. The voice of the immortal Jove comes to him from the throats of cannon:

[13] (Section III, p. 246.)
[14] (Section II, p. 88.)
[15] (Section III, p. 233.)
[16] Granville-Barker, *Prefaces*, 4th Ser., 1947, p. 182.
[17] G. Wilson Knight, 'The Othello Music', *Shakespeare Criticism 1919–35*, ed. A. Bradby, pp. 345, 347.
[18] Clemen, *The Development of Shakespeare's Imagery*, London, 1951, p. 127.
[19] Bradley, *Shakespearean Tragedy*, p. 189.

325

The trumpet and drum, the fife and the banners, were themselves tokens of the metaphysical world, in which Othello found his life's meaning.[20]

His is a narrow universe; and it is the narrower in that his personality partakes of the means of its mortal greatness, and founds itself upon the external. He gives little thought to his private emotions, and is scornful of emotion in others: it is the 'gravity and stillness' (II. iii. 188) of Montano's youth that has recommended him. To the inner world of his own nature he is something of a stranger; and emotion, when it is aroused in him, 'confuses and dulls his intellect'.[21]

It is therefore typical of him that, while remaining gravely courteous to Brabantio, he is unbending in the face of his distress. To him it can be little more than a 'spite'. He is convinced that the services he has done the state will 'out-tongue his complaints', as indeed they do; but they can have no effect upon a father's grief. Othello assumes that he can employ outward considerations against a private emotion, and the Duke, in the exigencies of the moment, must perforce fall into the same error. Brabantio's answer is a rebuke to both:

> I never yet did hear
> That the bruis'd heart was pierced through the ear
> (I. iii. 218–19).

In the failure to distinguish between the inner and the outer worlds lies the beginning of Othello's error: it denotes an ignorance of the means of love and trust, and foretells that the man who shields him against physical dangers will receive the same credence upon his claim to be protecting him in the realm of emotion.

Othello is supreme where all is objective and calculable, and preserves his supremacy by attributing to his fellow-creatures the constancy in which his own perfection seems to himself to lie. In part he is led to do so by a genuine freedom from the normal forms of vanity, self-seeking and distrust which makes it difficult for him to detect these vices in others.[22] He treats his fellow-men, as Hamlet would have them treated, after his own honour and dignity, and he wins them to him by adding to their self-respect. His instinct is to see the worthiness of those he governs: he who is quickly aware of 'great love' in the island's population will place a simple trust in the officer who serves him with outward deference and respect. Othello is essentially

> a free and open nature,
> That thinks men honest that but seem to be so
> (I. iii. 398–9).

[20] Granville-Barker, op. cit., p. 182.   [21] Bradley, op. cit., p. 189.
[22] Granville-Barker, *Prefaces*, 4th Ser., 1947, p. 173.

In assuming the power of goodness over the minds of his fellows, Othello is at one with the virtuous nature in all ages : a generous mind is inclined to trust, and predisposed to ignore or dismiss the worst, as Desdemona dismisses Iago's coarse jesting. Yet it is his ideal of himself rather than his natural inclination that must be held accountable for his rosy vision of the human scene : its assumed goodness and its external splendours alike are the means by which the soul of Othello can come into its own. The genesis of this vision in the will which entertains it may be inferred from the 'architectural stateliness of quarried speech', the 'noble cadence and chiselled phrase', in which both are given expression.[23] Othello fashions the world according to the needs of his own being, and may therefore be regarded as an example of a selflessness that ironically is not unselfregarding, no less than as an embodiment of 'the human will to see things as they are not'.[24] Nor is he a rarity in this respect. Many a nature which overcomes by a customary goodness, and which is quick to remark the kindnesses of others, may in truth be impelled by a deeper egoism of which it is not aware. Whatever the cause, it is certain that Othello is something of a 'romantic idealist' where human nature is concerned, and that his being so is a means of Iago's influence. Iago is able to express 'in some way a complementary view of life to Othello's',[25] and his power over him has been said to derive from there being projected in what he speaks

the half-truths that Othello's romantic vision ignored, but of which his mind held secret knowledge.[26]

Othello's credulity can thus be seen as the reverse side of a nobility that makes self-deception inevitable. Not every critic or beholder will see in the nobility itself, as F. R. Leavis does, the outward appearance of an 'obtuse and brutal egotism';[27] yet it must impress itself on many that Othello would be more in touch with the reality of others' natures and his own if he were less intent on exalting himself.

The power of love, no less than that of virtuous disposition or self-regard, is shown in the play to create an incapacity to take note of worser possibilities. In her devotion to her husband Desdemona can be described as 'a woman of faith'. The start of her love is a fascination by his noble qualities; she sees Othello's visage in her mind, and

It is in her fine faith in this vision of him that she goes forward[28] –

[23] G. Wilson Knight, 'The Othello Music', *Shakespeare Criticism 1919–35*, ed. A. Bradby, 1949, pp. 351, 354.

[24] T. S. Eliot, 'Shakespeare and the Stoicism of Seneca', ibid., p. 214.

[25] Helen Gardner, 'The Noble Moor', *Proc. Brit. Acad.* XLI, 1955, p. 195, citing M. Bodkin, *Archetypal Patterns in Poetry*, 1934, p. 333.

[26] M. Bodkin, *Archetypal Patterns in Poetry*, p. 223, quoted by H. Gardner, ibid.

[27] *The Common Pursuit*, 1952, p. 146, quoted by J. Bayley, *The Character of Love*, 1960, p. 129.

[28] Granville-Barker, op. cit., p. 179.

a faith that the sun where he was born had drawn all unworthy humours from him. She is thus rendered incapable of understanding his sudden suspicion, and responds to what is unaccountable with a fear which Othello misinterprets. Her instinct is to blame herself for idealizing her husband rather than the fault which belies the assessment : she will pray heaven to keep the monster of suspicion from Othello, but shrink from inquiring the cause of his transformation. After his infamous treatment of her she is 'Half-asleep', her mind faltering before the incomprehensible rather than being quickened by it. Emilia's clear deduction that the Moor must have been 'abused by some most villainous knave' holds no interest for her, since the Othello she loved would not have yielded to infamy. The very thought that he could be so changed would be a penance greater than she could bear. She has made her love for her husband, as he makes his own toward her, 'a part now . . . of the natural order of things',[29] and when that order is shaken can only cling the more resolutely to a belief as dear as her own existence, never allowing his unkindness to taint her love. The idea that she might be in danger does not enter her thoughts. In Desdemona and Othello there is the marriage of true minds. She believes in him precisely in the manner in which he believes in others : in neither mind does the worser possibility find acceptance.

It is fitting in one whose being is attuned to external event, that while the power of his 'new-found content' should impress itself upon him, its true nature should for the most part elude him. Othello speaks of his love for Desdemona as if it has been the decorous result of a ceremonious wooing; and though it may be true that he first loved her for her pitying him in the trials he had undergone in the past, the statement that

She loved me for the dangers I had pass'd

takes no account of the emotional depths of human love that Desdemona frankly acknowledges in her plea that she may not be bereft of 'The rites for which I love him'. The girl to whom Othello gives his heart is 'warmly human',[30] but his understanding of their relationship appears to be somewhat otherwise; and his own affection toward Desdemona has been judged

entirely unlike the love of Troilus for Cressida, it has no sensuality in it.[31]

Othello has a conscious contempt for what he terms 'the palate of my appetite', and is able to express a distinction between his newly-married state and the charge with which the Senators have entrusted him in the

[29] ibid., p. 71.   [30] G. Wilson Knight, *The Wheel of Fire*, 1949, p. 107.
[31] T. Spencer, *Shakespeare and the Nature of Man*, 1943, p. 127.

contrast between 'light-winged toys' and their 'great business'. The demands of a 'perfect soul' and those of passion are here seen as almost in principle opposed; and in his emphasis upon self-control Othello shows little respect at this point either for the rôle or for the strength of the emotions in marriage. Leavis's observation that 'his love is composed very largely of ignorance of self as well as ignorance of [Desdemona]'[32] can find ample justification from his attitude both early and late; and the fact, noted by Bradley, that

> his whole nature was indisposed to jealousy, yet such that he was unusually open to deception,[33]

can be explained by this ignorance of the emotional part of himself, as can the shock to his being and his unbridled vehemence when its forces come into their own. Their imperiousness has manifested itself from the start. Othello has renounced the 'free unhoused condition' that he would not otherwise have given up 'for the sea's worth', and love has moved Desdemona to a defiance of her father otherwise inconceivable.

Out of his marriage the self-sufficient Othello endeavours to create a new sufficiency principled upon his former being. He admits within its compass a novel potentiality and another person – and he 'finds in happiness with her a self unrealized before'.[34] That nobility in Othello which, according to Miss Gardner, lies in his capacity to recognize value and give loyalty,[35] finds magnificent expression in the vow he makes to Desdemona. He fashions his devotion into an all-embracing principle, and unites his very being with her : if their love should ever fail, chaos is come again. He can pledge his life upon her faith with confidence, for he is as sure of her as he is of his own soul. In these professions may be sensed the instinct of many a lover; but there may also be traced in them that incapacity for half-heartedness or compromise that constitutes the 'absoluteness of his character';[36] and well does Miss Gardner remark upon his idealization of the alliance, 'Let Othello remember that perfection is not to be looked for'. The exalted pitch of Othello's wooing may thus appear, not as a generosity but as an egoism – an attempt of the self-reflecting soul to incorporate its domestic joys within its transcendence, and to impose upon its love the pattern of the order it imposes upon the world of its imagination.[37] The true quality of Othello's love must be judged from the consequences of Iago's testing of it – with allowance being at the same time made for the satanic deception to which it is exposed. What must also be taken into consideration is 'the fact that

[32] *The Common Pursuit*, 1952, p. 145, quoted by J. Bayley, *The Character of Love*, 1960, p. 144.
[33] *Shakespearean Tragedy*, 1956, p. 186.
[34] Granville-Barker, 4th Ser., 1947, p. 179.
[35] 'The Noble Moor', *Proc. Brit. Acad.* XLI, p. 204.
[36] W. Clemen, *Development*, London, 1951, p. 130.   [37] (Section III, p. 249.)

329

great joy bewilders, leaving the heart apt to doubt the reality of its joy'.[38]
and the alarmingness of the sensation, between two people not yet
accustomed to each other, 'of the loved person suddenly seeming a total
stranger' – of a moment that is 'a dead spot in love',[39] when calumny
may speak to some effect. These things contribute to Iago's success; but
its chief cause must be found in the inability of Othello's love easily to
descend to the commonplaces of life where love must find embodiment.
From this point of view Othello indeed loves not wisely but too well. As
J. Bayley expresses it,

> Although love is by its nature absolute, its working out must be con-
> tingent on the relative and imperfect nature of human minds and
> human dealings. From Othello's refusal to recognize this the love idiom
> derives both its positive splendour, its firmness, colour and clarity of
> outline, and also its air of unreality.[40]

Othello's love for Desdemona is a thing of his own mind, 'a marvellous
revelation of himself rather than a real knowledge of her',[41] and the force
of her alleged betrayal comes, not from their relationship itself, but from
'the causeless and inexplicable withdrawal of his love vision'.[42] Sexual
love is often, as F. R. Leavis points out, 'a matter of self-centred and
self-regarding satisfactions';[43] but Othello's love, though it may admit
such small selfishnesses, is not truly compounded of them. For his Desdemona is an image of his own creating which is at the mercy of his secret
fears and suspicions, and exposed to any onslaught of intangible suggestion.[44] The perfection of love which he would assert and enjoy is part
of the endeavour toward the completeness of soul which is his true
delight; and there must therefore be found in him, as the explanation of
his later conduct, a concern, not with Desdemona as a woman in love, but
with the joy of his own soul.

Othello's heroic self-affirmation and conscious pursuit of an ideal of
a personal excellence can thus be held to blind him to the claims of
emotion, and to reality;[45] he lives in a dream of passionless integrity,
which his own passion is soon to dispel. Yet he is not without knowledge
of the irrational forces of man's inner world, for the relationship between
Desdemona and her father which forms the prelude of his own tragedy
is a miniature enactment of the entire play. Brabantio, moved by a love
which has degenerated into selfish possession, is confronted by forces
in his daughter's nature which he had not known to exist, and which

38 H. Gardner, op. cit., p. 197.
39 J. Bayley, *The Character of Love*, 1960, p. 167.
40 ibid., p. 170.   41 ibid., p. 146.   42 ibid., p. 174.
43 *The Common Pursuit*, 1952, p. 145, quoted by Bayley, op. cit., p. 144.
44 J. I. M. Stewart, *Character and Motive in Shakespeare*, 1959, p. 104.
45 (Section III, p. 239.)

overturn the ordered relationship upon which he had trusted. Desdemona's change of allegiance is seen as a treason to his soul; it transforms the despised Roderigo into an ally, and replaces a fond love by the limitless hatred of a betrayal. To what extent these happenings invade his consciousness cannot be judged; but the fact of the incalculable and the base in human behaviour is well established in other minds. It is present in Iago's purposeful protestations to others of his scruple, and in Brabantio's starting at a subversive idea that is not unlike his late dream. Cassio's laughing 'He speaks home, madam' at the witticisms which are slander in Desdemona's ears show an all-too-easy identification between cynicism and realism in the general awareness. And the storm can denote to Othello the disharmonies that lurk in human relationships, and draw from him the fervent wish, as he greets his wife, that

> this, and this, the greatest discords be
> That e'er our hearts shall make!
>
> (II. i. 198–9.)

Iago hints at Cassio's emotional indiscipline to bring him into discredit with his chief, and with other men; and it is by revealing to Othello the scope of the passionate and the irrational in the human soul that he triumphs. Othello is to follow with an almost sub-human respect in the footsteps of one who seems to have familiar knowledge of

> all qualities, with a learned spirit,
> Of human dealings
>
> (III. iii. 259–60);

and when Iago's treachery is at last revealed, it is the astounding course of his own viciousness that makes it impossible for Othello to resume his former shape.

That the realm of passion is the enemy of the idealized kingdom of Othello's own ordering is evident in the moment when it first invades his quiet in the figure of an incensed and brawling Cassio lost to all decorum, whilst a dreadful bell ministers to fear. Confronted with this revolt against his rule and the order of his island, Othello's instinct is to strike at the means of it; 'this vile brawl' challenges his own imperturbability, and in gathering passion he makes an example of the man who has shaken his self-confidence. In this respect he closely resembles his betrayer. What Bradley says of Iago can be seen to apply equally to his master:

Whatever disturbs or wounds his sense of superiority irritates him at once.[46]

[46] *Shakespearean Tragedy*, 1956, p. 221.

The effect of his anger is noteworthy: he is driven to defend as sacred the principle that has been violated, and to offer up as a sacrifice his own human sympathies. Even if the offender had been his own brother, 'Though he had twinn'd with me – both at a birth' (II. iii. 209), he would be cast off, as he discards Cassio in despite of 'the compunctious visitings of nature'. R. W. Battenhouse notes of Othello that

> Towards flesh and blood he has no pity when an ideal of moral deserving is to be served;[47]

but though an audience will see in this incident and its punishment a soldier's response to provocation, and will sense a depth of resentment, they will not apprehend in the present harshness the symptom of a will toward a creaturely absoluteness that may later be impressed on them.

At the commencement of his task of betrayal, Iago opposes against Othello's 'unquestioning self-confidence',[48] with a 'Ha! I like not that', a mere hint at depraved dealings. His master will stick to the principles of love's integrity, as he does in his resolve to deny his wife nothing when her pleas for Cassio first remind him of the hint he has received; and Iago's tactic is to appear to be ignoring the worst, and to indicate, by the echoing of words and by seemingly involuntary stops, the presence of a monster in his thought and emotion in his heart. Unwonted apprehension must lead Othello to the assertion that men should be as they seem; but Iago's quick application of the principle to Cassio now evokes an inevitable, and significant, 'Nay, yet there's more in this'. The unparalleled defiance of martial discipline by his subordinate for the sake of his own 'quiet', and Iago's very stubbornness in the act itself, further demonstrate to Othello the power of the emotions, and the helplessness of his ideal of integrity.

Once he has established in Othello's consciousness the potentiality of betrayal, Iago reverts to reasonableness on the subject of human frailty. He admits with shame to a prying disposition which can shape 'faults which are not' – for 'who has a breast so pure' that some 'uncleanly apprehensions' may not enter? There is no such thing as a perfect soul; and upon this consideration Iago swiftly introduces marital disloyalty as an accomplished fact, with moralizings of comfort to suit. Broad-mindedness is best; he 'Who dotes, yet doubts' inflicts agonies upon himself, whereas the cuckold may achieve contentedness in his poverty. By thus juggling with considerations of the dearest concern, Iago must generate passion; and by moralizing on the means to repress it, he makes doubly sure that it will arise. Othello's consequent assertion of his own

---

[47] 'Shakespearian Tragedy: A Christian Interpretation', *The Tragic Vision and the Christian Faith*, ed. N. A. Scott, N.Y., 1957, p. 87.

[48] Granville-Barker, 4th Ser., 1947, p. 40.

objectivity – that he will not 'turn the business of my soul' to giving credence to mere suspicion, but will proceed only upon proof – is in reality a token of his soul's trepidation, as his adversary perceives. He can now resort to the bluntly familiar[49] 'Look to your wife', linking the warning with recognition of his master's 'free and noble nature'; and, with the nearer proof that 'She did deceive her father, marrying you', can wring from the stricken Othello the indebtedness that his wife's father at a similar moment professed to the informer. In having to change his response to Iago's questioning from 'Not a jot, not a jot' to 'No, not much moved', he is led to recognize the thoughts that now exist within him; and the knowledge of his own lack of constancy impels him to the consideration that in humanity at large nature may err from itself. Iago has now only to conjecture a 'foul disproportion' and unnaturalness in the match, and his task is done.

His task has not been so much to poison Othello's mind against his wife as to reveal to him what cannot be comprehended into his soul ideal, and therefore into his world. What he has urged directly against Desdemona amounts to no more than the appearance of his own strong suspicion – yet its effect in its insubstantiality is far greater than would have been achieved by the production of detailed evidence. It is similarly to be noted that what is foremost in Othello's thought is not horror or rage relating to Desdemona's supposed act : the wrong she has done him must make way in his thoughts to the wrong he has done himself in marrying. Disgust at his wife's infidelity leads to a wider consternation at the newly-realized condition of his creaturely existence. What truly calls forth his revulsion is his vision of a human will so beset and implanted with incitements to inconstancy that it cannot be bound in honourable relationships; and the thought

> That we can call these delicate creatures ours,
> And not their appetites

(III. iii. 269–70)

provokes a loathing of the sexual impulse itself, 'the forked plague' which afflicts like a disease what is worthy and noble. Lear, who utters similar thoughts, has been struck down by manifest wickedness; but Othello is oppressed by the mere aspect of tendencies he had never admitted to his gaze, and the fact finds reflection in the play's imagery. As Miss Caroline Spurgeon has pointed out,

> In *Othello* we see a low type of life, insects and reptiles swarming and preying on each other, not out of special ferocity, but just in accordance with their natural instincts.[50]

[49] ibid., p. 48.   [50] *Shakespeare's Imagery*, 1935, p. 336.

The true victim of Iago's attentions is not Desdemona, but the world of Othello's self-esteem; and the inhumanity of the desire to 'whistle her off',
    Though that her jesses were my dear heart-strings
                                              (III. iii. 261),

derives not from the pangs of despised love, but rather from the disillusioning of a compulsive love of the self. It is with good reason that F. R. Leavis detects in the speed with which a faint mistrust is transformed into loathing and the rôle of lover into that of cuckold, evidence of the 'misgivings of angry egotism'.[51]

In the matter of Othello's discomfiture, writes J. I. M. Stewart, the 'main datum' is not Iago's diabolical intellect but Othello's readiness to respond:[52] he believes Iago's calumny because there is something in his nature which leads him to do so.[53] This verdict of a critic concerned with the psychological truth of the motives of Shakespeare's characters is in conformity with Augustine's thinking upon the nature of temptation. Unless there is stuff congenial to its working, temptation there cannot be:

> If a nature with its vice approaches another nature with a view to corrupting it, and finds in it nothing corruptible, it does not corrupt it. But if it does find something corruptible it effects the corruption of the other nature by the vice it finds in it. The stronger is not corrupted by the weaker if it refuses to be corrupted, but if it wills to be corrupted its corruption begins from its own vice rather than another's. Nor can an equal be corrupted by an equal if it refuses. When a vicious nature approaches another which is without vice in order to corrupt it, by that very fact it does not approach as an equal, but as weaker on account of its vice.[54]

This realization that the strength and initiative does not truly lie with Iago forms the basis of Stewart's appraisal:

> Iago's villainy draws its potency from Othello's own mind; it is invisible to others because it is, in a sense, *not there*; the devil in the play, like all devils, represents a projection upon some comparatively neutral or insignificant thing; Iago is a device of Othello's by which Othello hears an inner voice that he would fain deny.[55]

Nor is Stewart alone in this opinion. A. P. Rossiter, for example, quotes with approval F. R. Leavis's observation that Iago's power in the temptation scene is his representing something which is in Othello – that 'the essential traitor is within the gates'.[56]

[51] *The Common Pursuit*, 1952, p. 146, quoted by P. Ure, *Shakespeare and the Inward Self of the Tragic Hero*, 1961, p. 12.
[52] *Character and Motive*, 1959, p. 105.   [53] ibid., p. 103.
[54] *De Lib. Arb.* III. xiv. 39 (Pontifex tr.)   [55] op. cit., p. 102.
[56] *Angel with Horns*, 1961, p. 103; *The Common Pursuit*, 1952, p. 141.

These critics would probably not regard Othello's falling to temptation as being due to his possession of what, in Luther's terms, is a 'confounded, corrupt and poisoned nature' rather than a 'perfect soul'; nor would they see his downfall as the relapse that must come to the sick man following a presumption that he is healthy.[57] But they are alive nonetheless to Othello's imperfections, and can attribute the flawed nature of his love for Desdemona to its being deeply qualified by a concern for the self. If a thorough-going selfishness is indeed at work in him, he will have within himself – and intuitively know it – adequate prompting and reason for a partner's mislike : for generosity is the only true ground for attachment. Emilia's pragmatic principle for womankind, so considered, is in a sense the confirmation, if it is not the outcome, of such an attitude as is to be found in a man like Othello :

> The ills we do, their ills instruct us so
> (IV. iii. 102).

Emilia can be seen as the soul-mate of his worser soul, as Desdemona is of his nobler strivings; and indeed she can see in Othello's jealousy a passion and a purpose in no degree more distinguished than that she has known in her own husband. Iago's will to 'diet' his revenge is no more bloody than Othello's. He acts

> For that I do suspect the lusty Moor
> Hath leap'd into my seat; the thought whereof
> Doth like a poisonous mineral gnaw my inwards
> (II. i. 298–300);

but his imagination is little more prone to 'excitability by the most inadequate causes'[58] than Othello's, and no quicker to sense depravity, though it is less outwardly violent in its operation. Iago's awareness of superiority in Othello has its equivalent in Othello's grovelling respect for his ancient's skill in 'human dealing'; and thus, in the hero, 'A sense of inferiority, coupled with self-pity, leads at a bound to near-certainty'[59] in a manner that would be characteristic of the villain. They share the distinction of drawing a sword upon the woman who threatens discovery of their actions; though Othello does not use his, he shows some indication of being prepared to do so – and he does, after all, kill the mistress of the woman concerned. The unlooked-for resemblance between the two men is not strange if it be admitted that the two natures are possessed by different forms of inordinate self-seeking.

The tragic experience with which this play concerns itself is indeed, as Miss Gardner declares it to be, 'loss of faith'.[60] But in one profound

---

[57] (Section III, pp. 174, 252.)   [58] A. P. Rossiter, op. cit., p. 193.
[59] ibid., p. 194.
[60] 'The Noble Moor', *Proc. Brit. Acad.* XLI, 1955, p. 197.

sense it is an impossible faith that is in question, and reliance upon it is the spring of evil in the play: Othello's vain quest for his soul's nobility may be seen as the tragedy of the spirit that is the precursor to tragedy in the play's own world, and his yielding to Iago as the visible enactment of an alliance with perverse principle. There is thus further reason for his being corrupted by Iago's intellectual outlook before he is betrayed by the logic of evidence,[61] and, as the imagery shows, for his beginning in a sense to turn into the thing that betrays him. The closeness and kinship of the two minds in fact makes possible a symbolical solution of the temptation. Othello, as the human soul as it strives to be, and Iago, as that which subverts it from within, can appear as 'abstractions from a single, and, as it were, invisible protagonist', as 'interlocked forces within a single psyche'.[62] It might equally be argued that Iago's sinister presence in the play, and the inscrutability of his motives, may stem at the deepest level from his being the dramatic representation of the true nature of Othello's ideal, if not of the ulterior condition of his soul.

If the dominant force in Othello has been self-regard, the purpose of revenge against the person deemed to have destroyed his being is consistent and inevitable; and the loss of calm and dignity in the surrender to possessive emotion, which must seem to himself and to the spectator as his character's transformation, must in truth be its revelation. That the extent of his disillusionment, and his dedication to revenge, are alike the outcome of a compulsive love of the self, finds confirmation in the impressive farewell to his former greatness which he utters before turning finally to the inner world of his discomfiture. He takes leave of his own nobility as if divided from himself[63] – as if parting company for ever with the ideal he had honoured and served. 'He speaks', says Edith Sitwell, 'as a dead man might speak, watching the intolerable anguish of the living'.[64] The idea of his nobility has been life to him; and, feeling now the mutiny in his own soul, he must take leave of the tranquil mind together with the plumed troop and the big wars of his former external preoccupation, in such manner as betokens the annihilation of his own being. This conscious stepping down from the heights speaks of the heroic self-identification with a particular ideal or a limited good that is also the resort of the proud;[65] in the action may be seen 'a reflection of Othello's own god-pose, his refusal to see himself as ordinarily human',[66] and, at the same time, a consciousness that he has failed in the attempt to distance himself from human limitation. External achievement can no longer build his stature in his own eyes; he is subjected now to the frailties of

[61] J. Bayley, *The Character of Love*, 1960, p. 198.
[62] J. I. M. Stewart, *Character and Motive*, 1959, pp. 108–9.
[63] Granville-Barker, *Prefaces*, 4th Ser., 1947, p. 60.
[64] *A Notebook on William Shakespeare*, 1948, p. 98.
[65] (Section III, p. 239.)   [66] Stewart, op. cit., p. 104.

lf, and must fight the losing battle with the imagination that
's kisses on his wife's lips, and dissipates all possible means

1 the grip of passion, tends to accept whatever confirms his
a realize amidst his torture that he and Desdemona may be
ander, yet while demanding the proof of fact, he is slave to
igs of jealousy; and Iago, by hinting at what he most dreads,
Desdemona's guilt in his apprehension while urging the
.... of direct evidence. The sight of Cassio laughing, or a tale
.....at he had uttered in a dream, or even the idea of exposure to the
.....mptations of the senses, is now enough to denote 'a foregone conclusion'
to Othello's mind (III. iii. 429). The very tremblings of emotion within
him at the news of Cassio's supposed confession are proof in themselves:

> Nature would not invest herself in such shadowing passion without
> some instruction (IV. i. 39–41).

In the ruins of the world of his former glory, a universal sensuality takes
the place of all other truth, and overcomes all possibility of belief or
generous feeling. The tears that his violence evokes from his wife are a
'well-painted passion'; though he may ask her, 'Let me see your eyes',
neither in word or in look can he find confirmation of faithfulness.
Emilia's strenuous denials of her mistress's guilt must be held the response
of a 'subtle whore', for all that he has seen her kneel and pray; her
unexpected assertion is dismissed, not only because it contains 'the offer
of a comfort he can no longer take',[67] but because the new-found principle
of depravity exerts as strong a hold upon him as the earlier conviction
of his soul's integrity, and cynicism is more compatible with the dregs
of self-esteem. His awareness is now filled with the thought of the 'bawdy
wind' and the summer flies 'That quicken even with blowing'. Yet that
thought is death for Othello. The world's scorn he could bear 'well, very
well'; but he has entrusted his own being to another's love, and he cannot
distrust

> where I have garner'd up my heart,
> Where either I must live or bear no life
> (IV. ii. 56–7).

Othello's love is not for him a thing apart, but his whole existence; and
Desdemona's supposed unchastity, in dispelling a vision of rectitude and
making him the victim of jealous fears, must end all confidence in himself.
The idealized love which was valued for its contribution to a soul's self-
significance and self-content, rather than for itself, becomes, at the breath
of slander, an affront to the personality which has harboured it. The

[67] Granville-Barker, 4th Ser., pp. 94–5.

true depth and substance of Desdemona's loyalty – and his own – Othello had never understood; now passion combines with egotism to blind him to all but the outward form of the husband's authority and wifely obedience. Love is transformed into a principle of honour from which defection is treason; and, though the thought of killing may thereafter appal, the initial step of saying, 'All my fond love thus do I blow to heaven' (III. iii. 446) is all too easily taken.

That 'black vengeance' must, in Othello's very next words, replace 'fond love' may appear as the natural outcome of the extreme emotions of sexual jealousy. In the savagery of the wish that 'the slave had forty thousand lives' to accommodate his revenge may be recognized the horror of murderous intent. Yet these sentiments, in their immediacy and severity, may equally betray the accents of a towering awareness of the self; and in the very words of Othello's vow may be detected the tones of self-congratulation. The 'icy current, and compulsive course' of his pledged resolution is to be as inflexible as his own honour and former greatness; but the words are also eloquent of his compulsive aspiration to a creaturely absoluteness. That this, rather than the sexual jealousy in which it embodies itself, is the true cause of Othello's violence – that the 'darkened affections' of his inhumanity must indicate removal from God's presence[68] – a secular assessment cannot be expected to deduce. It can see, in his use of the commonplaces of religious belief, a Christianity that is rather 'a gracious demeanour and a habit of noble conduct' than a thorough-going belief; and it can be led, by Othello's ritual of swearing revenge, to discourse of the resurgence of the more primitive elements of his nature, and to recognize

> gestures and phrases which are dues of the reverence which belongs better to dim pagan cults than to any form of Christian worship.[69]

But such criticism, though aware of 'the paganism of the ritual', cannot consider its significance for the state of Othello's soul. Like Othello himself, it acknowledges the pity of his deed; but, like him, it does not apply the horror to the architect, or ponder the spirituality of a purpose that can express itself in the words, 'my great revenge', as Macbeth can speak of his 'great quell'. Nor does it readily explain the religious solemnity of Othello's address to his own soul as he approaches Desdemona's bed, or his consciousness of dedication to 'the cause'.

'The cause' is the cause which has directed Othello's thoughts and deeds throughout. It concerns his soul, since it has to do with his characteristic will of self-aggrandizement, and the overmastering desire to be sufficient in himself. It is a crusade against the source of confusion within his being,

---

[68] *Conf.* I. xviii. 28; Section III, p. 235.
[69] H. B. Charlton, *Shakespearean Tragedy*, 1952, p. 120.

and at the same time an attempt to restore the glory he had before grasped in imagination, by destroying the creature who has robbed him of it. Desdemona is now scarcely a person to him. She has become the symbol of the irrationality that corrupts the world of his ideal, and subjects the soul to littleness; and Othello can see himself as the instrument of a universal justice engaged in costly sacrifice rather than vengeance.[70] Not for nothing does he place himself beside the Creator in the supposed purity of his motive:[71] he is a pathetic example of that attempt to remake the world according to a creaturely righteousness by which tragic man, glorying in himself rather than yielding *'glory vnto him that makes him'*, seeks to usurp the rôle of Providence, and 'make the self seem the one beginning'.[72] The murder of Desdemona is an enactment of the perverse process whereby an erring soul, willing to make itself the measure of things, and for this purpose declining upon an excellence it presumes itself to possess, reacts with hatred against the being who confirms its creatureliness, shatters its sufficiency, and turns into absurdity the 'god-pose' with which it impresses itself and others. The consistency of Othello's action is implied in H. Granville-Barker's comment that, as he goes about the murder, he 'regains a satanic semblance of the nobility that was his'.[73] In proclaiming his purposes to his own ears and to the chaste stars, his words resume the cadences of old, and he is supremely himself again, just as he was when he commanded those scurrying about him to put up their bright swords.

With the death of Desdemona, 'the cause' vanishes like the illusion it was. The concern for greatness of soul gives place to dread; Othello is ashamed to admit his deed to his wife's servant, and the 'coarse-grained, conscienceless, light-minded'[74] Emilia is soon to show, by her true loyalty to another, the utter inadequacy of Othello's love for his wife, and the contemptible nature of the self-ideal on which his pride had rested. His response to the fact of his error is itself instinct with his soul's purpose of self-affirmation: it may indeed be said of Othello that nowhere in his life is he more consistent with himself than in the manner of his leaving it. His grief does not overwhelm him: he is equally taken up with the sense of his own guilt, and with amazed self-reproach; and he remains alone when all fly after Iago, contemplating the unprincipled course of his own conduct, and asking himself, 'why should honour outlive honesty?' Whether 'honesty' here refers to the dead Desdemona or to the quality of Othello's own intentions, it is clear that the phrase is a bitter admission of his own guilt, and at the same time a hint of his ultimate intention. His preoccupation – though now perhaps excusably –

[70] T. Spencer, *Shakespeare and the Nature of Man*, 1943, p. 130.
[71] Helen Gardner, 'The Noble Moor', quoted in Section III, p. 250.
[72] Augustine, *De Civ. Dei* XIV. xiii; Section II, p. 152.
[73] Granville-Barker, 4th Ser., p. 117.   [74] ibid., p. 197.

remains with himself. While Emilia breathes her last a few feet away from him his mind is elsewhere, and her death evokes from him no comment. His thoughts are occupied with the means by which he will at one stroke atone for his crime and recreate the Othello of the past; and his resolve enables him to play a 'grimly comic little practical joke'[75] on Gratiano in the process of rearming himself.

Othello's concern in his final utterance is to revive the image of himself that he and other men once believed to be true; and by his last action he seeks to vindicate the belief. The sense of his own guilt, as Miss Gardner observes, is overridden by 'The revival of faith in Othello which rings through his last speech'.[76] The 'word or two' of mention of his past services to the state reminds those in his presence of former glories; yet even now, as he stands disgraced, he wishes no excuse to be made for him, but can ask proudly to be spoken of as he is. The music in his words signifies the return to him of 'the old quiet authority'[77]—for in the last moments of his life he is able to resume once more the service of the ideal of his soul's integrity. The Othello who had been exalted in the conquest of his enemies in the field had turned aside to destroy the creature who had seemed to corrupt the excellence and order of his being from within. Now he knows the source of its shortcoming to have been in himself; and, by striking down what has marred the desired perfection, dies in that service of that soul-ideal which had been the means of his worldly greatness. In doing justice upon himself he is striking at the tyranny of those forces within himself and in human nature, personified in the 'turbaned Turk', which counter his aspiration toward purity of being, and undermine the integrity of the world of his creaturely greatness.[78]

In this consistency – and fortitude – there is much that is admirable; but, as T. S. Eliot declares, Othello has by now not only ceased to think about Desdemona in the concern with himself, but is also endeavouring to escape reality. He is engaged in a self-dramatization which takes in the spectator, but has the deception of himself as its primary intention. In Eliot's estimate, Othello takes pathetic refuge from the moral in the aesthetic.[79] Whether the term aestheticism can apply to whatever tendency it is that immediately precedes self-destruction may perhaps be questioned – though that purpose admittedly does not preclude the need for self-encouragement. But if Othello is 'trying to cheer himself up', he is pursuing a policy to which he has devoted his entire existence; for a faith in a human reality must ultimately be understood as a vain self-confidence that blinds the possessor to the stark tragedy of his situation. Othello has tried to gain life from a world that has no true life within

[75] ibid., p. 138. [76] op. cit., p. 202.
[77] Granville-Barker, op. cit., p. 148. [78] Helen Gardner, op. cit., p. 202.
[79] 'Shakespeare and the Stoicism of Seneca', 1927, *Shakespeare Criticism 1919–35*, ed. Bradby, 1949, p. 214.

itself; after a manner, he has sought a unity and an omnipotence, but in the realm of the temporal, where all things are transient like a shadow; he has looked for sublimities in creatures, and fallen into confusion and error.[80]

His death is thus at one with his life, and a tribute to what he has lived by: in the deepest sense, all that has gone before was an escape from reality – a feverish search for beatitude amongst things imperfect and perishing. It is not impossible to regard Othello as the embodiment of a will to righteousness in one whose loyalties are earthly, or as an example of that self-love which, cut off from the knowledge and the means of true righteousness, declines into a self-hate, and works its own ruin. And from the play itself there can be deduced a testimony to that paradox of the spirit whereby the things which may appear as virtues to the mind of man, 'if they be not all referred unto God, are indeed rather vices than virtues', and whoever perversely exults in the attaining of a good of nature 'is evil himself in this good, and wretched, being deprived of a better'.[81]

[80] (Section II, p. 101.) [81] (Section II, p. 94; Section III, p. 245.)

Chapter 23

KING LEAR

No hero is more clearly the architect of his own tragedy than King Lear. The love-test which he devises for his daughters, and the extreme of passion and policy which its failure drives him to, are evidences of blindness and folly; and Lear's actions are most readily explained as being the work of a wrathful temperament, perhaps assisted by the depradations of old age. Thus his behaviour at the beginning of the play is, as Dr Johnson sees it, 'hot, heady and violent';[1] and later criticism has been inclined to accept this estimate. A learned and cautious modern critic can see Lear's latter dealings as typical of 'a life composed of hasty imperious decisions', and Lear himself as incapable of acting sensibly :

> Even when he is sane, he is a man quite lacking in wisdom; nothing he does in the first act is good or sensible.[2]

It is but a step from this to the view that Lear is so completely the slave of uncontrolled emotion as to be both beyond the guidance of reason and unequal to the demands of moral obligation.[3] This reading of his character is well able to accommodate the love-test and all that is revealed by it; but it must also raise a question of Lear's suitability as a tragic hero. The degree of contrast which it makes with other of his recognized qualities, it could further be argued, 'appears too grossly'.

These qualities, together with a more sympathetic approach to Lear's initial conduct, make possible a very different impression. F. G. Schoff argues that for each instance of his anger there is adequate cause, and that from no one save Goneril and Regan is there a hint that he is wrathful by temperament. A lone act of folly is proof neither of stupidity nor senility; and there is subsequently to be noted in Lear a quickness of perception, a touch of humour and of magnanimity, a pitiless integrity in self-criticism, a capacity to learn from experience, an awareness of others' sufferings and an ability to win the affection of others which can only be indications of a 'greatness of spirit', and of a nature averse to

---

[1] *Johnson on Shakespeare*, ed. W. Raleigh, 1957, p. 155.
[2] T. Spencer, *Shakespeare and the Nature of Man*, 1943, p. 140.
[3] O. J. Campbell, 'The Salvation of Lear', *E.L.H.* XV, 1948, p. 101.

342

stupidity, vanity and egoism.[4] This conclusion, however, while making Lear acceptable as a tragic hero, makes his initial actions incomprehensible – and Schoff is prepared to accept them as a mere literary device. The Lear of Shakespeare's imagining, he argues, could not do what according to the story he must do; but in the situation itself, once it was past the initial postulate that these actions had occurred, there lay scope for that setting forth of the power of evil in the world that was Shakespeare's true dramatic intention. He therefore did not linger over the opening of the play, but 'got it out of the way as swiftly as possible; and got on to what mattered to him'.[5] Shakespeare's achievement in *King Lear*, therefore, rests upon its hero's inconsistency, and on his own.

That such widely differing appraisals of Lear should be possible, and that a firm judgement should have to run a perilous course between the Scylla of diminishing the hero's responsibility and the Charybdis of questioning the integrity of the author, points to a failing that is either literary or critical. The assumption, in an instance of this kind, that Shakespeare must be allowed to go free while others abide the question, is surely not to be made; yet the possibility remains that there is something which criticism, like the character it criticizes, has taken too little note of – a force which, like an engine, can wrench the frame of such a nature as Lear's from the fixed place of reasonableness and self-consistency which an art like Shakespeare's, schooled in human passions and motives to an unsurpassed degree, must have had fully in view. In this respect it may be suggested that Johnson's remark upon Shakespeare, that 'His story requires Romans or kings, but he thinks only on men',[6] has become too much of a commonplace for criticism. Lear certainly does not think of himself only as a man; but his word to those around him,

> come, come; I am a king,
> My masters, know you that
> (IV. vi. 200–1),

if it were addressed to literary critics, would receive most dubious response. They do not, upon the whole, bring to their appreciation of the man the conception of royal office which Shakespeare shared with his contemporaries, and do not write in awareness of the dangerous position a man faced when he attained to a throne, or of the habits of mind that the exercise of kingly power was likely to create in him. That an error which would be glaring in a man might almost be natural in a king is suggested in those productions of *King Lear* which emphasize the

[4] F. G. Schoff, 'King Lear : Moral Example or Tragic Protagonist?' *S.Q.* XIII, 1962 pp. 161–7.

[5] ibid., pp. 168–70.

[6] 'Preface to Shakespeare' (1765), *Shakespeare Criticism: A Selection*, ed. D. Nichol Smith, 1953, p. 83.

height of the royal throne above the actors on the stage, and thus combine the idea of an exalted level of awareness with an evident means of estrangement and imperception. Since it is possible that a certain insensitivity to the import of Lear's kingship has had a disabling effect upon criticism, the analysis of the play will here be preceded by a consideration of the contemporary understanding of the bearing of regal sway.[7]

The moralists of Elizabethan times were insistent that the natural and proper form of government was absolute authority of the one over the many. They were no less insistent, however, that the kingly prerogatives had the public welfare as their true aim : despite the claims that were made for monarchy, they knew that regal power was in fact founded upon the popular will, and that the dignity of the throne had therefore a strict dependence upon the whims and dispositions of the populace. The multitude, amidst whom regality was erected, were traditionally recognized to be debased, ignorant, and inherently rebellious. Lipsius lays down what is perhaps the main principle of monarchical rule in quoting Sallust and Caesar to the effect that *'no man doth willingly submit himselfe to be ruled by another'*, and when he insists that the way to govern effectively is to know what is in the thoughts of the people. For depravity is at the root of human affairs : the common people, he says,

> are vnstable. . . . They do cast off all passions, or else are out of measure affected. . . . They are void of reason. . . . They encline always to the greater part. . . . They are by nature enuious. . . . They are full of suspicions. . . . They are light of beliefe. . . . They cannot moderate or refraine their speech. . . . They are . . . desirous of new commotions. . . . They fauour these hot and fierie fellowes. . . . They neglect the publike profit. . . . They are fierce in words, and malapert by nature. . . . They are either cast downe with ouermuch feare, or raised vp with ouermuch hope.[8]

This damning – and generally accepted – indictment of the people as a ruler saw them was helped by the belief, no less widespread, that their appetites dominated over their understanding. In consequence they swarmed not only with errors, but with the vices that depended on them, and to gain their favour a man was under the obligation of forsaking his own reason. Arguments drawn from pleasure or utility were far more powerful with them than those drawn from honesty and virtue : they were concerned not with virtue itself, but with its reward.[9] All that was best in man was dashed to pieces on these barren shores: 'the lowest virtues draw praise from them', says Bacon; 'the middle virtues work in

---

[7] The section on monarchy that follows is based on the writer's article 'Cordelia and Lear', *S.Q.* VIII, 1957, pp. 146–9.

[8] *Sixe Bookes of Politickes or Civil Doctrine*, tr. W. Jones, 1594, IV. vi, p. 71; v, pp. 67–9.

[9] Sir T. Browne, 'Pseudodoxia Epidemica', *Works*, ed. Keynes, II, 27.

them astonishment or admiration; but of the highest virtues they have no sense or perceiving at all'.[10]

Such was the basis of power; but the man who held power was himself an imperfect and weak mortal, subject to the same infirmities as those he ruled. It was nearly always a man's place, not his greatness, that gave him eminence :

> Which PLACE, what is it but of reurence
> A throne rais'd on man's reason and affection?[11]

A king's authority, says Lipsius, is no more than the opinion the people conceive of him, 'a reuerent opinion of the King and his estate' :[12] to have the crown was not necessarily to have authority – an idea which readers of Shakespeare would find it hard to ignore. Being thus weak, a ruler might look for aid from powerful friends; but to do so would be a fatal mistake, for 'the conditiō of bearing rule as a king is such, that it cannot otherwise stād, but whē all authority is cōmitted to one'.[13] However great was his burden, a king had to take his own counsel. If he relied on his robes and furred gowns to hide his mistakes, he would be deceived; the people were the 'glasse of Power', and reflected its short-comings on all sides.[14] The men he called upon to do him service would desert him when he ceased to prosper,[15] and his enemies would take advantage of the inevitable grudge the people entertained against their ruler, for 'the enuy of a King /Makes people like reproofe of Maiesty'.[16] The estate of King was encircled by the insatiable desires of the ambitious : all too often a ruler was drinking in 'poison'd flattery' rather than 'homage sweet'. Because of the essential precariousness of his rule, the lot of a king was suspicion without end :

> Kings cannot safely raigne without mistrust,
> Because no state without Ambition is.[17]

Whoever is nearest to the throne in power or pretention, Lipsius declares, is always suspected and hated by rulers; they cannot even afford to trust their own children,[18] for normal values are only too easily abandoned by those who perceive the glistening of a crown. Thus a king could, through merely human weakness, commit the gravest errors : his private passions could become the instruments of evil-doers, for by understanding him they could control him and bring him to ruin.

A king was but an imperfect man; but he could secure himself in power so long as he kept in mind the two essential principles of rule. First,

[10] 'Of Praise', *Philosophical Works*, ed. J. M. Robertson, 1905, p. 799.
[11] Fulke Greville, *Treatise of Monarchy*, st. 34.   [12] IV. viii, p. 75; ix, p. 78.
[13] IV. ix, p. 81.
[14] Fulke Greville, *Alaham*, Chorus 4, 1. 43.   [15] Lipsius, IV. xii, p. 111.
[16] *Alaham*, I. i. 254–5.
[17] John Davies of Hereford, *Microcosmos*, p. 150.   [18] IV. vi, p. 71.

kings could be sure that their authority would not crumble, 'prouided, that an inward loue for their iustice and piety, accompany the outward worship giuen their places and power'.[19] Man's being was primarily a moral one, and it was by human virtue that his society was sustained; institutions – including that of kingship – existed in order that virtue might be protected. For this reason (as Sir Thomas Elyot makes clear) the governor was to bind his subjects to him with the chain of love that could be forged by a virtuous, just and benevolent mind. It was not simply the pomp of power, nor even the fact that a king filled a high place in the Divinely-ordained scheme of things, which made men ready to accredit authority as divine, to harbour the

> conceipt, that glory doth containe
> Some supernaturall sparke, or apparition,
> More than the common humour can attaine.[20]

There was also the fact that a man who was king was called to the exalted exercise of virtue; it was his task and his glory to overmaster the base, irrational tendencies of his own nature, and not only to cultivate his nobler qualities, but to make them the source of human actions and events. And was this not as it should be? for it was through the will of God that they were kings. High magistrates might have their faults;

> yet, being graced with the place of aucthority, they are and ought to be reuerenced of men accordingly, the person and not the function deseruing blame. They are to be called the speciall images of God, which being, they are lightned with knowledge, & indued with vnder-standing, they subdue affection, and follow reason, they excell in vertue, no lesse then they exceed in dignity, all other of other sort, how good, and how great so euer.

Indeed, princes who governed themselves as they ought

> are truly sayed to be Gods, and ought accordingly of men to be reuerenced, admired, and not to be compared with.[21]

The above words might well be Lear's estimate of his own nature, for he sees himself as a virtuous ruler. But virtue was only half of the picture of kingship. It was certainly a means of power for the ruler; but he would often find that the vices of the people he ruled over could not be contained by the use of virtue, and he had therefore to be able to resort to other means to preserve order. Even if a king were naturally inclined to the generous virtues, he was bound to realize that his goodness might be his ruin. The baseness of the populace and the ambitions of his nobles

[19] Raleigh, *History*, 1614, sig. C3.
[20] Fulke Greville, *An Inquisition vpon Fame and Honour*, st. 38.
[21] Sir George More, *A Demonstration of God in His Workes*, 1597, pp. 72-3.

were such that lenity was more likely to induce contempt than respect. Rulers had either to observe dark 'Scepter-mysteries',[22] or not be kings: government had to be founded on severity. And if harshness were not part of his nature, a king was to acquire it. This is how Lipsius refers to the first essential of kingly authority:

> First it ought to be *seueare*, because this ordinarie, and daylie lenitie induceth contempt, which is the very plague and ouerthrow of gouernment. In this corruption of manners and of men, *if wee haue not seueritie in vs to force feare, wee must seeke to purchase and vse it*; the rather because *the hope to escape vnpunished*, doth bring with it an *vnbridled liberty to do euill*. And who will stand in awe of him, *whose sword is alwayes in his scabberd so fast tyed that it can hardly be drawne out*? Who rather by negligence then clemencie, *doth suffer the edge of his authoritie to waxe dull*? Do not thou gouerne after this manner, and learne the nature of the common people, *for they are not such by nature, as to yeeld obedience to shame*, but to feare.[23]

A king – if we are to believe Lipsius and others – had to be prepared if occasion arose ruthlessly to destroy those who threatened his authority; to expiate the public hatred of the shedding of blood by the further sacrifice of the objects of public grievance;[24] to see to it that his subordinate officers were granted honours '*short* and *sweet*',[25] so that they never became too powerful, yet remained powerful enough for the 'insolency of inferiors' to be broken upon them before it could harm him.[26] And, if he saw policy and morality taking different paths, he was to console himself with the thought that he who had the common interest at heart never did ill.[27] There are many chapters in the book of policy to which a man like Lear would never have recourse; the Elizabethans were fully aware that

> to doe all that Policie doth will
> Must needes the *soule* with mortal *Sores* infect.[28]

But we can be sure that, faced with the need to apply severity, Lear would not shrink from the task.

If the matter of kingship is considered in terms of Elizabethan thought, the following conclusion seems inescapable. Whether a king chose virtue or severity, he would be fulfilling a god-like function – or at least, his conduct would set him apart from the ways of common men. For in either case he would find himself conquering his own passions and preferences. The less his rewards and punishments were alike impartial, the

---

[22] *Alaham*, V. i. 46.   [23] IV. ix, p. 79. See also *Microcosmos*, p. 114.
[24] See IV. ix, x, xi and VI. v, p. 197. See also *Microcosmos*, p. 109.
[25] *Microcosmos*, p. 114.
[26] Lipsius, IV. ix. p. 81; Bacon, 'Of Nobility', *Works*, ed. Robertson, p. 750.
[27] Lipsius, IV. xiii, pp. 112–14.   [28] *Microcosmos*, p. 107.

more his position would be weakened. And whatever line of policy he took, it was part and parcel of his office never to disclose his personal feelings, for in that event he showed himself more man than king. A king was not a god; yet he lived in a realm above humanity, and must ever keep himself beyond the reach of others' and even his own emotions. And yet, when all was said and done, this demi-god was no more than a man:

> A King [says Bacon] is a mortal god on earth, unto whom the living God hath lent his own name as a great honour: but withal told him, that he should die like a man, lest he should be proud and flatter himself, that God hath with his name imparted unto him his nature also.[29]

This, then, was the terrifying paradox of kingship, which Shakespeare well understood, and to which he gave incomparable expression in *King Lear*: that a king, though a mere man, could not be a king unless he continued to see himself as something more than a man, and to act in accordance with the kingly ideal that conferred a rare kind of mortal divinity upon him.

The difference between a private man and a king, declares Henry V, is comprised in the 'idol ceremony'; and he fittingly inquires of it,

> What kind of god art thou, that suffer'st more
> Of mortal griefs than do thy worshippers?
> (IV. i. 245-7.)

There is present in his question, however, a confusion of the man and his state: he cannot question his royalty without questioning himself. Both appear as objects of worship, and there persists a sense of the exalted distinction that sets a king above a commoner. A king is not to be separated from his kingliness: he must worship the 'idol ceremony' that he may himself receive the worship and obedience of those beneath him. Despite his protestations, King Henry must act in the uplifted self-awareness that alone makes possible monarchical rule, and be true to his destiny as 'a mortal god on earth'. The same may be said of King Lear. Though he is not without a prompting to forsake his office, there is nevertheless to be adduced from the play 'Lear's own assertion of kingship as something not far from godhead'.[30] No less than Othello, Lear is 'conscious of what he stands for'; but he has no need of Othello's deliberate cultivation of aloofness from his fellows in the process of proving to himself his own worth. Lear's worth is proved to himself by his office – by the destiny by which he was 'graced with the place of authority' and called to the exercise of the kingly virtues that seemingly

[29] 'Of a King', *Works*, ed. Robertson, p. 809.
[30] Granville-Barker, *Prefaces*, 1st Ser., 1949, p. 164.

raise him above the humanity he rules. He presumes – because he must – upon a greatness of soul that is inseparable from his calling, and makes his kingship his ideal and his divinity; but in kingship itself lies both temptation and the means by which a creaturely existence may aspire to a creaturely transcendence – by which it may become 'obsessed with inordinate glorie', and derive from its mastery of the limited good of rule the illusion of its omnipotence.[31] Lear may therefore be seen as having succumbed to the proud conviction that 'God hath with his name imparted unto him his nature also' – and as having in consequence to die like a man, that he may be disabused of his self-flattery.

It is possible from the very first to detect in Lear's peremptory and stern tones of authority the accents of a 'ferocious egotism';[32] and it is not difficult to catch a hint of the gratification derived by an imperious nature from the disposal of vast wealth and power. Similar impressions must arise from his inflexibility: Dr Johnson can find in his 'Nothing: I have sworn; I am firm' a culpable disposition 'to plead the obligation of a vow in defence of implacability'.[33] Yet it is a question in such instances as this whether Lear is the embodiment of 'perverse self-will'[34] or of the requirements of kingly rule. While it is not to be doubted that personal whim plays some part in Lear's reaction to Kent's demand that he should revoke the pronouncement he has made, Lear's fury arises in the main from the challenge to royal authority, and the attempt, in making a king break his own vow, to rend apart the personal and the political. A king who has sworn must be firm: the consciousness and the reality of power can only be maintained if the possessor identifies himself with the ideal which confers it. At moments of stress, therefore, Lear proclaims an absoluteness, for he must always keep before his eyes the picture of himself as a king: in the throes of madness he is still

> Ay, every inch a King:
> When I do stare, see how the subject quakes.
> I pardon that man's life
>
> (IV. vi. 108–10).

The 'pagan ferocity'[35] with which he meets opposition can be ascribed to the supreme need of his nature – and of his office – to assert his regality: if she defies the regal imperative, the child who is the joy of his heart will be 'as well neighbour'd, pitied, and reliev'd' as the barbarous Scythian. Lear will not shrink from the severity with which a king must respond to challenges to his position; but in his cruelty he may also be

[31] (Section III, pp. 240, 246.)
[32] L. C. Knights, *Some Shakespearean Themes*, 1959, p. 95.
[33] *Johnson on Shakespeare*, ed. Raleigh, 1957, p. 155.
[34] L. C. Knights, op. cit., p. 93.
[35] G. Wilson Knight, *The Wheel of Fire*, 1949, p. 183.

regarded as the victim of a lust for self-affirmation, breaking the bond of human kindness to gain the 'unlimited selfhood' which his soul covets, and which the bearing of absolute authority confers.[36]

A presumptuous self-will, and a blindness to human limitation may, as Bradley observes, be the products of a long life of absolute power;[37] Lear may in his imperiousness be an example of the 'petrification' that takes place when the arteries of habitual authority tend to harden.[38] In the manner of his dealings with others can be found an indication of his utter remoteness from them, and of his living in a world of his own. Thus W. H. Clemen points out that his failing to adapt himself to the person with whom he is speaking, but determining in advance the answers he will receive, is the reason for his misunderstanding of Cordelia. He takes no pains to understand what she is really trying to say, but catches up only the superficial form of her answer, and, because he had expected a different one, repels the person who is dearest to him.

> More and more Lear loses contact with the outside world; words become for him less a means of communication with others than a means of expressing what goes on within himself.[39]

Clemen's observation comes close to the perception that reality is for Lear assumed to be comprised within the bounds of the self; and, though he may not pursue the deeper implication of this judgement, Wilson Knight is doubtless led by the same impression to the conclusion that, if his speeches are any indication, Lear is 'more than a little of a tyrant'.[40] Lear's abruptness of command and insistence upon absolute obedience to his will may betoken the mere tyrant; but it is also possible to take a very different view of the bluntness of his speech, and to see in it – especially later in the play –

> the brusque familiar give and take which true authority never fears to practise with its dependents.[41]

For Lear is no jack in office. Through the harshness of assertion and the worship of his own regality emerges the presence of one who is every inch a king. The conscious irony in his reference to himself as crawling towards death freed of the burden of authority may be due to Lear's knowledge that he will remain a king to his last breath; and the wrath that Kent provokes in trying to come between his sentences and his power is eloquent of that

Which nor our nature nor our place can bear
(I. i. 172).

---

[36] (Section III, p. 248.) [37] *Shakespearean Tragedy*, 1956, p. 282.
[38] R. Speaight, *Nature in Shakespearian Tragedy*, 1955, p. 92.
[39] *The Development of Shakespeare's Imagery*, London, 1951, p. 134.
[40] op. cit., p. 164. [41] Granville-Barker, 1st Ser., 1949, p. 170.

In this respect, the fury that is occasioned by Cordelia's defiance of her father's power is possibly enhanced, as it is certainly pervaded, by a grief that arises from her affront to his royalty of nature. Cordelia has enjoyed the love of a king as well as a father; and her declining to give a royal heart the tribute it deserves must indicate to him that she is no nearer to him in nature than she is in obedience, and make it easier to see her as the 'stranger to my heart and me' that his own decree will pronounce her. Whether the strenuousness and savagery of the pronouncement itself are to be attributed more to Lear's pursuit of his soul-ideal than to the true nature of his soul must be held open to doubt, though the transformation of rebuff into betrayal, and devotion into the passion for revenge, is the familiar response of the self-affirming spirit. The 'war between the ordinary nature and the King-nature'[42] which has been remarked as a theme of the play may be regarded as going on within Lear's own mind, with his will to be true to his nature being fatally misdirected by his office towards his worser self.

The treatment of Cordelia can be viewed as an example of behaviour utterly abandoned and unrestrained, or as the rigid and unflinching adherence to the conditions of an agreed procedure. It can be seen as self-assertion, but also, in view of Lear's confessed attachment and real suffering, as a kind of monstrous self-restraint. Perhaps both categories are involved, for the one is to Lear the means of the other : it is only by a readiness to sacrifice his own emotions and preferences that Lear the king has been able to maintain his authority and attain to the supremacy of self-adulation. Evidence of such sacrificing is to be found elsewhere in the play. Bradley points out that Lear had noticed earlier how different were the characters of Albany and Cornwall, and objects that

> now he seems either to have lost this perception or to be unwisely ignoring it.[43]

The consideration does not come before him that, in ignoring his preferences and weighing equalities to a nicety in the apportionment of his land, Lear might be moved by a kingly ideal of impartiality, and that the scrupulous exactness here disclosed may be apparent elsewhere in his manner and dealings. Thus, as one son-in-law is addressed, the other is immediately assured that he is 'Our no less loving son of Albany'; and when Burgundy is the first of the wooers to be applied to, Lear must speak in consciousness of the fact. The two breaches of strict impartiality that occur in the first scene are made so exceedingly obvious as to cause

42 E. Sitwell, *A Notebook*, 1948, p. 60.
43 op. cit., p. 281.

some revulsion; but this fact is no indication of a mode of conduct that is habitual. Indeed, the advice to France to look elsewhere

> Than on a wretch whom nature is asham'd
> Almost to acknowledge hers
> (I. i. 213-14)

is equally an intimation addressed to Cordelia that her interests are now so unworthy of consideration as no longer to merit a kingly restraint. It is an extraordinary gesture, and is meant to appear so, for it is the outcome of strong emotion; but that it is not typical of Lear must appear from other evidence. The trial which he enacts during his madness is not conceived as a screen to hide a despotic vengeance; it is to be conducted with the gravity and reverence befitting one whose royalty is founded upon principle and service:

> Thou robed man of justice, take thy place;
> And thou, his yoke-fellow of equity,
> Bench by his side
> (III. vi. 37-9).

The earlier lines of the play have presented Lear the king; but there is soon to be 'the hint of another Lear, given us in the music of three short words'.[44] Those words are enough to affirm that in putting off his authority and its demands, he craves to enter into the humble – yet for him supremely real and desirable – joys of family life. That his kingship has placed him above the sphere of natural affection is evident both from the uninhibited proclamation of his love for his children and his assumption of the presence of love in them; and

> his complete blindness to the hypocrisy which is patent to us at a glance, his piteous delight in these protestations.[45]

must, if they are not to be characterized as the tokens of folly, be regarded as tribute to the encroachment which the years of rule have made upon his humanity. But if his delight is in one sense 'piteous', in another it is a sign of health. The glory that Lear derives from his kingship is not 'inordinate' – or, at least, not without limit: the authority with which he identifies his nature he does not make the measure of his being. On the contrary, he can prize other things – and very human things – above it, so that to a certain extent authority has become a burden. Yet if he finds any degree of pain in his kingship, he is also aware that it is his element: he cannot forget his own nature, or the calling with which he has identified it; even at his most unbending he is cautioning himself with 'For always I am Caesar'. The gesture that brings his authority to an end would reconcile the two main tendencies of his being: the last minutes of his reign will reward his children's love with lands and rule, and pro-

---

[44] Granville-Barker, 1st Ser., p. 165.   [45] Bradley, *Shakespearean Tragedy*, p. 281.

claim the warm affection that has for so long been hidden beneath his purple robes of state. But in the act of surrendering his regality he is not out of harness; indeed, it is at once his tragedy and his greatness that he never is. The error which would equate love and land, and attempt to 'measure in material terms what is not materially measurable',[46] has its origin in a clinging to the prerogatives, habits and calculations of tyrannical authority – a fact which Coleridge appreciates to the full. Lear, he says, eagerly wishes

> to enjoy his daughters' violent professions, whilst the inveterate habits of sovereignty convert the wish into a claim and positive right, and incompliance with it into crime and treason.[47]

Though wishing to act as a man, Lear bears the mind of a king, and must all unconsciously proceed in that exalted estimate of himself that must distort Cordelia's reluctance into betrayal. If human love may be said to appear to him as the very essence of righteousness, Lear can be described as facing a choice between the principle of righteousness and that of power; and, being, like the generality of men, a 'lover of might'[48] – and particularly so as a mortal ruler – he must pursue the latter.

That the principles which he tries to reconcile are in conflict within his own nature is clear from the way in which Lear announces the design of massive question and voluble answer by which he is to divide his kingdom:

> Tell me, my daughters, –
> Since now we will divest us both of rule,
> Interest of territory, cares of state, –
> Which of you shall we say doth love us most?
> (I. i. 48–51.)

In these words is to be seen an instant and fervent resort from the realm of policy to the human heart, from the status of king to that of man, which must indicate in Lear a disciplining and denial of spontaneous affection – a state from which the ending of rule will liberate him. The judgement of R. B. Heilman that Lear's surrender of power is an attempt to escape from 'the fettering of circumstance'[49] is in this respect important; it would mean that in his own initial purpose Lear anticipates the teaching of the play that those who are covered or disguised, either by their authority or by calculated falsehood, 'cannot manage by being candidly themselves', whereas those who renounce such protection, though suffering because of their nakedness, nevertheless have the means of sincerity and truth.[50] If this interpretation is correct, it points to an understanding

---

[46] R. B. Heilman, *This Great Stage*, Louisiana State University Press, 1948, p. 159.
[47] *Lectures and Notes on Shakespere*, ed. T. Ashe, 1904, p. 329.
[48] (Section II, p. 88.)   [49] op. cit., p. 34.   [50] ibid., pp. 68–9; 86.

in Lear that kings' 'priuate passions wound their publike States', and to a previous surrender on his part to the chilling demands of royal office which he has recognized as a thwarting of his humanity. Bradley's assertion that the abdication is

> a childish scheme to gratify his love of absolute power and his hunger for assurances of devotion[51]

is thus a half-truth which would do Lear a great injustice; the observation of H. B. Charlton that Shakespeare is the first teller of this tale to make the love-test coincidental with a will to abdicate is surely a better indication of Lear's intent.[52] Neither does Bradley do full justice to the quality of love which directs this action. The 'hunger for assurances of devotion' is obvious enough; yet Coleridge had been able to say of this 'intense desire of being intensely loved' that it was 'selfish, yet characteristic of the selfishness of a loving and kindly nature alone'.[53] The openness of Lear's preference for Cordelia, manifested in the words 'Now, our joy' no less than in a share of land 'more opulent' than her sisters', Bradley finds a source of both pitying contempt and painful embarrassment.[54] This is the other instance of Lear's breach of impartiality, made this time as a tribute to the force of his love rather than to his hate. Though admitting the open sentimentality of Lear's love for his youngest child, Wilson Knight is concerned to show how real it is; and in declaring that it is 'powerful and firm-planted in his mind as a mountain rock embedded in earth',[55] he gives a definition that is more conducive to a true assessment.

The decision to make the existence of family love a matter of public moment must be considered both unwisdom and indelicacy – though the identification of the personal and the formal is not without precedent in the lives of those bearing rule, and constitutes, in theory at least, the very essence of kingship. Having proclaimed his own love in his purpose, Lear does have the right to receive statements of his children's love; and he asks no more from them. But the staggering reply of 'Nothing', the flouting of his public proceedings, and the apparent defiance displayed in the presence of those whose respect is the means of his authority, must summon forth the instincts of the king rather than of the man and father – if they do not also conflict with the self-regarding aspirations of his very soul. Affronted regality seizes upon the terms of its bargain. By setting what she calls 'truth' above the claims of authority, Cordelia asserts, not only the slightness of her love for her father, but that the formality and power of his ideal is shallow and ridiculous. Lear is made to face the alternatives of rendering his kingship an absurdity by coming

[51] op. cit., p. 250.   [52] *Shakespearian Tragedy*, 1952, p. 195.
[53] *Lectures and Notes*, 1904, p. 329.
[54] op. cit., p. 281.   [55] *The Wheel of Fire*, 1949, p. 162.

to terms with the person who has challenged it, or breaking the bond of love which links him with his child – and which she appears already to have broken. His choice is terrible but predictable : she who forces it upon him has already foreseen it. Lear cannot believe other than that his office – and his will – are the means of order and happiness within the kingdom, and Cordelia's rebellion and defiance can only make her guilty in his eyes of 'pride, which she calls plainness'. Similarly, Kent's defiance of his command and assailing of his purposes is denounced as 'strain'd pride'. A king is a god on earth : and Lear is the centre of the universe of the state. That he should act with 'an unthinking acceptance of his own importance'[56] is rather a necessity of his situation than a basis for rebuke. And it is almost implicit in the nature of his calling that he should be claimed by the heroic compulsion of attempting to make a part of reality yield to the government of his own will – that instead of the submission and forsaking which are the means and accompaniment of the true virtue, his soul should be tempted into 'making trial of its own power' among those upon whom it is called to exercise power, and thus be in peril of producing a false imitation of the Almighty.[57] In the strenuousness of Lear's reaction there is indeed the appearance of something ill-moderated and perverse – a passionate clinging to prerogatives and appurtenances which might easily be taken away from him, the love of which might be understood as being full of menace to his true welfare, if not to his soul. There is perceptible in his dilemma those evidences of an incorrect self-love which have been described as loves which the mind cannot quell, and errors from which it can see no escape :[58] his attachment to kingly office, and all the 'large effects /That troop with majesty' he cannot forsake; and to the severest treatment of her upon whose kind nursery he had thought to set his rest he can recognize no alternative.

In the inhumanity of Lear, criticism as a whole does not recognize a soul being trodden down by its servant for want of obedience to its Master;[59] but in the casting off of Cordelia it does see a defiance of natural order.[60] Through stifling the promptings of kindness, and taking coldness to his heart, declares Dr Sitwell, Lear generates 'the endless cold of Goneril and Regan'.[61] Lear himself has set the precedent for Regan's later taunting Cordelia with her poverty : the bluntness with which Burgundy is asked to 'Take her, or leave her' after she has been described as

> Unfriended, new-adopted to our hate,
> Dower'd with our curse, and stranger'd with our oath
>
> (I. i. 204–5)

[56] T. Spencer, *Shakespeare and the Nature of Man*, 1943, p. 140.
[57] (Section II, p. 152.)   [58] (Section II, p. 92.)   [59] (Section III, p. 234.)
[60] R. Speaight, *Nature in Shakespearian Tragedy*, 1955, p. 95.   [61] *Notebook*, 1948, p. 58.

is a glorying in creaturely power which finds in present cruelty an expression that such dark aspiration can never avoid: the will which would make itself the centre of existence must offend against other life which has rightful place in the measure of things.[62] With word and action Lear flaunts a power that beggars and hurts the 'truth' that has been urged against him, and the person who trusts in it – and thereby gains a satisfaction similar to that Iago derives from mocking Cassio with the word 'lieutenant', the crude relish of mastery (II. iii. 256). It is not only Cordelia who suffers this treatment: Granville-Barker has noted 'the ironic last fling at Kent of "Away! By Jupiter, /*This* shall not be revoked" '.[63] In these tricks of arrogance which add insult to the injury he has decreed, as well as in the injury itself, is made evident 'the mentality common to the children of this world', who are quick to hurl their hatred where they find occasion for misliking.[64] In a quarrel for earth, Lear turns to earth – save that the quarrel, to a considerable extent, centres upon the matter of the presence of love. Cordelia's affirming of her sincerity, and incidental calling in question her father's judgement, is of no avail; it can provoke only a

> Better thou
> Hadst not been born than not to have pleas'd
> me better
>
> (I. i. 234–5).

Those accents resound with the proposition 'I am I' that marks the obsession of predominance. Lear is not inclined to fleer and jibe at sincerity; his respect for virtue and truth is absolute, but he must denigrate whatever detracts from his authority in the fixed belief that neither virtue nor truth can be in it. The qualities of the disguised Kent, who defends his dignity, call forth a respect from Lear which approaches that felt by Kent for his master.

Lear can find some comfort and gratification of soul in his cruelty; but the treatment of Cordelia does not outweigh, as it does not moderate, the reality of the grief to which her seemingly loveless answer has subjected him. The tyranny of that grief is to have a profounder effect upon him than the slight either to his authority or to his self-esteem. It is possible to blame the insensibility which receives as ultimately true formal statements of regard, to the point even of obscuring a better knowledge; and, to the extent that Cordelia's unexpected answer is a reflection of an absurdity in his own attitude, Lear may be accused of an incompetence of character, or even a blindness of soul to goodness and right. The power both to recognize and to effect what is good, further, may be held to have been diminished in him by the harshnesses of regal office;

---

[62] (Section III, p. 251.)   [63] 1st Ser. p. 165.   [64] (Section III, p. 236.)

and the passionate nature of his responses may be regarded as an ultimately questionable indulgence in the very means of imperception.[65] Yet what cannot be called in question is his sincerity and his love; if the beginning of the play does not make them sufficiently evident, everything that follows is a testimony to what reveals itself as a passion for righteousness. Nor is the righteousness that is sought purely moral, and human. Although there is that in Lear which seeks for a transcendence amidst mortality, he is also aware of the transcendental amidst his human experience. The perverse soul desires to be something more than a man, a cosmos in itself; but Lear can speak in consciousness of 'the power that made me', and even find his true self obscured and hindered by the very means of the power in which he takes pride. Though a 'will to self-assertion' may readily be seen to operate in Lear, therefore, it is by no means the will 'to unlimited selfhood' of the definition which A. P. Rossiter applies to Macbeth;[66] nor is it possible finally to regard him as endeavouring to impose upon the threatening incongruities of his situation the pattern of an order peculiarly his own.[67] If his concern is to exalt himself, his desire of eminence admits a conscious will to use it in the service of a purpose whose mercies to mankind are manifested to him in

> the orbs
> From whom we do exist and cease to be
> (I. i. 111-2).

Those who take Lear most strictly to task for selfishness are yet obliged to say of him that

> He naturally and invariably sees himself both in relation to large natural forces and to the gods that control them;[68]

and when his confidence in the human world is shaken, his relationship to the elemental powers is observed to be awakened.[69] He swears by these powers in casting off Cordelia, and appeals to them in the terrible curse upon her sister: Bradley notes of the earlier speech that 'the dramatic effect of this passage is exactly, and doubtless intentionally, repeated in the curse pronounced upon Goneril'.[70] At the very height of his tyrannical rage against his own kin, therefore, Lear is also, in principle at least, at his most impersonal, moved by considerations that may be termed both moral and religious in the appeal to a nature that he regards as 'a regulative principle, a restorer of moral equilibrium'.[71] It is precisely this devotion that leads T. Spencer to concur in Wilson Knight's description

[65] (Section II, p. 93.) [66] (Section III, p. 248.) [67] (Section III, p. 239.)
[68] T. Spencer, Shakespeare and the Nature of Man, 1943, p. 138.
[69] W. Clemen, The Development of Shakespeare's Imagery, London, 1951, p. 139.
[70] Shakespearean Tragedy, p. 283.
[71] Heilman, This Great Stage, Louisiana State U.P., 1948, p. 123.

of Lear as 'a tremendous soul';[72] and one may wonder whether they might both have done better to ascribe the origin and nature of his fury to outraged piety and horror at seeming human corruption – to all that constitutes the massiveness of soul they acknowledge – rather than to the effect of a 'puerile intellect'.[73] The best among men may be deceived, or deceive themselves, and one error, no matter how great, need not denote puerility; but that Lear's deception may be understood to have lain in the very monstrousness which ingratitude and lovelessness assume to his gaze is evident from Spencer's comment,

The *unnaturalness* of Goneril and Regan is what Lear cannot bear.[74]

The comment must be extended to cover Cordelia's inadequate and 'unhappy' speech;[75] and the further consideration must be kept in mind, whether one in whom is present so powerful a vision of a superhuman source of man's righteousness can at the same time be incited by the presumptuous trust of the proud in a righteousness of their own. Lear is not so entranced by the enormous powers with which kingship has armed him as to have lost the humility of reference to a system which creates both men and kings. There is every indication that Lear regards himself in his kingship as the champion of justice, love and kindness, as he is of order, within the state; and if this be true, his incomprehension that he may himself be doing evil is the more natural.

The above possibility may be thought to incur heavy qualification from a treatment of Cordelia and Kent that is traditionally regarded as wrathful and violent, and that may be thought to belie all manner of exalted protestations and awarenesses in Lear. The injustice to Cordelia and Kent is patent; but whether it is the outcome of 'uncontrolled anger' as Bradley asserts,[76] or even takes place in such an atmosphere, may be disputed. In both instances, Lear may be thought of as responding more as the man than as the king – or the tyrant. There is no outraged protest at Cordelia's answer. After the initial amazement, there are to be distinguished in Lear's words the tones of warning, but also of as near an approach to pleading as one of Lear's dignity may make, and of a questioning which in itself does not err:

> But goes thy heart with this?
> (I. i. 104.)

The words, 'So young, and so untender?' are almost a musing, and are certainly a lingering before the inevitable stroke. Astounded and heart-stricken as he is, he does his best in the solemnity of the moment to understand himself, and to make sure Cordelia knows what she is about.

[72] op. cit., p. 138; *The Wheel of Fire*, 1949, p. 162.
[73] G. Wilson Knight, ibid.   [74] op. cit., p. 142.
[75] Bradley, op. cit., p. 321.   [76] ibid., p. 281.

Anger is not immediate; and if it were the effect merely of wrath or pride, it would never admit the simultaneous confession,

> I lov'd her most, and thought to have set my rest
> On her kind nursery
>
> (I. i. 123–4).

Much the same considerations must apply to Kent's banishment. When Kent addresses his king so very meaningfully, Lear does not forbid him speech; he is evidently conscious both of the harshness of his previous action and of the struggle within his own soul, and does not silence the exponent of his own thought until that warfare becomes unbearable. If Lear had considered Kent's calling him an 'old man' to be 'in itself a blasphemous outrage' as he does in Granville-Barker's opinion,[77] there would surely have been an incensed exclamation and an instant end to Kent's speech – if not to his life: as F. G. Schoff argues, 'if Lear were the wrathful man sometimes pictured, the Earl might well be dead before his speech is out'.[78] If it is a king who has warned Kent, 'The bow is bent and drawn, make from the shaft', it is a man who pants – after he has let him have his say – 'Kent, on thy life no more'. That Kent is provoking, not the quivering fury of a despot, but the agony of soul of a king who is both sensitive and just, is clear from the manner of his banishment. The punishment itself is not vindictive; but Lear is careful to weigh it against the clear defiance of the offence with a kind of scrupulousness that is not new in him, though here it is applied perhaps as much to embolden himself as convince the onlookers or satisfy his principles. Kent's rebellion Lear can neither by nature nor place tolerate; but his action is not that of a despot. Indeed, if he were the monster of pride that many critics profess to believe him to be, then the question,

> How shall it be explained by what sublime genius this old King, so wilful, so terrible in his passions, is yet so near to our hearts,[79]

is scarcely to be answered. Suffering, it is true, can gain sympathy: and if we can identify ourselves with Macbeth, we can surely feel for one who is tortured and broken on the rack of this tough world. But only a goodness, and, humanly speaking, an innocence, can win our love.

From the moment of his reappearance after his abdication, it is clear that Lear is 'a mighty man, never a mere tyrant divested of power':[80] he retains the authority over the beholder's imagination that he exercises upon the disguised Kent. In giving away his powers he has presumed upon the royalty of nature that he is sure accompanies that of his office; and the rest of the play proves his presumption not to have been vain,

[77] 1st Ser., 1949, p. 164.
[78] 'King Lear : Moral Example or Tragic Protagonist?', S.Q. XIII, 1962, p. 164.
[79] Notebook, 1948, p. 66.   [80] Granville-Barker, op. cit., p. 165.

that in this respect he had known himself well. That the power of his innate worth is not identical with the powers of majesty, however, he has himself glimpsed in forsaking a throne which was proving a hindrance to what was best in him; the appalling extent of the difference he is destined to learn from the bitter lessons of the Fool and of his own kindred. The truth which the play enforces, that the power of human worth is not the same as that of authority, thus affirms Lear's kingliness of nature in the process of decrying the kingliness of office which he has attempted to put off, but which is still his pride. He finds he must still worship the 'idol ceremony' which has been the means of conferring upon him the god-like prerogatives and exaltation of earthly rule; and, still aspiring toward fullness of being, must struggle to possess, as if they were an ultimate good in themselves, the external dignities of the institution which has helped to create the eminence he bears. He will not submit to the dismissal of fifty followers, or to the politic consideration that many people under two commands cannot long hold amity in one house. In thus making an absolute of a good of the external order, Lear is not unlike many of his fellows who, in their illusions of creaturely greatness, turn to seeming realities of the temporal order and are doubly mocked and deceived. He finds, as they do, that these external goods not only cannot make a man better, but that their goodness depends entirely upon the manner in which they are desired, and exists only in so far as they are not made part of the soul of him who covets them.[81] In identifying himself with the trappings which can confer nothing upon him in pursuance of his ideal, Lear indulges in the service of this world and of himself; yet it must not be overlooked that these trappings, now that he has abdicated, are at the same time tokens to him of his children's love – for, so long as his regality is safe, it is always his will to accord human love pre-eminence over earthly power.

For the sake of his regality, and its remorseless demands upon his soul, he sacrifices his love for his child when it comes to the test. Goneril and Regan do similarly with regard to their father. The ingrained habits of rule appear to them as dispositions that transport him from what he rightly is; in the eyes of authority, the wisdom of one so old and reverend must be to conform to the wills of those holding power. They ask of Lear simply that, being weak, he should seem so – and thus repeat, in altered form, his own demand of Cordelia. Their compulsion to see him as a mere old man corresponds to his kingly view of Cordelia as a weak and dowerless girl; and their claim to know Lear's state better than he does himself is an echo of his own 'Nothing will come of nothing'. From the standpoint of what is politic they are not to blame: in being content to play the hypocrite for a kingdom they show failings of a kind that

---

[81] (Section II, p. 100.)

'have been known in the most reputable people';[82] and in first requesting Lear to appreciate his powerlessness, they 'are not, in their own view, nor from the world's point of view, wicked'.[83] At this stage they are no more than hard-hearted, though they are soon to surpass in cruelty their father's treatment of Cordelia. In calling Goneril 'a disease that's in my flesh', Lear speaks more truly than he knows : it is the perverse aspiration to earthly power that summons forth the hidden devils of man's being, and 'makes these hard hearts'. When he has doffed the protection of his place, he finds himself exposed to a climate that chills all that is generous and kindly in man and obliges him to cherish as his creed the bestial calculations of advantage :

> Have more than thou showest,
> Speak less than thou knowest
> (I. iv. 117–18).

In the frigid common sense of the Fool he comes to grips with that in himself against which the spirit of Cordelia has rebelled, and his own spirit must now strive :

> Nay, an thou canst not smile as the wind sits, thou'lt catch cold shortly (I. iv. 99–100).

His striving takes the form of a championing of the sincerity, love and kindness he had conceived his former authority as serving, yet recognized it to have hindered. Now that he is unburdened, 'the native genius of the man begins to show' :[84] the barren plainness of speech that had before been instinct with consciousness of power now proclaims a respect for nothing but human worth. His own imagination, no less than the Fool's grief, presents Cordelia's real deservings to him – and it is significant that his remedy should be to revert instantly to his former self :

> Lest it echo too loudly in his proud unhappy heart, with a quick turn he brings the old Lear to his rescue, rasps an order here, an order there, and – takes it out of Oswald.[85]

The sacrifice is the more painful now that its immediate cause has gone; for the authority that Lear is now concerned with, and upon which he places a supreme reliance, is that of the father and not of the king. His first words of bewildered response to Goneril's sudden ultimatum must be, 'Are you our daughter?'; and in asking her name, he indicates to her the degree to which she is 'stranger'd' by her coldness. But he is truly concerned by the more insistent question, 'Does any here know me?' – for if royal power and natural authority are departed from him,

[82] Granville-Barker, *Prefaces*, 1st Ser., 1949, p. 187.
[83] Edith Sitwell, *Notebook*, 1948, p. 61.
[84] Granville-Barker, op. cit., p. 165.   [85] ibid., p. 167.

he has lost his own identity. The fury of his curse upon Goneril proves to Bradley that 'the disposition from which his first error sprang is still unchanged';[86] but the disposition itself is to be determined less from the 'rash mood' than the horror from which it springs: the fact of the existence of creatures human in form, but not in sympathy – of 'seeming substances'. The monstrousness of ingratitude begins to possess his mind.

The outrage to Kent can provoke only a more fervent avowal of faith in the human heart. Lear will not listen to talk of tricks of character in those in office. He whose firmness had been his pride cannot bear the thought of a Cornwall 'unremoveable and fix'd' in his own course; he argues not in terms of individuals but of right, placing assurance in what he considers the undeniable fact that 'the dear father /Would with his daughter speak' (II. iv. 100–1), and reacting with a contemptuous 'You! Did you?' to a will that has violated natural respect. While the sincerity of his appeal to 'The offices of Nature, bond of childhood' is not to be doubted, however, the suspicion that it is not uppermost in his mind must arise from his dealings with those whose loyalty to these things is in question. The first reason he gives Regan for not returning to her sister – that she had abated him of half his train – outweighs the fact of her striking him 'upon the very heart' (II. iv. 158–60). Though he may invoke 'All the stored vengeance of heaven' upon Goneril for her unnaturalness, it is not long before he is engaged in hard bargaining with her; so great is the craving for the symbols of regality in him that he is ready to measure the human love he acclaims according to the number of the retainers that Goneril will allow him:

> not being the worst
> Stands in some rank of praise. I'll go with thee:
> Thy fifty yet doth double five-and-twenty,
> And thou art twice her love
>
> (II. iv. 257–60).

His state is at this moment to be pitied. It is evident to the spectator that no external prerogative can give Lear his greatness, and that in his blind conviction to the contrary he is reducing himself to a grovelling littleness that decries what he truly is – though he may not recognize the deeper meanings in the spectacle of one who, seeking through adherence to some temporal good to be made more, is so obviously being made less. Whether or not Lear can appreciate the extent of his humiliation, his readiness to batten upon the 'love' with which they are prepared to favour him is ended only by the triumphing of the 'unnatural hags' in their denial of a single follower. Enslaved by that which he has made his chiefest pleasure and his greatest good, Lear may be seen abjectly to follow

---

[86] *Shakespearean Tragedy*, p. 284.

withersoever it leads him, and to fear whomsoever seems to have power to rob him of it.[87] Yet in thus endeavouring to regain a meagre resemblance of the Lear of old, he gives evidence of a defeated stillness, a submissiveness almost, which is never to be seen in him again, and which denotes not a robust wish for assertion, but a desperate will to cling to reality against a rising flood of passion. Lear is a drowning man, and must clutch at his poor followers even if he knows they are naught but straws; and when even this much succour is denied him, he is submerged beneath the seething assaults of his truer self.

Madness breaks upon him in the passion for vengeance. The natural grief at the affront to himself, and what might be termed his spiritual grief at the loss of 'mutable things which the soul enjoyed or hoped to be able to enjoy',[88] drive the enraged Lear to the thought of an avenging justice that shall be of his own devising. But the unnaturalness which has revealed itself before him, and which is the truest cause of his sorrow, is beyond his power to repress as it is to understand; and at the moment of his helplessness it appears to him that a Divine justicier must have arisen in the storm on the heath to punish a perverse generation. The consciousness which has always seen itself in relation to the higher powers, and regarded itself in its kingship as their mortal instrument, can recognize its cosmic allies in the storm's 'high-engender'd battles', despite its being afflicted by their warfare. For the elements cannot be taxed with unkindness. Where the laws of love and sympathy between man and man cannot be infringed, he will recognize no tyranny : the only tyrant is he who will stifle the instincts of his own heart. Now that he is rid of the calling that inhibited love in him and made him insensitive to its presence or absence in others, he is alive to the 'pent-up guilts' concealed beneath the world's formalities, and asks the gods of a moral universe to set their agents upon their real enemies. For though he has hardened his own heart to grievous effect, Lear knows he was moved at least as much by horror at apparent unnaturalness as by unkindness of his own. He can claim to be a man more sinned against than sinning; and in the 'more than kingly dignity'[89] of his concern for the shivering wretch at his side there is testimony to the kindness of a nature truly royal.

The thought of an aged father cruelly abused, of a mouth tearing the hand that lifts food to it, now takes control of his mind; yet this inexorable vision, though it drives Lear to lunacy through the sheer weight of its pain, proves to be the beginning of an awakening of soul. It is 'a means of liberating for full flight an imagination that was hampered before',[90] and thus renders possible that clearing away of the

---

[87] (Section II, p. 91.)   [88] (Section II, p. 100.)
[89] Granville-Barker, 1st Ser., 1949, p. 174.
[90] R. B. Heilman, *This Great Stage*, 1948, p. 181.

untruth of appearances that enables the soul to attain to higher awarenesses within the external order and its own being.[91] One of the chief affirmations of the play, declares W. H. Clemen, is that we must first go through suffering before we can recognize our real selves and the truth; and

> it is . . . with his inner eye – in madness – that [Lear] penetrates to the very bottom of things and recognizes their true nature, whereas he formerly let himself be blinded by their outward appearance.[92]

The liberated imagination turns first to prayer; but the prayer is rather an utterance of infinite compassion upon the afflicted poor of that dark night, made by one whose bodily sufferings bring awareness of the harshnesses of the power he had before proudly and unthinkingly wielded. 'Take physic, pomp', he cries; 'Expose thyself to feel what wretches feel'; by this medicine of pity, authority will learn to cherish humanity, and not oppress it. 'To this haven of the spirit has he come, the Lear of unbridled power and pride'.[93]

Awareness of what should be makes the present reality the more unbearable, and in fantasy alone can Lear fulfil his nature. He can enact a trial of his daughters, and he can try to find out what he is in himself. In both endeavours his aim is a strict justice; and in the activity of his quest can be seen not only a disillusionment with the idols which ruled in his previous self-estimate, but a bursting forth of the spirit into full vitality.[94] With the sincerity that has always distinguished him, Lear wishes to be no more than he is: his passion now is 'for harmonizing inner and outer'.[95] The flatteries of man's institutions he has discarded; the illusions that stem from man's kindness to his fellows he would also eschew. In the past history of Poor Tom he surveys the whole range of the pride of life: the account is a series of 'images of concupiscence', and every syllable is charged with 'the nausea of possession'.[96] And in the unaccommodated wretch who now answers with his naked body to the extremity of the skies he discerns a true image of man: the poor bare forked animal before him is 'the thing itself'. He may not see in Tom the nature of humanity corrupted by its sin; but eagerly putting off with his clothes the old beliefs of his grandeur if not of his righteousness, he seeks, arrayed in the new truth manifested in his ragged 'philosopher', to become, like his mentor, 'a thing of elemental, instinctive life'.[97] Yet just as the impossibility of escape from his own sophisticated consciousness

[91] (Section III, pp. 184–5.)
[92] W. Clemen, *The Development of Shakespeare's Imagery*, London, 1951, p. 136.
[93] Granville-Barker, op. cit., p. 175.
[94] (Section III, p. 277.)   [95] Heilman, op. cit., p. 77.
[96] R. Speaight, *Nature in Shakespearian Tragedy*, 1955, p. 112.
[97] G. Wilson Knight, *The Wheel of Fire*, 1949, p. 184.

is implicit in the question, 'What is the cause of thunder?' so in the present squalor he cannot discard his kingliness. As R. B. Heilman points out, the command 'Pull off my boots; harder, harder; so' echoes the tones of his earlier authority.[98]

The Lear who appears wearing a crown of rank weeds, as if to scorn the regality which had once been his ideal and his delight, comes in his suffering manhood as the champion of humanity. The pomps and flatteries of office had hidden from him the deepest truth about himself; but the thorns of affliction have awakened him to self-discovery:

> When the rain came to wet me once and the wind to make me chatter, when the thunder would not peace at my bidding, there I found 'em, there I smelt 'em out. Go to, they are not men o' their words: they told me I was every thing; 'tis a lie, I am not ague-proof (IV. vi. 101–6).

Just as the sorrowing Cleopatra disclaims the title 'Empress' in the assertion that she is 'No more but e'en a woman', so the afflicted Lear proclaims that he is not a king, but a man. Whatever is truly and unashamedly human he will respect; and whatever tempts or impels man to forsake his kindness he will fly from. None shall die for adultery; he will let kindly procreation thrive rather than invoke the iron remorselessness of law. In this affirmation is evidence of the utter change in him: that 'from his cry for vengeance upon the wicked, he has now passed to . . . a deep compassion upon mankind itself'.[99] But in the very act of defending humanity from the earthly institutions which tyrannize upon it, he cannot but recognize that the temptation to inhumanity comes from within, and not from without: as Dr Sitwell has noted, his concept of procreation as 'the greater good' is spoiled by apprehension of 'the baseness of mankind'.[100] The naturalness of his own begetting has produced his pelican daughters: the means of life itself is the means of depravity, and of tyranny against its own flesh and blood. In crying out against all that can pervert the righteous and kindly will, Lear is led to denounce human sexuality; but his invective is really part of a frenzied awareness of the ineradicable evil of the human condition. The strength of the forces of bestiality that can invade the personality of man appals him. He knows in his soul that men move either 'by discipline toward spirit, or by indisciplined desire toward the animal';[101] and, enraged by the nearness of the means to depravity, can find in the sexual instinct a type of the brute passion in which evil is born. The lust of the senses Lear does not distinguish from the lust for worldly power and its exercise; as R. Speaight remarks,

[98] op. cit., p. 81.   [99] Granville-Barker, op. cit., pp. 180–1.
[100] *Notebook*, 1948, pp. 55–6.   [101] Heilman, *This Great Stage*, 1948, p. 92.

It is profoundly significant that as *King Lear* becomes more and more a play about power, it becomes more and more a play about lust; for lust is seen as just another variant of power.[102]

The denunciation of sex may be regarded as part of the process whereby Lear's deeper understanding presents to him as flawed and undesirable all the things of man's world,[103] and by its assurance of their corruption restores him in the end to sanity.

Its final assurance is of the delusive nature of the institution and calling which he had once thought to have raised him above mankind, and had drawn forth his unqualified endeavours. The god-like stature which kingship affords does not induce a corresponding nature in him whom it singles out; and the flatteries and compulsions of power tend to draw all love from his heart, and make him at the last an offense unto himself. The lure of self-importance can turn him into a beast; yet, imprisoned in his regality, he will persist in the illusion of grandeur – for 'a dog's obeyed in office'. He who wields the sword of justice is as abject as the wretch he punishes: robes and dignities hide what is evil in the one, while the tatters of abjectness enhance the sins that they disclose. Worldly authority is a pretentious edifice built upon the weak foundations of man's corruption:

> Plate sin with gold,
> And the strong lance of justice hurtless breaks;
> Arm it in rags, a pigmy's straw doth pierce it.
> None does offend, none, I say none
> (IV. vi. 166–9) –

for all are deep in sin. Having experienced in his personal world, and in his own deeds, the destruction of human right and order, he has thus gained insight into the common injustice and frailty of all mankind.[104] He now knows that

> The deep instinctive currents hold their old course, in earth, beast, and man. Man's morality, his idealism, his justice – all are false and rotten to the core.[105]

Human greatness and power are illusions; man's government puts into act the perversity that runs deep in the individual; and the great world itself is but a sounding-board to the vauntings of folly and the cries of the afflicted. Achievement or possession in it is a false beatitude;[106] its joys are but solaces to a state that is truly one of wretchedness;

---

[102] Speaight, *Nature in Shakespearian Tragedy*, 1955, p. 109.
[103] (Section III, p. 282.)   [104] Clemen, *Development*, p. 152.
[105] Wilson Knight, *The Wheel of Fire*, 1949, p. 192.
[106] Augustine, *De Civ. Dei* XIX. xx.

> When we are born, we cry that we are come
> To this great stage of fools
>
> (IV. vi. 183–4).

Lear is driven to the recognition that his tragedy is related to the condition of his own spirit and those of his fellow-men. He can see the whole life of mortal man as punishment; whether he sees that punishment as the chastisement of a higher power[107] must be a matter of conjecture.

What is beyond doubt, when Lear is restored to sanity in the presence of the child he has wronged, is that he has dismissed all thought of the prerogatives of kingship which he had once striven with all his soul to guard and possess. The preservation of any outward dignity is no longer an object; the age and folly which men and events had urged upon him are now acknowledged in the plainness of speech which would once have denied them: 'I am old and foolish'. In begging forgiveness of his daughter he can now resume the natural authority of a father that it had formerly been his highest aim to repossess; for the false glories of regality, and the distorting passions of self-regard which they had inflicted upon him, are now departed, and

> every defence of anger and pride that barriers his consciousness from his deepest and truest emotion . . . has been broken down.[108]

That emotion is love; for mortal man it is the ultimate emotion; and if his knowledge can go no further, his confidence must remain that the power of the natural bond, which binds soul unto soul, links him also to a reality that is above him.[109] In this emotion, at least, is accomplished Lear's renunciation of the world: he is one, declares Bradley,

> whose sight is so purged by scalding tears that it sees at last how power and place and all things in the world are vanity except love.[110]

Lear's forsaking and his loving are observed to produce in him, after his defeat in battle, a renunciation so perfect as to be 'serene':[111] Shakespeare has transported him, Granville-Barker affirms, 'beyond such issues as defeat, disgrace and disillusion'.[112] Lear's annihilation has been his strengthening; and if the 'radical transformation of consciousness' that has taken place in him has made him unsuited to the world of man, may we not wonder whether his experience has made him 'suited to God'?[113] Surely, Bradley exclaims, there is no figure in the world of poetry at once so grand, so pathetic, and so beautiful as Lear's – and all this he owes to the sufferings which have made us doubt whether life was not simply evil:

[107] (Section III, p. 177.)
[108] Wilson Knight, op. cit., p. 199.
[109] (Section III pp. 232-3.)
[110] *Shakespearean Tragedy*, p. 285.
[111] ibid., p. 289.
[112] *Prefaces*, 1st Ser., 1949, p. 182.
[113] (Section III, p. 283.)

Should we not be at least as near the truth if we called this poem *The Redemption of King Lear*, and declared that the business of 'the gods' with him was neither to torment him, nor to teach him a 'noble anger', but to lead him to attain through apparently hopeless failure the very end and aim of life?[114]

[114] op. cit., p. 285.

Chapter 24

HAMLET

Macbeth, Othello and Lear carry out the tasks they have set themselves in obedience to their own interests or the presumed requirements of their own souls; Hamlet's distinction is that he fails to sustain the purpose imposed on him. Like the others, he contributes to his own destruction; but whereas they may be said to create their tragedies out of what they do, Hamlet's tragedy must be judged to arise principally from his inaction: whether wisely or not, he cannot or will not do what they accomplish not wisely, but too well.

It is not surprising that this absolute difference in the nature of the tragedy should be accompanied by a certain uniqueness both in the character of the hero and in the quality of the drama. Instead of the familiar narrowing of outlook of the tragic hero – what Bradley calls a 'marked one-sidedness' and 'a fatal tendency to identify the whole being with one interest, object, passion, or habit of mind'[1] – there is to be found in Hamlet's 'many-sidedness and the extraordinary range of his ex-perience'[2] a positive surfeit both of natural endowments and of awareness. If his resulting tendency to introspection is morally a strength,[3] there is no doubt of its inhibiting him from action; and if his broad and quick sympathies make him the most appealing of Shakespeare's heroes, they also contrive that his resolve to become the embodiment of a single pur-pose, in the manner of the others, should be short-lived. This free-ranging awareness of Hamlet's, however, belongs to the state of mind of one who is borne along on the stream of events rather than involved in them.[4] Lear is plunged into happenings that must convince him amidst his toil of evils that his soul will not receive; Hamlet, arrested by the evils which the world reflects into his imagination, and preoccupied with their conse-quences for thought and feeling, yet remains apart from the world which is their origin.[5] Instead of the strenuous involvement which the action of tragic drama normally centres upon the life of the hero, in *Hamlet* there is detachment. As D. G. James expresses it,

[1] ibid., p. 20.   [2] Clemen, *Development*, London, 1951, p. 108.
[3] H. Levin, *The Question of Hamlet*, N.Y., 1959, p. 103.
[4] D. G. James, *The Dream of Learning*, 1951, p. 71.
[5] ibid., pp. 69–70.

369

Hamlet explores a mind arrested in dubiety before the awful problem of life; *King Lear* expresses life itself.[6]

This detachment is evidenced in Hamlet's first words in the play: he will be neither kindred nor courtier to the King of Denmark. His reluctance stems from a grief and disillusionment with life already sufficiently intense to be tragic, from an apprehension of a personal world overthrown; but the tragic sense of annihilation does not arise in this case from the subjugation of the aspiring self, but proceeds simply from

> The heart-ache, and the thousand natural shocks
> That flesh is heir to
>
> (III. i. 62–3)

that come as readily to afflict man's passivity as they do his heroism. Hamlet's despair has nothing to do with any action of his own. It finds expression in loathing of his uncle and in horror at the incestuous marriage, but its cause is to be sought in what Bradley terms 'the sudden ghastly disclosure of his mother's true nature'. Her new marriage has taken place in such a way

> that her son was forced to see in her action not only an astounding shallowness of feeling but an eruption of coarse sensuality;[7]

yet it would not be untrue to say that it is not the sensuality, but rather the insincerity which underlies it and which it comes to betoken for him, that affects him most deeply. The fidelity of persons that had appeared to him as the source of what was noblest in human life is now shown to have been fraudulent: the mother who now tells him that death is common has discarded with her robes of mourning the memory of her dead husband, and all sense of shame and principle. The scorn of insincerity that is present in his 'Seems, madam! Nay, it is; I know not "seems"' is no less profound than Lear's hatred of ingratitude; and the exclamations 'Let me not think on't' and 'Must I remember' witness to the compulsive quality of the thought: like Lear,

> He cannot prevent himself from probing and lacerating the wound in his soul.[8]

From the very beginning of the play, it has been remarked, Hamlet is seen to possess the 'noble obsession' of the kind that most tragic heroes attain at the end.[9] The shock which turns the world into an 'unweeded garden', revealing as misunderstandings all those previous understandings of the external order in which the soul might have sought reflection or assurance of itself[10] has happened before a word is spoken, and has been occasioned by the deeds of others.

[6] ibid., p. 77.   [7] op. cit., p. 118.   [8] ibid., p. 120.
[9] T. Greene, 'The Postures of Hamlet', *S.Q.* XI, 1960, p. 359.   [10] (Section III, p. 278.)

The shock is the greater in Hamlet because of his idealism. Bradley notes his tendency usually to see only what is good until he is forced to see the reverse, and observes that earlier, 'The world for him was *herrlich wie am ersten Tag*';[11] yet the goodness of the world did not depend for him, as it does for Othello, upon an exalted awareness of the self : extravagant personal attainment he has little use for. The highest term of praise, which he reserves for the memory of his father, is the plain, 'He was a man'. Goodness and simple humanity are Hamlet's ideal. More truly than the heroic, it is the moral that confers nobility on man; and the means of an ultimate distinction he sees to lie in being true to the promptings of kindliness – to the better part of one's nature :

> Persons who fail to live up to the level of men are beasts to Hamlet. Those who live above the level of men are gods.[12]

Like Othello and Lear, Hamlet is consciously pursuing a principle or means of excellence; but whereas they are concerned with what they themselves seem to be, Hamlet's vision is of what all men might be, but are not. Human excellence for Hamlet does not imply a self-aggrandizement, but rather the forsaking of an instinctive self-will, and the disciplining of the aspiring consciousness according to values which, though humble and familiar, are yet of a power to transcend. The chief passion of Hamlet's soul, therefore, is the precise antithesis of the heroic : it is not for nothing that Hazlitt saw him as a character marked by 'refinement of thought and sentiment' and thus 'as little of the hero as a man can well be'.[13] D. G. James similarly perceives that

> In the major issue of the play Hamlet is not heroic, and to keep him built up enough as a tragic hero was not easy; it must have been one of Shakespeare's most difficult tasks;[14]

while A. P. Rossiter is aware that the heroic 'steadfastness of mind' does not make its presence felt at the conclusion of the play.[15] To most critics, however, though Hamlet's humane regard is admirable, the resulting lack of the heroic ruthlessness in him must appear as a failing. They are not able to see in him one who – unlike his peers and indeed most of mankind – must cleave to the principle of righteousness before that of power, and who, if he is to conquer, must do so as a conqueror in truth rather than as a 'lover of might'.[16] The fact of moral scruple, and the extent even of moral dedication, they can appreciate; but to assess these

---

[11] Bradley, op. cit., p. 111.

[12] G. Coffin Taylor, 'Shakespeare's Use of the Idea of the Beast in Man', *Stud. Phil.* XLII, 1945, pp. 531–2.

[13] 'Characters of Shakespear's Plays', 1817, *Shakespeare Criticism : A Selection*, ed. Nichol Smith, 1953, p. 289.

[14] *The Dream of Learning*, 1951, p. 76.   [15] *Angel with Horns*, 1961, p. 181.

[16] Augustine, *De Trin.* XIII. xiii. 17; Section II, p. 88.

things in their ultimate meanings is not possible where the secular is the standard. Hamlet's pursuit of a greater good in the lively principles which subordinate humanity to a higher law will not be seen to preclude in him that inflexible pursuit of a lesser good which is the effect of the heroic self-love. The will to make trial of the soul's own strength, to impose upon outward fact the pattern of a false omnipotence, to assert unlimited selfhood with its accompanying recklessness – the pride in fact which underlies the heroic pretension[17] – Hamlet is unable to assume, because he does not possess it. The dramatic failure expresses the soul's initial failure in perversity.

The moral idealism which thus qualifies the heroic in Hamlet does so particularly by quelling in him the sense of his own integrity. The greatest claim he can make for himself is that he is 'indifferent honest'; the sense of his own shortcomings proves to him his relation to Gertrude, and to humanity at large. He knows himself to be affected by 'the defilement of living', and is readily able to regard himself as representative of all men, 'a being stirred by the loftiest aspirations but infected by life's evil'.[18] The sense of the loveliness that is possible for human nature alternates with a horror of the possible upsurge of what is vile; and this 'negative side of his idealism, the aversion to evil', whose vehement quality Bradley can liken only to that of Timon,[19] is only possible in one who apprehends his own nature to be, in Luther's terms, 'confounded, corrupt and poisoned'.[20] Through the mind of its protagonist, the play becomes receptive at all points to the idea of the good and the evil which struggle together in the world and in men's natures; the descent into animality is ever appallingly near; and Hamlet knows himself called upon not merely to revenge, but

> to rid the world of the satyr and restore it to Hyperion. Is it any wonder that he finds the task beyond him?[21]

Through an awareness of his personal deficiency, Hamlet is driven to an impersonality of vision that is utterly distinguished from the narrow self-concern and self-adulation of the other tragic heroes.

None of these heroes is a keener observer of the external world than Hamlet; but his gaze is directed, and its perceptions judged, by a consciousness entirely inward and detached from the appearances it apprehends. It is this withdrawn awareness – the conviction that 'there is nothing either good or bad, but thinking makes it so' (II. ii. 251–2) – that endows Hamlet with the 'gift of moral precision'.[22] A Lear will identify

---

17 (Section III, p. 240.)
18 H. Jenkins, 'The Tragedy of Revenge in Shakespeare and Webster', *S.S.* XIV, 1961, p. 48.
19 Bradley, *Shakespearean Tragedy*, p. 112.
20 (Section III, p. 174.)   21 H. Jenkins, op. cit., p. 48.
22 T. Greene, 'The Postures of Hamlet', *S.Q.* XI, 1960, p. 358.

his being with his kingdom's resources; but Hamlet can be bounded in a nutshell and count himself king of infinite space, provided his thoughts are free. He knows, as Lear does not, that external goods cannot add to his own worth and dignity: he cannot be tempted to seek a false beatitude amidst things that are evanescent,[23] nor seek to become conformed to what time or violence may take from him, being led wherever his supposed good leads him, and fearing whoever may take it from him.[24] Possession of the throne does not claim his soul's strivings; it is a moral perfection and power that he must first seek, and he will give unstinted praise to the man in whom he finds a freedom from the thraldom of passion that he cannot create in himself. His own inability to achieve what is best moves him to cherish in others all that is sincere, gentle and good: their achievement promotes, and in no way denigrates, his personal ideal – for that ideal is humanity itself. As Bradley observes, a king and a beggar are all one to him: 'He cares for nothing but human worth'.[25] Formality, the world's instrument of a distorted vision, he will brush aside, and change the title of 'poor servant' in the man he welcomes as his 'good friend'; unwillingness that authority should be founded on anything but true respect dictates that his answer to the soldiers' parting professions should be an impatient, 'Your loves, as mine to you'. His respect for human dignity enables him to engage in cheerful give-and-take with the Players and endure the insolence of the clown; and it makes him the sworn enemy of the false modesty that claims to do something 'indifferently', the 'garb' of mincing fashion and punctilious ceremony, and the smooth-faced pretence that relishes its hidden purpose. Though delighting in good, he is not blind to the fact that evil has part of its kingdom in the human soul: the observation that, if every man were used after his desert, few should 'scape whipping (II. ii. 533–5), is no distance removed from the conviction that the gladness of man is but wickedness unpunished.[26] Instead of the self-flattering preoccupations and pursuits of the ordinary tragic hero, which corrupt their natures by taking from them the means both of perceiving and doing what is good,[27] Hamlet's moral preoccupation can only strengthen this capacity within him.

It is impossible for Hamlet to proceed under the heroic illusion of adequacy, of the health of his own soul, or of the efficacy of some principle of personal excellence.[28] His hatred of what mars man's perfection and recognition that the means of corruption are ineradicably present in his nature is apparent in the 'dram of eale' speech. To Coleridge it is part of an 'unimportant conversation' – the attempt of a worried man to elude the pressure of his thoughts by turning aside to the trivial and

[23] Augustine, De Civ. Dei XIX. xx.
[25] op. cit., p. 113.
[27] (Section II, p. 93.)
[24] (Section II, p. 91.)
[26] (Section III, p. 175.)
[28] (Section III, p. 252.)

commonplace;[29] and a writer like W. Clemen does not seek beyond its hinting at Gertrude's sensuality and foreshadowing of the Ghost's tidings of murder.[30] Hamlet's thought is indeed commonplace : it recalls Nashe's warning to the drunkard, that

> that one beastly imperfection will vtterlie obscure all that is commendable in him; and all his good qualities sinke like lead down to the bottome of his carrowsing cups, where they will lie, like lees and dregges, dead and vnregarded of any man.[31]

But though Hamlet's thought is awakened by drunken revellings, it turns to the power of a single failing to destroy – in the 'general censure' – a perfection otherwise 'as pure as grace'. His meaning is closer to the commonplace that

> *oft the common people rude do vse, as voyd*
> *of wyt,*
> *The noble vertue to despise, if so be that they see*
> *With little spot of any vice defiled hir to bee.*
> *But what is hee vpon the earth, that liueth voide*
> *of crime?*
> *And from the true and beaten way departeth not*
> *sometime?*[32]

Hamlet's attention fixes itself upon the incorrectness that can dim the brightest human virtues, and he considers it not only in its public aspect but in terms of the constitution of man's own soul. The three faults he distinguishes – the 'mole of nature', the 'o'ergrowth of some complexion' and the tyrannous habit – are outside man's power to control; virtue and goodness are seen to be at the mercy of propensities that are at once alien and innate; and the conclusion is plain despair at a human redemptability. As R. Speaight observes, this is

> a most revealing speech. . . . The sense of it is that men are noted for their single faults . . . rather than for their many virtues; and these faults, being a part of *'nature's* livery', may lie beyond their remedy.[33]

The speech is eloquent of Hamlet's primary dedication, at the very moment of the Ghost's appearance to urge him to dedicate himself to the purpose of revenge. His taking mental refuge in the symbolic action of writing down the appalling significance of the Ghost's message, and the

---

[29] *Lectures and Notes on Shakespere,* 1904, p. 355.

[30] *The Development of Shakespeare's Imagery,* London, 1951, p. 115.

[31] 'Pierce Penilesse His Svpplication to the Divell', *Works,* ed. R. B. McKerrow, 1904, I, p. 205.

[32] M. Palingenius, *The Zodiake of Life,* 1531? tr. B. Googe, 1576, Scholars' Facsimiles & Reprints, N.Y., 1947, p. 15.

[33] *Nature in Shakespearian Tragedy,* 1955, p. 18.

subsequent frenzy of wild and whirling words, show a mind almost over-
whelmed, and preface a pretence of insanity that is in part due to fear
of the reality :[34] as Dover Wilson puts it,

> Shakespeare wishes us to feel that Hamlet assumes madness because
> he cannot help it.[35]

Yet it may be wondered whether the near approach of madness is the
effect not so much of horror at man's evil as of the confirmation of a deeper
sense of the helplessness it inspires. The Ghost's message has lengthened
the vistas of evil before which Hamlet has already found himself helpless
and despairing; and the urgent duty of revenge serves to demonstrate
the need of his deeper purpose while denying its feasibility. Any deed
must, in a time that is 'out of joint', seem valueless to one dedicated to
the principles of kindness, who can think only in terms of 'setting right'
a humanity grown corrupt. The Ghost's encouragement to revenge is to
the mind of Hamlet more truly an announcement of hopelessness; as
Dr Sitwell has finely remarked,

> From the moment when the message was given, the world turns to a
> ghost for Hamlet.[36]

He never doubts the act of revenge to be in the service of his ideal; but
he knows even in embarking upon his soul's quest that he is defeated from
the very start.

It is only by suppressing his truest and deepest thoughts that Hamlet
can go about his revenge. What is real to him is the inner vision; and
outward actions that do not correspond with this reality must seem as
the doings of a dreamer, or as 'actions that a man might play'. The image
of the theatre, present in 'the motive and the cue for passion' that
Hamlet protests are his, emphasizes how far he is removed from the
passion he seeks – as also does the spurious nature of the frenzy which
he works himself into, and which arouses his own contempt. He knows
he can act only in passion; but when it dies in him he returns to the
disillusionment that is now the true element of his being, and the inhibitor
of the emotions that are proper to vengefulness. A world possessed by
evil – by murder, lust, falsehood, treachery and self-seeking – is the real
object of his contemplation; and his instinct is not to clasp its uses unto
himself, but to fly from the 'mortal coil' that inspires his soul with
loathing.

Ophelia's apparent betrayal is part of the 'coil'; but her inconstancy
appears to Hamlet as the token of a corruption more far-reaching. He
sees in her 'the seeds of his mother's sin':[37] the undermining of fidelity

[34] Bradley, *Shakespearean Tragedy*, 1956, p. 120.
[35] *What Happens in 'Hamlet'*, 1935, p. 92.
[36] *A Notebook*, 1948, p. 83.   [37] ibid., p. 89.

375

and virtue in Gertrude has been the work of the senses; and Claudius's crime too is bound up with sensuality – he is a lecherous as well as a kindless villain. In the senses, therefore – in the 'compulsive ardour' that levels man with beast and can subvert what is worthy in him – Hamlet perceives a 'vicious mole of nature' that can confound the 'noble substance' in mankind; and in Ophelia herself he must recognize the agent and embodiment of these dark forces. Dover Wilson's view that his treating her as a prostitute is incomprehensible without such 'grounds for so doing' as his knowing her complicity in the eavesdropping[38] not only ignores the fact that sex becomes a symbol of depravity to Othello and Lear, but fails to apprehend that

> from the beginning of the play the whole pernicious process has been in train.[39]

As Charlton points out, Hamlet has before been living in an ideal world, 'a world fashioned in his own idea, a world in which chastity is a main prop'. Events have reduced this world to chaos; but Hamlet's cynical accusations, though 'pure fiction', are valid only in their relation to the ideal now dissipated.[40] Just as Othello's heroic vision of love is, after his disillusionment, replaced with a bitter certainty of universal lustfulness, so the force of sensuality now becomes Hamlet's new truth.

Dr Johnson declares of Hamlet that 'He plays the madman most, when he treats Ophelia with so much rudeness';[41] but even the intellect of a Polonius has been able to detect method in this behaviour. In counselling him not to let his daughter 'walk i' the sun' Hamlet broods on man's ever-present sensuality: if natural influence can breed in flesh that is dead, will not living flesh, with its innate passionateness, be subject to the tyranny of lust, and,

> lying by the violet in the sun,
> Do as the carrion does, not as the flower,
> Corrupt with virtuous season?[42]

The same thought is present in his incredulity at Ophelia's apparent virtue, first voiced in the sardonic alliance he makes between the 'pretentious expressions' nymph and orison. Ophelia is fair: therefore she must be corrupt:

> for the power of beauty will sooner transform honesty from what it is to a bawd than the force of honesty can translate beauty into his likeness (III. i. 111–14).

[38] *What Happens*, p. 103.
[39] H. Granville-Barker, *Prefaces to Shakespeare*, 3rd Ser. (rev.), 1937, p. 301.
[40] *Shakespearian Tragedy*, 1952, p. 91.
[41] *Johnson on Shakespeare*, ed. W. Raleigh, 1957, p. 196.
[42] *Measure for Measure* II. ii. 166–8.

The senses are the means of evil, and perpetuate a condition which is evil; Hamlet therefore could never truly have loved, and will not now either sin or be a breeder of sinners: in Granville-Barker's words, 'His spirit is in revolt against his natural affections'.[43] With the senses, however, he associates the whole imperfect state of humanity, 'crawling between heaven and earth', and also the imperfections he recognizes in his own nature; and in the desire to flee from their dominance that expresses itself in his consigning Ophelia to a nunnery, and his sense of women's bemonstering the race by seeking to enhance their sexual attractiveness, may be understood a process which – as in *King Lear*[44] – presents the corruption of man's condition to his deepest awareness in terms of the very means by which mankind is perpetuated.

The treatment of Ophelia is of a piece with that of Gertrude. Hamlet's view of both women is expressed in the reason he gives for declining Gertrude's invitation that he should sit by her: 'No, good mother, here's metal more attractive'. He professes openly and mockingly what he deems them to have entertained in their inmost thoughts, and taunts them with the insincerity to which he judges lust to have been the prelude. His cheerfulness in the play scene he concedes to have been styled upon that of his lately-widowed mother; and mention of the time that has elapsed since his father's funeral is greeted with mock astonishment that a dead spouse can be so long remembered. In his attitude to both women is to be seen a savage determination that they should know what he considers they are, or have done. The threatening roughness that he assumes towards his mother, however, belies, though it does not hide, his previous closeness to her in affection: 'it is with a kind of exasperated love', as Granville-Barker declares, 'that he rages at her'.[45] The ruthlessness of the disillusioned idealist, able to love only what is worthy, and hating what is not, is more evident in his dealings with Gertrude; and the ultimate kindliness of his purpose of wringing her heart is here also not obscured. She has acted so as to call virtue hypocrite and corrupt innocence, at the prompting of a 'Rebellious hell' that has sprung into horrifying activity in a matron's bones; but the recounting of her sin, though it be like daggers in her ears, is a blow struck for the good of her soul, and for the cause of righteousness. She is urged to confess herself to heaven, and to give 'rank corruption' no further opportunity to spread its infection; and as repentance appears, so do the glimmerings of Hamlet's respect and love. In this work of reclamation there is no lack of the passion and resolution so absent from the task of revenge; as Bradley says,

> while the rough work of vengeance is repugnant to him, he is at home in this higher work.[46]

[43] op. cit., p. 313.
[44] See p. 365 above.
[45] *Prefaces*, 3rd Ser., 1937, pp. 296–7.
[46] *Shakespearean Tragedy*, p. 138.

This higher work also gives Hamlet's awareness of the corrupting power of sense its proper limit and perspective:

> if his heart ever found relief, it was when those feelings, mingled with the love that never died out in him, poured themselves forth in a flood as he stood in his mother's chamber.[47]

The incensed harshness that seemed once to threaten Gertrude's life is gone, and his leavetaking of her is gentleness itself.

Hamlet's attitude to the senses is his attitude to the world. From both he is repelled; and his loneliness is the extent of his revulsion. The recognition of the world's wrong ensures that he should be a man isolated and alone in his thought:

> he is encircled away from the common humanity, even of a Court. He out-tops its knowledge and ascent to him is out of the question; he is a rare and estranged spirit.[48]

It is possible to see a fault in Hamlet's moody contrast with the 'robust' humanity of the Court of Elsinore;[49] but neither Hamlet nor, in the last resort, humanity itself can find a home where there is mirth in funeral and dirge in marriage, love lasts as long as the senses give warrant, and grief is summoned and dismissed by the power of the inky cloak. These dissonances proceed from a fallen human nature; but they are also the expression in personal terms of man's political achievement. The 'holy and religious fear' (III. iii. 8) with which Rosencrantz and Guildenstern prostrate themselves before the holder of kingly office is the clue to conduct in Elsinore: it is not through their action alone that we are able to 'breathe the mental climate of a Renaissance Court'.[50] The instruction to Ophelia that truth of affection is to be judged by compliance to the needs of the state, that a professed love holding no correspondence with those needs is but a 'fashion and a toy in blood', and that wariness and distrust, not generosity, is the prime requirement in matters of the heart, is the perverse wisdom of policy. Laertes is his father's son; and the great image of mortal authority is to be beheld in their cynicism, that reduces love to 'low-mindedness'[51] and honour to sniggering pretence. In his 'monumental complacency', his assumption that there can be no wisdom beyond his worldliness,[52] Polonius is the embodiment of Hamlet's Denmark; and Hamlet's limitless contempt is enforced by the plot of the play: he who prides himself on his skill in worming secrets out of men's hearts is revealed as a 'man wise in his own conceit who is wrong on every

[47] ibid., p. 119.   [48] James, *The Dream of Learning*, 1951, p. 73.
[49] See G. Wilson Knight, *The Wheel of Fire*, 1949, p. 30.
[50] R. Speaight, *Nature in Shakespearian Tragedy*, 1955, p. 34.
[51] H. Levin, *The Question of Hamlet*, N.Y., 1959, p. 27.
[52] Speaight, op. cit., p. 16.

point'.[53] That a counsellor of state, seeing a great one distracted by some matter, should proceed to 'beset a man with questions, and draw him on, and pick it out of him'[54] is a time-honoured practice; the scorn it arouses in Hamlet is the response of one who has consciously set himself apart from a society seen as inimical to human goodness. In the life of the Court,

> Meanness, craft, exploitation succeed : that is the point. Generosity, 'freedom from all contriving', and intelligent disinterestedness fail, or are impotent. That is why Denmark is the world, and a prison : a prison of the spirit controlled by minds of practical efficiency.[55]

From this prison Hamlet must try to escape; but his flight will be from something that lacks reality towards the sources of truth he knows to exist within himself. The temptation to shun action in the external sphere, and seek success in the realm of thought, is the greater because he knows the remedy for his world to lie in the minds that produce its disorder. Disillusion therefore drives him in upon himself and makes him

> a visionary, a seer, for whom the living things of the world about him embody and symbolize thought.[56]

Yet his isolation is by no means complete. The intellectual genius which distinguishes Hamlet concerns itself 'in the affairs of life'; and the necessity which drives him to think a thing to the end, to penetrate below the surface of things and to be ever unmaking his world and rebuilding it in thought, has as its outcome not the dissipation of truth, but 'a more intense experience of reality'.[57] It is to be observed of the images that Hamlet uses, that

> they do not waft the things of reality into a dream-world of the imagination; on the contrary, they make them truly *real*, they reveal their inmost, naked being . . . Hamlet is no abstract thinker and dreamer.[58]

The essential practicality that retains him within the world he despises is likewise to be seen in the readiness and success with which he engages in bursts of instinctive activity, whether in the sea-fight, his dealings with Rosencrantz and Guildenstern, or his seizing his revenge when chance offers it to him. So far is he from 'bestial oblivion', indeed, that when scruple inhibits him from action he both retains the desire to act and shows no recognition of the cause of inaction within him. The first of the

[53] L. B. Campbell, 'Polonius : The Tyrant's Ears', *J. Q. Adams Memorial Studies*, Washington, 1948, p. 312.
[54] Bacon, 'Of Simulation and Dissimulation', *Philosophical Works*, ed. J. M. Robertson, 1905, p. 741.
[55] Rossiter, *Angel with Horns*, 1961, p. 184.
[56] W. Clemen, *Development*, London, 1951, p. 106.
[57] ibid., p. 111.　　　　[58] ibid., p. 108.

two conflicts in which, according to Granville-Barker, Hamlet is involved – that between himself and the world he lives in – by no means brings about isolation; it is the other far more momentous battle

> between two selves within him, the one that could agree with this world, the other that cannot,[59]

that sets him apart from the scene which his consciousness continues steadily to regard.

Greater than the desire to act, in Hamlet, is the desire that he should act rightly; and in the moral prerequisite is the source both of division within the self and of alienation from the world. To a degree, as K. Muir points out, he is the prisoner of 'conscience' in its two senses of 'craven scruple' and of 'thinking too precisely': the highly developed sensibility from which right action can alone proceed makes the more difficult action of any kind. To do nothing is to be brutish; but to exercise reason and conscience to the full is to become aware of the moral complexity of the situation calling for action.[60] Moral passion amidst moral disorder turns into a pedantry;[61] and Hamlet can acquire neither passion nor a philosophy with which to overcome hindrances within or without :

> he inhabits a middle region where philosophy and passion, judgement and honour, reason and blood, annul each other, and leave him . . . helpless and angry, passive and violent.[62]

The world in which he must act repels him by its corruption, and appears as the place of uncertainty and doubt; and he must fear that even in his own clear purpose he may become 'a weapon in the service of unclarified cravings'.[63] He must therefore be 'torn and dragged between the betrayal of action and the failure of non-action'.[64] Since all acts falsify, his most sincere purpose may run into the condemnation of being 'insincerity toward oneself;[65] but inaction will not only result in detachment from the very situation which calls for his efforts, but create a disabling sense of 'the mind's own lack of togetherness and coherence' and bring about that acute self-awareness in which there is no self, but only selves.[66] The presence of this state in Hamlet is to be deduced from his puzzled ignorance of his own motives, and his alternation between excitement and depression, between irrelevant calculation and objectless passion. The

---

59 *Prefaces*, 3rd Ser., 1937, p. 290.

60 'Shakespeare and the Tragic Pattern', *Proceedings of the British Academy* XLIV, 1958, p. 153.

61 T. Greene, 'The Postures of Hamlet', *S.Q.* XI, 1960, p. 358.

62 James, *The Dream of Learning*, p. 62.

63 S. Kierkegaard, 'Man's Need of God Constitutes his Highest Perfection', *Edifying Discourses*, ed. Swenson, Minneapolis, 1950–3, IV, p. 23, quoted in Section III, p. 280.

64 A. P. Rossiter, *Angel with Horns*, 1961, p. 176, quoted in Section III, p. 288.

65 Kierkegaard, op. cit., p. 44, quoted in Section III, p. 284.

66 A. P. Rossiter, op. cit., pp. 172, 178, quoted in Section III, p. 287.

behaviour which baffles his enemies speaks of his own deeper bafflement: he is the true victim of his own

> impulsive or unpremeditated activity, activity in which he generally takes a keen delight, but which appears nevertheless to have very little to do with his volition.[67]

This division in the soul all critics must recognize as a sickness; but its symptoms are those in which the profounder appraisal may distinguish a sickness 'not unto death but unto life'. The conflict of selves is evidence not only of the disillusionment that is the prelude to spiritual health, but of the search for true autonomy of being that must ultimately lead to the source of being itself, if the voice of deeper self be not first 'drowned in the roar of the world's changes'.[68]

Its immediate effect is to render Hamlet unfitted for the world. His quick and relieved yielding to the 'distraction of a little intellectual cat-and-mouse play',[69] and the 'almost hysterical'[70] elation evinced by the success of his mental tricks, merely contribute to the impression Coleridge describes as that of

> a great, an almost enormous intellectual activity, and a proportionate aversion to real action consequent upon it.[71]

The strong evidence of excessive thought, however, as Bradley points out is not the direct cause of irresolution, but the guise in which a deeper malady presents itself.[72] How ineffectual Hamlet is rendered by his estrangement is evident from the fact that in the midst of the triumphant discountenancing of his opponents he is revealing his knowledge to them and faltering in his purpose. He can throw his full energies into the tormenting of guilty consciences: the images of the pipe and the sponge, like those of the ear and the Vice and the cutpurse he had used against Gertrude, are ones which 'seem in fact designed to unmask men'.[73] But the trenchancy of word and thought mask an aversion from action: Hamlet is never more remote from his world than when he is making its consciences writhe.

Whatever else may be thought of Hamlet's delaying his revenge, it is clear that revenge is out of keeping with his inmost understanding of life, if not with the code to which he consciously subscribes. A nature predominantly moral, recognizing in kindness and virtue alone the means of human excellence, which is plunged into despair by the vision of irremediable evil in his fellows and in his own soul, and which has forsaken

[67] Dover Wilson, *What Happens in 'Hamlet'*, 1935, p. 235.
[68] Kierkegaard, op. cit., p. 32; Section III, p. 281.
[69] Granville-Barker, 3rd Ser., p. 169.
[70] Bradley, *Shakespearean Tragedy*, 1956, p. 134.
[71] *Lectures and Notes*, (Bohn) 1904, p. 344.
[72] op. cit., pp. 107–8. [73] Clemen, *Development*, 1951, p. 109.

in spirit the world in which he can find no kinship or identity, is not that of an avenger.

Is there really anything mysterious about a man who has come to no clear and practical sense of life, and who in the face of a shocking situation which peculiarly involves him, shuffles, deceives himself, procrastinates?[74]

The fact that the beholder himself does not wish Hamlet to stab a defenceless, kneeling man is enough to show that Hamlet's opportunity is no opportunity at all;[75] and Hamlet's own words voice an apprehension that the day 'Would quake to look on' such 'bitter business' as the killing of Claudius must involve. Indeed, the exclamation which greets the sight of the praying Claudius – 'Now might I do it' – shows that 'he has no effective *desire* to "do it"'.[76] The wish to send his adversary's soul to hell, which Hamlet makes his excuse for delay, is in keeping with the code of revenge;[77] but in the sentiment which Dr Johnson found 'too horrible to be read or uttered',[78] others have found, with Coleridge, 'the marks of reluctance and procrastination'.[79] The thought that irresolution in an instance such as this can best be hidden by 'a refinement in malice',[80] that the strength of the expressed hatred can render the pretext more palatable, Bradley declares to be 'quite ludicrous'[81] – though later he is obliged to admit that Hamlet knows in his heart that the reason he gives is not the cause of his sparing Claudius. However, Bradley's being able to find

no reason whatever to doubt that Hamlet would have been very sorry to send his father's murderer to heaven, nor much to doubt that he would have been glad to send him to perdition,[82]

is not lightly to be dismissed. The observation is in keeping with Hamlet's never questioning his duty of killing the King: yet the testimony of the play is that he never advisedly and deliberately acts as he conceives that he should.[83] The matter is only to be resolved upon the theory of a divided conscience in Hamlet; and what his uncle says as he rises to his feet – his weary conviction that his words had not reached heaven because his thoughts remained on earth – is clearly intended to show the force of the scruple that dominates the better part of the mind opposed to him.[84]

[74] D. G. James, *Dream*, 1951, p. 47.
[75] H. Gardner, *The Business of Criticism*, Oxford Paperbacks, 1963, p. 46.
[76] Bradley, op. cit., p. 135.
[77] K. Muir, *Shakespeare : The Great Tragedies*, Longmans, 1961, p. 10.
[78] *Johnson on Shakespeare*, ed. Raleigh, 1957, p. 193.
[79] *Lectures and Notes*, 1904, p. 364.
[80] W. Hazlitt, 'Characters of Shakespear's Plays', 1817, *Shakespeare Criticism : A Selection*, ed. Nichol Smith, 1953, p. 290.
[81] op. cit., p. 100.   [82] ibid., p. 135.
[83] H. Levin, *The Question of Hamlet*, N.Y., 1959, p. 35.   [84] James, op. cit., p. 65.

The same may be said of Laertes and Fortinbras in the play : according to Bradley, either of them 'would have accomplished Hamlet's task in a day', and their personalities 'are evidently designed to throw the character of the hero into relief'.[85] The ferocity and directness of Laertes, coming after Hamlet's vacillation, can appear as 'a blast of fresh air';[86] but the seeming inflexibility which would sweep aside all conscience and principle to exact its vengeance, and 'dare damnation' to the extent of desecrating a church with his adversary's blood, quickly shows itself to be in reality a form of weakness. The vengeful man, who will submit to any course that speeds his purpose, 'becomes the patient of others' designs';[87] and the conclusion must be drawn that Laertes, whose cause is so similar to Hamlet's,

> is put in the play precisely for the purpose of showing us what a Hamlet who unhesitatingly carried out his father's wishes would be.[88]

Muir argues that if the gentlemanly ideal is in Laertes weighed in the balance and found wanting, the military ideal is similarly criticized in Fortinbras, and that the stoic or Senecal ideal, as it is exemplified in Horatio's calm, may be seen as having been achieved 'at the price of a certain inhumanity'.[89] What is not to be doubted, however, is that in Laertes – however impressive his tenacity at first sight – Shakespeare

> wished to show us what moral instability may really be, and to what sort of nature it properly belongs.[90]

Hamlet's failure to pursue his revenge may therefore be part of an integrity and firmness entirely different in quality from that which his world expects of him. He remains morally consistent. Though his hatred of falsehood may drive him to wounding scorn, and even to callousness, he can never consciously embrace what is wrong. To the very end, says Bradley,

> his soul, however sick and tortured it may be, answers instantaneously when good and evil are presented to it, loving the one and hating the other.[91]

Alone of Shakespeare's tragic heroes, he cannot find within himself the means of 'turning to earth':[92] for the ideal on which he sets his soul is far removed from the self-magnification which they practise. No will to self-aggrandizement determines in him a descent to the ruthless enact-

[85] op. cit., p. 90.
[86] G. Wilson Knight, *The Wheel of Fire*, 1949, p. 40.
[87] J. Lawlor, *The Tragic Sense in Shakespeare*, 1960, p. 49.
[88] K. Muir, 'Shakespeare and the Tragic Pattern', *Proc. Brit. Acad.* XLIV, 1958, p. 150.
[89] *Shakespeare : The Great Tragedies*, p. 14.
[90] Granville-Barker, 3rd Ser. (rev.), 1937, pp. 259–60.
[91] *Shakespearean Tragedy*, p. 112.   [92] (Section III, p. 236.)

ment of 'those things in which beasts delight',[93] to that harming of the other life around it which is the distinguishing mark of the life that seeks to transcend its creatureliness.[94] His overriding concern, on the contrary, must be that his heart should not lose its nature (III. ii. 399). The sacredness of the natural bond is his to protect, not to deny; and if the kindly and the moral is in truth dependent upon the spiritual condition of man – if ultimately it is 'nothing else than the divine reason or will issuing its commands to respect the natural order' – there exists a basis for asking whether this integrity in Hamlet proceeds from beyond the secular, and beyond himself: whether his soul's not being 'trodden down by its own servant' may be due to its service of its Master.[95]

Hamlet cannot transform himself into the instrument of the Ghost's command – albeit its purpose is achieved through his instrumentality. In a sense these two facts sum up the play; and they direct attention to the Ghost's appearance striking those who behold it with an uncertainty more insistent than their natural terror. Shakespeare seems determined not to commit himself to its true nature. Elements of the Roman Catholic and the Protestant faith, as well as a modern scepticism, are to be found in the reactions of the watchers; and the 'majestical' posture it first displays is soon confounded in the behaviour of an underground demon, the 'foul collier' of superstition. Dover Wilson, though able to account for this transformation, admits the grounds for the dread and distrust that Hamlet displays.[96] His first resolve is to speak to it 'though Hell itself should gape'; his first viewing it raises the possibility that it may bring 'airs from heaven' rather than 'blasts from hell'; but the conversation that follows indicates it to be a spirit in Purgatory. The moment it has vanished upon scenting the morning air, however, Hamlet in calling upon heaven and earth adds, 'And shall I couple Hell?' and his wonderment at this point is made good by the unqualified terror that the Ghost's subsequent appearance inspires in him. Throughout the play, its precise status continues a matter of mystery.

The Ghost is shown to be more than the 'illusion' to which Horatio's principle would reduce it, and it is also revealed to be 'honest' by Hamlet's device. His own response to it tends to instruct the beholder that 'we are meant in the play to assume that he *ought* to have obeyed the Ghost';[97] yet it must be questioned whether a 'spirit of health' could possibly have urged adherence to a 'barbarous principle, which . . . runs counter to both the Catholic and Protestant religions',[98] as well as to the pronouncement of the Homilies in which the age was schooled. J. J. Lawlor's attributing the hero's delay, in later revenge tragedies, to 'a scruple about

[93] (Section II, p. 152.) [94] (Section III, p. 251.)
[95] (Section III, p. 234.) [96] *What Happens*, pp. 52–86.
[97] Bradley, op. cit., p. 100. [98] Levin, *The Question of Hamlet*, p. 23.

384

revenge itself' can be disputed no more than his more general comment upon this principle :

> The avenger is one who takes it upon himself to say, 'Vengeance is mine; I will repay'. It is no mere device of the theatre that a purpose so dire should be, in all save the wicked or degenerate, not easily sustained. Equally, it is no accident that those who must come to whet the avenger's purpose rise from infernal regions, fresh from such sights as would 'harrow up' the soul.[99]

Through the very nature of the task to which he is summoned, therefore, we have in *Hamlet* a hero averse from the deed the play requires of him, endlessly seeking the cause of the aversion yet failing to know what it is, and a play that appears to bring into question the demand to which it owes its own existence. As W. M. Merchant argues, the prominence of the idea of the certain course of eternal justice cannot but affect the response of all concerned to 'the assumptions of revenge and its corollary, the stoic right to suicide'; and his conclusion is that

> the very revenge form itself is judged, even while it is the irreducible condition which Shakespeare accepts for his plot structure . . . [by] the very calculations of guilt and confession, of temporal and eternal justice to which the texture of the play . . . is committed.[100]

Such a conclusion is very far-reaching; and it is to be noted that Hamlet's own thoughts about the Ghost and its urging never quite reach to the possibility expressed so ominously by Banquo, that

> oftentimes, to win us to our harm,
> The instruments of darkness tell us truths,
> Win us with honest trifles, to betray's
> In deepest consequence (I. iii. 123–6).

Hamlet never seeks farther than to test the Ghost's immediate veracity; and, though the play powerfully queries its status, it never supplies an answer so adverse and explicit.

Yet it would in a sense be wrong to expect such explicitness in a play which so intently concerns itself with moral confusion and dilemma. The essence of *Hamlet* is its hero's having to make a moral decision in a complex situation where he cannot rely on cut-and-dried principles, or on the conventional code of the society in which he lives :[101] the more Shakespeare allows the play to leave the indeterminate and to approach definition, the more he must hazard his own purpose. As D. G. James argues, he was bringing an old, crude and violent story into majestic usage,

---

[99] *The Tragic Sense*, pp. 54–5.
[100] 'Shakespeare's Theology', *R.E.L.* V, 1964, p. 83.
[101] K. Muir, 'Shakespeare and the Tragic Pattern', ed. cit., p. 154.

controlling and amending it, so far as he could, to convey the tragedy of a man caught in ethical and metaphysical uncertainties.[102]

To this high purpose must be attributed Shakespeare's failing to make explicit what his successors did, with less skill – his laying upon his hero the duty of revenge without allowing him to discover the nature of his aversion.[103] Here also may lie the reason for his giving the Ghost that cold and solemn impersonality which puzzled Bradley,[104] and for leaving undetermined its own spiritual status, and the ethical quality of its demand upon Hamlet. This lack of definition, far from introducing the sense of artifice or unreality, brings the play closer to life and raises it to the highest level of significance. Freed from the inhibiting judgements innate in fixed ethical categories, it can treat of the conflict of soul in which man is ever engaged : that between his manifest worldliness of vision and his half-conscious understanding of spiritual truths and responsibilities. The substance of that conflict finds expression in what Hamlet does not do; the conflict itself would have been dissipated by the making manifest of what he ought not to have done.

To this higher level of significance the mind of the beholder is insistently challenged. No tragedy is more metaphysical than *Hamlet* : none contrives to bring so wide a range of human experience into question, or to question it with greater directness or urgency. Dr Johnson's solid objection that Hamlet forgets his princely dignity to mention ills and miseries 'to which inferior stations only are exposed'[105] finds its modern counterpart in the impression of a 'total effect of ambiguity' that can be created by the play's 'widely different levels of experience and insight'.[106] The turn of Hamlet's mind, as Hazlitt once observed, transfers its striking reflections on human life to the general account of humanity.[107] This unsubdued perceptiveness, and sensibility so diverse and acute, has led critics both of the nineteenth century and of the present to detect in Hamlet 'feelings that were personal to Shakespeare and not merely dramatically conceived',[108] something which Shakespeare did not 'manipulate into art';[109] yet at the same time there can be an admission that the play exhibits a consummate artistry, a 'high degree of self-possession on the part of the poet'.[110] The degree of Shakespeare's achievement in *Hamlet* is to be measured by the fact that his admission of the metaphysical, the philosophic and the subjective not only does not render its hero less real,

[102] *Dream*, 1951, p. 66. [103] J. Lawlor, *The Tragic Sense*, p. 57.
[104] op. cit., p. 174. [105] *Johnson on Shakespeare*, 1957, p. 192.
[106] L. C. Knights, 'Prince Hamlet', *Explorations*, 1946, p. 75.
[107] *Shakespeare Criticism*, ed. Nichol Smith, 1953, p. 288.
[108] Knights, op. cit., p. 73.
[109] T. S. Eliot, 'Hamlet', 1919 (*Selected Essays*, 1963, p. 144), quoted by Rossiter, *Angel with Horns*, 1961, p. 171.
[110] Knights, op. cit., p. 75.

but contributes to making him 'more real than any other being in any work made by man'.[111] So close is the beholder to him that Coleridge can declare it is we who are Hamlet; certainly the experience of the generations has been that

> his existence seems to reach out and touch ours, somewhat more intimately and more intensively than the kind of emotional involvement that the drama usually excites.[112]

The ready identification which the audience can make between the experience of Hamlet and their own – the extent to which he is the supreme Everyman of drama – becomes a point of assurance amidst the uncertainties of human existence to which the play itself directs the attention so powerfully; and in the very process of affirming that this is 'the most problematic of problem plays', the cautious critic finds it necessary to warn against a universal impression that an approach to the meaning of life may in some manner be made through the mind of its hero –

> as if, by somehow plucking the heart of Hamlet's mystery, we should come to know what God and man is.[113]

Against this caution may be urged the clear fact of the play's profundity, our inescapable awareness that 'Death and eternity have overshadowed this play from the beginning'.[114] As no other piece of drama, *Hamlet* is a human testament; but it is more. It is also, as no other, a perspective upon the world of man. The response of all sorts and conditions of humanity is comprehended in Dr Sitwell's penetrating utterance:

> Over the world of *Hamlet*, unlike the worlds of *Macbeth* and *King Lear*, reigns a perpetual and terrible light – the light of truth, dissolving all into its element.[115]

If truth reigns above the atmosphere of *Hamlet*, it is – if man's life terminates with the grave – a bitter truth: a secular view of this tragedy can point toward nothing that is not finally without meaning, or must not lead finally to despair. In *King Lear*, an affirmation is at least made even in the midst of chaos; but in *Hamlet*, all that is fine in human existence is seen to falter, painfully and haphazardly, into oblivion. In the musing words of Dr Johnson,

> The apparition left the regions of the dead to little purpose; the revenge which he demands is not obtained but by the death of him that was required to take it; and the gratification which would arise from the

[111] Edith Sitwell, *Notebook*, 1948, p. 81.
[112] Levin, *The Question of Hamlet*, N.Y., 1959, p. 6.
[113] ibid., p. 4.
[114] Speaight, *Nature in Shakespearian Tragedy*, 1955, p. 41.
[115] op. cit., p. 84.

destruction of an usurper and murderer, is abated by the death of *Ophelia*, the young, the beautiful, the harmless, and the pious.[116]

In human terms, the play can be categorized as an entire chronicle of despair; yet it possesses qualities which make it less tractable than the others to a strictly human assessment. One is certainly Hamlet's difference from the other tragic heroes – the absence in him of the heroic pattern of assertion. The ideal which, far from setting up a striving towards a personal predominance, tends to humble him into fellowship with mankind at its best, and leads him to the assertion, and not the defiance, of his human kindliness, must indicate health of soul, if it does not appear as evidence of spiritual vitality. But – perhaps in part because its tenor is that of despair – the whole drift of the play is away from that very finiteness of the human which its operation discloses. And in this movement toward the infinite – if it may be so termed without pretentiousness – it makes use of the clearest apparent references to the religious that are to be found in Shakespearian tragedy. As Bradley has observed,

> while *Hamlet* certainly cannot be called in the specific sense a 'religious drama', there is in it nevertheless both a freer use of popular religious ideas, and a more decided, though always imaginative, intimation of a supreme power concerned in human evil and good, than can be found in any other of Shakespeare's tragedies.[117]

Shakespeare's concluding reference in this play to another life, which Bradley notes in some puzzlement to be 'so much against his custom',[118] is part of a complex of comments evidently of theological significance which go up to the making of Hamlet's character, and which are especially noticeable in the lull before the fencing-bout.

The play therefore leads toward the metaphysical in a way that is individual and striking. In the matter of its meaning we are instantly taken to the boundary of the secular, and criticism is faced with Hamlet's own problem : whether to venture into

> The undiscover'd country, from whose bourn
> No traveller returns –

returns, at least, unchanged from what he was. *Hamlet's* uniqueness is that the presence – or otherwise – of the religious is the watershed of critical understanding; and to the secular critic its action can in this respect appear

> like a tedious argument
> Of insidious intent
> To lead you to an overwhelming question.

[116] *Johnson on Shakespeare*, p. 196.   [117] *Shakespearean Tragedy*, p. 174.
[118] ibid., p. 147.

388

His customary, and justifiable, decision that he is himself neither a prophet nor yet another Prince Hamlet is however too often masked by an insistence that there is no question to be answered : that the statements which Hamlet makes apparently of ultimate import are valid only in their testimony to pure world-weariness, and in other respects constitute no more than a piece of 'sublime mysticism and nonsense'. Thus, according to L. C. Knights, though they add to the nostalgia of the ending of the play, they provide at best an 'indulgence for some of our most cherished weaknesses', but are 'incapable of leading us far towards maturity'.[119] For D. G. James, the declared trust in Providence, appearing late in a play that gives no hint of its previous existence, comes from 'a defeated Hamlet who has given up the struggle'. They are the words of a 'secular soul' which, though nurtured in 'sweet religion', has long since ceased to regard it. In content they bear some relation to the religious; but of religion itself in the play James can declare, 'nowhere do we see it touching or inclining the soul of Hamlet'.[120] H. B. Charlton can indeed wax indignant that the atrophy in Hamlet of the will to act, and his consequent reduction to blank despair, should be varnished over with pious pretence – that, in the last moments of Hamlet's freedom,

> the recognition of the will's impotence is accepted as spiritual resignation; and the resignation is not seen as the moral abnegation, the *gran rifiuto*, which it certainly is; on the contrary, it is phrased as if it were the calm attainment of a higher benignity, whereas it is nothing more than a fatalist's surrender of his personal responsibility. This is the nadir of Hamlet's fall.

Whereas Bradley can postulate from the sufferings and failure that reveal the beauty of the soul of Lear a destiny that perhaps has led him to 'the very end and aim of life',[121] Charlton can see in Hamlet's professions of faith, and his graveyard survey of mortality, 'only processes which reconcile him to the last stage of failure'. And in the comments that follow from Hamlet's perceiving a 'special providence in the fall of a sparrow' this critic finds the limit of the irresponsible :

> This is absolute abdication : if Hamlet's duty is to be done, Providence will occasion its doing, as indeed Providence does in the heat of the fencing match when chance discloses more villainy, and stings Hamlet into a reflex retaliation. But Hamlet has failed. That is the tragedy.[122]

Are we to understand failure in Hamlet's impotence at the end of the play? Or are we to see in it the measure of a victory that takes its hero aloft with the wings and voices of angels? The answer lies in the prior

[119] Knights, 'Prince Hamlet', *Explorations*, 1946, p. 77.
[120] *The Dream of Learning*, pp. 63, 66.
[121] op. cit., p. 285.   [122] *Shakespearean Tragedy*, 1952, pp. 103–4.

question whether religious ideas and beliefs are actively present in the play. To the consideration of this question the play itself invites and challenges its critics; and, as is evident from the definite positions they tend to adopt, the challenge is of a kind that is not to be ignored. In spite of the perils inherent in the undertaking, therefore, the play's potentiality for religious interpretation must be assessed. If this potentiality exists, however, it will relate to a religion of the heart, not of the head; to a religion of vital experience, and not that of static formulation. It must thus accommodate the generalized, the inexact, the over-emphasized, and even the vague; and the sensitive critic will be he who proceeds, not upon the minutiae of academic definition, but upon the substance of a human response toward which these minutiae may direct him. Tragedy remains dedicated to the human and its vitalities; and any revelation which it succeeds in making of some higher truth, it must make, as it were, by default – for the transcendent to which it may point is inimical to its own nature. It is always to be borne in mind that the obvious appearance of the world by which it subsists is something 'which tragedy cannot dissolve without dissolving itself'.[123] Whatever may have been Shakespeare's own sense of ultimate issues, and to whatever extent he has conceived his hero as a Christian prince, and endowed him with evident awareness of a range of Christian principle, the very last thing he could do as a tragedian is to present Hamlet 'as a spokesman or propagandist for Christian doctrine'.[124]

The problem and all that devolves from it has been too little considered by R. W. Battenhouse in his important article on the religious content of *Hamlet*, in which he concludes that the hero's own universe is man-centred and therefore non-religious.[125] The conclusion is presumably based on the fact that religious concepts or attitudes do not in themselves constitute an explicitness in the dramatic sphere, where meaning is dependent upon the emphasis given to the verbal symbol which is otherwise merely part of the debased currency of a mundane awareness. Hamlet's emphasis is in general upon the human; and Battenhouse has therefore no difficulty in dismissing his 'sweet religion' as being

> founded in pagan naturalism and rationalism grown mystical but not supernatural in the Christian sense.[126]

Similarly, despite Hamlet's references to Providence and to the lawyer who would 'circumvent God', his assertion of his soul's immortality, and his consciousness of his own and Gertrude's depravity, Battenhouse can

123 Bradley, op. cit., p. 328.

124 R. M. Frye, *Shakespeare and Christian Doctrine*, London, 1963, p. 234.

125 'Hamlet's Apostrophe on Man : Clue to the Tragedy', *P.M.L.A.* LXVI, 1951, pp. 1073–113.

126 ibid., p. 1083.

assert that nature is viewed in the play without reference to a Creator, and man without mention of a divine image or of the concept of sin.[127] In these instances it is possible to see a conformity to sentiments that are natural rather than a grasping of what has been revealed; and in the same way a concept such as grace, so frequently upon Hamlet's lips, may be pressed into the service of a human ideal. In the expression 'as pure as grace', Battenhouse finds that

> grace is understood as a measure of nature's own perfection – and not (as for Aquinas) a gift from beyond nature for the perfecting of nature.[128]

Yet what escapes him is that the context makes clear the urgent need of such a gift from beyond nature : that the very sense of Hamlet's statement, particularly in its coupling of the notion of infirmity with the controlling sense of submission and subjection in the term 'undergo',[129] points both to human limitation and to the means by which it is to be overcome. Grace, while it is called upon as the 'measure of nature's own perfection', is revealed to be the only means of its salvation.

The interpretation Battenhouse offers is obviously based on what is defined rather than what is experienced; and he is also desiring an exactness of theological definition to which great drama can never attain. The 'grace' by which the soldiers swear their oath of secrecy may indeed have 'no Christian substance' for Hamlet;[130] and his use of the term in exhorting his mother to penitence may mean no more than that the 'code of nature and chivalry has been violated', and indicate a concept of 'moral beauty, but moral in the sense of the Greeks or of the Troubadors'[131] – though it is to be noted that Battenhouse makes no attempt to attribute the same sense to the accompanying words 'trespass', 'soul' and 'heaven'. These judgements proceed from an estimate of Hamlet's character, soon to be considered, that is derived from the famous apostrophe on man. But apart from showing the inadequacy of criticism by formulation, they call attention to the fact that the primary concern of drama with the human does not preclude the ability to suggest what is beyond it – especially in a context which underlines human inadequacy. And they indicate that a situation may come about where a denial of transcendental meaning in the conceptual utterances of a play's characters can only be made at the cost of a more or less strenuous assertion that they do not mean what they appear to say.

It is through his attitudes, however, rather than through his concepts, that the tragic hero is to be judged – a truth which liberates Hamlet's soul from a facile interpretation. For theological comments, as R. M.

[127] ibid., p. 1079.   [128] ibid., p. 1083.
[129] I. iv. 34; *N.E.D.*, 'undergo', 6.
[130] op. cit., p. 1081.   [131] ibid., p. 1082.

Frye has noted, occur with frequency in his characterization.[132] He is almost as quick to see the will of heaven in the act that kills Polonius as he is to invoke the 'angels and ministers of grace' in a moment of spiritual peril; and in his knowledge of the means by which diabolical 'abuse' may be practised upon man's senses, he displays an attitude no less traditional.[133] He knows his hands to be 'pickers and stealers' by the catechism,[134] and that, the predestinate and the reprobate being 'confused together, and commixed' in this world, it cannot grow honest 'until the general judgement make a separation'.[135] Yet these saws and maxims cannot denote him truly, except as they are perceived to be the outcome of an approach to life that must bring him within the province of faith. It is perhaps through his unfailing sense of human limitation that the beginnings of this approach in Hamlet are to be recognized. In the assurance to Horatio that there are more things in heaven and earth than philosophy has dreamt of we perhaps have what Frye asserts to be 'the central Christian denial of the validity of reason's operation in supernatural areas';[136] certainly Hamlet is affirming that we are 'but babes in understanding' so long as we remain but natural men.[137] The horror Hamlet experiences upon seeing the Ghost is such as anyone might feel; but R. Speaight is justified in calling our attention to the fact that it is 'primarily religious'.[138] He reacts in apparent awareness that there are matters 'unsearchable to human reason and understanding', where man's speculations are 'devilish';[139] that there is such a thing as inordinate curiosity,

> when a man studies to know the truth above the capacity of his own intelligence, since by so doing men easily fall into error.[140]

Hamlet appears zealous to heed this instruction that

> *The Godly wyse containes himselfe within*
> *Dame Natures wall;*[141]

and when this wall is breached by a return from the grave, his natural dread is surpassed by the speculations aroused by the event in creatures unfitted to sustain them, that have power to make

---

[132] op. cit., p. 223.
[133] See Aquinas, *Summa* I. cxiii. 1, 2, *ad R.*; cxiv. 2, 4, *ad R.*
[134] R. Noble, *Shakespeare's Biblical Knowledge*, 1935, p. 204.
[135] Augustine, *De Civ. Dei* I. xxxv.
[136] op. cit., p. 234.
[137] John Donne, *LXXX Sermons*, 1640, xxxi, p. 307.
[138] *Nature in Shakespearian Tragedy*, p. 19.
[139] *The Table-Talk of Martin Luther*, tr. W. Hazlitt, London, 1883, lxvi.
[140] *Summa*, IIa IIae clxvii. 1, *ad R.*
[141] M. Palingenius, *The Zodiake of Life*, 1531?, tr. B. Googe, London, 1576, Scholars' Facsimiles & Reprints, N.Y., 1947, p. 97.

> we fools of nature
> So horridly to shake our disposition
> With thoughts beyond the reaches of our souls
> (I. iv. 54–6).

A similar appearance of being 'Godly wyse' must arise from the manner of Hamlet's dealing with the potentialities of habit. His appealing to Gertrude 'for love of grace' to realize and arrest her habit of sin, and to throw away the worser part of a heart that is cleft in twain, echoes the traditional language that the soul in danger

> is to reflect on his lost peace and cry out for 'the Grace of God by Jesus Christ' to deliver him,

and deal inflexibly with the subject of a perverse love:

> *if it scandalize thee* – that is, if it blocks your road to true happiness, tear it out and cast it from yourself.[142]

His concern to overthrow the tyranny of what he terms 'damned custom' in his mother lest it should make her heart 'proof and bulwark against sense' is in accord with a religious realization that

> this is the dangerous slipperiness of sin, to slide by Thoughts and Actions, and Habits, to contemptuous obduration,[143]

and his driving her to repentance can be understood to devolve from a knowledge that only a true contrition can prepare the way for forgiveness – that

> He who hideth or excuseth his sinnes, struggleth against the streames of Grace;[144]

and that

> so long as contempt standeth, it is not possible that the sinne should bee remitted.[145]

For Granville-Barker, Hamlet's telling his mother to assume the virtue which she does not have is the resort of bitterness and despair. Having stripped one mask from her, he writes, Hamlet bids her wear another: 'for he has no faith, he finds, in her repentance'.[146] In seeing no more than cynicism in the course that is counselled, Granville-Barker is quite mistaken: its underlying assumption – that 'use almost can change the stamp of nature' – is in strict accordance with the traditional Christian

---

[142] Augustine, *De Serm. Dom. in Monte*, I. xii. 36. xiii. 37.
[143] John Donne, *XXVI Sermons*, 1661, vii, pp. 91–2.
[144] Sir John Hayward, *Davids Teares*, 2nd edn, 1623, p. 255.
[145] ibid., p. 166.
[146] *Prefaces*, 3rd Ser., 1937, p. 288.

view. Habits, Hamlet perceives, are caused by acts;[147] and just as a number of repeated acts set up a habit, so habit can be undermined or broken down through mere cessation from act[148] – one instance of refraining, in fact, will 'lend a kind of easiness' to the next abstinence. It is true that he can attribute a tyrannous habit to being 'nature's livery, or fortune's star'; but in so doing he follows an orthodox teaching which allows instances of a natural beginning to habit in both the apprehensive and appetitive powers of man, but which as a general rule attributes habit to acts rather than to natural disposition.[149] Hamlet's sense of the monstrosity of habit is a recognition of its capacity to become a 'complementary nature',[150] and take possession of the will; yet he is at the same time aware that habit remains within the dictate of reason, and can be altered by the operation of the same will which establishes it.[151] Both the virtues and the vices are thus constructed out of habit, and may even be regarded as forms of habit;[152] and the command to 'Assume a virtue, if you have it not' is in consequence the first necessity in the reconstruction of a soul's moral being. His assurance,

> That monster, custom, who all sense doth eat,
> Of habits devil, is angel yet in this,
> That to the use of actions fair and good
> He likewise gives a frock or livery,
> That aptly is put on
>
> (III. iv. 161–5),

states explicitly and forcefully what is at once orthodox doctrine and Elizabethan commonplace. In precisely the same terms John Davies of Hereford can argue that

> Sith *Custome* then is of such liuely force
> As it hath powre it selfe to overcome,
> How blest are they that doe themselves divorce
> From *Custome* ill, by force of good *custome*.[153]

The substance of agreement with Aquinas is scarcely acknowledged by Battenhouse, who demands a declaration from Hamlet that ultimately it is the grace of God, operating through the will, which effects deliverance from habit's domination[154] – in default of which he would pronounce

---

[147] Aquinas, *S.T.* Ia IIae li. 3, *ad R.*; E. Gilson, *The Philosophy of St Thomas Aquinas*, tr. Bullough, Cambridge, 1924, p. 247.

[148] *S.T.* Ia IIae li. 2, 3, *ad R.*; Gilson, op. cit., p. 248.

[149] *S.T.* Ia IIae li. 1, *ad R.*; Gilson, p. 247.

[150] Gilson, p. 246.

[151] *S.T.* Ia IIae liii. 1, *ad R.*; Gilson, p. 245.

[152] *S.T.* Ia IIae liv. 3, *ad R.*; lv. 1–4, *ad R.*; Gilson, p. 248.

[153] *Microcosmos*, Oxford, 1603, p. 82.

[154] *S.T.* Ia IIae cix. 2, *ad R.*

the speeches to be Pelagian in their mere rationality.[155] That he should father these speeches upon Pelagius, however, must follow from his having previously consigned the concept of grace, which in fact appears in them, to the mercies of the Greeks and the Troubadors – if not to the profoundest pit.

A similar correspondence with traditional Christian teaching may be adduced from Hamlet's championing of man's 'capability and god-like reason' as a principle of human excellence. Aquinas can define moral virtue as conformity to reason, and vice as what is contrary to it[156] – for by the operation of reason is rendered possible that accord with natural law which is a rational creature's participation in eternal law.[157] Hamlet's being attuned to the macrocosmic significance of reason is evident in his horror at its rejection: no less than Hooker, he is aghast at something which

> cannot be done without the singular disgrace of Nature, and the utter disturbance of that divine order.[158]

His sense of the balance or antithesis of passion and reason is appropriate to a doctrine which classifies passion as a disturbance of the soul when divorced from reason's control,[159] and gives to reason the task of assigning that right mean in the operations of the passions, equidistant from excess and deficiency, in which the moral virtues consist.[160]

This felicitous tension Hamlet defines as a 'commingling' of 'blood and judgement'; and in Battenhouse's view, the definition betrays an outlook that is 'naturalistic and fatalistic',[161] since the blessedness it would denote is not seen to relate to the condition of the will. Certainly Hamlet appears to be speaking somewhat physiologically; though in his attitude to others can be seen a full awareness that

> For man to act well, reason must not only be well disposed by the habit of intellectual virtue, but his appetite or faculty of desiring must be well disposed by the habit of moral virtue.[162]

The charge that in his conception of man's becoming 'A beast, no more' upon the lapse of reason Hamlet accepts the Renaissance emphasis of Ficino,[163] and shows an aspiration to become merely 'a rational or God-like animal',[164] is also to a certain extent justified – though it is to be noted that Hamlet's understanding of reason is no more out of keeping

155 'Hamlet's Apostrophe on Man', *P.M.L.A.* LXVI, 1951, p. 1095.
156 *S.T.* Ia IIae xviii. 5, *ad R.*; lxiv. 1, *ad R.*; lxxi. 2, *ad R.*; Gilson, p. 251.
157 *S.T.* Ia IIae xci. 2, *ad R.*; xciii. 3, *ad R.*
158 *Eccl. Pol.* I. vii. 7.   159 *S.T.* Ia IIae xxiv. 2, *ad R.*
160 Gilson, op. cit., p. 255; *S.T.* Ia IIae lxiv.1, *ad 1.*
161 op. cit., p. 1080.   162 Gilson, op. cit., p. 251.
163 Battenhouse, op. cit., p. 1093.   164 ibid., p. 1094.

with the contemporary religious consciousness than it is incompatible with Aquinas's teachings. Sir John Hayward writes in Hamlet's terms:

> GOD hath endued you with reason, to make you differ from beasts: vse it, and vse it well. If you doe not vse it, then you are beasts.[165]

Battenhouse's assertion that the view of man which would make his difference from the beast 'one of rationality only, and not of substance, can not claim the sanction of Christian philosophy as given precision by Aquinas',[166] must be placed beside Aquinas's definition that the form of man is his rational soul itself;[167] yet, despite all Hamlet's justification, it is to be admitted that he does try to make an absolute of his rationality. The essence of Battenhouse's objection to Hamlet's prizing of the rational principle is expressed in Augustine's definition that God's image in man is not man's rational nature, but rather man's power to use rationality to attain true knowledge in the partaking of the divine light.[168] Reason in man is validated by the creature's recognition of a principle beyond reason, a Person in whose image he is made; and this recognition, which at the same time validates and transcends rationality,

> yields a knowledge of the Divine Being, the *intellectualis visio Dei*, sufficiently clear and precise to make it possible for him to say that, 'next to myself, I know God'.[169]

This recognition, and this claim, do not exist in Hamlet for the larger part of the play; but the ending of his career reveals him as the possessor of both. The creaturely emphasis that he has before placed upon reason has manifested its deficiency; and reason in him – if his declared trust in God and in his purposes is true – has come to centre upon its proper object, and therefore proved through its ultimate test a general accord with religious principle. Hamlet's declaration, unfortunately, is according to Battenhouse fraudulent: we have his assurance that

> Hamlet's 'special providence' has no special provision for man; the 'readiness' it evokes is born of Classic despair, not Christian cheer.[170]

Hamlet's hatred of insincerity – his passionate wish that his relations with others, and theirs with him, should be 'even and direct' – is at one with his advocacy of reason. In both he gives evidence of that devotion to truth which, according to Aquinas, is the right mean for moral virtue, and which alone can confer it;[171] and by constantly appealing to the

165 *Davids Teares*, 1623, p. 169 (misnumbered 173).
166 'Hamlet's Apostrophe', p. 1093.   167 *S.T.* Ia IIae xviii. 5, *ad R.*
168 *De Trin.* XIV. iv. 6; see Section II, p. 126.
169 C. N. Cochrane, *Christianity and Classical Culture*, 1940, pp. 400, 406–7.
170 'Hamlet's Apostrophe on Man', *P.M.L.A.* LXVI, 1951, p. 1102.
171 *S.T.* Ia IIae lxiv. 2, 3, *ad R.*; Gilson, *The Philosophy of St Thomas Aquinas*, tr. Bullough, 1924 p. 255.

consciences of others in his scorn for the world's distortions reveals the work of conscience within himself. What alienates Hamlet from Denmark, and confers moral distinction upon him, is precisely that refusal to stand upon others' judgements, and that hearkening instead to truth's inward testimony, which Augustine declares to be 'the best virtue'.[172] His unerring grasp of the quality of men's purposes and acts – not least of his own – is due to the ability to penetrate beneath the surface of mortal affairs and achievements which, according to Augustine, only an awakened consience can confer. In considering the deeds of men, he certainly contrives to 'pay heed, not to the visible flowering but to the root beneath the ground';[173] and thus, in the process of detecting evil motives in others, he is able to confess, despite an 'indifferent' honesty in himself,

> I could accuse me of such things that it were better my mother had not borne me (III. i. 122–4),

and to see himself as implicated in a general knavery. This knowledge is the effect of that powerful working of conscience which exempts him from the condemnation Augustine would apply even to good men : their keeping aloof from evil-doers, and their failure to admonish or reform them for fear that they may 'lose their own vain temporalities'.[174] This fear never gains mastery over Hamlet : his readiness to challenge the perverse understanding often appears to the detriment of his worldly advantage. It is a readiness, indeed, which may form part of a religious calling. Conscience, for Shakespeare's age as for the theologian, is an agency neither passive nor secular; it is a 'dowrie naturall'[175] in man of Divine implantation, God's advocate within the heart.[176] By its activity a man may be assured that whatever is good in himself is present in God 'in a supereminent manner'.[177] Indeed, the strength and independence of its testimony is proof of the immediacy of God's presence –

> that there is a spiritual substance, most wise, most holy, most mightie, that sees all things to whome conscience beares record; and that is God himselfe.[178]

The religious quality of Hamlet's conscientiousness may likewise be seen in its creating in him the humility by which he is set apart from the other tragic heroes. Unlike them, he cannot relapse with the assurance of pride into the consciousness of his own merits, for he must be aware of

---

[172] *De Civ. Dei* V. xii (Healey tr.)
[173] *In Epist. Jo. ad Parth. Tract. decem* viii. 9.
[174] *De Civ. Dei* I. ix.
[175] Sir John Davies, 'Nosce Teipsum', 1599, *The Complete Poems*, ed. Grosart, 1876, I, p. 77.
[176] Sir W. Raleigh, *The History of the World*, 1614, Preface, sig. *A2*v.
[177] D. Person, *Varieties*, 1635, Bk 5, sect. 9.
[178] W. Perkins, 'A Discourse of Conscience', *Works*, 2nd edn, Cambridge, 1603, p. 621a.

his own weakness in the moral excellence to which he aspires; and, like the true Christian, far from desiring a uniqueness which that excellence might confer, grudging that another should be his equal in it, and striving thus to 'set himself up over other men',[179] Hamlet wishes that all men might be like himself in any good he attains. There can be observed in him that 'knowledge of one's own deficiency' which, according to Aquinas, 'belongs to humility, as a rule guiding the appetite';[180] and his inclinations are far removed from the 'craving for temporal things' and the 'boldness and haughtiness' in which Augustine detects the opposite of the state he declares to be the beginning of blessedness.[181] Humility, though it appear as manifest weakness in the world, is really an indication of strength, for it involves a readiness to depend on the true and unique source of power and harmony[182] – a readiness which the ending of *Hamlet* may be regarded as making evident.

It is true that the beauty which Hamlet wishes to see established in the human soul appears in the play as a whole to be of a natural rather than of a supernatural kind, and not to consist in a disposition of the will towards the content of revelation.[183] How such a disposition could be shown in him without destroying that obvious appearance of the world

> which tragedy cannot dissolve without dissolving itself[184]

is a consideration that fails to claim the attention of this critic. But the will toward human goodness and virtue, which is so strong in Hamlet, is not necessarily divorced from pious intent. If the status of man be defined by the rationality which raises him above the brutes, Augustine argues, so the excellence of his calling lies in his duty to excel 'the airy spirits in just living' :[185] beatitude, in Sir Walter Raleigh's words,

> doth not consist in the knowledge of diuine things, but in a diuine life.[186]

Above all else, Hamlet is dedicated to 'just living'. Where goodness exists, he pays faithful homage; where it is lacking, nothing can inhibit his scorn. To those whose authority is not the product of *'an inward loue for their iustice and piety'*[187] he must respond with loathing; and he is himself ready to forego the outward deference due to his rank if men do not respect him for what he is. In so far, however, as he seeks the ideal in men, and is prepared to accept goodness in them as an ultimate good, his

---

179 Augustine, *In Epist. Jo. ad Parth. Tract. decem* viii. 8.
180 *S.T.* IIa IIae clxi. 2, *ad R.*   181 *De Serm. Dom. in Monte* I. iii. 10.
182 C. N. Cochrane, *Christianity and Classical Culture*, p. 505.
183 Battenhouse, 'Hamlet's Apostrophe', p. 1080.
184 Bradley, *Shakespearean Tragedy*, 1956, p. 328.
185 Augustine, *De Civ. Dei* VIII. xv.
186 *History*, 1614, Preface, sig. C2v.   187 ibid., sig. C3.

fate must be that of disillusionment with the very humanity in which he seeks it; for

> *Mans* aye-searching *Sp'rite* with toil's opprest:
> Til it haue found that *Good* that giues it rest.[188]

Hamlet's inability to find in man the goodness which would give rest to his soul can denote, not an impious will, but a religious vocation. The search for justice and order in the soul does in fact make it plain to him that 'this is rather continually laboured after than truly attained in this life';[189] and he who is always 'weighing his own infirmity' by the standards of an exalted notion of righteousness cannot be one of those who 'dares to ascribe his purity and innocency to his own strength'.[190]

In the act of seeking within a human strength for an exalted good, Hamlet despairs of himself and others: the 'dram of eale' must ever confound the 'noble substance'. That this thought befits a religious consciousness is indicated by its presence in a context where Luther contemplates man's unperfectness. It behoves God's human creatures to care for their brethren who fall short of what they should be, Luther argues, and make good their failings through the commandment of love, curing human deficiency by supernatural means;

> *But so corrupted and blinded is nature by the devil's poison, that the children of this world, even though they know a man to be endued with many excellent gifts and virtues, yet if they discover but one spot or blemish in him, they have regard unto that only, and forget all his gifts and graces.*[191]

The observation which in Luther is part of a transcendental view, recognizing in the world

> *the kingdom of the devil, which securely despiseth faith and charity and all the works and words of God,*[192]

tends in Hamlet to be restricted – apart from the mention of grace – to the secular, and to the personal; but that it may be the beginning of a wider awareness, concerning both man's world and what is beyond it, is if anything confirmed by the remainder of the play. Hamlet's early acknowledgement that no man if used after his desert could escape whipping accords with the theologian's conception of human depravity: 'if you shall be paid what you deserve, you must be punished';[193] and the rest of his career may be seen as impressing upon him that in this mortal

[188] John Davies of Hereford, *Mirum in Modum*, 1602, sig. C2v.
[189] Augustine, *De Civ. Dei* XIX. iv.
[190] *Conf.* II. vii. 15.
[191] *A Commentary on St Paul's Epistle to the Galatians* (v. 14), ed. P. S. Watson, 1953, p. 491.
[192] ibid.
[193] Calvin, *Inst.* II. v. 2, quoted by Frye, *Shakespeare and Christian Doctrine*, 1963, p. 251.

life 'there shall neuer be any perfect soundness in vs', and that even the righteous of this world are 'so lame, that they dragge their legges and their wings after them'.[194] The misery which this knowledge brings to him is evident; what does not appear in the play is a realization, consequent upon his failure to find 'a full and complete righteousness in himself', that

> no human creature finds it in this life; it is altogether angelical, which shall fall unto us in the life to come.[195]

Similarly he voices no recognition that man's perfection and happiness depends upon theological as well as natural principles, and that the theological virtues are altogether distinct from intellectual or moral ones.[196] Yet the accents of faith itself – the theological virtue which according to Aquinas must precede the others[197] – are nevertheless eventually to proceed from Hamlet's lips. There cannot be detected in him the state of mind which would acknowledge the virtues that he has sought to be 'rather vices than virtues' while they remain undedicated to God's service;[198] yet on the other hand it is not within the realm of likelihood that an intellect as keen as Hamlet's, of necessity seeking a blessedness, but from things which by their nature cannot yield it, should long be withheld from perceiving both the essential absurdity of his situation and the means by which it may be restored – that the questing soul, in Augustine's words,

> truly commits a great error and enormity in not adhering to him.[199]

If, in placing a trust in the human and the mortal, Hamlet is claimed by the pride that must attend a 'conversion to creatures', his failing is to be deduced from his sense of the depravity of the senses and the passions, and his wish to fly from the corporality of his own condition. As Battenhouse justifiably observes,

> Brutalizing the body as a carcass, or flight from it as imprisoning, are alike anti-Christian . . . when stated in so unrelieved a fashion.[200]

He is able to note, however,

> the striking similarity some of Hamlet's utterances have to . . . Luther's and Calvin's views of human depravity[201] –

particularly those which make the world a sepulchre and the body a prison, or Calvin's image of human evil as a carcass which putrifies

---

194 *Calvins Sermons on Job*, tr. A. Golding, 1573, p. 3b.
195 Luther, *Table-Talk*, tr. W. Hazlitt, London, 1883, dcxxxvi.
196 Aquinas, *S.T.* Ia IIae lxii. 1, 2, *ad R.*
197 *S.T.* Ia IIae lxii. 3, 4 *ad R.*
198 *De Civ. Dei* XIX. xxv.   199 *De Civ. Dei* XII. i.
200 'Hamlet's Apostrophe on Man : Clue to the Tragedy', *P.M.L.A.* LXVI, 1951, p. 1103.
201 ibid.

beneath the salutary rays of the sun.[202] He is dealing with an emphasis which, far from denoting irreligion, is by no means novel – or inappropriate – in the history of Christian experience. The temptation in spiritual striving to impute human vices to the flesh rather than to the living according to the flesh is easily yielded to;[203] and the admissible horror at the flesh as the inheritor of original sin can at first impact hinder the recognition that the character of its evil belongs to punishment rather than to guilt,[204] and dim the soul's awareness of its own true responsibility for the evil it apprehends. This is particularly so in one who is to be conceived not as the assured possessor of faith, but rather as moving towards it. To him, and indeed to the average sincere Christian, the means of corporeal limitation upon man's perfectibility, which are present to the mind of the theologian in sufficient strength to place in hazard his categories of human responsibility,[205] must appear no less formidable. The spiritual content and utility of this kind of disillusionment will presently be considered; but that it involves some leaning towards the secular and the humanistic is not to be denied. The same might be concluded of Hamlet's praise of Horatio for his freedom from passion, in which Battenhouse is right to detect traces of what, in R. Speaight's words, is 'a humanist, a rather stoical ideal';[206] for by traditional Christian interpretation, moral virtue consists, not in the absence of passion, but in 'freedom from those passions *that are not as they should be as to manner and time*'.[207] It should be observed, however, that, in Hamlet's thought, liberation from slavery to passion is obtained through a balance of passion and reason rather than from passion's annihilation : the stoic emphasis is rather to be inferred than demonstrated, though its presence cannot be reasonably questioned.

Hamlet's humanism, and his disillusionment, is most evident when he comes to consider the brave o'erhanging firmament, and man, god-like in feature and capacity. It is his most characteristic utterance; and it illustrates better than any other what Santayana describes as the destructive, malicious and sterile quality that appears in the thought of one whose idealism is 'lame because it cannot conceive a better alternative to the things it criticizes'.[208] The apostrophe on man, upon which Battenhouse bases his assessment of Hamlet's character, does indeed show where his idealism has centred; and it indicates in him the grief that flows from loss of confidence in the mutable things upon which a soul has reposed

202 *Inst.* I. xvii. 5.
203 *De Civ. Dei* XIV. v.
204 Aquinas, *S.T.* Ia IIae lxxxiii. 1, *ad R.*
205 See Section II, pp. 109–11, 127–9.
206 *Nature in Shakespearian Tragedy*, 1955, p. 31.
207 Aquinas, *S.T.* Ia IIae lix. 2, *ad R.*
208 *Obiter Scripta*, 1936, p. 40, quoted by L. C. Knights, 'Prince Hamlet', *Explorations*, 1946 p. 67.

its trust,[209] and which it knows not how to replace with a good that is imperishable. Hamlet's triumphant thought that man is god-like terminates in the despairing conclusion that he is a 'quintessence of dust'. The reflection is not unbefitting the pulpit : John Donne can exclaim, in terms that recall Hamlet's,

> How abusively then doe men call the things of this world, Goods? . . . Health, and strength, and stature, and comelinesse, must be called Goods, though but of the body; The body it self is in the substance it self, but dust; these are but the accidents of that dust, and yet they must be Goods.[210]

These ideas, however, can be seen to drive Donne to the confirmation of his faith in the assertion that

> There is nothing good in this life, nothing in the next, without God.[211]

Once faith has been attained, man can be contemplated with untroubled admiration in the thought of the greatness of his Creator;[212] even a mind as conscious of human depravity as a Philip Stubbes can ask delightedly, in the consciousness of God's mercies,

> What Creature may be likened to man, either in proportiō of body, or gifts of the soule?[213]

Despair at human corruption and limitation, if persisted in, is recognized by the piety of every age to be 'nothing else but a want of true trust in the mercie of GOD to remit sinnes'.[214]

In a thorough and erudite analysis of Hamlet's speech, Battenhouse establishes without any difficulty the essential humanism of its main features. He detects the intrusion of the Renaissance concept of man as a span or link between heaven and earth into the traditional Christian view of man as occupying a state below the angels and above the animal creation. In the uncertain pointing of the articles in praise of man,

> in form, in moving, how express and admirable! in action how like an angel! in apprehension how like a god! (II. ii. 311–13.)

Battenhouse demonstrates a deeper confusion of thought, a 'blurring over distinctions at the upper end of the scale of nature',[215] by which the Renaissance, particularly in the writings of Pico and Ficino, sought by favouring the Neoplatonic at the expense of the Thomistic to ascribe to man an angelic status and function.[216] Hamlet's mood of 'reverence for man as God-like in his natural endowment of the contemplative faculty'[217]

---

209 Augustine, *De Vera Relig.* xii. 23.
211 ibid., p. 169.
213 *The Anatomie of Abuses*, 1583, sig. S2ᵛ
214 Sir J. Hayward, *Davids Teares*, 2nd edn, 1623, p. 261.
215 'Hamlet's Apostrophe on Man', ed. cit., p. 1091.
216 ibid., pp. 1086–7.
210 *LXXX Sermons*, 1640, xvii, p. 168.
212 Aquinas, *Summa Contra Gentiles* II. ii.
217 ibid., p. 1090.

is therefore taken as proof of a thorough-going humanism. In his concern
with the content of this speech, however, Battenhouse does not take into
account its tone. As H. Levin has commented, though the Folio's punc-
tuating the subsequent clauses with question marks rather than exclamation points is in itself nothing to go by, 'Hamlet's mood, at any rate, is
interrogative rather than exclamatory'.[218] The purpose of the speech is
in direct conflict with its philosophy :

> Hamlet utters the sentiment in order to qualify it, shifting his focus
> from the potentialities to the limitations of the species. If man is a
> matchless creature, he is 'the paragon of animals'. To complete that
> paradox, he is the last refinement, the 'quintessence of dust'.[219]

Battenhouse fails to acknowledge that the purport of the speech is destroyed by its ending; that, as R. Speaight declares, 'for Hamlet all this
exultant humanism is denied by the facts of life';[220] that Hamlet has built
up a case only bitterly and contemptuously to demolish it. So immersed is
he in the conceptual as to lose sight of the dramatic; and, having determined upon the condition of Hamlet's soul through an absoluteness of
analogy from disciplines by their nature remote from drama's liveliness,
he has proceeded to the confident disparagement of the evidences of
spiritual vitality which the play affords. His article, for all its undoubted
learning and real perceptiveness, is surely a notable instance of the depredations which conceptual thinking can make upon the critical sensibility.

The desire for non-existence is part and parcel of Hamlet's disillusionment with the existence he knows. As a desire it is of course eloquent of
the mind's mancentredness; but it might initially be remarked that the
immediacy and force with which the idea of life after death presents
itself to that mind can be shown to have a certain theological inevitability.
A right-thinking consciousness cannot – despite all efforts – entertain the
idea of its own annihilation. Augustine states the position in this way :

> A man who says, I should prefer this to that, chooses something. But
> non-existence is not something; it is nothing. Therefore you cannot
> possibly make a real choice, when there is nothing for you to choose.[221]

The object of the willed choice can only be of positive nature :

> Thus when a man wills to die, all that he desires is not non-existence
> after death, but rest. Though he falsely believes he will cease to exist,
> his nature seeks rest, that is, increase of existence. Hence, just as it is
> utterly impossible that anyone should take pleasure in non-existence, so it
> is utterly wrong that anyone should be ungrateful to the Creator's
> goodness for his existence.[222]

[218] *The Question of Hamlet*, N.Y., 1959, p. 31.   [219] ibid., p. 61.
[220] *Nature in Shakespearian Tragedy*, 1955, p. 26.   [221] *De Lib. Arb.* III. viii. 22.
[222] ibid., III. viii. 23.

In a matter so relatively tenuous it is well not to place too much weight upon any conclusion that is drawn; but the preoccupation with what form of experience may begin with 'this sleep of death' can betoken no unhealthiness of understanding, if Augustine's reasoning may be relied on. And certainly the stage is before long reached where Hamlet is considering his own existence by reference to that of his Creator.

It may be argued in disproof that the prospect of a life to come arouses dread in Hamlet rather than consolation; and that, though he appears to respect the canon of 'the Everlasting', it is

> Not merely intellectual recognition of a theological injunction, but a primitive fear of the unknown after-world[223]

that is uppermost in his thoughts, and restrains him from suicide. D. G. James has shown that an after-world which in Montaigne is both definite and benign becomes obscure and threatening in Hamlet's imagination, as if Hamlet is void of all assurance;[224] yet the same writer agrees with Dr Johnson that, in the 'To be, or not to be' speech, the thought both of suicide and of action is governed by the question of personal immortality, which in turn centres upon the existence of God.[225] Johnson summarizes the speech thus:

> Hamlet, knowing himself injured in the most enormous and atrocious degree, and seeing no means of redress, but such as must expose him to the extremity of hazard, meditates on his situation in this manner: *Before I can form any rational scheme of action under this pressure of distress*, it is necessary to decide, whether, *after our present state, we are to be or not to be.*[226]

In thinking of the multitudes of the troubles and fears which might all be done away by the simple act of a will resolute enough to confront all earthly troubles, 'and by opposing end them', and also in the dwelling, not upon death itself, but upon the state that is to follow after it, Hamlet's thoughts are entirely in keeping with what might occur – indeed, should occur – to the religious conscience. Augustine ponders as Hamlet does:

> And seeing that every mortal man, in the daily casualties of this life is threatened continually with innumerable sorts of death, as long as he is uncertain which of them he shall taste; tell me whether it were better to suffer but one in dying once for ever, or still to live in continual fear, than all those extremes of death? I know how unworthy a choice it were to choose rather to live under the awe of so many deaths, than by once dying to be freed from all their fear for ever. But it is one thing

223 Charlton, *Shakespearian Tragedy*, 1952, p. 92.
224 *The Dream of Learning*, 1951, p. 59.
225 ibid., pp. 39, 42.   226 *Johnson on Shakespeare*, ed. Raleigh, 1957, p. 191.

when the weak sensitive flesh doth fear it, and another when the purified reason of the soul overcomes it. A bad death never makes a good
life: for there is nothing that maketh death bad but that estate
which followeth death. Therefore let not their death that needs must
die be employed upon the manner of their death, but upon the estate
that they are eternally to inherit after death.[227]

That the concern with life after death should be a stumbling block on
the path to suicide thus shows a certain degree of conformity to a Christian sense of the natural and the appropriate, if it cannot be said more
certainly to represent an effort of 'the purified reason of the soul'. Hamlet
simply does not – and presumably cannot – express the sentiments of a
pagan: the threat of pending ills which at present 'we know not of' must
give him pause. This apprehension, according to Luther, must distinguish
the Christian from others:

It were a light and easy matter for a Christian to overcome death, if he
knew it was not God's wrath; that quality makes death bitter to us.
But a heathen dies securely; he neither sees nor feels that it is God's
wrath, but thinks it is merely the end of nature.[228]

For both Luther and Augustine, the Christian's faith in God's being and
mercies must through its assurance remove much of the horror of death.
In Hamlet's apprehension of death's imminence before the fencing-bout
there may be found some evidence of the ability of a professed faith to
'defy augury', and to assert of the approaching end of mortal existence,
'the readiness is all'.

A religious consciousness and potentiality is thus to be seen at work in
Hamlet; yet by no stretch of the imagination can it be said that the play
reveals him throughout as a man of faith. On the contrary, he is shown
both by nurture and desire to be a man of this world, one who has been
'The glass of fashion, and the mould of form'; and, though now driven
to despise the world, he consciously wills nothing more than adherence
to its fashions and forms in the pursuance of his sworn purpose. While
identifying freedom from passion with blessedness, he wills to be possessed by passion's tyranny, and cannot bear to be outfaced by the passion
of another. He can exult in the clash of the 'fell incensed points /Of
mighty opposites', and laugh at the conflict's striking down 'the baser
nature' in the persons of his schoolfellows; and his killing of Claudius
is ruthlessness itself, despite its stemming from the ruthlessness of others.
The passionateness he seeks is surely one of the '*darkened* affections' that
by Augustine's definition imply alienation from God;[229] and in his unqualified admiration for a Fortinbras stung into militancy by the vengeful assertion of a personal honour, there is to be found more than a mere

[227] *De Civ. Dei* I. xi.   [228] *Table-Talk*, dcclxxxviii.   [229] *Conf.* I. xviii. 28.

inclination of the aspiring self to bring the world into conformity with its own desire and edict.[230] The 'greatness' that does not scruple

> greatly to find quarrel in a straw
> When honour's at the stake
>
> (IV. iv. 55–6),

and is ready to sacrifice twenty thousand lives for 'a fantasy and trick of fame' concerning a piece of ground not big enough to contain the corpses of those who have died in its acquisition, though it indicate for Hamlet a 'spirit with divine ambition puff'd', has nothing to do with the stature of the soul. It relates instead to what Luther would have termed princely pride[231] – the ruthless quest for aggrandizement which is the madness that runs before the world's misery. Hamlet's will, it has been pointed out, is for purposive action, not reason: Fortinbras is admired for the very capriciousness and lack of moral justification with which he pursues to its violent end a piece of 'grandiose folly'.[232] For this reason J. M. Robertson considered that Shakespeare's writing of this soliloquy could not have been influenced by the following passage of the 'Apology of Raymond Sebond':

> This horror-causing array of many thousands of armed men, so great fury, earnest fervour, and undaunted courage, it would make one laugh to see on how many vain occasions it is raised and set on fire. . . . The hatred of one man, a spite, a pleasure . . . causes which ought not to move two scolding fishwives to catch one another, is the soul and motive of all this hurly-burly.[233]

But the fact that Hamlet's attitude is the object of Montaigne's ridicule increases rather than lessens the probability that Shakespeare knew this passage – for the ideal Hamlet exalts is ridiculous.

This extreme of self-regarding vengefulness, whose presence in Fortinbras Hamlet applauds, is for Augustine part of that endless 'conquering, or being conquered' which does no good, but 'only adds unto their intolerable vain-glory, who aim at such matters'.[234] The principle of revenge can find a cautious but sad acceptance in his thought, if the act concerned does not exceed the wrong done;[235] and Aquinas similarly can allow a revenge whose purpose is truly directed to some good rather than to the evil of the person affected.[236] But the mood of vengefulness must be inimical to the soul's health:

[230] (Section III, p. 239.)

[231] R. M. Frye, *Shakespeare and Christian Doctrine*, 1963, p. 228, citing 'A Treatise on Good Works'. See Section II, pp. 150–1.

[232] T. Greene, 'The Postures of Hamlet', *S.Q.* XI, 1960, p. 361.

[233] *Montaigne and Shakespeare*, 1909, pp. 60–1.

[234] *De Civ. Dei* V. xvii.

[235] *De Serm. Dom. in Monte* I. xix. 56.

[236] *S.T.* IIa IIae cviii. 1, 2, *ad R.*

'Are you not to have your revenge? Is he to tell the tale of what he has done to you? No, let him feel that he is dealing with a man.' . . . Such things are said only by those who love the world; and only by those who love the world are they listened to.[237]

This uncompromising judgement of the motive of revenge makes its appearance in Elizabethan drama in the 'universal condemnation of the person of the revenger',[238] and in *Hamlet* particularly in the contrast between the hero and the three true revengers whose actions are designed to exhibit 'to a superlative degree what the code of revenge demands'.[239] That code is condemned in the hero's inability to be governed by it:

> Hamlet's agony of mind and indecision are precisely the things which differentiate him from that smooth, swift plotter Claudius, and from the coarse, unthinking Laertes, ready to 'dare damnation' and cut his enemy's throat in a churchyard.[240]

His failure may be seen as the work of a 'kindness' which is 'nobler ever than revenge';[241] and the deadness of his conscience on the subject is perhaps to be understood as a consequence of that wiping from his memory of 'All saws of books, all forms, all pressures past' in order that a single command may live within the 'book and volume' of his brain. Certainly the manner of Hamlet's behaviour here shows a conformity to a religious understanding of mind and memory:

> The minde is the storehouse and keeper of all manner of rules and principles. It may be compared to a booke of law, in which are set downe the penall statutes of the land. The dutie of it is to preferre and present to the conscience rules of diuine law whereby it is to giue judgement.[242]

Hamlet may therefore be conceived – for so he conceives himself – as having flung aside the means of scruple and conscience. But it is impossible not to see in his will to champion the spirit and practice of revenge a characteristic inclination to worldliness and perversity – a desire to find a transcendence within his own existence, and invest his desires with an inhuman absoluteness, in the manner of the other tragic heroes. The desire is a fierce attempt by one who can truly identify himself with nothing in his world to wrest from it a principle of being and selfhood;[243]

[237] Augustine, *In Epist. Jo. ad Parth. Tract. decem* vii. 3.

[238] W. M. Merchant, *Creed and Drama*, 1965, p. 60.

[239] H. Jenkins, 'The Tragedy of Revenge in Shakespeare and Webster', *S.S.* XIV, 1961, p. 47.

[240] H. Gardner, *The Business of Criticism*, Oxford Paperbacks, 1963, p. 46.

[241] *As You Like It* IV. iii. 128.

[242] W. Perkins, 'A Discourse of Conscience', *Works*, 1603, p. 642a.

[243] (Section III, pp. 286–7.)

and its failure can be attributed to the hindrance occasioned to the gathering of a mundane identity and purpose by the surpassing quality of the quest for being that had first given rise to it – to the chosen posture's not fitting the universe it was to have affronted. It is perhaps admissible to speculate that its quality is tested and revealed upon Hamlet's sight of Claudius praying: that both the evaporation of purpose and the ruthlessness of assertion are a soul's response to a higher potentiality that drives it towards submission, or to the pettiness of defiance.

That this possibility can be no more than speculation, and can refer only to an impression that is momentary, is clear from its taking no immediate hold upon Hamlet's imagination. The failure of his worldly purpose, and of his ideal for humanity, does not attune him straightway to a different hope, but plunges him into unrelieved frustration, melancholy and despair. His attitude, declares Battenhouse,

> reflects the psychology of frustration in individual man whenever reason is cut off from Christian faith, and nature from Christian grace.[244]

The melancholy which he acknowledges, and which holds him in its grip almost throughout the play, is the measure of his disillusionment; it accompanies his forgetfulness of the task of revenge, but is at its most intense when he contemplates his own shortcomings – or rather, the human condition, which he sees mirrored in them. There can be no doubting the robust assurance of Luther that 'All heaviness of mind and melancholy come of the devil';[245] but it is not to be contested on the other hand that the diabolical activity is comprehended within the purposes of Providence.[246] It was well understood by Shakespeare's age that melancholy could be the effect of a condition of soul and mind, as well as of body and temperament – that it could arise from spiritual causes, and directly from the will of God. Timothy Bright's declared intention in his treatise is to explain

> what the difference is betwixt naturall melancholie, and that heauie hand of God vpon the afflicted conscience,[247]

and to make clear

> what part nature hath in the tragedy: & what cōscience of sinne driueth vnto. how one nourisheth another.[248]

A man might be afflicted with this disorder for the purpose of his spiritual reclamation, and might suffer by God's consent until such time as,

[244] 'Hamlet's Apostrophe on Man', *P.M.L.A.* LXVI, 1951, p. 1109.
[245] *Table-Talk*, ed. Hazlitt, London, 1883, dcxxxiv.
[246] (Section II, pp. 101–2.)
[247] *A Treatise of Melancholy*, 2nd edn, 1586, sig. *iii.   [248] ibid., sig. *v.

408

*being purified and cleared from that drosse of sinne which cleaveth so
fast, to our degenerate nature, you may make hereafter a more glorious
vessel, for his seruice and honour of his heauenlie maiestie.*[249]

The danger of applying the articles of a medical treatise to the consciousness of a Hamlet must be weighed against that of taking his malady
as necessarily indicating a state of separation from Christian truth and
experience. In what follows, the attempt is not to specify the condition
of his soul, but to consider the possibility of its health. The distinctions
are based on the arguments of Bright, and of William Perkins, the
divine,[250] which are very similar.

The affliction of conscience for sin is held to differ from ordinary
melancholy in that it does not come from 'meere fancy', but is seated in
the conscience.[251] The spiritual malady is due to 'the sight of sinne, and
the sense of Gods wrath';[252] it stems from the true conviction of a separation from Divine favour through an unrighteousness that merits punishment.[253] As Bright states the matter,

> whatsoeuer molestation riseth directly as a proper obiect of the mind,
> that in that respect is not melancholike, but hath a farther ground
> then fancie, and riseth from conscience, condemning the guylty soule
> of those ingrauen lawes of nature, which no man is voyde of, be he
> neuer so barbarous.[254]

Melancholy of the spirit can be present in a healthy body, for its cause
is rooted in the mind; ordinary melancholy can be cured by physical
means, but the healing of an afflicted conscience can only be achieved
by the assurance of God's grace and favour.[255] Whereas ordinary melancholy, since it is caused by physical deterioration, 'happeneth by degrees',
the afflicted conscience 'taketh of a sodaine like lightning.[256] Finally, the
truly melancholic man lives in apprehension of everyone and everything
through a causeless fear, but the sorrower for sin 'hath courage in many
other matters'.[257]

One of these conditions of spiritual vitality, at least, appears to be
fulfilled in Hamlet: his melancholy has come suddenly upon him. It is
also evident that his self-condemnation is not something entirely fanciful,
and thus constitutes 'a proper obiect of the mind'; and whether or not we
can regard him – or he can see himself – as one separated by God's
favour, there is no doubting his soul's conviction of its own unworthiness
and wretchedness, or the exalted nature of the ideal against which so

[249] ibid., sig. iiiiᵛ.
[250] 'The Whole Treatise of the Cases of Conscience', *Works*, 1609, II, pp. 1–176.
[251] Bright, op. cit., p. 183.   [252] Perkins, op. cit., p. 55a.
[253] Bright, op. cit., p. 180.   [254] ibid., p. 187.
[255] ibid., p. 184; Perkins, op. cit., p. 55a.
[256] Bright, op. cit., p. 189.   [257] Perkins, op. cit., p. 55a.

adverse a comparison can be made. And though Hamlet can accuse himself of a constant timorousness, no estimate of him can be true which denies the evidence of courage which the play affords. Amongst Hamlet's fears, that of Divine retribution makes no certain appearance; but the 'dread of something after death', of the ills that might attend him in the 'undiscover'd country', cannot be altogether unconnected with the thought of Divine justice. Allowance must be made for an apprehension of God which, if it be admitted to exist, must be a developing one.

No conclusive proof that Hamlet's melancholy is really sorrow for sin can be gained from comparisons of the type that have just been made. This is the more certain since the authorities of Shakespeare's time are themselves unable to make a final distinction between the two. As Perkins declares,

> And yet howsoeuer they are differing, it must be acknowledged that they may both concurre together : so that the same man which is troubled with melancholie, may feele also the anger of God for sinne.[258]

Bright describes the manner in which the one affliction could merge into the other through the mind's influence upon the body. The 'conscience terrified', he says,

> is of such nature, so beset with infinite fears and distrust, that it easily wasteth the pure spirit, congeleth the liuely bloud, and striketh our nature in such sort, that it soone becommeth melancholike.[259]

It is not impossible, therefore, despite the considerable indications to the contrary, that a natural melancholy is to be conceived as predominant in Hamlet. But it is not to be disputed that melancholic passions, whatever their origin, were for Shakespeare's age a means of putting the soul out of harmony with the body, and of causing a disease which could be the prelude, not only to a better, but to a truer, health. Hamlet's abandonment of the fleshly side of his nature and his absorption in the inner world of his own thinking correspond to the effect of melancholy as Bright describes it. Melancholic passions, he explains,

> depraue the most excellent and perfect actions, whereto the soule is bent in the whole order of mans nature, and by corruption of the Spirites, which should be the sacred band of vnitie, cause such mislike, as the soule, without that meditatiō, disdaineth the bodies longer fellowship, and betaketh it selfe, to that contemplation, whereto it is by nature inclined, and giueth ouer the grosse and mechanicall actions

---

[258] 'A Treatise Tending vnto a Declaration, Whether a man be in the Estate of Damnation, or in the Estate of Grace', *Works*, Cambridge, 1603, p. 435b.

[259] *A Treatise of Melancholy*, 1586, p. 189.

of the bodie, wherto by order of creation, it was allotted in the earthly tabernacle.[260]

Thus even a melancholia whose basis was purely physical might yet provide a means of spiritual advancement.

Amongst those who are most likely to fall into sorrow for sin Bright mentions naturally melancholy and contemplative persons who,

except they be well grounded in the word of God, & remoue not one haire therfrom,

become caught up in mysteries and profundities.[261] Indeed, 'ignorance and infidelitie'[262] is the chief cause of this condition – especially in those

who with neglect of Gods feare and hardnes of heart, against their conscience and knowledge, haue with desperate purpose gathered strength in the waies of sinne, and haue cast off all remorse, till the Lord's vengeance in this sort ouertake them.[263]

But sorrow for sin can also claim the consciences of those whose earnest wish is to live and act righteously,

when the inward feeling thereof doth not answere their desire.[264]

Hamlet would fit equally well into all three categories.

Once the salutary possibilities of melancholy are recognized, however, it would be unwise to pursue analogies with formal treatises. For melancholy and despair are bound to be occasioned in the process of an advance towards spiritual awareness; in such an advance, their sorrows and confusions become the tokens of the error the soul has made in having sought for sublimities in creatures.[265] That there is much of the worldling in Hamlet is evident not only from his dominant wishes, but from his response to other-worldly considerations : the thought of life after death dulls his lively intellect, inspiring him with dread rather than hope, and he can appreciate nothing but his own weakness in the thought that prevents him from destroying himself. The agonizing sense of the wretchedness and transience of mortal life owes its strength in him to the fact that he has been amongst 'such as found the perfection of felicity upon this life', whether placing it in body or mind, in pleasure or in human virtue. His dismay is exactly the conviction of 'the miseries of this life' which Augustine affirms must accompany the vain task of seeking happiness amidst mortality.[266] The apprehension of a 'vicious mole of nature' and the 'o'ergrowth of some complexion' finds its equivalent in the observation that

[260] ibid., p. 38.   [261] ibid., pp. 193–4.
[262] ibid., p. 197.   [263] ibid.
[264] ibid., p. 210.   [265] Augustine, *Conf.* I. xviii. 31.
[266] *De Civ. Dei* XIX. iv.

strength, beauty, health, vigour, and activity, are all subverted by their contraries, by loss of limbs, deformity, sickness, faintness, and unwieldiness. And what if a member fall into some tumour or other disease?[267]

Hamlet's feeling of life's afflictions, of the 'thousand natural shocks /That flesh is heir to', may be compared with the 'many forms and threatenings of death' which, according to Luther, man's miserable nature is doomed to endure,[268] or to the conviction of human frailty which arises in Calvin from the thought that,

If we consider well what the state of our life is: we shall find our selues subiect to a hundred thousand kinds of death, and that wee cannot treade one step, but we shall be wounded.[269]

The ills of human existence that Hamlet longs to 'shuffle off' are such as Augustine pronounces the good man must be ready to endure, without ever finding cause or mitigation in the anomalies themselves:

that he should have joy whose deserts we hold worthier of pains, and he pains whose good life we imagine to merit content: that the judge's corruption or falseness of the witnesses should send the innocent away condemned, much more uncleared; and the injurious foe should depart revenged, much more unpunished; that the wicked man should live sound, and the godly lie bed-rid; that lusty youths should turn thieves, and those that never did hurt in word be plagued with extremity of sickness . . . that the guilty should be honoured, and the godly oppressed, and such like as these; O who can stand to collect or recount them?[270]

But though Hamlet is alive to these evils, he appears to see no spiritual purpose in them. There is no overt recognition that the thousand forms of death which threaten man's life are a punishment of original sin which grace alone may overcome;[271] that afflictions instruct good men in patience, and that disproportion in worldly things is a warning against coveting them; that these crosses exist for the correction of the sins, or the augmentation of the virtues, of the elect.[272] Hamlet's despair betokens the state of a soul 'deprived of its pleasures and afflicted with grief': it is his response to the losing, in fact or in prospect, those 'mutable things which the soul enjoyed or hoped to be able to enjoy'.[273]

Despair must indicate sin to the theologian; yet theology recognizes

[267] ibid.
[268] 'Commentary on Genesis', quoted in *A Compend of Luther's Theology*, ed. H. T. Kerr, Philadelphia, 1943, p. 82. See also *Table-Talk*, cxxix.
[269] *Sermons on Job*, tr. A. Golding, London, 1573, p. 26a.
[270] *De Civ. Dei* XX. ii.
[271] Aquinas, *S.T.* Ia IIae lxxxv. 5, *ad R*; lxxxvi. 2, *ad R*.
[272] *De Civ. Dei* XX. ii.   [273] Augustine, *De Vera Relig.* xii. 23.

412

that despair may exist without unbelief. Despair, Aquinas argues, refers to appetite, unbelief to intellect; and a man can have a right faith in what is universal while failing in an appetitive inclination of the soul.[274] For despair of the creaturely must form part of the process of salvation: it is right that the world should for a time appear to the travailing soul 'like a beautiful flower, but stincking'.[275] The world's oppression must present itself in fearsome manner to the awakened sensibility; for,

> If it were not for that exceeding waight of glory, no other waight in this world could turne the scale, or waigh downe those infinite waights of afflictions that oppresse us here.[276]

The suffering which arises out of the sense of mortal inadequacy and affliction has to do with the health of the soul: 'despair', as Reinhold Niebuhr puts it 'has a greater affinity with repentance than complacency has with faith'.[277] The foolish arrogance of the spirit can only be beaten down, Calvin declares, by that proof of man's frailty which drives him to invoke the strength of God;[278] and the thought is commonplace in Elizabethan devotional literature that God permits his children to encounter evils on earth

> to the end that they dote not vpon a secure estate here, but rather through aduersity and affliction hee maketh them wearie of this world, that they may desire heauen: he maketh them to know themselves to bee but wretched men, as of themselues, and to haue all their helpe from him.[279]

Despair is the cradle of the awareness of God. Shakespeare's age was accustomed to accusations of depravity far more resounding than the accents of a stage-Hamlet, though strongly reminiscent of his own. While admitting his viciousness, Hamlet yet speaks hopefully of grace, and calls for the protection of its ministers; but a Donne in the pulpit can conceive of his imperfections as repelling the Divine mercy:

> Depart, in withholding thy Sacrament, for I am leprous inough to taint thy flesh, and to make the balme of thy blood, poyson to my soule; Depart, in withdrawing the protection of thine Angels from me, for I am vicious inough to imprint corruption and rebellion into their nature.[280]

The appropriateness of these sentiments lies in the fact that the consciousness of sin is at one with the consciousness of God.[281] It is only by

[274] *S.T.* IIa IIae xx. 2, *ad R.*
[275] Sir J. Hayward, *Davids Teares*, 2nd edn, 1622–3, p. 227.
[276] John Donne, *LXXX Sermons*, 1640, lxvi, p. 664.
[277] *Faith and History*, London, 1949, p. 175.   [278] *Inst.* III. viii. 2.
[279] John Norden, *A Pensiue Mans Practise* (1584), 8th edn, 1620, p. 56,
[280] *LXXX Sermons*, 1640, lviii, p. 589.   [281] (Section III, p. 289.)

413

the grace of God that a man becomes aware of the full extent and significance of his unworthiness; and in the very depth of that sense of unworthiness there is a message of rejoicing – for the primary condition of regeneration is being fulfilled in the sinner. To use Donne's own words,

> if this first beame of Grace enlighten him to himselfe, reflect him upon himselfe, *notum facit*, (as the Text sayes) if it aquaint him with himselfe, then, as the creatures in the Creation, then, as the new creatures at Nilus, his sins begin to take their formes, and their specifications, and they appeare to him in their particular true shapes. . . . This is our quickening in our regeneration, and second birth; and til this come, a sinner lies as the Chaos in the beginning of the Creation.[282]

The secular critic tends to see in Hamlet's attitudes of revulsion and of self-reproach no more than

> forms of escape from the difficult process of complex adjustment which normal living demands.[283]

But to the religious consciousness they may indicate that true activity of the spirit that is consequent upon a vision of the flawed and perverse condition of 'normal living', and of its own life. It may discern in the contempt for all creaturely potentialities the achieving of the state of repentance; for repentance can subsist in what Niebuhr has termed

> the simple process of recognizing the problematic character of all human virtues and the ambiguous character of all historic achievements.[284]

The process is as profound as it is simple. The soul's true knowledge of itself leads it to contemplate the goodness of God – indeed, no serious aspiration towards him is possible in the soul's self-ignorance; but on the other hand it is equally impossible for a human self-knowledge to be attained without a prior knowledge of God. As Calvin affirms,

> it is certain that man never achieves a clear knowledge of himself unless he has first looked upon God's face, and then descends from contemplating him to scrutinize himself.[285]

The clear and unrestrained confession by the soul of its inadequacy, which the purport of Hamlet's thinking may be held largely to constitute, must be regarded as 'inspired by that clear idea of absolute good which we know to measure our inadequacy'.[286] Repentance is, by Max Scheler's

---

[282] op. cit., p. 584.
[283] L. C. Knights, 'Prince Hamlet', *Explorations*, 1946, p. 71.
[284] (Section III, p. 293.)   [285] *Inst.* I. i. 2.
[286] M. Scheler, *On the Eternal in Man*, tr. B. Noble, London, 1960, p. 44.

definition, a 'God-intimating function'.[287] Even from the purely ethical aspect, it

> is a form of self-healing of the soul, is in fact its only way of regaining its lost powers. And in religion it is something yet more: it is the natural function with which God endowed the soul, in order that the soul might return to him whenever it strayed from him.[288]

Where repentance occurs in its profoundest form, it must gradually restore to the soul its full capacity for loving God;[289] for that frustrated love of good in itself is part of the soul's true love for the infinitely good. It has to do, not with the quality of past deeds, but with that of past being. As Scheler writes, quoting the dictum of Schopenhauer, 'the deepest state of repentance is not expressed in the formula "Alas! what have I done?" but in the more radical "Alas! what kind of a person I am!" ': it is not a mere *'repentance of conduct'*, but rather a *'repentance of Being'*.[290] The deeply repentant soul, in fact, might well exclaim,

> What should such fellows as I do crawling between heaven and earth?
> (III. i. 127–9)

and, taking regard of the quality of its living, decide it were better if it had never been born. Unlike lesser spirits, it will be able to see in the pains of its tragedy of the present some indication of its spiritual condition;[291] and in this respect it will not be able to persist in self-contemplation, but will see in its own afflictions others' woes, and indeed identify its own state with the condition of the whole race. In Scheler's words,

> Repentance is as fundamentally concerned with our share in all guilt as with our individual culpability; it is as fundamentally concerned with the tragic guilt to which we blamelessly fall a prey as with the guilt which we freely incur; with the collective and hereditary guilt of communities, families, peoples and all humanity as with individual guilt.[292]

The woes of all the world are upon its shoulders, as they are upon Hamlet's; and, like him, it is conscious of itself not only as a sinner, but as a breeder of sinners. The first stage of the soul's evolution in religious consciousness, therefore, is a sense of the partial nothingness and impotence of all relative or creaturely being, and of its own existence as part of such being – the state which Kierkegaard would call man's annihilation. The next stage, however, is an acquiescence in the limitation which first provoked despair, through the avowed recognition of that infinity whose presence to the soul first showed it the inadequacy of its creaturely being – the stage where repentance reveals the God by whom it has been decreed:

[287] ibid., p. 35. [288] ibid., p. 39. [289] ibid., p. 65.
[290] ibid., p. 46. [291] (Section III, pp. 175–6.) [292] op. cit., p. 58.

The second experience, of *createdness* or *creatureliness*, can enter only when we reflect on the positive entity which every thing still *is* and we as men still are – regardless of that partial non-entity and nothingness which we first apprehended in the presence of God . . . 'I am not utterly nothing, but a creature of God' is the sense of the second experience.[293]

After Hamlet returns to Denmark, as Bradley observes, he gives no direct expression to 'that weariness of life and that longing for death'[294] which marked his earlier utterance. There is 'a slight thinning of the dark cloud of melancholy';[295] and it is accompanied by

> a trait about which doubt is impossible, – a sense in Hamlet that he is in the hands of Providence.[296]

This new awareness of createdness or creatureliness, which is coincident with the idea of relationship to a Creator and of a being which is comprehended within His purpose, may be understood as the outcome of a despair which was ever religious in substance, and which has brought its possessor to that knowledge of the Divine being that is the 'second experience' of a true repentance.

In Bradley's view, this new development in Hamlet, apart from appearing to come too late, cannot create in the observer certainty as to its quality, despite its expressing a 'kind of religious resignation'.[297] The same difficulty must always characterize Hamlet's inaction in the task of revenge, which is open to a variety of interpretation. Its possible religious connotation may suggest – without being able in any way to prove – the presence in Hamlet of the charity which is not a natural constituent of the human soul, but can only be infused from beyond it. The fact that alone of the tragic heroes he is unable, despite himself, to dedicate himself to inhumanity – that he manages in the end

> to commit revenge, which is a crime, without ever committing himself to revenge, which would have enrolled him as a criminal[298]–

would suggest that he has been withheld from crossing to the wrong side of 'the great dividing mark' of love, which Augustine declares to be the only final distinction in this world between the sons of God and the sons of the devil.[299] No ultimate distinction between Hamlet and the other heroes is here intended, or could be made; but it is nevertheless to be noted that the love of God by definition cannot dwell in the heart

[293] ibid., p. 167. [294] *Shakespearean Tragedy*, 1956, p. 143.
[295] ibid., p. 144. [296] ibid.
[297] ibid., p. 145.
[298] P. Ure, *Shakespeare and the Inward Self of the Tragic Hero*, 1961, p. 7.
[299] *In Epist. Jo. ad Parth. Tract. decem* v. 7.

of him who 'shutteth up his bowels of compassion' from his neighbour.[300]
In the same way, a religious interpretation of Hamlet's career may postulate in it the activity of that patience of which charity is the direct
cause, but grace the ultimate origin.[301] He is forestalled in the undertaking
of violent actions by undetermined fears and uncertainties, and driven
to the passivity which

> makes us rather bear those ills we have
> Than fly to others that we know not of
> (III. i. 81–2).

The inhibiting of aggressive purpose may conceivably display a patience
susceptible of religious definition. The impatient among mankind, Augustine declares, are those who,

> while they will not suffer ills, effect not a deliverance from ills, but only
> the suffering of heavier ills. Whereas the patient who choose rather
> by not committing to bear, than by not bearing to commit, evil, both
> make lighter what through patience they suffer, and also escape worse
> ills in which through impatience they would be sunk.[302]

A similar possibility of religious explanation attends the process by
which Hamlet is withheld, as distinct from the deeds he is hindered from.
A pragmatic view will attribute Hamlet's inaction, and his own failure to
understand it, to the pressure of certain characteristic emotions, imperfections and uncertainties; but to those for whom the play has profounder
intimations, his failure in a matter of this kind must appear as in some
sense a triumph. Hamlet's unique revulsion from his own corruption of
nature will be seen as bound up with his revulsion from the task of
revenge: both constitute a rejection of the means of evil, and in both
the ulterior significance may be detected that

> it is one thing to be provoked of the flesh, and yet not willingly to
> yield to the lusts and desires thereof, but to walk after the leading of
> the Spirit, and to resist the flesh: and another thing to assent unto
> the flesh, and without all fear or remorse to perform and fulfil the
> works thereof.[303]

The unrecognized forces of resistance in Hamlet may be identified with
'the leading of the Spirit'. After that stage in the soul's development where
a man gains a full knowledge of his servitude to sin, Augustine affirms,
there follows the stage of his being prevented from sinning by the Spirit's
own intervention. If a man has gained God's favour, and trusts in His
help in the fulfilment of righteousness,

---

[300] ibid., v. 12.   [301] Aquinas, *S.T.* IIa IIae cxxxvi. 3, *ad R.*
[302] *De Pat.* ii. 2.
[303] Luther, *Galatians* (v. 19), ed. P. S. Watson, London, 1953, p. 511.

there ensues a lust against the flesh under the stronger power of charity; and thus, although man still experiences resistance from within himself so long as the whole of his sickness is not healed, yet as an outcome of faith the righteous man lives, and lives righteously, in so far as he does not surrender to evil concupiscence.[304]

To those other indications of the operation within Hamlet of a regenerate conscience, his strange inability to 'force his soul so to his own conceit' as to assassinate Claudius may be added. For the regenerate man is distinguished by an inability to act according to his own will, in matters both good and evil. He 'can not sinne at the time he desires to sin', declares William Perkins; and, if he does sin, he cannot do so

> with *full consent* of his will, or with all his heart: because the will so farre forth as it is regenerate, resisteth & draweth backe: yea, euen then whē a man is carried headlong by the passion of the flesh, he feeles some contrary motions of a regenerate conscience.

If he falls into sin, the grace in his heart makes him incapable of persevering in an evil course; similarly, an impotence manifests itself in the attempt to do good, since fleshly encumbrance will ensure that

> he can not doe it perfitly and soundly according to Gods will as he would.[305]

If these considerations may be applied to Hamlet, his inability to sweep to his revenge, and his disgust at his own evil condition, will be shown as all of a piece. The knowledge of his own and the world's corruption, of his incapacity either to set the world to rights or to champion his own cause, and of his growing alienation from the sphere of his own living, must then all appear as prelude to the experiencing of God.[306]

The Divine aid in the achievement of righteousness of living is dependent both on God's favour and on the believer's trust in His help. The former cannot be expressed in dramatic terms – unless Hamlet's entire dramatic career be regarded as evidence of it; and though Heaven's intervention is affirmed by Hamlet in his personal affairs and in man's destiny generally, there is no perceptible appeal to it in the matter of virtuous conduct. But towards the play's end a faith is declared; and the elements of it that are made clear, together with the movements in the direction of spiritual maturity that have been perceptible in his nature, form a sufficient basis in Hamlet for a religious trust. The immediate response to the judgement that he 'lives without faith and dies without

---

[304] *Enchiridion* xxxi. 118.
[305] 'Of the combat of the flesh and the spirit', *Works*, 1603, pp. 570–1.
[306] (Section III, pp. 282–5).

418

hope'[307] must consist in a referring of the criticism concerned to Hamlet's own words: throughout the play he is most forthcoming in speaking his innermost apprehensions, and consistency and commonsense in him and in his critics alike would indicate that he says what he means. Bradley, without condemning Hamlet for masking his failure in piety, finds that he must reject a religious resignation

> which, however beautiful in one aspect, really deserves the name of fatalism rather than that of faith in Providence, because it is not united to any determination to do what is believed to be the will of Providence.[308]

Bradley's saying that we are meant in the play to assume that he ought to have obeyed the Ghost[309] is an assertion which will not admit of proof, and which would produce a peculiar Providence and a Hamlet dressed in the vengeful virtues of Laertes, Fortinbras and Claudius. Without doubt Hamlet at this stage still experiences an inclination towards his purpose, and a weary incomprehension at his failure to carry it out; but the assumption that these things must preclude or invalidate spiritual activity in him would be a large one indeed – especially in view of his showing, in place of his previous determination, a

> sad or indifferent self-abandonment, as if he secretly despaired of forcing himself to action, and were ready to leave his duty to some other power than his own.[310]

Hamlet's inability to take revenge is the outcome of a struggle and involvement with a world which is hostile to his spirit. While the struggle continues, we can scarcely know him – and he can scarcely know himself – as he is: the real Hamlet can be known only at the point where that involvement ends, and the world's claims upon him fade away. As G. Wilson Knight observes, we properly know Hamlet himself only when he is alone with death – when he is at the frontier constituted by the Ghost's sudden appearance before him, by the discourse upon whether to be, or not to be, and above all in his musings in the graveyard. Here, according to this critic, and when he is dying, we glimpse 'the exquisite music of his soul'; and here may be occasioned in the beholder a thought in which death, not life, holds the deepest meaning for mankind.[311] Death is constantly before Hamlet in the play. He himself longs for it as a quietus; and the fact that it is 'as common as the most vulgar thing to sense' is proved to him in the course of events. The consideration of the dust to which the body of Polonius is kin, and the 'little patch of

[307] R. W. Battenhouse, 'Hamlet's Apostrophe on Man: Clue to the Tragedy', *P.M.L.A* LXVI, 1951, p. 1111.
[308] *Shakespearean Tragedy*, p. 145.   [309] ibid., p. 100.   [310] ibid., p. 145.
[311] *The Wheel of Fire*, 1949, pp. 45–6. See Section III, pp. 290–1.

ground' not big enough to receive the dust of those who are to die for it, leads properly to the graveyard scene, with its 'accumulation of images connecting death and dirt'[312] – where the imagined conversion of the noble Alexander's body into loam yields place in Hamlet's mind to the reality of Ophelia's funeral. He who has been tempted to idealize humanity now comes to the place of humanity's annihilation – to the full tragic experience of loss. The unearthly stillness of the corpse of the prating Polonius had earlier impressed him; now he considers the politician's cunning, the courtier's flattery, the lady's beauty and the conqueror's power from the place where all these things have end. The effects of this survey upon his thoughts are noteworthy. He smiles at the subjection to the power of death of one whose worldly purpose had been to 'circumvent God', and at the fate of another who had striven for earthly possessions:

> The very conveyance of his lands will hardly lie in this box, and must the inheritor himself have no more, ha? (V. i. 112–14.)

His derision might almost echo the pronouncement of Calvin, that

> wee haue a gulfe of couetousnesse in vs, so as wee could finde in our heartes to swallow vppe the whole earth. . . . And yet bee wee once deade, wee muste haue no more ground than oure owne lengthe, wherein to rotte and consume away to nothing.[313]

Hamlet's conclusion is that those who 'seek out assurance' in the world's transitory goods are as witless as the 'sheep and calves' whose skins are used for the parchment of their title-deeds. These thoughts upon the evanescence of worldly man and the things he trusts in can appear to the secular critic as 'wistful sentiment and idle fancy'[314] – as one of the tricks that sorrow shoots out of the mind. But a religious judgement will see the deepest meaning for humanity in the thought of death. The attitude of contempt for those who would be 'spacious in the possession of dirt' that comes to Hamlet from the lesson of death is close in spirit to the instruction,

> Lay not up for yourselves treasures upon earth, where moth and rust doth corrupt. (*Matt.* vi. 19.)

The alternative is to raise one's eyes to heaven: the contemplation of mortality, in Christian experience, must point directly towards faith. Nowhere else in Shakespeare does mortality receive so thorough a contemplation.

In Hamlet's preoccupation with the idea that man comes to dust,

312 R. H. Reno, 'Hamlet's Quintessence of Dust', *S.Q.* XII, 1961, p. 107.
313 *Sermons on Job*, 1573, p. 33b.
314 H. Granville-Barker, *Prefaces*, 3rd Ser., 1937, p. 159.

420

R. W. Battenhouse can see neither proofs of holy writ nor the influence of practices traditional in Christendom. The 'fine revolution' that blends the great and the lowly into earthy anonymity and oblivion denotes for him no more than the effect upon Hamlet of cynicism and bitterness;[315] and the quality of mind that must perceive beneath the appearance of woman's beauty the fleshless skull to which its mortality is destined is denounced, and dismissed, as 'the mental savagery of a disillusioned and hurt soul'.[316] Yet both conceptions are familiar in the contemporary pulpit, and are patently admissible as pious rebuke to man's inveterate worldliness. Hamlet's 'revolution' is to all effects and purposes the same as Donne's 'whirle-winde':

> when a whirle-wind hath blowne the dust of the Church-yard into the Church, and the man sweeps out the dust of the Church into the Church-yard, who will undertake to sift those dusts again, and to pronounce, This is the Patrician, this is the noble flowre, and this the yeomanly?[317]

Hamlet's reflection upon the dead lawyer's taking no action of battery against the knave who knocks him about the sconce with a dirty shovel may be compared to Donne's asking his hearers to stand with him by the body of a counsellor, and

> to see that brain produce nothing but swarmes of wormes and no Proclamation to disperse them.[318]

And his 'Now get you to my lady's chamber', in its scornful depiction of putrefaction, is even closer to Donne's accents:

> Those Gummes, and spices, which should embalme thy flesh, when thou art dead, are spent upon that diseased body whilest thou art alive: Thou seemest, in the eye of the world, to walk in *silks*, and thou doest but walke in *searcloth*; Thou hast a desire to please some *eyes*, when thou hast much to doe, not to displease every *Nose*; and thou wilt solicite an adulterous entrance into their beds, who if they should but see thee goe into thine own bed, would need no other mortification, nor answer to thy solicitation.[319]

There is in these considerations not merely disillusionment and disgust, but a recognition of the temporal and inadequate nature of all creaturely good that is the object of man's worldly desires. Of these inordinate loves and desires of sense, Augustine declares, Satan himself is prince; and through them he reigns in man, and takes possession of his heart.

[315] 'Hamlet's Apostrophe', *P.M.L.A.* LXVI, 1951, p. 1098.
[316] ibid.   [317] *LXXX Sermons*, 1640, xv, p. 148.
[318] ibid., xvi, p. 157.   [319] *Fifty Sermons*, 1649, xx, pp. 168–9.

Such are all those who love this world. But the devil is cast out, when with the whole heart renunciation is made of this world.[320]

The thought of man as a quintessence of dust is to be understood as part of the process of renunciation.

The strange transformation and irony that death makes can be seen to effect a 'revolution' in Hamlet's own mind: in some measure it induces a resignation that can only be termed religious. The development is sudden, but not inappropriate in him – particularly since the truth that 'a man's life's no more than to say "One" ' has so lately been impressed upon him. John Donne considered this fact the necessary clue to man's situation on earth:

> the womb and the grave are but one point, they make but one station, there is but a step from that to this.[321]

The realization of life's fleetingness is thus half of humanity's task:

> Those are the two great works which we are to doe in this world; first to know, that this world is not our home, and then to provide us another home, whilest we are in this world.[322]

In his last minutes Hamlet is to be understood as having provided himself with the 'home' and protection of faith. His saying, in face of the danger he apprehends, that

> the readiness is all. Since no man has aught of what he leaves, what is't to leave betimes? (V. ii. 222–4)

may be compared with Augustine's assertion, in distinguishing between the wealth of the Christian and the worldling, that 'we brought nothing into this world, nor can we carry anything out',[323] and Calvin's confidence that God does us no wrong 'to bereaue vs in one minute of an houre' of all earthly good whatsoever.[324] The readiness to accept death at whatever moment it comes may similarly be compared to sentiments in Augustine. The studied indifference of,

> If it be now, 'tis not to come; if it be not to come, it will be now; if it be not now, yet it will come (V. ii. 220–2),

may be found expressive of substantially the same attitude toward death that occurs in the words,

> This I know, that no man is dead that should not at length have died. For the life's ending, makes the long life and the short all one: neither

320 *De Agone Christ.* i. 1.
321 *LXXX Sermons*, 1640, xxvii, p. 268.
322 ibid., lxxii, pp. 735-6.   323 *De Civ. Dei* I. x.
324 *Sermons on Job*, tr. Golding, 1573, p. 34a.

is there one better and another worse, nor one longer, than another shorter, which is not in this end, made equal.[325]

Where all before was searching and doubt, there is now absolute trust. Hamlet's speculative questions 'have been reduced to the practical question of timing';[326] and the completeness of the assurance in a Divinity which pursues its just and benign purposes within man's own is made manifest by an echo from the new Testament which it would be difficult not to recognize:

there's a special providence in the fall of a sparrow.

In these things R. M. Frye, who is opposed to the idea of the theological explanation of this and the other tragedies, finds 'inescapable tokens of faith'.[327] The words speak for themselves; and if they are sincere, they are a confirmation, in the human terms of drama, of the truth that tragic circumstance through its very disharmonies can indicate a necessary harmony in things – that in a Divinely-ordained universe, everything finally 'suggests and proclaims the unity of the Creator'.[328] Hamlet's emergence in spirit from the arena of tragic helplessness that is this world may be seen to be the necessary and ultimate resort of a soul which, seeking a true being amidst the ruins of the idols of its earlier devotion,

turns from its whoremongering in spontaneous quest of its proper object, the idea of God.[329]

That faith in God should come to a nature like Hamlet's is not surprising; theologically speaking, it would be remarkable if such a perceptive intellect should fail to entertain it.[330] That the full awakening of faith, further, should be accompanied by a resignation that is unmistakable and appears to be complete is also entirely fitting; in Calvin's testimony,

we never truly glory in him unless we have utterly put off our own glory.[331]

If Hamlet's professions do not amount to the genuine faith of a Christian, they signify that something remarkable has happened. For evident cynicism and hopelessness have given way to intimations that are positive, and an estrangement of long standing has come to an end: in T. Spencer's estimate, Hamlet 'seems to have come to terms with his world'. He has

[325] *De Civ. Dei* I. xi.
[326] H. Levin, 'The Question of Hamlet', N.Y., 1959, p. 101.
[327] *Shakespeare and Christian Doctrine*, 1963, p. 232.
[328] *De Lib. Arb.* III. xxiii. 70; see Section II, p. 104.
[329] M. Scheler, *On the Eternal in Man*, tr. B. Noble, London, 1960, p. 268; see Section III, pp. 290–1.
[330] (Section II, p. 95.)   [331] *Inst.* III. xiii. 2.

been able to find identity in identifying himself with the order of which he is part:

> He is no longer *in* the tumult, but above it; he is no longer 'passion's slave', but a man who sees himself as a part of the order of things, even though his final view of that order, exhausted, resigned, and in a way exalted, is very different from the youthful rosy picture his Renaissance theoretical education had given him.[332]

The change that has come about is clear in the mood of acceptance – and of some evident exaltation – which it has made possible; and the interpretation that keeps closest to the text of the play must understand that change to consist essentially in a raising of outlook from the human to the divine. That the change, and the pronouncements associated with it, are very deliberately presented by Shakespeare may be gathered from the unoccasioned nature of the conversation that embodies them: it has been noted that Hamlet's waiting with Horatio before the fencing is 'a mysterious moment' having no 'objective correlative'[333] and unaccountable in terms of any situation in the play.

It might possibly be argued that, although the effects of a certain degree of assurance are making themselves felt in Hamlet towards the end of the play, they lack the serenity and amplitude that would be required by the category of faith. Yet faith in the lives of the majority of believers does not transform the conscience into a monolith of repose, but is rather an intimation of comfort that persists despite the constant assaults of the negative and the contradictory. Calvin, while of necessity teaching that faith ought to be 'certain and assured', must confess that 'believers are in perpetual conflict with their own unbelief'. The true substance of faith is to be sought in its tenacity rather than in its repose in the human spirit:

> He who, struggling with his own weakness, presses toward faith in his moments of anxiety is already in large part victorious.[334]

In similar manner Luther speaks of the two sorts of sacrifice that the spirit of man may offer towards its God. The first consists in fervent praise and witness; but the second occurs

> when a sorrowful and troubled heart in all manner of temptations has his refuge in God, calls upon him in a true and upright faith, seeks help of him, and waits patiently upon him.[335]

If this is the type of Hamlet's approach to his Creator, the reality of the assurance he finds is not to be doubted: his is then the offering of the

---

[332] *Shakespeare and the Nature of Man*, 1943 p. 108.
[333] R. H. Reno, 'Hamlet's Quintessence of Dust', *S.Q.* XII, 1961, p. 107.
[334] *Inst.* III. ii. 17.   [335] *Table-Talk*, tr. W. Hazlitt, 1883, cv.

troubled spirit, and the broken and contrite heart, that will not be despised.

A faith so grounded would not only help to explain the distance from past attitudes, but would also have reference to the impression of 'some forcing of his disposition' which the critic may gain from the Hamlet of the present. But if Hamlet's declarations are true, these changes of attitude are not to be considered simply in terms of the wishes or the character of him who entertains them. Faith in man is to be seen primarily as the work, not of a human power, but of a God who

> devises meanes, that . . . those whom sins, or death had banished, be not expelled from him.[336]

One of those Providential means is adversity, the bitter-sweet bringer of the self-knowledge which is at one with the knowledge of God;[337] but what enables men to walk by faith while they are as yet unable to walk by sight is properly to be attributed to the direct influence of the Holy Spirit. The God of faith is one who 'also helps those who do not help themselves in order that they may help themselves': His grace is ever to be thought of as prevenient to the creating of a good will in man.[338] It may be that we are meant to see in Hamlet's change of attitude the operation of Divine power; and in that event the advice which Timothy Bright gives to those who have been overtaken with melancholy is to be noted, that

> the spirit worketh without our leaue, and acquainteth vs not with his maruelous working more then is expedient at his pleasure.[339]

The change effected by the working of grace may be mysterious to the individual who is its subject, since, according to Aquinas, no one may have perfect assurance that he is its possessor.[340] And, human limitation and ignorance in matters spiritual being what they are, the effect of God's power upon it will be sudden: the justification of the godly 'takes place in an instant'[341]– or, as Luther puts it, 'there is no beginning, except where the king enters and is proclaimed'.[342] In more modern terms, it has been said that the highest forms of realization are not the result of human intention or calculation, but are rather the product within the human of a gracious movement or process

---

[336] LXXX Sermons, 1640, xxxi, p. 311.

[337] Raleigh, History, 1614, Preface, sig. D.

[338] Augustine, Retract. I. xiii. 4, 5, quoted by C. N. Cochrane, Christianity and Classical Culture, 1940, p. 453.

[339] A Treatise of Melancholy, 2nd edn, 1586, p. 226.

[340] S.T. Ia IIae cxii. 5, ad R.

[341] ibid., cxiii. 7, ad R.

[342] 'Gospel Sermon, First Sunday in Advent', quoted in A Compend of Luther's Theology, ed. H. T. Kerr, Philadelphia, 1943, p. 106.

which draws the self out of the self despite itself into the love of God and the neighbour.[343]

Hamlet's religious assurance and declarations, in their novelty and their suddenness alike, may readily be interpreted as in accord with a Christian understanding of man's striving towards God and of the effect of God's hand being laid upon him. If Hamlet's state fulfils the conditions of disillusion with idols and attainment of the soul's true spontaneity in the quest of being, then God must be with him 'as promptly as only He can be, who was already there',[344] and his spirit must necessarily attain

at one and the same moment, in an *indivisible and indestructible unitary experience*, to its substance in *God*, while in it the reality of God as a person becomes simultaneously discernible.[345]

It is therefore possible for the change in Hamlet to be 'out of character' while in keeping with his experience; but the possibility is unknown to the secular critic. Granville-Barker seems to attribute to the effects of strain the 'contempt for his own subtle brain and once devious ways' implied in Hamlet's trust in a divinity that directs human life,[346] and exclaims, at his seeing a special providence in the fall of a sparrow,

It is to no more than this, at the last, that the subtly questing mind has come.[347]

Hamlet appears to abandon the rationality he has prized; but this abandonment – if he has undergone a conversion bringing him into the Christian fellowship – is more apparent than real. For the rational, in the Christian understanding, is at its most supreme where it makes way for the Divine, and thus attains its true substance and validity.[348] The act which constitutes beatitude for our mortal natures, declares Aquinas, since it is a kind of participation in the perfect beatitude, belongs to the contemplative rather than to the rational.[349] In the same way, Calvin affirms that the knowledge coincident with faith is far above the sense-perception to which human rationality is necessarily limited:

For faith is so far above sense that man's mind has to go beyond and rise above itself in order to attain it. Even where the mind has attained, it does not comprehend what it feels. But while it is persuaded

343 R. Niebuhr, *Faith and History*, London, 1949, p. 198.

344 S. Kierkegaard, 'Man's Need of God Constitutes his Highest Perfection', *Edifying Discourses*, tr. Swenson, Minneapolis, 1950-3, IV, p. 43.

345 Max Scheler, *On the Eternal in Man*, tr. B. Noble, London, 1960, p. 28; see Section III, p. 277ff.

346 *Prefaces*, 3rd Ser., 1937, p. 166.

347 ibid., p. 172.

348 (Section II, pp. 125–28.)

349 *S.T.* Ia IIae iii. 5, *ad R*; E. Gilson, *The Philosophy of St Thomas Aquinas*, tr. E. Bullough, Cambridge, 1924, p. 262.

> of what it does not grasp, by the very certainty of its persuasion it understands more than if it perceived anything human by its own capacity . . . the knowledge of faith consists in assurance rather than in comprehension.[350]

Grace, which makes possible the recognition of unity between the individual consciousness and the external order in the process of creating unity between the soul and God, is a matter of direct experience, not discursive reasoning – of instant realization, like a child's awareness of its own consciousness and self-consciousness.[351] And the completed knowledge of God, which vigorously lays hold upon Him, is not a flight from reason to credulity, but a movement away from its own autonomy by a reason adhering to the principle of both its origin and true function, and becoming thus the soul's proper instrument in its will to submission and obedience to the Divine will.[352] It is not without significance that Dr Johnson should detect in Hamlet's trust in the Providential governance of the rashness of human acts 'a reflection upon the weakness of human wisdom':[353] Hamlet's relinquishing his pride in a creaturely rationality points to his attaining the stage where, the thought of God being established in him,

> *in the necessitie of this infinite power, all the reason of man ends and dissolues it selfe.*[354]

Hamlet's forsaking of creaturely reason expresses itself in resignation before a Providential destiny. According to K. Muir, the play itself exemplifies the constant opposition of the two themes of Fortune and Providence;[355] and Hamlet's uncompromising resolution of the matter provides a further confirmation of the reality of the faith which so moves him. Events in man's world, declares Calvin, must appear fortuitous,

> since the order, reason, end, and necessity of those things which happen for the most part lie hidden in God's purpose, and are not apprehended by human opinion.[356]

But if, to the conscience of faith, God's activity is evident in all happenings: if every success is God's blessing, and calamity and adversity are His curse, there can be no place now remaining for the purely contingent; and

[350] *Inst.* III. ii. 7.
[351] C. N. Cochrane, *Christianity and Classical Culture*, 1940, pp. 502–3.
[352] See R. E. Cushman, 'Faith and Reason', *A Companion to the Study of St Augustine*, ed. R. W. Battenhouse, N.Y., 1955, p. 310.
[353] *Johnson on Shakespeare*, ed. W. Raleigh, 1957, p. 194.
[354] Raleigh, *History*, 1614, Preface, sig. *D*3v.
[355] 'Shakespeare and the Tragic Pattern', *Proc. Brit. Acad.* XLIV, 1958, p. 151.
[356] *Inst.* I. xvi. 9.

'fortune' and 'chance' are pagan terms, with whose significance the minds of the godly ought not to be occupied.[357]

To a Christian persuasion, as Sir Thomas Browne observes, 'there is no liberty for causes to operate in a loose and stragling way';[358] and Hamlet's assertion of a special providence in the fall of a sparrow, taken together with his other references to the Providential direction of human affairs, must be taken as a statement to the same effect. The tendency of critics to quote Matthew's gospel as the source of this speech is objected to by Battenhouse as follows:

> But this is quite misleading. For the context of Jesus' utterance is that man is of 'more value than many sparrows', and needs therefore not fear to depend on God in seeking his end in God's Kingdom, since even the sparrow depends on Him while seeking its end in nature only.[359]

Whether these words assert that *Matthew* x. 29–31 is not the source of Hamlet's observation, or are intended to indicate a sparrow-like inclination or destiny in Hamlet, is not clear; it is more likely, however, that they show a mind's reluctance to being led in a direction it does not wish to go. The purport of Hamlet's words can be none other than confidence in the Providential ordering of mortal happenings. The thought that not an insignificant sparrow falls to the ground without conformity to the Divine will can have only one conclusion for the human understanding: in Calvin's words,

> Surely if the flight of birds is governed by God's definite plan, we must confess with the prophet that he so dwells on high as to humble himself to behold whatever happens in heaven and on earth (*Ps.* cxiii. 5–6).[360]

Hamlet's trust in Providence is therefore to be understood as belonging to that satisfaction of desire in the soul which betokens its homecoming in God – the recognition by the soul, at the journey's end, that it is God, and not itself, which has guided all its steps, and that all its steps have led it to Him.[361]

That this recognition is present in Hamlet in its fullness may be judged by the peculiar quality of his trust. For in it lies not only conviction, but repose. The true knowledge of God, Calvin affirms, is to know him both as the maker and as the ruler of the world,

> and further to know the nature of that direction. He does mercy and judgement and justice.[362]

---

[357] ibid., I. xvi. 8.   [358] *Religio Medici*, ed. G. Keynes, 1928, I, p. 28.
[359] 'Hamlet's Apostrophe', *P.M.L.A.* LXVI, 1951, p. 1101.   [360] *Inst.* I. xvi. 5.
[361] R. Hazleton, 'The Devotional Life', *A Companion*, ed. Battenhouse, N.Y., 1955, pp. 408–9.
[362] *Commentaries*, tr. Haroutunian, L.C.C. XXIII, 1958, p. 126.

The earlier apprehension of God startles and terrifies the human conscience through the very interposition of majesty and righteousness;[363]
but that sense of the Divine wrath and disfavour yields, upon the coming
of the Holy Spirit, to a new sense of God's graciousness, under which
mans' heart can become both 'happy' and 'bold'.[364] In Luther's words,

> That means to know God aright, if we apprehend him not by his
> power and wisdom, which terrify us, but by his goodness and love;
> there our faith and confidence can then stand unmovable and man
> is truly thus born anew in God.[365]

If the agonized apprehension of his unworthiness is deemed evidence of
the work of a spiritual principle in Hamlet, the comfort which the knowledge of his 'createdness' now brings may likewise be seen to point to a
certain maturity of spirit. It may be regarded as little short of that 'confidence of heart' in which Calvin would place assurance of the soul's
election.[366]

Such intimations of the spiritual as reach Hamlet, Battenhouse declares,
constitute 'only the shell of faith and none of its substance'.[367] The impression is created that nothing short of a recital of the Apostles' Creed by
the hero of this play would settle the critic's apprehensions; and yet, even
if great drama could yield place to the directness of 'eternal blazon', such
a recital would in itself denote no more than a knowledge of the Apostles'
Creed on the part of him who uttered it. In the criticism of great drama,
it is the quality of human personality which must tell; and it will do so
by bodying forth the ultimate in the human, not through the employing
the human to define the ultimate. But the question may be put, by
contrast, whether Battenhouse in his criticism is not himself applying the
shell of faith to the substance which Hamlet's career represents. For the
reality of faith lies in the experiencing of God, not in the formulations
by which the human intellect seeks to define the experience. In trying to
determine the reality of Hamlet's declared faith predominantly by the
measuring-rod of formal theological concept, Battenhouse is not only led
to forsake the dramatic which is the only basis of criticism, but tends to
neglect the experience which is the only basis of the conceptual – in
comparison to which, indeed, the conceptual, for all its impressiveness, is
a mere shell. The strict and consistent application of human definition
to intimations of the transcendent involves the danger of subjecting them
in their surpassing liveliness to considerations static and academic, and of

[363] Luther, 'The Babylonian Captivity of the Church', quoted in *A Compend*, ed. Kerr,
Philadelphia, 1943, p. 98.
[364] 'Gospel Sermon, Pentecost Sunday', quoted in *A Compend*, p. 67.
[365] 'Gospel Sermon, Good Friday', quoted in *A Compend*, p. 55
[366] *Inst.* III. xxiv. 7.
[367] 'Hamlet's Apostrophe', *P.M.L.A.* LXVI, p. 1110.

limiting the imagination's ability to see the growth of faith as the direct creation of God's Spirit within the recalcitrant spirit of man. Through his reliance upon definition rather than upon experience Battenhouse may be thought to position himself nearer the manward than the Godward end of the scale of operations;[368] and, while reproving Hamlet for his humanism, to reveal himself as the greater humanist of the twain. For Hamlet, despite his unexampled individuality and his embodiment of the humanist culture of the Renaissance, is to be regarded as a man more acted upon than acting: Dr Johnson's observation, that

> *Hamlet* is, throughout the whole play, rather an instrument than an agent,[369]

may be understood to apply most fully in the realm of the spirit. In *Hamlet* we have a rare, if not unique, phenomenon: a great play

> in which the fire and illumination that is the essence of religious experience becomes the central force,[370]

in a soul which, like most of mankind, is naturally impelled to the mundane. It is both cause and condition of the play's greatness that it should adhere to the common experience of mortality, and thus contrive to convey through the reticent and the negative the message which proclamation must, in the terms of great drama's existence, destroy. To the heart of worldly man it speaks all that it is able; and the rest is silence.

[368] See Section I, p. 58.
[369] *Johnson on Shakespeare*, ed. W. Raleigh, 1957, p. 196.
[370] Una Ellis-Fermor, *The Frontiers of Drama*, 1945, p. 5; see Section I, p. 57.

Conclusion

CONCLUSION

The discussion of literary problems with which this study began made apparent the difficulties in the way of a theological interpretation of Shakespearian tragedy. The basis for a theological criticism has however appeared, and the essays on *Macbeth, Othello, King Lear* and *Hamlet* are offered as evidence of its feasibility. Whether this kind of criticism, however cogent in itself, can merit acceptance as true literary appreciation would appear to depend upon its fulfilling certain conditions.

The first of them must concern the simple issue of the necessity of a religious approach to drama, and centre upon the reader's response. A theological assessment of tragedy, by whatever methods it is carried out, will be valid if its perceptions and judgements appear more incisive, profound and just, in their application both to the drama's detailed unfolding and to the wider significances which it evokes, than those attainable by a secular criticism. It must be able to bring into relation to itself, and to sustain, the findings of other categories of appreciation, and to give evidence, in cases of disagreement, of superior penetration. Not a jot or a tittle of what is substantial in a worldly appraisal is to be changed, far less distorted; and unless it can enhance meaning in a consciousness that has full recourse to secular judgements, it will have failed to justify its existence.

A second condition applies to the mode of application of theological insights to the study and evaluation of drama. Since the function of great tragedy is to make evident the natural human condition, and since the dramatic is by its inspiration averse to the conceptual, no criticism can be other than misleading which tries to found itself upon a framework of theological concept it contrives to distinguish within the play. Nor can a true appreciation result from the attempt to relate a play to some scheme of ultimate value outside it, on the basis of conceptual notions appearing, or judged to appear, within its tragic world. The beginning of a theological interpretation must not lie in formal pronouncement within the tragedy, but rather spring from the immediate apprehension of the mind which experiences it: only a living dramatic truth can usher in and entertain a theological one. The religious insights, therefore, must come not from the formulations of the intellect, but from the testimony of

433

the heart: it is not a conceptual theology, but rather a theological awareness, which must inform the conscience of the critic. Instead of applying
the terms of an abstract scheme, he must experience the tragedy in the
knowledge that he and his thoughts are comprised within that universal
order in which the playwright and the spectator, and the endeavours and
imaginations of both, are also involved – an order which will dictate the
terms and happenings of human life, and which infuses all thought and
art. He must see the theological potential of tragedy in its ability to reveal
the terms of that system as they appear to the secular consciousness of
man, and to show in the process the situation which man's soul must
transcend with the gift of power from above.

A further condition arises from the outcome of a theological interpretation of the tragic world – from what interpretation of this kind has power
to reveal. Here lies what is perhaps the greatest problem: for the truth
that comes to light is in large part a bitter and unwelcome one for mere
humanity. Man's characteristic affirmations have to do with what may
be called the pride of life: his energies and his hopes alike derive themselves from the visible glories and the assumed validities of his creatureliness and all its achievements. But theological interpretation of the tragic
scene must afflict and unnerve him; for

> Those mortall formes, moulded of humane error,
> Dissolve themselves by lookinge in this mirror.[1]

This type of criticism must make it possible for the reader not only to
find identity as a member of a fallen and self-worshipping generation,
but to conceive of every hero of great tragedy as an Everyman manifesting
in his own existence the whole effect of man's life without God – the
coveting of the journey rather than the return home. The tragic hero will
appear as a dweller in the outer darkness of inordinate desire, locked in
conflict with the errant wills of his fellows and with the compulsions his
own mind cannot master. In him, the virtues of an unregenerate conscience will turn to ashes; the wish of the incomplete to live according
to the idea of its completeness will be shown in its absurdity; and a trust
in things mutable and impermanent will enter upon its merited sorrow.
Beneath the apparent tragedy will be discerned the essential tragedy of
the soul's forsaking and being forsaken by the means of health and wholeness. The heroic endeavour will be transformed into the spectacle of self-
love declining upon limited good in the compulsive seeking of a mundane
omnipotence. What appeared as greatness in the protagonist will declare
itself the adjunct of 'an idolatry of some aspect of himself';[2] and he who

---

[1] Fulke Greville, 'A Treatise of Religion', st. 107, *The Remains*, ed. G. A. Wilkes, 1965, p.
229.

[2] R. W. Battenhouse, 'Shakespearian Tragedy: A Christian Interpretation', *The Tragic
Vision and the Christian Faith*, ed. N. A. Scott, N.Y., 1957, p. 84.

outwardly receives access of being, in truth will be known to have embraced a death-in-life. That pride, which in a mortal word is

a sinne of the soule, which is not seene and perceiued of any, but of God onely,[3]

will have become an open secret. And, like the hero, the reader will be summoned from the vain and defeated joys of creaturely assurance toward the surpassing happiness of creaturely submission to the eternal. Unless, therefore, a theological criticism can relate the tragic scene to the universal theatre of existence in the reader's consciousness, and constrain him to accept that vision in its compelling truth, as he would accept the presented vision of drama itself, it will have failed in its object and thrown doubt upon its own validity. And this necessary condition it must meet in the midst of its sensitive appraisal of the thought, word and act of drama's human pattern.

What is required of this kind of criticism in greater degree than is required of most others is therefore a genuine imaginative power. But, also unlike other criticism, it must found all it has to say upon two assumptions that are quite incapable of proof, the one regarding the universal scheme of being as it is known to human experience, and the other regarding its Author. The attitude of the theological critic toward his world must be that 'Whatsoever is, is good'.[4] This is a certainty that is normally beyond the approach of unaided reason and possible only to faith, to mysticism, and to the mystical reaches of poetry. But its intimations need not be unknown to the humble playgoer. The pleasure that is felt in the witnessing of literary tragedy, and the mood of enraptured acceptance that flourishes amidst its desolating conclusions, may well be thought part of

> that blessed mood,
> In which the burthen of the mystery,
> In which the heavy and the weary weight
> Of all this unintelligible world
> Is lightened : – that serene and blessed mood,
> In which the affections gently lead us on, –
> Until, the breath of this corporeal frame
> And even the motion of our human blood
> Almost suspended, we are laid asleep
> In body, and become a living soul :
> While with an eye made quiet by the power
> Of harmony, and the deep power of joy,
> We see into the life of things.[5]

[3] Robert Allot, *Wits Theater of the little World*, 1599, fol. 242.
[4] Augustine, *Conf.* VII. xii. 18.
[5] Wordsworth, 'Lines composed a few miles above Tintern Abbey'.

Together with the goodness of Creation is to be assumed the truth of Scriptural revelation, and the existence of a God who not only is, but whose gracious immediacy to the human spirit is a source of challenge, of comfort and of transformation to beings who are otherwise condemned to seeking a blessed life in the land of death. The theological interpretation of tragedy is a sophistry of deception if Kierkegaard's affirmation is false:

> O God, who art unchangeable, Thou art always and invariably to be found, and always to be found unchanged. Whether in life or death, no one journeys so far afield that Thou art not to be found by him, that Thou are not there, Thou who are everywhere. . . . And whenever any human being comes to Thee, of whatever age, at whatever time of the day, in whatever state: if he comes in sincerity he always finds Thy love equally warm, like the spring's unchanged coolness, O Thou who are unchangeable.[6]

However, if this testimony is indeed untrue, tragedy itself must appear as the faithful mirror of the deceptive appearance and true emptiness of life itself.

If there is a God, criticism cannot do full justice to what tragedy reveals without bringing a theological awareness into interpretation. Neither, it is believed, will theological criticism do justice to the tragedy if it fails to observe the conditions which have been stated. But just as human life need not, and generally does not, show forth the transcendental amidst the temporal, so a finality of understanding is not a manifest requirement of the interpretation of tragedy. Patterns of judgement of a secular kind are available for both areas of experience, and are valid and salutary within the scope and quality of the imagination which uses them. But to the mind of faith literary tragedy brings a message of joyous prophetic affirmation through the instrumentality of the very condition that imposes limitation upon its creatures. In its shattering of all mortal confidence, tragedy witnesses to the human spirit concerning a means of deeper assurance. It declares to every sort and condition amongst mankind:

> Then man! Rest on this feelinge from above,
> Plant thou thy faith on this celestiall way.
> The world is made for use; God is for Love;
> Sorrowe for sinne; knowledge, but to obay;
> Feare and temptation, to refine and prove;
> The heaven, for joyes; Desire that it may
>> Finde peace in endlesse, boundlesse, heavenly thinges;
> Place it else where, it desolation bringes.[7]

[6] 'The Unchangeableness of God', *For Self Examination*, tr. W. Lowrie, Oxford, 1941, p. 240.
[7] Greville, 'A Treatise of Religion', st. 114, ed. cit., p. 231.

436

Appendices

Appendices

Appendix A

HISTORICAL PROCESS AND
THEOLOGICAL CONSISTENCY

It is very tempting for the critic undertaking a theological interpretation of tragedy to see himself as applying standards which are timeless and constant to the form of art which more than any other demonstrates the unsureness of all that is mortal. Drama has to do with what is subject to time while theology exists by virtue of what is beyond it; yet the ultimate, to a Christian understanding, does not involve remoteness and inaccessibility, but reveals itself within temporal experience. A man has a poor conception of the Eternal, declares Max Scheler,

> if, merely grasping its contrast to the flow of time, he is unable to hear the soft voice of eternity in the most momentary demand which is made on the individual in the here and now. For, rightly conceived, the eternal is not sealed away from time in a simple juxtaposition : it timelessly embraces the content of time and its fullness, pervading each of its moments.[1]

But theology, however it be related to the eternal, is in no way to be identified with it; if the substance of its vision is changeless, the formulations which convey what is apprehended, and the mind which apprehends, remain within the province of the temporal, and are caught up in its fluctuations. In this respect there is no difference between theology and other intellectual achievements : it shares in

> the possibility of genuine evolution and growth, likewise genuine retrogression and diminution, of the rational human mind *in history* . . . because certain of the essential insights by whose functionalization its progress is controlled are attached to this or that particular locus in the concrete world-process and possible only at those points.[2]

Theology thus partakes of the ephemeral; and, equally, a particular age may succeed in penetrating to the ultimate in a manner which it is not open to another age to emulate. Considerations such as these, no less than

---

[1] *On the Eternal in Man*, tr. B. Noble, S.C.M. Press, 1960, p. 12 (Preface to the first German edn).   [2] ibid., pp. 206–7.

the abiding nature of the truth each age seeks to explore, constrain philosophers 'to discuss their problem, so to speak, *in common*', in a manner that is unknown to the scientist.[3] Despite differences of idiom, form and emphasis from age to age, therefore, and in one sense because of them, the truths of theology are more readily available to a gaze which sweeps across the centuries :

> it is in the very nature of the realm of essences and man's path of access to it that all philosophy, and even reflexive knowledge of the idea of the divine received in the religious act, is in general only possible through the *concert of peoples and ages* in the transactions of philosophy.[4]

The present study's seeking to arrive at a Christian estimate of the human condition by reference to the dominant thinkers of different ages may therefore be considered appropriate.

With such discursive reference as this, there is the danger that differences of concept and emphasis may be overlooked and agreement too readily assumed. But in the experiencing of God, which is the beginning of theology, there may be recognized a principle making for consistency, in that, while acting within man as a constituent of his being, it arises in its entirety from what is outside him, and thus must have salutary bearing upon his formulating of religious experience in any epoch. Just as the possession of word and reason is what first makes us man, Scheler writes, so

> man's connection with the divine through the religious act and divine manifestation is an inherent element in *essential human nature*[5]–

though it is possible for man to repudiate these native means of religious awareness. Through the religious act he is aware of an entity revealed to his consciousness in its attributes of absolute being and holiness; and in the sense of the impotence and the creatureliness of all relative being, including his own, which is present to his mind in the religious act lie reactions to the Divine reality which are open to observation.[6] Whatever his level of religious development may be, a man's religious experience is in origin utterly different from his experience of the empirical world, and can be derived from it neither through inference nor idealization;[7] however much it may be empirically occasioned, it is always negatively characterized by being as groundless as it is aimless :[8]

> In 'religious' hope we hope for something we have never experienced and of which we know that we *could* never have experienced it, and

---

[3] ibid., p. 207. [4] ibid., p. 208. [5] ibid., p. 174.
[6] ibid., pp. 163, 166. [7] ibid., p. 173. [8] ibid., p. 253.

we fervently hope what we hope, though there is within us no well-grounded confidence, founded in our calculation of earthly chance or prompted merely by an instinctive blind trust in life, that events will supply the substance of our hopes.[9]

The conclusion is, then, that despite the fact that his religious capability is integral to his creatureliness, only a real being with the essential character of divinity can be its cause.[10] From its world-transcending intention, which can only be fulfilled by the Divine entity which first revealed it, the basic principle of religious cognition holds good, that all knowledge of God is knowledge from God.[11] Religious faith, therefore, is best understood as self-identification with an object.

> The personality senses that the very nucleus of its existence and value is bound so closely to the object of faith that it is 'pledged' to that object, identified with it, as we say. 'I shall exist and have worth, and *wish* to exist and have worth, only in so far as thou, object of faith, art and hast worth' or 'we two stand or fall together' – these expressions render into words the relationship in which the person feels that it stands to the object of its faith.[12]

Man's awareness of God and approach to him, though a creaturely possession as it is a creaturely need, derives wholly from the realm of the eternal; and to the extent that theology devotes itself to making manifest what is both endowment and experience in man, it will retain an element that is constant from age to age.

Since the theologian and his work are both subject to historical process and all the subtle influences which create history and give direction to the human mind, theology experiences many of the historian's difficulties in the attempt to reach finality of statement. But the historian's quest of an estimate of happenings that should be fixed and timeless is made possible by the fact that his discipline is not evaluative in the final sense – that his concern is with the occurrence, and not with the approval of it: the theologian, on the other hand, is aware of a Divine initiative and control in history which an historical assessment cannot but falsify, and whose significance his own formulations must increasingly fall short of rendering with the passage of time. It must be the theologian's conviction, nonetheless, that the exalted wisdom which employs history's social and economic pressures to subject theology itself to the process of mutability does so with the object of remanifesting the same truth in accordance with the same purpose; and his work is therefore to be judged by its success in rationalizing religious experience so as to render it accessible

9 ibid., p. 252.   10 ibid., p. 261.   11 ibid., p. 250.   12 ibid., p. 268.

to his own generation.[13] In this task he is helped by the fact that the historical events relating to the Gospel are not mere occurrences embodied in time, but also realities which are continually being manifested in recurrent human situations.[14] They are part of the Divine absolute; but everything else, including the characteristic emphases of his own work, must share the relativity of the human condition. Unless it does so, indeed, his work cannot achieve its purpose. For the value of theological statement lies in an admissible subjectivity; that is to say, in its power to evoke the response of the human heart, to plumb the depths of what makes man most truly himself.[15] The terminology, idiom and concepts of theology may therefore differ from age to age; but the purpose it serves, the experience it sets forth and the predominant need to which it ministers do not alter.[16] From this it must be concluded that the theologies of different ages are most likely to be in accord where their formulations are not considered for what they are in themselves, but rather in their relation to that dynamic of man's need and recognition of God from which they have derived their existence. The attempt has accordingly been made in this study to view the theology upon which it is based from that point of apprehension of an ultimate order which it is believed literary tragedy constitutes.

It has been made in the belief that the human condition itself, which tragedy illuminates and to which theology bears a strict relation, also retains a constant identity within the process of flux of mortal affairs. Man, who creates history, is enabled through his freedom in some sense to transcend the temporal process; but he is himself subject to development through history because the incalculable extension of human power in the world which is its medium helps to create the very necessity he must serve.[17] The problem of how the freedom of human agents is related to historical change beyond the power of the human will is in Christian thinking resolved by a Providential mystery presiding over the world and time: the otherness of God at once validates history and man's rôle within it, giving aim to the freedom of which he is the possessor, and resolving the apparently anomalous within a unity which is to be perceived by faith alone.[18] Thus, while man and history are in process,

> there is a perennially valid truth in the Gospel which clarifies a perennial human predicament.[19]

The belief that the development of man's capacities radically alters the human situation is, according to Niebuhr, an exaggeration of the degree

[13] B. M. G. Reardon, 'History and Theology', *Anglican Theological Review* XLV, 1963, pp. 381–2.
[14] ibid., p. 383.   [15] ibid., p. 386.   [16] ibid., p. 387.
[17] Reinhold Niebuhr, *Faith and History*, London, 1949. p. 39.
[18] ibid., pp. 42, 55.   [19] ibid., p. 38.

of increase of creaturely freedom typical of human pride in any age, and most typical of modern times.[20] But

> Though all human capacities are subject to development and the cultural achievements and social institutions of mankind are capable of an indeterminate development, the extension of human power and freedom in either individual life or in the total human enterprise does not change the human situation essentially. Man remains a creature of nature on every stage of his development. There are certain bounds of finiteness which no historical development can overcome.[21]

Thus, although man may himself change, and change may occur within his mortal situation, the situation that is essential in his creaturely need for God does not alter. It has been the purpose of this study to investigate the human condition in its appearance, within both Christian theology and literary tragedy, as the unchanging basis of all human endeavours towards God.

The search for God amidst a process of unceasing change may be regarded as a condition of ultimate constancy in human experience. Man is the victim of process; but God in his eternity is the author and sustainer of process in his Providential purpose : change is the law of God – conceivably lest the human mind should undergo stagnation through one good custom's dominance. The challenge that existence makes to the human spirit may with theological and existential warrant be described as the search for the immutable – for true being – by the possessors of a limited being within a realm of evanescence :

> God is unchangeable. In His omnipotence He created this visible world – and made Himself invisible. He clothed Himself in the visible world as in a garment; He changes it as one who shifts a garment – Himself unchanged. . . . In each moment every actuality is a possibility in His almighty hand; He holds all in readiness, in every instant prepared to change everything : the opinions of men, their judgements, human greatness and human abasement; He changes all, Himself unchanged.[22]

Thus man may appear a different creature in different ages, or else as the same creature reacting to different problems in a different manner, but always with the unchanging task of realizing the being and seeking the presence of the God behind the phenomena. In the eternity and

[20] ibid., pp. 17, 96.   [21] ibid., p. 79.
[22] Søren Kierkegaard, 'The Unchangeableness of God', *For Self Examination*, tr. W. Lowrie, Oxford, 1941, pp. 230–1.

omnipotence of this God will lie the true and only hope of his mortal existence; for

> No matter how short we may fall, we can never frustrate His purpose, and despite the inescapable perpetual perishing which characterizes the temporal flux, nothing cherished is ever lost, for every accomplishment of value is contained forever in Him as an actualized fact.[23]

The supreme task for mankind, as Kierkegaard expresses it, is to attain to an understanding with a God whose unchangeable will it is that every human being should come to know Him and to fashion his life in accordance with an immutable purpose.[24] The religious experience is the ultimate experience for a dweller within the ephemeral, for it is the one which plucks him out of change; but it is also a seeking and an encounter that is most solemn and frightening to a mere creature.

> If then your will is not in harmony with His will, consider that you will never be able to evade Him. Be grateful to Him if through the use of mildness or of severity He teaches you to bring your will into agreement with His – how fearful if He makes no move to arrest your course, how fearful if in the case of any human being it comes to pass that he almost defiantly relies either upon the notion that God does not exist, or upon His having been changed, or even upon His being too great to take note of what we call trifles! For the truth is that God both exists and is eternally unchangeable; and His infinite greatness consists precisely in seeing even the least thing. . . . But then it is also true that *there is rest and happiness in this thought.* It is really true that when, wearied with all this human inconstancy, this temporal and earthly mutability, and wearied also of your own inconstancy, you might wish to find a place where rest may be found for your weary head, your weary thoughts, your weary spirit, so that you might find rest and complete repose : Oh, in the unchangeableness of God there is rest![25]

The foregoing study has been undertaken in the belief that within the tragic situation man's need for God is at its height, and God's closeness is most evident to man's spirit – whether it be the temporal tragedy mediated by the human condition, or the literary tragedy which is eloquent of that condition. It is held that there may be apprehended on the tragic stage a situation of constancy which exists amidst the flux of events in the world of temporal sequence; and that there, more than

---

[23] B. L. Clarke, 'God, Time and Human History', *Anglican Theological Review* XLV, 1963, p. 372.
[24] op. cit., pp. 231–2.   [25] ibid., pp. 235, 237–8.

in any other realm of man's experience, the literary imagination may be at one with a theological awareness.

A problem not unlike that of the attaining of finality in theological formulation exists in the endeavour toward a definitive interpretation of drama, in that appreciation is very strictly subject to all the changes which take place from age to age. Both disciplines seek to reveal higher significances to their times and to gain the profoundest of responses from man's being; and both centre upon what is elemental in his condition. From drama may be gained certain instinctive assurances concerning the permanence of human emotions and creaturely experience amidst the processes of temporal change : what appear to be differences in man and his condition are here often revealed as the product of essentially the same forces working in different contexts. And drama is able by the transmuting force of imagination also to transport the beholder into a bygone age : the spectator or the imaginative reader has, by the end of the play, in some sense lived in another epoch, breathed its air and rubbed shoulders with its people – no matter what subsequent interpretations or rationalizations he may put upon their actions and motives. Yet, as Miss Helen Gardner has pointed out, the affirmation that 'All good art is contemporary' needs to be balanced by the realization that 'All art, including contemporary art, is historical'.[26] For drama, perhaps more characteristically than other art, is the product of time.

The overriding importance of imaginative response to drama, however, places difficulties in the way of historical assessment. Tragedy presents to the imagination an exceedingly complex process, and interpretation depends upon subjectivity to a significant degree. As L. Abercrombie has stated the matter,

> To limit interpretation to what the play may have meant to Elizabethans is, frankly, to exclude the existence of the play as a work of art; for as a work of art it does not exist in what it may have meant to someone else, but in what it means to me : that is the only way it can exist.[27]

The difficulty arises, therefore, that while drama can only exist in minds historically conditioned and is to be experienced only in terms of that conditioning, its total meaning cannot be analysed historically despite the fact that it is approached in the continuum of history. Its

[26] *The Business of Criticism*, Oxford Paperbacks, 1963, p. 17.
[27] 'A Plea for the Liberty of Interpreting', *Proc. Brit. Acad.* XVI, 1930, p. 163, quoted by L. C. Knights, 'On Historical Scholarship and the Interpretation of Shakespeare', *Sewanee Review* LXIII, 1955, p. 230.

essentially extra-historical nature is attributed by Miss Gardner to the fact that

> it is the expression and creation of a human mind and personality and so is ultimately irreducible into anything but itself. The mystery of the survival of works of art brings one face to face with the mystery of the human personality.[28]

For Abercrombie, the existence of a work of art has spiritual rather than material connotation, for it comes into being out of the experience it continually creates;[29] and, according to M. Bewley, the experiencing mind's act of apprehension 'itself may constitute ontologically a part, and perhaps a large part, of the truth'[30] which an artistic work reveals.

To achieve a fully objective evaluation of drama, let alone a strictly historical one, is not possible. The varieties of interpretation which may exist within a single critical approach is in itself warning enough. When it comes to the point, therefore, the critic must look into his conscience and assert – he must, in fact, follow the advice which Luther gives to the experiencing Christian, and which the poet can give to himself. He may be able to feel so imaginatively at one with a work of another age as to be able to declare that

> The same life has clothed itself in different garbs; the same passions have spoken in different images;[31]

or he may on the contrary feel that only through a disciplined effort of the historical imagination can the assumptions of a mind of one age come to life in the mind of another. If imaginative identity between the different ages is at all conceivable through the medium of drama, it would appear most likely of attainment in the profoundest of its forms, where the human mind has in all the ages surveyed its mortal condition and the needs that arise from it.

[28] op. cit., p. 20.
[29] op. cit., p. 163, cited by Knights, op. cit., p. 232.
[30] *The Complex Fate*, 1952, p. 182, quoted by Knights, op. cit., p. 234.
[31] H. J. C. Grierson, *The Poems of John Donne*, 1912, vol. II, p. vi, quoted by H. Gardner, op. cit., p. 31.

Appendix B

THE INTERPRETATION OF TRAGEDY THROUGH CHARACTER

'The calamities of tragedy do not simply happen', A. C. Bradley wrote in 1904, 'nor are they sent; they proceed mainly from actions, and those the actions of men'. There was of course more to the story of a Shakespearian tragedy than human actions or deeds, but deeds were predominant in it; and they were deeds in the full sense of the word, being 'acts or omissions thoroughly expressive of the doer'. The conclusion which determined his approach to Shakespeare's plays was therefore that the centre of tragedy

> may be said with equal truth to lie in action issuing from character, or in character issuing in action.[1]

This conviction enabled Bradley to interpret the dramas by the principal method of treating their heroes as if they were living persons, and to seek the cause of disaster in the depth of the personality revealed in them. Yet his acute responsiveness to the dramatic helped to obscure a tendency which might otherwise have marred his interpretation: for – by Aristotelian standards – he was ostensibly giving major importance to what is a secondary principle in drama.

The dramatic character, according to Aristotle, exists not for his own sake, but primarily to speed the play's action; and the tragic hero necessarily stands in relation to the progress and the end of the action which reveals, tests and destroys him. Human character cannot be an end in itself, since its dramatic function is to be a means:

> character determines men's qualities, but it is by their actions that they are happy or the reverse. Dramatic action, therefore, is not with a view to the representation of character: character comes in as subsidiary to the actions. Hence the incidents and the plot are the end of a tragedy; and the end is the chief thing of all.[2]

To hold up for discussion the character of the heroes in isolation from event, as if the dramatic action had been suspended, would thus be to

---

[1] *Shakespearean Tragedy*, pp. 11–12.   [2] *Poetics* vi.

found criticism upon a false premiss, and to separate from the action what is in fact inseparable from it. But the action of a play as Aristotle defines it is inclusive of moral choice in the human agents of tragedy : character in the terms of drama itself lies for him not in personal qualities but in personal volition. Will, which forms the action and relates to its end, is of the essence of drama, whereas the appearances of personality are not.

In the drama of life, as Christian philosophy has interpreted it, the same degree of primacy has been accorded to human volition. Man is properly constituted neither by his intellectual powers nor by the complex of attribute and emotion which appears as character, but by the will's operation : the nature of personality is determined by the nature of the end to which the soul is striving. And since creaturely impulsions and external influences alike can prevail only through the consent of the will, and will's primacy is exercised in the soul's seeking for truth, it follows that what appears as personality, though it is expressive of the soul, has no reality in itself, and is meaningful only as it indicates movement towards an end. The will's relationship to the ultimate end of truth and God is determinative of character; and the essence of character is to be sought in the state of the will.[3] It has therefore been considered appropriate in a study linking the tragic and the theological that interpretation should proceed primarily by reference to the will of the tragic hero to the extent to which it may be ascertained through what has been termed character and action. This means that the heroes must be considered as persons, though the ultimate concern is not with personality; and it means also that character, through which the state of the will is approached, is, as expressive of will, a proper and valid object of critical appraisal.

For, as Bradley asserted, character in great drama does issue in action; to say character is not real in the sense of its being an artistic contrivance or agency is in fact to say no more than that there is nothing real in art itself, and that all apparent artistic liveliness is

> a false creation,
> Proceeding from the heat-oppressed brain.

What cannot be denied is that an impression of the liveliness and consistency of human personality is conveyed by drama; and the question is whether something that is so necessary and integral to the dramatist's purpose is to be disregarded. So to disregard it would be to do violence to the conditions of dramatic art, and blind oneself to its very operation. A 'decisive natural touch' that reveals the blending of character and action which is at the height of dramatic achievement is instanced by

[3] (Section III, pp. 214–5.)

J. Lawlor. Following upon his eavesdropping, Othello's angry certainty of Desdemona's unfaithfulness reaches the point of his striking her in Lodovico's presence. Now if ever, Desdemona must speak; but the play's action cannot admit expression on her part. What she does say is 'I have not deserved this' and 'I will not stay to offend you'; and she leaves Othello commenting ironically on her 'obedience', being now once more the master of the situation. Desdemona's 'obedience' at this uncertain moment, Lawlor declares, is not an attribute fastened upon her by a dramatic opportunism, but a consideration central in her nature, her love and her previous actions:

> 'Obedience', a deft touch that eases the fabric of the play at a point where the first assault is made upon a hapless victim, reveals a sure and steady hand. It is a natural touch, making a whole world kin; here, as throughout, the region of Shakespeare's consistent design and the wide area of our accidental, unpatterned experience are at one.[4]

Plot and character grow into a rich and strange unity.

It may be objected to the intensive study of character that it disrupts the priorities of a just appreciation. As Miss Ellis-Fermor observes, although the plot is by Aristotle's definition the first essential of drama, the common reader 'appears to reverse this order and approach instinctively through character'.[5] Once this order is reversed, declares R. Langbaum, the emergence to prominence of parts of a play which before were subordinated to unity destroys the play as an entity by violating the principles which relate events and characters to one another and to the whole. The logic of events themselves is annulled; and an upstart and 'unconditional sympathy to sheer vividness of character' robs much else of the sympathy that is its due. Indeed, sympathy becomes 'a law unto itself' apart from the play, and drama declines into dramatic monologue.[6] The possibility here set forth does exist, and the charge against criticism by character-appraisal is serious; but it could be more readily sustained if a play's events were not both created and interpreted through character, and if events by themselves were not inconceivable. The substantiality of character, far from denying reality to the plot, rather confers reality upon it; indeed, as has already appeared, Shakespearian tragedy is constructed upon the imagination of its hero, the logic of the action giving place to the primary need that the audience should share in the protagonist's experience.[7] Through this sympathetic identity Shakespeare is able to present the play's small universe of apprehension; and as meaning

---

[4] *The Tragic Sense in Shakespeare*, 1960, pp. 104–6.
[5] *Shakespeare the Dramatist and other papers*, ed. K. Muir, 1961, p. 21.
[6] 'Character Versus Action in Shakespeare', *S.Q.* VIII, 1957, p. 68.
[7] Una Ellis-Fermor, 'The Nature of Plot in Drama', *Essays and Studies* XIII, 1960, pp. 78–9; Section I, pp. 69–70.

is created and conveyed, so the heroic personality grows more distinct. How is it possible, in the circumstances of the theatre, for the beholder to stop himself responding to 'vividness of character'?[8] If he were able to do so, it would be in reproof of Hippolyta's reaction to the misfortunes of Bottom's Pyramus: 'Beshrew my heart, but I pity the man' (V. i. 288). The spectator, being subjected to an appeal that is purely imaginative, precisely does not distribute his sympathy systematically to every feature of the play. Sympathy will reach out to what occasions it; and it will be occasioned chiefly by personality. Nor is this surprising, in view of the fact, which Lawlor affirms, that the tragic artist's consistent aim is 'that the spectator should identify himself with the tragic hero'.[9] This identification is possible only where dramatic personality is received as real during the suspension of disbelief which is necessary for the full appreciation of the tragedian's art; and in no other way than by using the understanding of motive and behaviour gained from contact with personality in the everyday world can the emotions and deeds of a play's characters be interpreted by audience or by reader.[10] For them as for the mind which created the tragedy, the action which issues from character must be the basic element in drama.

It is possible to contradict this view through reference to the literary genesis and historical evolution of personages in Elizabethan tragedy – to the fact that criticism must sometimes be dealing not so much with character as with literary type. Thus the 'motiveless malignity' of an Iago has been explained in terms of the debt to his predecessor the Vice, and to the embodiment of the medieval tradition of the living metaphor into the *dramatis personae* of Elizabethan times.[11] Iago so considered needs no motivation for his enmity to what is lovely and of good report in mankind. This type of objection certainly applies to characterization in lesser drama, and to many characters who serve a stylized function in great drama; whether the same may be said of what a Shakespeare makes of an Iago is more doubtful. The literary type exists by virtue of a fundamental truth to nature within the limitation of art, and it may serve as well as anything else for the starting point of a creative imagination. The character-type may be in origin a mere personification or metaphor; but the human personality itself may develop toward a living metaphor, becoming the embodiment of a recognizable quality through the constraint of choice or custom. Ordinary experience must show that there is such a thing as an evil, or a covetous or wrathful man, and that such a person will display in himself a caricature of which life itself is

[8] R. Langbaum, op. cit., p. 68.   [9] op. cit., p. 59.

[10] V. Y. Kantak, 'An Approach to Shakespearian Tragedy : the "Actor" Image in *Macbeth*', S.S. XVI, 1963, p. 43.

[11] See B. Spivack, *Shakespeare and the Allegory of Evil*, N.Y., 1958, pp. 130–205; 415–53.

the artist. All art, and dramatic art particularly, must simplify and to a degree distort in order to capture reality; and the dramatist can derive from many realms of inspiration that vision of a personality in activity through which dramatic character makes its appearance. Where personality is so conceived, it is the vitality rather than the logic that is of the strictest account : it is the conviction of life which a dramatic character gives, rather than its possession of acceptable motive, which in the first instance qualifies it for the demands of great tragedy. The full depth of motive, indeed, can be no more exhibited in the swift passages of drama than they can in those of real life; but, like real life, drama provides the means whereby it may be inferred and understood, the imagination of the great playwright comprehending a wealth of human possibility. In Maurice Morgann's words,

> he boldly makes a character act and speak from those parts of the composition, which are *inferred* only, and not distinctly shewn.[12]

An absolutely motivated dramatic character could scarcely appear as a living one; and motive is subordinate to personality on the stage. The forms of literary tradition, therefore, may be quickened into life within the creative imagination; and wherever personality exerts its power upon the stage, it must be responded to.

There exists a type of critical sensibility which declines to surrender itself to the fascination of what is, like everything else in drama, literary artifice : the appearances of living character in the persons of a play, it affirms, cover a harsh reality of mere dramatic convention. With such determined objectivity there can be no discourse; but the same does not apply to the objectivity of approach which can point to varying degrees of evident inconsistency in the greatest of Shakespeare's characters. The prosaic fact that a Cleopatra goes through a process of ennoblement during the play does not preclude development in accord with a higher consistency of character; but demonstrable self-contradiction, in which a character's actions appear to belie his own nature or beliefs, is something of a very different order. The presence of this type of evident inconsistency in Shakespeare's heroes is to be admitted; but the consideration must at the same time arise whether they thereby appear less or more like real people. Thus for example the high degree of valour and imagination in Macbeth are, in K. Muir's estimation, sufficiently strong against the deed of Duncan's murder as to call in question veracity in Shakespeare and identity in Macbeth;[13] and A. P. Rossiter, finding it inconceivable that a man should commit a deadly sin in defiance of the clear and

[12] 'An Essay on the Dramatic Character of Sir John Falstaff' (1777), *Shakespearian Criticism: A Selection*, ed. D. Nichol Smith, 1953, p. 171.
[13] *Shakespeare : The Great Tragedies*, Longmans, 1961, p. 35.

powerful testimony of his conscience 'simply because he cannot endure to be called a coward', is driven to denying the entire conception of dramatic character. Macbeth and his wife, he declares, are

> parts of a pattern, a design : are images, are symbols; and while a human being cannot simultaneously be full of the moral awareness of evil *and* fully engaged in doing it, wholly aware that the only motive he can offer himself is inadequate, those symbols we call *dramatis personae* not only *can* be, but must be, if the full weight and pressure of their acts are to be felt by the readers' or audience's minds.[14]

Inconsistency, be it real or apparent, must of course point to the overall possibility of dramatic character's being without true substance. Whether in fact our senses are deceived by a literary magic or our minds intoxicated by poetry's *vinum dæmonum* into false apprehension of personality is a matter of assertion rather than of proof; but if from an ultimate point of view deception takes place, it would appear to matter little whether it come through a 'character' which is really a symbol or a symbol masquerading as 'character'. As to the immediate question, however, provided only that drama is allowed its latitude for demonstrating the significances of life in the process of its action, Rossiter's major premiss may be challenged. If men's actions did not habitually flout their better knowledge and conscience there would be no tragedy. Is it remotely possible to deny that those who do evil do so against their deeper awarenesses, and can go about their purposes only by closing their minds to the truth? What applies to real life becomes clearer in tragedy. The self-edifying scorn which enables Lear to blind himself to Cordelia's constancy of nature and to the harshness of his own dealings within the bounds of a telling speech –

> Better thou
> Hadst not been born than not to have pleas'd
> me better
> (I. i. 234–5) –

reveals by its very emphasis the underlying recognition of both these facts which is soon to express itself in the words,

> I did her wrong
> (I. v. 24).

The presence of inconsistency in Lear and Macbeth no more removes them from credibility than it does from humanity. It is for critics to learn – as many indeed have – that in Shakespeare there is

> no such thing as a fixed and thoroughly consistent character;

[14] *Angel with Horns*, 1961, p. 217.

452

that his characters, in the manner of all true personality,

> look at themselves as something strange and unknown, wondering what they themselves actually are, searching for causes and motive and not finding any.[15]

This observation of Clemen's does not only tend in its accuracy to sustain the concept of dramatic character in the heroes: it asserts the primacy of volition in the personalities that great tragedy sets before us. Actions, it is clear, are not merely the logical outcome of a particular cast or type of temperament as the playwright conceives it. Rather than specific qualities giving rise to actions in the hero, it is from will and deed that his qualities emerge into definiteness.

It is a very far cry from the charge of inconsistency to that of significance; but the latter has also been urged against the credibility of dramatic character. According to D. G. James, Shakespeare's overriding concern in his characterization is 'to exhibit certain moral ideas or states'.[16] It is not to be wondered at, in terms of this reasoning, that an Iago is motiveless: he has been made so, in the course of

> a poetical experimentation with life by the creation of extreme simplicities of both good and evil.[17]

The old Morality, far from being dead, survives into Shakespeare's greatest work to become 'a powerful instrument of discovery'; and what seems like personality really exists 'at the very limits of the human' in characters which

> reach beyond flesh and blood to brilliant spiritual significance.[18]

The life of a Cordelia is life drastically simplified, if not dehumanized, for the task of showing forth a surpassing truth. She and her sisters, far from having grown out of a preceding human situation,

> flare out and occur as the eternal powers which play for mastery in the human soul.[19]

Since they are the embodiment of spiritual forces, the characters tend to detach themselves from the plot and its exigencies. The unexplained silence of Kent makes clear the irreconcilability of the two; and the hesitancy of Cordelia, which brings down disaster, or the silence of Edgar, which heaps misery on himself and his father, are indications that their characters are part of the play's design 'to exhibit suffering and helpless virtue'. Harley Granville-Barker's comment that, after the third act of

[15] W. Clemen, 'Shakespeare and the Modern World', *S.S.* XVI, 1963, p. 58.
[16] *The Dream of Learning*, 1951, p. 116.
[17] ibid., p. 85. [18] ibid. [19] ibid., p. 103.

King Lear, 'the best will be incidental and not germane to the actual story', is held to confirm that Shakespeare is contemplating in Cordelia and Edgar 'figures of spiritual perfection' who cannot move at this level of the play's working.[20] A similar position is taken by I. Ribner, who argues that the characters of *Macbeth* are not shaped primarily to conform to a psychological verisimilitude, but rather to make explicit the intellectual statements with which the play is concerned in a function which is really choral and symbolic. The illusion of reality with which Shakespeare endows them serves merely to give emotional statement to these higher truths, and it is therefore futile to seek in them for such a thing as motive.[21]

The argument that dramatic characters exist in order to embody spiritual truth, and that in this function they must become dehumanized and unreal, cannot be confined to the literary. Literature is drawn from life; and human thoughts and actions are fraught with spiritual significance, if we have perception enough to see them. The pastime of dancing can reveal to the poet's eye the underlying harmony and joy of the created universe;[22] and the love of parent for child may teach mankind at large of the love of God.[23] Human conduct in high and low is expressive of transcendent meaning; and to a theological vision men and women indeed are the centres for 'the eternal powers which play for mastery in the human soul', what appears as motive in them being in reality subordinate to the manifesting in human terms of spiritual principles and agencies. To 'reach beyond flesh and blood to brilliant spiritual significance' is the making, and not the disabling, of humanity : and there can be no life in a Divine universe which is not in some sense 'choral and symbolic'. If the earthly ministry of Christ is in any way a guide to man's condition, his personality becomes more clearly symbolic of spiritual truth as it becomes more essentially human.

This of course is to deal with the objection on the theoretical level; but it is perhaps best answered by its own practical consequences. If a play is viewed strictly in terms of allegedly higher significance, the immediate dramatic significance by which it is constituted must fail in forcefulness and appeal. Thus, in Ribner's analysis of *Macbeth* according to its 'total conceptual pattern', the escape of Fleance is a representation of the truth that 'evil can never destroy the ultimate promise of good', and Lady Macbeth's suicide a reminder that 'evil inevitably breeds its own corruption' : in their actions these personages are, like 'Lazarus in the painted cloth', emblems suitable for embellishing a text. So are they in themselves. Malcolm is a mere portrait of an ideal king, while Macduff,

[20] ibid., pp. 107–13. Granville-Barker, *Prefaces*, First Series, 1949, p. 151.
[21] '*Macbeth* : the Pattern of Idea and Action', *S.Q.* X, 1959, p. 151.
[22] Sir John Davies, *Orchestra*, 1596.   [23] *Matt.* vii. 11.

despite his appearance as a fallible but good and brave man, is the personified nemesis of Macbeth's own evil. Banquo is a dramatic demonstration of the ordinary humanity which Macbeth must endeavour to destroy within his own nature; and Lady Macbeth, as the counter to Banquo, exists that her husband – if this is the correct word – may be placed between the representatives of good and evil like a Morality hero. Her reference to her children is 'a ritual statement'; but it is strange, in view of the symbolic function of her character, that she should be favoured with such a remark as,

No more than Macbeth can lightly break his bond with humanity, can his wife escape the woman in her.[24]

The last comment demonstrates that, despite the wealth of symbolic meaning the play supposedly embodies in its characters, a criticism which discounts or dismisses personality dismisses the essential means of judgement. The way to a play's meaning is to be sought through – not despite – what it presents to the beholder's imagination. All manner of impressions and profundities will arise to the experiencing consciousness, for life and the drama that reflects it in special intensity naturally suggest them. But the impressions of the theatre arise from the adequacy, and not the inadequacy, of the concept of personality which appears in it – and from everything else that is dramatically expressed and conveyed. That our imaginative involvement in the appearances of life is the condition for the apprehending of higher truth in drama is the theme of an article by V. Y. Kantak. He writes:

It is true that the characters are not 'real', but part of Shakespeare's artistry lies in convincing us that they are and in getting us emotionally involved with them. The symbolic function they seem to perform in the over-all pattern of the play does not exist independently. We have to create it in our minds by entering fully into the real lifelike situation of character and action.[25]

Thus the assertion that it is 'confusing real life with drama'[26] to credit Macbeth with the flights of poetic imagination that are really Shakespeare's own is to be countered with the fact of its being Shakespeare's aim in the theatre to produce this confusion, and the resulting impression of personality. And the occasional existence of a play's characters in some evident independence of the plot is not, as D. G. James takes it to be, a token of their unreality, but rather tends to denote their supreme

[24] op. cit., pp. 152–4.
[25] 'An Approach to Shakespearian Tragedy : the "Actor" Image in *Macbeth*', *S.S.* XVI, 1963, p. 44.
[26] K. Muir, ed., Arden edn, 1951, Introduction, p. lix.

importance for the play. To invest the main characters with a choric function, as Miss Ellis-Fermor has noted, may help to achieve a play's balance, especially in its creation of an 'inner action' made up by the apprehensions and attitudes of the characters' minds:

> The thought-world of Cordelia or of Kent has relatively little effect upon the course of those events in *King Lear* that are shaped by and shape the other characters; but it is of immense effect in our final impression of the universe revealed by the play.[27]

A certain non-realistic function in the characters of a drama does not automatically render them unreal, but only demonstrates that drama as a literary form is unreal in the sense that it is not ordinary life.

Personality must exist before it may symbolize. It is possible to contend that Shakespeare's predominant concern was with the ethical and metaphysical dimension that tragedy reveals; but to argue that in consequence Shakespeare's concern for character and its consistency must have waned is to assume that these significances can be contemplated apart from the mental experience of dramatic personality through which they are mediated. But this process of the mediation of larger awareness through personality is the condition of dramatic experience. As Kantak argues, it is through the dramatic personality's conflict with the forces of some ultimate dimension that the tension can be created from which tragedy itself is born:

> The moral order is there, but something has to run counter to it to produce that tension.[28]

The same perception leads A. Sewell to declare that character and moral vision must be apprehended together, and that 'when character is understood separately from moral vision it is in fact not understood at all'.[29] There is in each tragedy a conflict between metaphysical vision and the world of everyday; in personality the conflict is localised, and by personality higher truth is defined and interpreted: our concern in Lear, for example, is

> the manner in which, even in his madness, he addresses himself to the universe, and the manner in which, in that address, the universe is seen anew.[30]

All characters in tragedy are thus part of a metaphysical order, each play being a specific vision, and each character having his special address to the world.

It is through this interpretive function of character that will and choice

---

[27] *The Frontiers of Drama*, 1945, p. 132–3.   [28] op. cit., p. 44.
[29] *Character and Society in Shakespeare*, 1951, p. 59.   [30] ibid., pp. 84–5.

assume primary significance. From the very necessities of the dramatic action there must exist the 'free-will' which denotes the activity of choice – for, as J. Lawlor observes, 'drama is a doing'. Verisimilitude in character likewise must require scope for volition, for 'choice is proper to man; not to choose is not to be'. But it is from the will's essays into the medium of human existence, its seizing upon what is beyond it and its grappling with what is hostile to it, that any higher meaning is to be apprehended. It is this absolute need which imposes upon the writer of great tragedy the conditions which relate to the essence of personality:

> firstly, the character must be introduced as a particular sort of chooser, one more disposed to certain choices than to others: and secondly, he must be established as such, given a past field of choice in the evidence of confidants, acquaintances and the like, from whatever stand-point . . . they speak.[31]

In drama as in life, it is through the will's spontaneity that personality consists, and the contingent is transcended. This truth is not present to the minds of those who see dramatic character as a mere literary device, or as the rendering of the limited attributes of an earthbound creature. A view too restricted, as Miss Ellis-Fermor has argued, must tend altogether to disqualify dramatic character.

> The naturalists, in attempting to persuade us that a character in a work of art is a character in nature, lost touch with the deep, hidden wells of reality from which imagination draws its life, and the shallowness of their resultant rendering has at last forced itself upon our notice. And from this we unjustifiably conclude that 'character' in drama must always and necessarily be illusion. . . . Whereas, in fact, it is the great poetic dramatists whose sure, unerring technique alone makes character revelation possible, because it alone finds anything to reveal.[32]

Personality is not conveyed to us by a consideration of motive, or by a process of strictly rational appraisal: a great dramatic speech of one of the heroes works upon us

> not through our judgement but by direct appeal to that vast, hidden imaginative self which it alone can reach . . . such moments are the meeting-grounds of passion and inchoate thought that overwhelm characteristics and resolve the individual man into the eternal, the universal, the generic.[33]

[31] *The Tragic Sense in Shakespeare*, 1960, p. 112.
[32] *Shakespeare the Dramatist*, 1961, pp. 25–6.
[33] ibid., p. 31.

These words may be held to confirm a view of personality which regards it not as a matter of creaturely attribute and peculiarity, but rather as bound up with the end toward which the will is striving along a road which all men must travel in common. This concept, and Miss Ellis-Fermor's own in as far as it shares its emphasis, does not submerge individual difference and identity, but on the contrary provides it with the force by which it may assert itself. The passionate seeking by the tragic hero's will does at first seem to render void all the distinctions that exist between man and man :

> What we have here is the deep working of a half-hidden and half-articulative motive such as, in ourselves and other men, seems to overwhelm individuality. . . . Yet . . . the individuality is not utterly obliterated. Riding the torrent it cannot stem, it survives into a measure of choice, and what follows, in its action and thought, will have a power withheld in art or life from the 'character' that is rooted in its own consciousness.[34]

The verisimilitude and truth of dramatic character, and the truths that are bound up with its experience, have their origin in the will's dynamism within the life the play bodies forth.

It is this fundamental veracity, indeed, that makes it possible for great drama to be conceived. For its greatness is at one with its nearness to what is essential in human experience; and, as J. Bayley affirms,

> an author's love for his characters is a delight in their independent existence *as other people*, an attitude towards them which is analogous to our feelings towards those we love in life; and an interim interest in their personalities combined with a sort of detached solicitude, a respect for their freedom,[35]

such as we entertain for our friends. Modern criticism tends to discount even the possibility of this kind of relationship between an author and the persons created by his own imagination; it assumes instead that the author is 'a dictator rather than a constitutional monarch',[36] and that he will subordinate the individuality of his characters to the general atmosphere and purpose of his work. As an example of modern critical scepticism Bayley cites L. C. Knights's well-known article, 'How Many Children Had Lady Macbeth?'; but the question contained in the very title, in Bayley's opinion, testifies to Shakespeare's success

> in conveying the wider consciousness of his major figures as well as their dramatic and functional personality. There is a sense in which

34 ibid.
35 *The Character of Love*, 1960, p. 7.
36 ibid., p. 36.

the highest compliment we can pay to Shakespeare is to discuss his great plays as if they were also great novels. Of either the Ancients or the Moderns, observed Dryden, Shakespeare had the largest and most *comprehensive* mind, and one can be sure that somewhere in that mind the problem of Lady Macbeth's children would find its appropriate resolution.[37]

Thus A. C. Bradley's original question is justified; and the legitimacy of his considering the tragic characters as if they were real people is apparent in the fact that although his critical premisses are not today respected, his critical perceptions still are.[38]

According to Bayley, four distinct approaches to the characters of drama are possible. They may be treated as persons met with in real life or in the novel; or as pieces of dramatic and ethical convention; or as serving a dramatic function in relation to the plot; or as the embodiment of the metaphysical ideas of good and evil. The diverse possibilities of approach are a warning to us of the disproportionate havoc that may be caused by a judgement which is inadequate and unequal to the limitless clarity of Shakespeare's imagination. The articulation between the four *personae* may be occasionally disjointed, and they may not smoothly intermingle; but of the approaches, the first – 'the conventional and naturalistic idea of character' – is the master. For Shakespeare's characters have 'a richness of selfhood which is both inexhaustible and immediately recognizable': even from those lesser ones who speak only a few lines we learn 'far more than their dramatic status seems to require'. And in the great characters we may see a process of life itself in what Bayley calls the 'inside and outside effect', which is used to present

the subtlest kind of dramatic conflict – the conflict between the undefinable interior man and the *persona* that is required of him by society, or imposed on him by his own will.[39]

The true interpretation of great tragedy can only come through the consideration of what the play mainly presents to the beholder. The critic who seeks to plumb the depths of meaning can do no better than to concur in the judgement of Dr Johnson, and all that is implied in it, that Shakespeare is

the poet of nature; the poet that holds up to his readers a faithful mirrour of manners and of life. . . . His persons act and speak by the influence of those general passions by which all minds are agitated, and the whole system of life is continued in motion . . . it may be said, that he has not only shewn human character as it acts in real

[37] ibid., p. 42.   [38] ibid., p. 41.   [39] ibid., pp. 43–5.

exigencies, but as it would be found in trials, to which it cannot be exposed.[40]

In the fullest sense of which it may be said of dramatic creation, Shakespeare is the creator of character and personality; and the limitation of imaginative response to the personality which tragedy shows forth is nothing less than a disregarding of the tragedy itself.

[40] 'Preface to Shakespeare', 1765, *Johnson on Shakespeare*, ed. W. Raleigh, 1957, pp. 11–14.

Appendix C

THE INTERPRETATION OF TRAGEDY THROUGH POETIC IMAGERY

It has been for some time a dominant trend in Shakespeare criticism to approach the plays through the medium of their imagery. Their appeal to many critics, indeed, has appeared to lie not so much in their being drama as in their being a complex of poetic symbolism. The advice of G. Wilson Knight that the interpreter should 'see each play as an expanded metaphor'[1] has been taken to heart by the modern generation of critics; and one of the most distinguished of them speaks of something which has found wide acceptance in referring to 'the large metaphor which is the play itself'.[2] A definition in these terms will receive qualified acceptance from those whose approach is through the dramatic. Thus Miss Una Ellis-Fermor can acknowledge the work of imagery in increasing dramatic concentration, strengthening emotional experience, defining thought and event, creating mood, suggesting an accompanying universe of thought and experience, and making possible the rapid and significant revelation of character. But in all these functions the contribution of imagery is, for her, that it 'helps drama to overcome the limitations inherent in its brevity'.[3] It is a major element in a play; but it is neither the play's end nor its essence.

Certain advantages in the critical study of imagery are at once apparent, but the reality of what they contribute to assessment is not beyond question. J. Lawlor has argued that examination of imagery can make good the deficiencies of theatrical production, in that our imagination is 'given its true object';[4] but the literary study of the play as a play, rather than of imagery as expressive of it, might seem more likely to reveal its 'true object'. There is no doubt that in a play's imagery is to be found

> a conception which has the power to challenge us imaginatively, so that
> we are for the moment released from the prison of habitual assump-
> tion;[5]

[1] *The Wheel of Fire*, 1949, p. 15.
[2] R. B. Heilman, *This Great Stage*, Louisiana State University Press, 1948, p. 12.
[3] *The Frontiers of Drama*, 1945, pp. 78–87.
[4] 'Mind and Hand : Some Reflections on the Study of Shakespeare's Imagery', *S.Q.* VIII, 1957, p. 185.　　　　[5] Lawlor, *The Tragic Sense in Shakespeare*, 1960, p. 144.

461

but the danger of limiting meaning to a single or habitual aspect is balanced by a real (and unacknowledged) danger of finding in verbal echoes and affinities a source of such profusion of meaning as must hinder a response to drama's swift process. A further proffered advantage is our being led by imagery direct from Shakespeare's art to his mind : imagery

> helps us, as perhaps nothing else will, to share the authentic Shake-spearian experience which we may easily and involuntarily distort.[6]

The assumption that by penetrating closer to the creative experience we shall be better able to assess what is created is attractive, but in practice the case looks more doubtful. Macbeth's phrase 'this bank and shoal [or school] of time' conveys to Lawlor's imagination that

> Macbeth is at once an inattentive schoolboy and a prisoner on trial, and goodness reaches from a dusty classroom to the vast prospect of eternity;[7]

but it may be wondered whether the more immediate and commonplace image of Macbeth's treating as the foundation of assurance the flats and quicksands which are at the mercy of eternity's great tide is not more essential and penetrating. Again, the image of

> This guest of summer,
> The temple-haunting martlet
> (I. vi. 3–4)

as Duncan enters Macbeth's castle helps, apart from its irony, to enhance our sense of the 'enormity of evil' and the unnaturalness of Macbeth's course.[8] But that sense has been quickened in us by the play : the full significance inheres in the situation, and the imagery gives further expression and emphasis to what is already there. The same applies to Macbeth's image of the 'poor player'. It links with other imagery of the theatre in his utterance, and points to the artificiality in his career and in himself as its embodiment, as well as to his incompetence and failure.[9] But to call this imagery the 'master-conception that informs the whole'[10] is to ignore the fact that Macbeth's actions and thoughts have themselves established the adoption of pretence, the consciousness of artificiality, and the knowledge of failure within a rôle. The 'master-conception' is thrust upon us by the whole play, and imagery lends additional emphasis to the dramatic statement. As H. Weisinger declares of similar instances,

> it is after all no wonder that the images match the intent for the simple reason that the play is conveyed to us through poetry, that is to say,

---

[6] ibid., p. 143.   [7] 'Mind and Hand', op. cit., p. 185.
[8] The Tragic Sense, p. 136; 'Mind and Hand', op. cit., p. 184.
[9] 'Mind and Hand', op. cit., pp. 187–8; The Tragic Sense, pp. 138–42.
[10] The Tragic Sense, p. 142.

through a succession of images proper to the experiences being conveyed.[11]

Interpretations that are made through the study of a play's imagery are governed to a significant degree by the definition of imagery a critic employs, for it is by its nature imprecise. R. A. Foakes points out that Miss Caroline Spurgeon in her early study ignored what he terms the 'object-matter' of the image : the idea of sleep, for example, in Macbeth's 'ravell'd sleave of care' (II. ii. 38). He draws attention to a failure in criticism to classify imagery according to subject-matter so that images relating to the experiencing subject may be distinguished from those relating to the object, and to a general confusion of images present in Shakespeare's mind with those present in the reader's.[12] The dramatic importance of imagery – as opposed to other significance it may have – demands a careful distinction which it does not always receive, and the same may be said of the concentration and grouping of images that has predominant influence upon their meaning.[13] These considerations, and such other difficulties as the different appearance of images to different minds and the capacity of the term 'image' to include the iterative and the symbolic,[14] make the classification of dramatic imagery, according to Foakes, a formidable task. A discussion of dramatic imagery, he declares,

> would include reference to the subject-matter and object-matter of poetic imagery, to visual and auditory effects, iterative words, historical and geographical placing, and to both the general and particular uses of these things –

all of which are to be examined in relation to the

context, dramatic context, and to the time-sequence of a play.[15]

Foakes appears undeterred by the necessities he pronounces. But S. L. Bethell, having decided that there can be no rules to distinguish the possible uses of imagery, concludes that to isolate groups of images and deduce character and theme from them must be to produce a 'freak interpretation'. Imagery, he asserts, is not enough by itself : 'the various approaches need to be balanced one against another'.[16]

The difficulty of classification is perhaps one of the tokens of an untoward development in criticism. Through an 'excessive zeal' for the undertaking of imagestic studies, declares V. Y. Kantak, 'a dangerous

---

[11] 'The Study of Shakespearian Tragedy since Bradley', *S.Q.* VI, 1955, p. 389.
[12] 'Suggestions for a New Approach to Shakespeare's Imagery', *S.S.* V, 1952, pp. 83, 86.
[13] ibid., p. 84.   [14] ibid., pp. 87–8.
[15] ibid., p. 90.
[16] 'Shakespeare's Imagery : The Diabolic Images in *Othello*', *S.S.* V, 1952, p. 65.

separation between the poetry and the drama' has come about.[17] This may in part result from the fact that the approach through imagery readily develops from a mere technique into a frame of mind in the person applying it; but more responsibility may be seen to lie in the nature of imagery in abstraction. No one would doubt that, in Shakespeare's dramatic imagination, the situation of a Macbeth naturally expresses itself in the images of feasting, sleep, insomnia, milk, babes, blood and medicine;[18] but the converse does not apply : the images concerned do not naturally relate to the dramatic situation – and will lead the unwary critic far from it. A demonstration of this fact may be found in Cleanth Brooks's well-known interpretation of Macbeth's 'naked newborn babe' (I. vii. 21). This image, as well as revealing the nature of pity, is held to signify 'a future which Macbeth would control and cannot control'. But it also stands for 'all those enlarging purposes which made life meaningful' to Macbeth, and 'all those emotional and . . . irrational ties . . . which render him human'. But the babe is also able simultaneously to assume the sterner guise of 'an avenging angel'.[19] Miss Helen Gardner would put an end to this catalogue of similitudes. The naked babe 'strides the blast', she declares, simply because pity is to Shakespeare the strongest and profoundest of human emotions; and Brooks in this interpretation is said to be

> more interested in making symbols of babes fit each other than in listening to what Macbeth is saying.[20]

That Brooks is here being led toward irrelevance and away from immediacy of response may be considered evident; but his preoccupation is the effect of an underlying confidence as to the nature of imagery's function within drama. The error of judgement of which this instance is part, according to O. J. Campbell, results from the effort

> to force all the references to babes into one connected system of imagery to form a structural principle for the drama,

in the belief that in imagery may indeed be found thematic structures upon which the drama is built. Critics who proceed in this confidence, Campbell maintains,

> assume therefore that Shakespeare, like Donne, constructed an integrated system of connotation based on the iteration of certain words, to which the poet has given an arbitrary symbolic value. And they make the further assumption that in this system of sequence and repeti-

---

[17] 'An Approach to Shakespearian Tragedy : the "Actor" Image in *Macbeth*', *S.S.* XVI 1963, p. 43.
[18] See K. Muir, *Shakespeare : The Great Tragedies*, Longmans, 1961, p. 33.
[19] *The Well Wrought Urn*, London, 1960, pp. 42, 43, 45.
[20] *The Business of Criticism*, Oxford Paperbacks, 1963, pp. 60-1.

tion of images all the poetry of the play is fused into one intense impression.[21]

But Shakespeare's imagery is essentially metaphorical rather than symbolic; and its use is governed by necessities which are dramatic – the need to intensify the auditor's response and to create individuality upon the stage. The figurative language of the playwright, in fact,

> is designed to reveal and intensify the comprehensiveness and complexity of human life, not to adumbrate a gaunt metaphysical, ethical, or sociological proposition as the scaffolding on which his drama has been built.[22]

In reply to this view of the function of imagery, L. C. Knights points to what he terms a reverberation between the lines of the play's poetry. There is to be perceived, he declares,

> what I. A. Richards calls interanimation between the image on which we are focusing and some scores of others throughout the play. And this, surely, is one of the ways in which the poetic mind works when engaged at the deepest levels.[23]

Reverberations of this kind certainly exist; but to say this is not to show that their intimations may be schematized, and that formulations concerning the play's meaning may be made from them without primary regard to what is conveyed in the immediacy of response to the drama. The question of what 'reverberations' through imagery are for, and how they may legitimately be handled in themselves, is here not dealt with.

Part of the danger that lies in the 'separation' that can come about between a play and its poetry through undue concentration upon imagery is due to the ignoring of what is wrought upon the beholder's imagination by the totality of the dramatic structure under the governance of dramatic sequence. That this tendency is very real may be judged from L. C. Knights's assertion that

> the only profitable approach to Shakespeare is a consideration of his plays as dramatic poems.[24]

And despite an admission that the discipline of drama renders a play utterly different from a poem, G. Wilson Knight is prepared to conceive of Shakespeare's plays in 'spatial' terms, as 'small and great circles out-rippling from the same centre, the centre of life and creation',[25] in a

---

[21] 'Shakespeare and the New Critics', *J. Q. Adams Memorial Studies*, Washington, 1948, pp. 88, 93–4.
[22] ibid., p. 96.
[23] *Some Shakespearean Themes*, 1959, p. 17.
[24] 'How Many Children had Lady Macbeth?', *Explorations*, 1946, p. 81.
[25] *The Christian Renaissance*, Toronto, 1933, pp. 15–16.

manner that does not distinguish them from poems. To analyse the sequence of events in a play and the 'cause' linking dramatic motive to action and action to result in time, he declares elsewhere,

is a blunder instinctive to the human intellect.[26]

The capacity of the beholder to analyse the play in the way Wilson Knight deprecates is, for V. Y. Kantak, precisely what distinguishes a poetic drama like *Macbeth* from a dramatic poem like *The Waste Land*. To interpret drama chiefly through its imagery, he declares, must inevitably cause character, event, action and the motives behind the action to lose the sense that is normally attached to them, leaving the interpreter with a continuous dramatic poem in the absence of 'the shape of human activity' which is essential to drama's being. The poetic pattern of a play is not something which exists in its own right : it is

itself made up of the words uttered by characters and its logic is the logic of men expressing themselves in free activity[27]–

and, therefore, not that of the interrelationships of the words and images by which this activity is carried on. The words and images concerned, further, relate to a sequence of time and action to which they are more attached than they are to one another. Each image is to be interpreted in the context of character, action and visual patterns within the sequence if the dramatic is not to be dissipated; and, in view of the acknowledged importance of locality, O. J. Campbell may well be right in thinking that the contribution of the dramatic image is both subordinate and temporary – that Shakespeare's artistic imagination

usually finds release, not in an integrated structure of figures, but rather in a medley of metaphors, each one relevant only to some specific emotional situation.[28]

An integrating principle for imagery, in fact, may well exist only in dramatic character, to which all other dramatic phenomena are referred, and by which their significance is interpreted. Certainly, if imagery is assumed to be able to stand on its own, all that is dramatic, and to be inferred and known through the dramatic, must tend to fade away. T. R. Henn points to the necessary and perceptible outcome of a criticism that bases itself upon the image :

Does the plot now become merely a framework for the dramatic poetry, or rather for a particular aspect of that 'poetic content'? Are the ethical problems, the roots of will and choice in character, merged in a larger unity to which we are given no clue save our total 'poetic

[26] *The Wheel of Fire*, 1949, p. 5.
[27] 'An Approach to Shakespearian Tragedy', *S.S.* XVI, 1963, pp. 47–8.
[28] op. cit., p. 93.

response' to the play? And if that is so, are we committed to a new and subjective aestheticism in which the image becomes paramount; even though it is, in essence as in fact, a device for communicating intense passion in speech?[29]

The answer to all these questions, if the product of imagistic criticism is generally surveyed, appears to be in the affirmative.

The approach to drama, according to the devotees of this type of interpretation, is not to be made through the word as the medium of literature, but through the word as its substance. According to L. C. Knights, the critic starts with 'so many lines of verse on a printed page which we read as we should any other poem'. He proceeds to elucidate meaning and unravel ambiguities, and then turns to estimating the kind and quality of the imagery, and the 'precise degree of evocation of particular figures'. The next step is the exploration of the 'tentacular roots' of each word; and the progress towards meaning is complete when the critic has determined how the word controls and is controlled by the rhythmic movement of the passage.[30] What is necessary to the attaining of a 'total response' to a Shakespeare play is 'an exact and sensitive study of Shakespeare's handling of language'.[31] The fact that Shakespeare wrote drama for living presentation to the experience of an audience appears not to affect a critical purpose which would subordinate the theatre to the operating-theatre. It is true that a play consists of words as the body consists of cells; but just as it does not follow that the body's activity is best appreciated in terms of cellular structure, so it is by no means clear that the meaning and effect of a play can be reduced to what is verbal. L. C. Knights assumes the possibility and necessity of such a reduction. Of Macbeth's speech 'This supernatural soliciting', he declares:

> our recognition of the body – the very feel – of the experience, is a response to the poetry. . . . The equivocal nature of temptation, the commerce with phantoms consequent upon false choice, the resulting sense of reality . . . which has yet such power to 'smother' vital function, the unnaturalness of evil . . . and the relation between disintegration in the individual . . . and disorder in the larger social organism – all these are major themes of the play which are mirrored in the speech under consideration. They emerge as themes because they are what the poetry – reinforced by action and symbolism – again and again insists on.[32]

That the poetry is itself the expression of personality finely conceived can find no recognition in a theory which regards character as the incidental

29 *The Harvest of Tragedy*, 1966, pp. 153–4.
30 'How Many Children', *Explorations*, 1946, p. 16.
31 ibid., p. 10.   32 *Some Shakespearean Themes*, 1959, p. 121.

creation of word and image. Wilson Knight is not unaware of the force of dramatic character in Shakespeare, and can acknowledge what Maurice Morgann calls the 'roundness and integrity' by which their conduct may be recognized as the work of principles of their being undisclosed in the play itself. But this quality, we are assured, 'sprang from Shakespeare's use of words':[33] the perception inheres in the words which convey it. The verbal pattern is not to be seen as the outcome of a mind's observation of reality and event, of the effect of personality, of a conscience's striving with intimation and ideal: the critic can have no dealings with

> abstractions that have nothing to do with the unique arrangement of words that constitutes these plays.[34]

Criticism, in short, is to have as its primary task not the consideration of what the literary medium transmits, but the study of the details of transmission; by the same principle a painting could be looked upon primarily as 'a unique arrangement of paint', and its interpretation made a matter of a study of the quality, texture and interrelation of the brushstrokes which compose it. It is true that anyone judging a painting in this way would technically speaking be pointing to 'something that is actually contained in the work of art'[35] as, according to Knights, a good critic should; but meaning is 'contained' neither in a streak of paint nor in letters printed on a page. In its creation and its reception alike, it is the work of minds.

A less narrowly literal outlook would view a play's characters as coming into being through the same imaginative process which creates the imagery, and would concur with F. Fergusson in denying primacy to what is verbal. Drama, he declares, is

> at once more primitive, more subtle, and more direct than either word or concept.

Unlike the lyric, it is not essentially a composition in the verbal medium; the words may be understood to result from the underlying structure of incident and character. Just as the imagination grasps the quality of a human life not only through words, but actions and appearances, so

> We grasp the stage-life of a play through the plot, characters, and words which manifest it.[36]

It is the 'stage-life' alone which can lead us to a play's profounder meaning, and whose guidance must determine critical judgement – and stage-life centres upon the personality which the word conveys, and not the word itself. For the critic to settle down into a purely verbal preoccupation

[33] op. cit., p. 12.　　　　[34] ibid., p. 17.　　　　[35] ibid.
[36] *The Idea of a Theatre*, Princeton University Press, 1949, pp. 22–5.

must imply a refusal to accept the categories Shakespeare deliberately set out to create.

An outcome of such a refusal may be noted in a study of the tragedies by T. B. Tomlinson, whose primary assumption is that the 'fabric of the verse' constitutes 'the very substance of the play'. He rules out the possibility that the message of the plays is vitally concerned with some sort of 'spiritual journey' in their heroes.[37] Instead, he finds in the powerful impression of the vitality of nature conveyed by the poetic imagery a consideration of the profoundest importance. In the fabric of Shakespeare's verse, he affirms,

> the world of nature is given us as having an existence which, paradoxically, is at once independent of, and intimately related to, man's status and worth.[38]

The verse presents nature as 'exhibiting growth and life', and man as dependent upon this 'whole world of life and growth beyond the bounds of his personality'.[39] And so it comes about that, as Tomlinson sees it,

> the man-nature relationship in Shakespeare offers the truest insight into what part man – 'characters'– may play in the total complexity of the drama.[40]

In what precisely that part consists does not immediately become clear, but it appears to involve a rôle subordinate to that of nature, which becomes the true protagonist of the drama. Beyond all other assurances which spring from the interpretation of the plays is the dominating certainty that the vitality of the natural order transfuses the dramatic action. This order, as it appears in *King Lear*, for example,

> is a nature which includes and embraces both the 'eyeless rage' of mere destruction and also a fury which is vital even when threatening destruction . . . Lear's own protest against a seemingly hostile universe is in fact being put against, and modified by, this view of a natural order which is at once destructive and powerfully energetic.[41]

In this process lies the 'man-nature relationship' which is the centre of tragedy, and which must govern its interpretation. The problem of drawing conclusions from a relationship which is not between persons, as drama is more traditionally understood, but between man and nature, appears to be not inconsiderable : the profoundest intimations of the plays in effect can only have to do with the existence of the natural world itself. Thus we learn from the study of *Macbeth* that the play is 'packed with suggestions of firmness and growth',[42] and from *Antony and Cleopatra*

---

[37] *A Study of Elizabethan and Jacobean Tragedy*, 1964, p. 9.
[38] ibid., p. 11. [39] ibid., p. 16. [40] ibid., p. 12.
[41] ibid., p. 35. [42] ibid., p. 39.

that the play's images constitute 'a statement . . . that there is life and growth'.[43] *King Lear*'s images of the 'solid reality of the world' also 'can suggest growth, vitality and possibility'.[44] *Hamlet* and *Othello* are 'special cases for many reasons'[45] which are not discussed.

The approach through word and image must be credited with many excellent and valuable insights. But they may be thought to have been produced at the cost of a certain deadening of those natural and heart-felt sympathies which form part of an ordinary human responsiveness to drama's unfolding. Thus L. C. Knights is able to point out that the scene in which Lady Macduff and her son are murdered 'echoes the theme of false appearance' and 'shows the spreading evil'; but his comment on Lady Macduff's gallant reply to the Murderer's question about her husband's whereabouts –

> We recall the association set up in Act III, scene vi, a scene of choric commentary upon Macduff's flight to England, to the 'Pious Edward', 'the Holy King'[46] –

seems to take small account of an audience's natural horror at a murder and admiration for a woman's brave defiance. The scene that follows between Malcolm and Macduff does not appear to this critic as an interview between two men. Malcolm 'has ceased to be a person' and become part of a 'choric commentary'; but in announcing his innocence at the end he becomes 'once more a person'– though his words carry an 'impersonal overtone', since he speaks for the forces of order. His declared intention to invade Scotland, and his deliberate testing of Macduff's loyalty throughout the scene, are 'of subordinate importance'.[47]

But everything to do with personality, and the profounder issues that have their beginning in 'the roots of will and choice of character' are in fact all of 'subordinate importance' to this kind of criticism. *Macbeth* is a statement of 'ordered emotion', and the interests it arouses are 'heightened' and 'placed' in the last Act; but once this is acknowledged there is no more to be said:

> It is no use saying we are 'quietened', 'purged' or 'exalted' at the end of *Macbeth* or of any other tragedy. . . . It is no use discussing the effect in abstract terms at all: we can only discuss it in terms of the poet's concrete realizations of certain emotions and attitudes.[48]

The whole vocabulary of the moral nature of man – all that sets human activity in the context of 'values'– is, according to J. Holloway, inapplicable to drama. Critics who use it to form judgements 'are not speaking literally. They are speaking in metaphor.' All statements of moral ap-

43 ibid., p. 43.   44 ibid., p. 36.   45 ibid., p. 34.
46 'How Many Children', *Explorations*, 1946, p. 27.
47 ibid., p. 28.   48 ibid., p. 29.

praisal applied to a Shakespearian play must appear 'metaphorical'[49] – or in plain English unreal – to a criticism which confines meaning in drama to the verbal. To quote T. B. Tomlinson,

> The nature of the 'dramatic' means that truth and value as given in plays are only to be defined in terms of the structure and fabric of the writing in each play considered. Drama cannot be seen merely as working towards a lively illlustration, in 'human terms', of a truth about man or the universe held, in other terms, outside the given play or in other plays available.[50]

Tomlinson will not acknowledge the existence of dramatic irony in Banquo's reference to the 'temple-haunting martlet' as Duncan enters Macbeth's castle, or in Lady Macbeth's words of greeting and homage to the man whose murder is upmost in her thoughts, since in the imagery of these passages there is 'health and vitality given us', and verbal associations which 'assert life arising out of death and negation'.[51] The idea that King Lear undergoes in the latter part of the play a transformation of outlook which may be described as a redemption is dismissed as

> too vague and amorphous a value to put up against the (on the Bradley hypothesis) cruelly alien universe against which Lear had been fighting[52]–

a judgement which does not appear to concede the presence of good amidst the evil in the universe under discussion. All ethical values that are perceived, in effect, are suspect because they are illegitimate. For J. Lawlor to have stated the dominating themes of the tragedies 'exclusively in terms of the natural bond between man and man' amounts to 'a crippling limitation of Shakespeare's deeper insights';[53] and even L. C. Knights, in declaring that *King Lear* does make a positive affirmation of ethical truth – 'an affirmation *in spite of*'– is held to come

> dangerously close to oversimplifying the relation Shakespeare establishes between the valuable in nature and the tragically chaotic.[54]

For life, as Shakespeare's imagination apprehends it, is not a 'testing of values', but itself 'an indispensable source of value, an enriching of the artist's total vision'.[55] What 'value' there can be in a vision which lacks the means of distinguishing and testing the 'values' which appear within it, or which itself is unable to admit such 'values', is a question which must naturally arise. The vision would seem to be one of a certain moral nihilism.

[49] *The Story of the Night*, 1961, pp. 2–7.
[50] op. cit., p. 24. [51] ibid., p. 7.
[52] ibid., p. 28. [53] ibid., pp. 10–11.
[54] ibid., p. 32; *Some Shakespearean Themes*, 1959, pp. 116–19.
[55] ibid., p. 33.

But it is above all in the treatment of personality that the dehumanizing tendency of the verbal approach to drama is most strongly evident. As L. C. Knights argues, if personal implications are admitted into our response to Macbeth's last speech, they will destroy 'the system of values that gives emotional coherence to the play'[56] – Macbeth himself presumably contributing nothing toward that coherence. Indeed, from the viewpoint of this criticism Macbeth cannot exist: to imagine that one is watchng actual human beings in responding to the drama is to render oneself incapable of true appreciation.[57] The play is an 'expanded metaphor'; and

the persons, ultimately, are not human at all, but purely symbols of a poetic vision.[58]

Macbeth himself becomes a walking shadow or perambulating metaphor; and the drama is a tale providing a 'complex emotional experience'[59] but signifying nothing – apart from some predominately verbal 'values'. Our impressions of personality are the result, not of Shakespeare's genius, but of our poor taste: we should dismiss them from our consciousness as a 'sentimental indulgence', according to T. B. Tomlinson, and replace them with

the tough sensibility we feel to be there, behind and in the text as a whole.[60]

The personal and the ethical being denied to the criticism of the plays, appraisal is carried on by a species of categorizing, of moralistic tendency, that is based upon a play's images of life, and operates rather in the manner of allegorical 'explaining' of the Scriptures. Thus, as L. C. Knights sees it, *Macbeth* presents to us the themes of the reversal of values, of unnatural disorder, and of doubtful appearance.[61] The scene of the description of the battle against Cawdor is 'full of images of confusion'; that of Macbeth's meeting with the Witches represents 'uncertainty'; and the scene in which Duncan holds state signifies 'natural order'– a society in harmony with nature and ordered by law and duty.[62] The snake, in Macbeth's 'We have scotch'd the snake, not kill'd it' (III. ii. 13), though 'usually represented as the most venomous of creatures', nevertheless also 'stands for the natural order'.[63] As for the murder of Duncan, it 'is explicitly presented as unnatural';[64] and in that the banquet scene is a symbol of concord which dissolves into disorder, it is significant that 'The end of the scene is in direct contrast to the beginning'.[65]

[56] 'How Many Children', *Explorations*, p. 36.
[57] ibid.   [58] ibid., p. 4.   [59] ibid., p. 36.
[60] Tomlinson, *A Study of Elizabethan and Jacobean Tragedy*, 1964, p. 28.
[61] op. cit., p. 18.   [62] ibid., pp. 19–21.   [63] ibid., p. 24.
[64] ibid., p. 22.   [65] ibid., p. 25.

Malcolm's command of the disordered and unnatural at the end frees our minds 'from the burden of the horror', since 'this disorder has now a positive tendency' towards good.[66]

A similar type of allegorical commentary is exhibited in later writing. Thus the careers of Hamlet, Othello and Macbeth are characterized by J. Holloway as a progression or journey to isolation,[67] while *Hamlet* and *Macbeth* show Fortune developing into Destiny.[68] *Macbeth* conveys the sense of its hero's career 'as one of revolt against everything in the world';[69] he is the embodiment of that 'even-handed justice' which decrees that 'all they that take the sword shall perish by the sword' (*Matt.* xxvi. 52);[70] his career is like that of a Lord of Misrule; and also, 'Through his identification with the image of revolt he becomes an ikon of one of the great evil potentialities of life'.[71] The 'galloping of horse' which Macbeth hears and is declared by Lennox to have been occasioned by

> two or three, my lord, that bring you word
> Macduff is fled to England
>
> (IV. i. 141–2)

is attributed to either 'heaven's cherubim' or the Four Horsemen of the Apocalypse.[72]

Holloway's description of Othello as 'a protagonist who is undergoing, or has undergone, a distinctive experience'[73] is particularly meaningful for this type of criticism. For the end of drama, according to L. C. Knights, is 'to communicate a rich and controlled experience by means of words', or 'the use of language to obtain a total complex emotional response';[74] and it is to this, and not to the personal and the ethical, that criticism should properly address itself. The beholder's response to a great work of art, declares Holloway, produces in him

> a condition at once exuberant and reposed : the sense of having passed through a great experience, one which testifies . . . to the superb wealth and range of life, and to the splendid rather than the disastrous powers of man. . . . But before it is a source of insight, great imaginative literature is a source of *power*.[75]

The dynamism literature imparts shows itself within the experiencing imagination as

> a comprehensive excitement of the whole gamut of emotion, a general sharpening and broadening of all our powers of perception, and a

[66] ibid., p. 33.   [67] *The Story of the Night*, 1961, pp. 26, 51, 67.
[68] ibid., pp. 34–6, 71–2.   [69] ibid., pp. 60–1.
[70] ibid., p. 69.   [71] ibid., p. 73.
[72] ibid., p. 65.   [73] ibid., p. 53.
[74] 'How Many Children', *Explorations*, pp. 4, 6.
[75] *The Story of the Night*, p. 17.

473

joyous revitalization which operates at a profound level on the whole personality.[76]

This description of the essence and effect of artistic experience certainly conveys the excitement of both creation and response in art. But, until the question is answered why this power or revitalization comes about, Holloway's account must be regarded as akin in spirit to Falstaff's disquisition upon the properties of sherris. An 'experience' must be an experience of something; and if it is of life, of the world, of men, action, motive, personality, ideal, it is then an experience of those things, together with the significance that lies within them, and must be able to sustain objective description. This possibility Holloway is at pains to deny. Drama, he declares, partakes of the nature of myth; and myths, as may be seen amongst primitive societies,

> satisfactorily fulfil their function not by any appeal to the reasoning powers but by appealing through the imagination to the mind's affective powers –

they 'exercise power' rather than explain.[77] A new slogan in philosophy which applies also to myth, we are told, is: 'Don't ask for the meaning, ask for the use'.[78] The 'myth' of drama, it is conceded, can suggest meanings and answers as it were accidentally; but its true concern is to be 'a source of power, of sustained, renewed or enhanced vitality'.[79] The views it suggests are incidental: its value is in its offering 'a great experience'. The possibility that the power of myth lies in its conveying of meaning directly and intensely to the experiencing imagination – that the experience is 'great' in proportion to its significance – is not explored. A play, we are told, is

> a thing, offering a uniquely comprehensive and ordered experience of itself, in its own right.[80]

T. B. Tomlinson's definition of what drama has to offer is to the same effect. In Macbeth's soliloquy 'If it were done when 'tis done' (I. vii. 1) he finds 'the presence of values'; and in the words

> Here lay Duncan,
> His silver skin lac'd with his golden blood
>
> (II. iii. 112–13)

and the lines immediately following, there is also to be discerned 'the familiar assertion of values'. But the validity of the 'values' adduced lies in this: that they show forth

> the solid actuality and liveliness of experience itself.[81]

[76] ibid., p. 19.   [77] ibid., p. 171.   [78] ibid., p. 173.   [79] ibid., pp. 173, 176.
[80] ibid., p. 183.   [81] *A Study of Elizabethan and Jacobean Tragedy*, pp. 40–1.

From statements such as these it might be inferred that we are dealing with a kind of critical hedonism. To see drama not as the story of an action involving characters but as a developed pattern of words, and to rule out as invalid all considerations which do not relate to the verbal patterns and what is directly deducible from them, must in the end establish a single category – 'experience' rather than the hedonists' 'pleasure'– as the sole good, and deny the very existence of other categories relating to human experience. There may also be found in the attitudes that have been discussed the typical hedonistic confusion of attainable knowledge with immediate sensation, brought about by the despairing conviction that all other apparent truth is ephemeral. The hedonists' fundamental doubt as to what the sole good insisted upon really means and really is may also be adduced. And the depersonalizing effects of a depersonalizing philosophy, in which the individual's deeper perceptions and apprehensions can no longer count as criteria of reality, may also be suspected in the examples which have been given.

Whether or not the accusation of hedonism can be sustained, it is clear that the verbal approach to drama imperils an ethical evaluation. I. Ribner notes that Wilson Knight, in his imagistic preoccupation with the mood of evil which dominates *Macbeth*, sees all the play's characters as ensnared by it. The effect, he declares, is the critic's failure to note

the distinction among character functions which is part of the symbolism of the play, and in which its ethical idea is implicit.

As a further illustration of the dangers of a concentration upon poetic atmosphere 'which slights the logic of action and negates the factors of audience participation and sympathy',[82] he mentions Wilson Knights's interpreting Macbeth's resort to the Witches and his commitment to evil as a victory in its putting an end to the divided mind.

Knight, of course, denies that there are ethical implications in the play, but in such an artistic vision which ultimately negates the difference between good and evil and sets its seal simply upon a total commitment to either the one or the other, there is an inevitable ethic which is diabolic in its implications.[83]

A verbal interpretation which is consistent must inevitably come to challenge ethical values; and the fact that instances are not more frequent is due to the inability of the approach through word and image to exclude assumptions that derive from those wider realms of significance to which the experience of drama in truth both appeals and belongs. As L. Fiedler observes,

[82] '*Macbeth* : the Pattern of Idea and Action', *S.Q.* X, 1959, p. 155.
[83] ibid., p. 158.

The 'pure' literary critic, who pretends, in the cant phrase, to stay 'inside' a work all of whose metaphors and meanings are pressing outward, is only half-aware. And half-aware, he deceives; for he cannot help smuggling unexamined moral and metaphysical judgements into his 'close analyses', any more than the 'pure' literary historian can help bootlegging unconfessed aesthetic estimates into his chronicles. Literary criticism is always becoming 'something else', for the simple reason that literature is always 'something else'.[84]

A verbal criticism is one among various modes of specialized analysis which share a distrust of traditional standards and by their own operation help to question the very possibility of evaluation.

The act of evaluation remains . . . the vital center of criticism; but to practice it one must believe in the reality of the true, the good and the beautiful, as well as in the existence of men of taste, in whom a disciplined sensibility is capable of making discriminations among experiences in terms of those absolutes. Lacking these beliefs, one can only fall back on relativism, or make intrinsic, formal evaluations, that is, disguise the source of one's judgements in a scientific jargon or a parody of one.[85]

Miss Helen Gardner has remarked on the tendency of the study of images to disappoint that high estimate of the imagination's power to reach the profundities of experience from whence it arose, and, by ignoring the primary imagination, to degrade the creative imagination in criticism into an instrument for perceiving analogies and making connections. She expresses her uneasiness in these terms:

I cannot feel satisfied with a literary criticism which substitutes for the conception of the writer as 'a man speaking to men', the conception of the writer as an imagination weaving symbolic patterns to be teased out by the intellect.[86]

The study of the patterns of images, like the knowledge of the ideas, theories and beliefs current in a period of literature, is an effective tool in an interpreter's hand – but only if too much reliance is not placed on it.[87] Imagery presents, sustains, informs and diversifies human experience in drama, but is subordinate to the imaginative creation it helps to serve. For drama speaks to man's mind in the fullest and most challenging terms of his earthly experience and apprehensions; and it is personality, and not imagery, by which they are truly conveyed and received. It is for

[84] 'Toward an Amateur Criticism', *The Kenyon Review* XII, 1951, p. 564.
[85] ibid., p. 566.
[86] *The Business of Criticism*, Oxford Paperbacks, 1963, p. 125.
[87] ibid., p. 148.

this reason that Miss M. Lascelles has concluded, in her study of *Measure for Measure*, that

> for all the perils of misunderstanding with which it is beset, the study of the characters in their relation with one another – here conditioned by the given story, there, developing free of it – remains the right approach; and its alternative, a pursuit of phantoms.[88]

[88] *Shakespeare's 'Measure for Measure'*, 1953, p. 142, quoted by Miss Gardner, op. cit., p. 153.

Acknowledgements

The works of a wide range of authors receive mention in this study, and every effort has been made to ensure that each reference is acknowledged. For permission to quote extensively the author is indebted to : the Augsburg Publishing House, Minneapolis, Minn. (for Søren Kierkegaard, *Edifying Discourses* and *The Gospel of Suffering and The Lillies of the Field*, tr. L. F. and D. M. Swenson); Chatto & Windus Ltd and Stanford University Press (for L. C. Knights, *Some Shakespearean Themes*); Chatto & Windus Ltd and Harcourt Brace Jovanovich, Inc. (for J. Lawlor, *The Tragic Sense in Shakespeare*); The Longman Group Ltd (for A. P. Rossiter, *Angel with Horns and other lectures on Shakespeare*); Macmillan & Co. Ltd and St Martin's Press, Inc. (for A. C. Bradley, *Shakespearian Tragedy*); Methuen & Co Ltd (for Una Ellis-Fermor, *The Frontiers of Drama* and *Shakespeare the Dramatist*); James Nisbet & Co. Ltd (for Reinhold Niebuhr, *Beyond Tragedy* and *Faith and History*); and S.C.M. Press Ltd and Harper & Row (for Max Scheler's *On the Eternal in Man*). D. G. James's *The Dream of Learning* is quoted by permission of the Clarendon Press, Oxford.

List of Books and Articles Used

LIST OF BOOKS AND ARTICLES USED

i Literary and Philosophical: Primary Sources

J. Anouilh, *Antigone*, ed. W. M. Landers, London, Harrap, 1966.

Aristotle, *Poetics (Aristotle on the Art of Fiction)*, tr. and ed. L. J. Potts, Cambridge, C.U.P., 1953.

Francis Bacon, *The Advancement of Learning*, ed. W. A. Wright, London, O.U.P., 1920.

The Philosophical Works of Francis Bacon, ed. J. M. Robertson, London, Routledge, 1905.

Timothy Bright, *A Treatise of Melancholy*, 2nd edn, 1586.

Sir Thomas Browne, 'Religio Medici', *Works*, ed. G. Keynes, Faber and Gwyer, 1928–31.

Sir John Davies, *The Complete Poems of Sir John Davies*, ed. A. B. Grosart, London, Chatto and Windus, 1876.

Orchestra, 1596.

John Davies of Hereford, *Microcosmos*, Oxford, 1603.

Mirum in Modum, 1602.

W. Macneile Dixon, *The Human Situation*, Edward Arnold, 1938.

Sir Thomas Elyot, *The Gouernour* (1531), London, Dent (Everyman Edn.), 1937.

Fulke Greville, Lord Brooke, 'Alaham';

'Caelica';

'An inqvisition vpon Fame and Honovr';

'Mustapha';

'A Treatie of Humane Learning';

Poems and Dramas of Fulke Greville, ed. G. Bullough, Edinburgh, Oliver and Boyd, 1938.

Life of Sir Philip Sidney (1652), ed. Nowell Smith, Oxford, Clarendon Press, 1907.

'A Treatise of Religion', *The Remains: Poems of Monarchy and Religion*, ed. G. A. Wilkes, London, O.U.P., 1965.

Sir John Hayward, *Davids Teares*, 2nd edn, 1623.

K. Lorenz, *On Aggression*, tr. M. Latzke, London, Methuen, 1966.

Christopher Marlowe, 'Tamburlaine', *Works*, ed. C. F. Tucker Brooke, Oxford, Clarendon Press, 1946.

John Milton, 'Paradise Lost', *Poetical Works*, ed. D. Bush, London, O.U.P., 1966.

Friedrich Nietzsche, *The Birth of Tragedy*, tr. F. Golffing, New York, Doubleday, 1956.

M. Palingenius, *The Zodiake of Life* (1531?), tr. B. Googe (1576), New York, Scholars' Facsimiles & Reprints, 1947.

Sir Walter Raleigh, *The History of the World*, 1614.

Jean-Paul Sartre, *Existentialism and Humanism*, tr. P. Mairet, London, Methuen, 1966.

A. Schopenhauer, *The World as Will and Idea*, tr. R. B. Haldane and J. Kemp, London, Trübner and Co., 1883.

William Shakespeare, *The Comedies; The Histories and Poems; The Tragedies*, ed. W. J. Craig, The Oxford Edition, London, O.U.P., 1911–12, reprinted 1962. (Cited throughout.)

Sir Philip Sidney, *An Apology for Poetry*, ed. G. Shepherd, London, Nelson, 1965.

M. de Unamuno, *The Tragic Sense of Life*, tr. J. E. Crawford Flitch, London, Macmillan, 1931.

ii Literary and Philosophical: Secondary Sources

L. Abercrombie, 'A Plea for the Liberty of Interpreting', *Proc. Brit. Acad.* XVI, 1930, p. 137.

P. J. Adams, 'Analogical Probability in Shakespeare's Plays', *S.Q.* VI, 1955, p. 397.

H. Adolf, 'The Essence and Origin of Tragedy', *The Journal of Aesthetics and Art Criticism* X, 1951–2, p. 112.

I. W. Alexander, 'Jean-Paul Sartre and Existential Philosophy', *The Cambridge Journal* I, 1947–8, p. 721.

A. H. Armstrong and R. A. Markus, *Christian Faith and Greek Philosophy*, London, Darton, Longman and Todd, 1960.

L. Babb, 'On the Nature of Elizabethan Psychological Literature', *J. Q. Adams Memorial Studies*, Washington, 1948, p. 509.

S. Barnet, 'Some Limitations of a Christian Approach to Shakespeare', *E.L.H.* XXII, 1955, p. 81.

R. W. Battenhouse, 'Hamlet's Apostrophe on Man : Clue to the Tragedy', *P.M.L.A.* LXVI, 1951, p. 1073.

J. Bayley, *The Character of Love*, London, Constable, 1960.

J. W. Bennett, 'The Storm Within : the Madness of Lear', *S.Q.* XIII, 1962, p. 137.

M. A. Bernard, 'The Five Tragedies in *Macbeth*', *S.Q.* XIII, 1962, p. 49.

S. L. Bethell, 'Shakespeare's Imagery : The Diabolic Images in *Othello*', *S.S.* V, 1952, p. 62.

E. A. Block, '*King Lear* : a Study in Balanced and Shifting Sympathies', *S.Q.* X, 1959, p. 499.

G. Boas, 'Shakespeare and Christianity', *The Shakespeare Review* I, 1929, p. 90.

G. Bonnard, 'Are Othello and Desdemona Innocent or Guilty?' *English Studies* XXX, 1949, p. 175.

C. V. Boyer, *The Villain as Hero in Elizabethan Tragedy*, London, Routledge, 1914.

M. C. Bradbrook, 'The Sources of *Macbeth*', *S.S.* IV, 1951, p. 35.

A. Bradby, ed., *Shakespeare Criticism 1919–35*, London, O.U.P. (World's Classics), 1949.

A. C. Bradley, 'Hegel's Theory of Tragedy', *Oxford Lectures on Poetry*, London, Macmillan, 1941.
Shakespearean Tragedy, 2nd edn, London, Macmillan, 1905, reprinted 1956.

Robert Bridges, 'The Influence of the Audience on Shakespeare's Drama', *Collected Essays Papers &c I*, London, O.U.P., 1927

C. Brooks, 'The Naked Babe and the Cloak of Manliness', *The Well Wrought Urn*, London, Dennis Dobson, 1960.

L. B. Campbell, 'Concerning Bradley's *Shakespearean Tragedy*', *The Huntingdon Library Quarterly* XIII, 1949–50, p. 1.
'Polonius: The Tyrant's Ears', *J. Q. Adams Memorial Studies*, Washington, 1948, p. 295.

O. J. Campbell, 'The Salvation of Lear', *E.L.H.* XV, 1948, p. 93.
'Shakespeare and the New Critics', *J. Q. Adams Memorial Studies*, Washington, 1948, p. 81.

H. B. Charlton, *Shakespearian Tragedy*, Cambridge, C.U.P., 1948, reprinted 1952.

W. Clemen, *The Development of Shakespeare's Imagery*, London, Methuen, 1951.
'Shakespeare and the Modern World', *S.S.* XVI, 1963, p. 57.

S. T. Coleridge, *Lectures and Notes on Shakespere*, ed. T. Ashe, Bohn Classics, 1904.

H. Craig, 'The Ethics of King Lear', *Philological Quarterly* IV, 1925, p. 97.
'Ideational Approach to Shakespeare's Plays', *Philological Quarterly* XLI, 1962, p. 147.

D. G. Cunningham, 'The Characterization of Shakespeare's Cleopatra', *S.Q.* VI, 1955, p. 9.
'*Macbeth*: the Tragedy of the Hardened Heart', *S.Q.* XIV, 1963, p. 39.

W. C. Curry, *Shakespeare's Philosophical Patterns*, Baton Rouge, Louisiana State University Press, 1937.

J. F. Danby, '*King Lear* and Christian Patience', *The Cambridge Journal* I, 1947–8, p. 305.
Shakespeare's Doctrine of Nature, London, Faber and Faber, 1949.

W. Macneile Dixon, *Tragedy*, 3rd edn, Leeds, Edward Arnold, 1929.

T. S. Eliot, *Poetry and Drama*, London, Faber and Faber, 1951.
'Hamlet' (1919), *Selected Essays*, London, Faber and Faber, 1963.

483

G. R. Elliott, *Dramatic Providence in 'Macbeth'*, New Jersey, Princeton University Press, 1958.

'Shakespeare's Christian, Dramatic Charity', *Theology* LVI, 1953, p. 459.

U. Ellis-Fermor, *The Frontiers of Drama*, London, Methuen, 1945.

'The Nature of Plot in Drama', *Essays and Studies* (New Series) XIII, 1960, p. 65.

Shakespeare the Dramatist and other papers, ed. K. Muir, London, Methuen, 1961.

W. Farnham, *The Medieval Heritage of Elizabethan Tragedy*, University of California Press, 1936.

F. Fergusson, *The Idea of a Theatre*, New Jersey, Princeton University Press, 1949.

L. A. Fiedler, 'Toward an Amateur Criticism', *The Kenyon Review* XII, 1951, p. 561.

R. F. Fleissner, 'The "Nothing" Element in *King Lear*', *S.Q.* XIII, 1962, p. 67.

R. A. Foakes, 'Suggestions for a New Approach to Shakespeare's Imagery', *S.S.* V, 1952, p. 81.

C. S. French, 'Shakespeare's "Folly" : *King Lear*', *S.Q.* X, 1959, p. 524.

R. M. Frye, *Shakespeare and Christian Doctrine*, London, O.U.P., 1963.

Helen Gardner, *The Business of Criticism*, London, O.U.P. (Oxford Paperbacks), 1963.

'The Noble Moor', *Proc. Brit. Acad.* XLI, 1955, p. 189.

A. Gerard, ' "Egregiously an Ass" : The Dark Side of the Moor. A View of Othello's Mind', *S.S.* X, 1957, p. 98.

H. Granville-Barker, *Prefaces to Shakespeare*, London, Sidgwick and Jackson, 1st Ser., 1927; 3rd Ser. (rev.), 1937; 4th Ser., 1945.

T. Greene, 'The Postures of Hamlet', *S.Q.* XI, 1960, p. 357.

A. Harbage, 'Shakespeare's Ideal Man', *J. Q. Adams Memorial Studies*, Washington, 1948, p. 65.

R. B. Heilman, 'The Economics of Iago and Others', *P.M.L.A.* LXVIII, 1953, p. 555.

This Great Stage, Louisiana State University Press, 1948.

T. R. Henn, *The Harvest of Tragedy*, London, Methuen, 1966.

D. C. Hockey, 'The Trial Pattern in *King Lear*', *S.Q.* X, 1959, p. 389.

J. Holloway, *The Story of the Night*, London, Routledge and Kegan Paul, 1961.

David Hume, 'Of Tragedy', *Essays Moral, Political and Literary (1741–2)*, London, O.U.P. (World's Classics), 1966.

J. H. Jack, 'Macbeth, King James and the Bible', *E.L.H.* XXII, 1955, p. 173.

D. G. James, *The Dream of Learning*, London, O.U.P., 1951.

Karl Jaspers, *Tragedy is Not Enough*, tr. H. A. T. Reiche, H. T. Moore and K. W. Deutsch, London, Gollancz, 1953.

H. Jenkins, 'The Tragedy of Revenge in Shakespeare and Webster', *S.S.* XIV, 1961, p. 45.

Samuel Johnson, *Johnson on Shakespeare*, ed. W. Raleigh, London, O.U.P., 1957.

V. Y. Kantak, 'An Approach to Shakespearian Tragedy : the "Actor" Image in *Macbeth*', *S.S.* XVI, 1963, p. 42.

L. Kirschbaum, 'Albany', *S.S.* XIII, 1960, p. 20.

G. Wilson Knight, *The Christian Renaissance*, Toronto, Macmillan, 1933.
Principles of Shakespearian Production, London, Faber and Faber, 1936.
The Wheel of Fire, London, Methuen, 1949.

L. C. Knights, 'How Many Children had Lady Macbeth?' (1933); 'Prince Hamlet',
Explorations, London, Chatto and Windus, 1946.
'On Historical Scholarship and the Interpretation of Shakespeare', *Sewanee Review* LXIII, 1955, p. 223.
Some Shakespearean Themes, London, Chatto and Windus, 1959.

P. H. Kocher, 'Lady Macbeth and the Doctor', *S.Q.* V, 1954, p. 341.

M. Krieger, 'Tragedy and the Tragic Vision', *Kenyon Review* XX, 1958, p. 281.

R. Langbaum, 'Character Versus Action in Shakespeare', *S.Q.* VIII, 1957, p. 57.

J. Lawlor, 'Mind and Hand : Some Reflections on the Study of Shakespeare's Imagery', *S.Q.* VIII, 1957, p. 179.
The Tragic Sense in Shakespeare, London, Chatto and Windus, 1960.

F. R. Leavis, *The Common Pursuit*, London, Chatto and Windus, 1952.

C. Leech, 'The "Capability" of Shakespeare', *S.Q.* XI, 1960, p. 123.
Shakespeare's Tragedies, and Other Studies in 17th-Century Drama, London, Chatto and Windus, 1950.

H. Levin, *The Question of Hamlet*, New York, O.U.P., 1959.

F. L. Lucas, *Tragedy in Relation to Aristotle's 'Poetics'*, London, Hogarth Press, 1953.

O. Mandel, *A Definition of Tragedy*, New York University Press, 1961.

J. Markels, 'The Spectacle of Deterioration : *Macbeth* and the "Manner" of Tragic Imitation', *S.Q.* XII, 1961, p. 293.

J. C. McCloskey, 'The Emotive Use of Animal Imagery in *King Lear*', *S.Q.* XIII, 1962, p. 321.

W. M. Merchant, *Creed and Drama*, S.P.C.K., 1965.
'Shakespeare's Theology', *R.E.L.* V, 1964, p. 72.

485

J. Money, 'Othello's "It is the cause . . ." : An Analysis', *S.S.* VI, 1953, p. 94.

R. Morrell, 'The Psychology of Tragic Pleasure', *Essays in Criticism* VI, 1956, p. 22.

I. Morris, 'Cordelia and Lear', *S.Q.* VIII, 1957, p. 141.

K. Muir, 'Shakespeare and the Tragic Pattern', *Proc. Brit. Acad.* XLIV, 1958, p. 145.

Shakespeare: the Great Tragedies (Writers and their Work), London, Longmans, 1961.

H. J. Muller, *The Spirit of Tragedy*, New York, Knopf, 1956.

Allardyce Nicoll, *An Introduction to Dramatic Theory*, London, Harrap, 1923.

R. Noble, *Shakespeare's Biblical Knowledge*, S.P.C.K., 1935.

W. M. T. Nowottny, 'Lear's Questions', *S.S.* X, 1957, p. 90.

R. Ornstein, 'Historical Criticism and the Interpretation of Shakespeare', *S.Q.* X, 1959, p. 3.

R. H. Reno, 'Hamlet's Quintessence of Dust', *S.Q.* XII, 1961, p. 107.

I. Ribner, '*Macbeth* : the Pattern of Idea and Action', *S.Q.* X, 1959, p. 147.

P. B. Rice, 'Existentialism and the Self', *The Kenyon Review* XII, 1950, p. 304.

M. Rosenburg, 'In Defense of Iago', *S.Q.* VI, 1955, p. 145.

J. L. Rosier, 'The Lex Aeterna and *King Lear*', *J.E.G.P.* LIII, 1954, p. 574.

A. P. Rossiter, *Angel with Horns and other lectures on Shakespeare*, London, Longmans, 1961.

G. Santayana, 'The Absence of Religion in Shakespeare', *Interpretations of Poetry and Religion*, New York, Chas. Scribner's Sons, 1905.

E. Schanzer, 'The Problem of *Julius Caesar*', *S.Q.* VI, 1955, p. 297.

A. G. Schlegel, *Lectures on Dramatic Art and Literature*, tr. J. Black, rev. A. J. W. Morrison, New York, A.M.S. Press Inc., 1965.

F. G. Schoff, 'King Lear : Moral Example or Tragic Protagonist?', *S.Q.* XIII, 1962, p. 157.

L. L. Schücking, *Character Problems in Shakespeare's Plays*, London, Harrap, 1922.

R. B. Sewall, *The Vision of Tragedy*, New Haven, Yale University Press, 1965.

A. Sewell, *Character and Society in Shakespeare*, London, O.U.P., 1951.

P. N. Siegel, 'The Damnation of Othello', *P.M.L.A.* LXVIII, 1953, p. 1068.

P. Simpson, 'The Theme of Revenge in Elizabethan Tragedy', *Elizabethan Drama*, London, O.U.P., 1955.

Edith Sitwell, *A Notebook on William Shakespeare*, London, Macmillan, 1948.

H. Skulsky, 'King Lear and the Meaning of Chaos', S.Q. XVII, 1966, p. 3.

J. S. Smart, 'Tragedy', Essays and Studies VIII, 1922, p. 9.

D. Nicholl Smith, ed., Shakespeare Criticism: A Selection, London, O.U.P. (World's Classics), 1953.

R. Speaight, Nature in Shakespearian Tragedy, London, Hollis and Carter, 1955.

Theodore Spencer, Death and Elizabethan Tragedy, Cambridge (Mass.), Harvard University Press, 1936.

Shakespeare and the Nature of Man, Cambridge, C.U.P., 1943.

B. Spivack, Shakespeare and the Allegory of Evil, London, O.U.P., 1958.

C. F. E. Spurgeon, Shakespeare's Imagery and What it Tells Us, Cambridge, C.U.P., 1935.

J. Stampfer, 'The Catharsis of King Lear', S.S. XIII, 1960, p. 1.

G. Steiner, The Death of Tragedy, London, Faber and Faber, 1961.

J. I. M. Stewart, Character and Motive in Shakespeare, London, Longmans, 1959.

G. Coffin Taylor, 'Shakespeare's Use of the Idea of the Beast in Man', Stud. Phil. XLII, 1945, p. 530.

E. M. W. Tillyard, Shakespeare's Problem Plays, London, Chatto and Windus, 1957.

T. B. Tomlinson, A Study of Elizabethan and Jacobean Tragedy, Cambridge, C.U.P., 1964.

P. Ure, Shakespeare and the Inward Self of the Tragic Hero, University of Durham, 1961.

C. E. Vaughan, Types of Tragic Drama, Macmillan, 1908.

E. R. Wasserman, 'The Pleasures of Tragedy', E.L.H. XIV, 1947, p. 283.

M. Weidhorn, 'Lear's Schoolmasters', S.Q. XIII, 1962, p. 305.

H. Weisinger, 'The Study of Shakespearian Tragedy since Bradley', S.Q. VI, 1955. p. 387.

Tragedy and the Paradox of the Fortunate Fall, London, Routledge and Kegan Paul, 1953.

C. Williams, 'Two Brief Essays on Shakespearian Topics', The Image of the City and Other Essays, London, O.U.P., 1958.

J. Dover Wilson, What Happens in 'Hamlet', Cambridge, C.U.P., 1935.

W. B. Yeats, Plays and Controversies, London, Macmillan, 1923.

iii Theological: Primary Sources

Aurelius Augustine, Bishop of Hippo, 'Faith and the Creed' – De Fide et Symbolo;

'On Free Will' – De Libero Arbitrio (also consulted : St Augustine: The Problem of Free Choice, tr. M. Pontifex, The Newman Press, 1955);

487

'The Nature of the Good' – De Natura Boni;

'To Simplican : On Various Questions' – De Quaestionibus ad Simplicianum;

'The Teacher' – De Magistro;

'Of True Religion' – De Vera Religione;

'The Usefulness of Belief' – De Utilitate Credendi,

Augustine: Earlier Writings, tr. J. H. S. Burleigh, London, S.C.M. Press (Library of Christian Classics VI), 1953.

'Ten Homilies on the First Epistle General of St John' – In Epistolam Joannis ad Parthos Tractatus decem;

'The Trinity' – De Trinitate (also consulted : translation by A. W. H. Haddan in *Works*, ed. Marcus Dods, Edinburgh, T. and T. Clark, 1873);

'The Spirit and the Letter' – De Spiritu et Littera,

Augustine: Later Works, tr. J. Burnaby, London, S.C.M. Press (Library of Christian Classics VIII), 1955.

'Christian Doctrine' – De Doctrina Christiana, tr. J. F. Shaw;

'The City of God' – De Civitate Dei, tr. M. Dods;

'On the Gift of Perseverance' – De Dona Preseverantiae, tr. R. E. Wallis, rev. B. J. Warefield;

'On Grace and Free Will' – De Gratia et Libero Arbitrio, tr. P. Holmes, rev. B. J. Warefield;

'Homilies on the Gospel of John' – In Joannis Evangelium Tractus CXXIV, tr. J. Gibb and J. Innes;

'Our Lord's Sermon on the Mount' – De Sermone Domini in Monte secundum Matthaeum, tr. W. Findlay, rev. D. S. Schaff;

'On Nature and Grace' – De Natura et Gratia, contra Pelagium, tr. P. Holmes, rev. B. J. Warefield;

'On the Predestination of the Saints' – De Praedestinatione Sanctorum, tr. R. E. Wallis, rev. B. J. Warefield;

'On the Proceedings of Pelagius' – De Gestis Pelagii, tr. P. Holmes, rev. B. J. Warefield;

'On Rebuke and Grace' – De Correptione et Gratia, tr. R. E. Wallis, rev. B. J. Warefield,

The Nicene and Post-Nicene Fathers, Michigan, Eerdmans Pub. Co., 1956, vols. II, V, VI, VII.

'The Christian Conflict' – De Agone Christiano;

'On Continence' – De Continentia;

'The Enchiridion' – Enchiridion de Fide, Spe et Caritate (also consulted : *Enchiridion*, tr. E. Evans, S.P.C.K., 1953);

'On Patience' – De Patientia;

Seventeen Short Treatises of S. Augustine, tr. C. L. Cornish and H. Browne, London, O.U.P. (A Library of Fathers of the Holy Catholic Church), 1847.

The Confessions of St Augustine, tr. E. B. Pusey, London, Dent (Everyman), 1907 (also consulted : *Confessions*, tr. W. Watts

(1631), London, Heinemann (Loeb Classical Library), 1912.

The Morals of the Catholic Church, tr. R. Stothert, Edinburgh, T. and T. Clark, 1872.

St Augustine: The Greatness of the Soul. The Teacher, tr. J. M. Colleran, London, Longmans, Green & Co., 1950.

Sermons for Christmas and Epiphany, tr. T. C. Lawler, London, Longmans, Green & Co., 1952.

'Contra Secundam Juliani Responsionem Imperfectum Opus';
'De Genesi ad Litteram';
'De Quantitate Animae';
'Enarrationes in Psalmos';
'Expositio Quarumdam Propositionum ex Epistola ad Romanos';
'Retractiones';
'Sermones ad Populum',
Opera Omnia, Editio Parisina, Gaume Fratres, 1835–9, vols. I, III, IV, V, X.

Epistolae, Corpus Scriptorum Ecclesiasticorum Latinorum, vols. XXXIV, XLIV, LVII, Vindobonae, Lipsiae, 1895–1904.

D. M. Baillie, *God Was in Christ*, London, Faber and Faber, 1963.

J. Baillie, *Our Knowledge of God*, London, O.U.P. (Oxford Paperbacks), 1963.

John Calvin, *Calvin: Commentaries*, ed. J. Haroutunian, London, S.C.M. Press (Library of Christian Classics XXIII), 1958.

Calvin: Theological Treatises, ed. J. K. S. Reid, London, S.C.M. Press (Library of Christian Classics XXII), 1954.

Calvins Sermons on Job, tr. A. Golding, London, 1573.

Institutes of the Christian Religion, ed. J. McNeill, London, S.C.M. Press (Library of Christian Classics XX, XXI), 1961.

Instruction in Faith (1537), ed. P. T. Fuhrmann, London, Lutterworth Press, 1949.

John Donne, *LXXX Sermons*, 1640.

Fifty Sermons, 1649.

XXVI Sermons, 1661.

R. Hooker, 'Of The Laws of Ecclesiastical Polity', *Works*, ed. J. Keble, London, O.U.P., 1845.

Baron Friedrich von Hügel, 'Suffering and God', *Essays and Addresses on the Philosophy of Religion, Second Series*, London, J. M. Dent, 1930.

Søren Kierkegaard, *Edifying Discourses*, tr. D. F. and L. M. Swenson, Minneapolis, Augsburg Publishing House, 1950–3.

For Self Examination and Judge For Yourselves, tr. W. Lowrie, London, O.U.P., 1941.

The Gospel of Suffering and The Lillies of the Field (1847), tr. D. F. and L. M. Swenson, Minneapolis, Augsburg Publishing House, 1948.

489

Thoughts on Crucial Situations in Human Life (1845), tr. D. F. Swenson, Minneapolis, Augsburg Publishing House, 1941.

Martin Luther, *A Commentary on St Paul's Epistle to the Galatians*, ed. P. S. Watson, London, Jas. Clarke and Co., 1953.

A Compend of Luther's Theology, ed. H. T. Kerr, Philadelphia, Westminster Press, 1943.

The Letters of Martin Luther, tr. M. A. Currie, London, Macmillan, 1908.

Luther: Lectures on Romans, ed. W. Pauck, London, S.C.M. Press (Library of Christian Classics XV), 1961.

Luther: Letters of Spiritual Counsel, ed. and tr. T. G. Tappert, London, S.C.M. Press (Library of Christian Classics XVIII), 1955.

Martin Luther on The Bondage of the Will, tr. J. I. Parker and O. R. Johnston, London, Jas. Clarke and Co., 1959.

The Table-Talk of Martin Luther, tr. W. Hazlitt, London, George Bell, 1883.

Reinhold Niebuhr, *Beyond Tragedy*, London, Nisbet and Co., 1947.

Faith and History, London, Nisbet and Co., 1949.

'The Self' and the Dramas of History, London, Faber and Faber, 1956.

W. Perkins, *Works*, 2nd edn, Cambridge, 1603.

'The Whole Treatise of the Cases of Conscience', *Works*, Cambridge, 1609, vol. II.

Max Scheler, *On the Eternal in Man*, tr. B. Noble, London, S.C.M. Press (Library of Philosophy and Theology), 1960.

Thomas Aquinas, *Summa Contra Gentiles*, tr. English Dominican Fathers, London, Burns Oates and Washbourne, 1923–9.

The 'Summa Theologica', tr. English Dominican Fathers, 2nd (rev.) edn, London, Burns Oates and Washbourne, 1921–32.

'Opusculum VII In Librum Beati Dionysii De Divinis Nominibus';

'Quaestio Unica De Anima';

'Quaestiones Disputatae : De Malo';

'Quaestiones Disputatae : De Veritate',

Opera Omnia, Parma, P. Fiaccadori, 1852–72, vols. VIII, IX, XV.

iv Theological: Secondary Sources

R. W. Battenhouse, ed., *A Companion to the Study of St Augustine*, New York, O.U.P., 1955.

J. Burnaby, *Amor Dei*, London, Hodder and Stoughton, 1938.

B. L. Clarke, 'God, Time and Human History', *Anglican Theological Review* XLV, 1963, p. 358.

C. N. Cochrane, *Christianity and Classical Culture*, London, O.U.P., 1940.

490

H. S. Coffin, *The Public Worship of God*, London, Independent Press, 1950.

W. O. Cross, 'The Problem of Human Evil', *Anglican Theological Review* XLV, 1963, p. 1.

W. Cunningham, *S. Austin and his Place in the History of Christian Thought* (The Hulsean Lectures, 1885), Cambridge, C.U.P., 1886.

M. C. D'Arcy *et al.*, *A Monument to St Augustine*, London, Sheed and Ward, 1934.

J. N. Figgis, *The Political Aspects of S. Augustine's 'The City of God'*, London, Longmans, Green & Co., 1921.

B. A. Gerrish, *Grace and Reason: a Study of the Theology of Martin Luther*, London, O.U.P., 1962.

E. Gilson, *The Philosophy of St Thomas Aquinas* (3rd rev. edn of *Le Thomisme*), tr. E. Bullough, Cambridge, Heffer, 1924.
Introduction a L'Etude de Saint Augustin, Paris, Libraire Philosophique : J. Vrin, 1929.

Adolph Harnack, *History of Dogma*, vols. V, VII, tr. from 3rd German edn by J. Millar and W. McGilchrist, Williams and Norgate (Theological Translation Library X, XII), 1889, 1899.

G. S. Hendry, *The Holy Spirit in Christian Theology*, London, S.C.M. Press, 1965.

J. Laidlaw, *The Bible Doctrine of Man*, Edinburgh, T. and T. Clark, 1905.

D. M. Mackinnon, 'Theology and Tragedy', *Religious Studies* II, 1967, p. 163.

J. Morgan, *The Psychological Teaching of St Augustine*, London, Elliot Stock, 1932.

B. M. G. Reardon, 'History and Theology', *Anglican Theological Review* XLV, 1963, p. 372.

H. Wheeler Robinson, *The Christian Doctrine of Man*, 3rd edn, Edinburgh, T. and T. Clark, 1926, reprinted 1958.

N. A. Scott, 'The Tragic Vision and the Christian Faith', *Anglican Theological Review* XLV, 1963, p. 23.
ed., *The Tragic Vision and the Christian Faith*, New York, Association Press, 1957.

Paul Tillich, *The Courage to Be*, London, Nisbet and Co., 1955.

Index

492